THE ROUGH GUIDE TO

Yorkshire

This second edition written and researched by

Jos Simon

D0307910

roughgu

Contents

Introduction to
Yorkshire

Yorkshire, it has been said, is "a country in a county". The very name brings countless images to mind – wild moors, headlands and cliffs; rugged dales and enormous beaches; medieval cities, churches and monasteries; formal estates and vast steelworks; coal mines and woollen mills. This diversity is part of the county's appeal – its countryside and coast can compete with anywhere in Britain for beauty, its cities with any in the UK for shopping and dining and clubbing. And its pubs and breweries aren't half bad, either.

In area Yorkshire is by far England's largest county. Its geology and topography yield virtually every type of British landscape and habitat. And different stages of the nation's human **history** are etched on its landscape, layer upon layer – within these borders you can see prehistoric long boats, Roman walls and roads, medieval castles, monasteries and minsters, Edwardian mansions and Georgian resorts, and, with their own distinctive *jolie-laide* appeal, the iron and steel bones of heavy industry.

As a result, Yorkshire offers an unrivalled **range** of things to see and do. Its museums of science, history and industry are among the best in the world. It excels in ruined monasteries, proud cathedrals and humble rural churches. It boasts more than its fair share of enthusiast-run steam heritage railways, and a literary and artistic heritage that has left a number of evocative sights. The great outdoors is more than great here, in the dales and the moors, and along the craggy, dramatic coasts. Long-distance national trails including the Pennine Way and the Cleveland Way bring walkers and cyclists to **"God's own country"**, but there is also ample opportunity for caving and potholing, sailing and watersports.

Yorkshire **people**, too, have a distinctive identity. They'll quote the old saying "Yorkshire born, Yorkshire bred. Strong in't arm and thick in't 'ead", but it'll be said with a twinkle in the eye. Look at the writing of Alan Bennett and John Godber, the poetry of Simon Armitage and Ian MacMillan, the novels of Laurence Sterne and Kate Atkinson, the lyrics of Jarvis Cocker and Alex Turner – or almost anything said by Fred Trueman. You'll come across that dry, wry Yorkshire humour wherever you go.

ABOVE SCARBOROUGH **RIGHT** SWALEDALE

Where to go

If you are here to hike or cycle, then the obvious place to base yourself is in one of the **villages** of the Dales or the North York Moors. If it's the seaside you're after, then choose one of Yorkshire's fine coastal resorts, from the historic old fishing town of **Whitby** to the postcard-pretty **Robin Hood's Bay** or handsome old spa resort of **Scarborough**. And if you are after big city attractions, head for **Leeds** or **Sheffield**. Yorkshire's cities offer plenty of museums, shops, cafés and restaurants – Leeds in particular would be difficult to match anywhere outside London – along with good parks, and easy access to green spaces for when the urban attractions begin to pale.

South and **West Yorkshire** offer a range of spectacular **museums** – Magna in Rotherham, Kelham Island in Sheffield, Eureka! in Halifax, the National Coal Mining Museum and Yorkshire Sculpture Park in Wakefield, the Royal Armouries in Leeds and the National Media Museum in Bradford, among them – together with a host of smaller museums and art galleries often staffed by knowledgeable enthusiasts. In South and West Yorkshire in particular, the range of outstanding **industrial museums** and other heritage sites is impressive, as might be expected from one of the world's most important cradles of the Industrial Revolution.

At the heart of the county, the Vale of York boasts Yorkshire's single biggest tourist attraction – the historic city of **York** itself. Having played such a large part in the history of Britain from the time of the Celts, York has a huge concentration of tourist attractions. Prime among them is York Minster, of course, with Jorvik and Dig – two of the finest

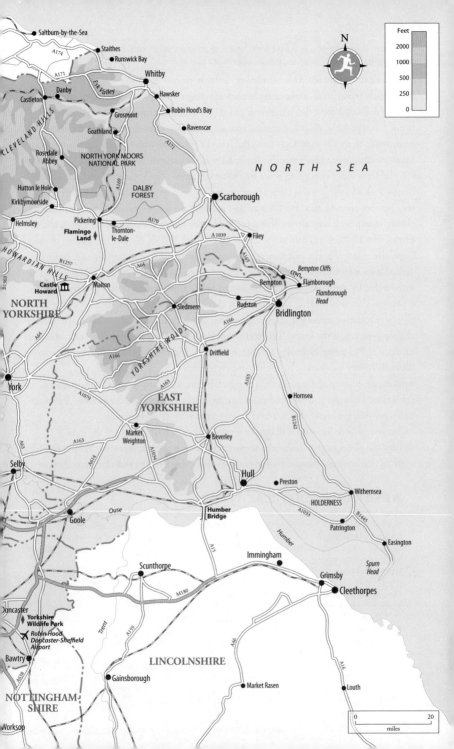

interactive museums you will find anywhere – as absolute must-sees, and the wonderful National Railway Museum, Yorkshire and Castle museums coming up fast behind. It's a great place to spend a few days, wandering aimlessly around its narrow lanes with their ridiculously picturesque overhanging houses, enjoying river trips or ghost walks, and treating yourself at lovely hotels, fine restaurants and shops. York has all you need for a perfect city break, but if possible, don't just confine yourself to the city – get out into the surrounding countryside to see the stunningly beautiful ruins of **Fountains Abbey**, and take time to get to know pleasant towns like Wetherby, Knaresborough, Harrogate and Ripon.

Yorkshire is lucky enough to boast two **national parks** – the Yorkshire Dales and the North York Moors, glorious stretches of rugged upland scenery, with fertile valleys and bare heather-covered hills. For fresh air and outdoor attractions you don't need to stick too closely within park boundaries, however. Nidderdale is one of the Yorkshire Dales, and the Howardian Hills are a continuation of the North York Moors. Neither is included in their respective national parks, but they are designated Areas of Outstanding Natural Beauty.

The **Dales** are rich in waterfalls, potholes and caves, with pretty stone villages surrounded by meadows, dry stone walls and field barns. Artisan crafts are thriving here – you can visit sites making anything from cheese to ropes, chocolate and beer. The Dales also have some astonishingly imposing **castles**, of which Richmond's, with its spectacular clifftop position, is the finest. The **North York Moors**, meanwhile, have their own share of castles – at Pickering, Helmsley and Scarborough – and the impressive, medieval **Rievaulx Abbey** overlooked by the elegant eighteenth-century Rievaulx Terrace. The working monastery of Ampleforth is another draw, and, across the north, the pastoral **Esk Valley**. Here too you will find the nostalgic **North Yorkshire Moors Railway**, its steam trains providing a lovely way to travel between the villages of the region.

One area of Yorkshire that is all easy to overlook, despite having some of the most worthwhile places to visit, is the area known as the East Riding, fringing the North Sea coast south of Scarborough. **Kingston-upon-Hull** (generally shortened to **Hull**) is a large sea port

---

WEIRD AND WONDERFUL ACTIVITIES

Never let it be said that Yorkshire doesn't have an eccentric side. In addition to mainstream and outdoor sports, you can try out a number of unusual activities at a variety of venues.

Cable waterskiing An electric cable instead of a boat drags you around the water at Rother Valley Country Park near Rotherham – where there's also fishing, golf and a number of other splendid outdoor activities on offer. See p.61.

Husky-trekking You don't need snow for this husky-trekking – you can become a "musher" on grass at Pesky Husky (Ⓦ peskyhusky.co.uk) in Staintondale between Scarborough and Whitby.

Mountain boarding Snowboarding, but not as we know it. This version uses boards with four wheels to whizz up and over the rocks. Try it at Another World Mountain boarding centre in the hills above Ogden Reservoir north of Halifax (Ⓦ anotherworldadventurecentre.co.uk).

Petanque The petanque court in the heart of Leeds allows you to indulge in the quintessentially French, and extremely civilized game of boules. And it's absolutely free. See p.88.

Via Ferrata Invented by the Italians to move troops around the Alps, Via Ferrata – meaning "iron road" – centres have spread across the world. In Yorkshire, the Via Ferrata at How Stean Gorge is the place for adrenalin junkies. One of just two in England, it offers a lengthy scramble along the chasm using fixed beams, cables and ladders. See p.206.

with a past reputation for being on the rough side but which is, with its designation as UK City of Culture 2017, finally able to show the world what a vibrant and intriguing place it is. With a vivacious, breezy city centre clustered around an attractive waterside, the city also boasts a terrific aquarium (The Deep) and one of the most successful regional theatres (The Hull Truck) in the country. **Beverley**, on Hull's doorstep, has its impressive Minster and its beautiful St Mary's Church, and a good range of shops and restaurants. Undulating prettily to the north, the **Yorkshire Wolds** offer numerous relics from past ages, from Rudston's monolith to the abandoned medieval village at Wharram Percy. East of the Wolds the east Yorkshire coast begins at **Flamborough Head**, with its colonies of seabirds, then plunges south through Bridlington and along the Holderness Peninsula to the weird and wonderful **Spurn Head**, the lonely territory of migrating birds, Humber pilots and lifeboatmen.

When to go

Yorkshire's climate is typical of that throughout the north of England, so although generally warm in **summer** (average Aug maximum 21°C) and cold in winter, the weather really can change from day to day. If anything, conditions are more changeable here because of the North Sea coast and the hills on its western and northern fringes. In **winter** the county gets a fair amount of snow in the Pennines, Dales and North York Moors. **Spring** and summer are even more changeable, and it can **rain** at any time, though Yorkshire's recorded rainfall is lower than many parts of the UK. The advice to visitors is, then, hope for the best, prepare for the worst, and bring lots of layers and waterproofs.

Author picks

Our author has spent many years living, working and travelling in Yorkshire. Here he shares some of his favourite experiences.

Real ale retreats Yorkshire has fine real ale pubs that still hold true to centuries of tradition. Try Sheffield's *Fat Cat* (p.55), *Mr. Foley's Cask Ale House* in Leeds (p.99), or *Nellies* in Beverley (p.291).

Splendid views Two of the best are from the top of the Buttertubs pass between Wensleydale and Swaledale (p.214), and from Middlesmoor at the top of Nidderdale (p.204). For urban views, the one of Richmond from its castle (p.216) takes some beating.

Quirky Yorkshire For offbeat attractions you'd be hard put to better the Forbidden Corner near Middleham (p.212), with its fantasy landscape and strange sepulchral voices, Eden Camp (p.241), a war museum housed in an old POW camp, and Skipton's Mart Theatre (p.196) – animal market during the day, theatre at night.

Gorgeous gardens Garden fans can take their pick: try the RHS's delightful 58 acres at Harlow Carr (p.165), and the spectacularly landscaped formal gardens of Studley Royal, next to Fountains Abbey (p.176).

Inspiring train journeys Yorkshire has some of the loveliest train journeys in the country. Two of the best are the Settle to Carlisle line in the west (p.186) and the North Yorkshire Moors railway (p.239) further east.

Foodie favourites For a taste of Yorkshire specialities, try Fodder, Harrogate's super-farm-shop-plus-café (p.167), the Wensleydale Creamery in Hawes (p.209) and, king of fish-and-chip shops, the *Magpie* in Whitby (p.253).

Great houses The whole of Yorkshire is studded with the flamboyant houses owned by the super-rich local families of the past. Wentworth Woodhouse (p.62), Harewood (p.96) and Castle Howard (p.236) will take your breath away.

> Our author recommendations don't end here. We've flagged up our favourite places – a perfectly sited hotel, an atmospheric café, a special restaurant – throughout the guide, highlighted with the ★ symbol.

LEFT BRONTË PARSONAGE MUSEUM (P.111)
FROM TOP WENSLEYDALE CREAMERY (P.209); BUTTERTUBS PASS (P.214)

15

things not to miss

It's not possible to see everything that Yorkshire has to offer in one trip – and we don't suggest you try. What follows is a selective but broad taste of the county's highlights: dramatic landscapes, stunning architecture, exciting activities and world-class museums. Each highlight has a page reference to take you straight into the Guide, where you can find out more. Coloured numbers refer to chapters in the Guide section.

1 WHITBY
Page 247
Yorkshire's finest seaside town, chock-full of history – the abbey, fishing, whaling, Captain Cook and, of course, Bram Stoker's *Dracula*.

2 BETTYS
Page 158
A select group of wonderful tea shops, *Bettys* has defied all attempts to open branches outside Yorkshire.

3 MALHAM
Page 191
The pretty village of Malham is an attraction in itself. Factor in the dramatic landscapes nearby – lofty limestone crags, a glacial lake and a plunging waterfall – and you have an unmissable destination, the perfect Yorkshire Dales base.

4 MASHAM BREWERIES
Page 213
Enjoy lashings of beer and the heady aroma of hops in Masham, one of the finest towns in the Dales.

9

5 SPURN HEAD
Page 301

Commanding the Humber Estuary, Spurn Head is an eerie finger of land occupied only by lifeboatmen, pilots and millions of migrating birds.

6 BRADFORD CURRY HOUSES
Page 107

Famed for its curry houses, Bradford offers hundreds to choose from and every local has their own particular favourite.

7 ROYAL ARMOURIES, LEEDS
Page 91

A spectacular space for a thrilling collection covering weaponry from Roman times – you might even see a tilting bout.

8 RIEVAULX ABBEY
Page 234

The picturesque ruins of one of Yorkshire's greatest Cistercian monasteries are set in a beautiful valley overlooked by formal eighteenth-century gardens.

9 HUMBER BRIDGE
Page 275

The epitome of elegant engineering, the Humber Bridge is the largest anywhere that you can walk across.

10 THE ESK VALLEY
Page 246

Lovely countryside away from main roads, accessible only by winding lanes or on the trains of the Esk Valley line.

10

11

12

Itineraries

Given Yorkshire's variety, you'll need to plan carefully if you want to get the most out of your stay. These itineraries will take you right across the region, from its great industrial cities to old fishing towns, pretty limestone villages to spanking new museums, taking in much glorious countryside along the way.

THE GRAND TOUR

This itinerary of big-hitting destinations will ensure that, after a week or ten days, you'll have sampled the very best of the county.

❶ **York** The best place to start, with a wonderful medieval Minster, meandering lanes, museums galore and great restaurants. **See p.138**

❷ **National Media Museum** On the edge of Bradford's city centre, this vivid interactive museum is a fabulous attraction – and don't miss the city itself, where you can stop off for a delicious curry. **See p.103**

❸ **Malham** A pretty village in an area abounding in them, Malham is a great base for exploring the Yorkshire Dales, with their rolling hills, caves, mountains and waterfalls. **See p.191**

❹ **Richmond** This handsome town, with its imposing castle perched on a bluff above the Swale, is worth a day to itself. **See p.216**

❺ **Helmsley** Use this attractive stone-built town as a base for exploring the wild North York Moors, and some fascinating castles, abbeys and stately homes. **See p.232**

❻ **Whitby** Stunningly pretty, with proud historical and literary associations, the old fishing town of Whitby is a glorious base for touring the Yorkshire coast. **See p.247**

❼ **Beverley** A characterful market town offering two of Yorkshire's most spectacular churches, a fine musical heritage and some excellent restaurants. **See p.284**

❽ **Hull** The UK's City of Culture for 2017, Hull has come into its own in recent years, with a redeveloped waterfront and The Deep aquarium heading a superlative group of museums. **See p.270**

LITERARY AND ARTISTIC TRAIL

Yorkshire has long been fertile ground for great writers and artists. But this itinerary, which could be covered comfortably in a week, is not only for fans – it also takes you to some of the most interesting and beautiful parts of the county.

❶ **Hebden Bridge** This appealing, arty canalside mill town is a good base for poetry fans, with easy access to Ted Hughes' birthplace and Sylvia Plath's grave. **See p.119**

❷ **Haworth** Yorkshire's main literary destination, Haworth is not only a pretty moorland village, but also offers poignant insights into the lives of the Brontës, and the wild landscape that so inspired them. **See p.110**

❸ **Saltaire** The magnificent Salt's Mill, a UNESCO World Heritage Site, boasts a large collection of David Hockney's works. **See p.107**

❹ **Yorkshire Sculpture Park** A truly lovely artistic experience, with pieces from all the greats displayed in the grounds of the beautiful Bretton Hall estate. **See p.132**

❺ **Hepworth Gallery** Wakefield's splendid new gallery is a temple to the work of Barbara Hepworth and to the sculpture and painting of other major contemporary artists. **See p.130**

ABOVE KELHAM ISLAND MUSEUM

❺ Thirsk Fans of the James Herriot books should stop at this pleasant market town to see where real-life vet Alf Wight, the books' author, lived and worked. **See p.226**

❼ Coxwold Eighteenth-century writer Laurence Sterne lived and died in this North Yorkshire village: visit Shandy Hall, where he wrote his most famous works, and the church of St Michael where he was the vicar. There are some nice places to stay and eat nearby. **See p.229**

❽ Hull Twentieth-century poet Philip Larkin was Hull's university librarian. The Larkin Trail gives you a quirky overview of this energizing waterfront city. **See p.270**

INDUSTRIAL HERITAGE

Yorkshire is a happy hunting ground for anyone interested in the UK's industrial heritage. The following itinerary should take a busy four days or a more leisurely week.

❶ Kelham Island Museum Start in Sheffield with this tribute to its one-time world domination in steel production. Here you can see the most powerful steam engine in Britain, a mighty Grand Slam earthquake bomb, a tiny "year knife" with 365 blades and much more, all "Made in Sheffield". **See p.50**

❷ Magna Housed in a gigantic decommissioned steelworks in the old industrial town of Rotherham, the hands-on Magna explores the large-scale production of steel and the science surrounding it. **See p.60**

❸ National Coal Mining Museum Moving into West Yorkshire and the old Caphouse Colliery, pick up your miner's lamp and hard hat and plunge deep underground to see how coal was extracted. **See p.131**

❹ Leeds Industrial Museum This was once the biggest woollen mill on Earth, and now displays fascinating displays of spinning and weaving machinery. **See p.94**

❺ National Railway Museum Among York's many attractions is the biggest and best railway museum in the world. Admire the steam leviathans of the past, and learn about the part Britain played in developing modern high-speed communications. **See p.154**

❻ Yorkshire Waterways Museum During the early Industrial Revolution, the heavy raw materials upon which it depended were moved not by rail, but by canal; this museum in the East Riding focuses on the canals and the lives of those who worked on them. **See p.284**

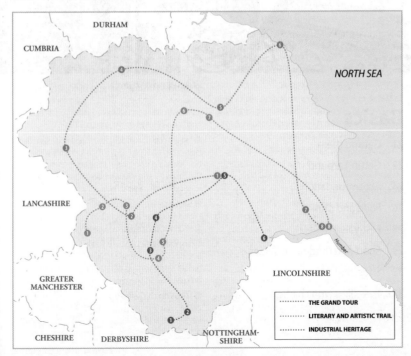

KIRKGATE MARKET, LEEDS

Basics

Getting there

Approximately half way up the island of Great Britain and stretching from the North Sea almost to the Irish Sea, Yorkshire is one of the easier places to get to in England. Major road and rail links between the south of England and Scotland pass through it, as do the principal northern cross-country routes from east to west. On a good day it can take around three hours to get to Sheffield or Leeds from London by car (between four and five hours by coach) and little more than two hours by train. Manchester, the north of England's biggest airport, is ninety minutes away by train or car, and Yorkshire has its own regional airports – Leeds-Bradford and Robin Hood Doncaster-Sheffield – which are steadily building up links with the rest of the world. Furthermore, Yorkshire has its own major deep-sea port – around a million passengers a year travel back and forth to the continent through the Port of Hull.

By car

England's main north–south motorway, the **M1**, intersects with its main northern east–west motorway, the **M62**, just south of Leeds. This means that Yorkshire is easily accessible from London, all points south, Liverpool and Manchester. Via the M6, the whole of the northwest, the Lake District and western Scotland is accessible. The other principal north–south route – the **A1** – also passes through Yorkshire, and is a very useful alternative to the M1; it is dual carriageway, with no roundabouts, from the outskirts of London to Yorkshire and beyond – indeed, much of it has motorway status and is designated **A1(M)**. The A1 merges with the M1 to the east of Leeds, and continues north all the way to Tyneside and Edinburgh.

By bus

Because of its excellent motorway system, travelling to Yorkshire by **bus** – long-distance services are known as "coaches" – is faster and more comfortable than to many other places in the UK. National Express (Ⓦ nationalexpress.com) routes link London with Leeds, Bradford, Huddersfield, Sheffield and York, at very low prices.

By train

As with the roads, Yorkshire benefits from being at the intersection of major rail routes – the **East Coast** line from London to Scotland; the **First TransPennine** line from northwest England into Yorkshire, the northeast and Scotland; **CrossCountry** from southwest and eastern England and the Midlands through Yorkshire to the northeast and Scotland; **East Midlands** from London to Sheffield; and **First Hull** from London to the East Riding. There are numerous high-speed trains from London to York, Leeds, Sheffield, Doncaster and Hull (1hr 40min–3hr or more). Fares vary, widely – book as early as you can, and be as flexible regarding travel times as possible. Using a booking site such as Ⓦ thetrainline.com can save money, but it is always worth trying the train companies themselves, too. For a full rundown of timetables, check National Rail Enquiries (Ⓦ nationalrail.co.uk). Note that many of Yorkshire's towns and cities offer a PlusBus option, a pass that gets you discounted bus and tram travel when you buy a train ticket; buy it at the station or at Ⓦ plusbus.info.

TRAIN LINES

CrossCountry Ⓦ crosscountrytrains.co.uk. From south, southwest and eastern England and the Midlands through Yorkshire to the northeast and Scotland.

East Coast Ⓦ eastcoast.co.uk. From London through Yorkshire to Newcastle and Scotland.

East Midlands Trains Ⓦ eastmidlandstrains.co.uk. From London to Sheffield.

A BETTER KIND OF TRAVEL

At Rough Guides we are passionately committed to travel. We believe it helps us understand the world we live in and the people we share it with – and of course tourism is vital to many developing economies. But the scale of modern tourism has also damaged some places irreparably, and climate change is accelerated by most forms of transport, especially flying. All Rough Guides' flights are carbon-offset, and every year we donate money to a variety of environmental charities.

First Hull Trains ⓦ hulltrains.co.uk. From London to Howden, the Wolds and Hull.

First TransPennine Express ⓦ tpexpress.co.uk. From Liverpool, Manchester Airport, Newcastle and Middlesbrough into Yorkshire and Scotland.

Grand Central ⓦ grandcentralrail.com. From London to Thirsk, Northallerton and York.

Northern Rail ⓦ northernrail.org. Runs extensive services across northern England, linking destinations in Yorkshire with Lancashire, the northeast and the Midlands.

By plane

With the growth of Yorkshire's two regional airports – **Leeds-Bradford** (ⓦ leedsbradford airport.co.uk) and **Robin Hood Doncaster-Sheffield** (ⓦ robinhoodairport.com) – plus nearby **Humberside** (ⓦ humbersideairport.com), which is in Lincolnshire, and **Manchester** (ⓦ manchester airport.co.uk), there are now many routes into Yorkshire from within the UK, a few cities in North America, and, in particular from other European destinations.

Flights from other parts of the UK and Ireland

Domestic air travel is never likely to be as popular in the UK as it is in big countries like the USA or Australia, and for most mainland routes when travel to and from the airports is taken into account it is often more convenient, quicker and cheaper by train, coach or car. It's certainly less harmful to the environment. However, there are **domestic routes** between Yorkshire and other parts of the British Isles, which include Aberdeen, Belfast, Bristol, Dublin, Edinburgh, Exeter, London Gatwick, Glasgow, Isle of Man, Knock, Newquay, Plymouth and Southampton to Leeds-Bradford as well as Belfast and Jersey to Robin Hood Doncaster-Sheffield Airport.

Flights from the USA and Canada

By far the greatest number of direct services linking the USA and Canada with the north of England fly into **Manchester airport** – it sees services from Atlanta, Chicago, Las Vegas, New York, Orlando and Philadelphia, plus Calgary, Toronto and Vancouver – which is close enough to Yorkshire, and has good enough motorway and rail links, to be convenient. The only route from the USA to one of Yorkshire's two regional airports is the New York to Leeds-Bradford route offered by Jet2 (ⓦ jet2.com).

Flights from South Africa, Australia and New Zealand

There are no direct flights from South Africa, Australia and New Zealand to Manchester or to Yorkshire's regional airports. The journey will therefore be **via London** with internal flights to or from Manchester or Leeds, or via European hubs.

By ferry

P&O car ferries run to **Hull** from **Rotterdam** (11hr 15min–12hr) and **Zeebrugge** (13hr 15min–14hr 30min). Voyages are overnight, so it is necessary to book a cabin, but this is a very civilized route – the ferries are like floating hotels, so you get a good night's sleep, and drive off the ferry in the morning with Yorkshire at your feet. See ⓦ poferries.com.

Tours and organized holidays

Package tours of Yorkshire, where accommodation and road transport are made on your behalf, are not only convenient, they can sometimes be cheaper than if you make the same arrangements yourself. They also allow you to tap into local knowledge and to get to know the county in depth.

ORGANIZED TOURS

Bespoke Tours of Yorkshire ⓦ theyorkshirechauffeurcompany .co.uk. Half- or full-day tours in chauffeur-driven Range Rovers. Drivers have a detailed knowledge of Yorkshire, and will construct a tour based on your interests and preferences.

Wold Travel ⓦ woldtravel.co.uk. Interesting bus tours, based on famous ex-residents (David Hockney, for example, or James Herriot) or on particular interests (Wensleydale Railway, perhaps), along with general-interest options.

Yorkshire Tour Company ⓦ theyorkshiretourcompany. Tours focusing on particular areas (Dales, moors and coast, Brontë country) or on interests (history, abbeys and minsters, gardens, golf), with a good choice of hotels and restaurants.

Getting around

For Yorkshire in general, the best way of getting to see and do the most in the least time is by car. In the most isolated parts of rural Yorkshire it's the only really convenient option. But in urban areas, particularly in South and West Yorkshire, integrated public transport systems, consisting of buses, trains and in some areas trams, is highly developed

and very efficient. Even in some rural areas – particularly in the Yorkshire Dales and North York Moors National Parks – extra routes and buses are run during the holiday season, and heritage railway lines run regular trains. In these areas, too, many visitors enjoy the countryside by bike or on foot. For help in route planning, go to ⓦyorkshire travel.net.

By car

Driving around Yorkshire is relatively easy, especially in South and West Yorkshire, where the national motorways double as interurban and suburban freeways – the main towns and cities of both hang from the M1, M62 and other motorways (eg M621, M606, M18, M180) like fruit from the branches of a tree. There being no toll, the local population use them continuously for short journeys – it's often quicker to use the motorway than to battle through traffic lights, roundabouts and one-way systems, even when it involves considerably greater mileage. If you're using satnav, go for the fastest, not the shortest, route. Away from the big cities, dual carriageways are rare and journey times are unpredictable – you might well end up stuck behind tractors pulling farm machinery, or in a convoy behind a slow driver. In the heart of the two national parks you might even be on single-lane roads with passing places.

Parking is plentiful and inexpensive in all but the biggest cities, and in these – especially Sheffield, Leeds and York – it might be as well to use the **Park-and-Ride** facilities. For visitors staying in city-centre hotels where parking isn't provided, hotels often have discount deals with nearby private car parks, though it can still be very expensive over an extended period.

Vehicle rental

Car rental is most conveniently booked online, either through one of the big international companies (Avis, Hertz, National, Budget and so on), from a company that works through other companies (ⓦauto-europe.co.uk for example), or from a local car rental firm. You can expect to pay around £30 per day (£50 at weekends) or anything from £120 to £200 a week, but look out for special deals. Check whether there are lower and/or upper age limits (often 21/70) and, if you want an

TOP FIVE YORKSHIRE RAIL JOURNEYS
Esk Valley Line See p.246
Keighley and Worth Valley Railway See p.110
North Yorkshire Moors Railway See p.239
Settle to Carlisle Railway See p.186
Wensleydale Railway See p.211

automatic, say so – it'll cost more, and may need to be booked earlier. Motorbike and motorhome (RV) rental is more expensive than car rental (try ⓦopen roadrentals.co.uk and ⓦjustgo.uk.com).

By bus and train

Bus and rail services in Yorkshire are run by a plethora of private companies – there are eleven companies operating buses in the **York** area alone (see ⓦyork.gov.uk). **West Yorkshire** has an excellent integrated bus and train system (ⓦwymetro.com), as does **South Yorkshire** (ⓦtravelsouthyorkshire.com), with the addition of **Sheffield**'s splendid Supertram network (ⓦsupertram.com). In **East Yorkshire** East Yorkshire Motor Services (ⓦeyms.co.uk) runs numerous bus routes, but train travel is more limited. In the Yorkshire **Dales**, DalesBus (ⓦdalesbus.org) run numerous routes, some all year, many during the summer only. The Moors Explorer service (ⓦeyms .co.uk/bus-services), meanwhile runs from Hull, Cottingham and Beverley into the **Vale of Pickering** and the **North York Moors**.

Train services within Yorkshire are provided by **First TransPennine Express** (ⓦtpexpress.co.uk), linking Leeds, York, Doncaster, Sheffield, Hull, Selby and Scarborough, and **Northern Rail** (ⓦnorthern rail.org), which runs trains across the north, including direct access to the North York Moors, Yorkshire Dales, the Peak District and the coast, and includes the service on the Yorkshire Wolds Coast Line from Hull to Scarborough.

In addition, North Yorkshire is blessed with some wonderful **heritage railways**, including the North Yorkshire Moors Railway (ⓦnymr.co.uk) from Pickering to Grosmont, where it connects with the beautiful Esk Valley Railway (ⓦeskvalleyrailway .co.uk) from Middlesbrough to Whitby, and the Settle to Carlisle Railway (ⓦsettle-carlisle.co.uk).

For **information** on local public transport, consult ⓦyorkshiretravel.net.

Rail passes

A bewildering number of **rail passes** are available. For visitors from overseas who intend to make extensive use of the rail network, a **BritRail England** pass, which can be bought only outside the UK, could save a lot on fares (🖥 britrail.net). They cover rail travel in England for from three to fifteen days in any two months – one child gets a free pass with every adult full-price ticket.

If you have been resident in a European country for more than six months, you can buy an **InterRail** pass (🖥 interrail.eu) allowing unlimited rail travel in European countries (except your own) for from three to eight days within one month.

A number of **domestic rail passes** are available to locals and visitors alike (🖥 nationalrail.co.uk). With Rover and Ranger passes you can have unlimited travel in a particular region for single, multiple or flexible days. For example, there's a West Yorkshire Day Rover (which covers rail and bus travel), a North Yorkshire Moors Railway Rover, a South Yorkshire PTE TravelMaster, a Yorkshire Coast Day Ranger, and others. Prices vary – the last, for example, which covers any journey between Hull and Whitby costs £19 for adults, £9.50 for children or £38 for families.

By boat

As a consequence of the major role it played in the Industrial Revolution, Yorkshire has numerous **canals**. Waterways that were built to carry heavy industrial raw materials and finished goods now offer a peaceful, often picturesque, way of getting around the county. Numerous companies offer anything from short trips to longer-term boat rental and canal boat holidays – for example Pennine Boat Trips (🖥 canaltrips.co.uk), Pennine Cruisers (🖥 penninecruisers.com) and Snaygill Boats (🖥 snaygillboats.com) in Skipton, Shire Cruisers (🖥 shirecruisers.co.uk) in Sowerby Bridge or Bronte Boat Hire (🖥 bronteboathire.co.uk) in Hebden Bridge. If you are staying near a canal, the chances are that there will be a boat rental company not far away.

By bike

If travelling by **bike**, you can follow sections of the National Cycle Network or smaller local routes. Most local authorities produce maps of their cycle network, which can be downloaded from their websites (for Sheffield, for example, you can download five PDF cycle maps on 🖥 sheffield.gov .uk/roads/travel/cycling/findir). If you haven't brought your own bike, you will be able to **rent** one in most large towns and even in small villages within the more scenic parts of the Dales and Moors. Rental costs are usually around £25 per day, more for specialist mountain bikes, less if you rent for several days or a week. Expect to have to leave some form of security – a deposit, credit card details or your passport. Most trains accept bikes, but regulations vary from company to company and you might need to book in advance – check beforehand (🖥 nationalrail.co.uk).

On foot

None of Yorkshire's cities is so large that their city centres cannot be explored thoroughly on foot. There are numerous marked **public footpaths** across towns and cities, and for short trips it's often far quicker to walk than bother with buses or cabs. And for getting around the county itself, there are many excellent **hiking trails** (see p.184).

Accommodation

Accommodation in Yorkshire is plentiful though, as you'd expect, range and capacity are far greater in the main holiday areas – York, the Dales, the North York Moors and the coast – than in industrial South and West Yorkshire, or more remote East Yorkshire.

The popular tourist areas offer the whole accommodation gamut – country house establishments with all the luxury bells and whistles; ubiquitous international and boutique chains; mid-sized family-owned and -run hotels; guesthouses and B&Bs; hostels (both YHA and independent),

---

ACCOMMODATION PRICES

For all accommodation reviewed in this Guide, we provide **prices** for high season (roughly July & Aug). In hotels and B&Bs, we give the lowest price for one night's stay in a double or twin room, for hostels it's the price of a bed in dorm accommodation (and of a double room if available) – note that for YHA hostels, prices quoted are for non-members (members get a £3 discount per night). For campsites we quote the cost of two people with a tent, unless otherwise stated.

bunkhouses and campsites. Look out too for pub accommodation – there has been a marked improvement, especially in the more rural areas, with many inns offering really well-appointed rooms at competitive rates.

In the industrial areas of South and West Yorkshire, the range of accommodation available outside Sheffield and Leeds is much narrower. Large chain hotels predominate, and these are usually located outside the town centres near motorway exits, since they depend on business clients and passing trade. Even if you're not driving this is not usually too inconvenient, since bus and taxi transport into the centres is relatively easy.

Hotels, guesthouses and B&Bs

Yorkshire has some of the most luxurious **top-end hotels** in the UK, and although they tend to be set out in the countryside, a number are dotted around in heavily populated areas. They are usually housed in beautiful historical buildings, often listed, with attractive grounds, plush public rooms and impressive restaurants, and have all the spas, pools, gyms and so on that you'd expect. Although their publicly quoted rates can be eye-watering, occasional discounts and special deals, which change from day to day, can put them within reach of most of us – a rate of around £80 for a double room is quite common if you choose your night carefully. A word of warning – many of the big hotels now make a lot of their income by hosting weddings and corporate events, and when these are in progress the service for ordinary guests can seem to suffer. It is worth asking if there are any such events scheduled when you book.

All the big **international chains** are well represented in Yorkshire, from the cheap and cheerful to the staid and the stately. You'd expect a pretty uniform experience – but in fact they can vary a lot, depending on the staff. We've detailed the best of them in the Guide.

There are, also, numerous privately owned and run **hotels**, **guesthouses** and **B&Bs** throughout Yorkshire. Many smaller establishments have taken a leaf out of the big hotels' books and now offer similar services – en-suite bathrooms and tea- and coffee-making facilities, wi-fi, complimentary newspapers.

And whatever accommodation you're considering, carefully check the availability of **parking**, especially in the city centres – it can be a real pain, and very expensive for all but the shortest stay.

TOP FIVE LUXURY HOTELS
Devonshire Arms See p.199
Feversham Arms See p.233
Middlethorpe Hall See p.158
Rudding Park See p.166
Swinton Park See p.214

Pubs

Across Yorkshire but especially in the rural areas, many **pubs** offer very acceptable accommodation. Two problems to look out for, though: they may be full – most have only a handful of rooms – and they may be noisy. So always reserve a room, check what time the bar closes and whether there's any live music or karaoke, and ask for a room as far from the public bar as possible.

Hostels

A variety of **hostels** and **bunkhouses** exist in Yorkshire, from the estimable establishments run by the **Youth Hostels Association** (Ⓦyha.org.uk) to the rough barns converted into bunkhouse and camping barn accommodation you find largely in the Dales (see Ⓦyorkshirenet.co.uk or Ⓦfindabunk house.co.uk). You don't need to be a member to stay at a YHA hostel, but you will be charged £3 extra per night. Membership (£15/year) is open to all EU nationals, can be bought online or at any hostel, and brings with it membership of Hostelling International (Ⓦhihostels.com) and its affiliated members.

Yorkshire also has a few **boutique hostels**, nicely turned out town-centre establishments containing multi-bunk dormitories. Two of the best are in York (see p.158).

Camping

Rural areas of Yorkshire (especially North Yorkshire) have long been dotted with **campsites**, from farmer's fields and pub back yards to full-on sites with comprehensive facilities. But look out too for sites attached to great houses, like Castle Howard and Burton Constable Hall – half close your eyes and you can imagine yourself lord of the manor. Industrial areas, too, have more sites than you'd perhaps expect, though to visit cities like Leeds and Sheffield you'll need to look outside the city centre – Leeds has several sites north of the centre in Bardsey, while for Sheffield your best bet is to stay in the neighbouring Derbyshire Peak District and commute. York is blessed with a fine site within ten minutes of the centre, and others from which you can get into the centre by boat. Note that camping **wild** is illegal in most national parks and nature reserves.

Self-catering

For extended stays **self-catering** is an eminently viable proposition, and can be a brilliant way of getting to know the real life of an area. Many farms in lovely locations supplement their income by converting no longer needed barns and workmen's cottages into self-catering accommodation. The so-called **apartment hotel**, with bedroom(s), bathroom, kitchen and lounge but minimal services are an increasingly popular option. They're often very luxurious, available on a nightly basis and can be surprisingly economical. There are many general self-catering websites that cover the whole of the UK and even abroad, and a number of good regional specialists

SELF-CATERING AGENCIES

Airbnb Ⓦ airbnb.com. Cool self-catering, with a huge variety of properties – seaside cottages to farmhouses, canal barges to warehouse apartments.

CouchSurfing Ⓦ couchsurfing.org. Huge worldwide directory listing people willing to let other members stay with them for free.

Country Hideaways Ⓦ countryhideaways.co.uk. Specialist in the Yorkshire Dales area.

Dales Holiday Cottages Ⓦ dales-holiday-cottages.com. Wide range of cottages in all the main Dales, both within and outside the national park.

Holiday Homes in Yorkshire Ⓦ selfcateringinthecity.co.uk. Big choice of top-end properties.

Yorkshire Cottages Ⓦ yorkshire-cottages.info. Covers the Dales, North York Moors, Vale of York and the Wolds.

Food and drink

Yorkshire has always been known for its high-quality, locally produced food – its lamb, beef, pork, hams, baked goods, cheese, pies, fish, chocolate, even extra virgin rapeseed oil. Yorkshire ham, Yorkshire pudding and Yorkshire ales are world famous, and everybody knows that the moon is made of Wensleydale cheese – well, according to Wallace and Gromit, anyhow. Increasingly, these wonderful ingredients get directly from producer to consumer, through farm shops and farmers' markets, and one of the joys of self-catering accommodation is searching out sources of good local produce. No wonder, then, that there has been a marked trend in the county for shops to sell locally produced food, and for restaurants to benefit from this cornucopia by increasingly using locally sourced ingredients.

In terms of **cuisine**, too, Yorkshire offers a huge range of dining experiences, catering for every taste and pocket. From internationally recognized top-end establishments to small local restaurants offering cuisine from all over the world to fish-and-chip shops, it is possible to eat well wherever you are in the county.

Look out for the **Deliciously Yorkshire** logo when shopping for food or choosing a restaurant. It's an initiative of the Yorkshire Regional Food Group, Deliciously Yorkshire (Ⓦ deliciouslyorkshire .co.uk), which seeks to promote the county's food producers, retailers and places to eat, and the logo is displayed by establishments that supply, sell or use Yorkshire produce. In addition, Deliciously Yorkshire awards – the county's food Oscars – are conferred annually in ten categories.

Food

The restaurant scene in Yorkshire has been on the up for many years. Fine dining has proliferated across the county – there are currently five Michelin-starred restaurants (two in North Yorkshire and one each in South, West and East Yorkshire) and many more establishments that offer similarly high quality. Named chefs are now being celebrated across the county – Tessa Bramley at the *Old Vicarage* in Sheffield, for example, or Frances Atkins at the *Yorke Arms* in Nidderdale.

Small independent restaurants and gastropubs can be found in virtually every city, town and

---

TOP FINE DINING SPOTS

Black Swan See p.231
Box Tree See p.194
Burlington Restaurant See p.199
Clocktower Restaurant See p.166
Old Vicarage See p.54
Pipe and Glass See p.291
Star Inn See p.234
Yorke Arms See p.205

village, and top-end chains like *Loch Fyne*, *Ask* pizzerias, *Café Rouge*, *Caffè Nero* and *Pizza Express* are well represented. In **Bettys tearooms** – in York, Harrogate, Ilkley and Northallerton – Yorkshire has a mini-chain of uniquely stylish establishments selling the most delicious cakes and puddings. **Whitby** boasts some of the most highly regarded fish restaurants in the country, including a splendid chippie in *The Magpie*, **Bradford** and **Leeds** some of the best offerings from the Indian subcontinent. And look out for little clusters of restaurants in particular places – Eccleshall Road in **Sheffield**, for example, much loved by the city's student population, or **Bawtry** near Doncaster, a small town with no fewer than fourteen establishments offering good food, including English, Chinese, Italian and Japanese cuisine, which draws in diners from Doncaster, Rotherham and beyond.

When visiting the county's restaurants, food shops and farmers' markets, make sure to try the

FARMERS' MARKETS

SOUTH YORKSHIRE
Doncaster Goose Hill; 1st and 3rd Wed
Sheffield Moor Market; 4th Sun
Wentworth Hague Lane; 2nd Sun

WEST YORKSHIRE
Halifax Russell St; 3rd Sat
Holmfirth Market Hall; 3rd Sun
Leeds Kirkgate Market; 1st and 3rd Sun
Otley Market Square; last Sun
Wetherby Market Place; 3rd Sun

NORTH YORKSHIRE
Grassington Town centre; 3rd Sun
Harrogate Market Place; 2nd Thurs
Leyburn Town Square; 4th Sun
Malton Cattle Market; last Sat
Northallerton Town Hall; 4th Wed
Pateley Bridge Nidderdale Showground; 4th Sat/Sun
Pickering Old Post Office Yard; 1st Thurs
Richmond Town Square; 3rd Sat
Ripon The Square; 3rd Sun
Skipton Canal Basin; 1st Sun
Thirsk Market Place; 2nd Mon
York York Auction Centre; 3rd Sat. Parliament St; last Fri
Whitby Old Market Place; every Thurs

EAST RIDING
Driffield Showground; 1st Sat
Humber Bridge Viewing area; 1st Sun
South Cave South Cave School; 2nd Sat

TOP FIVE PUBS
Blacksmiths Arms See p.244
Cod and Lobster See p.256
Flying Duck See p.194
Horseshoe Inn See p.244
Triton Inn See p.295

region's **local specialities**. The most famous is Yorkshire pudding. Not a pudding as such, though it can be served as a dessert, this savoury batter can be served with sausages, as toad-in-the-hole, or, even more commonly, with roast meats as a staple of Sunday lunches around Britain. Other highlights include Wensleydale cheese, much beloved by Wallace and Gromit; the dense oatmeal and black treacle cake known as parkin (though this is strictly a Lancashire as well as a Yorkshire delicacy); Pontefract cakes (not cakes, but discs of liquorice); and delicious rhubarb from Wakefield's rhubarb triangle.

Drink

Yorkshire ale and Yorkshire pubs have a nationwide reputation. Yorkshire has more than a hundred breweries, from the big boys like Samuel Smith's and John Smith's in Tadcaster to the small independent operators like Copper Dragon in Skipton or the Cropton Brewery in the North York Moors. Beerloving visitors to Yorkshire should try to make a pilgrimage to **Masham**, a pretty Dales town that supports two superb breweries, both of which have excellent visitor centres and brewery tours.

Similarly Yorkshire has a wealth of public houses. It's no coincidence that the Yorkshire section of the Campaign for Real Ale's *Good Beer Guide* is the longest – longer than the whole of London, longer than Scotland and Wales, much longer than Lancashire. Leeds and Sheffield have some terrific bars and pubs with wonderful selections of beer (look out for *North*, *Whitelocks* or *Mr Foley's Cask Ale House* in Leeds, or the *Devonshire Cat* in Sheffield), towns like Harrogate Wetherby, Ripon and Beverley have good old-fashioned town pubs (entering *Nellies* in Beverley is like stepping into the past), the coast has its share of smugglers' inns, and across the county almost every village has at least one country pub.

Less well known is the fact that Yorkshire has some of the most northerly **vineyards** in Europe – Leventhorpe Vineyard in Leeds, for example, and the Holmfirth Vineyard (appropriately located in the village where *Last of the Summer Wine* was filmed), who produce mainly white wines.

Festivals

Yorkshire cities, towns and villages host numerous festivals. Some have origins that are hidden in the mists of time; others owe more to local businesses trying to attract visitors during traditionally slow periods. Local tourist offices will have detailed lists for each area, but here are some of the more noteworthy annual festivals.

FEBRUARY–APRIL

Jorvik Viking Festival York; mid-Feb Ⓦ jorvik-viking-centre.co.uk. Nine days of Viking simulations, battle re-enactments, lectures and events in venues across the city.

Wakefield Festival of Food, Drink and Rhubarb West Yorkshire; towards end Feb Ⓦ experiencewakefield.co.uk. A weekend of street entertainment, cookery demonstrations, walks, tours, markets and visits to local rhubarb growers.

Huddersfield Literature Festival West Yorkshire; first half of March Ⓦ litfest.org.uk. Spread across ten days, with an emphasis on poetry, though a wide range of genres is covered via performances, masterclasses and workshops.

York Literature Festival End March Ⓦ yorkliteraturefestival.co.uk. An eleven-day event celebrating fiction and poetry with readings, signings, performances and workshops all over the city.

Harrogate Spring Flower Show Vale of York; towards end April Ⓦ flowershow.org.uk. A four-day weekend festival featuring competitions, displays and cookery demos.

Wath Festival of Music and Dance South Yorkshire; end April/ early May Ⓦ wathfestival.viviti.com. Largely folk music and dance, held in the Montgomery Hall and elsewhere, over a long weekend.

MAY

Late Music Festival York; May–Sept Ⓦ latemusic.org. Five-month series of Saturday evening concerts and recitals of the work of living composers, in York's St Saviourgate Unitarian Chapel.

Dales Festival of Food and Drink Leyburn, Yorkshire Dales; early May Ⓦ dalesfestivaloffood.org. Food hall, cookery and farming demonstrations, plus a beer festival, held over a weekend (Sat–Mon).

Whitby Moor and Coast Festival North Yorkshire; early May Ⓦ moorandcoast.co.uk. Weekend festival of music, dance, food and drink.

Holmfirth Festival of Folk West Yorkshire; first half of May Ⓦ holmfirthfestivaloffolk.co.uk. A weekend of folk music in pubs and on the streets.

Haworth 1940s Weekend West Yorkshire; mid-May Ⓦ haworth 1940s.co.uk. World War II re-enactments and films, music and other events.

Early Music Festival Beverley, East Riding; towards end of May Ⓦ ncem.co.uk/bemf. Music, talks and lectures, spread across five days (Wed–Sun).

Ryedale Folk Weekend Hutton-le-Hole, North York Moors; end May Ⓦ festivalonthemoor.co.uk/folkweekend/. Folk music and workshops in the Ryedale Folk Museum, held over a weekend.

Swaledale Festival Yorkshire Dales; last week May/first week June Ⓦ swaledale-festival.org.uk. Music (classical, choral, folk, jazz and world), talks and art throughout the dale.

JUNE

Bradford Mela West Yorkshire; mid-June Ⓦ bradford-mela.info. Weekend celebration of world cultures, with entertainment, food, street theatre, market stalls, children's activities and funfair rides in Peel Park.

Bramham Horse Trials Wetherby, Vale of York; mid-June Ⓦ bramham-horse.co.uk. Four-day (Thurs–Sun) equestrian and social event.

Beverley Folk Festival East Riding; second half of June Ⓦ beverleyfestival.com. Weekend festival, held in a marquee on Beverley racecourse.

Grassington Festival Yorkshire Dales; second half of June Ⓦ grassington-festival.org.uk. A fortnight of art, music and performance with walks and workshops on subjects as varied as beekeeping and dry-stone walling.

Hebden Bridge Arts Festival West Yorkshire; end June/early July Ⓦ hebdenbridge.co.uk/festival. A ten-day festival of comedy, music, dance, drama, literature and visual arts.

JULY

Harrogate International Festival Vale of York; all July Ⓦ harrogate-internationalfestivals.com. Major festival held in venues across town, encompassing music, drama and film (the Summer Festival) and the Old Peculiar Crime Writing Festival.

Morris Dance Festival Robin Hood's Bay, North Yorkshire; first weekend July Ⓦ yorkshirecoastmorris.org.uk/weekend-of-dance. Dancing in the village hall, on the streets and on the beach.

York Early Music Festival Vale of York; early July Ⓦ ncem.co.uk /yemf. A ten-day festival staged at various venues in the city.

Bradfield Traditional Festival of Music South Yorkshire; mid-July. Ⓦ bradfieldfestivalofmusic.co.uk. Classical and some jazz music at St Nicholas Church, High Bradfield, over a long weekend.

Great Yorkshire Show Harrogate, Vale of York; mid-July Ⓦ greatyorkshireshow.co.uk. One of the country's premier agricultural shows, held over three days mid-week.

Seafest Festival Scarborough, North Yorkshire; mid-July Ⓦ scarborough.gov.uk. Weekend festival including boats, cooking demonstrations, free live music and children's workshops and entertainment, held mainly on the West Pier.

Wetherby Food Festival Vale of York; mid-July Ⓦ wetherbyfood festival.co.uk. Weekend festival, offering a variety of food stalls and local entertainment.

York Mystery Plays Vale of York; mid-July Ⓦ yorkmysteryplays .co.uk. Medieval plays performed from wagons on two consecutive Sundays every four years. Last held in 2014.

AUGUST

Yorkshire Day Various; Aug 1 Ⓦ yorkshire.com. Instigated in 1975 as a slightly tongue-in-cheek protest against the 1974 local government reorganization, and hosted in a different Yorkshire town each year. Includes civic ceremonies, charity fundraising events and such like.

Proms Spectacular Castle Howard, North Yorkshire; mid-Aug Ⓦ castlehoward.co.uk. Classical music in the park, with picnic and fireworks; usually held on a Saturday.

Whitby Regatta North Yorkshire; mid-Aug Ⓦ whitbyregatta .co.uk. A long weekend of yacht and rowing races, air displays and fireworks.

Ilkley Summer Festival West Yorkshire; towards end Aug Ⓦ summerfestival.ilkley.org. Music, drama and dance. The main events are held across five days (Wed–Sun), with subsidiary events – including a jazz day – from the end of July onwards.

Whitby Folk Week North Yorkshire; towards end Aug Ⓦ whitby folk.co.uk. Held over a week (Sat–Fri) in venues across the town, with concerts, dances, workshops and street entertainment.

Leeds Festival West Yorkshire; Aug bank holiday weekend Ⓦ leedsfestival.com. Around 70,000 music fans descend on Bramham Park outside Leeds for this major music event – it's the sister to Reading Festival.

SEPTEMBER

Art in the Gardens Sheffield, South Yorkshire; early Sept Ⓦ sheffield.gov.uk. For one weekend, Sheffield's superb Botanical Gardens are transformed into an art gallery.

Sowerby Bridge Rushbearing Festival West Yorkshire; early Sept Ⓦ rushbearing.com. Weekend festival with a craft market and morris dancing, with a decorated 16ft-high cart pulled by men in clogs.

Harrogate Autumn Flower Show Vale of York; mid-Sept Ⓦ flowershow.org.uk. Garden shows, a giant vegetable competition, children's events and more, held over three days.

Hull Folk Festival East Riding; mid-Sept Ⓦ hull-folk.co.uk. Weekend festival of folk music at Hull Marina, Victoria Pier, Humber St and the Old Town.

National Book Fair York, Vale of York; mid-Sept Ⓦ yorkbookfair .com. Held at York's racecourse over a weekend (Fri & Sat).

St Leger Festival Doncaster, South Yorkshire; mid-Sept Ⓦ doncaster-racecourse.co.uk. This is more than just the last classic horserace of the season – there are markets, street entertainers, live music and more, spread over four days (Wed–Sat).

York Festival of Food and Drink Vale of York; second half of Sept Ⓦ yorkfestival.com. Ten-day festival with food, beer and wine markets, hands-on cookery displays, demonstrations and wine tastings.

Beverley Chamber Music Festival East Riding; late Sept Ⓦ beverleychambermusicfestival.org.uk. Held in St Mary's Church, with soloists, trios and quartets – one performance per night Wednesday–Saturday.

Scarborough Jazz Festival North Yorkshire; last weekend in Sept Ⓦ scarboroughspa.co.uk. Popular jazz festival, with some interesting acts, staged in the Spa Complex.

OCTOBER

Ilkley Literature Festival West Yorkshire; early Oct Ⓦ ilkley literaturefestival.org.uk. Authors' events, discussions, performances and workshops, with lots of big names, over more than two weeks.

Light Night Leeds West Yorkshire; early Oct Ⓦ lightnightleeds .co.uk. Avant-garde goings-on in theatres, galleries, shopping arcades, museums, prison cells and city streets on a Friday evening.

Marsden Jazz Festival West Yorkshire; early Oct Ⓦ marsdenjazz festival.com. Weekend festival with traditional and modern jazz in various venues.

Beverley Blues Festival East Riding; mid-Oct Ⓦ beverleyblues .com. Three-day festival that has featured headliners from the Dan Burnett Blues Band to Tom Attah and the Bad Man Clan.

Off the Shelf Literary Festival Sheffield, South Yorkshire; last three weeks in Oct Ⓦ offtheshelf.org.uk. Sheffield's ever-improving literary festival is held in various venues.

Ted Hughes Festival Mytholmroyd, West Yorkshire; late Oct Ⓦ theelmettrust.org. Weekend event, including poetry readings, talks, walks and a poetry competition in honour of the local writer.

York Ghost Festival Vale of York; end Oct Ⓦ yorkghostfestival .co.uk. Ghost-related and Hallowe'en activities in various venues.

NOVEMBER–DECEMBER

Christkindelmarkt Leeds, West Yorkshire; Nov–Dec Ⓦ christmasmarkets.com. Traditional German Christmas market, including fairground rides, in Millennium Square.

St Nicholas Fayre York, Vale of York; Nov–Dec Ⓦ yorkfestivals .com. Christmas events in Parliament St, Barley Hall, the National Railway Museum and other venues.

Grassington Dickensian Festival Yorkshire Dales; the three Sats before Christmas Ⓦ grassington.uk.com/Dickensian-festival. Street markets and activities on a Victorian theme.

Bradford Animation Festival West Yorkshire; second half Dec Ⓦ baf.org.uk. Hosted by the National Media Museum, and lasting a week (Mon–Sat).

Sport and outdoor activities

Yorkshire offers a wide range of interesting and exciting outdoorsy things to do and some really nice places to do them in, not least its two (and a bit) national parks. In a county that is famed for its landscapes, you can throw yourself around the skies above it, range far and wide across it, venture into the dim dark spaces beneath it, or enjoy the North Sea fringing it. And if outdoor activities don't float your boat, you can always watch some top-quality spectator sports.

Walking

Yorkshire is renowned for its walking. Most of the best-known routes are in the **Dales** and the **North York Moors** – the National Park Authorities for these two areas (see p.224) offer lots of advice, maps and other information at their visitor

YORKSHIRE'S NATIONAL PARKS

Yorkshire is home to two of the UK's great **national parks**, together with a small part of a third (⊚ nationalparks.gov.uk).

North York Moors National Park (⊚ northyorkmoors.org.uk). Taking up the northeastern part of North Yorkshire, the North York Moors park is bliss for hikers and cyclists, and has a rugged coastline that's excellent for watersports. The North York Moors can also be enjoyed from a train, either on the North Yorkshire Moors railway, or the Esk Valley line.

Peak District National Park (⊚ peakdistrict.org.uk). Most of this national park lies outside Yorkshire, but its northeastern edge occupies a sliver of countryside west of Sheffield. Travel west from Yorkshire's second city, and the transition from the heavily urban to the magnificently rural is startlingly immediate.

Yorkshire Dales National Park (⊚ yorkshiredales.org.uk). This park, which occupies much of the northwest of North Yorkshire, is heaven for walkers, cyclists and pony trekkers. You can also go potholing or visit famous show caves, and there are a number of waterfalls and castles. Those who want to see the countryside in relaxed mood can enjoy it from a train on the Settle to Carlisle line, or from the Wensleydale Railway.

centres – and there are spectacular walks along the coast. Some areas – Malham, for example – can get crowded, but it doesn't take much effort to get off the beaten track. Elsewhere too, even in the most heavily urbanized areas, there are walks galore. Every town and city, even in the most urban, industrialized areas, has its waymarked paths (ask for maps at the local tourist office, and for Leeds and Sheffield take a look at ⊚ walkit.com). There are numerous walks around Yorkshire Water's reservoirs and along canals, and circular walks around most Dales and North York Moors villages. Themed walks, too, are popular, adding interest to urban strolls. In rural areas organized walks include Ingleton Waterfalls Trail, Hardcastle Crags near Hebden Bridge, Ramsden Reservoir Walk in Holmfirth, and many more. Check at tourist offices or consult ⊚ yorkshire.com.

Several **long-distance national trails** cross parts of Yorkshire – the Pennine Way/Pennine Bridleway, the Cleveland Way and the Yorkshire Wolds Way, together with others like the Trans Pennine Trail, the Minster Way, the Wolds Way and many more. For details check ⊚ nationaltrail.co.uk and ⊚ yorkshire.com. You might also want to test yourself on the Yorkshire Three Peaks Walk (see p.190).

Cycling

Cycling is a popular pastime in Yorkshire, especially in the industrial areas – there are no fewer than sixty clubs in West Yorkshire alone. Indeed, the county's dedication to cycling led to the Tour de France mounting its high-profile start (*Le Grand Depart*) in Yorkshire in 2014.

Across the county you'll often see twenty or thirty cyclists bowling along in their full cycling gear, a study in ferocious dedication. However, for the weekend cyclist the least challenging cycling is in the Vale of York and East Yorkshire – it's far less hilly. Elsewhere, routes along canals and reservoirs can also be relatively gentle, or forest rides such as those in Dalby Forest.

The city of York lies at the intersection of two routes on the **National Cycle Network** – from Middlesbrough to Selby and Doncaster (National Route 65) and from Beverley and Pocklington to the east (National Route 66). At the time of writing the western section of this route (to Harrogate and Leeds) had not been completed. Other routes with sections in Yorkshire include National Routes 1, 6, 62, 67, 68 and 69, and regional routes 10 and 52. Check out the **Sustrans** website (⊚ sustrans.org.uk) – new routes and sections are being added all the time. Sustrans also publishes a good series of waterproof cycle **maps** (1:100,000) and regional guides.

Rock-climbing

Yorkshire offers a wide range of **rock-climbing** opportunities on both gritstone and limestone routes. Consult the Rockfax databases for both types of climbing (⊚ rockfax.com) – number and type of routes, range of grades, length and difficulty of approach and how sunny/shaded they are – and also the UK Climbing website (⊚ ukclimbing .com). If the weather's bad, you can climb indoors at Foundry Indoor Climbing Centre or Climbing Works in Sheffield (see p.57). Or if you just want to sit in comfort and watch other people doing all the work, get along to the Sheffield Adventure

Film Festival (ShAFF) at the Showroom Cinema, Sheffield, in March.

In addition, there are several activity centres in Yorkshire that involve **climbing wires** and swinging from poles. Try: Go Ape at Dalby (see p.244); Aerial Extreme at Bedale (see p.214) or How Stean Gorge's Via Ferata (see p.206).

Potholing and caving

Yorkshire's great **potholing** and **caving** region is the Yorkshire Dales where the area's geology has evolved to produce some dazzling natural phenomena. Where surface millstone grit and carboniferous limestone abut, the water cascading off the impervious former dissolves the soluble latter, creating elaborate formations of caves, gorges and chasms. Incomprehensible to claustrophobes, unaccompanied clambering about underground is not recommended for the untrained. But there are numerous show caves, including White Scar Cave at Ingleton near Ribblesdale and Stump Cross Caverns in Nidderdale, where you can enjoy the beauties of stalagmites and stalactites, travertine formations and so on as part of an organized tour. And you can arrange potholing and caving instruction from experts and accompanied expeditions through private companies such as ⓦyorkshiredalesguides .co.uk.

Fishing

Yorkshire offers good **fishing**, and enthusiasts of every type of angling will find places in which to indulge their sport. ⓦyorkshirefishing.net lists more than two hundred day-ticket fishing venues – rivers, reservoirs, lakes, canals and gravel pits – across the whole of South, West, North and East Yorkshire. For sea fishing, again there are lots of opportunities to get stuck into beach, boat and kayak fishing – check out ⓦwhitbyseaanglers.co.uk, ⓦwhitby-sea -fishing.co.uk and ⓦdiscoveryorkshirecoast.com, as well as numerous sites for boat charter companies. Or just stroll along the quays at any of Yorkshire's harbours and ports – fishing trips are advertised at them all.

Watersports

Yorkshire has a long **coastline** that falls into two sections – the headlands, cliffs and bays of the North Yorkshire coast, and the long gentle beaches of East Yorkshire. There are of places, then, to swim and snorkel, and not only the famous beaches of

Scarborough, Bridlington and Filey, but also lesser known resorts like Runswick Bay, Sandsend, Hornsea or Withernsea. Where more facilities are needed – for sailing, watersports and windsurfing, canoeing, sea-kayaking and jet skiing, there are numerous clubs and water sports centres, not only on the coast but on lakes and reservoirs as well.

Surfing and jet skiing

Yorkshire's broad beaches, while not able to compete with those in the premier surfing areas like the West Country, can still allow dedicated surfers to chase the waves. Best bet for surfers is **Scarborough** – try Cayton Bay Surf Shop and Surf School (ⓦscarboroughsurfschool.co.uk). Meanwhile, for jet skiing, Fosse Hill Jet Ski Centre (ⓦfossehill.co.uk) in East Yorkshire, between Beverley and Hornsea, is a good bet.

Sailing, windsurfing and sea kayaking

There are numerous clubs and watersports centres where enthusiasts can enjoy their hobby and beginners can arrange tuition.

SAILING CLUBS AND WATERSPORTS CENTRES

Allerthorpe Lakeland Park Near York ⓦallerthorpelakeland park.co.uk. More than 50 acres of lakes and grounds, offering a variety of watersports (pedalos, kayaks, canoes, windsurfing and sailing) and a campsite, children's playground and café. Instruction available.

Craven Sailing Club Embsay reservoir ⓦcravensailingclub.org.uk. Windsurfing, canoeing and kayaking, for beginners and the more experienced. Instruction available.

East Barnby Outdoor Education Centre Near Whitby ⓦoutdoored.co.uk. Activity centre that offers tuition in canoeing and sea kayaking (as well as climbing).

Filey Sailing Club ⓦfileysc.co.uk. At the base of cliffs north of the town, offering training in different types of sailing as well as a full calendar of racing.

Hornsea Mere ⓦhornseameremarine.com. Sailing, rowing and fishing based on Hornsea's famous mere. Café and putting green.

Thornton Steward Sailing Club Near Bedale ⓦthornton-steward -sailingclub.co.uk. Sailing (including tuition) and racing in pleasant surroundings with miles of footpaths and a comfortable clubhouse.

Yorkshire Dales Sailing Club Grimwith Reservoir, near Grassington ⓦyorkshiredales.sc. Sailing and windsurfing for old hands and beginners, together with a programme of racing.

In the air

Yorkshire has a number of good places to check out should you want to get up there into the wide blue yonder – be it by parachuting, gliding, hang-gliding, paragliding or ballooning.

AIR ADVENTURE OPERATORS

Active Edge Near Harrogate ⓦ activeedge.co.uk. Paragliding and paramotoring training.

Airborne Adventures ⓦ airborne.co.uk. Balloon flights over the Yorkshire Dales.

Airsports Rufforth Aerodrome, Vale of York ⓦ airsportstraining .co.uk. Training for microlight instruction.

Dales Hang-gliding and Paragliding Club ⓦ dhpc.org.uk. For experienced hang-gliders – lists 21 flying sites.

Sunsoar Paragliding West of Swaledale in Kirkby Stephen ⓦ sunsoar-paragliding.com. Paragliding courses just over the Cumbria border.

York Gliding Centre Rufforth Aerodrome, Vale of York ⓦ york glidingcentre.co.uk. Friendly club offering trial lessons and training.

Yorkshire Gliding Club ⓦ ygc.co.uk. On Sutton Bank, North York Moors (see p.228).

Football

Yorkshire's connection with **association football** (**soccer**) goes back to the game's very beginnings – **Sheffield FC** is recognized by the European and World administrators of the beautiful game as its birthplace. Despite near fanatical support in parts of the county, Yorkshire's many teams have in recent times been very disappointing in terms of their achievements – at the time of writing **Hull City** (officially Hull City Tigers, though many fans are contemptuous of the new title imposed by the owner in 2013; ⓦ hullcitytigers.com) was the only Yorkshire team to grace the game's top level, the Premiership, while arch rival Lancashire boasted five. Nonetheless, seeing a match played by teams such as Sheffield Wednesday (ⓦ swfc.co.uk), Leeds United (ⓦ leedsunited.com), Rotherham United (ⓦ themillers .co.uk), Huddersfield Town (ⓦ htafc.com), Sheffield United (ⓦ sufc.co.uk), Bradford City (ⓦ bradfordcityfc .co.uk), Doncaster Rovers (ⓦ doncasterroversfc.co.uk) and Barnsley (ⓦ barnsleyfc.co.uk) can be great fun when visiting this part of the world. **Tickets** can be bought in person at the ground, over the phone or online. Book as early as you can, and bear in mind that match-day prices are usually higher than pre-booked ones. Expect to pay in the region of £20.

Cricket

As for **cricket**, Yorkshire Cricket Club, the most successful in the sport's history, with more than thirty Championships – and famous for, until 1992, refusing to use any players not born in the county – is currently riding high again after some time in the doldrums. Great Yorkshire cricketing names abound: Len Hutton, Fred Trueman, Geoff Boycott,

Ray Illingworth and Brian Close are discussed, argued about and revered throughout the county. In Yorkshire, even an umpire – Dickie Bird – can become a star. Cricket is widely played across the county, with many local leagues and teams, and the fortunes of the national teams of England, India, Pakistan, Sri Lanka and Bangladesh are keenly followed. To watch an international or club match at the county's main ground, Headingley, near Leeds, choose which day(s) you want to attend and buy online at ⓦ yorkshireccc.com.

Rugby

The third of Yorkshire's great sporting quartet is **Rugby League**, invented in the county when breakaway Rugby Union clubs, fed up with the sport's strictly enforced amateurism, formed their own league in which players could be paid expenses. This took place in the *George Hotel* in Huddersfield. From then on, the rules of Rugby League and Rugby Union diverged – for example the lineout was abolished and the number of players reduced from 15 to 13. More recently, with the advent of the Super League, the season was moved from the winter to the summer, and clubs started to adopt American-style names like the Leeds Rhinos (ⓦ therhinos.co.uk). Tickets for games can be bought at the ticket office, by phone or online.

Horseracing and golf

Yorkshire has nine of the UK's most famous **racetracks**, which hold more than 170 meetings each year. Six of the nine – York (ⓦ yorkracecourse .co.uk), Beverley (ⓦ beverley-racecourse.co.uk), Pontefract (ⓦ pontefract-races.co.uk), Redcar (ⓦ red carracing.co.uk), Ripon (ⓦ ripon-races.co.uk) and Thirsk (ⓦ thirskracecourse.net) – hold only flat race meetings. Two are mixed – Catterick (ⓦ catterick bridge.co.uk) and Doncaster (ⓦ doncaster-racecourse .co.uk) – and one, Wetherby, specializes in National Hunt meetings (ⓦ wetherbyracing.co.uk).

Meanwhile, the county can also boast some of the finest **golf courses** in the UK.

GOLF COURSES

Alwoodley Golf Club Just north of Leeds ⓦ alwoodley.co.uk. Regularly hosts county and national tournaments.

Bradford Golf Club Near the village of Hawksworth ⓦ bradford golfclub.co.uk. One of Yorkshire's best-kept courses.

Fixby Golf Club Huddersfield, a mile from J24 on the M62 ⓦ huddersfield-golf.co.uk. "The Home of Yorkshire Golf" (the Yorkshire Union of Golf Courses is based here).

Fulford Golf Club A mile from York city centre Ⓦ fulfordgolfclub
.co.uk. Fulford has been played by, among others, Jacklin, Lyle, Torrance,
Norman, Weiskopf and Trevino.

Ganton Golf Club Vale of Pickering, between York and
Scarborough Ⓦ gantongolfclub.com. Gary Player called this "the only
inland course worthy of hosting the Open Championship".

Ilkley Golf Club Ⓦ ilkleygolfclub.co.uk. Deceptively difficult course
– with a par 69. The course record, held by Colin Montgomery, is only five
shots below this.

Moor Allerton Golf Club Just outside Leeds Ⓦ magc.co.uk. Many
world-class players have played the course during national and
international events, including Seve Ballesteros, Tom Weiskopf, Tony
Jacklin, Gary Player and Greg Norman.

Moortown Golf Club Leeds Ⓦ moortown-gc.co.uk. Created by top
course designer Dr Alister MacKenzie.

Pannal Golf Club Near Harrogate Ⓦ pannalgolfclub.co.uk. On
what was once part of the Harewood Estate.

Shopping

**In addition to the usual chains and many
out-of-town retail centres, every major
town in South and West Yorkshire has its
own covered market, some of which have
become bywords for inexpensive, good-
quality fresh meat and vegetables, and
for bargains in a range of clothes,
electronic equipment and more.**

Weekly **street markets** are often the best
places to pick up craft items – look out for railway
memorabilia, steel cutlery and pewter and even
Mouseman wood items (see p.229) – though you
may have to wade among a proliferation of
twee bric-a-brac to find anything truly original.
Markets are also the only places (apart from
antique shops and some secondhand shops)
where haggling is acceptable, even expected.
There are particularly good markets in Sheffield ,
Rotherham , Barnsley , Doncaster , Leeds , Halifax ,
Huddersfield and Wakefield .

Markets are good places to buy **Yorkshire food
specialities** including artisan cheeses, local meats
and other foods. There are also numerous **farmers'
markets** (see p.27) where good Yorkshire food
products are on offer. You'll also find similarly
authentic local items in **rural farmshops**, usually
signposted by the side of the road.

Retail villages and outlets are popular in
Yorkshire, where designer brands are available at
a fraction of the original cost – **Hornsea's
Freeport Outlet** (see p.299) claims to have been
the first in the UK. And for top-end, up-to-the-
minute designer shopping, you could hardly do

better than the **Victoria Quarter** in Leeds (see
p.101), which boasts the first Harvey Nichols to be
opened outside London.

Museum shops, too, can be a happy hunting
ground for shoppers, especially of good quality art
and craft, industrial artefacts and books. We've
mentioned some of the best in the Guide.

Most goods in the UK, with the chief exceptions
of books and food, are subject to 20 percent
Value Added Tax (VAT), which is included in the
marked price. Visitors from non-EU countries can
save money through the Retail Export Scheme
(tax-free shopping), which allows a refund of VAT
on goods to be taken out of the country. (Savings
will usually be minimal for EU nationals because
of the rates at which the goods will be taxed
upon import to the home country.) Note that
not all shops participate in this scheme (those
doing so will display a sign to this effect), and that
you cannot reclaim VAT charged on hotel bills or
other services.

Travelling with children

**Yorkshire is a wonderful area for family
holidays, with lots to do: beaches, theme
parks, child-friendly museums and
castles, petting farms and, for the older
ones, adventure activities.**

Accommodation options are rife, from campsites,
some with activities and kids' clubs, to self-catering
accommodation and child-friendly hotels; the old
seaside boarding house dragon-landlady is a dying
breed. Some hotels, B&Bs and campsites won't
accept children under a certain age (usually 12),
though in the big family holiday areas like Scarborough or Bridlington children are widely accepted –
it would be a bad business decision not to do so.

When you're travelling around, you'll find
attitudes to travellers with children in Yorkshire
similar to those in other areas of the UK – compared
to countries like Greece or Spain, parents with
young children can sometimes feel a little
unwelcome, though this varies with an increasing
number of places – pubs and restaurants, even
churches and cathedrals – providing boxes of
toys, colouring books and crayons to keep the
youngsters happy. A number of Yorkshire towns
and cities such as Rotherham and Hull have remodelled their public parks and now offer excellent
children's play areas. **Baby-changing apparatus** is

> ### TOP TEN FAMILY FUN
> **Eureka!** See p.113
> **Flamingo Land** See p.242
> **Forbidden Corner** See p.212
> **Lightwater Valley** See p.176
> **Magna** See p.60
> **National Railway Museum** See p.154
> **North Yorkshire Moors Railway** See p.239
> **Royal Armouries** See p.91
> **Tropical Butterfly House** See p.61
> **Yorkshire Sculpture Park** See p.132

usually available in shopping centres and train stations, while pharmacies and supermarkets stock a useful range of products (shops in rural areas will offer less choice). The situation as regards children in pubs varies – they are permitted where food is being served (and that includes at least one room in most pubs these days), and there are often family rooms or beer gardens (though since the total smoking ban the latter sometimes sit under a cloud of cigarette smoke). It all rather depends on the attitude of the landlord/landlady – some are vigilant in enforcing the letter of the law and see children as a nuisance to be kept at bay, others are as welcoming as anyone could hope. Under-5s generally travel free on **public transport** and get in free to attractions; 5- to 16-year-olds are usually entitled to **concessionary rates** of up to half the adult rate/fare. Don't expect huge discounts for children in the main commercial tourist attractions, though – it rarely amounts to more than a pound or two, though family tickets (which we have detailed, where they exist, throughout the Guide) can save money.

Travel essentials

Climate

Because of its size and topographical variety, the weather in Yorkshire can be changeable, with marked differences between places that are geographically close together. In particular, the weather on the North Yorkshire coast, on the heights of the Moors and Dales, in the Wolds, on the flatlands of East Yorkshire, and in the industrial south and west can vary between areas and from minute to minute. The advice would be to have lots of layers, and to hope for the best, prepare for the worst.

Costs

Yorkshire's as fine a place to live the good life as anywhere in the UK. You can stay at top-end hotels, eat at Michelin-starred restaurants and buy designer clothes and gifts to your heart's content. However, if you want to make a determined effort to keep costs down, that is perfectly possible too.

Your biggest cost is likely to be accommodation, so to get the best deal, always get online or phone around when looking for a **hotel**. Smaller hotels, guesthouses and B&Bs can be very reasonable, and even the big luxurious places, who have rates which change from day to day, can be surprisingly so if you catch them at the right time. **Hostels**, those of the YHA and others, often pan out at around £20 a night or less, and campsites are even cheaper.

As a rule, it's cheapest to use **public transport**, especially in the cities – it is fast, efficient and reasonably priced. However, if you're travelling in a group then **taxis** can be even cheaper, and far more convenient.

When it comes to **eating**, reckon on eating picnics for at least some of your meals, or opting for self-catering accommodation. There will always be good fresh and inexpensive food to be found in your local market, with especially good options at the farmers' markets (see p.27). For eating out, pub food is usually very good value, especially as publicans are aware that Yorkshire folk have a reputation for demanding value for money.

There are also several ways of keeping the bill for **attractions** down. Becoming a member of the **National Trust** (Ⓦ nationaltrust.org.uk) and/ or **English Heritage** (Ⓦ english-heritage.org.uk) will give you free entry to all their properties – between them they have nearly fifty properties in Yorkshire. Membership costs £58 (NT) and £49 (EH) per adult, while entry to sites for non-members ranges between £4 and £6. Within this Guide, National Trust and English Heritage properties are indicated with the initials NT and EH next to the price information.

Visitors to York can get hold of a **York Pass** (1–3 days, £36–58; Ⓦ yorkpass.com), which not only gets you in for free to more than thirty of the biggest attractions in the city and its surrounding area, but also gives you discount vouchers for lots of other sites, together with entertainment venues, restaurants and shops.

TOP TEN FREE ATTRACTIONS

Henry Moore Institute See p.90
Hepworth Gallery See p.130
Hull's Museum Quarter See p.277
National Coal Mining Museum See p.131
National Media Museum See p.103
National Railway Museum See p.154
Royal Armouries Museum See p.91
Weston Park Museum See p.51
Winter Garden and Millennium Galleries See p.46
Yorkshire Sculpture Park See p.132

Furthermore, some top-notch Yorkshire museums are free (see box above), and of course, many of Yorkshire's most popular pastimes, such as walking, cycling (if you've got your own bike), spending a day at the beach or at a local park, don't cost you anything.

Crime and personal safety

Crime in Yorkshire follows similar patterns to the rest of the country. Rural areas are relatively crime free, but in the big cities you should exercise some caution depending on which areas of town you're in. In the main tourist areas you should take the same precautions as you would anywhere else in the world – avoid the overt display of expensive cameras, watches and jewellery, don't flash wads of money, keep an eye out for pickpockets. It's not necessarily in the city centres that difficulties might be encountered – they are well policed, covered by CCTV and patrolled by community support officers. Away from the immediate centres, though, you should keep your guard up. In common with the cities, even relatively small towns can become raucous on Friday and Saturday nights, with local youth indulging in the binge-drinking that has become a national pastime. If you are robbed, you'll need to report it to the police in order to get a Crime Reference Number for your insurers.

Emergency numbers – for police, fire brigade, ambulance, mountain rescue and coastguard – are ☎999 or ☎112.

Electricity

The **electricity supply** in Yorkshire, in common with the rest of the UK, is 240 volts AC, delivered through sockets that accept plugs with three square pins. American appliances will need a transformer to step up the voltage, European, Australian and New Zealand only a plug adapter.

Entry requirements

Citizens of the European Union have the right to move freely throughout the UK armed only with a passport or ID card. Those from the USA, Canada, South Africa, Australia and New Zealand need only a valid passport to stay for up to six months without a visa. Citizens from the European Economic Union and Switzerland do not need visas, though there are regulations concerning permission to work. All other nationalities require a visa, which can be obtained from the British Consul's office in the country of origin. For detailed requirements, see ⓦ ukvisas.gov.uk.

Health

Citizens of EU and EEA countries are entitled to free medical treatment within the National Health Service (which covers most doctors and hospitals) on production of a **European Health Insurance Card** (ⓦehic.org.uk) obtainable before leaving home. Similarly, a number of countries have reciprocal agreements with the UK (Australia and New Zealand, for example), and their citizens too are entitled to free treatment. All others must pay for treatment, so holiday health insurance (see p.36) is strongly recommended.

For minor complaints, you can visit a pharmacist (known as **chemists** in Britain), though they can dispense only a limited range of drugs without a doctor's prescription. Most chemists are open standard shop hours, though some are closed at weekends and in large towns some stay open until 10pm – information will be posted on the shop doors. For generic, off-the-shelf pain-relief tablets, cold cures and the like, the local supermarket is usually the cheapest option.

More complicated complaints and injuries can be dealt with at a **doctor's (GP's) surgery** – any tourist office or hotel should be able to point you in the right direction, but you might have to wait a while for an appointment. For issues that require immediate attention, you can turn up at the 24-hour casualty (A&E) department of the local hospital, but will need to be prepared to wait. In an **emergency** – if you become seriously ill, can't move or are in extreme difficulties – call an ambulance on ☎999 or ☎112. And if you need

ROUGH GUIDES TRAVEL INSURANCE

Rough Guides has teamed up with WorldNomads.com to offer great travel insurance deals. Policies are available to residents of over 150 countries, with cover for a wide range of adventure sports, 24hr emergency assistance, high levels of medical and evacuation cover and a stream of travel safety information. Roughguides.com users can take advantage of their policies online 24/7, from anywhere in the world – even if you're already travelling. And since plans often change when you're on the road, you can extend your policy and even claim online. Roughguides.com users who buy travel insurance with WorldNomads.com can also leave a positive footprint and donate to a community development project. For more information, go to ⓦroughguides.com/travel-insurance.

medical help fast, and think you may need to go to the A&E – but it's not a ❶999 emergency – you can ring ❶111 for advice.

Insurance

Standard holiday insurance is perfectly adequate for most holiday visits to Yorkshire. However, more extreme sorts of activity and sport may need to be covered separately. So, if you're intent on gliding, parachuting, rock-climbing or any other activity that you're not sure of, consult your insurer.

Internet access

Many **public libraries** and **tourist offices** offer free internet access, and the availability of **wi-fi** is now widespread, with lots of hotels, guesthouses, B&Bs, hostels, pubs, cafés and even campsites now offering this facility. Chains such as *Starbucks*, *McDonald's* and *Wetherspoon's* increasingly offer wi-fi as a matter of course.

Mail

Controversially privatized in 2013, the Royal Mail (ⓦroyalmail.com) still provides a nationwide delivery service – consult its website for details of postal services and current postage costs. You can

DISTANCES, WEIGHTS AND MEASURES

Distances (and speeds) on English signposts are in miles, and beer is still served in pints. For everything else – money, weights and measures – a confusing mixture of metric and imperial systems is used: fuel is dispensed by the litre, while meat, milk and vegetables may be sold in either or both systems.

also find individual post offices and their opening hours by using its "branch finder" facility. In the big cities main offices stay open all day Saturday, while in small and rural communities you'll find sub-post offices operating out of a variety of retail outlets. Rural post offices are under threat, so if you can, use them or lose them. As well as in post offices, stamps are on sale at newsagents and other stores advertising them. Postage rates depend on the size and weight of the envelope or package, and when you want it to arrive – first-class should arrive next day, second-class within three working days. Airmail to European destinations, too, should arrive within three working days, and to countries outside Europe within five. Slower "surface mail" and express delivery services are also available.

Maps

Yorkshire is a relatively coherent area, though many of the **maps** which cover it are either too general (and include the rest of the North of England, for example) or concentrate on one particular part of Yorkshire: there are many tourist maps of the Dales and the North York Moors, including some very useful guides produced by the two National Park authorities (ⓦyorkshiredales.org.uk and ⓦnorth yorkmoors.org.uk). Maps for walks and cycle rides can also be downloaded from their websites. One of the most useful general maps to cover the whole county, and which includes a mass of information about attractions in the area, is the Philips Red Books *Leisure and Tourist Map of Yorkshire* (ⓦoctopusbooks.co.uk).

The principal producer of maps on a large enough scale for walkers and cyclists is the **Ordnance Survey** – their Landranger (pink, 1:50,000) and Explorer (orange 1:25,000) are the most useful. Landranger maps 98–101, 104–107 and 110–111 cover Yorkshire, the Explorer series are too numerous to mention, but look out for the ones (prefixed OL) that cover particularly popular holiday areas, like OL2 Yorkshire Dales Southern and Western Areas or OL26 North York Moors Western Area. The **National Cycle Network** produces excellent waterproof maps of their routes (Ⓦsustrans .org.uk) and also lists other local sources of cycling route maps – 24 for Yorkshire.

Otherwise, for general route-finding there are numerous road atlases: those published by the AA, RAC, Geographers A–Z and Collins for example, with scales of around 1:250,000. And there's always satnav, which is reliable in all but the deepest, steepest-sided valleys.

Most of these maps are available from large bookshops or specialist map and travel stores, either on site or online. In the UK main bookshops usually stock a good range of local/regional maps, while those passing through London should call in at Stanfords (Ⓦstanfords.co.uk), England's premier map and travel specialist. Yorkshire's tourist offices also stock a wide range of maps and guides, including some excellent locally produced ones detailing walks and bike rides in their areas.

Money

Britain's currency is the **pound** sterling (£), divided into 100 pence (p). Coins come in denominations of 1p, 2p, 5p, 10p, 20p, 50p and £1 and £2. Notes are in denominations of £5, £10, £20 and £50. Scottish and Northern Irish banknotes are legal tender throughout Britain, though some traders may be unwilling to accept them. If you're having difficulty getting rid of them, change them at a bank. Every sizeable town and village has a branch of at least one of the main high-street banks: Barclays, Halifax, HSBC, Lloyds, TSB and NatWest. The easiest way to get hold of cash is to use your debit card in an **ATM (cashpoint)**; there's usually a daily withdrawal limit, often around £250. You'll find ATMs outside banks, at all major points of arrival and motorway service areas, at most large supermarkets, some petrol stations and even in some pubs, rural post offices and village shops (though a charge may be levied on cash withdrawals at small, stand-alone ATMs). Depending on your bank and your debit card, you may also be able to ask for "cash back" when you shop at supermarkets.

Finally, **credit cards** can be used widely either in ATMs or over the counter. MasterCard and Visa are accepted in most hotels, shops and restaurants in Britain, American Express and Diners Club less so. Plastic is less useful in rural areas, and smaller establishments, such as B&Bs, will often accept cash only. Remember that cash advances from ATMs using your credit card are treated as loans, with interest accruing daily from the date of withdrawal. **Contactless payments** (ie made by simply holding your card over a card reader rather than punching in a PIN) are accepted at a growing range of outlets for sums of £20 or less – participating businesses display a logo similar to the wi-fi symbol, which is also marked on applicable cards.

Opening hours and public holidays

General **business hours** for most businesses, shops and offices are Monday to Saturday 9am to 5.30 or 6pm, although the supermarket chains tend to stay open until 8 or 9pm from Monday to Saturday, with larger ones staying open round the clock. Many major stores and supermarkets now open on Sundays, too, usually from 11am or noon to 4pm, though some provincial towns still retain an early-closing day (usually Wed) when most shops close at 1pm. Banks usually have core opening hours of Monday to Friday 9.30am to 4.30pm (though some, especially in big cities, open earlier and close later). Some branches also open on Saturday mornings. You can usually get fuel any time of the day or night in larger towns and cities (though note that not all motorway service stations are open 24hr). Full opening hours for specific museums, galleries and other tourist attractions are given in the Guide. Banks,

---

PUBLIC HOLIDAYS

Britain's public holidays (sometimes referred to as Bank Holidays) are:

Jan 1
Good Friday
Easter Monday
First Mon in May
Last Mon in May
Last Mon in Aug
Dec 25
Dec 26

Note that if Jan 1, Dec 25 or Dec 26 falls on a Saturday or Sunday, the next weekday becomes a public holiday.

CALLING ABROAD FROM ENGLAND

Australia ☎0061 + area code minus the initial zero + number.
New Zealand ☎0064 + area code minus the initial zero + number.
US and Canada ☎001 + area code + number.
Republic of Ireland ☎00353 + area code minus the initial zero + number.
South Africa ☎0027 + area code + number.

businesses and most shops close on public holidays, though large supermarkets, small corner shops and many tourist attractions don't. However, nearly all museums, galleries and other attractions are closed on Christmas Day and New Year's Day, with many also closed on Boxing Day (Dec 26).

Phones

The flimsy **BT phone kiosk** is still to be found throughout Yorkshire, though they're not as ubiquitous as once they were. Most will allow you to pay by coin, credit card or phone card. There are, too, quite a few surviving red phone boxes in rural areas (the iconic design by Sir Giles Gilbert Scott), and in Hull and Beverley you'll see the same ones but cream in colour, and minus the crown over the door. For **mobile phones** (cell phones), which are as common in Yorkshire than everywhere else, coverage is good in Yorkshire's cities but can be patchy in the Dales and the North York Moors.

Time

Greenwich Mean Time (GMT) is used from late October to late March, when the clocks go forward an hour for **British Summer Time** (BST). GMT is five hours ahead of the US Eastern Standard Time and ten hours behind Australian Eastern Standard Time.

Tourist information

Yorkshire's tourist industry is promoted by an umbrella tourist organization, **Welcome to Yorkshire**, made up of the relevant individual tourist authorities for the county, which cover everything from local accommodation to festival dates, attractions to food. Its well-organized website (Ⓦyorkshire.com) offers sophisticated bookmarking and itinerary-planning facilities, a mobile site for people using handhelds, and a twitter feed. **Tourist offices** (also called Tourist Information Centres, or "TICs" for short) exist in virtually every Yorkshire town, though they can vary from large, well-stocked, enthusiastically staffed offices in the principal tourist areas (York, say) to a bank of tourist leaflets and booklets in an unstaffed corner of the local council offices or the local library (Barnsley for example, or Huddersfield). Locations and opening hours of all the tourist offices are listed throughout this Guide. Opening hours vary, with no real pattern, though hours tend to be longer the more popular the area, and usually get shorter out of season. Staff will nearly always be able to book accommodation, reserve space on guided tours, and sell guidebooks, maps and walk leaflets. They can also provide lists of local cafés, restaurants and pubs, though they aren't supposed to recommend particular places. An increasing number of offices have internet access for visitors, but rarely have the space to look after baggage while you sally forth.

Yorkshire's two great **national parks** (Ⓦyorkshire dales.org.uk and Ⓦnorthyorkmoors.org.uk) have their own dedicated information centres, which offer similar services to tourist offices but can also provide expert guidance on local walks and outdoor pursuits.

Travellers with disabilities

All new public buildings in the UK – including museums, galleries and cinemas – are obliged to provide **wheelchair access**, though historic sights can be more problematic. Train stations and airports are generally fully accessible, many buses have easy-access boarding ramps, and dropped kerbs and signalled crossings are the rule in every city and town. The number of accessible hotels and restaurants is also growing, and Blue Badge parking bays are available almost everywhere, from shopping malls to museums. When it comes to accommodation, look out for the symbols of the National Accessibility Scheme, which rates accommodation regarding suitability for people with disabilities (Ⓦtourismforall.org.uk). If you have specific requirements, it's always best to talk first to your travel agent, chosen hotel or tour operator, or individual restaurants, attractions and venues you hope to use.

On the railways, blind, partially-sighted people and wheelchair-users are automatically entitled to **reduced fares**, and people with other disabilities can apply for a Disabled Person's Railcard (Ⓦ disabledpersons-railcard.co.uk), offering reductions of a third on the cost of most journeys. Buses, alas, offer no discounts for disabled passengers. Many tourist attractions offer concessionary rates, too: for reviews of leading attractions written specifically by and for disabled people, take a look at the *Rough Guide to Accessible Britain* (Ⓦ accessible guide.co.uk).

South Yorkshire

CONISBROUGH CASTLE

1

South Yorkshire

Decline in the iron, coal and steel industries hit South Yorkshire hard, leaving behind much economic and social deprivation. The region may not spring to mind as your main holiday destination, but it does have a surprising amount to offer. It's well endowed with medieval abbeys, castles and churches, and boasts a full spectrum of interesting industrial museums, from small, enthusiast-run places to the internationally renowned Magna science centre. There's even, in among the post-industrial grunge, some pockets of lovely countryside.

The decline of the traditional British heavy industries – iron and steel (mainly in Sheffield and Rotherham), coal (everywhere, but especially in Barnsley and Doncaster), and engineering – at the end of the twentieth century took away much of the region's identity and threatened to rob it of its soul. However, South Yorkshire has made sterling efforts to adapt to twenty-first-century realities, and with the help of national and European funding is making great strides in renewing its infrastructure and injecting a new lease of life.

Set in appealing Peak District countryside, **Sheffield** is the main city destination, metropolitan in ways that Rotherham, Doncaster and Barnsley are not. Though it lacks killer attractions, its big city buzz is unmistakeable, with a vibrant, largely pedestrianized centre focused on the impressive **Peace Gardens** and **Winter Garden** and a lively pub and music scene. **Rotherham**, though much more a traditional industrial town, has a world-class tourist attraction in the magnificent **Magna** science centre nearby; **Doncaster**, another largely industrial town, has one of Yorkshire's most famous **racetracks**; and **Barnsley** is well known for its **market** – and for producing Michael Parkinson, quintessential Yorkshireman and national treasure.

In between South Yorkshire's four great urban centres is some striking **countryside**, from the beginnings of the Dukeries on the Nottinghamshire borders south of Doncaster to the pockets of rolling parkland around Barnsley and the edges of the Peak District west of Sheffield.

Sheffield and around

SHEFFIELD, once the greatest manufacturer of high-grade steel in the world, is reinventing itself as a vital, modern, provincial city. Its vitality, culture and heritage make it a great day-trip or weekend break, and certainly an essential stopover on any visit to this part of Yorkshire. While the ebbing of the industrial tide has left behind its brackish pools of dereliction, Sheffield hasn't been slow to recognize the resulting opportunities, both in terms of industrial preservation – such as at **Abbeydale Industrial Hamlet**'s water-powered knife-grinding works or **Kelham Island Museum**'s collection of steel industry behemoths – and in the redevelopment of derelict land with the **Meadowhall** shopping complex. Within five minutes' walk of the centre are the giant

DONCASTER RACECOURSE

Highlights

❶ **Peace Gardens, Sheffield** Along with the neighbouring Winter Garden, this is the heart of South Yorkshire's greatest city, vibrant on a summer afternoon. **See p.46**

❷ **Fat Cat, Sheffield** Time-capsule pub, with real ale, good food and no gaming machines. **See p.55**

❸ **Magna, Rotherham** One of the best, most innovative industrial museums in the world. **See p.60**

❹ **Rother Valley Country Park** Wide open spaces with cable water skiing and a wakeboarding facility. **See p.61**

❺ **Barnsley markets** A rabbit-warren of bargain market stalls that have colonized the town centre. **See p.65**

❻ **Cannon Hall, Barnsley** Country house museum with a top-notch farm attraction in the grounds. **See p.69**

❼ **Doncaster Racecourse** Meetings and events throughout the year at the renovated home of the classic St Leger. **See p.74**

❽ **Conisbrough Castle** Great Norman keep that featured in Sir Walter Scott's *Ivanhoe*. **See p.76**

HIGHLIGHTS ARE MARKED ON THE MAP ON PP.44–45

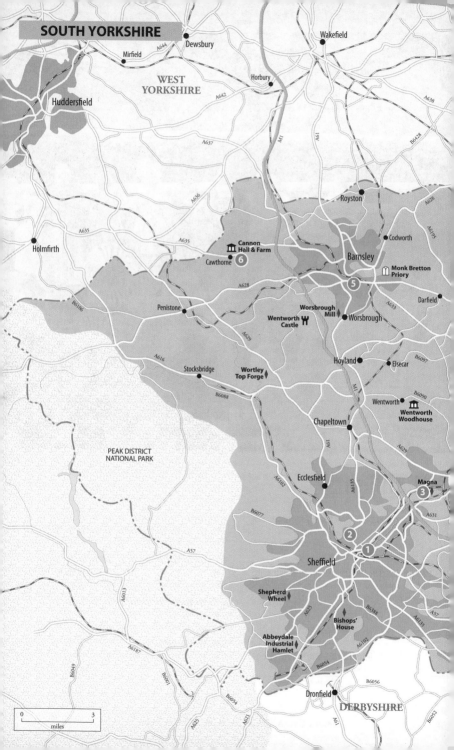

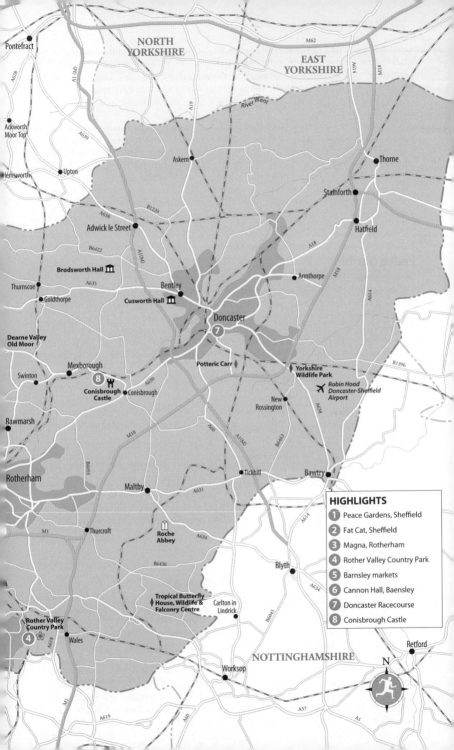

HIGHLIGHTS

1. Peace Gardens, Sheffield
2. Fat Cat, Sheffield
3. Magna, Rotherham
4. Rother Valley Country Park
5. Barnsley markets
6. Cannon Hall, Baensley
7. Doncaster Racecourse
8. Conisbrough Castle

1

wood-and-glass tent of the **Winter Garden**, full of tropical trees and flowers; the sparkling and oh-so-child-friendly **Peace Gardens**; the **Millennium Galleries**, with their permanent and travelling exhibitions; the **Graves Gallery**; and the **Lyceum** and **Crucible theatres** (the latter famous as the venue for the World Snooker Championships). Much of this city centre is pedestrianized, releasing it from the tyranny of traffic and giving it a relaxed, human scale.

With two huge universities slap-bang in the city centre, and a vibrant community of young professionals – many of them Sheffield graduates who couldn't bear to leave – the city is a bustling, youthful place. It has one of the best music scenes in the UK (the **Arctic Monkeys** are no fluke) with venues ranging from the intimate *Leadmill* and *Plug* through the resplendent **City Hall** to the colossal **Sheffield Arena**.

Being located in Yorkshire's extreme southwest corner, and fringing the Peak District National Park, the city also enjoys some spectacular **countryside** to the west, where Yorkshire gives way to Derbyshire – the transition from big city to hills, patchwork fields, dry-stone walls and pretty Peak District villages is startlingly abrupt.

Peace Gardens

Pinstone St • Daily 24hr • Free • Ⓦ sheffield.gov.uk

On sunny days the **Peace Gardens**, with huge bronze water features inspired by Bessemer converters pouring out molten steel, are crowded with people picnicking on benches or relaxing on the grass. Kids strip off and run in and out of the pulsing jets of the pavement-level fountain, float paper boats down the converging ceramic-lined rills (they represent the rivers that gave Sheffield steel mills their power) and giggle at their reflections in the surrounding steel balls that dribble water from their crowns. There's no nonsense about "Keep off the grass" or "Stay out of the fountains" here, either – the Peace Gardens are there for the people of Sheffield to use and to enjoy.

Winter Garden

Surrey St • Mon–Sat 8am–8pm, Sun 8am–6pm • Free • Ⓦ sheffield.gov.uk

Right next to the Peace Gardens, the **Winter Garden**, a twenty-first-century version of a Victorian conservatory on a huge scale – all unvarnished, slowly weathering wood and polished glass – offers a different kind of experience. At 230ft long, 73ft wide and high, with more than 2000 square yards of glass, it shelters fully grown eucalyptus trees and Norfolk pines, more than 2500 flowers and plants, paths that wind through verdant jungle and benches set beneath the soaring trees. A delightfully warm place in the depths of winter, it is kept cool in summer by a complex arrangement of automatically controlled fans and vents.

Millennium Galleries

Arundel Gate • Mon–Sat 10am–5pm, Sun 11am–4pm • Free • Ⓦ sheffieldgalleries.org.uk

Next to the Winter Garden, and opening into it, are the *Mercure St Paul's Hotel* on one side and the **Millennium Galleries** on the other. Although housed in a separate building fronting onto Arundel Gate, the Millennium Galleries' link with the Winter Garden is seamless, with a long corridor flanked by a series of display rooms. The **Ruskin Gallery** contains a collection of books, art and other artefacts assembled by the great nineteenth-century critic/artist John Ruskin as part of his drive to alleviate the suffering of the industrial poor through art and education. An eclectic mix (that is, a bit of a jumble), it includes among other things engravings by Dürer and J.M.W. Turner, Japanese enamelware, collections of coins and geological specimens and Ruskin's own sketches of birds, flowers and landscapes. The **Metalwork Gallery** features not only the city's collection of priceless silver and stainless steel, but also hands-on displays explaining the processes and development of the steel industry. In the corridor is an extensive shop, and an amusing interactive statue of a multi-headed monster, made entirely of cutlery, guaranteed to fascinate kids. At the end of the corridor an escalator drops down to Arundel Gate and the **Millennium Café**.

Graves Gallery

Leader House, Surrey St • Wed–Fri 10am–3pm, Sat 11am–4pm • Free • ☎ 0114 278 2600, ⓦ museums-sheffield.org.uk

The Central Library and **Graves Gallery** is the only part of a proposed 1920s redevelopment of Tudor Square that was ever actually built. It has an imposing Beaux Arts facade and many understated Art Deco details – note the relief of a primitive god-figure on the pediment on the corner of Surrey Street and Tudor Square. The gallery, on the top floor, is based on the collection of local mail-order magnate and philanthropist **J.G. Graves** (1866–1945). Highlights include several prints by J.M.W. Turner, and paintings from Cézanne (*Basin du Jas de Bouffan*) and Edward Burne-Jones (*Cupid Delivering Psyche*), together with later works by the likes of Vanessa Bell (*View of the pond at Charleston, Sussex*) and Gwen John (*A Corner of the Artist's Room in Paris*).

There are also some excellent temporary shows, from national travelling exhibitions to those that draw on Sheffield's art collection and concentrate largely on the art and natural history of this part of Yorkshire.

Fargate and around

Wide, busy and traffic-free, **Fargate** hosts a number of temporary structures such as amusement park rides, and usually echoes to the sound of buskers, *Big Issue* sellers, political rallies and the like. At its southern end stands the imposing **Town Hall** (appropriately enough, for this once industrial city, topped with the figure of the god Vulcan), which backs onto the Peace Gardens.

Orchard Square

Opening off Fargate is **Orchard Square**, a highly successful 1980s development that manages to blend old and new buildings into an agreeable public space. Look out for the modern clock tower out of which, when the clock strikes the hour, working figures of male and female knife-grinders emerge and rotate – a modern spin on a medieval tradition.

Sheffield Cathedral

Church St • Term time Mon 8.30am–5pm, Tues–Fri 8.30am–6.30pm, Sat 9.30am–3.30pm & Sun 7.45am–7.30pm; holidays Mon–Fri 8.30am–5pm, Sat 9.30am–4pm, Sun 7.45am–7.30pm • Free • ⓦ sheffield-cathedral.co.uk

Across the top of Fargate cuts another main shopping drag, Church Street/High Street, loud with trams and buses. Looming over it, **Sheffield Cathedral** – the Cathedral Church of St Peter and St Paul, to give it its full title – was a simple parish church before 1914, and subsequent attempts to give it a more dignified bearing have frankly failed. It's a mish-mash of styles and changes of direction, and you'd need a PhD in ecclesiastical architecture to make any sense of it. However, the magnificent **Shrewsbury Chapel**, at the east end of the south aisle, is definitely worth a look. Built around 1520, it contains the tombs of the fourth and sixth earls of Shrewsbury, adorned with their detailed alabaster effigies. The fourth earl's likeness lies between effigies of his two wives, Anne and Elizabeth, all of them dressed in sumptuous Elizabethan costume. The sixth earl, in full armour, lies alone – he became estranged from his second wife, Bess of Hardwick, partly perhaps because of the strains of the task he was charged with by Elizabeth I – looking after Mary Queen of Scots during her long captivity.

The area in front of the cathedral is paved with gravestones, many dating from the 1830s, when Sheffield suffered a major cholera epidemic.

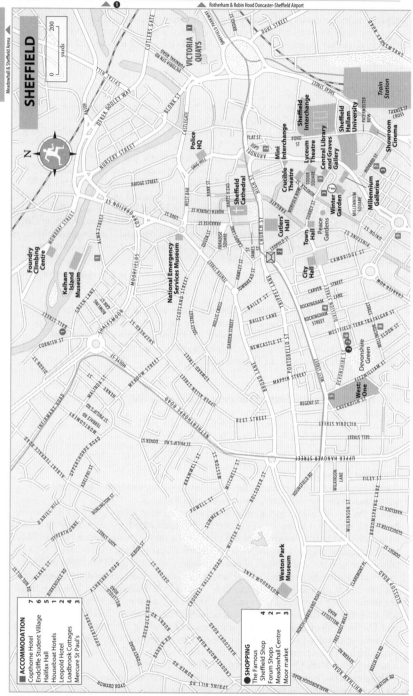

SHEFFIELD

Meadowhall & Sheffield Arena

Rotherham & Robin Hood Doncaster-Sheffield Airport

Train Station

Sheffield Interchange
Sheffield Hallam University
Showroom Cinema
Central Library and Graves Gallery
Millennium Galleries
Winter Garden
Lyceum Theatre
Mini Interchange
Crucible Theatre
Town Hall
Peace Gardens
City Hall
Cutlers' Hall
Police HQ
Sheffield Cathedral
National Emergency Services Museum
Foundry Climbing Centre
Kelham Island Museum
Devonshire Green
West One
Weston Park Museum

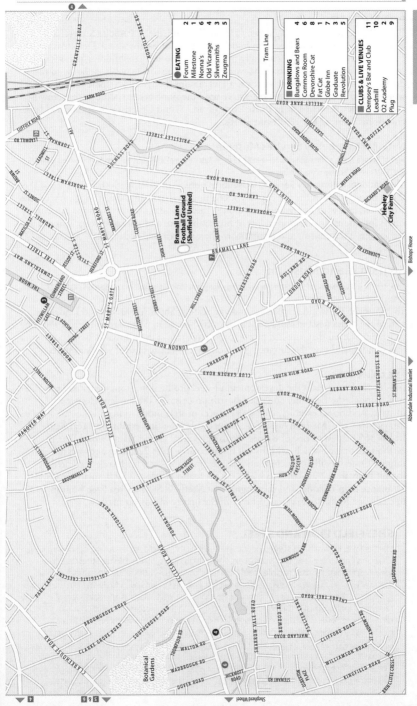

EATING
Forum	2
Milestone	1
Nonna's	6
Old Vicarage	4
Silversmiths	3
Zeugma	5

— Tram Line

DRINKING
Bungalows and Bears	4
Common Room	6
Devonshire Cat	8
Fat Cat	1
Globe Inn	7
Graduate	3
Revolution	5

CLUBS & LIVE VENUES
Dempsey's Bar and Club	11
Leadmill	10
O2 Academy	2
Plug	9

Bramall Lane
Football Ground
(Sheffield United)

Heeley
City Farm

Botanical
Gardens

Bishops House ▶

Abbeydale Industrial Hamlet ▶

Shepherd Wheel ▼

1

Paradise Square

Behind the cathedral, sloping downward off Campo Lane, is **Paradise Square**, as beautiful an ensemble of Georgian houses as can be found anywhere. Despite its coherence and harmony, it is actually the result of two separate building periods and much renovation, though none the worse for that. The square has been home to the doctor who delivered Queen Victoria, a Freemasons' Lodge and a home for fallen women, and various public speakers have used the slope here to address large crowds – John Wesley preached from the balcony of no.18, and Chartist orators inspired large crowds here during the 1830s and 1840s.

National Emergency Services Museum

North of Paradise Square, on the roundabout between West Bar and West Bar Green • Wed–Fri 10am–2pm, Sat & Sun 11am–5pm • £5 • ☎ 0114 249 1999, ⓦ emergencymuseum.org.uk

The **National Emergency Services Museum** is housed in an old (1900) fire station – the doors through which the fire engines once thundered are still there. Though it's a niche attraction, and with limited opening hours, the enthusiasm with which the museum is run is infectious. In addition to lots of fire, ambulance and police vehicles, you can also see various old uniforms and equipment. There's also a café and shop.

Kelham Island Museum

Alma St (on an artificial river island just north of the city centre) • Mon–Thurs 10am–4pm, Sun 11am–4.45pm • £5 • ☎ 0114 272 2106, ⓦ simt.co.uk

To appreciate the world importance and vast scale of Sheffield's historic steel industry a visit to the **Kelham Island Museum** is a must. It's housed in what was, until the 1930s, the generating station that supplied power to the city's trams; the colossal Bessemer converter that stands guard over the entrance gives you an immediate taste of what's in store.

The collections

Inside, displays explain the development of steel production, from blister and crucible steel through the Bessemer and open-hearth processes to the modern electric arc furnace. Additional exhibits cover every aspect of steel production and the vast array of things that were "Made in Sheffield". Look out for the tiny exhibition "Year Knife" (it has 365 blades) to one of Barnes Wallis's gigantic "Grand Slam" World War II earthquake bombs which, with its tail fin, was more than 22ft long and weighed 10 tonnes. Other highlights include an early ceramic-and-steel flush toilet invented by Joseph Bramah (1748–1814), a hydraulic press also developed by Bramah for Royal Ordnance map-making, and the magnificent Sheffield Simplex roadster, built in 1920 to challenge Rolls Royce's stranglehold on the luxury motor car market.

SHEFFIELD IRON AND STEEL

Sheffield was known for its **steel** production as early as the Middle Ages – it is mentioned in Chaucer's *Canterbury Tales*. Two types of expensive, high-quality steel – **blister steel** from the seventeenth century and **crucible steel** from the eighteenth – were made in Sheffield, with manufacture tending to congregate along the fast-flowing streams coming down from the Peak District into the west of the city. Cutlery and weapons that were "Made in Sheffield" were renowned for their quality throughout the world. Then, in the nineteenth century, the development of the Bessemer and open-hearth processes of producing cheap steel in large quantities by burning all the impurities out of the pig iron, then adding the correct amount of carbon, moved the industry to the east of the city, where steel for buildings, railways, shipping and so on was manufactured. Such steelworks as remain are still to be found on the eastern side of the city, but for further insights into Sheffield's industrial past you can visit Kelham Island Museum (see above), Abbeydale Industrial Hamlet (see p.52) and the Shepherd Wheel (see opposite).

Star of the collection, though, is undoubtedly the **River Don engine**, the most powerful surviving steam engine in Britain. As high as a three-storey house, it was built in 1905 and has been used at different times in the production of armour plate, nuclear reactor shields and North Sea oil rigs. You can usually see it in steam at noon and 2pm (and Sun 4pm), a magnificent combination of power, economy and elegance, a symphony in hissing steam and ringing metal. Running times are not guaranteed, however – if it's important to your visit, check with the museum first.

Weston Park Museum

Weston Bank, 1 mile west of the city centre • Mon–Fri 10am–4pm, Sat 11am–5pm, Sun 11am–4pm • Free • ☎ 0114 278 2600,
ⓦ museums-sheffield.org.uk • Bus #51 or #52 from city centre, or Sheffield University tram

Set in the park of the same name, the family-friendly **Weston Park Museum** is a superb attraction, with a varied collection of objects and interactive displays offering insights into natural, scientific and artistic aspects of Sheffield's history. The "Natural Connections" section covers the sort of wildlife to be found in north Sheffield's Greno Wood, including a giant food web (who eats whom) and an examination of small creatures through an interactive microscope. You can also trace the history of the city through ten objects, visit a "history lab" in which children can try to answer questions thrown up by the city's history, explore "Arctic World" (inspired by the museum's popular Polar Bear, Snowy), investigate the traditions of the Punch and Judy show, and marvel at curious treasures such as a man-eating crocodile skull brought back from India. With verve and imagination, the museum takes the inevitably random and arbitrary nature of its collections and turns it into a plus. There's a café and a picnic area, and several activity areas, along with five "trails" for kids aged 4 to 11.

Botanical Gardens

Clarkehouse Rd • Summer Mon–Fri 8am–dusk, Sat & Sun 10am–dusk; winter Mon–Fri 8am–4pm, Sat & Sun 10am–4pm • Free •
☎ 0114 268 6001, ⓦ sbg.org.uk • Bus #10, #30 or #505 from city centre

Opened in 1836 by the Sheffield Botanic and Horticultural Society, the nineteen acres of the **Botanical Gardens** were designed along Gardenesque principles – with an informal layout – on a site that slopes down from the main entrance on Clarkehouse Road to other entrances on Thompson and Botanical roads. Following a £7million restoration, the gardens and their associated buildings are now in mint condition, and they're a delight. A series of themed plots, including Rose, Woodland, Prairie and Asia gardens, intersperse lawns and meandering paths, and interest is added by a bear pit, a statue of Pan and a fossilized tree. Like a diamond tiara across the top of the gardens stand the superb **pavilion glasshouses**, consisting of a central seven-bay pavilion flanked by two of three bays. Within the classically columned main entrance to the gardens is a gift shop, and next to it, in the Curator's House, a café with an attractive terrace.

Shepherd Wheel

Whiteley Woods, just off Hangingwater Rd, a couple of miles southwest of the city centre • Sat, Sun & bank holidays 10am–4pm •
☎ 0114 236 7731, ⓦ simt.co.uk • Bus #83 or #83a from the centre

In many ways more typical of Sheffield's early steel industry than Abbeydale Industrial Hamlet (see p.52), the **Shepherd Wheel**, set in woodland and using the power of the Porter brook, was used to power just one process – sharpening cutlery. An 18ft-high wheel powered twenty grindstones and several glazing stones, which are all now contained in two restored workshops, together with all the various tools of the trade. The wheel has limited opening hours, there are no facilities and no parking – the nearest parking is on Rustlings Road. One for aficionados, then.

1

Heeley City Farm

Richards Rd, just off the A61 to Chesterfield, about 1 mile south of the city centre • Daily: summer 9am–5pm; winter 10am–4pm • Free • ☎ 0114 258 0482, ⊛ heeleyfarm.org.uk • Bus #47, or walkable (20min) from the centre

Like most city farms, **Heeley City Farm** is somehow incongruous. Livestock and piles of manure seem a little out of place in a pleasant suburb so close to a modern city centre – very *The Good Life*. A registered charity, the farm allows children (and adults) to get close to a variety of domestic animals, including poultry, large black pigs, Soay sheep, goats, an Exmoor pony and a cow. But it's not just a petting farm: it takes its responsibility to the environment very seriously. There's a peat-free **garden centre**, a **café** selling a range of delicious organic food, herb gardens and vegetable plots, renewable energy displays, a **children's playground** and information about recycling and composting. It lacks the slickness of some commercial farm attractions, but is none the worse for that. The views across the relentlessly urban city centre contrast intriguingly with the farm's animals, wellies and smellies.

Bishops' House

Meersbrook Park, just off the A61 to Chesterfield, about 2 miles south of the city centre • Sat & Sun 10am–4pm • Free • ☎ 0114 278 2600 • Bus #19, #20 or #53 from the city centre

A rare survival from pre-Industrial Revolution Sheffield, and the city's best-preserved Tudor building (stone on the ground floor, half-timbered above), the **Bishops' House** sits on a substantial hill above the city centre. Although some parts of the house date from around 1500, its interiors owe more to the early seventeenth century, with oak panelling, wooden floors and ornate plasterwork. There's no evidence that bishops ever lived in the house – indeed, for many years before it became a museum in 1976, it was the formal residence of the various park keepers. The views of the city's tower blocks from the garden make a quirky contrast with the off-centre character of this lovely old building.

Abbeydale Industrial Hamlet

A621, 4 miles southwest of the city centre • Mon–Thurs 10am–4pm, Sun 11am–4.45pm • Free • ☎ 0114 236 7731, ⊛ simt.co.uk • Bus #97, #98 or #218 from the city centre

As an industrial museum, **Abbeydale Industrial Hamlet** is the equal of, but very different from, Kelham Island (see p.50). A metal-working site from at least 1200 AD, it became an important steel-making community, specializing largely in scythes, from the early eighteenth century onwards. It finally closed in 1933, though it briefly reopened during World War II to help with the war effort.

Preserved more or less complete, and donated to the city by J.G. Graves, of Graves Art Gallery fame (see p.47), it sits on the banks of the River Sheaf. Powered by four water wheels (and, from 1855, a secondary steam engine) it became a sort of one-stop-shop for scythe blades and other edged tools, with all the processes needed for making steel and then using it to make edged blades taking place on this one site.

Beyond the crucible steel furnace, where the steel was made, you'll see a tilt **forge** built in 1785. These two huge tilt hammers, driven by the main waterwheel, were used to make blades, sandwiching the expensive steel edge between two layers of (much cheaper) wrought iron. A grinding hull of 6ft-high stones and two glazing stones, hung in water to keep them wet, sharpened the new blades, while a boring shop drilled holes in them for the rivets and a blacking shop painted them to prevent rust. Together with the manager's house, the counting house and workmen's cottages, sitting below the works dam, the whole cluster of buildings forms an interesting and atmospheric whole worthy of an industrial landscape painter. The **dam**, used to power the wheels, is now a haven of peace and wildlife, usually dotted with colourful anglers' umbrellas.

There's a timber-clad café, a shop, craft displays and relevant courses, and ample car parking at the site. Take care on wet days – the bricks underfoot can get very slippery.

ARRIVAL AND DEPARTURE SHEFFIELD

Sheffield must be one of the easiest cities in the country to get to. The Robin Hood Doncaster-Sheffield **airport** has links with many parts of the world, while by car the city is approached along 6 miles of **dual carriageway** from the M1's junction 33. There's ample parking, including eight large Park-and-Ride sites around the city's perimeter that link with the trams. The city's excellent bus, coach and train **interchange** is right in the city centre on Sheaf Street; the train station is nearby, though to transfer between buses and trains requires some walking.

By car Though driving around the city can be a nightmare, Park-and-Ride schemes allow you to leave your vehicle on the outskirts and catch a tram into the centre. There are Park-and-Ride sites at Middlewood Rd, Nunnery Square, Halfway, Malin Bridge, Meadowhall, Attercliffe, Abbeydale and Dore.

By train Sheffield train station is on the eastern edge of the city, about a 5min walk from the Sheffield Interchange. Destinations Barnsley (every 12–20min; 25min); Doncaster (every 10–20min: 27–40min); Leeds (every 30min; 40min–1hr); London King's Cross/St Pancras (30min; 2hr 10min); Rotherham (every 10–20min; 12min); York (every 30min–1hr; 52min–1hr 9min).

By bus The bus station is part of the Sheffield Interchange at Pond Square on the eastern edge of the city centre. Regular buses depart for all parts of the city and South Yorkshire, and National Express coaches for the rest of the country. Destinations Barnsley (every 15min; 1hr); Birmingham (every 2–4hr; 2hr 20min); Doncaster (every 10–20min: 1hr 20min); Liverpool (hourly; 3–4hr); London (every 2–3hr; 4hr); Manchester (every 1–2hr; 1hr 30min–3hr); Rotherham (every 5–15min; 30min); York (every 30min–1hr; 52min–1hr 9min).

By plane Robin Hood Doncaster-Sheffield Airport (robinhoodairport.com) lies 25 miles from the city centre, near Doncaster.

GETTING AROUND

Getting around Sheffield is a doddle – most of the city centre is eminently walkable, the integrated **bus** and **tram** system makes longer hops easy, and, for journeys in and out, the bus/tram Sheffield Interchange is butted right up to the city centre near the train station. Don't bank on using a car for exploring the city, though – its labyrinthine one-way system will defeat all but the most knowledgeable local.

By tram The Supertram system (supertram.com) connects the city centre with the Meadowhall shopping centre (see p.56), Halfway, Herdings Park, Malin Bridge and Middlewood, with the stations in between giving comprehensive access to most of the city and connections to the Park-and-Ride scheme.

By bus The bus system is comprehensive and efficient, though not as transparent as the tram system.

By bicycle There is an extensive network of marked and unmarked cycle routes within Sheffield and reaching far

out into the surrounding countryside. Route maps are available online at sheffield.gov.uk.

By car Sheffield's city-centre roads, riven by one-way streets, are a challenge to all but the stoutest of hearts. Far better to use public transport, or the Park-and-Ride scheme, which links well with the tram system.

Transport information Excellent guides to the urban transport systems are available at the Sheffield Interchange and at the tourist office (see below).

INFORMATION

Tourist office Unit 1, Winter Garden, Surrey St (Mon–Fri 9.30am–1pm & 1.30–5pm, Sat 9.30am–1pm & 1.30–4pm; 0114 221 1900, welcometosheffield.co.uk).

Listings Useful online resources include exposed magazine.co.uk, sheffieldtelegraph.co.uk/lifestyle and thestar.co.uk/what-s-on.

ACCOMMODATION

As befits the biggest conurbation in South Yorkshire, Sheffield has the best choice of **accommodation**, including large modern chain hotels, old building conversions, guesthouses, vacation-use of university hostels and houseboats. Rotherham, close to Sheffield, has a number of country house hotels and makes an alternative base.

Copthorne Hotel 1 Bramall Lane 0114 252 5480, millenniumhotels.co.uk/copthornesheffield. The *Copthorne Hotel* occupies a modern high-rise building next to Sheffield United's stadium. It offers a range of stylish rooms, from standard to penthouse, a bar, restaurant and fitness room, and friendly, unfussy but attentive service. **£87**

Endcliffe Student Village Endcliffe Crescent, Endcliffe Ave, Oakholme Rd 0114 289 3500, conference withus.com/bookingspage. Self-catering student rooms in the University of Sheffield's Endcliffe Student Village, within a 10min walking distance of the city centre. Mid-July to late Sept only. **£44**

1

Halifax Hall Endcliffe Vale Rd ☎0114 222 8810, ⓦhalifaxhall.co.uk. Located on the western slopes of Sheffield and within walking distance of the centre, *Halifax Hall* is the former home of a Victorian Sheffield steel magnate and has also seen time as a women's hall of residence. It is now an impressive and luxurious boutique hotel, well placed for exploring the city. **£85**

★**Houseboat Hotels** ☎01909 569393, ⓦhouse boathotels.com. An interesting alternative to ordinary hotels, offering quality accommodation with all mod-cons in three houseboats – *Ruby*, *Lilly-May* and *Mallard* – moored at Victoria Quays near the *Hilton*, a 5min walk from the city centre. You get exclusive use of your own boat in any combination of one to four people, and for an extra charge you can use the *Hilton* pool, sauna and gym. Breakfasts are available (but you have to cook them yourself). **£79**

★**Leopold Hotel** 2 Leopold St ☎0114 252 4000, ⓦleopoldhotel.co.uk. Sheffield's first boutique hotel, the *Leopold* occupies a Grade II listed building, once a boys' grammar school. The keynote is solid luxury with a quirky edge – many original features have been kept and whimsical touches added. Centrally located, the hotel backs onto tiny, beautifully remodelled Leopold Square, which boasts eight places to eat; the *Leopold* itself has a highly rated restaurant. **£99**

Loadbrook Cottages Game Lane, Loadbrook, 7 miles west of Sheffield ☎0114 233 1619, ⓦloadbrook.co.uk. Rural Peak District idyll just a 15min drive from the city centre, *Loadbrook Cottages* offers varied accommodation – B&B and self-catering – in an eighteenth-century farmhouse. Delightfully homely, in a beautiful area, with lovely views. **£75**

Mercure St Paul's 119 Norfolk St ☎0114 278 2000, ⓦmercure.com. Sandwiched between the Peace Gardens and Tudor Square, this modern hotel couldn't be more central. Indeed, the bar opens directly into the palm-thronged Winter Garden, giving it a distinctly tropical feel. Comfortable rather than innovative, with understated (if a little anodyne) decor and all the usual high-end pool, fitness centre, sauna, and wi-fi bells and whistles. Its 163 rooms are supremely well appointed, and the higher you go the better the view. Look out for deals, especially at weekends. Parking service. **£94**

EATING AND DRINKING

Sheffield has become a regional centre for eating and drinking, and there is lots of choice. While wherever you are you'll never be far from a good place to eat, a number of streets in and on the edge of the city centre have made a name for themselves for the range and quality of their pubs and restaurants – Division Street, West Street, London Road and **Ecclesall Road**. The last, in particular, is known for its pubs and bars, frequented not only by students but also by twenty- and thirty-somethings and older locals. Other good areas to explore include Broomhill, west of the city centre, and Heeley Bottom, Nether Edge and Woodseats to the south. Most of the pubs we list below also serve food.

CAFÉS AND RESTAURANTS

★**Forum** 127–129 Devonshire St ☎0114 272 0569, ⓦforumsheffield.co.uk. A vibrant mix of bar, café, music venue and boutique (see p.56), the *Forum* attracts a lively crowd of students, office workers and shoppers who use it as a breakfast joint, lunch spot, after-work bar and evening restaurant, comedy club and disco. Snacks (sandwiches, nachos, wraps, burritos and burgers) and main meals (fish and chips, risotto, half chickens, fish, steak; around £5–15) are served. There are three areas – a main bar, a sunny conservatory and a multihued terrace overlooking Devonshire Green, with deckchairs in summer. Check the website for music and comedy nights, barbecues and special events. Sun–Thurs 10am–1am, Fri & Sat 10am–2am; food served Mon–Fri until 10pm, Sat & Sun until 8pm.

Milestone 84 Green Lane ☎0845 201 3179 or ☎0114 272 8327, ⓦthe-milestone.co.uk. Close to Kelham Island, and in an attractive listed building, the award-winning *Milestone* offers gastropub and upmarket restaurant menus at reasonable prices (starters around £4.95–6.95; mains £10.95–23.95; lunches £12 for two courses, £14.50 for three). Gastropub main courses might include caramelized polenta, slow-cooked pork loin, Yorkshire sausages, Hereford beef or whatever fish was good in the market that morning. All meat is locally sourced, all vegetables fresh and seasonal, all food home-made, and the whole place has a lovely atmosphere. They also host cocktail and cookery classes. Mon–Sat 11am–11.30pm, Sun 11am–10.30pm.

Nonna's 535–541 Ecclesall Rd ☎0114 268 6166, ⓦnonnas.co.uk. Open since 1996, and a Sheffield institution, Italian *Nonna's*, on the lively, student-dominated Ecclesall Rd, is the place to be seen throughout the day. There's a long bar, café, two dining rooms and a deli, and the atmosphere is noisy, informal and congenial. Prices are moderate – antipasti around £5–6, secondi £12–18. Daily 8.30am–11pm.

Old Vicarage Ridgeway Village, 5 miles from Sheffield centre ☎0114 247 5814, ⓦtheoldvicarage.co.uk. As the only Michelin-starred restaurant in the region, the *Old Vicarage*, out in Sheffield's southeast suburbs a 10min drive from the centre, is not cheap, though set menus – three-course lunch menu £40, four-course dinner menu £75 – makes it less daunting. It is beautifully housed in (yes) an old vicarage, and the atmosphere, food and wine are all spot on, making it a wonderful venue for a special occasion. Food is inventive and delicious, from rope-cultured mussels, local lamb and Gressingham duck to Whitby cod or Aberdeen Angus beef. Tues–Fri lunch from 12.30pm, dinner from 6pm, Sat dinner from 6pm

★**Silversmiths** 111 Arundel St ☎0114 270 6160, ⓦsilversmiths-restaurant.com. A "kitchen nightmare" turned around in 2008 by Gordon Ramsay, city-centre *Silversmiths* supplies top-notch Yorkshire food from locally sourced ingredients in a 200-year-old ex-silversmith's workshop. Menus change weekly or fortnightly, depending on season – look out for venison sausages and pies or spinach tart with Yorkshire Blue cheese. Tuesday is pie night (£8.50) and there's a three-course set menu Wed–Sat (£15). Reservations recommended. Tues–Thurs 5.30–11.30pm, Fri & Sat 5.30pm–midnight.

Zeugma 146 London Rd ☎0114 258 2223, ⓦzeugmaiki.com. Cracking Turkish restaurant within a stone's throw of Sheffield United's football ground. Known for its big portions, lively atmosphere and a good selection of meats cooked on open grills, the restaurant now has a second branch, *Zeugma Iki* (☎0114 275 6666), also on London Rd. Prices are reasonable – main courses £9.50–14.95, wine £10.95–28.50, and you can take your own bottle for £3.95 corkage. Daily noon–11pm (Fri & Sat two sittings at 7pm and 9pm).

PUBS AND BARS

Bungalows and Bears Old Fire Station, 50 Division St ☎0114 279 2901, ⓦbungalowsandbears.com. A bar in an old fire station, with comfy sofas and floor-to-ceiling mirrors. It's an ideal venue for a daytime drink and bite to eat, or an off-the-wall, retro start to a night out. Regular DJ nights. Sun–Thurs noon–midnight, Fri & Sat noon–1.30am.

Common Room The Forum, 127–129 Devonshire St ☎0114 280 8221, ⓦcommon-room.co.uk. There are thirteen full-sized American pool tables, and a quiz and nine-ball knockout competition, in this American sports

bar, pool bar and diner. Sun–Thurs 11am–midnight, Fri & Sat 11am–1.30am.

★**Devonshire Cat** Wellingtons St, off Devonshire Green ☎0114 279 6700, ⓦdevonshirecat.co.uk. Big, busy and functional, the *Devonshire Cat* is all about beer. There's a dizzying range of draft and bottled beers, ciders and barley wines from all over the world, plus robust food (£8.95–9.95) – burgers, steaks, sandwiches and pub favourites like fish and chips. Strategically placed between Sheffield's two universities but not confined to a student clientele, it can be chaos at weekends and on weekday nights, but remains pleasant (and good value) the rest of the time. Mon–Thurs 11.30am–11pm, Fri & Sat 11.30am–1am, Sun noon–10.30pm.

★**Fat Cat** Alma St ☎0114 249 4801, ⓦthefatcat .co.uk. Stepping into the *Fat Cat*, just around the corner from the Kelham Island Museum, is like travelling back in time. Bought by real ale enthusiasts in 1981 after a brewery sell-off, it now offers a wide range of bottled and draft beers, ciders and country wines, and a hearty pub-grub menu (meals around £4.50). With its open fires, polished mahogany bar and etched mirrors, and its total absence of flashing gaming machines and piped music, this is pub-going as it used to be. Sun–Thurs noon–11pm, Fri & Sat noon–midnight.

Globe Inn 54 Howard St ☎0114 276 3124. Situated directly opposite Sheffield Hallam University, this is inevitably an archetypal student pub. Rock music and cheap, basic food and drink. Daily noon–12.30am.

Graduate 94 Surrey St ☎0114 275 3767. You can guess the target market. Pool, cheap drinks and a good Sunday lunch. Quiz night Wed. Daily noon–late.

Revolution 1 Fitzwilliam St ☎0114 273 9469, ⓦrevolution-bars.co.uk. Lots of leather, polished wood and vodka, just as you would expect from this quality chain vodka bar. Quite pricey, unless you're a member of their loyalty scheme. Sun–Wed 11am–12.30am, Thurs–Sat 11am–1am.

NIGHTLIFE AND ENTERTAINMENT

Sheffield is by far the best place in South Yorkshire for nightlife. Not only do the **students** of its two huge universities ensure a good range of pubs and top live music venues – as you'd expect from the city that produced the Arctic Monkeys, Pulp, Richard Hawley (plus of course Def Leppard) to name but a few (see p.56) – but the city's healthy social and intellectual mix supports a fine regional **theatre** and a flourishing independent **cinema**.

LIVE MUSIC AND CLUBS

Dempsey's Bar and Club 1 Hereford St ☎0114 275 4616, ⓦdempseys-sheffield.com. Established gay venue, licensed until the small hours. Mon, Tues, Thurs & Sun 9pm–4am, Wed 9pm–1am, Fri & Sat 9pm–6am.

Leadmill 7 Leadmill Rd ☎0114 221 2828, ⓦleadmill .co.uk. Large venue for live music and club nights. Music spans funk to reggae, industrial to forged beats/krautrock.

Mondays are "Shag" – student night – featuring r'n'b and pop in the main room, with indie, rock and punk in room two. Various nights 11pm–3am.

O2 Academy 37–43 Arundel Gate ☎0114 253 7777, ⓦo2academysheffield.co.uk. Large live music venue catering to a wide audience, from fans of Basement Jaxx to The Pogues. As well as live music, the *Academy* hosts "Propaganda", a huge Indie night every Friday from 10.30pm till 3am. Hours vary according to event.

1

SHEFFIELD AND POPULAR MUSIC

It may not be as famous as Liverpool for its contribution to popular music, but Sheffield can hold its head high when it comes to both the number and quality of its musical offspring. Here, in roughly chronological order, are our top five Sheffield bands and singers:

Joe Cocker Gravelly-voiced blue-eyed-soul singer, active from the 1960s. Standout song: Lennon-McCartney's *With a Little Help from my Friends*.

Def Leppard Heavy-metal mega-stars, formed in 1977, most active during the 1980s and early 1990s, with a huge following on both sides of the Atlantic. Standout song: *Pour Some Sugar on Me*.

Pulp Formed in 1978 and popular locally during the 1980s, Pulp only hit the national and international heights during the Britpop explosion of the 1990s. Known for their whip-smart lyrics and the bohemian charisma of lead singer Jarvis Cocker. Standout song: *Common People*.

Richard Hawley The musos' musician – a highly rated guitarist, session musician, singer-songwriter and producer, with a pure voice and retro crooner appeal. His work often references his home town. Standout song: *Don't Get Hung up in Your Soul*.

Arctic Monkeys The young Arctic Monkeys broke new territory in the early 2000s when a groundswell of local support and online word-of-mouth led to their first album becoming the fastest-selling debut in history. Lead singer Alex Turner's strong rock-star presence, and their clever, witty social-realist wordplay, engaging with the band's Sheffield roots, has won the band several Brit awards. Standout song: *I Bet You Look Good on the Dancefloor*.

Plug 14 Matilda St ☎0114 241 3040, ⓦthe-plug.com. Mid-sized music venue featuring everything from live acoustic folk to diverse club nights, including the award-winning "Jump Around" every Thursday from 10.30pm. Box office Mon–Fri noon–5.30pm.

THEATRE AND CINEMA

Crucible Theatre Tudor Square ☎0114 249 6000, ⓦsheffieldtheatres.co.uk. In a listed building next to the Lyceum, the Crucible offers not only theatrical productions, but also the annual World Snooker Championships. Usually Mon–Sat 10am–8pm (6pm if no performance).

Lyceum Theatre Tudor Square ☎0114 249 6000, ⓦsheffieldtheatres.co.uk. Built in the 1890s, this late Victorian gem is the only work of theatre and music hall designer W.G.R. Sprague to survive outside London (his most famous theatre is the Aldwych) –all gilded rococo plasterwork and plush boxes inside, and decorated stucco on the outside. It hosts touring West End and Opera North productions, as well as plays put on by local companies. Usually Mon–Sat 10am–8pm (6pm if no performance).

Showroom Cinema 7 Paternoster Row ☎0114 276 3534, ⓦshowroomworkstation.org.uk. This independent cinema and creative hotbed, in a beautifully renovated 1930s structure near Sheffield train station, screens everything from current releases to classics, family films and world cinema, and hosts regular festivals and special events. The café/bar is worth a visit on its own. Box office: Mon–Fri from 10am, Sat & Sun from 10.30am; café/bar Mon–Thurs 10am–11pm, Fri 10am–midnight, Sat 11am–midnight, Sun noon–10.30pm; food served Mon–Sat until 9pm, Sun noon–4pm.

SHOPPING

Sheffield city centre has all the national chain stores and other **shops** you'd expect, with top-end options concentrated particularly along Fargate and High Street on one side of the Peace Gardens and budget alternatives along The Moor on the other, with large department stores dotted around on both sides. Boutiques and specialist shops are concentrated on the western side of the city, around Devonshire Green and along Ecclesall Road as far as Hunter's Bar.

The Famous Sheffield Shop 475 Ecclesall Rd ☎0114 268 5701, ⓦsheffield-made.com. The perfect place to pick up Sheffield souvenirs, with a wide variety of stainless steel cutlery and jewellery, plus pewter tankards, flasks and goblets. Mon–Fri 9.30am–5.30pm, Sat 9am–5.30pm.

Forum Shops 127–129 Devonshire St ☎0114 272 0569, ⓦforumsheffield.co.uk. Ten small independent boutiques under one roof, mainly selling clothes, accessories, shoes and hats, but also gifts, with a tattooist/piercer and skate shop. There's food and drink, too (see p.54). Mon–Sat 10am–6pm, Sun 11am–5pm.

Meadowhall Centre Meadowhall Way, 3 miles east of Sheffield city centre ☎0845 600 6800, ⓦmeadowhall .co.uk. Since it opened in 1990 on the site of a derelict steelworks, the Meadowhall Centre, an easy tram ride east of the centre, has dominated Sheffield shopping like a colossus, pulling in thirty million shoppers a year from all over the north of England. Blamed from the start for urban decay as far away as Scunthorpe, it was expected to decimate city-centre shopping in the rest of South Yorkshire. Twenty-five years later, the jury's still out. With hundreds of shops under one roof, it's either Meadow-heaven or Meadowhell, depending on your point of view. But even those who hate it find its weatherproofing and free parking hard to resist. Mon–Fri 10am–9pm, Sat 9am–8pm, Sun 11am–5pm.

Moor market 77 The Moor. Covered market south of the city centre, with 190 stalls selling fruit and veg, meat, fish, clothes and jewellery. There are artisan, Russian and Jamaican food stalls, handmade cakes, crafts and a lot more. Mon–Sat 8.30am–5.30pm.

SPORTS AND OUTDOOR PURSUITS

Lying partly inside the Peak District National Park, Sheffield has a number of centres where you can hone your bouldering or **rock-climbing** skills. It also has a strong footballing legacy, boasting the world's oldest club, **Sheffield FC** (founded 1857), who since 2001 have been playing at the Coach and Horses Stadium in Dronfield, Derbyshire. The city has two other football clubs, once among the greatest in the land, but now laid relatively low – **Sheffield Wednesday** (at the time of writing in the Championship, English football's second tier) and **Sheffield United** (at the time of writing in League 1, English football's third tier). Though both are relatively well supported compared to other teams in their respective divisions, tickets are easy to get, at the ground or online.

STADIUMS AND SPORTS CENTRES

Ice Sheffield Coleridge Rd ⓦ icesheffield.com. Hosting many national ice-skating championships including the British Ice Dance Championships and the British Ice Figure and Dance Championships, this large complex is open to the public for various sessions. £3–5, family tickets from £20.50. Opening hours vary day to day according to what sessions are on; consult website.

Ponds Forge International Sports Centre Sheaf St ⓣ 0114 223 3400, ⓦ ponds-forge.co.uk. Olympic-standard swimming and diving pools and sports hall in the city centre. Membership from £5.

Sheffield United Bramall Lane ⓣ 0871 995 1889, ⓦ sufc.co.uk. Tickets to see the "Blades" cost from £10 at the gate, £1 extra if bought by phone or online. Season Aug–May.

Sheffield Wednesday Hillsborough ⓣ 0871 900 1867, ⓦ swfc.co.uk. To see the "Owls" costs from £25; £2 extra if ordered by phone. Season lasts Aug–May.

CLIMBING CENTRES

Climbing Works Off Abbeydale Rd, 2 miles south of Sheffield centre ⓣ 0114 250 9990, ⓦ climbingworks .com. In a cluster of commercial buildings south of the centre, Climbing Works has a huge bouldering wall, together with mini-versions for children and novices. The admission fee (£7) gives you a full day's access. There's a small café and a shop. Mon–Fri noon–10pm, Sat & Sun 10am–8pm.

Foundry Indoor Climbing Centre Mowbray St, just off junction 9 of the inner ring road ⓣ 0114 279 6331, ⓦ foundryclimbing.com. A 10min walk from the city centre, offering full climbs and bouldering. There's a substantial café and a well-stocked climbing shop. You must be experienced and will have to sign a form to that effect, or you can book ahead to receive instruction. £7. April–Oct Mon–Fri 10am–10pm, Sat & Sun 10am–6pm; Nov–March Mon–Fri 10am–10pm, Sat & Sun 10am–8pm.

Rotherham and around

While the main attraction in **ROTHERHAM** is the superb, multi-award-winning science adventure centre, **Magna**, a couple of miles southwest, the city itself is worth a look for its magnificent Gothic **Minster**, appealing **Clifton Museum** and the lively **Rotherham Markets** – indoor, outdoor and, on certain days, on the streets. Other highlights include two open spaces: the **Crofts** and, with its superb children's playgrounds, **Clifton Park**. Throughout the day the town centre is flooded with students from Rotherham College, and there's a lively outdoor pub-and-café society – largely courtesy of the smoking ban. Easily accessible from the centre, meanwhile, are some good attractions: England's largest country house, **Wentworth Woodhouse**; **Rother Valley Country Park** with its cable waterskiing; the excellent **Tropical Butterfly House**; the **Wildlife and Falconry Centre**; and the atmospheric **Roche Abbey**.

Rotherham developed in Saxon times as a market town at a ford across the River Don, and flourished as a coal and steel town during the Industrial Revolution. Today it looks like a typical victim of **post-industrial** decline – a quarter of a million people stranded by the ebbing economic tide, overshadowed by nearby (and resurgent)

1

Sheffield, with high unemployment, social deprivation and manifest poverty. Look deeper, though, and you'll see the great strengths of this indomitable community, which has a fierce pride in its heritage. While much of the centre is dominated by what can only be described as brutal yawn-to-horrible early postwar buildings – and there's no excuse, as Rotherham largely escaped Sheffield's pounding by the Luftwaffe – and much of the hinterland has been scarred by heavy industry, there are treasures to be found. Embedded in the mid-twentieth-century cityscape you'll find **architectural gems** like the **Imperial Buildings** (now a small café/bar/shop complex) and the **Old Town Hall**, along with the **Chapel of Our Lady**, a rare example of a chapel built on a bridge.

Rotherham Minster – Church of All Saints

All Saints Square • Mon, Tues, Thurs & Fri 9am–1pm & 2–4pm, Wed & Sat 9am–noon • Free • ☎ 01709 364737, Ⓦ rotherhamminster.co.uk

A fine ecclesiastical building, **Rotherham Minster** dominates the town's central All Saints Square – the best views of the building are from the Minster Gardens beside it. The Minster's 180ft-high spire, topped by a 7ft-high gilded weather vane, is not only impressive, it's a useful navigational aid. Though churches have occupied the site for at least a thousand years, in its current Perpendicular Gothic form it dates from the early fifteenth century. The Minster is welcoming to visitors, with a coffee bar to the right (mornings only) and a clear, easily absorbed history of the church to the left as you enter through the porch, and a useful single-sheet guide. Look out for the Green Men hidden among the stone foliage at the top of the pillars in the nave, the attractive "wine glass" pulpit dating from 1604, and, in the chancel, the poppyhead (bench end) carvings of nativity figures (Archangel Gabriel, Mary and Joseph, the Three Wise Men) dating from 1480. Make sure, too, to search out the 77 individually carved oak roof bosses in the nave, the great 1420 fan-vault under the tower, and the organ, installed in 1777 by star organ builder Johann Snetzler, with an impressive black-and-gold case and – a Snetzler signature – a keyboard with the black and white keys reversed.

The Crofts

Behind the Minster, at the top of Moorgate Street and easily missed, lies the **Crofts**, an open area that was once Rotherham's main cattle market. Now a pleasant paved square with two reasonable pubs, the *High House* and *Cross Keys*, it was one of the region's biggest animal marts until the mid-nineteenth century, when it was first closed by an outbreak of rindpest (don't you hate it when that happens?) and then later eclipsed by the new market in Sheffield. The handsome building taking up its east side was built in the 1920s as the West Riding Courthouse and converted in the 1990s into Rotherham's **Town Hall**, outside of which is a reminder both of one of the town's great industries and of one of its greatest families. The **Walker Cannon**, an 8ft-long muzzle loader weighing a tonne and a quarter, dates from between 1790 and 1820, and was made in the local factory of Samuel Walker and Company, one of Britain's premier gun manufacturers. At the time of the American War of Independence and the wars against France they produced a quarter of all the guns used by the Royal Navy, including 79 of the 105 guns aboard HMS *Victory*.

Chapel of Our Lady

Frederick St • Tues 11am for communion • Free

If you're in Rotherham town centre, it's worth a quick visit to the fourteenth-century **Chapel of Our Lady**, one of only three or four surviving medieval bridge chapels in the country. Said to have housed Mary Queen of Scots (she did get about) when it was briefly used as the town prison, it is now open only once a week for communion, or by arrangement for weddings. Though fine in architecture and detail, it now looks a little sad and neglected.

Clifton Park

Clifton Lane • **Park** Daily 10am–8.30pm **Amusements** Mon–Fri 11am–3pm, Sat & Sun 11am–5pm (term time); daily 11am–5pm (school holidays) • Free • ☎ 01709 254588, ⓦ cliftonparkrotherham.co.uk

A five-minute walk east of the town centre, **Clifton Park** is a delightful green space, crisscrossed with paths, ablaze with flowerbeds, and featuring a rock garden, bandstand and cenotaph. Pride of place goes to its superb **play area**, with a series of interconnected zones for different ages – a modern playground for very young children;

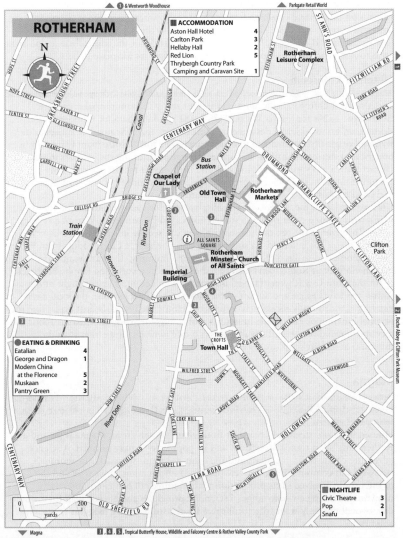

1

ROTHERHAM MARKETS

Rotherham markets, with **indoor** and **covered outdoor** sections, are an integral part of the town centre, housed in a bleak brick and concrete building on Effingham Street (indoor: Mon–Sat 8.30am–5pm; outdoor: Mon, Fri & Sat 8.30am–4.30pm, though some stalls close earlier). There's also a weekly **street market** (Tues) and a monthly **farmers' market** (last Wed of the month) on Effingham Street. The setting might be dowdy, yet the spirit is in keeping with Rotherham's venerable history as a market town. Prices are incredibly low – dresses for a fiver, phones unlocked for £10, huge Desperate Dan breakfasts (at *Robert's* café) for £2.20. And get a look at the Smoking Joint ("Roll your own specialists") offering a bewildering choice of pipes, papers, tips, matches and lighters – for the smoking of unfashionable tobacco.

an impressive adventure playground with high towers, a zipwire, tubular slides, suspension bridges and climbing frames; an exciting water play area for all ages; an amusement park; and a gigantic sand pit. There's also the opportunity to practise skateboarding and cycling skills at the Skate Park, while for the adults there are pleasant areas to just sit around, read or chat. If you've got kids, it's the place to be.

Clifton Park Museum

Clifton Lane • Mon–Fri 10am–5pm, Sat 9.30am–5pm, Sun 1.30–4.30pm • Free • ☎ 01709 336633, ⓦ cliftonparkrotherham.co.uk/museum

The history of **Clifton Park Museum** is typical of many such municipal museums. Built in the 1780s for Joshua Walker (1749–1815), son of Samuel, founder of the Rotherham ironworks, and designed by John Carr of York, the house is Palladian in style and originally commanded fine views across the town. Rotherham Corporation bought it in the second half of the nineteenth century, turning the grounds into a characteristically Victorian park in 1891 and the house into a characteristically Victorian museum in 1893. Having been updated over time, it is now a stimulating and child-friendly place, full of quirky treasures.

Just to the left of the entrance is a small playroom for young children (the Lion's Den), with, among other things, a stuffed lion called Nelson and a Victorian rocking horse. Throughout the rest of the museum, you can see the inevitable miscellany of artefacts that it has inherited – a stuffed bear and pheasant, a canoe paddle from Papua New Guinea, odd shells, a piece of wrapping for a mummy. There's a wealth of information about Rotherham's history – the Walker ironworks and family, Ebenezer Elliot the Corn Law Rhymer (a local iron dealer who became a leading light of the Anti-Corn Law League and author of the radical *Corn Law Rhymes*), the local canal network – and, a really nice touch, a series of "House Detective" boards explaining the original function of each of the museum's rooms, together with information about servants drawn directly on the walls. There's a café (which closes earlier than the museum) and a gift shop.

Magna

Sheffield Rd, 2 miles southwest of Rotherham town centre and 1 mile from M1 exit 34, and well signposted from both • Daily 10am–5pm • Museum £10.95; family £27.95–52.45; Sci-Tek & Aqua-Tek day passes £6.50, adults £2 • ☎ 01709 720002, ⓦ visitmagna.co.uk • Bus #69 from Rotherham or Sheffield

Housed in an old steelworks between Rotherham and Sheffield, **Magna** is far and away Rotherham's main tourist attraction, and its popularity is fully justified. A science adventure centre built in and around the giant decommissioned Templeborough steelworks, it combines imaginatively presented information about steel and the lives of the people involved in its production with hundreds of hands-on, interactive displays illustrating a whole range of scientific principles and effects. Plan for a whole day – you'll not only want to get full value for the stiffish entry fees, but you really will need it.

1

Having entered through a cavernous, dark and echoing **Face of Steel**, designed to set the scene, you climb to a central walkway that travels the length of this colossal building. Along the walkway touch-screen computers fill you in on life among the steelworkers (in their own dialect, Yorkshire, with English subtitles), and "Steel Reveal" units explain the functions of the huge shadowy machines and equipment that you see around you – direct the beam of a powerful spotlight, and a concise illustrated explanation of what you're illuminating comes up on the attached screen.

From the walkway, a lift and stairs mounted in the **Transformer House** gives access, above and below, to four separate pavilions dealing with earth, air, fire and water. The highest of these, of course, is **air**, appropriately housed in an enormous blimp that floats up near the ceiling. Then comes **fire**, **water** and finally, in the basement, **earth**. Hundreds of exciting interactive displays illustrate the principles of practical science – air cannons, speaking tubes, a hydrogen rocket, a hot air balloon, a fire tornado, a blue whirlpool – and you can do hundreds of interesting things: have a steel-saver race using electromagnets to ferry cans, operate a JCB, blast rock in a quarry, fire water cannons, sit on a gyroscopic chair, and many, many more.

Across the road from the entrance are a huge, modern children's playground (**Sci-Tek**) and water play area (**Aqua-Tek**), part of the museum but for which there is an extra charge. The *Red Hall Café* offers refreshment and there's a gift shop.

Rother Valley Country Park

Mansfield Rd, Wales Bar, 7 miles south of Rotherham and 10min west of the M1 (exit 31) and well signposted • Daily: April & Sept 8.30am–7pm; May–Aug 8.30am–8pm; Oct 8.30am–6pm; Nov–March 8.30am–5pm • ☎ 0114 247 1452, ⓦ rvcp.co.uk • Bus #29 from Rotherham, with a 25min walk from the bus stop

Rother Valley Country Park is a good bet for a family day out. Opened in 1983, the park was the result of the redevelopment of a large open-cast coal mine, and was designed not only to provide recreational facilities, but also to develop wildlife habitats and to control flooding. Extensive **footpaths** and **cycle tracks** encircle a series of lakes, a **watersports centre** offers bike, boat, canoe and windsurf rental, there's a grass skislope, a narrow-gauge railway, a play area for 2–14 year olds, **fishing**, a **golf centre**, a **café** and an information point. The park is also one of the few places in the country that offers **cable waterskiing** (ⓦ sheffieldcablewaterski.com). An electric cable (imagine a ski-lift that goes around a lake instead of up a mountain) pulls up to eight waterskiers or wakeboarders at intervals around a shallow lake, at speeds that can be varied from 16 miles/hr (beginners) to 36 miles/hr (experts). It's environmentally friendly, and costs a fraction of what you'd pay for speedboat-towed skiing. All equipment can be rented at the ski centre, and there are full facilities – toilets, changing rooms, showers, a café/bar and even a campsite.

Tropical Butterfly House, Wildlife and Falconry Centre

Woodsetts Rd, North Anston, 9 miles southeast of Rotherham, and 5min east from exit 31 of the M1 • Mon–Fri 10am–4.30pm, Sat, Sun & school holidays 10am–5.30pm • £9 • ☎ 01909 569416, ⓦ butterflyhouse.co.uk • Bus #19A from Rotherham

The **Tropical Butterfly House, Wildlife and Falconry Centre** may not exactly bear a snappy title, but it accurately reflects what the attraction is all about. At its heart is the steamy **Tropical House**, warm and damp, with a bunch of snakes, birds, crocodiles, terrapins, frogs, insects, snails, crabs, bats, hedgehogs and lush tropical greenery, as well as a huge variety of multicoloured butterflies that flap disconcertingly around your head. Look out in particular for the speckled caiman (it's a crocodile), the three iguanas that roam free, White's tree frog (it's brown, hardly moves, and looks surprised), the big, knobbly stick insects, giant African snails and hermit crabs, and the green tree python, pygmy hedgehogs and leathery fruit bats of the nocturnal room. Some of the insects are the stuff of nightmares – just dare to look at the domino and death's head

1

cockroaches, the scorpions, the assassin bugs – but it's altogether a riveting experience. When you arrive you're handed a list of events for the day – parrot shows perhaps, along with bird of prey displays, ferret roulette, and the chance to handle exotic species or even milk a goat.

Roche Abbey

Maltby, 9 miles east of Rotherham • April–Sept Thurs–Sun 10am–5pm • £3.60; EH • ⓦ english-heritage.org.uk • From junction 1 on the M18 head for the pit village of Maltby – as you arrive, at the White Swan, bear right (signposted East Retford) and, after 1.5 miles, turn right down the cobbled lane to the car park; there are buses from Rotherham to Maltby (#1), but it's a 30min walk from the village

Established in 1147 by Cistercian monks from Northumberland, **Roche Abbey** is an unexpected delight – the medieval elegance of its Gothic remains, the intricate outline of its ground plan, bisected by a fast flowing stream, are set in parkland of ethereal loveliness.

It owes its beauty, oddly, to two acts of vandalism. First it was despoiled and looted in 1538, during the dissolution of the monasteries, when locals grabbed whatever was left after Henry VIII had taken first pick. Then, having been inherited by the Earl of Scarborough in the eighteenth century, it was developed by famed landscape gardener Capability Brown, who pulled down buildings, earthed and turfed over much of the site, and created the wonderful parkland that now surrounds it. Excavation in the 1920s resurrected the remains of the abbey, thus creating the winning combination of medieval ruins and elegant parkland you see today.

After wandering around the ruins, turn right and follow the fence onwards and to the right. This will take you on a delightful, fifteen-minute **walk** that encompasses a waterfall, stepping stones, a lake, and wonderful views of the abbey, bringing you back to the abbey entrance.

Wentworth Woodhouse

Wentworth, 5 miles northwest of Rotherham, a couple of miles from the M1 (exit 35) • **House** For tour dates, consult the website • £10 (basic tour), £15 (basic tour plus rooms associated with the 1st Earl of Strafford), £25 (the "full experience") **Kitchen Garden** Daily: April– Sept 10am–5pm; Oct–March 10am–4pm • ☎ 01226 351161, ⓦ wentworthwoodhouse.co.uk • Bus #227 from Rotherham.

The village of **Wentworth**, with its stone-built houses and attractive pubs, seems a million miles away from Rotherham's urban sprawl. Just outside the village stands what is thought to be England's largest stately home – **Wentworth Woodhouse**. Originally built for Thomas Wentworth, 1st Earl of Strafford, one of Charles I's most important advisers (who was executed in 1641 with the King's reluctant connivance), the house was completely rebuilt and developed between 1725 and 1750 for the 1st Marquis of Rockingham, creating what are in effect two great houses back to back: one in the Baroque and the other in the Palladian style. It is certainly big – the great east elevation is more than 600ft, and the house as a whole covers a total of more than three acres. For sixty years closed to the public as a result of an inheritance squabble, it is now, since being bought in 1999 by Clifford Newbold, open for organized tours.

You get good views of the house's frontage from the public footpath that crosses its 250-acre deer park, and you can examine its renovated kitchen garden, now maintained by Wentworth Garden Centre, with its ornamental statues, maze and bear pit. Numerous events are held in the grounds, such as police dog trials and classic car rallies.

ARRIVAL AND INFORMATION   ROTHERHAM

By car Rotherham town centre lies in the angle between the M1 and the M18, and can be accessed from junctions 33 and 34 on the M1, or junction 1 on the M18. There is lots of public parking in the town centre, and you're strongly

recommended to use it – one-way streets and pedestrianization make town-centre driving a nightmare.

By train Rotherham train station lies on the western edge of the town centre, separated from it by the River Don and

CLOCKWISE FROM TOP SHEFFIELD PEACE GARDENS (P.46); ROTHERHAM MINSTER (P.58); ROTHER VALLEY COUNTRY PARK (P.61) >

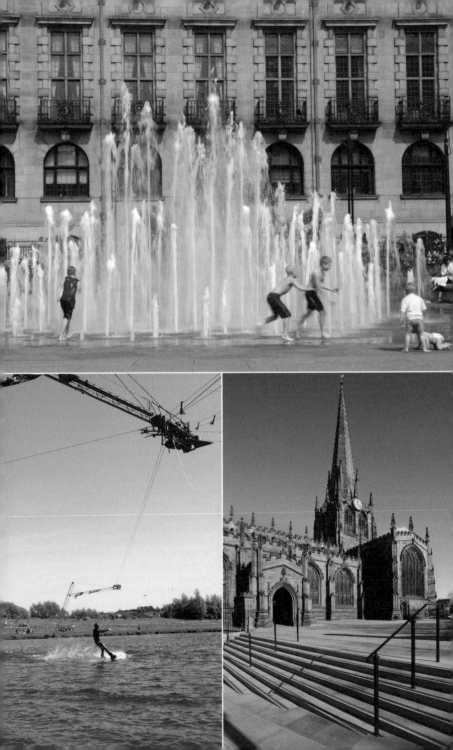

1

accessible across the Chantry Bridge. While not on a main line, it offers regular services from Rotherham to Sheffield and Doncaster, which have good connections.
Destinations Doncaster (every 30min; 20min); Sheffield (every 3–35min; 15min); Wakefield (hourly; 45min).
By bus The well-organized bus station lies on the northern edge of the centre, with frequent services to surrounding towns and villages, and to Doncaster and Sheffield.

Destinations Barnsley (every 10–20min; 1hr); Doncaster (every 10min; 45min); Maltby (every 10min; 35min); North Anston (every 15min; 50min); Sheffield (every 5–15min; 30min).

Tourist office There's a well-stocked and helpful tourist office (Mon–Fri 9am–5pm, Sat 9.30am–4pm; ☎01709 835904) facing the Minster, on the corner where Bridgegate enters All Saints Square.

ACCOMMODATION

There is little accommodation in Rotherham town centre – most of the bigger hotels, which rely on corporate and private events and the passing trade rather than tourism, are close to motorway exits. However, there are several **country house hotels** which are well placed for any exploration of Rotherham, or even for Sheffield and other parts of South Yorkshire.

★**Aston Hall Hotel** Worksop Rd, Aston, 5 miles south of Rotherham and 1 mile from M1 junction 31 ☎0114 287 2309, ⑩astonhallhotel.co.uk. An eighteenth-century country house set in its own 55-acre park, where the individually designed and named rooms are all refurbished, boasting lovely decor and good facilities. It is much used for weddings (the parish church is right next door) and corporate events. **£89**

Carlton Park 102–104 Moorgate Rd, between M1 junction 33 and Rotherham town centre ☎01709 849955, ⑩carltonparkhotel.com. Clean, modern and comfortable, with a bar and restaurant and small but comprehensive leisure facilities. Frequent buses (or a 15min walk) into Rotherham town centre. **£61**

★**Hellaby Hall** Old Hellaby Lane, Hellaby, near junction 1 of the M18, 5 miles east of Rotherham ☎01709 702701, ⑩hellabyhallhotel.co.uk. Four-star luxury and seventeenth-century character, with smart, understated decor and all the in-room, hotel-wide and health club bells and whistles you'd expect, at a surprisingly

reasonable cost. Although next to an industrial estate, it's screened from it by attractive grounds. **£93**

Red Lion Sheffield Rd, Todwick, 1 mile from M1 junction 31 and 6 miles southeast of Rotherham ☎01909 771654, ⑩redlion-todwick.com. This early nineteenth-century farmhouse (oak beams, stone floors) is comfortable and cosy. It's easy to get to by car, and there are regular buses to Rotherham and Sheffield. There's a good restaurant, too, serving a wide range of pub-style food – burgers, steaks, bangers and mash and so on. Look out particularly for the beef and ale pie. **£50**

Thrybergh Country Park Camping and Caravan Site Doncaster Rd ☎01709 850353, ⑩rotherham.gov .uk. Off the main Rotherham–Doncaster road and attached to Thrybergh Country Park, this site has 24 caravan pitches (with electricity) and twelve tent pitches, and a shower and toilet block. There's a small visitor centre and café next to the site. Regular buses into Rotherham and Doncaster town centres leave from immediately outside the site. One pitch and up to 4 people **£17**

EATING AND DRINKING

Eatalian 29a High St ☎01709 820150. Good Italian food, largely Neapolitan, in intimate surroundings (so it can feel a little crowded). Expect to pay around £15 for the meal, with wine starting at around £10 a bottle. No parking, as it's in the town centre. Booking advisable on Fridays and Saturdays. Mon–Sat dinner only.

★**George and Dragon** 85 Main St, Wentworth, 5 miles from Rotherham ☎01226 742440, ⑩georgeand dragonwentworth.co.uk. A lovely old pub in a lovely old village, the *George and Dragon* offers superior pub grub (mains £7.95–13.95 with wine starting at just under £12 a bottle). There's a snug and cosy two-level bar downstairs, with the restaurant upstairs, and a large garden; children are welcome. Food is nicely cooked pub grub – steaks, pork ribs, scampi and the like, with a particularly tasty red snapper. Mon–Wed 11am–11pm, Thurs 11am–11.30pm, Fri 11am–midnight, Sat 10am–midnight, Sun 10am–11pm.

Modern China at the Florence Moorgate Rd ☎01709 360606, ⑩newmodernchina.co.uk. A short distance beyond the Croft, this Chinese restaurant is well regarded by locals, and provides the usual range of Cantonese food. Set menus start at £23. Mon–Thurs & Sun 5.30–11pm, Fri & Sat 5.30–11.30pm.

Muskaan 3–5 Corporation St ☎01709 839955. Specializing in Bangladeshi meat curries, especially chicken and lamb tikka, and fish dishes – look out for *begun fishwala* and tandoori king prawn – in a smart modern interior. A starter and main course with drinks is likely to come to around £20. Daily from 5.30pm.

Pantry Green Red Lion Yard ☎01709 364077. Tucked away behind the *Red Lion* (the entrance to the yard is on Effingham St), *Pantry Green* provides comfortable seating at which you can eat your sandwiches or baguettes, cooked meals or salads away from the bustle of the main thoroughfares. Mon–Sat 8am–4.30pm.

NIGHTLIFE AND ENTERTAINMENT

1

Civic Theatre Catherine St; box office 40 Bridegate ☎01709 823621, ⊛ rotherhamtheatres.co.uk. Stand-up, amateur and touring theatre, live music, dance and pantomime. Box office Mon–Fri 10am–5pm, Sat 10am–4pm.

Pop 8–13 Ship Hill ☎01709 720124, ⊛pop -rotherham.com. A mix of club nights, including student

night ("Project") on Thursday, "Hustle" on Friday and "Houseparty" on Saturdays. Thurs–Sat 10.30pm–3am.

Snafu 1–8 Westgate Chambers St ☎01709 836991, ⊛ snafurotherham.co.uk. Live rock venue showcasing local bands every Thursday night and hosting an annual battle of the bands. Thurs 9pm–3am, Fri & Sat 8pm–3am.

Barnsley and around

BARNSLEY is a little different from the rest of South Yorkshire. People speak differently here, with an accent that's renowned for being impenetrable. And if outsiders comment on the strength of a Barnsley resident's accent, they are likely to be told that, on the contrary, "it's posh for Barnsley".

Barnsley itself expects few visitors, but it's well worth taking a look at this bustling and unpretentious place, thronged most days with shoppers, families and students from the town-centre **Barnsley College**, a campus of the University of Huddersfield. The town centre boasts a creative hub in the shape of the **Civic** arts centre and the **Cooper Gallery**, and, famous throughout South Yorkshire, the **Barnsley markets**. If the range of **shopping** opportunities in the centre comes as a surprise, so too might be the beauty of the surrounding area; here you'll find a handful of worthwhile attractions including **Wentworth Castle and gardens**, **Cannon Hall and farm**, **Monk Bretton Priory** and the **Worsborough Mill Museum**.

Brief history

Though old enough to have appeared in the Domesday Book, Barnsley started growing to regional prominence in the seventeenth century, becoming an important meeting of the ways between the other South Yorkshire towns of Sheffield, Rotherham and Doncaster and those of what is now West Yorkshire, especially Leeds and Wakefield. Then, when the **Industrial Revolution** gathered impetus in the eighteenth and nineteenth centuries, it developed into a centre for the production of glass, and more particularly for the extraction of coal – flanking the shield on the town's coat of arms are a glass worker and a coal miner. Despite the efforts of local firebrand Arthur Scargill, the coal industry has since disappeared, though Barnsley nevertheless retains a strong sense of community.

Following its fair share of industrial decline and economic recession, at the beginning of the millennium the town's "Remaking Barnsley" project created much excitement. Though the plans to become a sort of "Tuscan hill town", drawn up by controversial postmodern architect Will Alsop in 2003, might have been the source of much mirth elsewhere in the country (or even in other Yorkshire towns) and eventually foundered when one of the principal partners withdrew, early progress was made with the building of the new **Gateway Plaza** development (including a hotel, bar and restaurant), a refurbishment of the **Civic** building, and a redeveloped transport interchange.

Barnsley markets

Between Kendray St and Cheapside; markets office on Upper May Day Green Arcade • Main hall (meat and fish) Mon–Wed, Fri & Sat 8.30am–5pm; open market (everything else) Tues, Wed, Fri & Sat 8.30am–5pm; Sun car boot • ⊛ barnsley.gov.uk

Barnsley has had a regular **market** ever since receiving royal approval in 1249, and the current one is, apart from the impressive list of celebrities who come from the area (most notably Michael Parkinson), the town's chief claim to fame. A maze-like

1

sprawl of 100 open, 119 semi-open and 110 indoor stalls sell meat, fish and vegetables, along with everything from books to bedding, fishing tackle to flowers, wigs to watches, home-brew equipment to homeopathic medicine, paste jewellery to picture frames to pet supplies, clothing to cooked foods to craft equipment. There's even a stall that just sells Barnsley memorabilia. There are numerous cafés and street-food kiosks, and access to the **Alhambra** shopping mall next door (Mon–Sat 9am–5.30pm, Sun & bank holidays 10am–4pm), and also to a large multistorey car park. On Sundays car-boot-sale stalls spill out onto nearby pedestrianized streets, parking is free throughout the town, and street performers enliven the scene. The architecture may be modern, but the atmosphere is vibrantly medieval.

Cooper Gallery

Church St • Mon–Fri 10am–4pm, Sat 10am–3pm • Free • ☎ 01226 242905, ⓦ cooper-gallery.com

In a sympathetically modernized stone house near the town hall, bearing a blue plaque with the name of the great railway engineer Joseph Locke, who attended the grammar school here, the **Cooper Gallery** opened at the start of World War I to display the art collection of local philanthropist Samuel Joshua Cooper. While his collection of paintings by Corot, Ruskin and others still forms the heart of the gallery, works by Turner, Henry Moore, Vanessa Bell and Paul Nash are also now on view, and there are periodic exhibitions of contemporary works. There's also a café and shop.

The Civic

Hanson St • ☎ 01226 327000, ⓦ barnsleycivic.co.uk

The Civic, built in 1877 but now completely remodelled, is a multi-use building designed to support creative activities. It includes the **Assembly Room**, which hosts theatre, music, dance and comedy performances (see p.71) and the **Gallery@** (Mon–Sat 10am–5pm), which puts on art exhibitions and has workspaces for local artists. The adjacent Mandela gardens, with water-wall fountain, open lawn and steel-rod benches, is a pleasant congregating point and beautifully lit at night.

Monk Bretton Priory

Cundy Cross, 1 mile east of the town centre • Daily 10am–3pm • Free; EH • ⓦ english-heritage.org.uk • Bus #31, #57 or #59 from Barnsley

Monk Bretton Priory is one of the few Cluniac monasteries in England. A tenth- to twelfth-century back-to-basics breakaway Benedictine group, the Cluniacs were pledged to clean up the order and rid it of corrupt practices such as the buying and selling of religious office (simony) and openly sexual relationships between monks and women (concubinage). Run by English Heritage, the ruins can be traced on an easy to follow site plan, and you can also see the remains of a later, fifteenth-century gatehouse.

Maurice Dobson Museum and Heritage Centre

Vicar Rd, Darfield, 4 miles east of the town centre on the main A635 road to Doncaster • Nov–March Wed 1–4pm, Sat 10am–2pm; April–Oct Wed 1–4pm, Sat 10am–4pm, Sun 2–5pm • Maurice Dobson room free; other rooms £1 for both • ☎ 01226 753440, ⓦ darfield.co.uk • Bus #218, #219 or #X19 from Barnsley

The **Maurice Dobson Museum and Heritage Centre** in **Darfield** is one of several village museums in the Barnsley region. While not worth a special trip, it's an interesting half hour if you happen to be passing during the very restricted visiting hours. And it's not just the miscellaneous local memorabilia – of the mining industry, World War I, domestic and village life and so on – that appeals, but the palpable enthusiasm of the volunteers who staff the place.

Worsbrough Mill Museum and Country Park

Worsbrough Bridge, 2.5 miles south of Barnsley • Sat–Wed 11am –5pm, • Free, though charges for some events • ☎ 01226 774527, ⓦ worsbrough-mill.com • Bus #66 from Barnsley

Worsbrough Mill at Worsbrough Bridge is both a museum of flour milling and a country park. If you arrive by car, leave it in the off-road **car park** (pay and display) and take the pleasantly tree-shaded five-minute walk to the mill, a picturesque cluster of buildings sitting below the modern Worsbrough Reservoir. The first, and oldest, part of the mill you come to dates from the eighteenth century, when it ground corn for local farmers, with the miller taking his toll of the flour. All the original machinery, including cogs, drive shafts and the water wheel itself, would have been made of wood, though this was replaced with cast iron after a new steam mill was built next to the original one in the early 1840s – that's the three-storey building that now holds much of the museum. By the early twentieth century the traditional mill was being replaced by commercial roller mills nearer the ports and the population centres, and the steam engine was sold for scrap. The water mill, however, continued milling crops for local farmers right up to the 1960s. Tracing the structures and processes used to grind the corn is fascinating: from the millpond that sits above the mill, fed by a modern reservoir above it, to the 14ft-high water wheel which drives the internal machinery, right through to the tail race that returns the water to the river. It's a model of environmental friendliness, all explained in the excellent booklet *Worsbrough Mill Museum* by Martin Watts, available in the museum shop. Also on sale are pamphlets outlining three graded **walks** in the country park, from just over one mile to just over three miles.

Elsecar Heritage Centre

Wath Rd, Elsecar, 5 miles southeast of Barnsley • Daily 10am–5pm; opening times of shops and businesses vary • Free • ☎ 01226 740203, ⓦ elsecar-heritage.com • Bus #66 from Barnsley

Housed in the former ironworks and colliery of the Fitzwilliams of Wentworth Woodhouse (see p.62), the **Elsecar Heritage Centre** represents an interesting marriage of conservation and commerce in a historical setting. Here you can see the only Newcomen atmospheric engine in the world to still be on its original site – invented by Thomas Newcomen in 1712, these engines were widely employed in

---

FIVE SOUTH YORKSHIRE HAVENS OF PEACE

In a small, crowded and largely industrial area like South Yorkshire, it can be a blessing to find a place to relax, listen to the birds and smell the flowers. Five of the best include:

Botanical Gardens, Sheffield A mini-Kew in the heart of Sheffield, with a variety of garden areas and beautifully restored glass pavilions. See p.51

Brodsworth Hall Gardens, Doncaster English Heritage have done a sterling job in rescuing and renovating Brodsworth Hall and Gardens, which now offer a wealth of paths, tunnels and bridges. See p.76

Potteric Carr Nature Reserve, Doncaster A Yorkshire Wildlife Trust site that offers peaceful paths through a variety of habitats, and loads of birds, butterflies and flowers. See p.320

Roche Abbey, Rotherham Despite being close to a large pit village, the ruins of Roche Abbey, set in a landscape designed by Capability Brown, are stunningly peaceful. See p.62

Wentworth Castle, Barnsley Their 60 acres of recently renovated garden, with associated follies and two marked walks, offer a virtual history of British gardening. See p.68

1

eighteenth-century coal mines, using atmospheric rather than steam pressure to pump out water. In addition to the engine, the listed buildings and the **steam railway** built to haul coal from the mine (☎01226 746746, ⓦelsecarrailway.co.uk), there are craft shops, an antique centre, artists' studios, a children's indoor play area and pleasant tearooms.

Wentworth Castle

Lowe Lane, 3 miles southwest of Barnsley · **Stainborough Park** Daily · Parking £3 **Wentworth Castle Gardens** Daily: April–Sept 10am–5pm; Oct–March 10am–4pm · £6.50, parking included · ☎01226 776040, ⓦ wentworthcastle.org · Bus #23 or #24 from Barnsley

Wentworth Castle, actually a country house, was built in the eighteenth century by Thomas Wentworth, a cousin of the family who owned Wentworth Woodhouse (see p.62), its opulence and scale a result of rivalry between the two. The house itself is now the home of Northern College Adult Education, and is not open to the public, though its surrounding parklands, the 600-acre Stainborough Park, which consists of landscaped park and woodland, are a delight. The formal **Wentworth Castle Gardens**, are also appealing, and like the house they are Grade I listed.

Two trails are available. The **Garden Trail** includes Stainborough Castle, a folly with superb views, and different landscaped areas – the Stumpery (full of, yes, stumps), the Fernery, the Wilderness, the Victorian Flower Garden, the Union Jack Gardens and the John Arnold Garden – together with the restored Victorian conservatory, which featured on Griff Rhys Jones's TV series *Restoration*. The two-mile-long **Parkland Trail**, meanwhile, takes in the beautiful estate surrounding the house, stopping by a number of restored follies, including the Duke of Argyll Column (built in 1742 by Thomas Wentworth to honour his wife's father), along with the Queen Anne Monument (a recognition of the extent to which Wentworth owed his rise to the patronage of the Queen), and all the other paraphernalia of the typical eighteenth-century park – a Rotunda, several lakes, a Palladian Bridge and a Corinthian temple, with striking views of the house itself.

Victoria Jubilee Museum

Taylor Hill, Cawthorne, 4.5 miles west of Barnsley, just off the A635 · Easter–Oct Sat 1–4pm, Sun 2–5pm · £1 · ☎01226 790545, · Bus #92 from Barnsley

The pretty stone village of **Cawthorne** is home to the **Victoria Jubilee Museum**, a volunteer-run jewel. Interesting for its own history as well as for its collections, it was founded in 1884 by the formidable local vicar Charles Tiplady Pratt to encourage the village's young people to take an interest in their surroundings. He gathered stuffed birds, birds' eggs, wild flowers, butterflies, moths, fossils and a wide range of domestic paraphernalia and memorabilia, a collection that continued to grow as local people donated items of interest.

As it threatened to outgrow its original premises, Pratt persuaded the local squire, Sir Walter Spenser Stanhope of Cannon Hall (see p.69), and his artist brother Roddam, that the village needed a purpose-built museum. Roddam in turn roped in a number of his Pre-Raphaelite Brotherhood friends (including John Ruskin) to help with the design, and true to the Arts and Crafts tradition, Cannon Hall estate craftsmen were used to build the museum's current rather splendid home. Splendid too are the typically Victorian **exhibits** – a two-headed lamb, a stuffed mongoose fighting a stuffed snake, a 9.5lb stone removed from a horse's intestine, a figure of John Wesley carved out of whalebone and a man-trap among them.

Cannon Hall

1

Bark House Lane, Cawthorne, 4.5 miles west of Barnsley • April–Oct Mon–Wed, Sat & Sun 11am–5pm; Nov, Dec & March Sun 11am–4pm; garden and park open all year • Free • ☎ 01226 790270 • Bus #92 from Barnsley

Just on the edge of the village of Cawthorne is **Cannon Hall**. A house on the site was bought by local iron founders the Spencers (later the Spencer-Stanhopes) in 1660, was developed into a splendid country house during the eighteenth century, and was sold to Barnsley Council in 1951, who now maintain it. It consists of a museum housed in the Hall itself, a fine walled garden and greenhouses, and acres of elegant parkland. The **Cannon Hall Museum** contains an extensive collection of ceramics, paintings and furniture. In particular, try to see the Victorian glass sculptures of ships, fruit and animals, a rare portrait by landscape painter John Constable, many original bookcases (one of which came from *The Times* newspaper offices in London's Printing House Square), a fascinating Victorian bedroom from whose windows there are fine views of the surrounding countryside, and, on the top floor, the Regimental museum of the 13th/18th Royal Hussars and the Light Dragoons, most famous for their part in the Charge of the Light Brigade, with interesting displays on the Charge itself and on the Crimean War in general.

In the grounds, well-served by information boards, the **walled garden**, next to the house and close to the stables, includes glasshouses, some parts of which may date back to the eighteenth century, truly enormous espaliered pear trees, some of which are nearly two hundred years old, and the remains of a hothouse that was used from the eighteenth century onwards to grow exotic plants, including the much-prized pineapple. Half way up the drive is a deer shed – much finer than it sounds – with stone walls and a slate roof held up by four enormous yew trunks, designed to offer shelter to the herds of ornamental deer, along with a ha-ha (a hidden wall) to stop them wandering up to the house.

Cannon Hall Farm

Bark House Lane, Cawthorne, 4.5 miles west of Barnsley • Mon–Sat 10.30am–4.30pm; Sun 10.30am –5pm • £5.95 • ☎ 01226 790427, ⓦ cannonhallfarm.co.uk

Right next to Cannon Hall is the privately owned **Cannon Hall Farm**. Once Cannon Hall's home farm, it was developed by its current owner Roger Nicholson, after he inherited it in 1958 at the age of 16, into one of the region's biggest attractions. It's still a working farm, but also now has an extensive collection of domesticated animals from around the world. There are numerous opportunities for children to handle the animals and to milk (artificial) cows, plus a huge adventure playground, with a separate section for the under-3s, delicatessen, tearooms and an ice-cream parlour. Look out in particular for the Hungarian mangalitza pigs, which, disconcertingly, have thick white fleeces like sheep, the huge metal Roundhouse that allows you to climb up onto a central gantry to view the cattle in the segmented enclosures below, and the panorama walk from where you can see the animals relaxing in large paddocks against an extensive countryside backdrop. Most of the food on sale in the shop and tearooms is produced on the farm.

Penistone

Eight miles west of Barnsley • Bus #20, #21 or #92 from Barnsley

Penistone is a good centre for exploring the nearby villages and moors. As you approach the town from the east past the elegant 29-arch **viaduct** that carries the Sheffield-to-Huddersfield line, it nestles invitingly in the valley of the River Don. There's a weekly **market** (Thurs), a monthly **farmers' market** (second Sat), and the joyously old-fashioned Paramount Cinema, in a building dating back to 1914 (see p.71).

1

There's good **walking** in the surrounding area, especially the Thurgoland Boundary walk, a nine-mile circular route taking in open fields, woodland, disused railway lines and country lanes, and the Trans Pennine Trail, which runs through the parish. A recently constructed viewing point at Royd Moor, four miles northwest of Penistone, overlooks extensive vistas across rolling countryside and the thirteen turbines of Royd Moor wind farm.

Wortley Top Forge

Forge Lane, Wortley, 6.5 miles southwest of Barnsley • Easter–Nov 5 Sun & bank hols 11am–5pm • £3 • ☎ 0114 288 7576,
ⓦ topforge.co.uk • Bus #23 from Barnsley

Though of limited appeal to non-specialists, anybody interested in the nuts and bolts of industrial history will find **Wortley Top Forge** a wonderful day out. The dam, races and sluices designed to control the water power, the wheels, drop hammers, cranes, bellows and furnaces associated with the forging of wrought iron, and the domestic buildings are all on show. It's run by volunteer enthusiasts, so opening hours are limited, and you might find some of the displays slightly obscure, but industrial archeologists will be in seventh heaven.

ARRIVAL AND INFORMATION   BARNSLEY AND AROUND

An efficient and architecturally interesting **transport interchange** on the northeast edge of Barnsley town centre gives access to local and national travel by train, coach, bus and taxi.

By car Barnsley lies just east of the M1, about halfway between Sheffield and Leeds. The town centre is only a mile from junction 37, but junction 36 can be used for the south of the borough, and 38 for the north. There are numerous well-signposted car parks throughout the town (free at weekends).
By train Trains and buses leave from the interchange.
Destinations by train Leeds (every 30min; 36min); Sheffield (every 10–20min; 22–32min).

Destinations by bus Cawthorne (hourly; 24min); Doncaster (every 30min; 49min); Elsecar (every 10min; 33min); London (every 3–6hr; 5hr); Penistone (every 10–30min; 33–43min); Rotherham (every 5–15min; 50min–1hr); Worsbrough (every 10–20min; 12min).
Tourist information Although there's no staffed tourist office in Barnsley, pamphlets are available in the Civic Hall on Eldon St and in many pubs and hotels.

ACCOMMODATION

Apart from the *Barnsley Central Premier Inn*, accommodation in the Barnsley area tends to be in chain hotels near motorway junctions that rely on corporate and private events and the passing trade rather than tourism. For more atmosphere, head to the **country house hotels** hereabouts.

Barnsley Central Premier Inn Gateway Plaza, Barnsley ☎0871 527 9204, ⓦpremierinn.com. Hundred-bed hotel, part of the town centre redevelopment, offering affordable cleanliness and comfort in the heart of town. Coffee shop and restaurant. **£39**
★**Cubley Hall** Mortimer Rd, Cubley, 8 miles west of Barnsley ☎01226 766086, ⓦcubleyhall.co.uk. Just south of Penistone, *Cubley Hall* is a handsome, ivy-covered ex-moorland farm that has been converted into a delightful inn. It offers comfortable rooms with Victorian features, pleasant gardens, a wrought-iron pavilion which is much used in weddings, and lovely views. There's a popular pub, restaurant and carvery, too (see opposite). **£75**
Fairway Hotel Elmhirst Lane, 2 miles west of Barnsley centre ☎0871 200 2289, ⓦnewcountryinns.com. The *Fairway Hotel* is an excellent budget option, especially if you've got children – there are family rooms with pull-out

beds, the bar and restaurant are very child-friendly, and there's crazy golf in the car park. **£48**
Greensprings Touring Park 2.5 miles south of Barnsley, just over 1 mile from M1 junction 36 ☎01226 288298. *Greensprings Touring Park* has sixty pitches (22 caravan, 15 tent and 23 mixed) set in pleasant countryside. Open April–Oct. Pitches from **£12**
Tankersley Manor Church Lane, Tankersley, 5 miles south of Barnsley ☎01226 744700, ⓦqhotels .co.uk/hotels/tankersley-manor-barnsley.aspx. A seventeenth-century manor house, all mellow stone and oak beams, sitting in well-maintained grounds a couple of minutes from junctions 35A or 36 on the M1, with a high level of modern comfort, a choice of where to eat (*The Brasserie* or the *Pennine Restaurant*) and a swimming pool and spa. Rooms are comfortable and tasteful. **£119**

EATING AND DRINKING

Aroma Café/Bar 8–10 The Arcade ☎01226 321293, ⓦaroma-cafe-bar.co.uk. Choose from comfortable leather sofas or tables and chairs on two floors, and an all-weather outside seating area – you've got the arcade roof above your head. Modern café decor, and a wide selection of food – sandwiches, light snacks, burgers, main courses and sizzlers, with a specials board that changes daily. Food comes in at £6–9, or there's a set menu at £15. Daily 8.30am–4pm.

Chilli Indian Restaurant 66–68 Market St ☎01226 290333, ⓦchillirestaurant.co.uk. Modern storefront restaurant at the end of traffic-free Market St, with clean, uncluttered lines, a good-value one-/two-course lunch menu (£5.95/£7.95) and evening meals with starters around £5, mains from £7.50–10.95 and six or seven vegetarian options for around £6. Try the *hyderabadi gosht*, the chicken tikka *chasni* or the *paneer makhani*. Daily noon–3pm & 6–11pm.

Cubley Hall Mortimer Rd, Cubley, 8 miles west of Barnsley ☎01226 766086, ⓦcubleyhall.co.uk. On the edge of Penistone, *Cubley Hall* offers a wide range of sandwiches, snacks, pizzas and pasta dishes in the hotel/bar and conservatory at very reasonable prices – only the steaks and the mixed grill cost more than £10 – and carvery meals in a splendid restaurant with massive oak beams, slate floors and rustic furniture (set price £9.75 a head). Bar daily 11.30am–11pm; food served until 9.30pm.

Pinocchio's 15–17 New St ☎01226 770121, ⓦpinocchios-restaurant.co.uk. Highly rated locally for value, authenticity and friendly informal surroundings.

Pinocchio's starters vary from an olive and asparagus dip at £3.50 to king prawns at £7.25, and main courses from around £11.95–17.95. There's a children's menu from which children can eat free up to 7pm (one/adult). Limited parking. Mon–Fri 11.30am–2pm, 6–10pm, Sat 11.30am–2.30pm, 5–10pm.

★**Royal** Barnsley Rd, Barugh Green ☎01226 382363. With a handsome nineteenth-century building and a understated but comfortable interior, the *Royal* pub manages to combine the welcome of a traditional local with great food in attractive surroundings. Authentic tapas includes delicious cheese croquettes, hot prawns and deep-fried squid; a la carte varies according to what fish and meat are good in local markets. Mains £10–30; tapas (£3–6) in the bar. Allow longer than usual for visits to the loo – there are extensive displays of saucy postcards, a tribute to the local company that produced them. Pub Tues–Fri 5pm–midnight, Sat & Sun noon–midnight; tapas Wed–Sat 5–10pm, Sun 5–9pm; restaurant Fri & Sat 7pm–late (bookings only).

Spencer Arms Cawthorne, 4.5 miles west of Barnsley ☎01226 792795, ⓦspencerarms.co.uk. Beautiful, award-winning old (1720) pub in a pretty village. You can eat in the traditional beamed-and-panelled bar areas or in the linen-tablecloth luxury of the restaurant. Extensive lunch and a la carte menus, with pizzas, salads and desserts on the former (nothing's more than £10), and main courses on the latter starting at £13 (salmon and chicken). Top price, sirloin steak at £22. Extensive parking. Daily noon–11pm.

ENTERTAINMENT

Assembly Room Hanson St ☎01226 327000, ⓦbarnsleycivic.co.uk. Venue at the Civic (see p.66) hosting performances of all sorts including theatre, music, dance and comedy. Mon–Fri 10am–6pm (5pm school holidays), Sat 10am–5pm, Sun (when there's a performance) 10am–4pm.

Lamproom Theatre Westgate ☎01226 200075, ⓦbarnsleylamproom.com. Occupying an old Non-conformist chapel, a Grade II listed building dating from 1780, this theatre hosts a variety of performances, from national touring productions to local am dram, "Evenings with..." and panto. There's a theatre bar on performance nights, and parking in the car park across the road is free

after 6pm. The front of the building doesn't look like much, but the opposite side is a delight. Box office Mon–Sat 10am–2.30pm.

Paramount Cinema Shrewsbury Rd, Penistone, 8 miles west of Barnsley ☎01226 767532, ⓦpenistone paramount.co.uk. Wonderfully old-fashioned cinema hosting a combination of films, live shows, comedy and music.

Parkway Cinema 62–68 Eldon St ☎01226 248218, ⓦbarnsley.parkwaycinemas.co.uk. Barnsley has a small (two-screen) town centre cinema – something of a rarity these days. Mon–Fri 5–9pm, Sat 1–9pm, Sun 2–7.30pm.

Doncaster and around

DONCASTER has always made things – from mighty steam locomotives (both the world-record holding *Mallard* and the *Flying Scotsman* were built here) to sweets that became household names (Parkinson's butterscotch, Nuttall's Mintoes, Murray Mints). Under the Romans Doncaster was an important town known as Danum. It played a

1

prestigious part in aviation history when the first air display in Britain was held here in 1909 and it became renowned for coal extraction. But perhaps above all the town is known for its **racecourse**, home since the eighteenth century to the classic race the St Leger, which gives the place a certain raffishness that is missing from other South Yorkshire towns.

A number of town-centre sites are worth a visit – in addition to the **Doncaster Racecourse**, there's **St George's Minster**, **Doncaster Market** and **Doncaster Museum**, together with the redeveloped **Lakeside** area. However, the area around Doncaster arguably has more going for it than the town itself, not least two lordly country houses open to the public – **Brodsworth** and **Cusworth** halls – the magnificent Norman castle at **Conisbrough** and a fine children's attraction at Brockholes Farm – the **Yorkshire Wildlife Park**. Worth a visit too is the small town of **Bawtry**, which has become the pub, restaurant and car-buying capital of the area.

Doncaster Minster

Church St • Mon–Fri 10.30am–3.30pm, Sat 11am–noon • Free • ☎ 01302 323748, ⓦ doncasterminster.org

Though it can't compete in age with Rotherham's Minster (see p.58), **Doncaster Minster Church of St George** is just as interesting in its own way. Considered to be one of the finest examples of Gothic Revival architecture in Britain – "Victorian Gothic at its very best", according to John Betjeman – it was designed by Sir George Gilbert Scott, the architect of, among many other edifices, St Pancras Station and the Albert Memorial in London. The original church having burnt down in 1853, Scott's hugely impressive cathedral-like parish church was completed five years later. Externally it is cruciform, with a massive 170ft-high Perpendicular tower and a nave and chancel in the early Decorated style. Inside, it boasts good Victorian stained-glass windows, a clock by Dent (who also designed Big Ben) and a huge five-manual organ by Edmund Schulze. Though at a distance it dominates its surroundings, it is unfortunately isolated from the rest of the town centre by the swirling traffic of an inner ring road and a new bridge across the Don – by far the best view of the Minster is from the *Costa Coffee* in the Frenchgate Centre's Waterstones.

Doncaster Market

Market Place • Tues, Fri & Sat 9am–4pm; farmers' market 1st & 3rd Wed of the month

Established in 1248, **Doncaster Market** is based in and around the Corn Exchange, just across from the Minster. One of the biggest markets in the north of England, with around four hundred indoor and two hundred outdoor stalls, it sells fresh food, clothes, crafts and gifts, with a fortnightly farmers' market. Within the Corn Exchange building, in the **Forum**, above the stalls, arts and crafts traders produce goods on the premises and offer them for sale; there's a balcony tearoom, too.

Mansion House

45 High St • Group visits can be arranged on ☎ 01302 734032

Worth a quick look in the town centre is the **Mansion House**, an elegant civic building designed in 1749 by James Paine, who was already at work in the area restoring Nostell Priory. Doncaster Mansion House is one of only three such buildings in the country – the others being the mansion houses of London and York – and is still used for civic functions by the mayor. Public access is limited to several open days throughout the year (two per month), plus group tours. On show are numerous rooms used by the mayor and council – the civic parlour, the great kitchen, the salon, several committee rooms and the impressive ballroom and council chamber.

FROM TOP MAGNA, ROTHERHAM (P.60); WINTER GARDEN, SHEFFIELD (P.46) >

1

Doncaster Museum and Art Gallery

Chequer Rd, just south of the town centre • Wed–Fri 10am–4.30pm, Sat & Sun 10.30am–4pm • Free • ☎ 01302 734293, ⓦ doncaster.gov.uk

Doncaster Museum and Art Gallery has some fascinating displays relating to the town's ecclesiastical, coal mining, engineering and sporting history, the geology and wildlife of the surrounding area and much else besides. Kids in particular will enjoy the roaring bears as you enter, the nightmarish sea lamprey, the huge stuffed sturgeon, a coin minted at the time of Alexander the Great, a crocodile skull and jaw, the fossilized ichthyosaurus, a Micronesian sword inlaid with sharks teeth, the samurai armour and a host of everyday objects from the past. Displays of ceramics and art include a beautiful Swinton loving cup, a display of racing cups going back to 1779 and numerous paintings of Doncaster races. Attached to the museum is the **Regimental Museum of the King's Own Yorkshire Light Infantry**. There's a small shop, and coffee is available.

Doncaster Racecourse

The Grandstand, Leger Way • Reception Mon–Fri 8am–6pm • Tickets generally £7–39, more for the St Leger • ☎ 01302 304200, ⓦ doncaster-racecourse.co.uk

One of the oldest and largest in Britain, **Doncaster Racecourse** has hosted horse racing since the sixteenth century. One of nine racecourses in Yorkshire, and the only one in South Yorkshire, the course was first marked out in 1614 and is today state-of-the-art for both flat and jump racing. Two famous races were established in the eighteenth century – the **Doncaster Cup** in 1766 and the **St Leger** in 1776. Both are still held to this day, and are run during the St Leger meeting in the second week of September. Look out in particular for the "Go Racing in Yorkshire" festival in July, family days in the summer, Championship days throughout the year, and in particular the St Leger, the last classic race of the flat season. Great fun too is Ladies Day in St Leger week, when women dress up to the nines, attend the races, then throng pubs throughout the area in their finery. At other times, the Racecourse is used as a venue for acts such as Status Quo, the Kaiser Chiefs and James Blunt.

Lakeside

Access mainly from Bawtry Rd and White Rose Way • Mon–Wed & Fri 10am–6pm, Thurs 10am–8pm, Sat 9.30am–6pm, Sun 10am–4.30pm, bank holidays 10am–6pm • ⓦ lakeside-village.co.uk

Lakeside, lying between the town centre and the M18, is a mixed development built around a man-made lake. The lake itself is nicely laid out, with islands linked by wooden bridges, an artificial beach and miles of paths for walking. Around the town end of the lake stand a **multiplex cinema** and a **bowling alley**, while at the far end is a discount retail outlet with nearly fifty shops offering up to sixty percent discounts on a range of famous brands, together with indoor and outdoor children's play areas, cafés and plentiful parking. Beyond this lies the **Keepmoat Stadium**, home to the town's league football team Doncaster Rovers, and to the Doncaster Belles, one of the country's premier women's teams.

Dome

Lakeside • ☎ 01302 370777, ⓦ the-dome.co.uk

At the entrance to the Lakeside development is the **Dome**, a leisure complex that includes a two-level ice-skating rink, a large leisure pool with a wave machine, a variety of slides and an open tube that swings out into the fresh air, a health club and spa, a concert venue and a number of food outlets. They often have special offers available so it's well worth checking their website.

1

Aeroventure

Dakota Rd • Wed–Sun plus bank hols & Tues during school hols: April–Oct 10am–5pm; Nov–March 10am–4pm • £5 • ☎ 01302 761616, ⓦ aeroventure.org.uk

Tucked behind the multiplex and bowling alley in the Lakeside development, on what was once RAF Doncaster (follow the brown propeller signs), **Aeroventure** aircraft museum occupies – and spills out of – a group of hangars and huts. Run entirely by enthusiastic volunteers, it's a great hotchpotch of planes, aircraft parts, helicopters (a particular strength), engines, missiles, bombs and airfield vehicles and equipment. With aircraft of all sorts suspended from the hangar ceiling, it looks like an adolescent giant's bedroom. For enthusiasts it's well worth browsing in the excellent model and gift shop and chatting to the knowledgeable attendants.

Yorkshire Wildlife Park

Brockholes Lane, Branton (signposted off the A638 Bawtry road, 5 miles south of Doncaster) • Daily 10am–6pm, last entry 5pm • £15.50 • ☎ 01302 535057, ⓦ yorkshirewildlifepark.com • Bus #91 from Doncaster

Yorkshire Wildlife Park provides a fine day out for families with young children. A well-organized and up-to-date wildlife facility that makes full use of its rural setting, it has a clutch of attractions just inside the entrance, including a large café/restaurant, a play barn and outdoor play area, a gift shop, aviary and a petting zoo. Beyond, a trail loops out into open grass and woodland, with enclosures of well-kept animals and birds – both common domesticated animals such as dogs, chickens, ducks and geese, and more exotic racoons, meerkats, lamas, red river hogs and painted hunting dogs. There's a huge **African Plains** enclosure, with zebra, antelopes called lechwe (which can run and swim well, and can escape predators by submerging themselves in water, leaving only their nostrils above the surface), ankoli cattle, with hollow horns that can span up to 12ft, and ostriches. They are often, alas, a long way away, but there is a coin-in-the-slot talking telescope that helps you to see them while telling you all about them. Beyond the African Plains enclosure, two fenced areas allow the public to mingle with animals after passing through a double gate – the wallaby walkabout, and the lemur woods. Elsewhere are Leopard Heights, Land of the Tiger, giraffe and giant anteaters enclosures and a South American village. And everywhere there are picnic spots and information boards with details on the wildlife.

Bawtry and around

Eight miles south of Doncaster • Bus #21, #25, #29 or #99 from Doncaster to Bawtry; #22 to Tickhill

On the Yorkshire/Nottinghamshire border, two satellite towns have become popular as day-trip destinations. **BAWTRY**, which owes its existence to travel – as a port on the River Idle, a staging post on the Great North Road, a base for bomber command

---

TOP FIVE FAMILY DAYS OUT IN SOUTH YORKSHIRE

Clifton Park, Rotherham Well-organized museum and the biggest play area in Yorkshire, with separate areas for different ages. See p.59

Magna, Rotherham A terrific hands-on industrial museum, with excellent wet and dry play areas outside. See p.60

Tropical Butterfly House, Sheffield Not only butterflies, but birds, meerkats, insects and snakes, with birds of prey and parrot displays, skunk feeding and much more. See p.61

Weston Park, Sheffield Fine museum covering the history of the city, with plenty of opportunity for dressing up. See p.51

Yorkshire Wildlife Park, Doncaster A succession of imaginatively planned animal enclosures, all in acres of space. See above

(RAF Finningley) and the site of England's newest airport – Robin Hood Doncaster-Sheffield – has become the pub and restaurant capital of the region. It also attracts evangelicals to the Christian centre in Bawtry Hall, browsers to its numerous independent shops, and wheeler-dealer tyre-kickers to its thrice-weekly **car auctions**. Nearby **TICKHILL**, meanwhile, clustered around its 1777 Buttercross, grew up around a motte-and-bailey castle, whose remains are still there, indistinct from the ground but clearly visible in aerial shots. It boasts a beautiful millpond, the superb twelfth-century **St Mary's church** – a mainly Perpendicular structure with some traces of Norman style – and its own fair share of pubs and restaurants.

Conisbrough Castle

Six miles southwest of Doncaster on the A630 • May– Sept daily 10am–6pm; Oct daily 10am–5pm; Nov–March Sat & Sun 10am–4pm • £4.70; EH • ☎ 01709 863329, ⓦ english-heritage.or.uk • There's a free car park on the main road at the bottom of the hill, from where it's a 5min climb up to the castle; bus #x78 from Doncaster and Rotherham

CONISBROUGH, a picturesque and heavily wooded village, is dominated by **Conisbrough Castle**, particularly the magnificent Norman keep. Built in around 1180 on the site of an earlier motte-and-bailey castle, it stands 90ft high, with walls 15ft thick at the base, and is universally recognized as the finest of its type (circular, with buttresses) in England. The castle featured (if somewhat unhistorically) in Sir Walter Scott's medieval tale *Ivanhoe*, and is now jointly maintained by English Heritage and the Ivanhoe Trust. The information available in the castle is spot on – informative, but not too detailed. There's an excellent single-sheet colour guide on sale in the modern **visitor centre**, where there's also an informative display on the castle's history, and individual parts of the complex are clearly posted with information boards. Views from the roof of the keep are extensive.

If you have the time, it's worth taking the short walk to **St Peter's church** in the village – it's the oldest stone building in South Yorkshire, parts of which date from as early as 750 AD, and one of the ten oldest in England.

Cusworth Hall and Park

Back Lane, 3 miles west of Doncaster • **Museum** Mon–Wed 10am–4.30pm, Sat & Sun 10.30am–4.15pm • Free **Tearoom** Daily 10am–4pm • ☎ 01302 782342, ⓦ cusworth-hall.co.uk • Bus #41 or #42 from Doncaster

Cusworth Hall and Park stands on a hill surrounded by trees overlooking an ornamental lake and, in the distance, the sprawl of Doncaster. Its story is a familiar one – built in the eighteenth century for a local merchant family, it declined over time until, in the early 1960s, soaring maintenance costs and stiff death duties forced its owner to sell it to the local authority. Now a council-run **museum**, it has an interesting hotchpotch of displays of artefacts from various aspects of the region's social and industrial history – costume, jewellery, toys, coal mining, transport – all with enlightening information boards. The building itself is of interest, with lots of Georgian plasterwork and a kitchen, bakehouse, library and chapel. There's a **tearoom** and a shop.

Brodsworth Hall

Brodsworth, 5 miles northwest of Doncaster• **House** April–Oct daily 11am–5pm • £9.70 including gardens; EH **Gardens and tearooms** April–Sept daily 11am–6pm; Oct daily 11am–5pm, Nov–March Sat & Sun 10am–4pm • Gardens only £5; EH • ☎ 01302 724969, ⓦ english-heritage.org.uk • Bus #203 from Doncaster

Brodsworth Hall is a mid-Victorian house with a fascinating history. On the death of its creator Theophile Thellusson in 1797, the original estate became enmeshed in a complicated legal dispute that rumbled on for over half a century. Finally the matter was resolved in the 1850s, when local industrialist Charles Thellusson inherited it, knocked down the original house, and built the present one as a home fitting for one of the county's wealthiest landowners and father of six children. After his death in 1885, the estate, and its declining income, were inherited by each of his four sons in turn, and then, since they were all childless, by his daughter Constance. By the 1980s her granddaughter Pamela and her husband were camped out in a single room with an oil heater, unable to maintain the crumbling and increasingly leaky edifice. She finally gave the house to English Heritage in 1990, and the house and gardens were sympathetically and gently renovated to give an excellent impression not only of how the landed classes lived in the mid-nineteenth century, but also of how room-use could change over time. It is, in many ways, an interestingly untypical house. Rooms are more intimate, less grand than in many similar mansions. Instead of being stuck in the attics, the servants had their own wing – it's the lower one on the right as you face the main entrance and porte-cochère. The magnificent mainly grass and evergreen **gardens** are worth visiting at any time of year. Look out in particular for the fern dell; the archery range and the target house, used to store archery equipment; the west lawns, set up with croquet hoops; the eye-catcher, a deliberately created ruined wall; the summer house; and the long rose pergola. There's a café and a children's playground.

ARRIVAL AND INFORMATION   DONCASTER AND AROUND

Doncaster's connections with the rest of the country are excellent – it's no wonder that so many companies have distribution warehouses in and around the town. It lies in the angle between the M18 and A1(M), giving it access not only to those two motorways but also to the M1 and M62. Rail links too are first-rate, since Doncaster sits astride the main east–coast rail route between London and Scotland, and also the Transpennine line to Manchester and the northwest. For local transport, buses and trains head off to Sheffield, Leeds, York, Hull, Grimsby, Worksop and Mansfield, from the very well-organized **Doncaster Interchange** – and if you have to wait, you can shop in the Frenchgate Centre upstairs.

By car Doncaster lies off M18 exits 3 and 4 and the Warmsworth exit on the A1(M). There are numerous multi-storey car parks in the town centre, though not much on-street parking.

By train Doncaster train station is in the Doncaster Interchange, next to the bus station and the Frenchgate centre. Destinations Leeds (every 15–20min; 35–50min); London Kings Cross (every 5–15min; 1hr 45min); Sheffield (every 10min; 20–30min); York (every 5–40min; 20–25min).

By bus Doncaster's main bus station is at Doncaster Interchange.

By plane The UK's newest airport, Robin Hood Doncaster-Sheffield, lies 5 miles southeast of Doncaster; there are frequent shuttle services from the airport to Doncaster Interchange.

Destinations Barnsley (every 30min; 45min); London (2 daily; 4hr 10min); Rotherham (every 5–25min; 53min); Sheffield (every 10min; 1hr 24min).

Tourist office Blue Building, 38–40 High St, Doncaster (Mon–Fri 9.30am–5pm, Sat 10am–3.30pm; ☎01302 734 309, ⍜ visitdoncaster.co.uk).

ACCOMMODATION

Crown Market Place, High St, Bawtry, 8 miles south of Doncaster ☎01302 710341, ⍜ crownhotel-bawtry .com. Bawtry's only surviving coaching inn, this venerable posting house looks from the outside just as it did in the late eighteenth century. Inside it's a different matter, with all the modern decor and facilities of a twenty-first century refit. It's a good medium- to top-end business and wedding hotel, with 76 rooms of varying standards. And with a range of restaurants (see p.78) and food pubs on the doorstep, you needn't always eat in at the hotel. __£135__

Danum Hotel High St, Doncaster ☎01302 342261, ⍜ danumhotel.com. Slap-bang in the centre of Doncaster,

the venerable Edwardian *Danum* has been a feature of the town for a century. Though some rooms are rather tired, the old-fashioned atmosphere is in keeping with its history. Wonderful location right in the thick of things, but it can be noisy, especially at weekends. Look out for deals – it can be remarkably cheap. __£50__

★**Grand St Leger** Racecourse Roundabout, Bennetthorpe, Doncaster ☎01302 364111, ⍜ grand stleger.com. Directly across a large roundabout from Doncaster Racecourse, the *Grand St Leger* occupies a solid 1810 Grade II listed building that has housed, at different times, the *Turf Inn* and accommodation for stable lads.

1

Not big – with twenty executive, deluxe and standard rooms – the hotel offers understated comfort. It's getting a bit down-at-heel, but a large expansion is planned. Drinks and snacks are available in the *Paddock* bar, and fine dining in *Carrington's* restaurant. **£65**

Mount Pleasant Great North Rd, 6 miles south of Doncaster ☎01302 868696, ⊛ mountpleasant.co.uk. The *Mount Pleasant*, out towards Bawtry, is an attractive mix of traditional architecture and up-to-the-minute modern facilities. Public areas are sumptuous, rooms are luxurious, there are three bars, an excellent restaurant, a health and

wellness centre, and the grounds are extensive. Frequent buses from outside the hotel run to Doncaster, Robin Hood Doncaster-Sheffield airport and Bawtry. **£89**

★**Regent** Regent Square, Doncaster ☎01302 364180, ⊛ theregenthotel.co.uk. In the town centre, the *Regent*, a boutique-style hotel, occupies a cluster of eighteenth-century buildings looking out onto a pleasant Georgian square. Its bars, restaurant, public areas and rooms can seem labyrinthine, but services are good, rooms contemporary and comfortable, and there's often live music – in the *Abbey Road* bar (yes, the Beatles stayed here in the 1960s). **£65**

EATING AND DRINKING

The centre of Doncaster is a good place to eat and drink, though it can get very boisterous on Friday and Saturday nights. The small towns of **Bawtry** and **Tickhill**, south of Doncaster, are better bets for anyone seeking a quieter ambience.

DONCASTER

Black Bull 12 Market Place ☎01302 361661. A large, traditional pub that's packed with punters on market days (Tues, Fri & Sat). A good choice for Sunday lunch if you have a large appetite – their roast dinners are gigantic. Mon–Sat 10am–11.30pm, Sun noon–10.30pm.

Hare and Tortoise 329 Bawtry Rd, a few miles south of the town centre ☎01302 867329, ⊛ vintageinn .co.uk/thehareandtortoisedoncaster. A typical *Vintage Inn*, in an interesting building – in this case eighteenth century, once an inn attached to a toll house, with the mismatched furniture, open fires, exposed beams and pleasant garden giving it a welcoming country atmosphere, despite its location on a busy road junction. Good variety of food, from classics such as fish and chips, gammon and hunter's chicken to steaks and burgers and a variety of pies (the beef and Merlot is well worth a try). Starters cost around £3.50–5.95 and mains £7.95–17.99. Ample parking, and it's on the main Bawtry and Robin Hood bus routes. Mon–Sat noon–11pm, Sun noon–10.30pm.

White Swan 34 Frenchgate ☎01302 366573. A small, long-established inn that's popular with the real ale drinkers due to the superior range of reasonably priced beer, served across what is said to be the highest bar in Britain. It also does food. Mon–Wed 10am–11pm, Thurs 11am–1am, Fri & Sat 10am–1am, Sun 11.30am–10.30pm.

BAWTRY

★**China Rose** 16 South Parade ☎01302 710461, ⊛ chinarose.co.uk. This large, family-owned and -run Cantonese restaurant is well known throughout South Yorkshire for the quality of its food and service. Standout dishes include duckling in orange sauce, fillet steak Cantonese style and Szechuan chicken. The decor is smart, with plenty of room between tables and a warm atmosphere. Booking is essential at peak times; if you arrive early you can relax with a drink in the comfortable bar area and

order your food. Parking is limited, so you might have to leave the car in the centre of Bawtry – a 2min walk from the restaurant. Starters £6–11, main courses £9.50–15.50, set menus for two to six people £20–26 per person. Daily 5.30–11pm.

Crown Market Place, High St ☎01302 710341, ⊛ crown -hotel-bawtry.com. An eighteenth-century coaching inn in contemporary clothes, this stylish if dark restaurant offers a range of grills, pastas and fish. Look out in particular for the sharing platters – Asian, American, Mediterranean, seafood and antipasti. Daily noon–10pm.

Dower House Market Place ☎01302 719696. In a large building on the market place adjoining Bawtry Hall, the *Dower House* attracts diners from all over the area for its good, varied Indian menu. Tandoori cuisine is a speciality. The bar is often thronged with takeaway customers and people waiting for their tables. Starters £3.50–5.20, main courses £8.50–14. Daily 6–11pm.

The Ship Gainsborough Rd ☎01302 710275, ⊛ theship-bawtry.com. On the edge of Bawtry, this is a typical local whose owners have, since taking over in 2007, re-invented it as a hugely popular food pub without alienating its long-term customers. The lounge bar largely caters for diners and the public bar for people just having a drink. There's a long chalkboard menu, generous portions of well-prepared food – the chicken in cheese sauce is to die for – and a good choice of beautifully kept real ales. It's child-friendly, too. Mains £7.95–16.95. Mon–Thurs noon–10.30pm, Fri & Sat 11.30am–11.30pm, Sun noon–10.30pm.

Zinnis 1 Market Place ☎01302 711115. Tuscan cuisine in cool modern surroundings. It's popular at lunchtime and in the evenings, but can get manic at weekends. Don't miss the *ravioloni di ricotta bufala* and the *saltimbocca alla Romana*. The pizzas are good, too. Starters £2.75–9.95, Mains £13.95–22. Mon–Sat 11am–11pm, Sun noon–10.30pm.

NIGHTLIFE

★**The Leopard** 2 West St, near Doncaster train station ☎01302 363054, ⓦmyspace.com/theleopard doncaster. The dowdy, brown-tiled exterior hides a treasure of a grungy music venue. Live bands every Friday and Saturday, and a surprisingly diverse clientele drinking a good range of fine ales. Thurs 4pm–midnight, Fri–Sun noon–midnight.

The Priory Club Lazarus Court, Bradford Row, Doncaster ☎01302 768204, ⓦtheprioryclub.com. A compact nightclub with a strong focus on guest DJs and club nights. A wide range of genres is featured throughout the week, from house on Saturdays to indie on Fridays and metal on Wednesdays. Tues 11.30pm–3am, Wed 11pm–3am, Fri & Sat 11.30pm–4.30am.

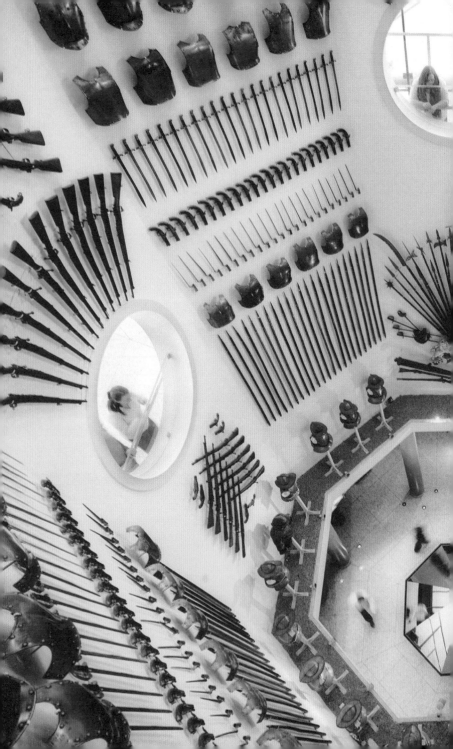

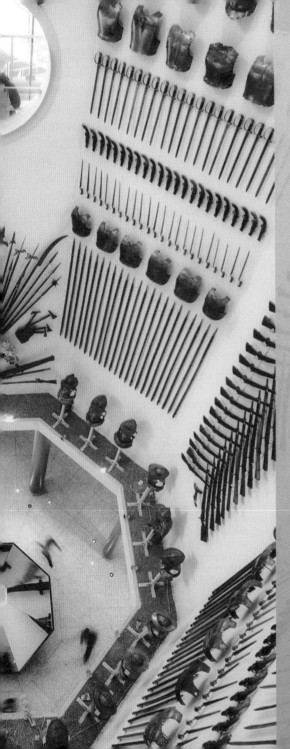

West Yorkshire

ROYAL ARMOURIES MUSEUM, LEEDS

West Yorkshire

The population of West Yorkshire – the area spreading from Lancashire in the west to the A1 in the east – accounts for more than half the population of Yorkshire as a whole. The area's wealth and power traditionally arose from wool and coal – roughly, textiles to the west (Halifax, Huddersfield and Bradford) and coal to the east (Wakefield), while regional capital Leeds had a foot in both camps. With the decline of textiles and coal in the late twentieth century, many areas have struggled to develop alternatives; without doubt, the most successful has been Leeds, a popular destination for recreational and business tourism and a major centre for financial services. However, the whole region is doing its best to bring in visitors, and there are many worthwhile attractions, including industrial heritage sites, castles, monasteries, great houses, gardens, museums, villages and market towns.

While there are wide **open spaces** to enjoy in West Yorkshire – in particular, the lovely Calder Valley to the west of Halifax and the South Pennine moors to the west of Haworth and Keighley – these are more of a recreational space for the population of the industrial cities than a major tourist draw for visitors. Pretty as they are, they're not in the same league as the Yorkshire Dales National Park to the north.

In **Leeds** the main draws include the Royal Armouries, the Thackray Medical Museum, the great house of Temple Newsam and a number of Victorian arcades. The city also takes pride of place in the region for interesting places to stay, eat and go out. **Bradford** is known for its excellent **National Media Museum**, and for the flourishing community of people of Asian origin whose clothes emporia, food shops, restaurants and places of worship invigorate certain parts of the city. In the surrounding area the big draws are **Saltaire**, with its model village and magnificent mill, containing, among other things, the Hockney gallery, and the world-famous Brontë parsonage at **Haworth**. **Halifax** boasts Eureka!, the only museum in Britain to be aimed specifically at primary-age children, while the nearby **Calder Valley** features a succession of mill villages, once grimy with coal dust, now basking in a post-industrial tranquility – chief among them is the pretty canalside town of **Hebden Bridge**. In **Huddersfield** check out the charming Red House Museum and the rather more splendid Oakwell Hall, and near **Wakefield**, the **National Coal Mining Museum**, with its opportunity to go underground, and the genuinely splendid open-air **Yorkshire Sculpture Park**.

YORKSHIRE SCULPTURE PARK

Highlights

❶ Royal Armouries Museum, Leeds
World-class collection related to war, peace and hunting, with hands-on displays. **See p.91**

❷ Thackray Medical Museum, Leeds The horrid history of disease shouldn't be this entertaining, but it is. **See p.92**

❸ National Media Museum, Bradford
Interactive introduction to photography, television, film and animation. **See p.103**

❹ Bradford curry houses Britain's curry capital offers everything from fine Indian restaurants and cheap and cheerful canteen-style diners. **See p.107**

❺ Saltaire Sir Titus Salt's Victorian factory town and mill now contains a range of galleries, cafés and shops. **See p.107**

❻ Hebden Bridge Pretty mill town, now an artistic and new age destination, sitting astride a canal. **See p.119**

❼ National Coal Mining Museum A working coal mine until the mid-1980s, now a museum that includes subterranean visits. **See p.131**

❽ Yorkshire Sculpture Park Art and nature come together in wide-open spaces dotted with beautiful sculptures. **See p.132**

HIGHLIGHTS ARE MARKED ON THE MAP ON PP.84–85

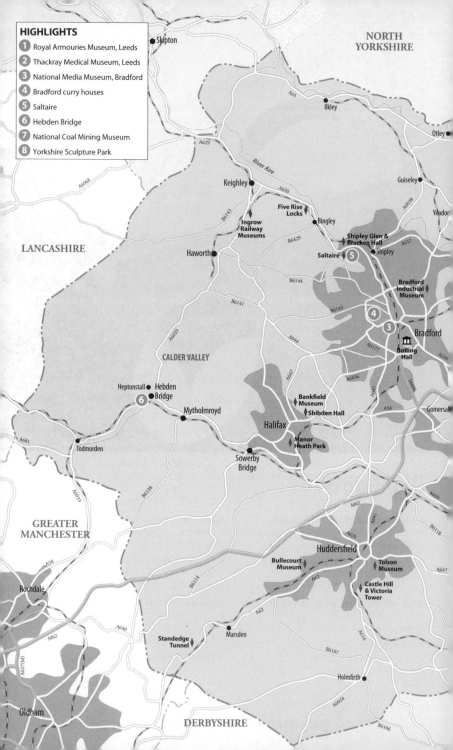

HIGHLIGHTS

1. Royal Armouries Museum, Leeds
2. Thackray Medical Museum, Leeds
3. National Media Museum, Bradford
4. Bradford curry houses
5. Saltaire
6. Hebden Bridge
7. National Coal Mining Museum
8. Yorkshire Sculpture Park

NORTH YORKSHIRE

LANCASHIRE

Skipton

Ilkley

Otley

Guiseley

Yeador

A65

A629

A6068

Keighley

Five Rise Locks

Bingley

River Aire

A650

B6143

Ingrow Railway Museums

Haworth

B6429

Shipley Glen & Bracken Hall

Saltaire (5) Shipley

A657

Bradford Industrial Museum

B6144

B6141

B6145

(4)
(3) Bradford

A6177

Bolling Hall

A6036

A641

A6056

A658

A650

CALDER VALLEY

A6033

A644

A647

Heptonstall ● Hebden Bridge

(6)

Mytholmroyd

Bankfield Museum

Shibden Hall

Gomersa

Todmorden

A681

Halifax

A58

Manor Heath Park

A644

Sowerby Bridge

B6138

A6033

GREATER MANCHESTER

A58

M62

A629

M62

A641

B6118

Rochdale

Huddersfield

Bullecourt Museum

Tolson Museum

A642

A62

Castle Hill & Victoria Tower

A640

A62

A616

Oldham

A627(M)

M62

Standedge Tunnel

Marsden

B6107

B6024

Holmfirth

B6106

DERBYSHIRE

Leeds and around

LEEDS is Yorkshire's greatest city. The inhabitants of Sheffield, York and Hull, even Bradford, may deny it, but they know in their hearts that it's true. Just as Manchester owed its huge industrial expansion to the development and mechanization of the Lancashire cotton industry, Leeds grew up as the power behind the similar growth of the Yorkshire woollen industry – between them, nineteenth-century Manchester and Leeds clothed the world.

As soon as you arrive in Leeds, you feel the metropolitan buzz of its burgeoning culture and commerce, its successful redevelopment and the in-your-face chutzpah of its magnificent Victorian architectural heritage. It's the home of the regional studios

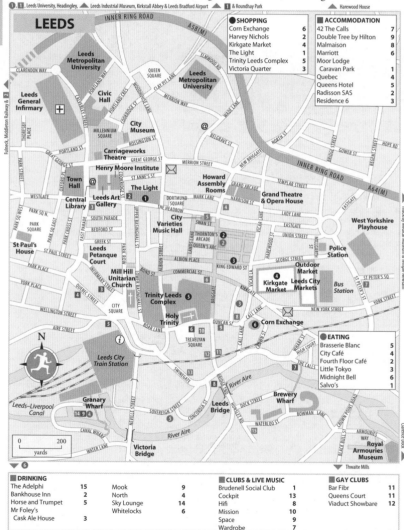

LEEDS

● SHOPPING	
Corn Exchange	6
Harvey Nichols	2
Kirkgate Market	4
The Light	1
Trinity Leeds Complex	5
Victoria Quarter	3

■ ACCOMMODATION	
42 The Calls	7
Double Tree by Hilton	9
Malmaison	8
Marriott	6
Moor Lodge Caravan Park	1
Quebec	4
Queens Hotel	5
Radisson SAS	2
Residence 6	3

■ EATING	
Brasserie Blanc	5
City Café	4
Fourth Floor Café	2
Little Tokyo	3
Midnight Bell	6
Salvo's	1

■ DRINKING			
The Adelphi	15	Mook	9
Bankhouse Inn	2	North	4
Horse and Trumpet	5	Sky Lounge	14
Mr Foley's Cask Ale House	3	Whitelocks	6

■ CLUBS & LIVE MUSIC	
Brudenell Social Club	1
Cockpit	13
Hifi	8
Mission	10
Space	9
Wardrobe	7

■ GAY CLUBS	
Bar Fibr	11
Queens Court	11
Viaduct Showbare	12

of the BBC and ITV, its Grand Theatre hosts Opera North and gets regular visits from Northern Ballet, and it has a range of top-end shops, fine restaurants, good pubs and museums and art galleries galore. Forget flat caps and whippets – Leeds is up there, if not with London, then certainly with Manchester and Birmingham as a bright and fast-moving modern city that has built on its august industrial past.

City Square seems to capture the history and flavour of the city – an island of Victorian municipal statuary standing at the centre of a swirl of heavy traffic, surrounded by modern tower blocks. The two other major squares also sum up aspects of Leeds history – **Park Square**, the early days of eighteenth-century growth, **Millennium Square**, a mixture of Victorian (City Museum), inter-war (Civic Hall) and twenty-first-century (Mandela Gardens). Just down the road there's a cracking fine arts complex made up of the **Library**, the **City Art Gallery** and the **Henry Moore Institute** – all free. Though Leeds didn't avoid the excesses of urban planning and redevelopment in the 1960s, since the 1980s a great deal of sympathetic regeneration has taken place, including the renovation of the **Corn Exchange**, the conversion of older buildings such as **The Light**, the renovation of the **Victorian Arcades** and the development of the areas along the Leeds and Liverpool Canal and the River Aire – especially the dock upon which the **Royal Armouries Museum** is built.

Outside the city centre, too, there is much of interest. **Roundhay Park**, the largest municipal open space in Leeds, offers fine walking and the excellent **Tropical World**. The museum opposite **Kirkstall Abbey**'s gaunt medieval remains offers an insight into the world of Cistercian monks whose medieval wool dealings laid the foundations of Yorkshire's all-conquering textile industry. The **Thackray Museum** on the massive St James's Hospital (known as "Jimmy's" to Leeds residents) site, which deals with nineteenth-century medical practices and public health, is one of the best of its kind in the world. **Temple Newsam** Elizabethan/Jacobean mansion is a wonderful introduction to sixteenth- and seventeenth-century history; **Harewood House**, one of Britain's foremost stately homes, to that of the eighteenth century. And a trio of industrial museums – **Thwaite Mills**, **Middleton Railway** and **Armley Mills** – gets down to the nitty-gritty of what made the city of Leeds great.

City Square and around

At first sight **City Square**, just north of the train station, looks like a glorified traffic island. It's worth, though, a more careful look and half an hour's exploration. Built between 1893 and 1903 to mark the elevation of Leeds to city status, it features a large and impressive **equestrian statue** of Edward, the Black Prince, whose connection with the city seems obscure; a semi-circle of eight rather sexy **nymphs**; and four life-sized **statues** of great men from the city's past: James Watt (again, connection obscure, though his steam engines were important in the growth of the woollen industry), John Harrison, an early woollen cloth merchant and builder of St John's, Dr Hook (an ex-vicar of Leeds, not the band) and Joseph Priestley, who lived in the city from 1767 to 1773. Immediately behind the statues and a contemporary pavement fountain stands the former General Post Office, built in 1896, which now houses, among other things, two upmarket restaurants and a stylish hotel. Other buildings were added over time: the 1921 Majestic Cinema, a Grade II listed building that is currently being redeveloped, and the 1937 **Queen's Hotel**, facing the square with its back to the station, which is worth popping into for the Art Deco interior. The only building on the square to predate its late nineteenth-century remodelling is the **Mill Hill Unitarian Church**, which was built in 1847 to replace the one where Joseph Priestley was a minister. The whole square works despite the thundering traffic – it has the air of a Victorian dowager who has fallen asleep and woken to find herself surrounded by towering modern descendants.

> ### LEEDS OWL TRAIL
>
> Owls are significant to Leeds. There are three of them in the city's coat of arms, and they can be seen on many carvings and stained-glass windows. A fun way to get to know the place, especially if you have children in tow, is to follow the **Owl Trail**. The map, downloadable from ⓦleedsowltrail.com and sold at the information office, leads you to 25 owls dotted around Leeds centre, with information on each introducing a different aspect of the city's history.

Leeds Petanque Court

Bond Court

Near City Square is a little area called Bond Court – it's a short cut from Infirmary Street to East Parade. Here is the delightful, if little heralded, **Leeds Petanque Court** – a wedge of gravel overlooked by a noticeboard bearing the rules of petanque, or boules. There are tables and chairs around the court for spectators, but the nicest touch of all is the statue of a man squatting, boule in hand, considering his next shot, and another of a family group watching the game. The court is now popular with the numerous petanque clubs that have sprung up in West Yorkshire; there has been a perhaps unlikely surge of interest in this sport that is more commonly associated with sunny afternoons in the south of France.

Park Square

Park Square, on the western edge of the city centre, is something of a Georgian surprise in largely Victorian-and-later Leeds. The fact that it wasn't conceived and built as a unified whole adds to its charm, with slightly varying styles and roof-lines. An interesting exception to the largely eighteenth-century architecture is **St Paul's House**, built in 1878 as a factory and warehouse for John Barren, pioneer of ready-made clothes. Having seen circular saws being used to cut wood veneer, he adapted the idea to cloth-cutting, and never looked back. By the time of his death in 1905 he was employing three thousand people. The building, now an office block, is in what might be called Moorish style, and though heavily restored (the little minarets, apparently, are made of fibreglass) it's still rather impressive.

Millennium Square

The largely modern and sloping **Millennium Square**, towards the northern edge of the city centre, stands at the heart of a cluster of important buildings and attractions. On its northern edge is **Civic Hall**, looking like a bull with gold wing mirrors, and beyond it **Leeds Metropolitan University**, which, together with the **Colleges of Art and Technology**, ensure that the square seems permanently thronged with students. The west of the square is dominated by the Victorian **Leeds General Hospital**, a typically grandiose affair designed by Sir George Gilbert Scott. The square itself hosts a variety of events – fun-fairs and concerts, for example, and an annual temporary ice rink. At the southern end are the new **Mandela Gardens**, a patchwork of lawns, fountains and statues created in honour of both the great man and of the city's partnership with Durban in South Africa.

City Museum

Millennium Square • Tues, Wed & Fri 10am–5pm, Thurs 10am–7pm, Sat & Sun 11am–5pm • Free • ⓣ 0113 224 3732, ⓦ leeds.gov.uk/citymuseum

The impressive **City Museum**, which was the Mechanics Institute until 2005, takes up the eastern side of Millennium Square. Designed by Cuthbert Broderick (see opposite), the stern Victorian building holds a typical Victorian collection of artefacts, invigorated by a modern hands-on approach. Galleries cover subjects including ancient civilizations, life on earth, costume, domestic life, fossils, military history and ethnography. Look out particularly for the numerous stuffed animals, including the famous **Leeds tiger**, which started its life at the museum as a tiger-skin rug, was stuffed amateurishly with straw, has survived suggestions that it be thrown away (seen off by a local newspaper campaign) or given the attention of modern taxidermists, and is now retained as a sad and sagging example of the triumph of enthusiastic Victorian collecting at the expense of good taste. Another standout is the **Leeds mummy**, which has survived not only three thousand years of history but also a German air raid in 1941, while at the heart of the museum is the **Leeds Arena**, a huge interactive map of the city that you can walk on or observe from the circular balcony.

2

Leeds Town Hall
Westgate

On Westgate stands **Leeds Town Hall**, one of the most splendid municipal buildings in the UK. The Leeds Improvement Society, formed in 1851 by a group of prominent industrialists and businessmen, bought the site and drew up a specification for an architectural competition, to be judged by Sir Charles Barry, the nineteenth-century architect best known for designing the House of Commons. Of the sixteen submissions, one by a virtually unknown young architect – **Cuthbert Broderick** of Hull – was chosen. He would go on to design the Mechanics Institute (now the City Museum) and the Corn Exchange. A stroll around the outside of the Town Hall will reveal much of its grandeur – the ranks of stately columns, the 225ft-high clock tower – and many interesting details, such as the carved faces looking snootily down at the wheelie bins along the west (Oxford Place) side. The inside is equally magnificent, though is only open to the public for concerts and civic functions.

The Headrow

The Headrow is the city centre's main east–west thoroughfare, and holds some of Leeds' most important institutions – the **Central Library**, the **City Art Gallery** and the **Henry Moore Institute** – and a host of large shops arising from its redevelopment in the 1930s and 1940s. **The Light** (see p.101), consisting of two blocks dating from 1930 joined together by overarching glass roofs and new structures, is a modern shopping mall that is airy and light (hence the name), and which has retained its original character. It includes shops, a health and fitness club, a multiscreen cinema and a luxury hotel. As the Headrow dips downwards, in the distance you'll see a building that looks like something out of a science fiction B movie, and whose forbidding exterior has led it to be known locally as the Kremlin. Opened in 1993, it is home to the Department of Health and also several arts-related organizations, including the West Yorkshire Playhouse (see p.100).

Central Library and Leeds Art Gallery
The Headrow • Mon, Tues & Thurs–Sat 10am–5pm, Wed noon–5pm, Sun 1–5pm • Free • ☎ 0113 247 8256, ⓦ www.leeds.gov.uk/artgallery

Immediately east of the Town Hall stands the **Central Library and Leeds Art Gallery**. Opened in 1884, the library is housed in what was once the Municipal Buildings, while the art gallery occupies an extension dating from 1888. **Leeds Art Gallery**, where Alan Bennett used to potter around as a break from doing his homework in the library, has an important collection of largely nineteenth- and twentieth-century paintings, prints, drawings and sculptures, some on permanent display, others rotated. It also hosts a constant stream of visiting exhibitions, together with numerous talks, workshops and classes. As you would expect, there are works by Barbara Hepworth and Henry Moore, both Yorkshire born and bred, who studied at Leeds School of Art (now the College of Art) – Moore's *Reclining Woman* stands just to the right of the Art Gallery entrance. Look out, too, in the entrance lobby for Antony Gormley's *Brick Man*, a scale model for a proposed 100ft-high statue to stand near Leeds train station. It was never built, its rejection by the then city council, due, according to Gormley, to a "lack of nerve".

The Library and gallery are joined by the tearoom and shop in the magnificent **Tiled Hall**, with granite pillars, tiled walls – particularly good examples of the exuberant tiles to be found in buildings all over Leeds, with relief portraits of Homer, Milton, Burns and others – and a beautifully vaulted ceiling with hexagonal coloured bricks forming a mosaic and gold bosses, part of the original ventilation system, that are still working today. You'll not find a more palatial place to have a cup of tea and a bun anywhere in the country. If all this art and beauty leaves you wanting to own some, head to the downstairs **Craft Centre and Design Gallery** (Tues–Sat 10am–5pm; free; ☎0113 247 8241, ⊚craftcentreleeds.co.uk), which has lots of modern jewellery, glass and metalwork for sale.

Henry Moore Institute

The Headrow • Tues–Sun 11am–5.30pm • Free • ⊛ henry-moore.org/hmi

Next to the Library and Art Gallery, and joined to them by a walkway, is the **Henry Moore Institute**, created in 1993 out of a disused warehouse – the facade, which on first sight might seem to be glass, is in fact highly polished igneous rock. Dedicated to the study of sculpture, it has galleries, a library and a sculpture archive and mounts extensive exhibitions. It also oversees the sculpture collection of the Leeds Art Gallery next door, though has no permanent collection of its own and, particularly surprisingly, no Henry Moore sculptures. For those you'll need to travel to the Yorkshire Sculpture Park in Wakefield (see p.132).

Briggate and the Arcades

Though between them **New Briggate** to the north and **Briggate** to the south feature a trio of excellent theatres (see p.100), it is not primarily for the arts that the street is world famous, but for **shopping**. Pedestrianized, thronged with shoppers and buskers, Briggate is the trunk off which the city's famous arcades branch. The two oldest, **Thornton's Arcade** (1877) and **Queen's Arcade** (1889), both have impressive clocks – the former (the Ivanhoe Clock, where almost life-sized figures based on characters in Sir Walter Scott's novel move as the clock strikes) is at the end of the arcade, the latter at the entrance. Most famous, though, is the **Victoria Quarter** (see p.101) where between 1898 and 1904 the slums around the shambles, or meat market, were cleared. The two cross streets between Briggate and Vicar Lane – Queen Victoria and King Edward streets – were entirely enclosed by high glass roofs, creating three blocks divided by two main east–west lanes and a number of cross lanes. The buildings themselves are riots of brick and terracotta, with arches, domes, urns, gables and turrets, and the shop-windows prosperous in shiny mahogany and glass. It's a beautiful setting for the plethora of top-end names – Vivienne Westwood, Nicky Clarke, Mulberry, Louis Vuitton, Harvey Nichols and a host of others – who ply their trade here.

Kirkgate Market

Kirkgate • Mon–Sat 8am–5.30pm • ⊛ leedskirkgatemarket.co.uk

Southeast of the Victoria Quarter, between parallel Vicar Lane and St Stephen's Street, lies **Kirkgate Market**, consisting of covered and outdoor areas. With entrances on Vicar Lane, Kirkgate and George Street (the signs say "Leeds City Markets"), this is said to be the largest marketplace in Europe, containing more than eight hundred stalls inside and out. The building dates from 1904, and incorporates remnants of the 1857 structure that it replaced; its exterior is a symphony of balustrades, steeples and domes, while inside you'll see cast-iron and steel columns and girders supporting glass

THE MARKS & SPENCER ARCHIVE

The history of Marks & Spencer, Britain's historic department store, is heavily bound up in the history of Leeds. Fans of the brand can follow an **M&S Heritage Trail**, which starts at the company's heritage stall in Kirkgate Market (see p.90), and takes in many sites important to the store's story. Maps are available from the stall or from the **M&S archive**, in the Michael Marks Building, Western Campus, University of Leeds (Mon–Sat 10am–5pm; free; Ⓦ marksintime.marksandspencer.com). The archive, set up in 1984 to mark the company's centenary, has an ever-growing collection of artefacts and documents and is open to all.

clerestory windows, lantern roofs and a central octagon. It has the whole gamut of stalls, together with a specialist Butchers' Row, Game Row and Fish Market. In the **outdoor market**, which stretches across to Leeds bus station, Michael Marks, a Polish Jewish immigrant, set up his first stall (with a sign saying "Don't ask the price – it's a penny") – in 1884. From such humble beginnings grew the household name of **Marks & Spencer**. Today, a heritage stall next to the M & S clock offers information, M&S walking tour maps, branded goods and coffee.

Corn Exchange

Call Lane • Mon–Wed, Fri & Sat 10am–6pm, Thurs 10am–7pm, Sun 10.30am–4.30pm • Ⓦ leedscornexchange.co.uk

Just south of Kirkgate Market, one of Leeds' most iconic buildings rises above the surrounding roofs – the **Corn Exchange**, designed by Cuthbert Broderick (see p.89), a rare oval domed building home to numerous **independent shops**. On the exterior, note the diamond-pointed stone which gives the building an incredibly rich texture, especially when the sun is low in the sky; the two rows of arch-topped windows separated by what looks like mini-millstones; and the rosettes above the second row of windows (a Broderick signature), which look very like Yorkshire roses. Inside, a flagstoned open basement is reached down wood-and-iron steps, with similar steps leading up to a cast-iron balcony. Over the whole space arches a wonderful elliptical iron and wood dome with large glazed openings. At one end, where the ribs converge, is a clock flanked by sheaves of corn; at the other end the city's civic arms.

Royal Armouries Museum

Armouries Drive • Daily 10am–5pm • Free • ☎ 0113 220 1999, Ⓦ armouries.org.uk • Bus #28 from city centre

A fifteen-minute walk southeast from the city centre, via the Centenary Footbridge just below the Calls, will bring you to the tower blocks and nascent office/apartment/shopping development Clarence Dock, of which the **Royal Armouries Museum** is the centrepiece. Built in 1995–96 to house the relocated collection of the Tower of London, it's a modern take on a medieval fortress in grey brick, with an imposing entrance and a huge octagonal glazed tower. The core contains a comprehensive display of weapons and armour (the Hall of Steel) around which twists an octagonal spiral staircase that serves the museum's galleries. There are, thank heavens, lifts as well. To make the most of your visit pick up a *What's On Today* leaflet from the admissions desk (free), which gives details of that day's events and live interpretations, or a *Royal Armouries Souvenir Guide* (£5, and worth every penny).

This is one of the best museums of its type in the world, with five enormous galleries containing beautifully displayed weapons for war, tournament and hunting, armour and other artefacts dating from as far back as Roman times. Particularly spectacular are the fabulously decorated ceremonial suits of **full plate armour** (from the fifteenth century onwards), the reconstruction of a tiger hunt, the eighteenth-century Indian **elephant armour** consisting of 8500 iron plates (the heaviest armour in the world), and a Sikh **quoit turban** from the same century which carried a blood-curdling array of throwing quoits,

2

garrotting wires and knives. Look out also for the Samurai and Mongol armour and weapons, and many ornate **guns**, from a reconstruction of an enormously long Essex punt gun to an exquisite Tiffany-decorated Smith and Wesson .44 Magnum.

Outside is the tiltyard, which mounts **jousting**, military skills and falconry exhibitions, plus a **menagerie** where the birds and horses used in the tiltyard are kept and a **craft court** where you can see a gun-maker and armourer at work. There's also a shop, bistro and restaurant. Some may think that the museum glorifies war – it doesn't. In its own words "Learn from the past, hope for the future". The Royal Armouries Museum is an absolute gem, and would justify a trip to Leeds by itself.

Thackray Medical Museum

Beckett St • Daily 10am–5pm, last admission 3pm (open till 8.30pm on 3rd Thurs of the month) • £7 • ☎ 0113 244 4343, ⊕ thackraymuseum.org • Buses #16, #42, #49, #50, #50A or #61 from the city centre all stop outside the museum (all around 15min)

Next to the giant St James's Hospital (aka Jimmy's), the **Thackray Medical Museum** cannot be over-praised. It's different, it's imaginative, it's interactive and it's vastly entertaining. Appropriately set in a Victorian workhouse building (from which Jimmy's hospital grew), the museum takes as its starting point the horrendous problems suffered by people in one particular place and time – Leeds in 1842 – and follows the processes by which these problems were solved. The account of **public health issues**, cholera, TB and the like are enough to turn the stomach, not to mention the weird and wonderful remedies that were applied to cure diseases. You get not only the sights and sounds, but also the smells, so the pie-seller resting his tray on the edge of a midden, the butchers' shop, the little girl having her leg amputated (without anaesthetic) after a mill accident – all these will stay with you for a long time. You can pick up a card with details of a real person (Alice Finch, a 7-year-old bookseller's daughter, perhaps, or Mary Holmes, 27-year-old dressmaker, along with many others), follow their fortunes through the museum – and then find out how they died.

The displays are not, however, confined to 1842 Leeds. Other striking exhibits include large and small iron lungs (for adults and children), prosthetic limbs, the "Iron Man" made entirely of metal plates used in surgery, a canvas "boobs and belly" suit to give dads an insight into the discomforts of pregnancy, and two large mannequins showing modern replacement joints and acupuncture points. The **Life Zone** gallery is aimed towards young children but adults will enjoy it as well – it deals with everything from the length of human intestines (29ft) to how muscles work and how different teeth do different jobs. And where else could you enjoy the experience of being a pea travelling from the mouth through the intestinal tract?

Roundhay Park

Ring Rd, Shadwell, 3 miles northeast of Leeds city centre • Daily 24hr • ⊕ roundhaypark.org.uk • Bus #2 or #12 from city centre

At 700 acres, **Roundhay Park** is Leeds' largest public open space and one of the largest public parks in Europe. Owned by Leeds City Council, it consists of an impressive early nineteenth-century **mansion** and extensive landscaped **parkland**, with gardens, lawns and trees, two lakes and a castle folly, together with a golf course, bowling green and tennis courts. Much used by local people, yet big enough to offer peace and quiet, it has two watering holes – a lakeside café and a restaurant in the mansion. There's a shop, plenty of parking and a good food pub.

Tropical World

Princes Ave, Roundhay Park • Daily: summer 10am–6pm; winter 10am–4pm • £3.50 • ☎ 0113 237 0754, ⊕ roundhaypark.org.uk • Bus #2 or #12 from city centre

On the eastern edge of Roundhay Park is **Tropical World**. Developed from a set of conservatories built in 1911 for tropical plants, it now consists of a beautifully thought-out series of tropical habitats – rainforest, desert, swamp, jungle – through which wooden walkways meander. There's a nocturnal section, the largest collection of tropical plants in the UK outside Kew Gardens, a substantial artificial waterfall – where you can stand behind the flow of water – and a variety of birds, reptiles, fish and mammals, some of which roam freely within their own enclosures (though not the crocodiles, thankfully, who have an enclosure to themselves). There's also a shop, and, in its own building, the *Explorer's Café*.

2

Temple Newsam

Off Selby Rd, 4 miles east of Leeds city centre • **House** Tues–Sun: summer 10.30am–5pm; winter 10.30am–4pm • £4.50 **Rare breeds farm** Tues–Sun: summer 10am–5pm; winter 10am–4pm • £3.50 • ☎ 0113 336 7461, ⓦ leeds.gov.uk/templenewsam • On Sun bus #63a runs to the house from central Leeds; during the rest of the week #19 and #19a run to Colton, from where it is less than a mile's walk; in summer holidays, #10 bus runs directly to the house

The manor of Newsam dates at least from the time of the Domesday Book, and a fine mansion was built on the present site in early Tudor times by Thomas Darcy, a chum of Cardinal Wolsey – and it was in this house that Lord Darnley was born, later to become second husband of Mary Queen of Scots and father of King James I of England. Both came to a sticky end – Darcy on the Tower Hill scaffold, Darnley when he was strangled in Scotland at the age of 21, many thought by his wife's lover (and in due course, third husband) Lord Bothwell. The house was bought and completely rebuilt in 1622 by Sir Arthur Ingram, a Yorkshire financial tycoon, and, as **Temple Newsam**, has remained largely untouched since then, a fine example of a Jacobean mansion. Architecturally important, aesthetically beautiful, stuffed with priceless paintings, porcelain and furniture, set in wonderfully landscaped parkland, with a visitor centre, shop and tearooms in the stable block, it will engender wonder or envy, depending on your nature. Around the parapet of the house, in 2ft-tall letters, is the following invocation, given here in full to save you from a stiff neck: "all glory and praise be given to god the father, the son and holy ghost on high, peace on earth good will towards men, honour and true allegiance to our gracious king, loving affection amongst his subjects, health and plenty be within this house".

In the grounds stands Europe's largest **rare-breeds farm**, where the whitefaced woodland sheep, red poll cattle and golden Guernsey goats can give the kids a break from history and art.

Thwaite Mills

Thwaite Lane, Stourton (less than 2 miles southeast of Leeds city centre) • Sat & Sun 1–5pm, plus Tues–Fri during Leeds school holidays 10am–5pm • £3.60 • ☎ 0113 378 2983, ⓦ leeds.gov.uk/thwaitemills • Bus #110 from Leeds city centre

Though there have been water mills on this site since the seventeenth century, the current **Thwaite Mills** complex was built in 1823–25 on an island between the River Aire and the Aire and Calder Navigation, and originally consisted of the mill building, warehouse and workshop, stables, rather fine late Georgian house and (now demolished) workmen's cottages. The water wheels, of course, only provided the power – how that power was used changed over time, from turning rapeseed into oil, through grinding flint for glazes, to grinding chalk into putty. The mill closed in 1975 when the weir that directed the water along the mill races collapsed, but the machinery is in working order. At the heart of the complex are the two giant wheels – 18ft in diameter, and more than 14ft and 8ft wide respectively, each revolving once every five seconds and driving all the other machines in the building. The whole site was a model of well-organized, sustainable industry. Nowadays, surrounded by water, it's a wildlife haven with a variety of water birds, mammals, insects and plants.

Middleton Railway

Moor Rd, 2 miles southeast of Leeds city centre • April–Oct (and on certain other dates) Sat & Sun 11am–4pm, also Aug Wed 10am–5pm • £2.50 single • ☎ 0113 378 2983, ⓦ middletonrailway.org.uk • Bus #110 from Leeds city centre

The **Middleton Railway** claims to be the oldest working railway in the world, having started as a horse-drawn colliery railway in 1758, with steam power being used from 1812. Never used as a passenger railway, and only just surviving after the closure of the Middleton Colliery by hauling for local industry, it was taken over by Leeds University students during Rag Week in 1960 and after that it never looked back. The students and other volunteers, while preserving engines and rolling stock, increasingly tried to attract recreational passengers as industry declined. Finally, with lottery funding, it celebrated a grand opening in its present form in 2007. It isn't the slick final product you'll get at some other volunteer-run railways – opening hours are extremely restricted (check the website for details), though there is a small café and shop, and ample free parking – but for railway buffs, anyone interested in industrial history, or families with kids who want a day out, it's fun – a 1.25-mile trip on standard gauge rails, steam or diesel hauled, with the option at the other end of coming straight back or having a wander around Middleton Park. The park itself, covering 470 acres of mixed park and woodland, has a café, bowling greens, a playground and a fishing lake.

Leeds Industrial Museum

Canal Rd, Armley, 2 miles northwest of Leeds city centre • Tues–Sat 10am–5pm, Sun 1–5pm • £3.60 • ☎ 0113 378 3173, ⓦ leeds.gov.uk /armleymills • Bus #5 from Leeds city centre to the museum or #33, #33A, #508 or #757 to the Vue cinema complex just across the river – there's a footbridge next to *Frankie and Benny's*

Leeds Industrial Museum occupies the buildings of Armley Mills, a nineteenth-century woollen mill in the Kirkstall Valley. Having started as an eighteenth-century fulling mill – basically a set of water-powered hammers bashing the finished cloth to consolidate the fibres – Armley Mill became, following rebuilding after a fire in 1805, the biggest woollen mill in the world, introducing machine mass production and steam power. Although it includes displays on the history of cinema and on printing in Leeds, most of its collection reflects the dominance of the wool industry in the city, from the days of the huge spinning mules and power looms to the later production of off-the-peg clothing for famous names such as Hepworth and Burton. There's a shop, and dressing-up clothes are available for kids.

Abbey House Museum

Abbey Walk, about 3 miles northwest of Leeds city centre • Tues–Fri & Sun 10am–5pm, Sat noon–5pm • £4 • ☎ 0113 230 5492, ⓦ leeds.gov.uk/abbeyhouse • Bus #33, #33A or #757 from Leeds city centre

Directly across the main road from the ruined **Kirkstall Abbey** is the **Abbey House Museum**, once the gatehouse to the abbey, then, after the Dissolution, a private residence, and finally, from 1927, a museum. Particularly child-friendly (and there's a children's playground in the park on the other side of the car park as well), it concentrates on aspects of Victorian life in Leeds, with reconstructed shops and streets, pubs and homes, costume and toys. There's a shop and restaurant, and pleasant gardens.

Fulneck

FULNECK, on the edge of the market town of Pudsey, lies seven miles west of Leeds, around half way to Bradford. The village, strung out along a single main street on a hillside overlooking pleasant pastoral countryside, has a Grade I listed chapel, a private school (once attended by an unhappy Diana Rigg) and an interesting village museum. Nice, you might say, but nothing special. Notice, however, the signs as you enter the village from either end – "Moravian Settlement Fulneck". *This* is what makes Fulneck special.

FROM TOP NATIONAL MEDIA MUSEUM, BRADFORD (P.103); SALTAIRE (P.108); VICTORIA QUARTER, LEEDS (P.90) >

Brief history

Fulneck was established by the followers of **Jan Hus** (or John Hus) of Moravia, now part of the Czech Republic, who believed in a simple, rather austere religion free of pomp and ornament. He was martyred in 1415, and his followers left the Roman Catholic Church in 1457 to form their own church. The present Moravian church (Unitas Fratrum or Unity of the Brethren, to give it the correct title) started when a group of Moravians settled on land given to them by Count **Nicholas von Zinzendorf** in Saxony. They called the settlement **Herrnhut** (roughly "under the watch of the Lord"). From 1727, missionaries streamed out of Herrnhut to spread the word, especially in the West Indies and America, where there are still Moravian settlements. Many of the missionaries stayed in Britain, and there are to this day numerous settlements in Yorkshire and Lancashire, near Bristol and in London.

Moravian Fulneck

Today, **Moravian Fulneck** is a delight. The church is beautifully simple, though when it was built there was much grumbling that the architect hadn't followed the brief and had added too much frippery. **Fulneck Moravian Museum** (55 Fulneck; Easter–Oct Wed & Sat 2–4pm; free; ☎0113 256 4828, ⓦfulneck.org.uk) is interesting in a rather understated way, with Moravian memorabilia featuring lace and embroidery and objects from around the world, such as Tibetan brass work and Inuit carvings. Plaques commemorate two of the village's famous sons: **Benjamine H. La Trobe** (1764–1820), one of the architects of the White House in Washington DC, and **Sir Len Hutton** (1916–90), Yorkshire and England batsman, and one of the country's greatest-ever cricketers.

The simple stones in the **Moravian burial ground** in the centre of the village are laid flat, in line with the Moravian belief that all are equal in the sight of God. The absence of extravagant monuments and obelisks emphasizes rather than diminishes their poignancy – "Harriet Angell, died November 15, 1823. Aged 16 years. No. 1404" says it all.

Harewood House

Harewood, 7 miles north of Leeds city centre • Opening hours vary widely according to day and season; check website for full details • Freedom ticket, covering all parts of house and gardens £14, £7.50 in winter • ☎ 0113 218 1010, ⓦ harewood.org • Frequent buses run to Harewood from Leeds, including the #36 (every 15min, every 30min on Sun)

Harewood House is one of the UK's greatest country mansions, created in the mid-eighteenth century by an all-star cast: designed by John Carr of York, interiors by Robert Adam, furniture by Thomas Chippendale, with paintings by Turner, Reynolds, Titian and El Greco, all sitting in beautiful grounds landscaped by Capability Brown. It doesn't get any better than that. Tours of the house include the below-stairs kitchen and servants' quarters as well as the innumerable galleries, halls, reception rooms and staircases, dripping with antiques and priceless art treasures.

It's a wonderful family day out, with an adventure playground, gardens – including the **bird garden** with its variety of habitats – special interest tours and talks on subjects from bee-keeping to photography and food. Regular events include craft fairs, concerts, car rallies and kite-flying festivals, and there are good refreshment areas, from the *Terrace Café* to the *Courtyard Café*. Although this is the private home of the Earl and Countess of Harewood, the whole experience is warm and welcoming, an invitation to admire the achievements of a past age. Incidentally, the village is pronounced "Harewood" as it is spelt, while the house is pronounced "Harwood".

ARRIVAL AND DEPARTURE   LEEDS

By car Sitting astride the intersection of the UK's main north–south (M1) and east–west (M62) routes, and with the A1(M), M621, A58(M) and A64(M) all nearby, Leeds is well served by motorways.

By train National and local trains use Leeds City train station, at the edge of the centre on City Square.
Destinations Bradford (every 20min; 20min); Carlisle (every 2hr; 2hr 40min); Harrogate (every 30min; 34min);

Hull (hourly; 1hr); Knaresborough (every 30min; 45min); Lancaster (4 daily; 2hr); Liverpool (hourly; 1hr 50min); London Kings Cross (every 30min; 2hr 20min); Manchester (every 15min; 1hr); Scarborough (every 30min–1hr; 1hr 20min); Settle (every 2hr; 1hr); Sheffield (every 20min; 40min–1hr 25m); Skipton (every 15–30min; 45min); York (every 10–15min; 25min).

By bus The bus station occupies a site to the east of town, behind Kirkgate Market, on St Peter's St, and there's a comprehensive set of bus stops outside the train station.

Destinations Bradford (every 20min; 35min); Halifax (every 30min; 1hr 15min); London (hourly; 4hr 15min); Wakefield (every 10min; 31min).

By plane Leeds–Bradford airport (ⓦ leedsbradfordairport .co.uk) lies some 7 miles northwest of the city centre; it is neither as accessible nor as busy as Manchester Airport.

GETTING AROUND AND INFORMATION

By car There's a complicated one-way system in the city, but the central "loop" at least gives you the chance, if you've missed your destination, to go around again. Parking is at a premium, but clearly signed.

By bus Leeds has an efficient and reasonably easy-to-use bus system, centred on the bus station (see above).

By taxi There's an efficient cab rank right next to the train station on City Square, and lots of ranks across the city centre.

Tourist office The Arcade, at the train station (Mon 10am–5.30pm, Tues–Sat 9am–5.30pm, Sun 10am–4pm; ☎ 0113 242 5242, ⓦ visitleeds.co.uk). They offer a good range of published material and gifts, and an accommodation booking service (☎ 0800 808050).

ACCOMMODATION

Leeds has a number of city centre **chain hotels**, luxury and budget, most of them within a few minutes' walk of the train station. There are also some interesting **boutique hotels**, though small-scale guesthouses and private establishments are few and far between. Parking can be a problem, and except for the rare hotel with its own, most places have arrangements with nearby commercial car parks, which guests can use at subsidized rates (around £12/24hr).

★**42 The Calls** 42 the Calls ☎ 0113 244 0099, ⓦ 42thecalls.co.uk. *42 The Calls* is in an eighteenth-century corn mill, with many original features allied to top-quality modernist decor and fittings. It goes out of its way to be quirky – fishing rods in rooms overlooking the canal, twelve varieties of sausages for breakfast, a late-night trust-the-customer bar. Being next to the Centenary footbridge, it can sometimes suffer from noisy passers-by. **£105**

★**DoubleTree by Hilton** Granary Wharf ☎ 0113 241 1000, ⓦ doubletree3.hilton.com. Beautifully located on Granary Wharf, 5min walk from the train station. Luxurious rooms, friendly, committed staff, and a choice of ecstatically reviewed restaurants – *Granary Lounge* and *City Café* (see p.98). Parking is limited (first come, first served) under railway arches, or at reduced rates in the nearby commercial car park. **£119**

Malmaison 1 Swinegate ☎ 0113 398 1000, ⓦ malmaison-leeds.com. One of a string of thirteen city- and town-centre hotels named after the Paris chateau that once housed Josephine, Napoleon's consort. The emphasis is on luxury accommodation in interesting old buildings – in this case, the Leeds tram and bus company office just east of the train station, decorated in dark browns, creams and maroons. Gym, brasserie, bar and – a nice touch – local musicians performing on Sunday nights. **£113**

Marriott 4 Trevelyan Square ☎ 0113 236 6366, ⓦ marriott.co.uk. Highly regarded by all types of guests, the Leeds *Marriott*, a large hotel with comprehensive facilities, combines city-centre location (just off Boar Lane) with the tranquillity of Trevelyan Square. There are two in-house restaurants and plenty of places to eat nearby. **£79**

Moor Lodge Caravan Park 103 Blackmoor Lane, Bardsey, 6 miles north of Leeds ☎ 01937 572424, ⓦ moorlodgecaravanpark.co.uk. One of the best campsites within striking distance of Leeds, *Moor Lodge* is well kept, with immaculate facilities. Buses #X98 and #X99 run to Leeds (30min; 30min), and Wetherby and Harrogate are easily accessible. Pitch plus two people **£20**

Quebec 9 Quebec St ☎ 0113 244 8989, ⓦ theeton collection.com. Part of the same group of boutique hotels as *42 The Calls*. Ornate 1891 ex-Liberal Club boutique hotel with superb terracotta exterior, Victorian interior trappings and rooms of understated opulence, just off City Square. Very limited parking (six spaces) – phone just before arrival to try to bag one, though they're not cheap. Otherwise there is commercial parking nearby. **£110**

Queens Hotel City Square ☎ 0113 243 1323, ⓦ qhotels.co.uk. Huge hotel backing onto the train station and looking out onto City Square. The *Queens Hotel*'s Portland stone gravitas and refurbished Art Deco interior would make Fred and Ginger feel at home – 1930s style, twenty-first-century mod cons. The bar and restaurant are much used by local business people, so you feel at once a part of the metropolis and a favoured guest. **£89**

Radisson SAS 1 The Light, the Headrow ☎ 0113 236 6000, ⓦ radissonblu.co.uk. At the western end of the Headrow, next to the Henry Moore Institute, the *Radisson* is spacious and well appointed, with a modern

Art Deco-influenced style, and with immediate access to the pools, fitness suite, shops and cafés of The Light. Rooms vary in size, so check before committing yourself. **£97**

★ **Residence 6** 3 Infirmary St ☎ 0113 285 6250, ⊛ residencesix.com. Centrally located in the old Post Office building just off City Square, *Residence 6* offers superb accommodation with free wi-fi, games console and fully equipped kitchen/dining rooms. If you don't want to cook you can order in. Very limited parking – otherwise reduced-rate parking nearby. **£125**

EATING AND DRINKING

Leeds has the greatest concentration of highly rated and popular restaurants in the region, together with a plentiful supply of chain restaurants and gastropubs. You'll find good places to eat throughout the city centre – the area around **Granary Wharf** is perhaps particularly rewarding – and out in suburbs such as Headingley.

CAFÉS AND RESTAURANTS

Brasserie Blanc Victoria Mill, Sovereign St ☎ 0113 220 6060, ⊛ brasserieblanc.com. One of the seventeen restaurants established by French celebrity chef Raymond Blanc throughout the UK, the Leeds branch is a 5min walk from the train station. Housed in an old mill, with plain brick walls, vaulted ceilings and iron pillars, it offers good food (pan-fried pork sirloin, say, or lemon- and date-stuffed lamb heart) in smart but unstuffy surroundings at unthreatening prices. Set two-course menus from £11.95 (lunch) and £14.45 (dinner). Mon–Fri noon–2.45pm & 5.30–10pm, Sat noon–10.30pm, Sun noon–9pm (bar open all day).

★ **City Café** 2 Wharf Approach, Granary Wharf ☎ 0113 241 1039, ⊛ doubletree3.hilton.com. The restaurant of the *Doubletree by Hilton Hotel* on the canal side at Granary Wharf, the *City Café* offers fast friendly service, tasty food (potted shrimp with prawn toast; rack of lamb and the like) and an extensive wine list, half of which is available by the glass. Starters £6–9, main courses £11–25. Mon–Fri noon–10pm, Sat & Sun 1–10pm.

Fourth Floor Café Harvey Nichols, 107 Briggate ☎ 0113 204 8000, ⊛ harveynichols.com. As you'd expect from the famous top-end department store, this restaurant is something special. Traditional meat and fish dishes – lamb rack, pork shoulder, rib-eye steak – are served in light, elegant surroundings with good views across the rooftops. The restaurant shares the top floor with a wine shop, deli and sushi bar and is accessible through the store or, in the evenings, via an express lift. Set lunch menus £17.50–20. A la carte and bar menus also available. Tues–Sat noon–3pm & 5.30–10pm, Sun & Mon noon–3pm.

Little Tokyo 24 Central Rd ☎ 0113 243 9090, ⊛ littletokyo-leeds.co.uk. Popular Japanese restaurant in the city centre, with a variety of noodle, sushi and sashimi courses and bento "four-course meals in a box" £12.99–15.99. Lively atmosphere and good service, but no booking, so you take your chances. Sun–Thurs noon–10pm, Fri & Sat noon–11pm.

★ **Midnight Bell** 101 Water Lane ☎ 0113 244 5044, ⊛ midnightbell.co.uk. A 10min walk south of the train station, the *Midnight Bell* is one of six pubs owned by the 2007-established Leeds Brewery – the largest in the city – whose standout beers include Yorkshire Gold, Midnight Bell and Gathering Storm. Here the focus is on the food, with locally sourced dishes (fish and chips, gammon and eggs, sea bass, steaks and burgers, ranging from £11.50–16.95) served in a converted Grade II listed foundry building with contemporary decor. Food served Mon–Sat noon–9pm, Sun noon–5pm.

Salvo's 111–115 Otley Rd, Headingley a mile or so north of Leeds ☎ 0113 275 5017, ⊛ salvos.co.uk. Probably the best-known Italian restaurant in Leeds, winner of "best local Italian restaurant" in Gordon Ramsay's *The F Word*, it's worth the trip out to Headingley to eat quality favourites at prices that don't exclude students. Pizzas and pasta dishes go for around £8.50–10.95 and main courses (*brasato al vino rosso*, for example, or *calamari alla brace*) £15.95–19.50. Lovely atmosphere and friendly service. Mon–Thurs noon–2pm & 6–10.30pm, Fri & Sat noon–2pm & 5.30–11pm, Sun noon–9pm.

BARS AND PUBS

The Adelphi 3–5 Hunslet Rd ☎ 0113 245 6377, ⊛ theadelphi.co.uk. Joshua Tetley's first pub, just south of the river across the Leeds Bridge. The splendidly Victorian *Adelphi* is all things to all men (and women), offering four bars, a wide range of draft beers, ciders, wine and food – snacks, pub grub and full meals. Sun–Thurs noon–11pm, Fri & Sat noon–12.30am; food Mon–Sat noon–10pm, Sun noon–9pm.

Bankhouse Inn Bankhouse Lane, Fulneck, 7 miles west of Leeds ☎ 0113 256 4662, ⊛ thebankhouseinn.co.uk. The *Bankhouse Inn*, just beyond the end of Fulneck village, offers a range of pub meals, with starters from £3.95 to £5.95 and mains from £8.45 to £9.95, as well as sandwiches and salads. Mon 5–11pm, Tues–Fri noon–3pm & 5–11pm, Sat & Sun noon–11pm; food served Tues & Wed noon–2.30pm & 5–8.30pm, Thurs & Fri noon–2.30pm & 5–9pm, Sat noon–9pm, Sun noon–5pm.

Horse and Trumpet 51–53 the Headrow ☎ 0113 243 0338. A no-nonsense city drinking establishment, divided into small areas with wood panelling and unbelievably cheap food – burgers, pies, fish and chips – with two meals for £7.95 "all day, every day". They offer grill nights, curry nights and Sunday roasts. No admission to children under 18. Mon–Thurs 10am–11pm, Fri 10am–midnight, Sat 9am–midnight, Sun 11am–10.30pm; food served Mon–Sat noon–10pm, Sun noon–8pm.

★ **Mr Foley's Cask Ale House** 159 the Headrow ☎ 0113 242 9674. Super Victorian pub near the Town Hall, with several bars on different levels, draught beers listed on a blackboard with strengths and tasting notes, and bottled beers from around the world. Mon–Thurs 11am–11pm, Fri & Sat 11am–midnight, Sun noon–7pm.

Mook 3–5 Hirst's Yard ☎ 0113 245 9967. Situated down an alley just off Call Lane, *Mook* is hard to track down but well worth the hunt. It's cool, relaxed and friendly, with a daily happy hour (4–9pm) that includes their excellent range of cocktails. The back bar is generally quieter than the front, and there is a sizeable dance floor resounding to cleanly mixed funk and electro. It's right next to *The Space* (see p.100), so makes an ideal start for a night out. Sun–Wed 4pm–2am, Thurs–Sat noon–3am.

North 24 New Briggate ☎ 0113 242 4540. Just north of the Headrow, *North* is a long, narrow bar with wooden floors, small tables and chairs (except for the much-prized Chesterfield at the back) and, on the wall opposite the bar, the names of hundreds of beers from all over the world – including Arrogant Bastard and Kelpie Seaweed Ale. It may not serve them all, but there's a broad selection. Mon & Tues 11am–1am, Wed–Sat 11am–2am, Sun noon–midnight.

Sky Lounge Doubletree by Hilton, Granary Wharf ☎ 0113 241 1000, ⓦ doubletree3.hilton.com. Situated on the thirteenth floor of the *Doubletree by Hilton* hotel, the *Sky Lounge* is very popular with Leeds' young professional crowd. Often busy, and certainly expensive, but well worth a visit for the wide range of exquisitely prepared cocktails served with the city's best views from its wraparound terrace. Mon–Thurs 5pm–midnight, Fri–Sun noon–2am.

★ **Whitelocks** 4 Turks Head Yard ☎ 0113 245 3950, ⓦ whitelocksleeds.com. *Whitelocks* is not easy to find (go down Briggate from the Headrow and it's in the first alley on the right after the Commercial St/Kirkgate junction) but it's well worth tracking down. A pub dating (probably) from 1716, with an interior that is all polished brass and copper, tile-inlaid counters and engraved mirrors dating (definitely) from 1886. Good selection of real ales. Mon–Thurs 11am–midnight, Fri & Sat 11am–1pm, Sun 11am–11.30pm.

NIGHTLIFE AND ENTERTAINMENT

Leeds has a fair range of **clubs** and live music, dance and comedy venues where you can experience anything from one-off performances to regular world-famous events. Most of the **gay** venues are clustered in the area around Lower Briggate, which is widely known as the Leeds Gay Quarter. There's a flourishing **comedy** scene, in venues from the largest hall to the smallest, most intimate pub, and a thriving **dance** culture (ⓦ cityofdance.co.uk) focusing on the Balbir Singh Dance Company (☎ 07790 919398, ⓦ balbirsinghdance.co.uk), Northern Ballet (☎ 0113 220 8000, ⓦ northernballet.com), Phoenix Dance Theatre (☎ 0113 236 8130, ⓦ phoenixdancetheatre.co.uk), RJC Dance (☎ 0113 239 2040, ⓦ rjcdance .org.uk), the Northern School of Contemporary Dance (☎ 0113 219 3000, ⓦ nscd.ac.uk) and Yorkshire Dance (☎ 0113 243 9867, ⓦ yorkshiredance.com). Finally, there are several popular **outdoor venues** in and just outside the city, including Millennium Square (see p.88) and Roundhay Park (see p.92). For all the latest **listings** and information, check out ⓦ leedsguide.co.uk.

LEEDS MUSIC: FOUR BIG EVENTS

Leeds' vibrant live music scene is reflected in its big-name festivals and competitions. Some of the best-known events held in the city include:

Live at Leeds ☎ 0113 244 3446, ⓦ liveatleeds.com. Contemporary, indie-focused music festival, held at various venues during the first bank holiday weekend in May. Performers have included the Macabees, Mumford and Sons, Scroobius Pip and Ladyhawke.

Leeds Festival ☎ 0115 912 9000, ⓦ leedsfestival.com. Held over the August bank holiday weekend at Bramham Park, the Leeds Festival is up there with Reading and Glastonbury. It attracts around seventy thousand people with big-name acts such as the Arctic Monkeys, Queens of the Stone Age and Jake Bugg.

Leeds International Concert Season ☎ 0113 224 3801, ⓦ leedsconcertseason.com. A biennial programme organized by Leeds City Council, with a hundred or so concerts – including brass band, orchestral, choral and chamber music – held throughout the year in venues across the city.

Leeds International Piano Competition ☎ 0113 244 6586, ⓦ leedspiano.com. Attracting entrants from all over the world, this competition is held every three years, over two and a half weeks in late August/early September. Venues include the Great Hall of the University and the Town Hall.

2

CLUBS AND LIVE MUSIC

★ **Brudenell Social Club** 33 Queen's Rd ☎0113 275 2411, ⊚ brudenellsocialclub.co.uk. Most famous for hosting secret gigs for bands like Franz Ferdinand and the Kaiser Chiefs, the *Social Club* emphasizes live music and is a great supporter of up-and-coming bands. Originally a working men's club, it has been a primary cog in the Leeds music scene for a number of years. Cool and inexpensive with great sound. Sun–Thurs noon–11pm, Fri & Sat noon–midnight.

Cockpit Bridgend House, Swinegate ☎0113 244 1573, ⊚ thecockpit.co.uk. Independent live music and club venue, 5min by foot from the train station, under three railway arches. Gigs take place on their three stages most nights of the week showcasing local and international bands. Friday nights see "The Session" with guitar and electro tracks in the main room, backed up by retro indie in room 2, and everything else from 1980s pop to hip-hop in the last. Saturdays play host to "The Garage" – wall-to-wall rock in its various guises. Room 3 is reserved for a cycle of different nights throughout the month. Doors usually open daily 7pm unless otherwise stated.

Hifi 2 Central Rd ☎0113 242 7353, ⊚ thehificlub.co.uk. Perennially popular little club offering everything from Motown to drum'n'bass, with live music on selected days. Regular nights through the month cater to lovers of jazz, funk, soul, rock and hip-hop. "The Sunday Joint" is also popular, with a live band to accompany your Sunday roast, and more music running on into the evening. Comedy on Saturdays at 8pm. Tues–Sun 10.30 or 11pm–3am.

Mission 8 Heaton's Court ☎0870 122 0114, ⊚ clubmission.com. *Mission* is a large venue with enough space for 1500 clubbers. A great range of nights feature big-name DJs every weekend. The Thai beach party "Full Moon" runs on Thursday nights, with house/electro and hip-hop/r'n'b in arenas 1 and 2 respectively. Thurs until 3am, Fri until 4am, Sat until 5am.

Space Hirst's Yard ☎0113 246 1030, ⊚ facebook.com /SpaceLeedsClub. Literally an underground club, the *Space* is a well-established leader in the Leeds dance music scene. It focuses strongly on house and electro, shunning the mainstream in favour of darker sounds and richer beats. It's perhaps best known for the full-on Sunday club night "Funky Dory", which bangs out high-octane mixes until 5am on Monday morning. Tues 10am–4am, Thurs–Sun 11am–5am.

Wardrobe 6 St Peter's Square ☎0113 383 8800, ⊚ thewardrobe.co.uk. Stylish and cool, *The Wardrobe* is east of the centre near the bus station. Excellent food upstairs (Tues–Thurs noon–2.30pm & 5.30–9pm, Fri & Sat closes at 10pm), with soul and funk on Friday and Saturday nights, often with a live band thrown in for good measure, in the club room downstairs. Free entry upstairs; varying entry charges downstairs for club nights and live acts.

Sun–Wed 11am–11pm, Thurs 11am–midnight, Fri & Sat 11am–2am (3am when there's live music).

GAY CLUBS

Bar Fibre 168 Lower Briggate ⊚ barfibre.com. Leeds' finest gay bar comes with plenty of attitude. There's food during the day at *Café Mafiosa*, and regular alfresco parties in the courtyard outside (summer) and roaring fires inside (winter). Sun–Wed noon–1am, Thurs & Fri noon–3am, Sat noon–4am.

Queens Court 167 Lower Briggate ⊚ queenscourtleeds .com. On two floors in the same courtyard as *Bar Fibre* (with which it has wild monthly summer parties), this bar has cool yet comfortable contemporary design, a basic menu, and an upstairs nightclub (*The Loft*). Mon noon–2am, Tues, Wed & Sun noon–midnight, Thurs–Sat noon–4am; food daily noon–8pm.

Viaduct Showbar 11 Briggate ☎0113 245 3255, ⊚ viaductshowbar.com. Traditional pub converted into a gay venue with live music, "cabaret spectaculars", drag artists and tribute acts. Mon–Thurs noon–1am, Fri & Sat noon–3am, Sun 1pm–1am.

THEATRES AND VENUES

Carriageworks Theatre Millennium Square ☎0113 224 3801, ⊚ carriageworkstheatre.org.uk. Along the southern edge of the square, housed in a small development called the Electric Press, the Carriageworks Theatre puts on a variety of plays, shows and festivals, many of them for children.

City Varieties Music Hall Swan St ☎0113 391 7777, ⊚ cityvarieties.co.uk. Built in 1865. Harry Lauder, Charlie Chaplin and Harry Houdini all appeared here (older Brits will remember it as the venue for television's *Good Old Days*, from 1953 onwards), and Dara O'Briain still reckons it to be "the best venue for stand-up in the nation".

Grand Theatre and Opera House 46 New Briggate ☎0870 121 4901, ⊚ leedsgrandtheatre.com. The regular base of Opera North (⊚ operanorth.co.uk) and Northern Ballet (⊚ northernballet.com) also puts on a full range of theatrical productions.

Howard Assembly Room New Briggate ☎0844 848 2727, ⊚ operanorth.co.uk/howard-assembly-room. Between them, the Grand Theatre and Opera House and the splendidly restored Howard Assembly Room offers an eclectic range of performances, from the high culture of Opera North and Northern Ballet productions to one-man/-woman shows, stand-up comedy, spectacular musicals and children's productions.

West Yorkshire Playhouse Playhouse Square, Quarry Hill ☎0113 213 7700, ⊚ wyp.org.uk. Based in the "Kremlin" (see p.89), the West Yorkshire Playhouse is one of the best regional theatres in the UK, putting on a variety of new and classic plays – many of its productions have transferred to the West End.

SHOPPING

When **Harvey Nichols** opened their Leeds store in 1996 (their first outside London) it only went to show that the city is one of the very best for shopping outside the capital. In addition to the usual high-street chains and mall developments that you get in all big cities, Leeds has numerous independent shops, the classy emporia that throng the city's beautifully restored **Victoria Quarter** and other arcades, the shopping and entertainment complex of **The Light**, the new Trinity Leeds complex, and the eight hundred traders housed in the Edwardian City Markets in Kirkgate.

Corn Exchange Call Lane ☎0113 234 0363, ⓦleedscornexchange.co.uk. The Corn Exchange is home to numerous independent shops, including the wonderfully named Alice Found Treasure, Little Pink Wardrobe and Mad Elizabeth. Mon–Wed, Fri & Sat 10am–6pm, Thurs 10am–7pm, Sun 10.30am–4.30pm.

Harvey Nichols 107–111 Briggate ☎0113 204 8888, ⓦharveynichols.com/store/leeds/ Top-end department store, complete with uniformed commissionaire at the entrance. Mon–Wed 10am–6pm, Thurs 10am–8pm, Fri 10am–7pm, Sat 9am–7pm, Sun 10.30am–5pm.

Kirkgate Market Kirkgate ⓦleedskirkgatemarket .co.uk. More than eight hundred traders housed in the renovated Edwardian covered market and in the open air (see p.90). Mon–Sat 8am–5.30pm.

The Light The Headrow ☎0113 218 2060, ⓦthelightleeds.co.uk. Imaginatively adapted historic building (see p.89) that contains not only shops such as Benetton and Ark but also a health and fitness club, a cinema and a hotel. Mon–Fri 6am–12.30am, Sat & Sun 8am–12.30am.

Trinity Leeds Complex Albion St ☎0113 394 2415, ⓦtrinityleeds.com. The latest mall development in the city centre, with shops from Adidas and Apple to Warren James and Wilkinson. Mon–Sat 9am–8pm, Sun 11am–5pm.

Victoria Quarter Main entrance on Briggate; stretches along King Edward St to Vicar Lane ⓦv-q.co.uk. Beautifully renovated, adapted and extended Victorian arcades packed with high-end designer shops such as Louis Vuitton, Mulberry, Diesel, Ted Baker and Vivienne Westwood, along with some nice places to eat. Mon–Sat 9am–6pm, Sun 11am–5pm.

Bradford and around

BRADFORD lies nine miles west of Leeds, in a shallow depression surrounded by hills. Though it was not well treated by the twentieth century, there is still plenty to see in the city centre, and even more in the surrounding area. Despite often unsympathetic development, some handsome late nineteenth-century buildings remain – the **Town Hall**, the **Wool Exchange** and **St George's Hall**, for example – and "**Little Germany**", an area of warehouses associated with the influx of German-Jewish entrepreneurs, has survived almost intact. The **Alhambra Theatre**, meanwhile, built in 1914, has been restored to its previous glory. While the excellent **National Media Museum**, on the edge of the city centre and overlooking it, is reason enough to visit, there are a number of interestingly offbeat museums (such as the **Peace Museum**) and art galleries in Bradford itself. And with substantial immigration from Germany in the 1820s and 1830s, Ireland in the 1840s, Poland and Ukraine immediately after World War II, and the Asian subcontinent from the 1950s onwards, Bradford is one of the most culturally diverse cities in the UK; if you like good **Asian food**, this is the place to be.

Bolling Hall, a medieval manor much altered over the years and now a museum, is less than a mile from the centre, and as you'd expect from this area, there are numerous interesting industrial attractions: **Bradford Industrial Museum**, **Ingrow Railway Museums** and the **Keighley and Worth Valley Railway**.

Brief history

A village that mushroomed during the early nineteenth century as it became the world leader in the production of **woollen worsted cloth**, Bradford was, until the 1850s a byword for filth and squalor. As the untrammelled operation of the free market sparked an unplanned building free-for-all, factories sprang up across the city, their chimneys creating a permanent pall of smoke, and dwellings, which quickly became slums, were flung up to house a workforce sucked in from surrounding areas. Little survives from this period.

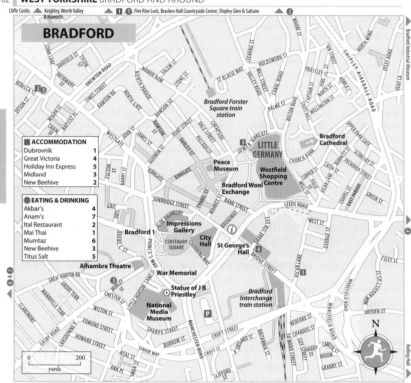

From around 1850, though, and especially in the 1860s and 1870s, growing prosperity, coupled with the work of the council and the Street Improvement Committee, secured an improvement in housing and public health, and a number of impressive city-centre buildings were commissioned: **St George's Hall** in 1851–53, the **Wool Exchange** in the 1860s, the **Town Hall** in the 1870s, and a host of schools and warehouses of notable splendour. Bradford became a Victorian city with a centre appropriate to its wealth and success.

Although boosted by the need for uniforms during the world wars, the general trend for the worsted industry in the twentieth century was downward. In the second half, particularly, Bradford reeled from the double whammy of the decline of its staple industry and a city-centre redevelopment plan that destroyed great swathes of the nineteenth-century city, replacing dignified factories and warehouses with dull offices, shops, and windswept and bleak residential developments. Twenty-first-century developments only compounded the damage, but the city's traditional vigour and entrepreneurial flair, which served it so well in the nineteenth century, seem set to start things moving as the new millennium progresses.

Centenary Square

Dotted around central **Centenary Square** are several memorials that together give a fair insight into Bradford's history. The **Bradford City Fire Memorial** remembers the 1985 Valley Parade disaster, in which 56 people were killed and more than three hundred injured when fire engulfed the main stand during a Third Division football match. In the Memorial Garden, the **Bradford Pals** headstone commemorates the 16th and 18th battalions of the West Yorkshire Regiment, among the many so-called "Pals Battalions" raised across the country during World War I. The idea was to keep volunteers from the same towns and cities together, on the grounds that they would be more likely to sign up if they were among familiar faces. It certainly worked, and towns and cities vied with each other to see who could contribute the most recruits. The **Workers' Memorial Day Plaque** was erected in memory of the 1984 Bhopal disaster, when a chemical leak in that Indian city killed around twenty thousand people; another commemorates the help given to **Balkan states** during the Bosnian war; the **Hiroshima and Nagasaki Plaque** does the same for the one hundred thousand-plus people who died as a result of the dropping of the two atom bombs on Japan; and the **Bob Cryer Memorial Tree and Plaque** recalls the Bradford MP and peace campaigner who died in a car crash in 1994. These last memorials indicate the strong links between Bradford and the peace movement – it's no coincidence that Bradford's most famous son, J.B. Priestley, was a staunch anti-racist and CND supporter, that Bradford University is the only one in the country with a Peace Studies Department, nor that Bradford has the only Peace Museum in Britain. In Centenary Square, too, are the modern **Impressions Gallery** (Tues, Wed & Fri 11am–6pm, Thurs 11am–8pm, Sat & Sun noon–5pm; free; ☎01274 737843, ⓦimpressions-gallery.com) and **Bradford 1** (Tues, Wed & Fri 11am–6pm, Thurs 11am–8pm, Sat & Sun noon–5pm; free; ☎01274 437800, ⓦbradfordmuseums.org), both attractive venues for temporary art shows.

National Media Museum

Pictureville, Little Horton Lane • Daily 10am–6pm • Free, screenings £7.70 • ☎ 0844 856 3797, ⓦ nationalmediamuseum.org.uk

On the southern edge of the city centre, and overlooking it, is the best reason for visiting Bradford – the **National Media Museum**. Part of the same group as London's Science Museum, it shares with it a terrific, hands-on approach; you'll need the best part of a day to do the place justice. First pick up the daily *What's On* guide and the seasonal *Family Guide*, then plunge straight in. The first two floors house temporary exhibitions, while the top three have permanent displays. The third floor is about television, and offers you the chance to see how well you can read the news (it's not as easy as it looks), perform pratfalls on a sitcom set, or use a blue screen to see yourself against a variety of backgrounds. There are also loads of vintage tellies on display. The Magic Factory on the fourth floor contains interactive activities involving lenses, prisms and mirrors, demonstrating the science behind film, photography and television – shake hands with yourself in the convex mirror, for example, or look out across the city centre through a pinhole camera or a TV zoom lens. Other highlights include the Kodak Gallery, devoted to a history of popular photography, and Life Online, the world's first gallery dedicated to the internet.

As well as visiting the exhibits, try to fit in a film: there are three **cinemas**, from the small and intimate Cubby Broccoli through the Pictureville Cinema to the giant IMAX (whose projection booth you can see on the sixth floor). There's also a good-sized restaurant (and a picnic area) and an excellent shop.

Outside the museum, note the large bronze **statue of J.B. Priestley**, bareheaded, pipe in hand and coat tails flying. Unveiled in 1986, it commemorates the famous novelist, playwright and man of letters who was born in Bradford, and wrote very perceptively about it in *English Journey*, an account of a trip taken through England in 1933.

War Memorial

Victoria Square

Bradford's **War Memorial** stands on Victoria Square near the landmark **Alhambra Theatre** (see p.107) – a cenotaph flanked by two bronze soldiers carrying guns. When it was erected in 1922, peace-loving city that Bradford was, there was a big reaction against what was seen as the overly aggressive stance of the soldiers, in particular the "crude and mistaken symbolism" of the bayonets attached to their guns. In response, the bayonets were removed, only, oddly, to be replaced each year on Remembrance Day.

Bradford Wool Exchange

Hustlergate

Bradford Wool Exchange was the third of the big three city-centre Victorian projects designed by Lockwood and Mawson (see box below) – St George's Hall for culture, the Town Hall for local government, and the Wool Exchange for Bradford's dominant industry. The Wool Exchange is particularly interesting – almost triangular in shape, as determined by its plot – and in a Venetian Gothic style, with pointed arches on the ground floor and double- and triple-arched windows on the first and second storeys. Its clock tower features statues of Bishop Blaize, patron saint of wool-combers, and Edward III, and around the building, between the ground-floor arches, are medallions portraying figures considered important one way or another to the development of Bradford. Here you'll spot Richard Cobden, radical liberal statesman and hero of the free trade movement; Sir Titus Salt, local manufacturer and power behind the construction of Salt's Mill and Saltaire (see p.108); inventors Robert Stephenson, James Watt, Richard Arkwright and J.M. Jacquard; and politicians William Gladstone and Lord Palmerston. Also making an appearance are various explorers with no clear connection with the city apart from having expanded the known world (and therefore markets for Bradford's woollen cloth). The side of the Wool Exchange facing Hustlergate has been partly rebuilt in glass, and now houses a group of shops including Waterstones on the ground floor.

Peace Museum

10 Piece Hall Yard • Wed –Fri 10am–4pm • Free (donations welcome) • ☎ 01274 780241, ⦿ peacemuseum.org.uk

One of around a hundred museums worldwide dedicated to the twentieth-century peace movement, but the only one in Britain, Bradford's **Peace Museum** is hard to find, tucked away in Piece Hall Yard, immediately opposite Waterstones, and hard to reach (the notice on the door says "there are several flights of stairs" and they are emphatically not kidding; there's no lift). But persevere – it's worth it. In three rooms at the top of a fine Victorian bank building, the museum contains more than five thousand posters, banners, photographs, letters, pieces of film footage, newspaper cuttings and works of art, all related to the peace movement.

BRADFORD'S ARCHITECTS: LOCKWOOD AND MAWSON

Rarely can a city have owed its appearance and atmosphere so completely to the vision, expertise and hard work of two men – **Henry Francis Lockwood** and **William Mawson**. Yorkshiremen through and through – Lockwood, the senior partner, was born in Doncaster in 1811, Mawson in Leeds in 1828 – they were partners in the architectural firm that designed, in both Gothic and Renaissance styles, the majority of the city's most impressive buildings. Between 1850 and 1875 they won the contracts for their great triumvirate – **St George's Hall**, their first success (see p.107), the **Town Hall** and the **Wool Exchange** (see above) – together with a host of less famous structures including churches and chapels, hospitals, workhouses, political clubs, schools and colleges, mills, and several warehouses in Little Germany (see opposite). Most of these buildings have survived and can still be seen, though often their usage has changed. Lockwood and Mawson were responsible, too, for the whole of Saltaire (see p.107), the mill and model village built for Sir Titus Salt.

Bradford Cathedral

1 Stott Hill • Mon–Sat 9am–4.30pm (except during organ recitals) • ☎ 01274 777720, ⓦ bradfordcathedral.co.uk

Bradford Cathedral started life as a lowly parish church before being elevated to cathedral status in 1919, and even with considerable rebuilding between 1951 and 1965 its humble origins are apparent. The resulting design is confused, neither medieval fish nor twentieth-century fowl. Climbing up to the churchyard from Forster Square gets you a very pleasant overall impression of the green and the cathedral staff housing – you would also have fine views across the city were it not for the huge hole of the Westfield development project. The two splendid **Pre-Raphaelite stained-glass** windows are among the building's great glories; you should call ahead if visiting especially to see them, however, as access is restricted during public recitals on the magnificent **organ** – the cathedral's other highlight.

2

Little Germany

Near Bradford's cathedral is the one area of the city that has largely avoided the wrecking ball. **Little Germany**, between the cathedral and the main Leeds road, earned its name from the many German wool exporters who moved into the district in the second half of the nineteenth century. Palatial **warehouses** were designed, many of them by Lockwood and Mawson (see opposite), to emphasize the power and success of the woollen companies – many survive intact, especially along Well Street, Vicar Lane and Currer Street. This is still a business district, so none of the buildings, as yet, are open to the general public.

Bolling Hall

Bowling Hall Rd, 1 mile south of Bradford city centre • Wed–Fri 11am–4pm, Sat 10am–5pm, Sun noon–5pm • Free • ☎ 01274 431814, ⓦ bradfordmuseums.org • Bus #624 from Bradford Interchange (5min plus a walk)

Bolling Hall has been continuously occupied for at least five hundred years. During that time it has been built on and modified to such an extent that it now offers a vivid illustration of the changes in architecture and fashion since the end of the fifteenth century. A fine medium-sized manor house, once the seat of two important local families – the Bollings and the Tempests – it has a total of fifteen rooms open to the public. The oldest part of the house is the southwest tower, which dates from the Middle Ages – the southeast tower was built in the seventeenth century to balance it. Each room is furnished in the style of its time; look out in particular for the large bed made for Harewood House in Leeds (see p.96) by Thomas Chippendale and the interesting array of seventeenth-century stained glass. The house also claims to be the residence of Bradford's most famous **ghost**. The story goes that when Roundhead Bradford was under siege by Cavalier forces the Royalist commander, the Earl of Newcastle, stayed with Sir Richard Tempest at Bolling Hall. Infuriated by the town's continued resistance, the earl vowed that when it fell he would put the whole population to the sword. That night, woken by a ghostly figure who wailed "Pity poor Bradford", he was so shaken that when the town finally succumbed, he spared the civilian population. There's a public park and a children's playground across the road.

Bradford Industrial Museum

Moorside Rd, Eccleshill, 3 miles northeast of Bradford city centre • Tues–Fri 10am–4pm, Sat & Sun 11am–4pm • Free • ☎ 01274 435900, ⓦ bradfordmuseums.org • Bus #640 or #641 from city centre (10min)

In the suburb of **Eccleshill** stands the impressive 1875 Moorside Mills, originally a worsted spinning mill and now the council-run **Bradford Industrial Museum**. The approach to the mill takes you past the mill-owner's house and the **workers'**

2

cottages, with their interiors set up to look as they would have in the nineteenth century. The **stables** are given over to equine exhibits, with a good few horse-drawn vehicles (including a fire engine), and a "Horse Power Emporium" full of the paraphernalia associated with working horses – collars, bits and bridles. To one side is the paddock, and there are always working horses to be admired (but not fed). Inside the mill you can see excellent **displays** on the local woollen industry, from traditional spinning wheels and hand looms to tools used in mechanized cloth production, and biographies of great Bradfordians, including Sir Edward Appleton, winner of the 1947 Nobel Prize for Physics for his work on the ionosphere. Particularly interesting is the huge "Coat of Many Cultures", made of silk, worsted and linen cloth from all over the world, and "From Mirpur to Manningham", about the great influx of people from South Asia and East Africa in the 1950s and 1960s. Elsewhere are collections of steam engines of all types, printing presses and a wonderful collection of vintage motor vehicles, plus Bradford's last surviving tram and trolley bus. Most afternoons there are also horse-drawn rail tramway rides.

ARRIVAL AND INFORMATION   BRADFORD

By plane Leeds-Bradford International airport (ⓦleedsbradfordairport.co.uk) lies 6 miles north of the city centre.

By car Just 2 miles from junction 26 of the M1 (and joined to it by motorway spur M606), Bradford is easy to get into and out of by car. There are plenty of Pay-and-Display car parks, but they tend to be just out of the city centre.

By train There are two train stations – Bradford Forster Square (in the north of town) for services to Skipton, Ilkley and Leeds, and Bradford Interchange (in the south of town, off Bridge St) for services to Halifax, Huddersfield and Manchester. A free city bus links the city centre with both.

Destinations from Forster Square Ilkley (every 30min;

31min); Leeds (every 30min; 23min); Skipton (every 30min; 48min).

Destinations from Bradford Interchange Halifax (every 20min; 12min); Huddersfield (hourly; 45min); Manchester (every 30min; 1hr).

By bus The Bradford Interchange (see above) also handles buses, with services linking all parts of the city and the rest of West Yorkshire (ⓦfirstgroup.com). It also has a National Express coach station.

Destinations Huddersfield (every 15–20min; 49min); Leeds (every 20min; 31min); London (every 50min–1hr 30min; 5–6hr); Wakefield (every 30min; 1hr 7min).

Tourist office Britannia House, Broadway (April–Sept Mon–Sat 10am–5pm; Oct–March Mon 10.30am–4pm, Tues–Sat 10am–4pm; ☎01274 433 678).

ACCOMMODATION

Dubrovnik 3 Oak Ave, 1.5 miles north of the centre ☎01274 543511, ⓦdubrovnik.co.uk. On a pleasant suburban street a 2min walk from Lister Park, one of the city's largest green spaces, the *Dubrovnik* is a capacious, privately owned hotel. Pleasant public rooms, friendly, helpful staff, well-appointed accommodation, good food and ample free parking make this a good alternative to the all-pervasive hotel chains. **£57**

★**Great Victoria** 39 Bridge St ☎01274 728706, ⓦtomahawkhotels.co.uk. A Victorian station hotel, the work of Lockwood and Mawson (see p.104), the architects who designed the Town Hall and St George's Hall, the *Great Victoria* offers solid comfort and individually designed and very smart rooms right in the heart of the city. It has a good restaurant, a popular bar, and that Victorian spaciousness you don't get in many modern hotels. Free parking. **£50**

Holiday Inn Express Vicar Lane ☎0871 423 4878, ⓦihg.com. Standard *Holiday Inn* accommodation and

facilities, within walking distance of the city centre. It's in a leisure complex, with cinema, casino, bowling and restaurants, yet quiet, with the reception and rooms upstairs above all the noise. Paid parking in the leisure complex's multistorey. **£43**

Midland Foster Square ☎01274 735735, ⓦpeel hotels.co.uk. Right in the centre, directly across from the Westfield Broadway development site, this is another updated railway hotel combining Victorian roominess with old-fashioned elegance and designer chic. Free on-site parking. **£97**

★**New Beehive** 171 Westgate ☎01274 721784. For a change from the run-of-the-mill, try this terrific pub (see p.107) bursting with character and with more accommodation than you'd expect (seventeen rooms, all en suite). It's still essentially a drinking destination so it can get noisy: ask for a top-floor room, or one of the two across the courtyard. Free car park adjacent. **£48**

EATING AND DRINKING

Bradford is famous for the range and quality of its **Indian restaurants**. Most Bradfordians have their own favourites – the online curry guide at ⓦwebsite.lineone.net/~bradfordcurryguide features a lively debate about the delights or otherwise of a range of restaurants. Though it would seem a shame to visit Bradford and not try its Indian cuisine, there are other types of restaurant in the city.

Akbar's 1276 Leeds Rd, Thornbury ☎01274 773311, ⓦakbars.co.uk. Near the ring road to the east, this is the original of a chain that now has branches across the north of England (and one in Birmingham). It's famed for the quality of its south Asian cuisine, offering a wide range of chicken, lamb and prawn curries, and is hugely popular – at weekends you may end up waiting, even when you've booked. Most dishes cost well under £10. Mon–Fri 5pm–midnight, Sat 4pm–midnight, Sun 2–11.30pm.

Anam's 211 Great Horton Rd ☎01274 522626, ⓦanams.co.uk Newish chrome-and-steel Indian restaurant with buffet and a la carte. The usual range of masala, rogan josh and so on, but also less common *cocony*, all at around £6.95. Daily noon–4pm & 5pm–midnight.

Ital Restaurant 626 Bolton Rd ☎01274 626254, ⓦitalrestaurant.co.uk. A classy, long-established Italian place, boasting excellent service and a lively atmosphere. Try the calzone, and the chef's speciality, the *filetto alla Griglia*, or fillet steak. Starters £3.50–7.50, mains £10.80–20.50. Mon–Fri 5.30–10.30pm, Sat 6–10.30pm.

Mai Thai 198–200 Keighley Rd ☎01274 499088, ⓦmaithairestaurant.co.uk. Out beyond Lister Park, just under 2 miles north of the centre, and popular for its laidback atmosphere and fresh, tasty Thai food. Expect to pay between £10 and £20 per person, without wine. Mon–Sat 5–9.30pm.

★**Mumtaz** 386–410 Great Horton Rd ☎01274 522533, ⓦmumtaz.co.uk. *Mumtaz* is probably even more well regarded than *Akbar's* (there's another one at Clarence Dock in Leeds), with plaudits from everyone from Dawn French and Amir Khan, through Shilpa Shetty and Frank Bruno, to Queen Elizabeth II herself (or so its website claims). With its delicious Kashmiri food – a range of *karahi* and biryani dishes, with meat, fish and vegetarian options – and smart decor, it's always busy with locals and visitors from all over the country. Remember, though – no alcohol. Expect to pay around £30 per person for a meal. Sun–Thurs 11am–midnight, Fri & Sat 11am–1am.

New Beehive 171 Westgate ☎01274 721784. Excellent Edwardian CAMRA-rated pub with five gaslit bars (three with open fires), live music at weekends and lots of microbrewery real ale. They offer good accommodation, too (see opposite). Mon–Thurs 1–11.30pm, Fri & Sat 1pm–1am, Sun 6–11pm.

Titus Salt Unit B, Windsor Baths, Morley St ☎01274 732853. You couldn't ask for cheaper food in better surroundings than the *Titus Salt* just up from the Alhambra, a Wetherspoon's where they have excelled themselves by converting an interesting building (the swimming baths) and choosing to name it after one of the colossi of the city's history (see p.108). Mon–Thurs & Sun 8am–midnight, Fri & Sat 8am–1am; food served all day.

ENTERTAINMENT

Alhambra Morley St ☎01274 432000, ⓦbradford-theatres.co.uk. One of the glories of Bradford's city centre, built on the eve of World War I. The Alhambra's splendidly pillared and domed exterior, echoed in the 1980s steel-and-glass extension, is more than matched by its plush auditorium – all rich colours, ornate gilded plasterwork and luxurious boxes, with a beautifully painted domed ceiling. Among those who have graced its stage are Helen Mirren, Terence Stamp and Michael Caine; it was also used, evocatively, as a location in the 1983 film *The Dresser*, starring Albert Finney and Tom Courtenay.

It stages a wide variety of productions, from the Northern Ballet and Royal Shakespeare Company to pantomime and the *Rocky Horror Show*.

St George's Hall Bridge St ☎01274 432000, ⓦbradford-theatres.co.uk. Jointly managed with the Alhambra, St George's Hall, another landmark structure, was the first of Bradford's big mid-nineteenth-century public buildings, designed by Lockwood and Mawson (see p.104) in 1851–53. Renowned for its excellent acoustics and audience-friendly intimacy, it seats up to 1500 for orchestral concerts, stand-up comedy, variety and rock concerts.

Saltaire and around

SALTAIRE, five miles northwest of Bradford city centre, is an early example of a Victorian **mill complex** and **model village**, still remarkably intact after more than a century and a half. The complex – its name combines that of its founder, **Titus Salt**, and the River Aire upon which it stands – has been designated a UNESCO World Heritage Site by virtue of its architectural unity and as a prime example of Victorian philanthropic paternalism. In addition to its industrial heritage, it also holds a major exhibition of works by **David Hockney**.

Brief history

Saltaire was built in the 1850s and 1860s by **Sir Titus Salt**, one of Bradford's great wool entrepreneurs. Having made a fortune by the age of 40, largely by introducing alpaca and other new fibres into worsted manufacture, he wanted to build a new factory clear of the shambolic mess that Bradford had become during its massive expansion in the first half of the nineteenth century. He chose a greenfield site near Shipley that had excellent transport links with the rest of the country – a river (the Aire), a canal (the Leeds and Liverpool) and a railway – with which to bring in raw materials and despatch finished cloth. He also wanted to provide housing and other services for his workers, hoping that such things would guarantee a stable and sober workforce, and employed Bradford's foremost firm of architects – Lockwood and Mawson (see p.104) – to design it all.

Salt's Mill

Victoria Rd, Shipley • Mon–Fri 10am–5.30pm, Sat & Sun 10am–6pm • Free • ☎ 01274 531163, ⓦ saltsmill.org.uk • Bus #662 from Bradford Interchange (every 10–20min; 23min); train from Bradford Forster Square (every 35min; 7min)

The enormous **Salt's Mill** – the biggest industrial building in the world when it opened in 1853 – has, since its closure in 1986 and its subsequent redevelopment, become a multi-use art and design centre, with shops selling arts and crafts, flowers, music, textiles, antiques, jewellery, clothes, furniture and books. You can also see an exhibition on the mill's history (in Gallery 2) and, in the **1853 Gallery**, one of the biggest displays of the work of **David Hockney** in the world. The artist, who was born in Bradford in 1937 and trained at the Bradford School of Art before transferring to the Royal College of Art in London, was a close friend of the late Jonathan Silver, the man responsible for the conversion of Salt's Mill into the great art and design complex it is today. There is also a collection of Hockney's opera sets on the top floor (which is open only Wed–Sun). Refreshments are available in the mill's diner.

Saltaire model village

A walk around **Saltaire model village**, built between 1851 and 1872 to house the mill workers, takes between one and two hours, and is fascinating. Half a mile square (including the mill and the park), it is laid out on a grid plan, with houses that differ in size and grandeur depending on the status of the people they were built for. Even the humblest mill hands had two bedrooms, a living room, a kitchen and a cellar pantry, together with a small garden, and all houses were supplied with drainage, water and gas. Public buildings included the Congregational Church, almshouses for the elderly, public baths, an imposing education institute, a school and a hospital, plus a park – with, naturally, a statue of Sir Titus Salt. In line with Salt's deeply held Christian beliefs there were no pubs, though he wasn't fanatical – there was an off-licence, and he had no objections to families having a barrel of beer in their cellars. Apart from Victoria Road and Albert Road, all the streets are named after members of the Salt family – Titus, his wife Caroline, their children, grandchildren and daughter-in-law. The village is still a living community, so visitors have to content themselves with looking at, but not entering, the houses.

Opinion over Saltaire model village was then, and is now, divided. On the one hand, Salt's workers and their families had far better working and living conditions than other mill workers in West Yorkshire. However, their lives were stiflingly regimented, with a paternalistic employer who frowned upon any dissent towards management – trade unions were banned, for example.

Shipley Glen

Above Saltaire is an area that owed its nineteenth-century popularity to its proximity to the Saltaire mill and to Shipley, Bingley and Keighley. **Shipley Glen**, a beautiful, wooded gash-and-shoulder of moorland, became a local beauty spot, thronged with walkers at weekends and holidays, with fairground rides and temporary tearooms set up in farmers' barns – you can still see faded signs on walls or roofs. Still popular today, the Glen is a great deal quieter than it must have been when thronged with Victorian mill workers.

Tramway

Sat & Sun noon–4.30pm, weather permitting • £1; £2 for day ticket • ☎ 01274 589010, ⓦ glentramway.co.uk

In 1895 a local entrepreneur – Sam Wilson – who'd already built several fairground rides on the Glen, decided to spare visitors from Saltaire the long walk up, and built the Shipley Glen Cable Railway, a tramway with two 0.25-mile-long, 20-inch tracks with a gradient of 1 in 7 and two opposing trams. The fairground rides that occupied the so-called Pleasure Grounds have now gone, but the **Tramway** – which climbs to the Glen from just north of Roberts Park in Saltaire – survives, owing to the unbelievably dedicated support of local people and the Bradford Trolley Bus Association.

2

ARRIVAL AND DEPARTURE   **SHIPLEY GLEN**

By bus Buses #626 and #677 run from Bradford Inter-   Shipley Glen is a 10min walk.
change to Baildon (every 15–20min; 35min), from where

EATING AND DRINKING

Old Glen House Prod Lane, Baildon ☎ 01274 597777,   noon–11pm, Fri & Sat noon–11.30pm, Sun noon–
ⓦ theoldglenhouse.co.uk. The nearest pub to Shipley   10.30pm; food served Tues–Sat noon–2.15pm & 5.45–
Glen, serving good pub grub (starters £5, mains £10) with   9.30pm, Sun noon–6pm.
sandwiches and soups ideal for walkers. Tues–Thurs

Five Rise Locks

Bingley, 6 miles northwest of Bradford • Bus #662 from Bradford Interchange (5–10min; 37 min), then a 15min walk

The **Five Rise Locks** are worth a quick visit if you're in the area. Built in 1773–74 and contributing 59ft to the 487ft rise that the Leeds and Liverpool Canal needs to manage in order to cross the Pennines, they represent one of the great masterpieces of early canal building, and are an excellent example of a "staircase", where the lower gate of each lock is the upper gate of the next lock downhill (not to be confused with a "flight", where the locks are separate, but happen to be in close proximity). There's a café on the quayside at the top, and fine views across Bingley.

Keighley and around

Around eleven miles northwest of Bradford, Keighley is a traditional mill town that owed its growth to the booming nineteenth-century cotton industry. The **Cliffe Castle Museum** is one of the excellent local authority museums with which Yorkshire is blessed, while on the outskirts of town is a cluster of enthusiast-run **railway attractions**.

Cliffe Castle Museum

Spring Gardens Lane • Tues–Fri 10am–4pm, Sat & Sun 11am–4pm • Free • ☎ 0153 618231, ⓦ bradfordmuseums.org • Bus #662 from Bradford Interchange to Keighley (every 10min; 56 min), from where you can walk for 15min or change on to bus #25, #66, #762 or #903 (every 10–15min; 5–11min)

Cliffe Castle Museum occupies a house that was built in the 1830s for a wealthy lawyer, passed through the hands of a millionaire textile manufacturer, and was finally

2

KEIGHLEY: A TRAINSPOTTER'S GUIDE

The Keighley and Worth Valley Railway, with terrific memorabilia shops at Ingrow and Haworth, is a popular pilgrimage for **rail enthusiasts**. Add that to the Loco Museum and the Museum of Rail Travel, both of which sit next to the railway's Ingrow West station, and you have the perfect day out – and not just for trainspotters.

Keighley and Worth Valley Railway Next to Keighley mainline station (all year Sat & Sun, July & Aug daily, check website for timetable; rover tickets £15, family tickets £35 – ordering through tickets at mainline stations is cheaper than buying separate tickets for the KWVR; ☎01535 645214, ⓦkwvr.co.uk). Though it was built in the 1860s, to serve both the mills in the area and the burgeoning Brontë tourism industry (see p.112), KWVR, which closed in 1962, is now run to capture the atmosphere of a 1950s branch line. It has such a comprehensive range of features – five miles of track, six stations, including Haworth (see below), four signal boxes, two tunnels, two level crossings, a turntable, several bridges and a viaduct – that it is in constant demand for film and television programmes. Its credits include the 1970 film *The Railway Children*, plus, on TV, Victoria Wood's *Housewife 49*, *A Touch of Frost*, *The League of Gentlemen* and a Tetley Bitter advert among many others. It even makes an appearance in the 1982 movie The *Wall*.

Museum of Rail Travel Ingrow Bridge (daily 11am–4pm; £2.50; ☎01535 645214, ⓦvisitbradford .com). Numerous carriages and station paraphernalia packed into a large shed. The museum is run by the Vintage Carriages Trust (ⓦvintagecarriagestrust.org) charity.

Ingrow Loco Museum Ingrow Bridge (Sat, Sun & selected days 11am–4.30pm; free entry with Museum of Rail Travel ticket, otherwise £1.50; ☎01535 690739, ⓦingrowlocomuseum .com). Run by the Bahamas Locomotive Society (named after its first project, a Jubilee class steam locomotive called *Bahamas*), the museum displays four engines, a breakdown van and a breakdown crane.

developed into a museum by Keighley Corporation in the 1950s. It's an eclectic collection, beautifully displayed. One gallery is devoted to the geological formation of the Airedale valley, with masses of rock and mineral samples. You can also see several Egyptian mummies and the 3000-year-old "black coffin", along with exhibits on local reptiles, amphibians and, especially, birds – including a display case of thirteen of the most common species, which allows you to test your knowledge of their song. Local agriculture, industry, costume and dolls houses are also highlighted, and, in an octagonal room with a gallery, there are temporary exhibitions and a history of the building. Look out for the "Hen Peck'd Husband's Wife-Taming Cradle", designed in the 1860s to rock nagging wives to calm and soothe them, the animal heart stuck full of pins (a charm against witchcraft), the lamb with two faces, the scrying ball for telling the future (more commonly known as a crystal ball), and the glass walking sticks (said to ward off bad luck).

Haworth

On the moors above the Worth Valley, ten miles west of Bradford, **HAWORTH** is one of Britain's major tourist destinations. An attractive stone village with steep cobbled streets, its pulling power arises solely from its connection with the hugely talented but ultimately tragic **Brontës** (see box, p.112).

Haworth's two main streets, **Main Street** and **West Lane**, are full of cafés, gift shops and guesthouses, and get chock-a-block with tourists. And yet however crowded Haworth becomes, however sick you get of the Brontë names being used inappropriately for all manner of commercial enterprises, however sternly literary critics tell us that it is the works that are important not the lives, a visit to Haworth – the **Parsonage** where the family lived, the **church** where they worshipped, the *Black Bull* where Branwell drank or the chemist where he got his laudanum, and, perhaps above all the wild surrounding **moors** where the sisters got their inspiration – is a moving experience for anybody who admires their work or knows about their lives.

Brontë Parsonage Museum

Church St • Daily: April–Oct 10am–5.30pm; Nov–March 10am–5pm • £7.50 • ☎ 01535 642323, ⓦ bronte.org.uk

A visit to the **Brontë Parsonage Museum**, at the top of the hill next to the church, is a must. This rather forbidding house was where the newly appointed vicar of Haworth, Patrick Brontë, came to reside in 1820, and where his four children lived from 1820 until their deaths, and from where their imagination took flight. You can see the toy soldiers that are said to have sparked their earliest attempts at storytelling (see box, p.112), the little books that they made for the soldiers to read, the rooms and furniture they used – including the stool Emily used to sit outside on, and the bed she died in. The **church** next door (controversially totally remodelled in 1879) is where Patrick Brontë preached, where Charlotte was married, and where all but Anne are buried.

2

The moors

Out on the **moors** you can walk to the Brontë Falls and Bridge and, just over a mile beyond, to the ruins of **Top Withens**, said by many, wrongly, to be the Wuthering Heights of the novel. Less than a mile beyond that Ponden Hall (now a hotel) has perhaps a little more of a claim to be Thrushcross Grange. The countryside is bleak but beautiful, redolent with the spirit of the Brontë sisters and the characters who peopled their novels. It can get crowded, though.

ARRIVAL AND INFORMATION   HAWORTH

By train It's more fun to arrive in Haworth on the Keighley and Worth Valley Railway (see opposite); you can transfer from the main line at Keighley.

By bus From Bradford Interchange you can take the #662 to Keighley (every 10min; 56 min), and change there for the #665 (hourly; 13min), which stops at Haworth station.

Tourist office West Lane, at the top of Main St (daily: April–Sept 10am–5pm; Oct–March 10am–4pm; ☎ 01535 642 329, ⓦ visithaworth.com).

ACCOMMODATION AND EATING

Apothecary 86 Main St ☎ 01535 643642, ⓦ theapothecaryguesthouse.co.uk. Traditional guesthouse opposite the church, in a seventeenth-century building with oak beams, millstone grit walls and quaint passages, whose rear rooms, breakfast room and attached café have splendid moorland views. **£55**

Fleece Inn 67 Main St ☎ 01535 642172, ⓦ fleeceinnhaworth.co.uk. Busy stone-built pub/restaurant on the hill, with attractive rooms. Booking is advisable, and it's likely to be noisy until closing time. Pub Mon–Thurs 11am–11pm, Fri 11am–11.30pm, Sat 10am–11.30pm, Sun 10am–10.30pm; food served Mon–Fri noon–9pm, Sat 10am–9pm, Sun 10am–7pm. **£75**

Old Registry 2–4 Main St ☎ 01535 646503, ⓦ theoldregistryhaworth.co.uk. At the bottom of Main St, offering nine rooms, most with four-poster beds and fine views. Two-night minimum stay at weekends. **£75**

River Street Café 429 River St ☎ 01518 273 2740. Friendly bistro-type café with a solid local clientele enjoying a good range of pastas, frittatas, paninis, steaks, omelettes and an excellent full English breakfast. Mon–Fri 7am–3.30pm, Sat 8am–3.30pm.

Rosebud Cottage Guest House 1 Belle Isle Rd ☎ 01535 640321, ⓦ rosebudcottage.co.uk. Beautiful stone house on a terrace in the centre of the village, with comfortable rooms and friendly service. **£85**

Wilsons of Haworth 15 West Lane ☎ 01535 643209, ⓦ wilsonsofhaworth.co.uk. Top-end B&B with five luxurious rooms (four doubles and a single) and the feel of a boutique hotel. It's located in a converted row of weavers' cottages near the Brontë Parsonage museum. Minimum two-nights stay at weekends. **£89**

YHA Haworth Longlands Hall, a mile or so from the centre of Haworth, off the Keighley road ☎ 0870 770 5858, ⓦ yha.org.uk/hostel/haworth. YHA hostel in a former Victorian mill owner's mansion overlooking the village. Bradford buses stop on the main road nearby. Closed Mon–Fri Nov to mid-Feb. Dorms **£15**; doubles **£49**

2

THE BRONTËS

The Brontë family moved into Haworth Parsonage when Patrick Brontë became vicar there in 1820. **Patrick Brontë** (originally Brunty), an Irishman from a humble background who'd done well for himself by going to Cambridge University, was, in addition to being a clergyman, himself a published writer, with several collections of poems, short stories and a single novel to his name. Nine months after the move to Haworth his wife Maria died of cancer, leaving him with five daughters and a son to raise with the help of his sister-in-law Elizabeth Branwell, who moved up to Yorkshire from Cornwall.

The four older girls were sent away to school, but after the eldest two, **Maria** and **Elizabeth**, were sent home sick and died (in 1825), the surviving two were brought home to join their brother and youngest sister. While living in the parsonage, the four siblings – **Charlotte** (1816–55), **Branwell** (1817–48), **Emily** (1818–48) and **Anne** (1820–49) made up stories for each other (many involving a box of toy soldiers given to Branwell by his father) to keep themselves entertained. Patrick Brontë, whose own history made him a great believer in the power of education, encouraged the children to read widely, and during this time they produced the famous **"little books"** – tiny, perfectly made volumes with minuscule writing, small enough for the toy soldiers to read.

It was clear that, since Patrick Brontë had no private income, the girls would have to be prepared for life as teachers and governesses, the only socially acceptable employment for well-brought-up young women. First Charlotte, then Emily and Anne, were sent away to school and, as they grew into young women, became teachers, with varying degrees of success (Emily, in particular, hated teaching, apparently telling her charges in one school that she much preferred the school dog to any of them). Dissatisfied with the role of governess, the girls decided to set up a school of their own at the Parsonage, and Charlotte and Emily went to Brussels for a year (paid for by their aunt Elizabeth) to brush up their foreign languages. Their aunt, however, died in 1842, and Emily returned to Haworth to look after her father, with Charlotte joining her two years later, and Anne the year after that. The reuniting of the three young women and their brother seems to have recreated their childhood, and they started to write. The scene was set for one of the most spectacular literary debuts in history.

In 1846 the three young women used some of the money left to them by their aunt to publish a selection of their poems, under pseudonyms that were to become famous: **Currer** (Charlotte), **Ellis** (Emily) and **Acton** (Anne) **Bell**. The book (*Poems*) was quite favourably reviewed, but sales were disappointing – two copies. Under the same pen-names, all three sisters had novels published in 1847 – **Jane Eyre** by Charlotte, **Wuthering Heights** by Emily, and **Agnes Grey** by Anne. A feeding frenzy of interest in the authors soon identified them as women, and Charlotte in particular became the toast of literary England.

The family's happiness at their success was short-lived. First Branwell, who'd initially been considered the most talented of the siblings, but who'd been laid low by his addictions to alcohol and laudanum, died in September 1848 at the age of 31. In December of the same year, Emily, aged 30, died of tuberculosis. Anne, also consumptive, travelled to Scarborough to try a sea cure in May 1849 – four days later, she too was dead. She was 29. Charlotte had time to further develop her career as one of the country's foremost authors, to get married to her father's curate, and to become pregnant. Then she too died, together with her unborn child, in 1855. She was not yet 40. All of the Brontës are buried in a family vault in Haworth church except Anne, whose grave is in Scarborough (see p.260).

Halifax and around

After Leeds, **HALIFAX** is the West Yorkshire town that is probably adapting most successfully to the twenty-first century, retaining many of its notable early buildings but still altering to meet the needs of the present. Halifax is the most westerly of West Yorkshire's main towns, and the hilliest – in 1933 J.B. Priestley thought that at night the trams (now alas gone) looked like "luminous beetles swarming up and down a black wall". As you approach the town, downhill from whichever direction you're travelling, you will see before you a forest of perpendiculars – factory chimneys, tower blocks, church spires – interwoven with sinuous roads carried on soaring flyovers and iron bridges, the whole lot cupped by the surrounding hills. It could have been a mess, yet it seems to work.

Perhaps the town's biggest appeal is outside it – the fifteen-mile-long **Calder Valley** (see p.118), which stretches west to the Lancashire border. In town, however, there are a few key sights: the Parish Church, a **Minster** since 2009, is well worth a visit, as is the magnificent **Piece Hall**, built while England was involved in trying, and failing, to keep hold of the American colonies. **Eureka!**, Britain's only museum aimed entirely at children, is fun for the kids. Other notable buildings include the **Square Chapel**, now a performance venue – the **arts scene** in Halifax makes good use of its stock of nineteenth-century wool-town buildings – and the **Town Hall**, the **Victorian covered market** and **Dean Clough Mill**. Look out too for the modern recreation of the **Halifax Gibbet**, which long predated Dr Guillotine's more famous contraption, and the town's handsome 1855 train station.

Away from the centre the slightly old-fashioned **Bankfield Museum**, stately **Shibden Hall** and **Manor Heath Park** with its "Jungle Experience" are all within a ten-minute car ride, while further afield are the mighty **Wainhouse Tower**, outdoorsy **Ogden Water**, **Hardcastle Crags** and **Gibson Mill**.

Piece Hall and around

Blackledge • Mon–Fri 9am–5pm, Sat 9.30am–6pm, Sun 11am–5pm • Free • ⓦ thepiecehall.co.uk

The **Piece Hall** was opened in 1779, financed by a group of cloth manufacturers. A fine Georgian building, it is almost square in shape and consists of four colonnaded sides enclosing a central space. It's built on a hillside (there's a 16ft fall), so the side at the top of the site has two storeys, the one at the bottom of the site has three, and the two sides that join them go from two to three storeys halfway along. To give access to the upper storeys there are staircases at each corner (and one next to the Westgate entrance), and a lift in the southeast corner. Within the hall are 315 rooms in which handloom weavers would display and sell their pieces of cloth, consisting of 24-yard by 27-inch strips, each one of which was the result of a week's part-time work – the rest of their time would have been devoted to farming. At the time of writing, the Piece Hall was closed for a major refurbishment, and is likely to remain closed until Spring 2016.

Square Chapel and Square Church

10 Square Rd • Mon–Fri 9.30am–5pm, Sat 11am–3pm • ☎ 01422 349422, ⓦ squarechapel.co.uk

Downhill from the Piece Hall are the **Square Chapel**, a former Nonconformist chapel (1772) that is now given over to an art gallery and performance venue, and where plans are in hand for a new extension. Nearby is the **Square Church**, a nineteenth-century structure that burned down in 1971 leaving an interesting, brambly ruin. The "square" doesn't refer to their shape, incidentally, but to their location.

Eureka!

Discovery Rd • Tues–Fri 10am–4pm, Sat, Sun, hols & bank hols 10am–5pm • Adults and children older than 3 pay £11.95 for an annual pass • ☎ 01422 330069, ⓦ eureka.org.uk

The only museum of its kind in Britain, **Eureka!**, next to Halifax's train station, is a modern, purpose-built museum directed towards under-11s and based upon the principle that learning should be fun. Spread out across two floors, its galleries are packed with high-quality interactive displays – "Living and working together" (a child-sized town including banks and supermarkets), "SoundSpace" (all about music), "SoundGarden" (in which kids can experience the sounds of a garden from the point of view of an insect) and "Desert Discovery" (based on the Mojave desert) among them. The giant mouth (with wobbly tooth) and cycling skeleton are perennial favourites.

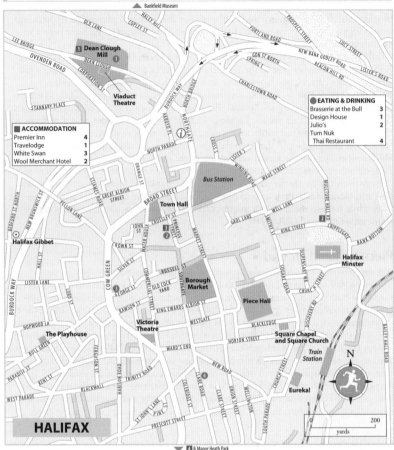

Everything is in the vivid primary hues of a child's colouring book – great for kids, though adults may feel like they've been indulging in illegal mind-altering substances. And everything is in immaculate condition and working order

There's a gift shop and café, and masses of play equipment outside, including a huge sandpit. Set aside several hours – you'll have to drag the kids away, kicking and screaming.

Halifax Minster

Causeway • Daily: summer 10am–4pm; winter 10am–2pm • Free • ⓦ halifaxminster.org.uk

Though the thirteenth-century **Halifax Minster** looks a bit smoke-grimed on the outside, its exterior has plenty of interest – look out for the sundial (on the wall next to the porch) and the gargoyles just below the roof. Inside, you should make for the intricately carved font cover suspended from the ceiling; the beautifully rich seventeenth-century pews (shortened, alas, by 2ft in the nineteenth century); the figure of Old Tristram, a life-sized carved wooden effigy of a man with a poor-box in front of him ("Pray remember the poor"); and the clear glass windows in the chancel, where the absence of stained glass, enforced by the Puritan church authorities, is subverted by the beautiful intricate patterns of the leading.

Borough Market

Southgate St • Mon–Sat 9am–5pm

On Southgate Street is the entrance to Halifax's large covered **Borough Market**. Opened in 1896, and declared a Grade II listed building in 2011, it has all the usual food and clothes stalls, as well as a wide range of other goods. Raise your eyes from the bargains and the circular fruit-and-veg stall to examine the intricate iron-and-glass roof, with its central dome and clock.

2

Halifax Town Hall

Crossley St

Halifax Town Hall, a stately building designed by Houses of Parliament architect Sir Charles Barry, was opened in 1863 by the Prince of Wales (later Edward VII) in a ceremony that attracted seventy thousand spectators. The clock is more than 6ft in diameter, with the largest of its bells weighing more than 4 tons, but it has been silent since 1918, when famous opera singer Dame Nellie Melba, staying in the nearby *White Swan*, complained that the striking of the hours was keeping her awake.

Halifax Gibbet

Gibbet St

Just across the inner ring road west of the city centre stands a reconstruction of the **Halifax Gibbet**. This is not the familiar gibbet of the children's "hangman" game, but a machine for beheading criminals very similar to the French guillotine: an axe head, embedded in a heavy lead-weighted block, descended in a frame onto the neck of the felon, separating the head from the body. It is this horrendous punishment that led to the felon's prayer: "from hell, Hull and Halifax, good lord deliver us". Used especially as a punishment for theft, its severity is explained by the fact that woollen cloth, having been soaked in urine to bleach it, had to be left out on frames to dry, making it particularly easy to steal. Daniel Defoe, in his *Tour through the Whole Island of Great Britain*, said that he could find no record of such a machine being used in Hull. He also tells of a story where a woman, driving a cart to Halifax market, was passing next to the gibbet while an execution was taking place. The blade descended with such force that the miscreant's head flew off into one of the hampers in the cart, to be discovered later by the horrified countrywoman when she came to unpack her goods. Defoe noted so many improbabilities, though, "that 'tis reasonable to think the whole tale is a little Yorkshire, which I suppose you will understand well enough!"

It's not easy to find – there are no signposts from the town centre, and it's perched on a little park, backing onto a motor repair garage, the only plaque giving the names of sponsors (of the reconstructed gibbet, not the executions themselves), rather than an explanation of its historical context.

Dean Clough Mill

Dean Clough • ☎ 01422 250250, ⊛ deanclough.com

Clearly visible off the A58 on the northern edge of Halifax, and within walking distance of the centre, the enormous **Dean Clough Mill** complex was built in the mid-nineteenth century to manufacture John Crossley's carpets and was once the biggest carpet factory in the world. When the mill closed in 1983, the opportunity to develop the site for community use was seized, and the Grade II listed building was adapted to include several art galleries and display spaces, the *Viaduct* café/bar, which often hosts stand-up comedy, the *Design House* restaurant (see p.118), numerous small businesses including an excellent home design shop, and the highly regarded **Viaduct Theatre** (see p.118).

2

Manor Heath Park

Skircoat Moor • Daily: summer 10am–4.30pm; winter 10am–4pm • Free

Manor Heath Park, less than a mile south of the town centre, is what's left of the home of Halifax's great carpet manufacture John Crossley (of Dean Clough Mills). The house was demolished in 1958 after becoming derelict, but the park remains as a leisure area with pleasant views of the surrounding hills, well-tended lawns, a sunken garden, water garden and rather good children's play area. It is in this park that all the plants and saplings needed to decorate the town are grown (any surplus supply is sold off to the public at very reasonable prices). Also here is the **Jungle Experience**, a series of rather shabby greenhouses stuffed with tropical plants, flowers, birds, terrapins, fish and butterflies. Though it's superficially unprepossessing, you should persevere – they've packed a lot of good things in, including some rather savage-looking carnivorous plants.

Shibden Hall and estate

Lister's Rd • Mon–Thurs 10am–5pm, Sat & Sun 11am–5pm • £4.50 • ☎ 01422 352246 or ☎ 01422 321455 • Bus #508, #548, #549 or #681 from Halifax, and then a 15min walk; it's well signposted from the town centre and has two adequate car parks

Located on a hill above the main road (A58) from Halifax to the M1, **Shibden Hall** is a fine house whose earliest parts date to 1420 and whose most famous resident was **Anne Lister** (see box below). The estate includes a wilderness garden, a cascade, a mere and a lodge plus a boating lake, a miniature railway, children's play equipment and a pitch and putt. The house itself illustrates the furniture and styles of different ages in period room settings, and there's a fine folk museum, with a collection of horse-drawn vehicles (in the house's seventeenth-century barn), interiors of craftsmen's workplaces – a blacksmith, a wheelwright, a cooper – and a reconstruction of the nineteenth-century *Crispin Inn* (noted for meetings of Luddites). There's a pleasantly intimate café (the cheese toasties are terrific) and a small shop.

Wainhouse Tower

King Cross • The tower is open to the public on most bank holidays; phone to check • £2.50; family ticket £7 • ☎ 01422 288001

Resembling a giant asparagus stalk, the **Wainhouse Tower** dominates the skyline a mile southwest of Halifax town centre. Built in the early 1870s by local dye magnate John Edward Wainhouse in response to the 1870 Smoke Abatement Act, the structure was originally intended as a chimney to disperse smoke from his factory. However, before it was finished, Wainhouse sold the works, and the new owner refused to take on the expense of completing it. Wainhouse retained ownership of the chimney and in 1875 his architect transformed it into a 275ft-high tower, with an octagonal shaft on a square base and 403 steps climbing up to a viewing platform set among florid decoration. As for Wainhouse's motives in building it, all is conjecture. The world's tallest folly? An

ANNE LISTER (1791–1840)

Famous at the time, and since, for her open lesbianism (she was known in the area as "Gentleman Jack"), **Anne Lister** inherited **Shibden Hall** from her uncle in 1826. She was a tireless traveller, mountaineer, academic and businesswoman. Her portraits clearly show a woman of masculine dress and demeanour, and her four-million-word diaries contained fascinating accounts of her life and adventures, and (in code) graphic descriptions of her many passionate love affairs with women ("I love and only love the fairer sex and thus beloved by them in turn, my heart revolts from any love but theirs", she wrote on October 29, 1820). When she inherited Shibden Hall, she managed the estate, including farms, a quarry and a coalmine, herself. She travelled widely until, in 1840, she died of a fever in Russia. Her body was brought back to Yorkshire by her companion and lover Ann Walker and buried near Halifax.

astronomical observation tower? A platform built to annoy Sir Henry Edwards who'd boasted that his estate, on neighbouring land, was the most private in Halifax? Whatever the truth of the matter, it has achieved iconic status.

Bankfield Museum

Akroyd Park • Tues–Sat 10am–4pm • Free • ☎ 01422 352334 • Bus #576 from Halifax bus station

Bankfield Museum, around a mile north of Halifax town centre, is a curiously old-fashioned museum that is interesting more, perhaps, for its place in the town's history than for what it now contains. The home of Victorian local mill owner Edward Akroyd (1810–87), it started as a relatively modest town house but was increasingly transformed after he inherited money from his father, and as his career progressed from successful businessman, through early supporter of the Yorkshire Penny Bank and Halifax Permanent Building Society, to Lieutenant Colonel of the 4th Yorkshire Halifax Rifle Volunteers to Member of Parliament. By the time of his death Bankfield Mansion was a very substantial Italianate mansion that became, shortly afterwards, the museum it is today.

Edward Akroyd was that typical Victorian mixture of local benefactor and muscular Anglican entrepreneur, with an interest in improving the lot of working people. In particular, he encouraged his employees to progress by their own efforts, saving money, worshipping God and investing in decent housing. He developed Akroyd Park surrounding the mansion, the church of All Souls, and across the Boothtown Road, the model village of **Akroydon**. Designed by George Gilbert Scott, and similar to in date and function, though on a smaller scale than, Saltaire (see p.107), Akroydon has houses, a square and a burial ground, much of which remain relatively untouched. There are excellent guides to the area available in the museum, which gives a real feeling for the nineteenth-century development of Halifax.

The museum itself has good collections of furniture, art and costume (on the top floor), and the well-presented **Duke of Wellington's Regimental Museum**.

ARRIVAL AND INFORMATION   HALIFAX

By car Halifax is a 10min drive north of junction 24 on the M62. There's ample parking in and around the town centre – perhaps the most convenient car park for exploring the town is on the southeastern edge, right next to Eureka! (Discovery Rd/Horton St).

By train The train station lies off Discovery Rd.
Destinations Bradford (every 13–18min; 14min); Huddersfield (hourly; 25min); Leeds (every 13–18min; 38min);

London Kings Cross (every 15–30min; 3hr 10min).
By bus The bus station is a 10min walk from the train station, on the northern edge of the town centre on Winding Rd.
Destinations Bradford (every 5–10min; 40min); Huddersfield (every 10min; 39min); Leeds (every 10–30min; 1hr 20min).
Tourist office Central Library, Northgate (Mon, Tues, Thurs & Fri 9.30am–7pm, Sat 9.30am–5pm; ☎ 01422 368725).

ACCOMMODATION

Premier Inn Broad St Plaza ☎ 0871 527 9348, ⓦ premierinn.com. This *Premier Inn* is a good option – cheap, clean and friendly, and with ample free parking. There's a *Beefeater* restaurant on site. **£29**

Travelodge Gate 9, Dean Clough Industrial Park ☎ 0871 984 6144, ⓦ travelodge.co.uk. In the town centre, cheap, and in a lovely building with all Dean Clough's facilities on the doorstep. **£58**

White Swan Princess St ☎ 01422 355541, ⓦ whiteswan halifax.com. Comfortable, 1858-built traditional hotel in the city centre, within walking distance of all attractions. Dining is at *Julio's* restaurant in the basement. **£89**

★**Wool Merchant Hotel** 5 Mulcture Hall Rd ☎ 01422 368783, ⓦ woolmerchanthotel.co.uk. Refurbished budget hotel in a fine nineteenth-century building – a wool merchant's warehouse. Clean and friendly, with a large car park. **£40**

EATING AND DRINKING

Brasserie at the Bull 5 Bull Green ☎ 01422 330833, ⓦ brasserieatthebull.co.uk. Gastropub on the western side of the town centre, with a good Modern British menu

(twice-cooked belly pork, poached haddock), a healthy wine list, smart unfussy decor and big windows from which to watch the world go by. It's not too expensive, and there are fixed-price menus (two courses £11.95, three courses £13.95). Service can be slow at busy times. Mon–Thurs 11.45am–3pm & 5–11pm, Fri & Sat 11.45am–12.30am. **Design House** Dean Clough Mill ☎ 01422 383242, ⓦ designhouserestaurant.co.uk. Highly regarded restaurant in the Dean Clough Mill complex (see p.115), an ideal place to dine when taking in a play, concert or exhibition. Decor is so cool as to be verging on the icy. If you'd prefer informal snacks, go for the *Viaduct* café in the same complex instead. Tues–Fri noon–2pm & 5.30–9.30pm, Sat 5.30–9.30pm.

Julio's 2 Princess St ☎ 01422 349449, ⓦ julios.co.uk. Popular town-centre Italian restaurant offering good, unpretentious food, excellent service and a convivial atmosphere. Starters £3.95–7.50, mains £10.95–17.50. Mon–Sat 5–10pm, Sun 5–9pm.

ENTERTAINMENT

Square Chapel 10 Square Rd ☎ 01422 349422, ⓦ squarechapel.co.uk. Mounts a mixture of theatre (amateur and touring), comedy, poetry and music, much of it with a local focus. Mon–Fri 9.30am–5pm, Sat 11am–3pm.

Viaduct Theatre Dean Clough Mill ☎ 01422 250250, ⓦ deanclough.com/arts/theatre.asp. Home to Barrie Rutter's highly rated Northern Broadsides Theatre Company (☎ 01422 255266), which has made a huge name for itself with its innovative approach to Shakespeare and the classics (its 2009 version of *Othello* starring comedian Lenny Henry was a triumph). The theatre also stages classical and popular music.

Victoria Theatre Fountains St ☎ 01422 351158, ⓦ calderdale.gov.uk/victoria. Puts on largely light entertainment and community events and activities. Box Office March–May & Sept–Dec 10am–6pm; Jan, Feb & June–Aug 10am–4pm.

Calder Valley

A beautiful and atmospheric post-industrial landscape, the **Calder Valley** meanders some fifteen miles west from Halifax towards the Lancashire border. The valley came to prominence when the local woollen industry abandoned farmhouse, cottage and hill village in favour of large water mills along the River Calder. When the mills switched to steam, chimneys sprouted along the riverbank and transport improved, with the road, canal, and eventually railway forming a multistrand link between Yorkshire and Lancashire.

Clear of smoke and grime since the decline of the woollen industry, today the valley is a lovely spot, with interesting mills and cottages modernized and repurposed, canal boats puttering between steep-sided hills, and dry-stone walls, tussocky grass and scribbles of woodland climbing up to heather uplands. The main settlement is the vibrant, artsy town of **Hebden Bridge**, while within a couple of miles of it and each other are the birthplace of **Ted Hughes** and the grave of his wife **Sylvia Plath**.

GETTING AROUND CALDER VALLEY

By train There are train stations at Sowerby Bridge, Hebden Bridge, Mytholmroyd and Todmorden, with Northern Rail services running hourly from Halifax.

By bus Though the train is by far the quickest way to visit the Calder Valley towns, buses #590 and #592 travel along the valley from Halifax.

OUTDOOR ACTIVITIES IN THE CALDER VALLEY

There are many fine **walks** in the Calder Valley, many starting and ending in Hebden Bridge, but with others starting in all the main villages. They vary from easy strolls along the canal to tough forays into the surrounding hills. Visit ⓦ walkingbritain.co.uk, ⓦ walkinginyorkshire.co.uk or ⓦ walkingenglishman.com for descriptions and downloadable maps, and ⓦ calderdale.gov.uk for guided walks run by the local authority. Worth looking at too is ⓦ calderdaleheritagewalks .org.uk, which details guided walks from April to October, following a variety of themes.

Cycling, too, is well catered for. The council (ⓦ calderdale.gov.uk) offers a free download of the authority's cycle network, summarizing routes through the valley (National Cycle Routes 66 and 68 and the Hebden Trail), as well as routes that cut across the valley (the West Yorkshire Cycle Route and the Pennine Bridleway). It's also worth looking at ⓦ cyclecalderdale.co.uk.

Sowerby Bridge

Around three miles west of Halifax, **SOWERBY BRIDGE** lies just off the main road. Not to be confused with Sowerby itself (a little further south), the town has many impressive mill buildings, and apart from being an important wool town, also produced steam engines used all over Yorkshire and Lancashire. This is where the Rochdale Canal joins the Calder and Hebble Navigation – the eighteenth-century canal basin and its associated buildings are all listed.

2

Mytholmroyd

Four miles west of Sowerby Bridge, **MYTHOLMROYD** (pronounced "My…" not "Myth…") is notable mainly for being the birthplace of **Ted Hughes**, poet laureate from 1984 to his death in 1998. Little is made of the fact – there don't appear to be any obvious signs to help you find the house, and there is certainly no "Ted Hughes" café or "Ted Hughes" guesthouse.

Walkley Clogs

Midgley Rd • Tues–Fri 10am–5pm, Sat 10am–4pm • ☎ 01422 885757, ⓦ clogs.co.uk

Walkley Clogs occupies a unit in Mount Pleasant Mills just off Mytholmroyd's main street (follow the brown sign); you can see the clog-maker at work, browse in the factory shop, or just breathe in the heady aroma of leather and wood. If you don't want to be lumbered with carrying around your purchases for the rest of your holiday, you can order online when you get home, choose a style, then achieve the right fit by sending off paper patterns and measurements of the feet to be clogged. Some of the clogs are very pretty and colourful, but a remarkable number are heavy-duty work clogs, even in this day and age. And they'll last, too, until – well, until you pop your clogs.

Ted Hughes's birthplace

1 Aspinall St (off Zion St, which is off Midgley Rd, which runs north from the main A646)

Ted Hughes's birthplace is not easy to find. It's a small end-terrace house (still privately occupied), distinguishable from its neighbours only because of the blue plaque on the wall. This simple place, with little fanfare or fuss, brings home how humble the great poet's origins were.

Hebden Bridge

A couple of miles beyond Mytholmroyd is the Calder Valley's main town, **HEBDEN BRIDGE**, something of a Yorkshire anomaly and probably the best place to stay if you're exploring this region. A characteristic mill town, it was just a hamlet before the need for water power brought the woollen industry down the hill from Heptonstall (see p.121) which stands high above it. Today it has earned a reputation as a place where dyed-in-the-wool Yorkshire folk live in harmony with faintly left-wing **green enthusiasts** and **gay activists**, a place with smart cafés and bars, upmarket independent shops, and lots of nice traditional pubs. It has developed a substantial tourist industry, both for itself and as a centre for **walking** on the surrounding hills.

The town is pretty as a picture. The Rochdale Canal arrows straight through the centre, as does the River Calder and its tributary Hebden Water, ensuring lots of bridges and mill buildings which have been converted into hotels, restaurants, shops and lots more. While wandering around Hebden Bridge there's a lot to look out for. At the heart of the town is pleasantly pedestrianized **St George's Square** (more a triangle), with shops, cafés and pubs dotted around it and, just off it, the quaint **Old Packhorse Bridge**.

Old Packhorse Bridge
Off St George's Square

The **Old Packhorse Bridge** dates from around 1510, but with repairs made (and commemorated in the parapet) in 1602 and 1657. The triangular alcoves were to allow

WEST YORKSHIRE'S GIANTS OF LITERATURE AND ART

West Yorkshire has long been fertile ground for the imagination of writers and artists, and visitors to the area are blessed indeed to have giants of literature and art to interpret it for them. The Haworth of the Brontës, the Bradford of J.B. Priestley, Ted Hughes's Calderdale – the connections between these writers and their little bits of West Yorkshire are palpably strong. Among local artists, too, the inspiration can be deduced – there's something of the grandeur of moorland rocks in the work of Henry Moore and Barbara Hepworth, and David Hockney's stay with his sister in Bridlington led to some wonderful large-scale paintings of both Bridlington itself and of woodland in the nearby Wolds.

THE BRONTËS

The superstars of Yorkshire literature are undoubtedly the **Brontë sisters** (see p.112), whose home village Haworth has become a major tourist attraction. Haworth and the wild surrounding moors are clearly the setting of Emily Brontë's *Wuthering Heights*, while other titles, including Anne's *The Tenant of Wildfell Hall* and Charlotte's *Jane Eyre* rely heavily on the landscape and atmosphere of the region.

TED HUGHES AND SYLVIA PLATH

Perhaps unsurprisingly, little is made of the story of **Ted Hughes** (1930–98) and **Sylvia Plath** (1932–63) in Calderdale. Of the two it was only Hughes who was inspired by West Yorkshire; this working-class Yorkshireman, who rose to be one of the foremost poets of his generation, owed much of the passion for nature that defines his work to the first six years of his life, when he roamed the moors of the Calder Valley with his gamekeeper brother. Plath, also a wildly talented poet, who had come from the USA to study in England, didn't share his love for this wild stretch of English countryside – when Hughes brought her to the valley in the early years of their marriage, she hated it. Today you can see the humble end-terrace in Mytholmroyd where Ted Hughes was born (see p.119), and, less than two miles away, the understated grave in Heptonstall where Sylvia Plath is buried (see p.122), despite her lack of feeling for the region.

J.B. PRIESTLEY

The reputation of **J.B. Priestley** (1894–1984) has had its ups and downs since his death. A prolific novelist, playwright and essayist, he is probably best remembered today for his travel book *English Journey*, an account of a tour of England he made in 1933 in which he considered at length what it meant to be English. His left-wing humanitarianism – he was a founder member of the Campaign for Nuclear Disarmament – makes him a particularly typical Bradfordian. His birthplace in that city (34 Mannheim Rd) is blue-plaqued and his statue stands outside the National Media Museum.

DAVID HOCKNEY

Though probably best known for his Californian paintings, much-travelled artist **David Hockney** (born 1937) has a considerable body of work portraying his native Yorkshire. Having painted scenes from around his home in Bradford during the 1950s, from 1997 he made a series of paintings of the Wolds while staying with his elder sister Margaret in Bridlington. Look out for the exhibitions of his work at Salt's Mill, Bradford (see p.108) – he was a great friend of its visionary developer Jonathan Silver.

HENRY MOORE AND BARBARA HEPWORTH

By far Britain's most famous sculptors, **Henry Moore** (1898–1986) and **Barbara Hepworth** (1903–75) both hailed from West Yorkshire – Moore from Castleford, Hepworth from Wakefield. Both trained at Leeds School of Art, both studied at the Royal College of Art from 1921, and both became internationally famous. Their names are honoured by the Henry Moore Institute in Leeds (see p.90) and the Hepworth Gallery in Wakefield (see p.130), and examples of their work can be seen in the Yorkshire Sculpture Park (see p.132) and elsewhere.

pedestrians to get away from the packhorses if a line of them was crossing the bridge. One of the three spans now has no water beneath it, but it used to cross the "tail goit" or mill race that carried water back to the river after it had driven the wheel in Bridge Mill, upstream. Next to the bridge are the recently added "wavy steps", usually host to ducks, geese, pigeons and crows. Beyond the bridge a path rises steeply upwards – the old packhorse route (the "Buttress") to **Heptonstall** (see below), which will take about thirty minutes, depending on how fit you are, and which is worth the effort for the superb views on the way up.

2

Alternative Technology Centre

Unit 7, Victoria Works, Victoria Rd • Mon–Fri 10am–5pm, Sat & Sun phone ahead • Free, with charges for guided tours and workshops • ⊤ 01422 842121, ⓦ alternativetechnology.org.uk

The **Alternative Technology Centre** is exactly what you'd expect from its title. It's a large space, devoted to sustainable communities and showcasing local projects – including small-scale microhydropower, community energy projects and bike recycling and other bike-related activities. They also run many hands-on workshops and courses on all aspects of sustainability. Don't expect a slick concern – they're either visionary enthusiasts putting dreams into practice or a bunch of hippies, depending on who you talk to.

ARRIVAL AND INFORMATION — HEBDEN BRIDGE

By car There are six car parks tightly grouped in the centre of Hebden Bridge, several of them free.

By train Hebden Bridge train station is across the canal at the eastern edge of the village, about a 10min walk from the centre.

Destinations Burnley (hourly; 19min); Halifax (every 5–15min; 13min); Leeds (every 15–20min: 50min); Todmorden (every 10–25min; 8min).

By bus Hebden Bridge has no bus station, but there are stops all along the main street. Timetables tend to give the train station as the destination.

Tourist office Visitor and Canal Centre, Butlers Wharf, New Rd (mid-March to mid-Oct Mon–Fri 9.30am–5.30pm, Sat 10.15am–5pm, Sun 10.30am–5pm; mid-Oct to mid-March Mon–Fri 10am–5pm, Sat & Sun 10.30am–4.15pm; ⊤ 01422 843831, ⓦ hebdenbidge.co.uk) in the Marina (actually a canal wharf and dry dock). Here you can consult the knowledgeable staff and pick up excellent guides – in particular the *Discover Hebden Bridge Town Centre Trail*, produced by the local history society (ⓦ hebdenbridgehistory.org.uk).

ACCOMMODATION AND EATING

Angeldale Hangingroyd Lane ⊤ 01422 847321, ⓦ angeldale.co.uk. Clean, comfortable and well set-up guesthouse in an imposing Victorian building with nice gardens, 2min from the centre. **£75**

★ **Organic House** Market St ⊤ 01422 843429, ⓦ organic-house.co.uk. Freshly prepared food including breakfasts, main meals (organic house platters, bean burgers and the like, but also meat and chicken burgers, and pies and peas), cakes and the best coffee for miles. Mon–Sat 8.30am–5pm, Sun 10am–5pm.

Rim Nam Thai Restaurant Butlers Wharf ⊤ 01422 846888, ⓦ rimnamthairestaurant.co.uk Next to the visitor centre, right on the canal. Meals, including curries, stir fries, duck steak and seafood dishes, go for around £10–20, and they do a very good early bird, four-course menu (Sun & Tues–Fri 5–7pm). Tues–Sun 5–11pm.

Shoulder of Mutton Bridge Gate ⊤ 01422 842585. Pretty stone pub in the town centre, with real ale, pub grub and a nice convivial atmosphere. Sun–Thurs 11.30am–11pm, Fri & Sat 11.30–midnight,

White Lion Hotel Bridge Gate ⊤ 01422 842197, ⓦ whitelionhotel.net. Mid-seventeenth-century farmhouse next to the town square, and possibly the oldest building in the town. Smart accommodation in seven individually decorated rooms. **£115**

Heptonstall

Less than a mile above Hebden Bridge is **HEPTONSTALL**, a beautiful stone village on and just below the hilltop, which once housed the handlooms that were replaced by Hebden Bridge's water-powered mills in the valley below. It is well worth visiting, not only to soak up the atmosphere of a pre-Industrial-Revolution Yorkshire village and to enjoy the wonderful views down across Hebden Bridge and west along the meandering Calder Valley, but also to pay respects to American poet **Sylvia Plath**, who is buried here.

Though it may seem to comprise little more than a couple of pubs, a tiny post office, and two churches sharing a graveyard, there are a lot of interesting things to see in the village. Take a look at **weavers' square**, with its rows of weavers' cottages; note the rows of windows on the first floor, built to give plenty of light for the weavers to be able see the fine threads. You can also see an octagonal **Methodist chapel** (built in 1764 after a visit by John Wesley), and the **village stocks** nearby.

Dominating the village is a ruined church, damaged by a gale in 1847, dedicated to St Thomas Becket and, in the same churchyard, a newer one – the church of **St Thomas the Apostle**. The churchyard is paved with uneven tombstones.

Sylvia Plath's grave

Becketts Close

American poet **Sylvia Plath**, who committed suicide in 1963 at the age of 30, is buried in the "New Graveyard" – to find it, turn left at the top out of the old one, and it's just down the lane. Her simple **tombstone** is in the third row back from the lowest tier, about eight graves in from the far edge – there's little except a throng of mementos left by fans (pens, pebbles, seashells, plastic jewellery, toys) to indicate which is hers. The enigmatic inscription on the gravestone ("Even amidst fierce flames the golden lotus can be planted") was chosen by her husband, though few know where it originates – the best guess seems to be the Chinese epic, *Monkey*, by Wu Ch'Eng-En.

The very presence of Sylvia Plath's body in this graveyard has been a cause for controversy – an American, who died in London, she was buried here by her estranged husband Ted Hughes, at whose door many laid the blame for her suicide (it occurred shortly after he left her). Even more controversial was the fact that she is called "Sylvia Plath Hughes" on the gravestone – her supporters felt that this added insult to injury, and the "Hughes" has been chiselled off, and replaced, a number of times.

ARRIVAL AND DEPARTURE   **HEPTONSTALL**

On foot One of the nicest ways to arrive is by walking up the Old Packhorse Route from Hebden Bridge – but bear in mind that it's a stiff climb.

By car There's a visitors' car park in season, and at other times you can just park on the street.

By bus Bus #596 from Hebden Bridge takes 7min.

Huddersfield

As you drive into **HUDDERSFIELD** you might at first think that there's little to detain you. But persistence brings its own reward. J.B. Priestley observed in *English Journey* when he visited in 1933 that "Huddersfield is not a handsome town", going on to say "but yet is famous in these parts for the intelligence and independence of its citizens". And there are still signs to support this. Though it's not the only town in the Kirklees Metropolitan region – there's also Batley, Dewsbury, Holme Valley and others – Huddersfield is certainly the biggest, yet its residents have persistently refused to apply for city status. And although the town features plenty of undistinguished postwar architecture, there are many interesting things to see, in particular where efforts have been made to find new uses for beautiful old buildings.

Huddersfield's **train station**, for example, a Grade I listed building, is host to two excellent watering holes and overlooks **St George's Square** with its clutch of stately Victorian buildings. One of these is the imposing **George Hotel**, birthplace of **Rugby League**, sadly closed at the time of writing. The **Town Hall** is an excellent music venue, **St Paul's** church is now a concert hall and part of **Huddersfield University**, the 1819 **Wesleyan chapel** is the **Lawrence Batley Theatre**, and the **Parish Church of St Peter** has a rather nice restaurant in the crypt. A plaque on the iron-and-glass **open market** says it all: "Built 1888, restored 1980, repainted 1998, refurbished 2008". The people of Huddersfield believe in looking after what's left of their heritage.

Away from the town centre, the hilly area around Huddesfield is much disfigured by industry, yet achieves a kind of majesty, with valley floors full of ribbon development, factories, sewage works, railway lines, reservoirs and viaducts, steep hillsides covered in terraced houses, and narrow lanes bounded by dry-stone walls climbing up on to the surrounding empty moors. In this hinterland there's a good balance of attractions. The most prominent feature, visible for miles around, is **Castle Hill**, topped by the **Victoria Tower**, built to commemorate the queen's Diamond Jubilee. To the west of the town is the **Bullecourt Museum**, tracing military history from 1815 to the present; to the east, the **Tolson Museum** covers many aspects of Huddersfield's history.

Huddersfield Library and Art Gallery

Princess Alexandra Walk, at the bottom of Ramsden St • Mon 9.30am–6pm, Tues, Thurs & Fri 9.30am–7pm, Sat 9am–4pm • Free • ☎ 01484 221959

First stop in Huddersfield, if only because it houses the tourist office (see p.125), has to be the **Library and Art Gallery**, an impressive lump of Art Deco architecture opened in 1937, with paintings, drawings and sculptures from the Kirklees Collection, including work by well-known artists such as L.S. Lowry, Francis Bacon and Henry Moore.

Parish Church of St Peter

On the angle of Kirkgate and Byram St • Mon–Fri 9am–4pm, most Sats 10am–2pm • ☎ 01484 427964, ⓦ huddersfieldparishchurch.org

The original structure on the site of the **Parish Church of St Peter** is said to have been built by a certain Walter de Laci, who when thrown from his horse into a swamp some time around 1100 AD promised God that he would build a church if he could see his way clear to sparing him. He was spared, and the church was built. The current church, however, dates from 1503–06, and a subsequent rebuilding was undertaken in 1830 when a larger, more impressive structure was deemed appropriate to reflect the growing wealth of the town. Designed by James Pigott Pritchett of York, the new church was consecrated in 1836, but hasn't, alas, stood the test of time – the external walls have weathered very badly in places. The crypt, created in the 1830 rebuilding, is now home to the popular *The Keys* restaurant (see p.125).

Open Market

On the intersection of Byram and Brook Sts • Mon, Thurs & Sat 9am–4pm (general), Tues & Sat 9am–3.30pm (secondhand), 2nd Sun of the month ("Upmarket Sunday"; antiques and bric-a-brac) 10am–4pm.

Marked by a gantry that bears its name, the quaint **Open Market**, brightly painted in blue and red, isn't really completely open, since it boasts an ornate wrought-iron and glass roof over a tiled floor, but it's well worth a visit for the architecture and for the detail (much use is made of the town's coat of arms), if not for the rather limited range of stalls.

St George's Square

The best-preserved part of Huddersfield town centre is undoubtedly **St George's Square**, dominated by the imposing bulk of **Huddersfield train station**, designed by James Pigott Pritchett, the architect of the rebuilt parish church. Built between 1846 and 1850, and much admired by John Betjeman, the station is a Grade I listed building of great magnificence, which is odd in that Huddersfield's links with the rest of the railway system are not that good – you need to change in Manchester, Leeds or Wakefield if you want access to the main routes. The steps of the station, at the high end of the square, host open-air performances, and the two single-storey wings on either side of the imposing two-storey classical facade are occupied by two excellent real ale **pubs** – the *Head of Steam* (see p.125) and the *King's Head*.

2

HAROLD WILSON: HUDDERSFIELD HERO

When walking around Huddersfield's St George's Square, you won't be able to miss the splendid statue of **Harold Wilson** (1916–95), British prime minister from 1964 to 1970 and from 1974 to 1976. He was born and raised in Huddersfield, became an academic, and gained quick promotion within the Labour party in Attlee's postwar government. Looking as if he's hurrying from the station to some unnamed political meeting, the statue was unveiled by Tony Blair in 1999, and caused some comment at the time because there's no sign of Wilson's trademark pipe. This was, apparently, at the insistence of his widow – she couldn't prevail upon him to give up smoking during his lifetime, but had the last word after his death.

Victoria Tower

Castle Hill (off Lumb Lane) • Noon–4.30pm on certain days, phone or check website for details • £1.75 • ☎ 07968 426312, Ⓦ kirklees.gov uk • Bus #341

By far the most obvious feature in Huddersfield, south of the centre, is the **Victoria Tower** on top of **Castle Hill**, built to commemorate Queen Victoria's Diamond Jubilee in 1897 and opened in 1899. With a top just short of 1000ft above sea level and despite renovation in 1960 it still isn't in very good condition. It should, however, provide a splendid viewpoint when planned further renovations – renewal of paths, repair of erosion, provision of viewing platform and seating, the construction of a bridge – are carried out.

Bullecourt Museum

Milnsbridge, a mile or so west of Huddersfield • Sat, Sun & bank holidays 2–4pm • £2 • ☎ 01484 461029 • Bus #301, #302 or #30

The **Bullecourt Museum**, in the old drill hall of the 7th Battalion, Duke of Wellington Regiment, covers military history from 1815 to the present. Named after a World War I battle in which the 7th Battalion were involved, it contains displays, uniforms, weapons and vehicles from all the major campaigns involving the Duke of Wellington's regiment. Look out for the Anderson shelter, the American jeep, a copy of *Mein Kampf* liberated from Hitler's Berlin bunker at the end of the war, and a German map of Huddersfield with all the strategic places marked, ready for the occupation.

Tolson Museum

Wakefield Rd (visible from the road as you travel east on the A629 Wakefield Rd about 1 mile out of the town centre) • March–Oct Tues–Fri 11am–5pm, Sat & Sun noon–5pm • Free • ☎ 01484 223830, Ⓦ kirklees.gov.uk • Bus #81 or #232

The **Tolson Museum** is a Victorian mansion standing in its own grounds. It covers the history of Huddersfield, and has displays on local history and archeology, textiles, birds, insects and plants, music, weapons, science, toys, dolls and transport. The best-known item in the "Going Places" section is the three-wheeled LSD car, manufactured in Huddersfield between 1919 and 1924 – nothing to do with drugs or money, L S and D were the initials of the vehicle's designer (Longbottom), manufacturer (Sykes) and accountant (Dyson) responsible for its production. Surely the only time an accountant has been immortalized in such a way. The museum hosts visiting exhibitions and events – check online for details.

ARRIVAL AND INFORMATION

By car Huddersfield sits just south of junction 23 of the M62 and the road system around the town – a clearly defined ring road with ample signs telling you where the car parks are and how many cars they can take.

By train The train station is on St George's Square. Destinations Barnsley (hourly; 47min); Bradford (hourly; 42min); Leeds (every 10–15min; 20min); Manchester (every 10–20min; 34min); Sheffield (hourly; 1hr 16min); Wakefield (hourly; 44min).

By bus There's a well-organized bus station (☎ 0113 245 7676) on the western edge of the town centre, just inside the ring road on Upperhead Row.

Destinations Bradford (every 20min; 39min); Halifax (every 10min; 40min); Manchester (every 10–20min; 40min).

Tourist office In the foyer of the Library and Art Gallery in Princess Alexandra Walk (Mon–Wed 9.30am–5pm, Thurs & Fri 9am–5pm, Sat 9am–4pm; ☎01484 223200).

ACCOMMODATION

Briar Court Hotel Halifax Rd, Birchencliffe, 2 miles from Huddersfield ☎01484 519902, ⓦbriarcourt.co.uk. Modern stone-built hotel on the road from Huddersfield to the M62, and convenient for both. The decor is all clean lines, and rather severe, but there's a cheerful Italian restaurant with a wood-burning pizza oven. Good value. **£95**

★ **Huddersfield Central Lodge** 11/15 Beast Market ☎01484 515551, ⓦcentrallodge.com. As you'd expect from the name, the privately run *Huddersfield Central Lodge* is centrally located, on the eastern edge of the town centre inside the ring road. It's hugely popular and boasts a startlingly long list of awards and celebrity guests. A real gem in these days of huge hotel conglomerates. **£74**

Pennine Manor Hotel Nettleton Hill Rd, Scapegoat Hill, about 5 miles from Huddersfield, close to the M62 ☎01484 642368, ⓦthedeckersgroup.com. The *Pennine Manor*, owned by the small but select *Decker* group of hotels, gastropubs and grills, is a pleasant medium-sized hotel with all mod cons, fine views, good food and friendly service. **£48**

Titanic Spa Apartments Low Westwood Lane, Linthwaite ☎01484 843544, ⓦtitanicspa.com. Billing itself as the country's first eco-spa, occupying a massive old woollen mill, *Titanic Spa Apartments* offers a full range of treatments and products, and has become known through word-of-mouth and national press attention. Aiming to be carbon-neutral, it offers guilt-free pampering, and although individual treatments can be pricey, a number of packages bring the cost right down. However, it is not possible to book a room without a treatment. **£119**

EATING AND DRINKING

Batter Sea Fish Bar 1316 Manchester Rd ☎01484 843585. Traditional fish-and-chip shop with superb, award-winning fish and chips and a variety of other stuff on offer, too, including gluten-free and vegetarian options. They deliver, too. Mon 4–7.30pm, Tues & Wed 11.30am–2pm & 4–7.30pm, Thurs–Sat 11.30am–2pm & 4–8pm.

Botafogo 37 John William St ☎01484 535440, ⓦargentosteakhouse.com. Named for a beachfront neighbourhood in Rio de Janeiro, *Botafogo*, just east of the train station, specializes in South American food – not only steaks and fish, but also sausages, chicken thighs and much else. You can help yourself to unlimited side dishes. Busy and popular, with a cheerful interior. Mon–Sat 5.30–10pm, Sun 4–9pm.

Bradleys Restaurant 84 Fitzwilliam St ☎01484 516773, ⓦbradleyshuddersfield.co.uk. Starters are often Mediterranean in flavour, while mains focus on classy traditional favourites, from confit duck leg to grilled hake with caper butter. It's good value, with low prices (two-course dinner £15.95, three courses £19.95). Standards of service can decline during busy periods, and with loads of special offers, tribute nights and so on, there are lots of these. Tues–Thurs noon–2pm & 6–10pm, Fri noon–2pm & 5.30–10pm, Sat 5.30–10pm.

Head of Steam St George's Square ☎01484 454533, ⓦtheheadofsteam.co.uk. Located in the train station, this pub consists of four rooms – the bar, lounge, family room and buffet (which also serves as the station buffet) – arranged around a central server. Food includes pub classics, burgers, hot dogs and ciabattas, with a buffet menu at £7 per head. There's a huge range of genuine railway memorabilia on show – train spotters' heaven. Mon & Tues 11am–11pm, Wed & Thurs 11am–midnight, Fri & Sat 11am–2am, Sun noon–10.30pm.

The Keys Byram St ☎01484 516677, ⓦkeysrestaurant .com. A daytime-only restaurant in the crypt of the parish church of St Peter, serving a big selection of breakfasts, lunches and snacks, including sandwiches (toasted and otherwise), jacket potatoes, quiches and salads costing between £5 and £12, in warm surroundings, with beautifully lit columns and vaulted ceilings. It's a smart, busy place, with open-plan kitchens. Mon–Fri 9am–2.30pm, Sat 8am–3.30pm.

Thai Sakon 5 St John's Rd ☎01484 450159, ⓦthaisakon.co.uk. One of several restaurants in and around the railway arches north of Huddersfield train station, the *Thai Sakon* has earned universally good reviews both from diners and the local press. Smart surroundings, excellent food, and staff who have the time and inclination to help out less knowledgeable customers. Mon–Fri 5.30–10.30pm, Sat 6–11pm, Sun 6–10pm.

ENTERTAINMENT

The **University of Huddersfield**, which has campuses in Oldham and Barnsley as well as in the centre of town – and whose Chancellor is *Star Trek and X-Men* actor Patrick Stewart – has done much to put Huddersfield on the map, and to enliven its social scene. There are lots of lively pubs and clubs, as well as the world-famous **Contemporary Music Festival** (ⓦhcmf.co.uk) consisting of around fifty new and experimental music events held over ten days every November, including concerts, musical theatre, dance, multimedia, talks and film.

Huddersfield Town Hall Ramsden St ⓣ01484 221900, ⓦkirklees.gov.uk. Built between 1875 and 1881, with excellent acoustics, the Town Hall seats up to 1200 people for classical and choral music. Events are advertised in, and are bookable through, tourist offices in Huddersfield (see p.125) and Holmfirth.

Lawrence Batley Theatre Queens St ⓣ01484 430528, ⓦthelbt.org. The LBT occupies what was, when it opened in 1819, the biggest Wesleyan chapel in the world, accommodating around two thousand worshippers. It now hosts a variety of plays, dance, music gigs, pantomime and comedy, and has an elegant bar and bistro. Box office Mon–Sat 9.30am–5pm (unless there's a performance, in which case the box office closes 15min after it starts)

St Paul's Queensgate ⓣ01484 422288, ⓦkirklees.gov.uk. Built in 1829 as a church, and now a concert hall owned by the University of Huddersfield, St Paul's seats 400 and hosts the university's awards ceremony as well as the Huddersfield Contemporary Music Festival. Concerts and recitals are advertised in the library and around town.

2

SHOPPING

Piazza Shopping Centre Princess Alexandra Walk ⓣ01484 534594, ⓦpiazzacentre.co.uk. Next to Huddersfield's library and art gallery, with a wide range of shops that are generally visited along with the neighbouring Queensgate Market. Mon–Sat 9am–5.30pm, Sun 10.30am–4.30pm.

Queensgate Market Princess St ⓣ01484 223732, ⓦqueensgatemarket.co.uk. The market next to the Piazza shopping centre has many covered stalls and an open space that hosts a Christmas ice rink and various other entertainments over the course of the year. Mon–Fri 9am–5.30pm, Sat 8.30am–5.30pm.

Around Huddersfield

Beyond Huddersfield are the **Red House Museum,** illustrating life in the 1830s, and **Oakwell Hall** with its country park, while in an arc about six miles south of town are three popular attractions: the **Standedge Tunnel and Visitor Centre**, **Kirklees Light Railway** in Clayton West and the village of **Holmfirth**, whose connection with TV's **Last of the Summer Wine** brings in hordes of visitors.

Red House Museum

Oxford Rd, Gomersal, 8 miles northeast of Huddersfield, close to the M62 • March–Oct Tues–Thurs 11am–5pm, Sat & Sun noon–5pm; Nov–Feb Tues–Thurs 11am–4pm, Sat & Sun noon–4pm • £2.50 • ⓣ01274 335100 • Numerous buses from Huddersfield town centre (5min)

In **Gomersal** the charming **Red House Museum** occupies a cloth-merchant's residence (the family were appropriately called the Taylors), with 1830s period rooms, tableaux showing the family at work and play and formal gardens that complement the house but contrast oddly with the modern properties you glimpse through the trees. An early resident was **Mary Taylor**, one of the many indomitable women that Yorkshire seems to produce – feminist writer, businesswoman and leader of women's mountain climbing expeditions. She was a great friend of Charlotte Brontë's, who, in her novel *Shirley*, used both the house ("Briarmains" in the book) and the area (Gomersal) as a setting.

Oakwell Hall

Nutter Lane, Birstall, 9 miles northeast of Huddersfield • March–Oct Tues–Thurs 11am–5pm, Sat & Sun noon–5pm; Nov–Feb Tues–Thurs 11am–4pm, Sat & Sun noon–4pm • £2.50 • ⓣ01924 326240 • Bus #255

Birstall is the location of the 1583-built **Oakwell Hall**, bedecked with period rooms, modelled on the 1690s, and featured, like the house now occupied by the Red House Museum (see above) in *Shirley* – as the eponymous heroine's home Fieldhead. Rather more splendid than the Red House, it is surrounded by an arboretum, walled gardens and delightful parkland. There's a play area, a café and a shop. A fine Elizabethan house with, internally, many late seventeenth-century features (in particular the Great Parlour) and a mixture of original and reproduction furniture, it only just escaped being exported to the USA in the early twentieth century, and is now often used for filming – including for the story of Anne Lister (see box, p.116), shown on British TV in 2010.

Kirklees Light Railway

Park Mill Way, Clayton West, about 7 miles southeast of Huddersfield · Check website for operating days · £7; family ticket £22 · ☎ 01484
865727, ⓦ kirkleeslightrailway.com · Bus #80 or #81 from Huddersfield

Southeast of Huddersfield, in **Clayton West**, the **Kirklees Light Railway** is a narrow-
gauge (15in) railway built by enthusiasts on the route of a discontinued branch line
that had served local coalmines. Four diminutive steam engines (*Hawk, Owl, Fox* and
Badger), together with one diesel and one tram, pull passengers along the nearly four
miles of track between Clayton West and Shelley, a trip that takes about 25 minutes
across rolling countryside, with views of Elmley Moor transmitting station, Britain's
tallest freestanding building. All but one of the engines were built by Brian Taylor, the
driving force behind the whole enterprise. The **Clayton West** station has a café and
shop, an indoor play area and an even smaller miniature railway (7¼in gauge; 50p)
running around a duck pond. The Shelley station also has a café.

Holmfirth

Six miles south of Huddersfield is the town of **HOLMFIRTH**, famous now as the setting
for popular and long-running TV series **Last of the Summer Wine**. You can see, and take
refreshment, in Sid's café and numerous other places that will seem familiar. But things
are not always where you expect them to be – the programme-makers ranged far and
wide for locations, and by no means all of them are in the town.

Apart from the *Last of the Summer Wine* connection, the town is a mixed bag.
Surrounded by the attractive moorland countryside across which the programme's
elderly delinquents roam while enjoying their second childhood, the town itself is a
mixture of the quaint and the scruffy. There's a lot of nice Pennine architecture with
attractive stone cottages, terraces of houses that picturesquely line the banks of the
river, nice independent shops, the neat 1912 Picturedrome, the solid *Old Bridge Hotel*
and steep flights of stone steps that rise beside the church to the maze of narrow alleys
above it. But there's also the large nonentity of the Riverside Shopping Centre, the busy
bus station right in the centre of town and ugly concrete walls that guide the turbulent
stream through the town centre – either taking the edge off Holmfirth's attractiveness,
or making it real and unpretentious, depending on how you look at it.

Last of the Summer Wine Exhibition

30 Huddersfield Rd · April–Oct daily 9am–4pm; Nov–Feb Sat & Sun 11am–2.30pm; March Fri–Mon 11am–3pm · £2.50 ·
ⓦ summerwine-holmfirth.co.uk

Nora Batty's house is now the site of the **Last of the Summer Wine Exhibition**,
opened by Bill Owen ("Compo") in 1996, with photos, props, memorabilia, video
clips (including out-takes), a timeline and list of episodes, and a great deal more.
There's a pleasant tearoom (inevitably called *The Wrinkled Stocking*), and a gift shop.
The exhibition is pretty comprehensive, as you'd expect since the BBC gave its full
support to the venture.

EATING AND DRINKING   HOLMFIRTH

Farmer's Arms 4 Liphill Bank Rd ☎ 01484 683713,
ⓦ farmersarmsholmfirth.co.uk. Pretty-as-a-picture
traditional pub serving superior old-fashioned pub food
(mains £10–14) and a range of sandwiches (£4–5). There's
an open fire in winter, and a pleasant back garden
with views. Mon & Tues 5pm–midnight, Wed–Fri
noon–2.30pm & 5pm–midnight, Sat noon–midnight,
Sun noon–11pm; food served Tues–Fri noon–2pm
& 6–9.30pm, Sat noon–3pm & 5–9.30pm, Sun
noon–8pm.

Spiced Pear Sheffield Rd, New Mill, Hepworth,
a mile southeast of Holmfirth ☎ 01484 683775,
ⓦ thespicedpearhepworth.co.uk The *Spiced Pear* offers
a small menu of top-quality locally sourced food (red deer
venison, for example, or Yorkshire lamb) with mains
around the £20 mark, all artfully plated by chef Timothy
Bilton. There's a roaring fire in winter, a balcony with fine
views, a tearoom and a cocktail bar. Wed–Sat noon–2pm
& 6–9.30pm, Sun noon–5pm; tearoom Wed–Sat
11am–5pm.

Standedge Tunnel and Visitor Centre

Waters Rd, Marsden • Mon–Fri 11am–4pm, Sat & Sun 10.30am–5pm • Free; boat trip £4.50 and £15 • ⓦ standedge.co.uk • Bus #183 or #184 from Huddersfield; by car, note that the official free car park, which is signposted, is next to Marsden train station, a good 15min walk along the canal from the tunnel entrance – there is some parking across the canal from the visitor centre for blue badge holders, and on summer weekends volunteers run a water ferry (50p) from the car park to the tunnel (☎ 01484 844298, ⓦ canalrivertrust.org.uk /standedge-tunnel)

Some twelve miles southwest of Huddersfield is the **Standedge Tunnel and Visitor Centre**, near the mill town of **Marsden**. The tunnel, which takes the **Huddersfield Narrow Canal** through the Pennines, is, at just over three miles long, the longest in the country. The superlatives don't end there – it's also the highest above sea level, and the deepest underground. You can take a thirty-minute trip by narrow boat into the tunnel, or you can book a through trip. There isn't, of course, much to see in the dark, and it isn't suitable if you're claustrophobic. The **visitor centre** tells the story of the tunnel and the canal, and there's a shop, some excellent information boards and a café.

Wakefield and around

WAKEFIELD, like several other major towns and cities in Yorkshire, is experiencing serious challenges in terms of urban development. Faced with the decline in its traditional industries, especially coal during the Thatcher years, and more recently suffering the effects of global recession, its attempts at urban regeneration have met with mixed success, with the massive Trinity Walk development around the old market hall in particular grinding to a halt as the developers hit the financial buffers.

That said, there are still many good things to see, starting with the impressive **Cathedral** right in the centre and the group of grand Victorian civic buildings north of the **Bull Ring**, plus two small but interesting museums – the **Gissing Centre** and the **Mental Health Museum** – though the opening hours of both are very restricted. The **Wakefield Bridge** to the south of the centre has a rare **Chantry Chapel**, and beyond it, the riverside continues to develop into an attractive waterside area that includes the fabulous **Hepworth Gallery**, devoted to the work of sculptor Barbara Hepworth. However, apart from the Hepworth, the real draws in the district are in the wider area: outside town, in the surrounding metropolitan district, Wakefield has three of West Yorkshire's biggest attractions – the **Yorkshire Sculpture Park**, the **National Coal Mining Museum** and **Nostell Priory**. Consequently, the city attracts far more visitors, both domestic and foreign, than you might at first expect.

Wakefield Cathedral

Westmorland St • Mon–Sat 9am–4pm plus service times • Free • ☎ 01924 373923, ⓦ wakefieldcathedral.org.uk

At the heart of the town centre is **Wakefield Cathedral**, whose 247ft spire is the tallest in Yorkshire. The earliest part of the present building (some of the nave's north arcade) dates from 1150, and bits have continued to be added ever since – the south arcade in 1220, the western tower and spire between 1409 and 1420, and much else during the rest of the fifteenth century. The seventeenth century saw the addition of the south porch sundial (1635), the quire screen (1636) and the font (1661, to replace one vandalized during the Commonwealth). Major remodelling and rebuilding was undertaken by Sir George Gilbert Scott between 1857 and 1874. Following its promotion to cathedral status in 1888, a new east end was added early in the twentieth century. And throughout the second half of the nineteenth century and up to 1907, stained glass by Charles Eamer Kempe (1837–1907) was added – 23 windows in all. A recent restoration of the nave has turned a fusty, dark Victorian

space into one that is light and airy. As you go around the cathedral, look out for the many carved animals and green men typical of medieval churches, and for Kempe's emblem – the golden wheatsheaf – on the stained-glass windows. Or better still, do the "Discovery" **audio-guide tour** (free, but donation welcomed); there are separate versions for adults and children.

Wakefield Museum

Burton St • Mon & Tues 9am–6pm, Wed 9am–8pm, Thurs & Fri 9am–7pm, Sat 9am–5pm • Free • ☎ 01924 305356, ⓦ wakefield.gov.uk

North of the centre, **Wakefield Museum**, behind County Hall in the Wakefield One building, is a good local history museum. It's a great spot for kids, who can follow one of the "digitrails", using a hand-held gizmo to guide them through a particular theme – animal exhibits, for example, or clothing through the ages. Highlights include the Story of Wakefield gallery, organized thematically, a Front Room, which contains a Victorian kitchen, and a 1940s living room, where children can dress up, displays on life in Roman Wakefield and the part played by the town in the Civil War, a social history of the Victorian town, an account of the miners' strike, and a display on local explorer and eccentric **Charles Waterton**. Waterton, who travelled widely and wrote *Waterton's Wanderings in South America*, which influenced the young Charles Darwin, collected animals and plants, many of which are on view in the museum – his method of preserving animals was unique, leaving them hollow and remarkably true to life. On his return to his estate – Walton Hall – he built a three-mile-long, 9ft-high wall around it, and turned it into the world's first nature reserve. He also invented the nesting box. His alleged eccentricities included buzz-cutting his hair when longer locks were fashionable, growling like a dog and biting his guests, and creating tableaux with his preserved animals that made fun of people he didn't like.

Hepworth Gallery

Gallery Walk • Tues–Sun 10am–5pm • Free • ☎ 01924 247360, ⓦ hepworthwakefield.org • Free citybus Mon–Fri off peak, train from Leeds to Wakefield Westgate (about 25min), then within walking distance of Wakefield's two railway stations, with numerous buses stopping at Doncaster Rd (5min walk) or Bridge St (next to the gallery)

A cuboid concrete riverside building designed by Sir David Chipperfield, the huge **Hepworth Gallery** has ten display areas housing a wonderful collection of Dame Barbara Hepworth's work – not only finished sculptures like the 1934 *Mother and Child*, but also working models in plaster and aluminium, and lithographs. You can even see her original workbench and tools. Other contemporary artists such as Jackson Pollock and Paul Klee are represented too, as is the work of leading British artists – Roger Fry, for example, along with Paul Nash, Nigel Henderson and Ben Nicholson. And a constant flow of new exhibits is assured by the museum's close relationship with the Arts Council, the British Council and the Tate. There's a café and shop, and a children's playground within its pleasant surroundings.

Mental Health Museum

Fieldhead Hospital, Ouchthorpe Lane • Wed–Fri 10am–4pm • Free • ☎ 01924 328654, ⓦ southwestyorkshire.nhs.uk

The **Mental Health Museum**, once housed in what was originally the West Riding Pauper Lunatic Asylum, was later moved to its current location in Fieldhead Hospital, and offers a salutary lesson in how far we've come in terms of the treatment of mental ill-health. The collection traces the history of treatments from the early nineteenth century onwards; the restraining, medical and surgical equipment, the horrible padded cell and the early ECT equipment (looking like something out of a *Frankenstein* film) is enough to freeze the marrow.

Gissing Centre

2–4 Thompson's Yard, just off Westgate • May–Sept Sat 2–4pm • Free • ☎ 01484 663645, ⓦ wakefield.gov.uk

The **Gissing Centre** is a museum dedicated to late nineteenth-century Wakefield writer George Gissing, sometimes mentioned in the same breath as George Meredith, Arnold Bennett and even Thomas Hardy, and author of many novels, including the highly regarded *New Grub Street*, published in 1891, about the difficulties of novelists and journalists trying to earn a living by writing. He died of emphysema in 1903. Given the limited opening hours, it's a good idea to call first.

2

National Coal Mining Museum

Caphouse Colliery, Overton, about 10 miles south of Leeds, halfway between Wakefield and Huddersfield (on the A642, signposted from M1) • Daily 10am–5pm; last tour 3.15pm • Free • ☎ 01924 848806, ⓦ ncm.org.uk • Trains from Leeds to Wakefield Westgate; from the station #128 goes right past the museum, while #232 passes nearby

Whether you're from the UK or abroad, if you want to understand modern Britain, the **National Coal Mining Museum** is an essential stop. Coal mining encapsulates everything that made Britain a world power – the entrepreneurial nous of the early coal owners (and, later, it has to be said, their greed), immense engineering ingenuity, the social solidarity of the mining communities, and the brave political intervention of governments stirred by admirably national outrage over conditions to solve hitherto unknown problems. Government had a less positive influence during the 1980s when pit closures and the miners' strike destroyed the British coal industry. The National Coal Mining Museum was established in 1988 in what was, up to its closure, the Caphouse Colliery.

Set aside at least half a day for the full experience. When you arrive, first book in for the underground tour (90min) and then fit the rest of your visit around it. Start with the **visitor centre**, which has excellent displays on a host of aspects of the history of the coal industry – the lives of the miners and their families, work at the coal face, child labour and mining disasters.

Caphouse Colliery and Hope Pit

The whole **Caphouse Colliery** (it was a working pit from the 1770s until its closure in 1985) is one giant museum – the winding engine house, the screening plant and weighbridge, the pit ponies in their stables (two of them called Eric and Ernie), the pithead baths, the medical room. A smaller colliery – the **Hope Pit** – has exciting interactive displays covering the science behind mining: you can walk there (it's about 0.25 miles), or ride on the narrow-gauge railway. In addition, there are nature trails, bird hides and reed beds.

Underground tour

The highlight of any visit to the National Coal Mining Museum has to be the **underground tour**. The brass token you're given is an exact replica of one of those that every miner had to hand over before going underground, and which they were given back when they returned to the surface – a simple way of ensuring that nobody got forgotten. Having picked up your miner's lamp and hard hat you enter the cage and plummet 440ft into the **New Hards Seam**. This is the only part of the tour that might bother claustrophobes – once you are underground, the mine is surprisingly spacious. The tour involves walking along the tunnels or "roadways" with an ex-miner guide, who offers a detailed and often hilarious commentary that covers methods of extraction from the early hand-hewing days to the big cutter-loaders and modern shearers, and details the dangers of mine collapse, gas explosion, carbon monoxide poisoning and flooding. Though the big disasters created all the headlines, there was a constant trickle of underground accidents – at the start of the twentieth century, around a thousand men and boys died every year.

Yorkshire Sculpture Park

West Bretton, 6 miles southwest of Wakefield, a mile from the M1 (junction 38) • Daily 10am–6pm (galleries, restaurant and café 10am–5pm) • ☎ 01924 832631, ⓦ ysp.co.uk • Bus #96 (Sun #435/#436) from Wakefield city centre (Kirkgate) – it's then a 15min walk from the bus stop

The splendid **Yorkshire Sculpture Park** is an inspired idea. A stunning estate, designed in the eighteenth and nineteenth centuries around Bretton Hall, has become an outdoor art gallery where work from some of the finest names in modern sculpture is displayed in glorious English parkland. Over time indoor spaces have been added, too – **Bretton Chapel**, **Underground Gallery** and **Longside Gallery**, for instance. The outdoor sculptures, although on loan, are virtually permanent, while the indoor galleries host ever-changing visiting exhibitions – previous shows have included Ai Weiwei and Roger Hiorns. The excellent free maps detail the park's eight areas and some of its main highlights – Anthony Caro's *Dream City*, for example, or Antony Gormley's *One and Other*, Barbara Hepworth's *Family of Man*, or a host of Henry Moore sculptures. There is also work by Elisabeth Frink, Andy Goldsworthy, Julian Opie, Isamo Noguchi – even a rare open-air sculpture from Tracey Emin – along with many more. If you want detailed background, then fork out for the *Essential Sculpture Guide* (£5, and worth every penny). The park is huge, though some of it is private land, and there's a **visitor centre**, a café/restaurant and a shop. You'll need at least half a day to get the most out of it, and ideally longer – there's a great deal to see.

Nostell Priory

Doncaster Rd, Nostell • **Priory** March–Oct Wed–Sun 1–5pm; mid-Dec Sat & Sun 1–4pm • £9.45 with gardens; NT **Gardens** Daily • £5.90; NT • ☎ 01924 863892, ⓦ nationaltrust.org.uk • Arriva bus #496 Wakefield–Doncaster, or #485 or #495 from Wakefield

Nostell Priory was built in the mid-eighteenth century on the site of a medieval priory for Sir Rowland Winn. He'd married into money and wanted to celebrate. Notable for the contributions of a number of big names – James Paine, and then Robert Adam, in the design of the house, Thomas Chippendale (himself a Yorkshireman) in its furnishing – the house has been continuously occupied by the same family since. Until World War I it was run as a typical "great house" – after that it went into something of a decline, until it was handed over to the National Trust in 1953. The Trust now maintains Nostell Priory, though the family still uses part of it.

The house contains many treasures, and boasts one of the biggest collections of **Chippendale furniture** in the world, most of it designed specifically for this very spot. In the billiard room, look out for the 1717 **long case clock** made by John Harrison, whose father was probably a Nostell Priory estate carpenter, and who solved the problem of how to work out longitude at sea by inventing the marine chronometer – you can still see it at the Royal Observatory, in Greenwich, London. Probably the most famous of Nostell's treasures, though, is the **dolls' house**, in the south passage. Made at the time that the house was built, it provides a perfect scaled-down version of an eighteenth-century country house, complete with ornate beds, elaborate staircases and perfect miniature furniture. The surrounding parkland has an adventure playground, **garden** and lakeside walks and a picnic area.

ARRIVAL AND INFORMATION

WAKEFIELD

By car Tucked as it is into the horseshoe formed by the M1, the M62 and the A1, Wakefield's road connections are excellent. The town is well signposted from all three roads, and there are numerous car parks encircling the city centre – the most convenient is the multistorey in the Ridings Shopping Centre.

By train Wakefield has two train stations, of which Westgate, on the western edge of the city centre, is the

most important, being on the main East Coast line with services south to London and north to Scotland. Kirkgate, to the south of the centre, handles local routes. Both stations are within easy walking distance of the town centre.

Destinations Doncaster (every 45min–1hr; 35min); Edinburgh (hourly; 3hr 20min); Huddersfield (every 10min; 29min); Leeds (every 15–30min; 13–20min); London

King's Cross (hourly; 2hr–3hr 20min); York (hourly; 40min).
By bus Wakefield bus station stands on Union St, at the northern edge of the town centre, just beyond the new market hall.
Destinations Barnsley (every 15–30min; 36min); Bradford (every 15–30min; 1hr); Huddersfield (every 10min; 29min);

Leeds (every 30min; 31min); Pontefract (every 20–35min; 33min); Wetherby (every 2hr; 1hr 37min).
Tourist office Wakefield's well-stocked and helpful tourist office (Mon, Tues, Thurs & Fri 9am–4.30pm, Wed 9am–3.45pm, Sat 10am–3pm; ☎ 0845 601 8353, ⓦ wakefield.gov.uk) is on the Bullring.

ACCOMMODATION

Holiday Inn Leeds Wakefield Queens Drive, Ossett, less than 2 miles from Wakefield, near Junction 40 on the M1 ☎ 0870 400 9082, ⓦ holidayinn.com. Slightly more upmarket than the *Premier Inn*, with lots of free parking and a restaurant (*Traders*). There's a pub serving food nearby. **£54**
★ **Waterton Park Hotel** Walton Hall, Walton, 4 miles from Wakefield ☎ 01924 257911, ⓦ watertonparkhotel .co.uk. If distance from the city centre and cost are no

object, then this is surely worth a look. One of the most beautifully located hotels in the country (the hotel is modern, but attached to Georgian Walton Hall by a bridge), with a range of comfortably furnished and smartly turned out rooms with peaceful views of the lake or countryside. There's a swimming pool and gym on site, and a championship golf course nearby. Frequent good offers bring the price down. **£175**

EATING AND DRINKING

Bella Roma 63 Northgate ☎ 01924 371059, ⓦ bella romawakefield.co.uk. Something of a decor time-warp, but serving good Italian food and robust wines. There's an ever-changing specials board. Tues–Sat noon–2pm & 5.30–10pm, Sun 1–9pm.
★ **The Cow Shed** 53 Northgate ☎ 01924 291044, ⓦ cowshed.uk.com. A lovely little restaurant and grill housed in an interesting half-timbered, sixteenth-century Grade II listed building just up from the Bull Ring. With many original features and wooden tables, it has the feel of a medieval banqueting hall, but the food is anything but – it's Modern European, confined to a limited choice done well, with an emphasis on steak, and an extensive wine list. Typical dishes include venison and black pudding (£18.95), salmon wrapped in Parma ham (£13.95) and rib-eye steak with blue

cheese (£18.95). Mon–Sat noon–2pm & 6–9.30pm.
Six Chimneys 41–43 Kirkgate ☎ 01924 239449. Standard *Wetherspoon* pub, which means low prices, no music and no-nonsense, reasonably priced food. Children are welcome, and there's wi-fi available. Sun–Thurs 8am–midnight, Fri & Sat 8am–1am.
Thai on the Square 3–9 Cross Square ☎ 01924 298555, ⓦ thaionthesquare.co.uk. Though the unprepossessing entrance has been likened by some to that of a massage parlour, the first-floor *Thai on the Square* is a pleasant mixture of Thai and English design, the service is discreet but attentive, the food is excellent and the prices reasonable – most main courses come in at between £8 and £12.50. Tues–Fri noon–2pm & 6–10.30pm, Sat 6–10.30pm, Sun 5–9.30pm.

ENTERTAINMENT

Wakefield is rather short of permanent venues for music and theatre, so its several **festivals** depend upon a variety of temporary venues across the district – usually pubs. The prestigious **Wakefield Jazz** (ⓦ wakefieldjazz .org.uk), for example, uses Wakefield Sports Club for its Friday night sessions. Otherwise, there are one-offs such as occasional concerts or exhibitions at the Yorkshire Sculpture Park, the National Coal Mining Museum or the Wakefield Museum.

Theatre Royal Drury Lane (just off Westgate) ☎ 01924 211311, ⓦ theatreroyalwakefield.co.uk.

The only large venue in Wakefield for music, dance, theatre and comedy.

Pontefract

PONTEFRACT is a handsome town that sits in the western angle between the M62 and the A1 about twelve miles east of Wakefield. Gathered on a hillside around a spacious **Market Place**, the town centre has lots of blue-plaqued historic buildings, the longest racecourse in Europe, an interesting half-ruined church in All Saints and the remains of **Pontefract Castle**, which played a decisive part on several occasions in English history. The town is also known for its historical importance in **liquorice** farming, and hosts an annual liquorice festival each summer.

Market Place

Pontefract's wide, irregular **Market Place**, thronged every Wednesday, Friday and Saturday with market stalls, is dominated by its **Buttercross**, a sturdy structure consisting of a stone roof supported by stone columns built in 1734 to shelter dairy traders and still today offering protection from the sun and rain. The massive wooden bench inside it and the timber-encased water pump just outside are both probably original. Facing the Buttercross is **St Giles' Church**, built in the twelfth century as a chapel-of-ease to the church of All Saints (see below), which it replaced as Pontefract's parish church after All Saints was damaged during a bombardment of the nearby castle during the Civil War.

The names of the surrounding streets and the surviving historic buildings attest to Pontefract's origins as an important and prosperous market town – Beastfair, Cornmarket, Shoemarket, Salter Row – as does the large water-trough at the top of Beastfair next to the War Memorial.

Pontefract Castle

Castle Garth • Summer Mon–Fri 8.30am–5pm, Sat & Sun 9.30am-6.15pm; winter Mon–Fri 8.30am–4.30pm, Sat & Sun 9.30am–4.30pm • Free; tour of ammunition cellars £2.20 • ☎ 01977 723440

On the east side of town, **Pontefract Castle**, described by Edward I as "the key to the North", and by Oliver Cromwell as "one of the strongest inland garrisons in the kingdom" was once one of the most formidable strongholds in the country, and its remains, explained in a series of excellent context boards, are well worth an hour or two of your time. Built just after the Norman Conquest as a wooden motte-and-bailey fort, the structure passed to the Lancaster family in the early fourteenth century and became a royal castle when the Dukes of Lancaster became Kings of England from 1399 onwards. That there's so little of it left is down to Parliamentary forces during the Civil War and their comprehensive bombardment after its doughty resistance to no fewer than three Roundhead sieges. However, today the original conical motte estate (the artificial hill on which the Norman wooden fort stood) can still clearly be seen – it was progressively strengthened during the twelfth and thirteenth centuries, with kitchen and bakehouse added in the fifteenth century. Look out in particular for the Gascoigne Tower, in which the deposed King Richard II was imprisoned by his usurper Henry IV. Richard was dead within a few months, possibly of starvation. Guided tours of the cellars, used as a magazine, are worth it for the commentary alone.

All Saints Church

South Baileygate • Free • ⓦ allsaintspontefract.co.uk

There can be few more atmospheric ruins in West Yorkshire than **All Saints Church**, which stands at the foot of the hill crowned by the castle. From when it was built, during the thirteenth to fifteenth centuries, up until the Civil War, All Saints was Pontefract's parish church. However, it was so severely damaged by Parliamentary bombardment of the Royalist-held castle that the status of parish church passed to St Giles. Though much of the church is still ruined (signs warn "Danger of falling debris"), the tower and transept were restored in 1831 and a new nave was included within the old ruins in 1967. The result is a fascinating (and photogenic) half-ruined, half-working church that still hosts services and weddings.

Kirkebi Anglo Saxon Church

The Booths • Daily 24hr • Free

Across the road from All Saints you can see what's left of **Kirkebi Anglo Saxon Church**, excavated in the mid-1980s. Though little remains bar the footprint of the building, its survival is truly remarkable – the church is mentioned in the Domesday Book,

PONTEFRACT LIQUORICE

Pontefract has at least four centuries of historical connection with the **liquorice plant**, from which at first medicine and later sweets were made. Thought to have been introduced to the area by Crusaders and later cultivated by Spanish monks, it was grown for its purported ability to ease sore throats, coughs and colds, and to take the edge off thirst when no water was available. In the eighteenth century a local chemist called George Dunhill started to mix liquorice with sugar to make it more palatable, creating small liquorice sweets ("Pontefract cakes") and setting off the town's liquorice manufacturing industry. Liquorice fields at one time surrounded the town, with thousands of the low-growing shrubs being cultivated for their roots, harvested from the second or third year after planting; cultivation died out in the early twentieth century in the face of stiff competition from imports. There is talk of reintroducing liquorice production on a small scale to Pontefract; meanwhile, a little of the atmosphere of the fields can be found in John Betjeman's poem *The Liquorice Fields at Pontefract*, which tells us that "In the liquorice fields of Pontefract /My love and I did meet", and with perhaps a touch of tongue-in-cheek humour includes a description of the plants and the town.

2

and it is where, in 947AD, King Eadred of England accepted the allegiance of the Northumbrians and Archbishop Wulfstan of York.

ARRIVAL AND INFORMATION   PONTEFRACT

By car Pontefract is easily accessible and is well signposted from the M62 and from the A1(M).

By train Pontefract has three rail stations – Monkhill, the main station; Tanshelf, which serves Pontefract racecourse; and the sleepy Baghill.

Destinations from Monkhill Castleford (hourly; 9min); Leeds (hourly; 34min) Wakefield (hourly; 21min); London King's Cross (every 1hr 30min–2hr; 2–3hr).

Destinations from Tanshelf Wakefield (hourly; 20min).

Destinations from Baghill York (2 daily; 42min).

By bus Pontefract bus station is on Horsefair, between the town centre and the castle.

Destinations Barnsley (hourly; 1hr); Castleford (every 5–15min; 22–29min); Doncaster (hourly; 1hr 19min); Leeds (every 30min; 50min); Wakefield (every 15min; 35min).

Tourist information Town library, Shoemarket (Mon–Wed & Fri 9.30am–7pm, Sat 9am–4pm; ☎01977 727692, ✉ pontefractlibrary@wakefield.gov.uk).

ACCOMMODATION, EATING AND DRINKING

King's Croft Hotel Wakefield Rd ☎01977 600550, ⓦ kingscrofthotel.com. A privately owned hotel housed in a Grade II listed building in extensive grounds on the hill about a mile west of Pontefract's town centre, the *King's Croft* offers character and comfort at very reasonable rates. It hosts weddings, proms and entertainment, but these impact very little on ordinary guests. **£58**

Robin Hood 4 Wakefield St ☎01977 702231. Good old-fashioned town-centre pub highly rated by locals. The unique selling point – they brew their own ale. Mon–Thurs 5–11pm, Fri & Sat noon–1am, Sun noon–midnight.

Shuhag 79 Station Lane, Featherstone, 5 miles west of Pontefract ☎01977 699999, ⓦ shuhag-restaurant .co.uk. The finest Indian restaurant in the area, serving excellent Bangladeshi food in convivial surroundings.

Specialities include *nagha tarkaari* (chicken and mince) and *begum bahar* (chicken or lamb tikka with a sweet and sour sauce). Mains £7–10.95. Sun–Thurs 6–11pm, Fri & Sat 6am–midnight.

Skyline Restaurant 27 Ropergate ☎01977 600659, ⓦ ruankumrai.co.uk. Top-notch Thai restaurant in the town centre. The surroundings are stylish, with lots of Thailand-themed decorations. Main courses £8.95–14.95. Daily noon–3pm & 5–10.30pm.

Spread Eagle Estcourt Rd, Darrington, a couple of miles east of Pontefract ☎01977 699698. Traditional pub serving a nice range of beers and good home-cooked pub grub at under a tenner for a main course. Daily noon–3pm & 5–11pm; no food served on Sun evenings or Mon.

The Vale of York

YORK MINSTER

The Vale of York

The Vale of York, loosely defined, is the long strip of prime farming land that stretches from the city of York north to the Tees and south to the Humber. Flanked to the west by the Dales and to the east by the North York Moors, the Howardian Hills and the Wolds, it has always been a main north–south route, funnelling road and rail communications from the south of England to the north and Scotland between North Yorkshire's two upland areas. Dotted with villages and market towns, it has some of the county's top destinations, of which by far the most popular is the walled City of York itself, a fascinating slice of history sitting right in the centre of the valley.

3

One of the biggest tourist hot spots in Britain, **York** combines a wealth of fascinating history with all the buzz of a contemporary city. With its superlative Gothic **Minster**, its inventive museums and its narrow, meandering lanes reflecting its medieval street plan, it also has a solid infrastructure – from hotels and restaurants to open-topped buses and sightseeing boats – and is also clearly a real city, buzzing with students and with a local life.

But it's not only York that merits a visit. Twenty miles to the west, classy **Harrogate**, large and rather grand, is a once-famous spa town that has adapted well to the modern world without sacrificing its Regency and Victorian heritage. Nearby, the riverside market town of **Knaresborough**, with its gorge, ruined castle and its petrifying well, is one of the prettiest places in the county. The idiosyncratic model village of **Ripley** is also worth a look, while **Boroughbridge** is famed for its Roman connections and its prehistoric monoliths. Some fifteen miles north of Harrogate, the pleasant market town of **Ripon** has a lower profile but is well worth a visit for its hornblower – following a tradition that dates back to the ninth century – and its intriguing cathedral. Above all, the town makes an excellent jumping-off point for the World Heritage Site of **Fountains Abbey**, one of Yorkshire's major attractions, with its Cistercian monastery, lovely old mill and beautiful water gardens set in the Skell Valley. **Wetherby**, meanwhile, just a few miles southeast of York, actually just inside West Yorkshire and a short hop from Leeds, is a peaceful little town that grew up to service travellers on their way to and from Scotland.

York and around

With its great stock of medieval, Tudor and eighteenth-century buildings, **YORK** has a place in the history of England, and in its affections, out of all proportion to its size. Now a world-famous attraction pulling in around four million visitors annually, only 140,000 people actually call it home, putting it in the same bracket as Blackpool, Ipswich or Peterborough. The city has developed catering for tourists down to a fine art, and there are plenty of places to stay, eat and drink. It's not cheap, and in July and August it can become uncomfortably crowded, but don't let this put you off – the city is popular because, quite simply, it's a wonderful place chock-full of treasures.

A weekend in York p.144
York ghost tours p.148
Dick Turpin (1706–39) p.153

Agatha Christie's lost ten days p.165
Blind Jack of Knaresborough p.168

STUDLEY ROYAL

Highlights

❶ York Minster Britain's greatest Gothic cathedral. Prepare to be awed, but also amused – the guides will fill you in on lots of interesting and entertaining details. **See p.145**

❷ Dig, York Jorvik's sister attraction takes you through simulated archeological excavations, led by bona fide archeologists. See p.150

❸ Jorvik Viking Centre, York Tenth-century Viking York as seen, heard and smelt from your very own time capsule. **See p.151**

❹ National Railway Museum, York The world's best museum of railway transport, in the country that invented it. **See p.154**

❺ Bettys Retro splendour, crisp starched linen and cakes to die for in these gloriously nostalgic tearooms. **See p.158, p.165 & p.166**

❻ Turkish Baths, Harrogate Sweat it out in this beautiful Victorian spa. **See p.164**

❼ Fountains Abbey and Studley Royal, Ripon Spectacularly beautiful ruined medieval abbey set in extensive eighteenth-century water gardens. **See p.176**

HIGHLIGHTS ARE MARKED ON THE MAP ON PP.140–141

THE VALE OF YORK

N

HIGHLIGHTS

1 York Minster
2 Dig, York
3 Jorvik Viking Centre, York
4 National Railway Museum, York
5 Bettys tearooms
6 Turkish Baths, Harrogate
7 Fountains Abbey and Studley Royal, Ripon

NORTH YORK MOORS NATIONAL PARK

NORTH YORKSHIRE

DURHAM

Saltwick Bay
Whitby
Guisborough
Great Ayton
Middlesbrough
Darlington
Scotch Corner
Richmond
Scorton
Bedale
Masham
Northallerton
Ripon
Boroughbridge
Helperby
Easingwold
Thirsk
Knayton
Helmsley
Kirbymoorside
Hovingham
Pickering
Malton
Norton-on-Derwent

River Tees
River Wiske
River Swale

Lightwater Valley

Fountains Abbey & Studley Royal

A171
A171
A173
A172
A19
A684
A167
A66
A67
A1
A684
A6108
A6136
B6271
B6265
B6267
B6268
B6108
A61
A170
A168
A19
A168
A1
A61
A59
A170
B1257
B1257
A169
A170
A64
A171
A169
A174
A684
B6275
B6274
B1263
B1303
A66
A167
A19

The top attractions are part of the fabric of the city – individual buildings such as the Gothic **Minster**, **Clifford Tower**, the **Fairfax House**, **Barley Hall** and the **Merchant Adventurers' Hall**, but also nearly three miles of thirteenth-century **city walls** that surround the city centre, and the narrow, cobbled lanes within it such as the picturesque **Shambles**, overhung by teetering medieval houses.

These are supplemented by a clutch of world-class museums. Perennial favourites include the innovative **Jorvik Viking Centre** and its even more hands-on partner **Dig** – the group that runs those two big-hitters also manages museums dedicated to Kings **Richard III** and **Henry VII**, and **Barley Hall**, a medieval townhouse. Other excellent choices include the mighty **National Railway Museum**; the **Yorkshire Museum**, in its own beautiful gardens; the **York Castle Museum**, which occupies what was once the county jail; and the chilling **York Cold War Bunker**. Scattered around the city centre are numerous other attractions, all within walking distance of each other – the **City Art Gallery**, the **Grand Opera House**, the **Theatre Royal** and **Friargate Theatre** among them. There's even a **Quilt Museum,** occupying a venerable old guildhall, and the remains of **Roman Baths** in the basement of a pub of the same name.

Brief history

York jumped on to the national stage with a bang in Roman times – before then it was a small marshy settlement of the locally dominant Celtic Brigantes tribe at the confluence of the Ouse and the Foss. Then, in 71 AD, the Romans arrived and built a garrison from which to subdue the locals. Around it grew the town of **Erboracum**, which in due course became the capital of the Roman Empire's northern territories. From here Hadrian masterminded the pacifying of the north and the building of his famous wall. Here it was, too, that Constantine was proclaimed Emperor in 306 AD.

When the Romans withdrew their army from Britain in the fifth century AD, York was conquered by the Anglo-Saxons, who made it the capital of the kingdom of Northumbria – **Eoforwic**. Not long afterwards, York added to its undoubted and growing political clout a religious dimension: in 627 AD, bishop Paulinus, pushing the Christian envelope northwards, baptized King Edwin of Northumbria in a specially built wooden chapel. Within six years, that humble church had become the first Minster, and Paulinus the first **Archbishop of York**.

Fast-forward a couple of centuries, and in 867 AD the city of York fell to the Vikings. They renamed it **Jorvik**, and it became the capital of the Viking-dominated Danelaw. Their hundred-year occupation ended in 954 AD when York was regained by the Anglo-Saxon King Eadred of Wessex. This is how things remained until the Annus Horriblis of 1066. The year kicked off well for the English King Harold, who defeated a combined invasion-cum-insurrection jointly led by Harald Hardrada of Norway and Tostig, King Harold's half brother, at Stamford Bridge just outside York. But then news arrived that William of Normandy had landed in the south. The exhausted English army returned to the south, only to be defeated at the Battle of Hastings.

Norman rule started badly for York – the city was destroyed during William the Conqueror's ferocious "harrying of the north", punishment for having had the temerity to oppose his occupation of the country. As the dust settled, however, York prospered. A new **cathedral** was built by the Norman Archbishop Thomas, starting in 1080, and this sparked the development of the city as the principal religious centre of the north of England, with the establishment of many religious houses. Economic recovery followed, with York becoming a major trading hub, importing from, and exporting to, France and the Low Countries. The city's many medieval buildings are the result of this combination of religious growth and economic prosperity during those years.

It didn't last. **Tudor times** brought economic recession caused by a downturn in the fortunes of the woollen industry, and the effects of the split with the Roman Catholic faith sparked by Henry VIII's desire to divorce Catherine of Aragon and marry Anne Boleyn. The subsequent northern rebellion in support of the Pope and the Catholic

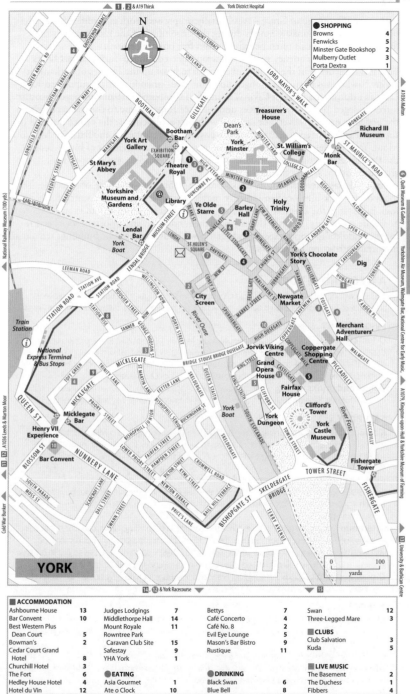

York District Hospital

1, **2** & A19 Thirsk

SHOPPING

Browns	4
Fenwicks	5
Minster Gate Bookshop	2
Mulberry Outlet	3
Porta Dextra	1

3

YORK

0 — 100 yards

■ ACCOMMODATION

Ashbourne House	13	Judges Lodgings	7	Bettys	7	Swan	12
Bar Convent	10	Middlethorpe Hall	14	Café Concerto	4	Three-Legged Mare	3
Best Western Plus		Mount Royale	11	Café No. 8	2		
Dean Court	5	Rowntree Park		Evil Eye Lounge	5	**■ CLUBS**	
Bowman's	2	Caravan Club Site	15	Mason's Bar Bistro	9	Club Salvation	3
Cedar Court Grand		Safestay	9	Rustique	11	Kuda	5
Hotel	8	YHA York	1				
Churchill Hotel	3					**■ LIVE MUSIC**	
The Fort	6	**● EATING**		**● DRINKING**		The Basement	2
Hedley House Hotel	4	Asia Gourmet	1	Black Swan	6	The Duchess	1
Hotel du Vin	12	Ate o Clock	10	Blue Bell	8	Fibbers	4

faith – the Pilgrimage of Grace – was brutally suppressed. York also suffered from the plundering of the monastic houses during the dissolution of the monasteries which followed (though locals often benefitted from free building stone).

York's regrettable tendency to pick the wrong side continued during **Stuart times**. First it was involved in the 1605 Catholic plot to blow up the Houses of Parliament – Guy Fawkes was born and brought up in the city – then it strongly supported King Charles I during the English Civil War. In 1644 combined Parliamentary and Scottish forces besieged York. Royalist forces under Prince Rupert came to the rescue, driving the besiegers out. However, not satisfied with that achievement, the prince pursued the superior Parliamentary forces west of the city, then was routed at the Battle of Marston Moor. York was left defenceless, and owes its survival to an accident of birth – one of the Parliamentary commanders, Lord Fairfax, was from York, and stopped his victorious troops setting fire to the city.

During the **eighteenth century** York's prestige went into something of a decline. The focus of the Yorkshire woollen industry moved west and south as the search for power took it first into the Pennine hills (water power), then into the west and south Yorkshire coal fields (steam). The city remained, however, an important social centre for the middle and upper classes, and their town houses and public buildings remain an important attraction for visitors.

3

A WEEKEND IN YORK

York is a wonderful place for a weekend **city break**, with enough attractions and places to eat and drink to fill far longer than that. The following itinerary gives you a taster of all the highlights.

FRIDAY NIGHT

Orientation Get a first view of this beautiful city by walking the walls (they're open until dusk), or, if you're feeling less energetic, then take an open-top tourist bus (see p.157). For the rest of the evening, join one of the ghost tours (see box, p.148) – or take a look at York by night from one of the tour boats that ply their trade on the River Ouse (see p.157).

Dinner and drinks Perhaps a light meal at *Café Concerto* (see p.158) or a more robust English meal at *Café No. 8* (see p.159), then a few drinks at the nearby *Three-Legged Mare* (see p.159).

SATURDAY

Morning Devote your morning to York's past. Both the Yorkshire (see p.149) and the Castle (see p.152) museums are lively and informative. Even more user-friendly and innovative are Jorvik (see p.151) and Dig (see p.150) – at the first you travel in a time capsule across Viking York, experiencing the sights, sounds and smells of the city a thousand years ago; at the second, hard hat on head and trowel in hand, you'll be guided through a simulated archeological dig. Don't overdo it, though – any one of these four could fill your morning.

Lunch Try *Bettys* (see p.158), a Yorkshire institution, with staff in starched white aprons and a lovely retro atmosphere.

Afternoon During the afternoon, explore the centre's winding lanes and myriad independent shops, which draw people from all over the north of England and beyond. But if shopping fills you with dread, make your way to York Minster (see p.145) – you'll have to pay to get in (unless you're just going to worship) but then you can join a free and fascinating guided tour.

Dinner and drinks To save any further wear and tear on your feet, why not eat at *Mason's Bar Bistro* (see p.159), then cross Fossgate for drinks at the delightful *Blue Bell* (see p.159)?

SUNDAY

Morning Catch the road train the short distance out to the National Railway Museum (see p.154) and wander around the biggest collection of bygone locomotives, rolling stock and memorabilia in the world.

Lunch You can have lunch at one of the museum's cafés/restaurants.

Afternoon Return to Museum Street then stroll along the river from Lendal Bridge or in the nearby Museum Gardens until it's time to go home.

Things looked up with the coming of the **railways** in the nineteenth century. York became an important rail centre, and also, through the Rowntree and Terry dynasties, a great manufacturer of **confectionery**. By the time these two industries went into twentieth-century decline, York's future prosperity was assured by its burgeoning tourist industry.

York's walls

Dawn to dusk • Free

A great way of orienting yourself when visiting York is to walk the **walls**. One of the glories of the city, York's walls date mainly from the fourteenth century, but contain bits of earlier construction, especially the Roman section along Museum Street. The walls are complete, except for a section on the eastern edge where marshland and fish ponds made defence unnecessary, and in the south where the city was already protected by its castle. Where the river prevented the building of walls, chains would be slung across during times of danger. Particularly fine are the several surviving medieval gatehouses – the **Bootham Bar** to the northwest near Exhibition Square, **Micklegate Bar** to the southwest, **Monk Bar** to the northeast and **Walmgate Bar** (the only one to retain its protective barbican) to the southeast. There are numerous access points to the walls apart from these gates, and walking the walls is one of the great pleasures of York, offering ever-changing views of the city and its surroundings.

York Minster

Minster Yard • Mon–Sat 9am–5pm, Sun 12.45–5pm; free guided tours (1hr) take place Mon–Sat 10am–3pm (subject to availability) and include access to the "Revealing York Minster" and the Orb visitor attractions • £10 (including undercroft); combined ticket with tower £15; admission ticket valid for 12 months, and up to four children 8 to 16 admitted free with one adult • ☎ 01904 557200, ⍟ yorkminster.org

York Minster – first built as a temporary wooden structure in 627 AD, destroyed and rebuilt many times over succeeding centuries, and finally erected in its current splendid form from 1220 onwards (but not declared complete until its consecration in 1472) – is one of England's great Gothic churches. It's awe-inspiringly grand but also remarkably easy to comprehend, and with so many human-scale foibles that, on closer acquaintance, it becomes almost endearing. A full tour will take at least half a day, but could spark a love affair that will last you a lifetime.

The **main entrance** to the cathedral leads you into the **south transept**. As you take in the stupendous scale of the building, stand with your back to the entrance, look around and get oriented. Ahead is the crossing below the **central tower**, beyond which is the **north transept** and, in the far right-hand corner, the entrance to the **Chapter House**. Left at the crossing is the **nave**, while to the right is the **quire** and the east end of the cathedral.

Nave

In medieval times the **nave** was the less religious part of the building, a general meeting place thronged with people and animals, stalls selling religious items, even choirboys playing football – a duel was once fought here.

Imagine it without the two aisles on either side – that was the size of the original Norman cathedral. Most of the current nave was built between 1280 and 1350, in the Decorated style. The aisle roofs are made of stone, while that of the nave itself is made of wood, and painted to look like stone, following an 1840 fire. All bar one of the new roof bosses were copies of the originals. The one that was changed showed the Virgin Mary breast-feeding the baby Jesus – in the primmer Victorian version she uses a bottle.

Jesse window

As you walk down the **south** (left) **aisle**, past the memorial to anti-slave-trade campaigner William Wilberforce, you can examine the lovely medieval stained-glass windows. The most famous is third from the end – the **Jesse window**, showing the claimed descent of Jesus from Jesse (Jesse at the bottom, Jesus at the top). The three dates are of the window's installation and subsequent restorations.

Great West Window

At the west end of the church is the Great West Door, above which is the **Great West Window**. It consists of eight lancets and complicated tracery in which can be seen the shape that gives the window its nickname – the "Heart of Yorkshire". Notice in the range of niches that line up with the middle of the doors an interesting modern addition – twelve figures representing saints. Made of MDF, they are headless (a reference to the effigies defaced during the Reformation), and are using their halos to spell out, in semaphore, "Christ is here". Any feeling that these "semaphore saints" look like people playing with Frisbees must be sternly resisted.

North aisle

As you return towards the central tower along the **north aisle** of the nave, notice the door that once led to the chapel of St Sepulchre. After the chapel was demolished, the only place that the door led to was an inn, making York probably the only cathedral in the world with its own pub entrance. (The inn, alas, has also been demolished.) Next, up in the roof is a **red and gold dragon**, which swivels on a pivot; it's thought to be a counter-weighted crane for lifting the heavy lid of a long-gone object – either a font or a reliquary containing the head of St William of York. The best-known window along this aisle is the sixth – the **bell-founders window**. It shows scenes of bell-founding and bell-tuning, together with a representation of the miracle of the Ouse Bridge in 1153 when the bridge collapsed under the weight of the crowds assembled to welcome St William of York to the city, yet nobody was killed.

North transept

Turning left at the central tower crossing brings you into the **north transept**, built in 1220 to 1260 in Early English style, and the giant **Five Sisters Window** – the largest lancet window in the world. Made of five lancets of muted grey-silver Grisaille glass, each 57ft high by 5ft wide, it is largely non-representational, except for a colourful circle at the bottom of the central lancet which is glass recycled from the Norman cathedral. The window was rededicated after World War I to the memory of all the women who'd died during that conflict (the ceremony was performed by the Duchess of York, who later became the Queen Mother), and the roll-call of those who died can be seen behind the doors around the **astronomical clock**. The clock itself is a memorial to RAF air and ground crew who served in the area during World War II, and the picture in its centre represents York as seen from the air – you can see the Minster and the medieval walls. The other clock in the north transept strikes at each quarter hour – the face dates back to the eighteenth century, while the figures of knights who strike the metal bars are fifteenth century. The clocks have traditionally been wound by members of the same family for the last century and a half.

Chapter House

Walking through the vestibule – looking out for carvings of green men hidden among the tracery – brings you into the octagonal **Chapter House**, which dates from the same period and is of the same style as the nave, built in 1290 to accommodate meetings of the cathedral's governing body. It's still used today, and you can see the names of the Canons above each of the 44 seats around the walls. Unusually, York's Chapter House doesn't have a central pillar holding up the roof – it's made of wood, and suspended from a complicated system of beams above it (there's a model to show you how this works). Above the seats is a riot of carving where the masons who did the work were given a degree of leeway in what they depicted. So for example, one is of a pig, which were often used by working people to convert food scraps and waste into meat. This leeway has been extended to modern masons doing restoration work – elsewhere in the cathedral, at the east end, there's a man rudely mooning, and two figures from *Star Trek* on the external arch of the Great West Door.

Quire

In the main body of the cathedral, take a look at the **quire**, a wooden room-within-a-room in which day-to-day services are held and choristers sit. The screen through which you enter the quire has effigies of fifteen kings who have reigned during the existence of the cathedral, from William the Conqueror on the left to Henry VI on the right. Within, the choir stalls face each other, and on the right at the far end is the throne (cathedra) of the Archbishop of York. All the woodwork in the quire is Victorian – in 1829 a man called Jonathan Martin, taking exception to the way that services were celebrated, made his displeasure known by coming out of hiding after the cathedral was shut, piling all the medieval choir stalls around the organ, and setting fire to the lot.

East end

Beyond the quire is the **east end** of the cathedral, the newest part, built between 1361 and 1472 in the Perpendicular style. Beyond the quire and the high altar, the **Lady Chapel** is dominated by the gigantic **Great East Window**. Or it will be when the window's restoration, started in 2008, is complete (estimated for 2016). In the meantime the space is covered by a full-sized replica of the window on a printed banner – at the size of a doubles tennis court, it's the largest high-res graphic in the world. Nearby you can see an ever-changing selection of the window's most famous stained-glass panels in the odd, inverted-cauldron-shape of **the Orb**.

Returning towards the central crossing along the south aisle, look out for the **Archbishop Lamplugh monument**, carved in 1691 by Grinling Gibbons – in particular at the ends of his legs where he appears to have two right feet. This is thought to be either because left and right shoes weren't differentiated in those days, or, much more fun, that Gibbons went off on a break and told an apprentice to "carve the left foot exactly like the right".

Central crossing

At the **central crossing** underneath the tower, stand on the lozenge-shaped stone and look upwards. You are now directly below the central boss hundreds of feet above you. To give an idea of scale, consider that the central boss is the same size as the flagstone you're standing on, and that the tower windows, foreshortened high above you, are in fact the same size as the massive lancets of the Five Sisters Window in the north transept (see opposite).

South transept and tower

The **south transept** is dominated by the rose window above the cathedral entrance, installed to celebrate the wedding of Henry VII and Elizabeth of York, which finally ended the Wars of the Roses. From here you can climb to the top of the **central tower** – for which there is an extra charge – if you've got the lungs for it and suffer neither from claustrophobia or vertigo. The views from the top are spectacular.

Undercroft

In the Minster foundations is the **undercroft**, a museum with an excellent exposition of the history of the building as told by the different bits of the foundations that remain. Many of these were discovered when, in 1967, the tower was in danger of collapse. Massive engineering work was carried out to underpin the foundations (you can see the huge concrete blocks, studded with massive bolts, everywhere), and the foundations of the Norman cathedral, and before that the Roman principia, or fortress, that once stood on the site. They even found a Roman culvert along which water was still flowing to empty into the Ouse. A new, interactive gallery, **Revealing York Minster** has utilized space uncovered during emergency excavations in the 1970s to explore the history of the cathedral's subterranean underpinning, from the Roman barracks which predated the Minster to its Norman foundations.

Treasury and crypts

Beyond the undercroft is the **treasury**, full of ceremonial gold, silver and pewter objects. The most famous is the Horn of Ulf, a carved elephant tusk that belonged to a Viking nobleman. Finally you come to the **crypts**, with their many sarcophagi (including one that holds the remains of St William of York), and the Doomstone of the Norman cathedral, carved to depict lost souls being herded into hell by demons.

Treasurer's House

Minster Yard • March–Oct Sat–Thurs 11am–4.30pm; Nov–Feb Sat–Thurs 11am–3pm • £6.36; family £15.90; NT • ☎ 01904 624247,
ⓦ nationaltrust.org.uk/treasurers-house-york

Just behind York Minster (take the footpath past the Great West Door across Dean's Park) is the National Trust-run **Treasurer's House**, a fine seventeenth-century mansion. Much restored by its owner from 1897, industrial magnate Frank Green, and organized into period rooms to display his various art and antique collections, it tells far more about the late Victorian and Edwardian taste of the house's reconstruction than of its Jacobean origins. That said, its opulence makes for a diverting visit, as does the famous story of the ghost of Roman legionaries marching through its basement, and anecdotes about Green's increasingly eccentric and obsessive tidiness – creeping down to the kitchen at the dead of night to check that cutlery was laid out in rows, insisting that the renovation workmen wear slippers, having glass fronts fitted to cupboards so that he could check the organization of their contents. There's a small shop and a licensed tearoom, and it's remarkably child-friendly.

Richard III Museum

Monk Bar, Goodramgate • Daily: April–June, Sept & Oct 10am–5pm; July & Aug 10am–8pm; Nov–March 10am–4pm • £3.50, joint ticket with Henry VII Experience (see p.154) £5, "pastport" to all five Jorvik group attractions £17.50; family tickets available • ☎ 01904 615505,
ⓦ richardiiiexperience.com

Monk Bar, east of the Minster and the tallest of York's medieval gatehouses, contains the imaginative **Richard III Museum**, run by the Jorvik group. The approach, in

---

YORK GHOST TOURS

No doubt because of its venerable history, York has given birth to a lot of "horrible histories"-type stories of torture and murder, with the consequent tales of unquiet spirits that rise up at the dead of night. You can either enjoy a fixed-site dollop of gore and horror at the York Dungeon (see p.152), or join one of the **ghost tours** of the city centre. You don't need to book, and they can be fun, depending on your willingness to suspend disbelief and the narrative powers of your guide, most of whom are Equity card-holders. Pick up leaflets from the tourist office (see p.157), or choose one of the following:

Ghost Creeper ☎ 07947 325239, ⓦ ghostdetective .com. Starts outside the Jorvik Viking Centre at 7.30pm. No booking required. £5. Nov–June Fri–Sun, July–Oct daily.

Ghost Hunt of York ☎ 01904 608700, ⓦ ghosthunt .co.uk. Starts at the bottom of the Shambles at 7.30pm. No booking required. £5. All year.

Ghost Trail of York ☎ 01904 633276, ⓦ ghosttrail .co.uk. Starts at the Minster's west door at 7.30pm. No booking required. £4. All year.

The Original Ghost Walk of York ☎ 01759 373090, ⓦ theoriginalghostwalkofyork.co.uk. Starts outside the *King's Arms*, near the Ouse Bridge at 8pm. No booking required. £5. All year.

common with the other Jorvik attractions, is wonderfully unstuffy and populist. King for just two years (1483–85), and defeated in the Battle of Bosworth by Henry Tudor, Richard is an intriguing figure: there has been much debate as to whether he was actually the malformed fiend who murdered his own nephews – the Princes in the Tower – depicted by Shakespeare, or whether this is all propaganda designed to please the Tudor dynasty that succeeded him. He continues to cause controversy to this day – the 2013 discovery of his skeleton underneath a Leicester car park has provoked a squabble between the rival claims of that city and York as to where his last resting place should be. The museum offers multimedia presentations and displays illustrating his life, reign and death.

York Art Gallery

Exhibition Square • Daily 10am–5pm • Free • ☎ 01904 687687, ⓦ yorkartgallery.org.uk

York Art Gallery houses an extensive collection of early Italian, British and northern European paintings. The gallery puts on a year-round series of special exhibitions and events, and is noted for its collections of British studio pottery and twentieth-century British painters. It was closed for redevelopment at the time of writing, but should be open by the time you read this; hours and admission charges are likely to remain the same.

Yorkshire Museum and Gardens

Museum St • Daily 10am–5pm • £7.50 • ☎ 01904 687687, ⓦ yorkshiremuseum.org.uk

The **Yorkshire Museum**, housed in a majestic Grade I listed building, has plenty of appeal. Galleries include "History of York", a multiscreen, audiovisual display; "Extinct", which covers dinosaurs and more recently extinct creatures; "Meet the People of the Empire" (Roman York); "Capital of the North" (York's medieval history); and "Enquiry", exploring how archeology and science can uncover the past. Highlights include Iron Age gold torcs, the fifteenth-century gold and sapphire pendant known as the Middleham Jewel, the ornate Anglo-Saxon Ormside Bowl, two stuffed Great Auks (now extinct) and the fossil of a giant ichthyosaur.

The **Museum Gardens** slope attractively westwards down towards the River Ouse. Here you'll find the neat **Victorian gatehouse** and the **Multangular Tower**, which is, along with the attached section of wall, the only surviving part of Roman Erboracum – the fortress. The garden also contains the ruins of Benedictine St Mary's, established shortly after William the Conqueror's harrying of the north, and dissolved by Henry VIII, and the oldest working observatory in Yorkshire, built in 1832–33 (Thurs & Sat 11.30am–2.30pm).

Barley Hall

Coffee Yard (off Stonegate and Swinegate) • Daily: April–Oct 10am–5pm; Nov–March 10am –4pm • £5.50; joint ticket with Jorvik (see p.151) £14, with Dig (see p.150) £10; "pasport" to all five Jorvik group attractions (see p.151) £17.50; family tickets available • ☎ 01904 615505, ⓦ barleyhall.co.uk

Medieval townhouse **Barley Hall** (off Stonegate, down an alley near a little carved red devil), one of several innovative historical attractions managed by the Jorvik group, offers a real taste of the Middle Ages. Only the floor tiles and some timbers are original, the rest is reconstruction and replica, but it's accurate and doesn't confine itself to the building itself – you'll also get insights into all sorts of aspects of medieval life from food preparation, drink and sanitation to burial practices, heating and lighting, and more than you probably ever wanted to know about illness, disease and hospitals. Barley Hall is delightfully unstuffy – you can sit on the chairs, handle the objects and take as many photographs as you like.

The Shambles and around

Radiating from **King's Square** are many of the picturesque streets and lanes for which York is renowned. Most famous among them is the **Shambles**, once a street of butchers, now narrow, pretty and photogenic, the old timber-framed buildings leaning towards each other above a cobbled passage. Running parallel to the west of the Shambles is **Newgate Market**, a little street market that the residents of Barnsley or Leeds would scoff at, but nice enough. Just beyond it, in St Sampson's Square, the **Roman Bath** pub has a small museum in the basement, designed around the remains of the legionary bathhouse that stood just inside the Roman fortress (daily 11am–4pm; £2.50).

York's Chocolate Story

King's Square • Daily 10am–6.30pm (last tour 5pm) • £9.95; family £29.50 • ☎ 0845 498 9411, ⓦ yorkschocolatestory.com

Caravanners and campers can't help but notice something about the city of York. Its Caravan Club site is called Rowntree Park, and it's on Terry Avenue. And as anybody brought up in Britain will know, Rowntree and Terry's were two of the country's major producers of chocolate. To celebrate this aspect of the city's history, take a guided tour of **York's Chocolate Story**. The **Story Zone** describes the development of chocolate from the rainforests of Central America to eighteenth-century York and the great Quaker families (not only Rowntree and Terry, but also the Tukes and the Cravens) who adopted the manufacture and sale of chocolate. The **Factory Zone** outlines the production methods, and introduces a host of famous brands while also allowing you to create your own chocolate bar to eat or take home. The third area – the **Indulgence Zone** – lives up to its name with its variety of chocolate sweets and drinks. It can get a bit hectic during high season, but if you want to know about chocolate and you like eating it, it's worth the effort.

Dig

St Saviourgate • Daily 10am–5pm, last admission 4pm • £6; joint ticket with Jorvik (see opposite) £14.45, with Barley Hall (see p.149) £10; "pastport" for all five Jorvik attractions £17.50; family tickets available; pre-booking advised • ☎ 01904 615505, ⓦ digyork.co.uk

In the church of St Saviour is one of the most remarkable attractions in York – indeed, anywhere in the country. Run by the Jorvik group, **Dig** starts where other museums leave off: most are designed to display historical artefacts, this one shows you how the artefacts are discovered, and how we learn about the past from them. But it's not just what it does that is different – it's how it does it. When you get to the museum, you join a **tour** run by young and enthusiastic experts. An initial session in the "briefing hut" allows your guide to get a feel for the interests and level of knowledge of the group – you may be asked probing questions or, for example, to put pottery shards into chronological order. Then you grab your trowels, head for the four excavation pits – Roman, Viking, Medieval and Victorian – and start digging. As you reveal bones, masonry, pottery or other artefacts, your guide will ask you questions – what sort of bones are they? Is this the inside or outside of the house? What did these people eat? You might then have a go at sorting finds – just as real archeologists do – into bone, antlers, metal, glass and so on. At the end of the formal tour (it lasts about 45 minutes), you can then use a bank of computers to do more research, or investigate the working methods of archeologists in three areas – the "study zone" deals with historical research, such as using documentary evidence to supplement the archeological finds, "lab works" covers the scientific perspective, while "in the field" takes you through the practicalities of organizing a dig. In each area, your guide is a hologram. Finally, "York Revealed" gives you a holographic and 3D cinematic summing-up. The whole experience is an absolute delight – don't miss it.

Merchant Adventurers' Hall

Fossgate (best approached through the Tudor arch off Fossgate, just before the bridge over the Foss) • March–Oct Mon–Thurs
9am–5pm, Fri & Sat 9am–3.30pm, Sun 11am–4pm; Nov–Feb Mon–Thurs 9am–4pm, Fri & Sat 10am–3.30pm • £6 • ☎ 01904 654818,
Ⓦ theyorkcompany.co.uk

The **Merchant Adventurers' Hall** is York's biggest and best-preserved half-timbered
building. Pictures of the Hall don't prepare you for how beset by other more recent
buildings it is, but once you're inside the medieval atmosphere is palpable. The
Merchant Adventurers, investors who risked their capital in overseas trade, were
the premier craft guild in York, and controlled imports and exports, especially of
wool. The hall was built by them in 1362, and consists of three main rooms,
corresponding to the three functions of the guild – business, charity and religion.
The upstairs **Great Hall**, dating from the mid-fourteenth century, has a bowed
wooden floor and ornate open-beamed roof, and was used for meetings of the guild.
On the same floor are three small anterooms leading to the governor's parlour,
where you can see some interesting furniture and silverware. This floor was the
business-end of the building. Below it stands the **undercroft**, with flagged stone
floor, massive wooden posts that support the rest of the building, and a brick
fireplace that faces in several directions. This room was used, right up until 1900,
as a hospice for the poor and infirm, especially members of the guild who were
down on their luck. Finally, off the far end of the undercroft is the **chapel**, which
dates largely from the mid-seventeenth century – look out for the "Prayer of the
Merchant Adventurers" on the right. You can pick up a handset for the excellent
audio-tour as you enter the hall – it's included with entry.

Jorvik Viking Centre

Coppergate Square • Daily: April–Oct 10am–5pm; Nov–March 10am–4pm • £9.95; combined ticket with Dig (see opposite) £14.45,
with Barley Hall (see p.149) £14; "pastport" to all five Jorvik attractions £17.50; family tickets available • ☎ 01904 615505,
Ⓦ jorvik-viking-centre.co.uk

In 1976 the remains of a Viking street were found while clearing the site of an old
confectionery factory to make space for the Coppergate Shopping Centre. The **York
Archaeological Trust** excavated the site, then decided to recreate what they'd found
– the houses, shops, markets and workshops – furnishing them with the figures, sights,
sounds and smells of this part of the Viking city of Jorvik, and open the whole thing to
the public. Predictably, many people sneered at the reconstruction, feeling that it was
simultaneously sexing-up and dumbing-down an important archeological site. The
public didn't agree: since its opening by Prince Charles in April 1984 the **Jorvik Viking
Centre** has become one of the country's biggest attractions.

Honed and updated over several refurbishments to take account of subsequent
research, the latest in 2010, the centre is a superb evocation of life in a York street in
975 AD. As you swoop and swerve across the Viking city in your **time-pod**, listening to
a commentary (choice of languages and age level), you see the sights, hear the sounds
and smell the smells of a thousand years ago. And remember, this isn't some brash
fairground attraction – everything you experience is historically accurate, even the
animatronic people whose bodies (including the faces) are reconstructed from skeletons
and skulls found during the excavation. When your trip is finished, you're free to
explore a vast array of **exhibits** that fill you in on the methodology that lies behind the
reconstruction of the street, and on the forty thousand Viking objects yielded by the
dig. An archeologist will take you through the life of a Viking warrior as reflected in
the many injuries you can see on his skeleton, you can work out if you have any Viking
blood in your veins, be instructed by holographic Vikings, and lots more. If you
combine it with a visit to the Jorvik group's other big attraction, Dig (see opposite),
you'll get a vivid picture not only of what we know about Viking York, but also how we
know it. During school holidays **pre-booking** is advised.

York Dungeon

12 Clifford St • Daily: there are 14 different sets of opening hours, with minor variations on 10am–5pm; check the website • £15.95 • ☎ 01904 632599, ⓦ thedungeons.com

The **York Dungeon** offers a cross between a ghost train and pantomime, in which you pass through a series of tableaux (a medieval inn, a Viking battlefield, a torture chamber and so on), regaled with blood-curdling stories by actors dressed for the part. The special effects are cheesy, the emphasis on pain, gore and horror relentless, but the whole thing is done with humour and tongue-in-cheek gusto by the young actors, who ad lib merrily in response to customer repartee. For an hour's entertainment, though, it's quite pricey – look out for special deals online.

Fairfax House

Castlegate • Mon entry on tours only 11am & 2pm (no booking required), Tues–Sat 10am–5pm, Sun 12.30–4pm; closed Jan • £6 (group, evening and "connoisseurs" tours available at £5, £12 and £25) • ☎ 01904 655543, ⓦ fairfaxhouse.co.uk

Fairfax House is one of the most spectacular Georgian townhouses in the country, and its survival is nothing short of a miracle. Built between 1755 and 1762 by John Carr, it had by the 1920s fallen into disrepair, and it was used first as a dance hall, then as the foyer and toilets of the St George's Hall cinema, opened in 1921 (you can still see the facade). With an interior restored to full splendour in the 1980s, and containing the Noel Terry – he of York's famous chocolate family – collection of Georgian furniture, porcelain and, especially, clocks, Fairfax House is an utter delight, a tour-de-force of English Rococo stucco, classical columns, coved ceilings, palms and swags, busts of Newton and Shakespeare and ornate Georgian decoration. Even the presentation – formal, with hushed attendants keeping an eye on you – seems appropriate.

Clifford's Tower

Tower St • Daily: April–Sept 10am–6pm; Oct 10am–5pm; Nov –March 10am–4pm • £4.30; family £11.20; EH • ☎ 01904 646940, ⓦ english-heritage.org.uk

Clifford's Tower, together with the section of wall just south of the Castle Museum and Crown Court buildings, is all that's left of **York Castle**. The castle, built by William the Conqueror during the harrying of the north, started its days as a motte and bailey with a wooden keep. Major events in its chequered history included the burning of the old wooden tower in 1190 AD, when it was being used as a refuge by hundreds of Jews trying to escape anti-Semitic riots in the city, and the execution, ordered by Henry VIII, of Robert Aske, leader of the Catholic "Pilgrimage of Grace" rebellion against the Reformation.

Of a rare quatrefoil (clove-leaf) design, perhaps an experiment to improve sight lines between the top of the keep and the base of the walls, the tower once had two floors with a supporting central column. What you see now is the **shell** of the mid-thirteenth century structure, with subsidence-weakened walls leaning dizzyingly outwards, excellent information boards and a model to explain the tower's history. Standing as it does at the top of 55 steps from the car park, the **views** of the city from the top of the keep are spectacular.

York Castle Museum

Eye of York (south of Clifford's Tower) • Daily 9.30am–5pm • £8.50 • ☎ 01904 687687, ⓦ yorkcastlemuseum.org.uk

Immediately south of Clifford's Tower are three eighteenth-century buildings – the one in the middle built as early as 1705 as a debtors' prison, those on either side by **John Carr** in 1773–77 as a women's prison (on the left as you face them) and Assize Court (on the right). Today the right-hand building is the **Crown Court**, while the other two form the superb **York Castle Museum**.

At the start, you pass a series of period rooms, set up to look as they would in different eras from the seventeenth century to the 1980s. Every item in each is genuine,

DICK TURPIN (1706–39)

The amazing thing about the myth of **Dick Turpin** is how little of it is true. First the legend – he was a dashing and debonair highwayman, a crack shot, who relieved rich travellers of their money and jewellery, rode from London to Yorkshire in less than 24 hours, and when finally caught and convicted, went to his death on the gallows with great devil-may-care dignity.

The truth is somewhat different. An Essex butcher who turned to cattle-rustling, smuggling and robbery with violence in the London area, he operated with a gang that terrorized isolated farmhouses, using torture to discover where their victims had hidden their valuables. He wasn't very good at any of this – at one point he fired at constables who had arrested one of his accomplices and missed, fatally wounding the accomplice – and often had to live rough in Epping Forest until the heat had died down. With his gang dispersed, he turned to highway robbery, and committed several murders. Eventually, when capture seemed a certainty if he stayed in the southeast, he left the capital for Yorkshire. He didn't do it in less than 24 hours (that was another highwayman, John "Swift Nick" Nevison, in the previous century), and he didn't do it under his own name – he took the alias John Palmer. Finally arrested for horse theft, and identified as the notorious southern highwayman Dick Turpin, he was hanged at York racecourse.

It wasn't until a century later that the myth of Dick Turpin, highwayman extraordinaire, started to gain ground, largely as a result of fictionalized accounts of his purported exploits by author William Harrison Ainsworth. One thing is true though. Thuggish low-life that he undoubtedly was, he did go to his death bravely, and with great swagger, putting on a show of nonchalance for the crowd, bowing to spectators as he passed and even paying for five professional mourners to accompany him to the gallows. The condemned cell in which he spent his last night can be seen in the York Castle Museum, and his grave can be tracked down in what was St George's churchyard in Fishergate.

and the attention to detail is remarkable. Older visitors will be thrust down memory lane by the decor, furniture and hundreds of objects in the twentieth-century rooms. Another large room is devoted to Victorian attitudes to birth, marriage and death, followed by a wonderful reconstruction of the sights and sounds of York's Kirkgate during the final years of the nineteenth century, often staffed by people dressed in authentic costume. There are displays, too, of period kitchens – who'd have thought that state-of-the-art equipment from the 1980s could look quite so out-of-date – and on historical attitudes to hygiene, costume through the ages, toys and World War II. There's also a superb re-creation of the fashion, music and news stories of the 1960s.

Finally, the **cells** in the basement of the prison building contain an affecting series of real-life stories, told by video-recordings of actors projected onto cell walls, gleaned from the prison's records. Most notable is the case of celebrity highwayman **Dick Turpin**, executed in 1739 (see box above), but there's a clutch of others including Mary Burgan (reprieved and released because she became pregnant by the jailer in 1710), William Petyt (a debtor who died of his injuries after being beaten by warders, 1741) and Elizabeth Boardingham (the last woman to be executed in Yorkshire by strangulation and being burned at the stake in 1776).

Quilt Museum and Gallery

Peasholme Green • Jan–early Dec Mon–Sat 10am–4pm • £6 • ☎ 01904 613242, ⓦ quiltmuseum.org.uk

To the east of the city centre, housed in one of York's oldest buildings, the **Quilt Museum and Gallery** is well worth a visit. The combination of the slightly esoteric nature of its subject matter, the enthusiasm of its staff and the beauty both of its exhibits and of its setting are a winning combination. Grade I listed St Anthony's Hall, a fifteenth-century guild hall in Peasholme Green, is home to the collection of the 1979-formed Quilters' Guild of the British Isles – not only beautiful quilts from the eighteenth century to the present day, but also the templates, tools and equipment associated with the craft.

National Railway Museum

Leeman Rd • Daily 10am–6pm • Free • ☎ 0844 815 3113, ⓦ nrm.org.uk • You can get to the museum on a road train from Duncombe Place (April–Oct; every 30min 11.15am–4.15pm; £2 each way)

The most groundbreaking innovation of the Industrial Revolution, one that in a matter of decades changed first Britain and then the world forever, was the development of the railway system. The **National Railway Museum**, a little way west of the town centre, tells the story of this development, not only through the display of its hundred locomotives and two hundred items of rolling stock, but also through videos, sound recordings, photographs, posters, paintings, station equipment, timepieces and a hundred other things associated with the history of rail travel.

The heart of the museum lies in the exhibitions of the steam leviathans of the past and their modern equivalents in the **Great Hall** (through the tunnel on the right of the museum shop) and the rolling stock and associated exhibits in the **Station Hall** (straight ahead). Look out for *Mallard*, still the world speed record holder for steam locomotives, the beautiful *Duchess of Hamilton*, which looks as though it has jumped out of an Art Deco poster, the Japanese Bullet Train (the only one outside Japan), the assorted Royal trains, including Queen Victoria's carriage, and the great turntable. Don't miss either the **Warehouse**, with its huge collection of railway memorabilia, the **Works**, where you can see restoration in progress, or the **South Yard** with its miniature railway, play and picnic areas. There's also a range of talks, activities, demonstrations and events put on each day, plus an excellent shop, a restaurant (in the Station Hall) and a café (in the Great Hall). Entrance to the museum, and even the handy map, are free. It's a truly wonderful day out, even if you're not a railway nerd.

Henry VII Experience

Micklegate • Daily: April–Oct 10am–4pm; Nov –March 10am–3pm • £3.50; joint ticket with Richard III Museum (see p.148) £5; "pastport" to all five Jorvik attractions £17.50; family tickets available • ☎ 01904 615505, ⓦ richardiiiexperience.com

The **Henry VII Experience**, in Micklegate Bar, is run by the Jorvik goup. It concentrates on Richard III's nemesis, Henry – his early life, what it was like to live in York during his reign and, in conjunction with Terry Deary, some of the "Horrible Histories" aspects of Tudor England. There are lots of information boards for the adults, and *Horrible Histories* screenings, board games, dressing-up opportunities and colouring-in activities for kids.

Bar Convent

17 Blossom St • Tours Mon–Fri 10am–3.30pm • Free • ☎ 01904 643238, ⓦ bar-convent.org.uk

Just outside Micklegate stands the **Bar Convent**, the oldest still-functioning convent in England. Housed in a Grade I listed building, it was established in 1686 by the followers of Mary Ward (1585–1645), the founder of the Institute of the Blessed Virgin Mary (now called the Congregation of Jesus). The **museum**, on two floors of the convent, tells the story of Mary Ward and the dark days (for Roman Catholics) between the English Reformation under Henry VIII and the repeal of the penal laws in 1777 – a sorry tale of secret worship (there's an altar disguised as a bedstead), heroism and martyrdom. An affecting display deals with Margaret Clitherow (there's a shrine in her memory in the house she lived in on the Shambles), and also on local man Guy Fawkes. Upstairs displays cover the Roman Catholic religion and the convent's history as a school. An introductory video, narrated by York native Dame Judi Dench, covers the history of the convent and the collections in the museum. While you're visiting the museum, you can also admire the beautifully tiled Victorian entrance hall and the chapel. You can even stay the night.

CLOCKWISE FROM TOP LEFT JORVIK VIKING CENTRE, YORK (P.151); TURKISH BATHS, HARROGATE (P.164); BETTYS, YORK (P.158) >

Cold War Bunker

Monument Close • April–Oct Fri–Sun 10am–6pm; Nov–March Sun 10am–4pm; visits by tour only, every 30min, last tour 1hr before closing • £6.60; EH • ☎ 01904 646940, ⊛ english-heritage.org.uk

The **Cold War Bunker**, about a mile west of the city centre, is one of 29 command centres that were set up across the country in case of nuclear attack. This one was in commission from 1961 (the year before the Cuban Missile crisis) until the signing of the East–West non-aggression treaty in 1991. The bunker was designed to house a sixty-strong No. 20 Group, Royal Observer Corps, working in three shifts to monitor nuclear explosions in the region and the resulting fallout.

Tours lead you to the operations room, with all the original communications equipment, decontamination rooms (with air filters and sewage ejection systems), officers' room, telephone exchange and dormitories. There's a ten-minute film about the policy of overwhelming nuclear response to attack (appropriately called Mutual Assured Destruction, or MAD) – bear in mind as you go around that if the bunker had ever been used for its purpose, most of the country's population would have been dead. Chilling for those who remember the Cold War, almost incomprehensible for those who don't.

Yorkshire Air Museum

Elvington, about 5 miles southeast of the city centre • Daily: April–Oct 10am–5pm; Nov–March 10am–4pm • £8; family £22 • ☎ 01904 608595, ⊛ yorkshireairmuseum.co.uk • By car, it's clearly signposted off York's southern bypass; by bus, take #195 from Merchantgate

For anybody interested in the war in the air, or in aircraft generally, the **Yorkshire Air Museum** is a must. It occupies **RAF Elvington**, a World War II bomber station, and its control tower, hangars, Nissen huts, ops room, radio operators' room, airman's billet and NAAFI provide an evocative context for the forty-plus aircraft and mass of equipment such as gun turrets, searchlights and bombs. A series of displays outline the role of Bomber Command during the war. Uniforms, military vehicles including jeeps and ambulances are also on show, plus accounts of the pioneers of aviation and of associated units, such as the Red Berets, the United States Army Air Force and the Royal Observer Corps. As regards the stars of the show – the aircraft – as well as the Spitfire, Hurricane, Messerschmit, Halifax, Wellington and Lancaster, there's also a good selection of less-known World War II planes like the Mosquito and the Dakota, prewar planes that look as if they're made of string and sealing wax, and postwar planes – the Victor, the English Electric Lightning, the Javelin, the Meteor and the Harrier. The links with Allied countries such as the US, the Commonwealth countries and Poland are evident, but the strongest connection was with the French – their only two heavy bomber squadrons operated from the airfield, and it was the only base operated by French personnel. A Mirage jet, donated by the President of France, is the only one of its kind in Britain, and in the nearby village is a French war memorial.

Yorkshire Museum of Farming

Murton Lane, about 5 miles northeast of the city centre • April–Oct daily 10am–5pm • £6; family £16 • ☎ 01904 489966, ⊛ murtonpark .co.uk • Bus #10 from Merchantgate

Clearly signposted off York's southern bypass, the **Yorkshire Museum of Farming** in Murton Park is one of the many British museums that have evolved from the activities of enthusiasts, in this case the Farm Machinery Preservation Society. What's particularly useful is its blend of theory, explanation and hands-on practicality. There's an excellent display on the farming year, and the Livestock Gallery introduces the tools and equipment used by farmers raising sheep, cows, pigs and horses. There's also a small display of personal gear belonging to celebrity vet and author James Herriot, who practiced in Yorkshire. The highlight of any visit to the museum, though, is its livestock, with many rare or historical breeds of goats, pigs, sheep, poultry and ponies.

ARRIVAL AND DEPARTURE

By car York lies around 15 miles east of the A1, the main north–south route on the eastern side of the Pennines; the connecting road (the A64) is a fast dual carriageway that becomes the southern part of the York ring road. The city has numerous well-signposted car parks, and (a very sensible alternative) comprehensive Park-and-Ride facilities.

By train The station is on the western edge of the city centre, just outside the walls – a 10min walk to the centre, if that.

Destinations Harrogate (hourly; 32min); Leeds (every 10–20min; 23min); London (every 30min; 1hr 55min–2hr 22min); Northallerton (every 30min; 20min); Scarborough (hourly; 49min).

YORK

By bus There is no central bus station in York: most routes start at the train station, Exhibition Square and Piccadilly. York is served by East Yorkshire (☎ 01482 222222) for Hull, Beverley and Bridlington, Yorkshire Coastliner (☎ 01653 692556) for Leeds, Castle Howard, Pickering, Scarborough and Whitby, and National Express (☎ 0871 781 8178) for London.

Destinations Bridlington (every 10–40min; 1hr 53min); Hull (every 2hr; 1hr 40min); Harrogate (every 2hr; 54min); London (3 daily; 5hr 20min); Pickering (hourly; 1hr 10min); Scarborough (hourly; 1hr 22min); Whitby (every 1hr 30min–2hr 30min; 2hr 20min).

GETTING AROUND

On foot The city centre (broadly, the part of the city enclosed by the medieval walls) is easily walkable.

By bicycle Get Cycling, 22 Hospital Fields Rd (Mon–Fri 8.30am–6.30pm, Sat 8.30am–6pm, Sun 10am–4pm; ☎ 01904 636812, ⓦ getcycling.org.uk) rents out town bikes at £10/4hr, £15/day.

By taxi There are several taxi ranks, including at Rougier St, Duncombe Place, Exhibition Square and the train station; or call Station Taxis (☎ 01904 623332).

By road train A regular road train links the National Railway Museum with the city centre (see p.154).

INFORMATION AND TOURS

Tourist office 1 Museum St (July & Aug Mon–Sat 9am–5.30pm, Sun 10am–4pm; Sept–June Mon–Sat 9am–5pm, Sun 10am–4pm; ☎ 01904 550099, ⓦ visityork .org). There's a small but useful tourist information point in the train station, too.

York Pass A York Pass, covering more than thirty attractions in York and the surrounding area (one day £36, two days £48, three days £58; ⓦ yorkpass.com), can be a good

investment – it's available from the tourist office, and includes numerous discount vouchers for dining, evening entertainment, activities and shopping.

Bus tours Numerous open-topped bus tours start in Exhibition Square (£12; family £25; ⓦ yorkbus.co.uk).

Boat tours Boat tours provide a nice way to see the city from the River Ouse (April–Oct daily from Kings Staith and Lendel Bridge; £7.50; family £20; ⓦ yorkboat.co.uk).

ACCOMMODATION

HOTELS AND B&BS

Ashbourne House 139 Fulford Rd ☎ 01904 639912, ⓦ ashbournehouseyork.co.uk. Hotel-standard facilities at guesthouse prices, halfway between the city centre and southern bypass (it's a 20min walk or 5min bus ride into the city). Delicious Yorkshire breakfasts and free off-street parking. £95

★**Bar Convent** 17 Blossom St ☎ 01904 643238, ⓦ bar-convent.org.uk. Here's a unique opportunity to stay in a convent, a grand Georgian building housing a museum and café as well as nine inexpensive single rooms, three twins, two doubles and a family room, along with a self-catering kitchen and guest lounge. Some rooms have shared bathroom facilities. Pay-and-display parking over the road. Continental breakfast included. £80

Best Western Plus Dean Court Duncombe Place ☎ 01904 625082, ⓦ deancourt-york.co.uk. A stylish, medium-sized hotel slap-bang in the middle of the city and around the corner from the Minster. There's a nice bar/café-bistro (mains £8.75–14.50) and attractive restaurant offering Modern European cuisine (mains £18.50–22.50).

Don't be put off by the clunky website. Bar Mon–Sat 9am–10pm (last food order 9pm), Sun 10am–7pm. £180

Bowman's 33 Grosvenor Terrace ☎ 01904 622204, ⓦ bowmansguesthouse.co.uk. Six spotless rooms in friendly renovated Victorian terrace B&B off Bootham, within easy reach of city centre. They provide a permit for free on-street parking. £40

★**Cedar Court Grand Hotel** Station Rise ☎ 01904 380038, ⓦ cedarcourtgrand.co.uk. York's only five-star hotel, 10min walk from the train station, is housed in what was the 1906 headquarters of the North Eastern Railway. It has bags of character, wonderful views of the walls and the Minster, luxuriously unique rooms, a fine dining restaurant and a relaxing bar. Pricey, but look out for special deals online. £300

Churchill Hotel 65 Bootham ☎ 01904 644456, ⓦ churchillhotel.com. Housed in an early nineteenth-century mansion within walking distance of the city centre, the *Churchill* is historic on the outside, smart and contemporary within. There's a piano bar and upmarket restaurant

3

looking out through tall windows on the front garden. Free parking for all guests. **£119**

Hedley House Hotel 3 Bootham Terrace ☎01904 637404, ⊛headleyhouse.com. Friendly, comfortable small hotel 10min walk from the train station. It's best in summer – there's an outdoor area with sauna/aqua spa on a garden deck – but rooms can be chilly in the winter, especially in the (separate) annexe. Free car parking on first come, first served basis. **£108**

Hotel du Vin 89 The Mount ☎01904 557350, ⊛hotel duvin.com. One of the slick boutique-hotel-and-bistro chain, close to the centre of town. The style is as classy as you'd expect, and there's alfresco dining in the courtyard. Wide selection of malt whiskies. Limited parking. Breakfast not included. **£129**

Judges Lodgings 9 Lendal ☎01904 638733, ⊛judges lodgings.com. Beautifully renovated Grade I listed building in the centre of York, which housed Assize Court Judges for more than a century and a half. Luxurious accommodation, attentive but discreet staff, and a bar in the basement. There is some pay parking, which you need to book. **£110**

Middlethorpe Hall Bishopsthorpe Rd ☎01904 641241, ⊛middlethorpe.com. A grand eighteenth-century mansion next to the racecourse. Antiques, wood-panelling, superb rooms (some set in a private courtyard), gardens, parkland, a pool and spa, and fine dining in the formal restaurant. **£140**

Mount Royale The Mount ☎01904 628856, ⊛mount royale.co.uk. Lots of antiques, super garden suites (and cheaper rooms) and a heated outdoor pool in summer. There's also a hot tub, sauna and steam room, and a well-regarded restaurant. **£135**

HOSTELS

★**The Fort** Little Stonegate ☎01904 639573, ⊛thefortyork.co.uk. A "boutique hostel" offering rooms/dorms of from two to eight beds – individually decorated on themes such as log cabin or deep sea creatures – in the city centre at a knockdown price. In the words of the owner, "luxury, funky and easy on the pocket". Dorms **£36**; en-suite doubles **£85**

Safestay Micklegate House, 88–90 Micklegate ☎01904 627720, ⊛acehotelyork.co.uk. Handsome 1752 building in the centre of the city, with many impressive features – stone-flagged entrance hall, wide staircase, panelled rooms, vaulted cellar and ornate plaster ceilings. All are en suite, and rates include continental breakfast. Dorms **£16**; doubles **£80**

YHA York Water End, Clifton ☎0845 371 9051, ⊛yha.org .uk/hostel/york. Large Victorian mansion, a 20min walk from centre. Mainly dorms, with some private rooms that need to be booked well in advance. There's also a licensed café, large garden, parking and discounted tickets for attractions. Buffet breakfast included in rates. Dorms **£21**; doubles **£59**

CAMPSITE

★**Rowntree Park Caravan Club Site** Terry Ave ☎01904 658997, ⊛caravanclub.co.uk. A wonderful site, the best located in the city, 10min walk from the centre, with a back gate that opens onto a street of takeaways, pubs and shops. Open to nonmembers. It's mainly for caravans and motorhomes, but with a small tent enclosure – anyone with a tent must arrive on foot. Advance booking essential, especially at weekends. Two adults plus pitch **£23.20**

EATING AND DRINKING

There are plenty of **restaurants** and cafés to suit all tastes in the city centre. As for **pubs**, for a major eighteenth-century coaching town, the number of good options is disappointing: a lot of the old coaching inns have been demolished.

TEAROOMS, CAFÉS AND RESTAURANTS

Asia Gourmet 61 Gillygate ☎01904 622728. Small, cheerful restaurant in the city centre with prompt service. Mainly Japanese food (sushi is a speciality) though other Asian cuisines are available. Sushi £2.20–5.80. Tues & Sun 5–10pm, Wed–Sat 5.30–10pm.

Ate o Clock 13a High Ousegate ☎01904 644080, ⊛ateoclock.co.uk. Dreadful name, but excellent lunches (largely sandwiches, burgers, omelettes and steaks) and dinners, which they describe as being Mediterranean with a twist of Scouse (though it's tricky to see the Scouse influence in risotto of blue crab with lemon syrup and pea shoots or breast of Gressingham Duck with walnut potato cake and beetroot tart). Good food, attentive service and relaxed atmosphere. Two-course lunch £9.50, main dishes £14.25–20.50. Mon 5.30–9pm, Tues–Fri noon–2pm & 6–9.30pm, Sat 5.30–9.30pm.

★**Bettys** 6–8 St Helen's Square ☎01904 659142, ⊛bettys.co.uk. Famous across Yorkshire, *Bettys* now has branches in Harrogate, Ilkley, Northallerton and Harlow Carr as well as two in York. This is the original, serving tea, coffee, cakes and pastries like mother used to make (or not) – try the pikelets or the Yorkshire fat rascals – plus hot dishes and puddings to die for, in elegant Art Deco surroundings. You can't book, and the queue sometimes snakes around the block, so try to visit off-peak. And visit the basement where there's a mirror with the signatures of the hundreds of Allied airmen – mainly Canadians – who used *Bettys* as an unofficial mess during World War II. English breakfast £11.25; afternoon tea from £9.25. Daily 9am–9pm.

Café Concerto 21 High Petergate ☎01904 610478, ⊛cafeconcerto.biz. Independent bistro with sheet-music-papered-walls, waiting staff in robust aprons and a Belle Epoque feel. Facing the Minster, with papers to browse and a busy relaxed atmosphere. Mains (roast butternut squash lasagne, say, or a Concerto cottage pie) £12.95–16.95, with breakfasts and coffee on offer too. Daily 8.30am–10pm.

★**Café No. 8** 8 Gillygate ☎01904 653074, ⓦcafeno8 .co.uk. A short, well-selected menu using excellent locally sourced produce (Masham sausages and beer, Yorkshire beef and lamb, Ryedale ice cream) in unpretentious surroundings. Mains around £10 during the day, £14–17 in the evening; or £16.50 for two courses midweek. The heated garden is a popular spot. Mon–Fri noon–10pm, Sat & Sun 10am–10pm.

Evil Eye Lounge 42 Stonegate ☎01904 640002, ⓦevileyelounge.com. Colourful café-bar with Indochinese food – Malaysian, Vietnamese, Thai, Tibetan, Japanese, Indonesian. A relatively cheap night out, with all dishes being £7.90–12 and a huge range of cocktails and beers. Mon–Fri noon–9pm, Sat noon–7pm.

Mason's Bar Bistro 13 Fossgate ☎01904 611919, ⓦmasonsbarbistro.co.uk. An all-day bar/bistro which offers atmosphere and simple breakfast, lunch and dinner menus. The food is good, with generous portions at medium prices – all burgers (from lamb and mint to Portobello mushroom and halloumi) are under £10, light bites £4–8 and main courses (sausage and chips, salmon fishcakes, chicken skewers) £8.95–13.95. Mon–Thurs noon–3pm & 5.30–9pm, Fri noon–3pm & 5.30–9.30pm, Sat noon–9.30pm, Sun noon–7.30pm.

Rustique 28 Castlegate ☎01904 612744, ⓦrustique york.co.uk. French-style bistro serving excellent-value Gallic food and wine. There are a couple of set menus (two courses £13.95, three £15.95); a la carte features all the classics, including steak frites, moules marinieres and confit de canard. Mon–Sat noon–10pm, Sun noon–9pm.

PUBS

Black Swan 23 Peasholme Green ☎01904 679131, ⓦblackswanyork.com. Imposing half-timbered, sixteenth-century pub (York's oldest) across the road from the Quilt Museum. It has wonderful internal detail – flagstones, period staircase, inglenook – and the beer's good. There are jazz and folk nights, too (see ⓦblackswan folkclub.org.uk for details of gigs). Mon–Sat noon–11pm, Sun noon–10.30pm.

Blue Bell 53 Fossgate ☎01904 654904. Built in 1798, the *Blue Bell* is a tiny local whose interior has been given Grade II listing by virtue of its perfect Edwardian decor – oak-panelling, engraved and frosted glass and original fittings. Good real ales, too. Mon–Sat 11am–11pm, Sun noon–10.30pm.

★**Swan** 16 Bishopgate ☎01904 634968. Lovely local, a Tetley Heritage Inn that offers convivial surroundings, well-kept real ales and a really friendly atmosphere. Mon–Wed 4–11pm, Thurs 4–11.30pm, Fri 4pm–midnight, Sat noon–midnight, Sun noon–11pm.

Three-Legged Mare 15 High Petergate ☎01904 638246, ⓦyork-brewery.co.uk. York Brewery's airy outlet for its own quality beer in a converted shop. No kids, no juke box, no video games. It's named after a three-legged gallows – it's there on the pub sign, with a replica in the beer garden. Mon–Sat 11am–midnight, Sun noon–11pm.

NIGHTLIFE AND ENTERTAINMENT

For a city that isn't renowned as a top clubbing or live music centre, York in fact does very well, with a range of relatively intimate venues and some good **clubs** catering for locals, students and tourists.

CLUBS

Club Salvation 3 George Hudson St ☎01904 635144, ⓦclubsalvation.co.uk. A larger club with two rooms, plus a large heated rooftop smoking terrace. Big on hen and birthday parties. Thurs & Sun 10pm–3.30am, Fri & Sat 10pm–4.30am; plus Tues 10pm–4.30am for "Student Night" during term time.

Kuda 12 Clifford St ☎01904 647947, ⓦgalleryclub .co.uk/york. York's main nightclub, with rooms on three floors of a Grade II listed building. There's a South-Pacific-themed Tiki Bar, Mambo VIP Lounge with waitress service, and private booths. Wed, Fri & Sat 10.30pm–4.30am.

LIVE MUSIC

The Basement 13–17 Coney St, below City Screen cinema ☎01904 612940, ⓦthebasementyork.co.uk. An intimate venue with a variety of nights – from music to comedy to arts events. The first Wednesday of every month is Café Scientifique – a free evening of discussion surrounding current issues in science, while Sunday night sees stand-up comedy. Live music events are scattered through the week, along with cabaret, burlesque and club nights. Most nights 8–11pm; comedy club 7–10.30pm.

The Duchess 7 Stonebow House ☎01904 641413, ⓦtheduchessyork.co.uk. A spacious, single-room venue in the centre of town that plays host to bands most nights of the week, varying from the latest in indie to high-end tribute bands. Fridays and Saturdays often have club nights blasting out anything from indie to electro. Doors open 7.30pm; tickets available from venue Mon–Sat 10am–4pm and on show evenings.

Fibbers 3–5 Toft Green ☎01904 620203, ⓦfibbers .co.uk. York's primary live music venue, *Fibbers* regularly puts on bands of both local and national standing in a lively atmosphere along with club nights featuring everything from 1990s pop to rap and indie disco. Club nights 10.30pm–3.30am, gigs doors open at 7.30pm.

THEATRE AND CINEMA

City Screen 13–17 Coney St ☎0871 902 5726, ⓦpicturehouses.co.uk. The city's Picturehouse cinema, with three screens, a riverside café-bar and the *Basement Bar* with regular live music, events and a comedy club. Daily 11am–11pm.

Grand Opera House 4 Cumberland St ☎0844 871 7615, ⓦagtickets.com. An unstuffy diet of musicals, ballet, pop and family entertainment. Box office Mon–Sat 9am–10pm, Sun 10am–8pm.

National Centre for Early Music St Margaret's Church, Walmgate ☎01904 632220, ⓦncem.co.uk. Not just early music, but also folk, world and jazz. Times of events and workshops vary. Check website for times.

Theatre Royal St Leonard's Place ☎01904 623568, ⓦyorktheatreroyal.co.uk. Musicals, mainstream drama and seasonal panto. Box office Mon–Sat 10am–8pm (closes 6pm on non-performance nights).

SHOPPING

York is famous in the North of England for its shops. It has a full range of the usual high-street chains and three main out-of-town shopping centres – **Clifton Moor** (bus #6 from York train station), **Monks Cross** (bus #9 from York train station) and **McArthur Glen** (bus #7 from York train station). But it's for its range of stylish department stores and independent shops that York is best known. Book-lovers should visit the **York National Book Fair**, a two-day antiquarian book fair held every September at the Racecourse (first day noon–7pm, second day 10am–5pm; free shuttle bus from the train station every 20min; ⓦyorkbookfair.com).

Browns Davygate ☎01904 611166, ⓦbrownsyork .co.uk. Classy family-owned department store (one of four in the region) selling a wide range of designer and other goods. Mon–Fri 9am–5.30pm, Sat 9am–6pm, Sun 11am–5pm.

Fenwicks Coppergate Centre ☎01904 643322, ⓦfenwick.co.uk. This high-end department store sells fashion, beauty and homeware products, gifts and so on, with spa and restaurant. Mon–Thurs 9am–5.30pm, Fri & Sat 9am–6pm, Sun 11am–5pm.

Minster Gate Bookshop 8 Minster Gates, off High Petergate ☎01904 621812, ⓦminstergatebooks .co.uk. Five floors of secondhand and antiquarian books, plus prints and maps. Mon–Sat 10am–5.30pm, Sun 11am–5pm.

Mulberry Outlet 23–25 Swinegate ☎01904 611055, ⓦmulberry.com. Top-end bags and clothes, at discounted prices. Mon–Sat 10am–6pm, Sun 11am–5pm.

Porta Dextra 1A High Petergate ☎01904 673673. Contemporary jewellery specialists, with a modern art gallery and shop selling handmade crafts and gifts. Mon–Sat 9.30am–5.30pm, Sun 10.30am–5pm.

Selby Abbey

The Crescent, Selby, 14 miles south of York • Daily 9am–4pm • Free • ☎01757 703123, ⓦ selbyabbey.org.uk

Selby is a workaday sort of place, known in the past largely for shipbuilding and as an inland port. However, it is reputed to have been the birthplace of King Henry I, the son of William the Conqueror, and it appears to have been this connection with the Norman royal family that led to its one undoubted claim to fame – **Selby Abbey**.

Established in 1069 by one Benedict of Auxerre, the monastery of Selby received its charter jointly from William the Conqueror and his wife Matilda. It granted the fledgling monastery generous land holdings, privileges and tax exemptions. Despite structural problems caused by the fact that it was built on just 3ft of sand, Selby Abbey is still a fine church – one of the biggest and best non-cathedrals in the country.

After its foundation, Selby's wealth and power expanded, and the building was extended, despite a great fire in 1340. The relatively favourable terms it enjoyed during the Dissolution – all the monks received pensions – were probably due to the Abbot supporting Henry VIII's divorce from Catherine of Aragon and playing no part in the Pilgrimage of Grace, the great northern rebellion against the religious changes. The monastery church – the Abbey – survived the Dissolution's destruction, and in 1618 became Selby's parish church. Over succeeding centuries much restoration was carried out, only for a disastrous fire to destroy much of the edifice in 1906. Today, the Abbey is worth visiting for its overall beauty and proportion, and for one particularly magnificent survival – the **Jesse Window**, tracing the ancestry of Christ. Created after the fire of 1340, it is a beautiful example of medieval stained glass.

Wetherby

Though it's just inside West Yorkshire, some fourteen miles north of Leeds and a popular dormitory town for that city, **WETHERBY** feels more at one with Knaresborough, Harrogate and Ripon in North Yorkshire. It's pleasant and pretty without having specific attractions – a good place for an hour's stroll, say, or even a possible base for exploring this part of Yorkshire.

Mentioned in the Domesday book, Wetherby grew to prominence as a crossing point on the River Wharfe (especially after 1233 when the ford was replaced by a bridge), a market town and, in the eighteenth century, as a staging post for traffic on the Great North Road. Its prosperity continued into the **Industrial Revolution** – the bridge was twice widened, once in the eighteenth century and again in the nineteenth. Most of the surviving buildings date from this era, as do the pubs, of which there are far more than you'd expect in a settlement of this size.

The **Blue Plaque Trail**, available from the tourist information point in the library (see below), takes you around eighteen sites. Look out for the fine collection of old **coaching inns** along the High Street and its continuation North Street – particularly splendid are the *Angel*, which could once stable a hundred coach horses, and the *Swan and Talbot* (see p.162).

Wetherby bridge

Any exploration of Wetherby has to start with its raison d'etre – the **bridge** across the River Wharfe, which stands at the southern edge of the town, its six arches carrying the road across 50–100yd of fast-flowing water. From the bridge, upriver you can see the **weir** that used to divert water into the town mill – at different times it milled corn, fulled cloth and pressed rape seed. The mill was demolished in the 1960s – its position is marked by a cog wheel and a modern sculpture of two fish – but the weir has been renovated and a salmon leap added. Downriver, next to the bridge, is a small park with a bandstand, car park, seats and picnic tables, all linked by a riverside walk that goes under the final town-side arch of the bridge.

Market Place and around

North of Wetherby's bridge, across the Wharfe River, is the **High Street**, off which, to the left, runs **Market Place** (more of a street than a market place) which climbs up the hill to the imposing 1845 **Town Hall**. There are numerous fine **Georgian** buildings along Market Place, one of the best being Wetherby House. Opposite the Town Hall, parallel with and between Market Place and the High Street, is the **Shambles**, an eleven-bay covered market erected between 1811 and 1824 – the end facing the Town Hall was smartened up in 1911 to celebrate the coronation of George V.

ARRIVAL AND INFORMATION   WETHERBY

By car Wetherby is just off the A1(M), and parking in the town is largely free. The main car park is right at the mini-roundabout by the bridge.

By train The nearest train stations are in Knaresborough (8 miles) and York (14 miles).

By bus The tiny bus station is near the Wetherby Bridge.

Destinations Harrogate (every 5–30min; 25–33min); Leeds (every 30min; 45min); York (hourly; 40min).

Tourist information Wetherby Library (Mon–Fri 9/10am–6/7pm, Sat 9/10am–4pm; ☎01937 582151, ⓦ wetherby.co.uk), at the top end of Market Place where it becomes Westgate.

ACCOMMODATION

Days Inn Junction 46, A1(M), Kirk Deighton, just over a mile from Wetherby centre ☎01937 547557,

ⓦ daysinn.com. A reliable, newish option that is more useful perhaps as a stop-off than for a lengthy stay. **£59**

★**Wood Hall Hotel and Spa** Trip Lane, about 3 miles from Wetherby ☎0845 072 7564, ⒲handpickedhotels .co.uk. Set in peaceful countryside at the end of a long drive, the *Wood Hall Hotel* is on another plane entirely – beautiful old building, luxurious rooms, well-appointed spa, magnificent views, a fine dining restaurant and lots of attention to detail (you can borrow wellies and umbrellas if you fancy a walk). **£140**

EATING AND DRINKING

Wetherby abounds in places to eat, with some **takeaway** options on Market Place and several pubs serving food. If you want to push the boat out try the restaurant at the *Wood Hall Hotel* (see above).

The Gourmet Café 9 The Shambles ☎01937 586031, ⒲thegourmetcafe.co.uk. Attractive coffee shop with a good reputation, serving all-day breakfasts, sandwiches, jacket potatoes and the like. Snacks and sandwiches, including toasties and paninis, are very good value at around £5. Mon–Fri 9am–4pm, Sat 8.30am–4.30pm, Sun 9.30am–3pm.

Swan and Talbot 11 North St ☎01937 582040, ⒲swanandtalbot.com. One of Wetherby's finest historic coaching inns, dating back more than four hundred years. Along with offering no-nonsense and good-value rooms, it also serves large portions of good pub food – fish and chips, steak and ale pie and the

like – with a few fancier options. It can get busy. Mains £9.95–18.95. Food served Mon–Sat noon–9pm, Sun noon–8pm. **£65**

★**Windmill Inn** Main St, Linton ☎01937 582209, ⒲thewindmillinnlinton.co.uk. Just outside Wetherby, the gorgeous *Windmill Inn* in Linton is not only a super pub in a lovely village, but does excellent food. Mains such as Thai chicken curry, harissa chicken and cajun surf 'n' turf go for £8.95–17.95. Mon–Thurs 11am–3pm & 5.30–11pm, Fri & Sat 11am–11pm, Sun noon–10.30pm; food served Mon–Thurs noon–2pm & 5.30–9pm, Fri 11am–2.30pm & 5.30–9pm, Sat noon–9pm.

ENTERTAINMENT

Wetherby's Cinema Crossley St ☎01937 580544, ⒲wetherbyfilmtheatre.co.uk. Originally opened in 1915, this lovely old cinema reopened after closure in the 1990s with a single auditorium, seating 150, and a Wurlitzer organ.

Harrogate and around

HARROGATE folk have a reputation in the rest of Yorkshire for thinking themselves "a cut above", and the town's property prices are certainly among the highest in the north of England. That's not to say it's a snooty place, however: here is a sizeable modern town – eighty thousand people or so – that has successfully reinvented itself as its circumstances have changed. Though it is famous as a spa town, its famous **mineral springs** now account for few of its substantial visitor numbers; that said, the beautiful Victorian **Turkish baths** remain a major draw. Other attractions include its splendid collection of Victorian and Edwardian buildings dating back to its glory days as a spa town, its extensive **gardens**, and the range of exhibitions and conferences it hosts.

Sitting just twenty miles west of York, the centre of Harrogate falls into four main areas, all within walking distance of each other. Immediately west of the train and bus stations, sandwiched between **Station Parade** and **Parliament Street** lie most of the big shops and chain stores, especially in and around the Victoria Shopping Centre – Oxford Street, Cambridge Street, James Street, Albert Street. On the other side of Parliament Street lies the triangular area known as the **Montpellier Quarter**, a fashionable district of boutiques, cafés, restaurants and pubs. Most of the streets here are Montpellier something – Hill, Parade, Street, Road, Gardens, Mews, Walk. At the bottom of the hill, cutting across the north end of the Montpellier Quarter and the main shopping area are **Valley Gardens**, the **Crescent** and **Kings Road**, along which are most of the public buildings – among them the **Royal Pump Rooms**, **Mercer Art Gallery**, **Royal Baths**, Exhibition Hall and International Centre. Finally, along the southern edge of this area, on the other side of York Place and Knaresborough Road, is the **Stray**, a 200-acre stretch of open grassland.

Beyond the town centre lie the **Gardens of the Royal Horticultural Society** and the **Great Yorkshire Showground**, both of which are worth a trip.

Brief history

In the Middle Ages the town consisted of two separate settlements – **High Harrogate** up on the hill, and **Low Harrogate** in a valley about a mile to the west. Although Sir William Slingsby discovered the Tewit Well in 1571, the town was slow to capitalize on its springs: partly because the main landowner, the Duchy of Lancaster, was reluctant for it to become the new Cheltenham or Leamington, but also because they were so scattered. From the late eighteenth century onwards, however, Harrogate capitalized on its iron and sulphur rich waters, attracting growing numbers of wealthy visitors who flocked to the town to take the waters. Many of its public buildings were erected during the first half of the nineteenth century to accommodate and service this well-heeled influx. In 1860 an impressive new town centre was developed on the land between High and Low Harrogate, and the railway was extended into town. Many of Harrogate's palatial Victorian hotels date from this period.

During the twentieth century, as belief in the healing powers of spa waters declined, Harrogate seemed in danger of going into serious decline. However, the occupation of many of its hotels by government departments during World War II offered a hint of things to come, and from the 1960s onwards Harrogate became a player in the corporate conference and exhibition field.

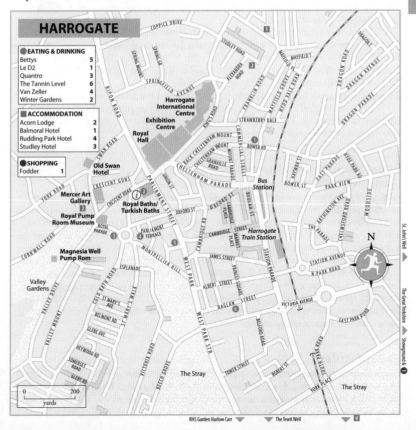

Royal Baths

Crescent Rd

Harrogate's colossal **Royal Baths**, built over two of the town's many mineral springs, opened in 1897 to provide luxurious access to the healing waters. On offer were more than ninety treatments for all sorts of ailments, based on different combinations of the two main types of water – sulphide and iron waters – together with many other trace elements such as barium, potassium, sodium and magnesium. Anyone suffering skin diseases like eczema, psoriasis and acne would take a saline sulphur bath; those who were bunged-up might opt for a nasal douche and water spray; people with colitis and constipation might benefit from the Harrogate intestinal lavage treatment; and rheumatism, lumbago and sciatica could be treated with a variety of peat baths. During the twentieth century, as modern medicine came increasingly to grips with chronic ailments and diseases, faith in water treatments declined, and visitor numbers dropped. By the late 1960s all the facilities, except the **Turkish Baths**, had closed. The building has since been colonized by the tourist office (see p.166), the *Royal Baths Chinese Restaurant*, and the *Winter Gardens* pub around the back – this part of the building was added in the 1920s to allow visitors to relax among the potted palms in any weather, and it's worth a look just to admire the Art Deco interior – a riot of columns and staircases, iron and glass.

Turkish Baths

Entrance on Parliament St • Daily, hours vary, with a complicated timetable of mixed and single-sex sessions (no under-16s); a minimum of 90min is recommended • £13–19; there are various tariffs – standard, off-peak (Tues) and peak (weekends); towels are included • ☎ 01423 556746, ⓦ turkishbathsharrogate.co.uk

The far end of the Royal Baths houses the magnificent and still-functioning **Turkish Baths**. The most complete example of Victorian Turkish baths in the country, they have an elaborate Moorish design complete with Islamic-style arches and screens, lovely glazed brickwork walls and colourful floors and ceilings. You can enjoy the traditional Turkish Bath experience of progressing through the steam room, the plunge pool, the Tepidarium (warm), Calidarium (hot) and Laconium (ferocious), perhaps several times, then cooling off in the Frigidarium, along with more modern facial and body treatments, reflexology, hot stone therapy and massages. For women, there's also waxing, eye and nail treatments and tanning.

Royal Pump Room Museum

Crown Place • Mon–Sat 10.30am–5pm, Sun 2–5pm • £3.95; family £11 • ☎ 01423 556188, ⓦ harrogate.gov.uk

A stone octagon with a dome built in 1842 over the Old Sulphur Well – the original covering building was moved to the Tewit Well (see p.163) – the Royal Pump Room is one of Harrogate's exquisite spa buildings. In its iron-and-glass annexe, added in 1912–13, the **Royal Pump Room Museum** deals largely with the history of Harrogate as a spa town, illustrating the types of treatments that were available, some of which were less than pleasant – the nasal douche, for example. Other aspects of the town's history are also covered – links with the Russian royal family, World War I, costume and jewellery – and there is also a display, reflecting the mid-Victorian fascination with all things Egyptian, of ancient Egyptian artefacts. Up to 2012 you could, if you had the stomach for it, taste the foul-smelling waters, but in that year an EU directive found them unfit for human consumption.

Valley Gardens

Corner of Cornwall Rd, Valley Drive and Royal Parade • Daily 24hr • Free • ⓦ friendsofvalleygardens.co.uk

In a widening wedge southwest of Royal Parade lie the Grade II listed, typically Victorian **Valley Gardens**. Look out for the magnificently domed and colonnaded Art Deco **Sun Pavilion**; the pretty babbling brook dropping down through a series of mini-waterfalls; and, dotted around among lawns and flower beds, a bandstand (concerts May–Aug Sun afternoons), children's boating and paddling pools, tennis courts, crazy golf, pitch-and-putt and a play area. The café occupies the **Magnesia Well Pump Room**, built in 1895 over one of the celebrated springs.

Mercer Art Gallery

31 Swan Rd • Tues–Sat 10am–5pm, Sun 2–5pm • Free • ☎ 01423 556188, ⓦ harrogate.gov.uk

The Assembly Rooms on Swan Road, one of Harrogate's many recycled Victorian buildings, now houses the **Mercer Art Gallery**. The gallery mounts touring exhibitions of paintings, photographs and sculptures – recent shows have included "Art and Yorkshire: From Turner to Hockney" – as well as rotating selections from the town's own two-thousand-strong collection of mainly nineteenth– and twentieth-century works, with paintings from Sir Edward Burne-Jones and Alan Davie among many others.

The Stray

The **Stray**, the great swathe of rough grass on the south side of town, is usually dotted with people walking dogs, flying kites and enjoying other outdoor activities. At the western end of the park you'll find the **Tewit Well**, the quality of whose water was first recognized, and compared with the water of Spa in Belgium, by Sir William Slingsby in the 1570s, and which started the town's long rise as a place for the upper and middle classes to "take the waters". Until 1842 its covered open dome, with twelve Tuscan columns, stood over the Old Sulphur Well. To the east, another of Harrogate's famous springs, **St John's Well**, is marked by a small 1842-built kiosk.

RHS Garden Harlow Carr

Crag Lane, 1.5 miles southwest of Harrogate centre • Daily: March–Oct 9.30am–6pm; Nov–Feb 9.30am–4pm • £7.95; family £23.70 •
☎ 01423 565418, ⓦ rhs.org.uk • Bus #6 or #6A from Harrogate bus station

The delightfully informal **RHS Gardens Harlow Carr** are a pleasure for anybody, but sheer unadulterated heaven for keen gardeners – not only the 58-acre gardens themselves, but also the super-environmentally friendly Learning Centre, the glass Alpine Centre, the separate historical gardens and the shop stuffed with plants, gifts and books related to gardening. And the tearooms are run by *Bettys* (see p.166) – life doesn't get any better.

AGATHA CHRISTIE'S LOST TEN DAYS

Established around 1700 and much rebuilt since then, the handsome **Old Swan Hotel**, which stands at the junction of York Road and Swan Road, was made forever famous by a mysterious interlude when **Agatha Christie** stayed here, anonymously, for ten days in 1926.

On December 3 that year, the popular 36-year-old novelist disappeared from her home in Surrey; her car was found later the same day hanging over the edge of a cliff. For eleven days police, reporters and civilians scoured the country looking for her. Even aircraft were roped into the search. The story was a sensation across the country, and newspaper coverage put even the celebrity obsession of the modern tabloid press in the shade.

Then, on December 14 Christie was found in Harrogate safe and well, apparently enjoying the social whirl of the town. She had signed in to the *Old Swan* as Theresa Neele, the name of her husband's mistress, and was finally recognized by the banjo player in the hotel band. It emerged that she had travelled to London, then Harrogate, by train. A number of possible explanations for her extraordinary behaviour have since been put forward – perhaps it was the result of amnesia caused by the crashing of her car, or depression brought on by her mother's recent death and her husband's infidelity. Many at the time suspected that it was a publicity stunt. Agatha Christie herself never offered an explanation, though the fact that she divorced her husband two years later may be significant.

ARRIVAL AND INFORMATION

HARROGATE

By car Sitting astride the A61, 14 miles north of Leeds and nearly 7 miles from the A1(M), Harrogate is reasonably accessible by road and, being so spread out, there's plenty of on-street and off-street parking.

By train The train station is on the eastern edge of the town centre on Station Parade.

Destinations Leeds (every 30min; 38min); York (hourly; 40min).

By bus The bus station is a little way north of the train station.

Destinations Leeds (every 15min; 40min); Ripon (every 15min; 32min); Wetherby (every 10–20min; 20–30min).

Tourist office Royal Baths building, facing onto Crescent Gardens (April–Oct Mon–Sat 9am–5.30pm, Sun 10am–1pm; Nov–March Mon–Sat 9.30am–5pm; ☎01423 537300, ⊛enjoyharrogate.com).

ACCOMMODATION

Because of its history as a popular spa town, and its modern incarnation as a conference and exhibition venue, Harrogate has a huge range of hotels and B&Bs. Some of the great early hotels are perhaps past their prime, waiting patiently for refurbishment. There are also plenty of modern chain hotels.

★**Acorn Lodge** Studley Rd ☎01423 525630, ⊛acornlodgeharrogate.co.uk. A guesthouse with big-hotel ideas (luxury fittings, individual decor, Jacuzzi, massage available in room) but B&B tariffs and friendliness. Well placed for the town centre (5min). **£89**

Balmoral Hotel Franklin Mount ☎01423 508208, ⊛balmoralhotel.co.uk. Upmarket boutique hotel occupying a rather grand terrace of three Edwardian houses. Fixtures and fittings are luxurious, rooms are spacious and individual, staff are pleasant and helpful. **£110**

★**Rudding Park Hotel** Follifoot, 3 miles southeast of Harrogate ☎01423 871350, ⊛ruddingpark.co.uk.

Top-end hotel in Grade I listed building, set in extensive parkland and with its own golf course. The rooms and facilities are luxurious, the service is terrific and the restaurant is immaculate – the whole experience is impossible to fault. The rates make it a special-occasion type of place, but check the website for some excellent offers. **£239**

Studley Hotel Swan Rd ☎01423 560425, ⊛studley hotel.co.uk. Medium-sized independent town-centre hotel with attached Thai restaurant. The attractive rooms vary in size and cost, and service is good, though the restaurant can sometimes get very busy. Rates can be surprisingly good if you shop around online. **£119**

EATING AND DRINKING

In addition to the excellent **hotel restaurants** – *The Orchid* at the *Studley Hotel*, the *Clocktower* at *Rudding Park Hotel* – and the café/restaurant at Fodder in the Great Yorkshire Showground (see opposite), there's a very good selection of eating places in Harrogate.

Bettys 1 Parliament St ☎01423 502746, ⊛bettys.co.uk. A Yorkshire institution with branches in several North Yorkshire towns (they've refused to open any outside the county), *Bettys* has a uniquely old-fashioned air, with exterior wrought-iron canopy, large bowed windows, a light airy room, waiting staff in starched linen and cooking and baking that harks back to more leisured times (though not alas in prices – afternoon tea, served Fri–Sun, will set you back £26.95). Reservations are essential for afternoon tea but aren't taken at other times, so you may have to wait for a table (often for quite a while) – it's worth it. Daily 9am–9pm.

★**Le D2** 7 Bower Rd ☎01423 502700, ⊛led2.co.uk. Quality French-accented and Mediterranean food (from grilled goats' cheese to coq au vin and *vignole*, an Italian veg stew) and excellent service in unpretentious surroundings, at affordable prices – two courses for £12.95 at lunch and £21 in the evening. Tues–Sat noon–2pm, Tues–Thurs 6pm–late, Fri & Sat 5.30pm–late.

Quantro 3 Royal Parade ☎01423 503034, ⊛quantro .co.uk. Highly rated Modern European town-centre restaurant with stylish, if slightly regimented, decor. Dishes

might include confit of duck leg with a mango and kiwi mash, sauteed lamb kidneys with leek and apple risotto or squash and goats cheese pudding with pea tagliatelle. Two/three courses at dinner £14.50/ £16.90, with slightly cheaper lunchtime/early bird options. Mon–Sat noon–2pm & 6–10pm.

The Tannin Level 5 Raglan St ☎01423 560595, ⊛tanninlevel.co.uk. Popular brasserie, smartly under-stated, with a Michelin-trained cook and super, locally sourced food. Try the potato, brie and asparagus gratin or the slow-braised lamb shank with chorizo, tomato and chickpea cassoulet. Early bird two courses £12.95, a la carte mains £14.75–24.95. Mon–Thurs noon–9pm, Fri & Sat noon–9.30pm, Sun noon–8pm.

Van Zeller 8 Montpellier St ☎01423 508762, ⊛vanzellerrestaurants.co.uk. Terrific restaurant in the heart of the fashionable Montpellier district, serving very fine food in cool and classy surroundings. Highlights on the regularly changing menu might include saddleback piglet with gooseberries, cauliflower and spiced aubergine, or salmon with bacon jam, avocado and watercress.

Three-course menu £50; ten-course tasting menu £85 (vegetarian £75). Tues–Sat noon–2pm & 6–10pm.
Winter Gardens Royal Baths, Parliament St ☎ 01423 877010, ⓦ jdwetherspoon.co.uk. For rock-bottom prices, you can't beat *Wetherspoon's* pubs, whose menus will tell you not only how much each meal costs, but also how many calories it contains. The *Wetherspoon* chain is renowned for revitalizing interesting buildings, and the *Winter Gardens* is one of their best – all wrought iron, glass and ornate staircases. Daily 7am–11pm.

SHOPPING

★**Fodder** Great Yorkshire Showground ☎ 01423 541000, ⓦ fodder.co.uk. Championed by the Yorkshire Agricultural Society, Fodder sells more than one hundred top-quality locally sourced products from all over the county – meat, bread, cheese and other dairy, veg, fruit, wine, preserves, pies – in a light, airy, environmentally friendly building. There's a café/restaurant where you can eat fresh, locally sourced food while reading your complementary newspaper (the *Yorkshire Post*, naturally). Mon–Sat 8.30am–6pm, Sun 10am–4pm.

Knaresborough

3

At first sight **KNARESBOROUGH**, just four miles northeast of Harrogate, might seem pleasant but unremarkable – a nice little market town clustered around its L-shaped square, worth perhaps a short stop and an aimless wander. Explore more thoroughly, though, and you'll find that it's one of Yorkshire's prettiest, most interesting towns, perched on an escarpment above a gorge through which the **River Nidd** flows. The views from its castle, either of its two bridges or its railway viaduct are stunning.

The main part of town sits on top of the hill, clustered around the **Market Place** and **castle**. Below the castle, and accessible via steps that zig-zag downwards from it, is the river. The rest of town lies down here, between the High and the Low bridges (it's nothing to do with their height – the first's upriver, the second downriver), with the railway viaduct in between.

Market Place

In the **Market Place**, L-shaped because of the encroachment of the Town Hall, are two reminders of the town's most famous son – John Metcalfe, or **Blind Jack of Knaresborough** (see box, p.168). The first is a statue of the great eighteenth-century road engineer, slouching on one of the square's benches, his measuring wheel beside him, looking for all the world as if he has just stopped for a breather during his incessant pacing of the surrounding countryside. Immediately beyond is **Blind Jack's**, a lively and historic Georgian brick pub named after the engineer – look out for the trompe l'oeil figure of Jack leaning out of an upstairs window.

Knaresborough Castle

Castle Yard • April–Sept 11am–4pm • £3.30; family £9 • ☎ 01423 556188, ⓦ knaresborough.co.uk/castle

Just off Market Place, perched high above the River Nidd, **Knaresborough Castle** stands in ruins; it is well worth visiting, but more for its atmosphere and its splendid views than in its own right. The remains – St John's Tower and a few bits of the curtain wall – became a public park in 1897. The **ruins** are peaceful and atmospheric, in sharp contrast to their history. From the far end of the inner ward (the war memorial end), the upriver **views** of the town – the houses climbing steeply from a bend in the river, the elegant railway viaduct with the parish church behind it, the surrounding woods – are almost too good to be true. Indeed, when there's a train crossing the viaduct, the whole aspect has the miniature perfection of a model railway layout.

Built intermittently over the two hundred years up to 1312, the castle consisted of a keep to the north, where the largest part of the remains, **St John's Tower**, now stands, an outer ward on the town side, and an inner ward along the cliff top towards the west.

3

BLIND JACK OF KNARESBOROUGH

John Metcalfe is one of the great characters of the early Industrial Revolution. Born in Knaresborough in 1717, the son of a horse breeder, he was blinded at the age of 6 by smallpox. He spent his early adult years earning a living by playing the fiddle, dealing in horses and even acting as a guide to visitors. According to his autobiography, which was written towards the end of his long life (and which, perhaps, needs to be taken with a pinch of salt), he certainly didn't let his lack of sight impede his enjoyment of life, learning to swim, play cards, ride and hunt, as well as attending cock fights. Throughout he capitalized on aristocratic contacts he made while playing in Harrogate, often staying on their country estates or in their fashionable London houses. During the Jacobite Rebellion of 1745 he recruited soldiers in the Knaresborough area, accompanied them to Scotland, and was involved in the logistical problems of moving artillery around on the battlefield.

His love life was equally eventful, getting engaged to a local girl when he was in his early 20s, getting another girl pregnant, and clearing off to the Yorkshire coast to keep his head down. When he heard that his original girlfriend was getting married, he rushed back and married her himself, snatching her from under the prospective groom's nose the night before the wedding. In due course they had four children.

So far, then, a picaresque eighteenth-century tale made even more remarkable by his blindness. It is, however, as a **road builder** that Blind Jack made his name. Even before he went to Scotland he'd made a start as a carrier. On his return he started a stone carting business, which grew into a stagecoach company. When the government, in a desperate attempt to improve transport to facilitate the early stirrings of the Industrial Revolution, started to pass Turnpike Acts, devolving road improvements to groups of businessmen who could invest in building a new section of road and then charge for its use, there was a shortage of road engineers. Blind Jack stepped in, surveying and building good-quality roads across the north of England. He became a familiar sight, striding across the moors with his measuring wheel and his two sticks – one for feeling his way, the other for poking into the ground to assess its properties. After retirement he moved in with his daughter and her husband in Spofforth, where he eventually died at the age of 92. His grave is in Spofforth Church.

Historical figures associated with the castle include Hugh de Moreville and his gang, who in the 1170s took refuge in an earlier incarnation of the castle after they'd assassinated Thomas Becket in Canterbury Cathedral, and John of Gaunt, who took possession of the castle in 1372. The castle came to a spectacular end during the English Civil War when the town sided with King Charles; the Roundheads laid siege and took the castle in 1644. Finally, as a result of a general Parliamentary order that Royalist castles should be "slighted" (rendered defensively useless), the castle was demolished in 1648, the coup de grace being delivered by opportunist townsfolk who helped themselves to the masonry.

Courthouse Museum

Located in the castle grounds and housed in what was once the town's courthouse, the **Courthouse Museum** is aimed largely at children. An exhibition explains what life was like for those who lived in the castle, and there are medieval and Civil War costumes to try on, games from the Middle Ages and accounts of food, drink and education at that time. The original Tudor courtroom has survived and contains a tableau and other exhibits about Tudor law and order.

Knaresborough Mill

If you walk down the steps from the castle and look downriver, you will see a double weir swinging the River Nidd around a curve. The eighteenth-century **Knaresborough Mill**, which the weir was built to serve, has at different times pumped water from the river up into the town, worked as a paper mill and been involved in a variety of cloth-making processes – cotton and flax spinning, and, right up to its closure in 1972, weaving flax. The buildings are now residential.

River Nidd

As you walk upriver from Knaresborough Mill along attractive **Waterside**, you will pass several cafés, one of which – *The Marigold Café* – rents out boats (daily 10am–4pm; boats £6/person/hr; ☎01423 869773, ⓦmarigoldcafe.co.uk) To the right of the café are the remains of the **Old Dye House**, built in 1610, where dye was made to supply the local textile factories up to 1840.

Fifty yards or so beyond, after a pleasant riverside terrace, the road passes under the **railway viaduct**. Built by Thomas Grainger of the East and West Yorkshire Junction Railway, it was finally completed in 1851, after an earlier attempt had collapsed. Made up of four arches at a maximum height of nearly 80ft, it is either an eyesore or a fine piece of civil engineering, depending on who you talk to. The view of Knaresborough from the castle would certainly be the poorer if it wasn't there.

Old Manor House and around

Just upriver from the viaduct stands the black-and-white-painted **Old Manor House**, built as a hunting lodge for King John, and believed to be where Oliver Cromwell received the formal surrender of the Royalist forces defeated at Marston Moor, the biggest and most pivotal battle of the English Civil War, held around eight miles west of York on July 2, 1644. You'll see a number of buildings in town decorated in this **black-and-white chequerboard style**. Continuing along Waterside brings you to the **High Bridge**, which is medieval in origin though was extensively repaired in 1773.

Mother Shipton's Cave

Prophecy Lodge, High Bridge • Feb Sat & Sun 10am–4.30pm; March Sat & Sun 10am–5.30pm; April–Oct daily 10am–5.30pm • £6; family £18 • ☎01423 864600, ⓦ mothershiptonscave.com

Set in parkland that stretches along the riverbank from the High Bridge down to the Low Bridge, **Mother Shipton's Cave** claims to be England's oldest purpose-built tourist attraction. The site, which includes an adventure playground, a woodland adventure trail, refreshments and picnic areas, offers views of the viaduct, the weir and the town on the opposite bank, together with walks laid out by Sir Henry Slingsby in 1739. The **cave** itself is said to be where soothsayer Ursula Sontheil (aka Mother Shipton, her married name) was born in 1488. The story of Mother Shipton's ability to predict the future is doubtless hokum, but since her death in 1561 the legend of her uncanny prophecies has grown, carefully tended no doubt by the people for whom it has provided, over the years, a decent living.

Petrifying Well

The park also features a so-called **Petrifying Well** – a spring that deposits minerals on anything immersed in it, petrifying them immediately. As early as the 1720s Daniel Defoe dismissed any claims to its being the only one of its kind in the country, saying that it was "nothing extraordinary" and that he'd come across others in Derbyshire. But the well is certainly great fun, with objects on display such as the headwear placed there in 1853 by a couple on their way to York races, one of Queen Mary's shoes and various objects from celebrities like Agatha Christie (handbag), John Wayne (hat) and numerous cast members of British soaps. And the well, with its curtains of tufa and travertine, has a strange beauty all of its own.

St John the Baptist church and around

Church Lane • Daily dawn to dusk • ☎ 01423 869209, ⓦ knaresboroughanglicanteam.org.uk

One of the first things you'll notice as you enter **St John the Baptist church** is the sixteenth-century octagonal **font**, which has an ornate lid so heavy that it requires a crane to raise and lower it. The **Slingsby Chapel** to the left of the chancel has monuments to many members of the prominent local family. The oldest, dated 1601, features effigies of Francis and Mary Slingsby, strangely thin and awkward-looking, especially Mary. Sir William Slingsby (1638) is commemorated by an upright statue in a niche – leaning on his sword, with his legs nonchalantly crossed, looking as if he's waiting for a bus. Sir Henry Slingsby's effigy is headless – he was executed by Oliver Cromwell in 1658. Sir Charles Slingsby (1869) tragically drowned – the nautical West Window is dedicated to his memory. Note also the two attractive Pre-Raphaelite **stained-glass windows** installed by Morris and Co (William Morris's company) and designed largely by Ford Madox Brown – one at the west end of the south aisle, the other the right-hand one of two on the south side of the chancel.

Having left the church, notice the blue-plaqued cottage across from the main door – it's where, it is claimed, **Blind Jack** (see box, p.168) was born (though some say that his birthplace was demolished).

Chapel of Our Lady of the Crag

Abbey Rd • Open most Suns 2–4pm • Free • ⓦ stmarysknaresborough.org/shrine.html

Just beyond the Low Bridge is the **Chapel of Our Lady of the Crag**, an oratory or wayside shrine built, so the story goes, by a certain John the Mason in 1408 in thanks for his son being saved from falling rocks. It has since been conjectured that it might also have been a bit of masonic showing off, designed to drum up trade for his business. Climbing a flight of steps (which can get very slippery when wet), you come to a small leaded window and tiny doorway, with a knight in armour (added later) hewn out of the rock. The chapel itself, also carved into the rock face, is tiny – 13ft by 8ft – and is decorated with gargoyles. Above the shrine is a rock dwelling called variously the **House in the Rock** or Fort Montague, which was built in the eighteenth century by a local weaver – interesting, but not open to the public.

Spofforth Castle

Four miles south of Knaresborough on the Wetherby Rd • Daily: April–Sept 10am–6pm; Oct–March 10am–4pm • Free; EH • ⓦ english-heritage.org.uk

The village of **Spofforth**, south of Knaresborough, is notable both as the burial place of **Blind Jack**, Yorkshire's most famous road builder (see box, p.168), and for **Spofforth Castle**. The castle, a fortified manor house most of which dates from the fourteenth and fifteenth centuries, once belonged to the powerful Percy family. It's strong on atmosphere, with an undercroft built up against a rock face, but otherwise doesn't offer much of interest.

ARRIVAL AND INFORMATION
KNARESBOROUGH

By car Well signposted from the A1(M) and all other directions, Knaresborough is easy to find by road, but is so close to its larger neighbour Harrogate that you could end up there if you're not careful. There are several pay-and-display car parks, including one in the centre of town and another on the riverside next to the High Bridge.

By train The train station is off Kirkgate, a 2min walk from the Market Square.

Destinations Harrogate (every 30min; 8min); Leeds (every 30min; 47min); York (hourly; 30min).

By bus The bus station is very near the train station.

Destinations Harrogate (every 30min; 20min); Ripon (every 2hr; 50min).

Tourist office 9 Castle Courtyard, between the Market Place and the Castle (April–Oct Mon–Sat 10am–5pm, Sun 10am–1pm; Nov–March Wed & Sat 10am–4pm; ☎ 01423 866886, ⓦ visitharrogate.co.uk).

ACCOMMODATION

Best Western Dower House Hotel Bond End ☎01423 863302, ⓦdowerhouse-hotel.co.uk. Just on the edge of the town centre, a few hundred yards from Mother Shipton's Cave, this is a beautiful Grade II listed building with fourteenth-century origins, though most of what you see today dates back to the seventeenth and eighteenth centuries. Although blessed with great character, friendly and attentive staff, a pool and a spa, some parts of the hotel itself are rather tired and in need of refurbishment. **£112**

EATING AND DRINKING

★**Blind Jack's** 19 Market Place ☎01423 869148. A good spot for a few drinks, *Blind Jack's* is a lovely traditional pub, named after the famous local character (see box, p.168). Daily.

Bonney's in the Courtyard 10 Castle Courtyard ☎01423 869091. Pretty café in a covered, glass-roofed courtyard. Excellent coffee, sandwiches, scones and Italian ice cream. Mon–Sat 8am–6pm, Sun 9.30am–6pm.

Carriages 89 High St ☎01423 867041. Atmospheric little wine bar/bistro with tapas and an a la carte menu. Expect to pay anything from £10 to £30. Tues–Thurs 6–9.15pm, Fri & Sat noon–2.15pm & 6–9.15pm, Sun noon–4pm & 6–9.15pm.

The Mitre 4 Station Rd ☎01423 868948, ⓦwww .themitreinn.co.uk. Mediterranean-style brasserie serving a good range of mains – home-made fishcakes, falafels, fancy macaroni cheese – mostly under £10, with antipasti, meze or a Yorkshire platter to start. Mon–Thurs noon–2.30pm & 6–9pm, Fri noon–2.30pm & 5.30–9pm, Sat noon–9pm, Sun noon–4pm.

Ripley

Three miles north of Harrogate, the attractive model village of **RIPLEY** lies just off the main A61 road to Ripon. It owes much of its interest to its history, inextricably tied up with the prominent local **Ingilby** (sometimes spelt Ingleby) family, who have dominated the village since the early fourteenth century, and have lived in Ripley Castle for seven hundred years. **All Saints Church**, across the road from the castle, is filled with many of their family monuments.

The **village** itself has a remarkable unity, with all the houses constructed in gritstone, with hipped roofs and pointed sash windows. It was rebuilt as a piece between 1820 and 1835 by Sir William Amcotts Ingilby, who, following a European trip decided to remodel the place to resemble the villages he saw and admired so much in Alsace. Look out for the **Ripley Endowed School**, founded in 1707, rebuilt by Sir William in 1830, and still ringing in term time to the shouts and laughter of children, and the **Hotel de Ville** (the name's above the front upstairs bay window), started in 1854 and completed after Ingilby's death in that year by his widow. In the market place you'll find the **Market Cross** (probably seventeenth-century) and the village **stocks**.

Ripley Castle

Ripley • Guided tours only: April–Oct Sat, Sun & school holidays hourly 11am–3pm; term time Mon–Fri 11am, 12.30pm & 2pm; March & Nov Tues, Thurs, Sat & Sun 11am, 12.30pm & 2pm; Dec–Feb Sat & Sun 11am, 12.30pm & 2pm • £10.50; family £24; gardens only £7; family £16.50 • ☎01423 770152, ⓦripleycastle.co.uk

Built seven hundred years ago, **Ripley Castle** is actually a house rather than a castle; the current occupant, Sir Thomas, is the 26th generation of the Ingilby family. During the tour of the house, the oldest part of which is the 1450 gatehouse, you'll hear how the family won its boar's head crest (an Ingilby saved King Edward III from an injured boar), see the well-hidden priest's hole, learn about Ingilby links with most of those involved in the Gunpowder Plot, be told tales about "Trooper" Jane Ingilby who apparently held Oliver Cromwell hostage at gunpoint in the library, and hear all manner of stories about the Ingilbys' service to the kings and queens of England. There's a pleasant tearoom and shop, and the gardens are beautiful.

★ **Boar's Head Hotel** Ripley Castle estate ☎ 01423 771888, ⓦ boarsheadripley.co.uk. Named in honour of the Ingilby family crest, this old coaching house has a quirky layout and attractive decor. It serves a good choice of beers and wine and excellent pub grub (mains around £14) all with fast, friendly service. Rooms are comfortable and individually designed by Lady Ingilby. Food served Mon–Sat noon–2.30pm & 6.30–9pm, Sun noon–8pm. **£100**

Boroughbridge and around

BOROUGHBRIDGE was established in Norman times next to the old Roman settlement at Aldborough after a bridge was built to replace the ford across the River Ure. It later became an important staging post on the Great North Road between London and Edinburgh. Now consisting of three main streets, two squares and the eponymous **bridge** (which shows obvious signs of having had a new, wider surface put, in 1949, on top of a much earlier structure – part Tudor, part Georgian), Boroughbridge is an attractive place, with most of its buildings dating from its Georgian coaching heyday. In **Hall Square** you will find the small **Butter Market Museum** (daily; free), which contains everyday artefacts donated or loaned by residents – a bread oven, a butter churn, railway memorabilia – and an old coaching inn, the *Crown,* which was once able to stable a hundred horses. **St James Square**, meanwhile, features a delightful **Market Well**, put up in 1875 in memory of an Andrew Lawson of Aldborough Manor, and operated by an iron wheel. However, along with the Roman site at nearby **Aldborough**, it is the ancient monoliths known as the **Devil's Arrows** that are the real draw here. Few of the photographs you'll come across give any hint of their scale.

Devil's Arrows

Along Roecliffe Lane, on the way to the A1

The three **Devil's Arrows** represent one of the most astonishing survivals from prehistory you're likely to encounter anywhere. Gritstone monoliths that date from the late New Stone Age or early Bronze Age, they are gigantic – one is 18ft, one 21ft and one 23ft high, and each extends a further 5ft below the ground. It is thought that there may have originally been four or five stones, but their function, if any, is obscure. The name dates from an eighteenth-century legend that the devil was throwing them at local rivals Aldborough, but they fell short.

Aldborough Roman Site and Museum

Aldborough, just off the B6265, about a mile east of Boroughbridge and 15 miles northwest of York • April–Sept Sat & Sun 10am–6pm • £3.60; EH • ☎ 01423 322768, ⓦ english-heritage.org.uk

A pretty village centred on a triangular green and maypole, **Aldborough** was originally a Roman town, probably built to protect a ford where Dere Street crossed the River Ure. The capital of the Romanized tribe the Brigantes – Isurium Brigantum – and home of the Ninth Legion, it settled into obscurity after the Romans left, and especially after it was overshadowed by nearby Boroughbridge in Norman times. Today the **Aldborough Roman Site and Museum** features two superb Roman mosaic pavements, remains of a Roman house and some of the fort's defences. In the museum, look out for a selection of fine Roman pottery, stylii for writing on wax tablets, needles, coins and a piece of brick with a stamp identifying it as the property of the Roman Ninth Legion.

Tourist office 1 Hall Square (March–Oct Mon–Fri 9am–4pm, Sat 10am–4pm; Nov–Feb Mon–Wed 8am–1pm, Thurs & Fri 9am–1pm, Sat 10am–1pm; ☎ 01423 323373, ⓦ boroughbridge.org.uk).

FROM TOP KNARESBOROUGH (P.167); NATIONAL RAILWAY MUSEUM (P.154) >

EATING AND DRINKING

The Dining Room 20 St James Square ☎01423 326426, ⓦthediningroomonline.co.uk. Highly rated restaurant housed in a Grade II listed building in the centre of town, with a stylish formal restaurant on the ground floor, a comfortable bar/lounge upstairs and a terrace for fine-weather eating and drinking. The menu usually has a choice of three or four main courses (two courses £14.95, three courses £18.95) – it's simple food, stylishly cooked. Tues–Sat 7pm onwards (last orders 9.15pm), Sun noon–2pm.

Ripon and around

Technically a city, England's fourth smallest, **RIPON** is in reality an agreeable small market town with a population of around sixteen thousand. From the twelfth century onwards Ripon had an important part to play in England's wool trade, first as a market for raw wool, then for finished cloth. It was also an ecclesiastical centre, based on its cathedral, but after being hard hit by the Reformation, it took advantage of the Tudor fashion for ornately worked spurs and reinvented itself as the spur capital of England. However, the Industrial Revolution largely passed Ripon by, and it became the pleasant little place it is today. Visitors come to see its fascinating **cathedral** and to use it as a base for the beautiful **Fountains Abbey** and **Studley Water Gardens** (see p.126). Other nearby attractions include the great English house **Newby Hall** and the **Lightwater Valley Theme Park**.

A knot of narrow lanes clustered around a large **market place**, Ripon is a pleasure to explore, with everything worth seeing within walking distance of the central square. The Ripon Civic Society has done a grand job pointing out all sorts of historical snippets on the numerous green plaques erected around the town. There is also pleasant walking in the **Spa Gardens** just west of the centre, and along the rivers and canal just to the south – the **Canal Basin** has several shops and a café, and offers canal boat tours.

Market Place

The **Market Place** is used as a car park except on market days (Thurs and Sat) and farmers' market days (third Sun of the month). Interesting features include a 90ft **obelisk** dating from 1781 and a quaint little **cabmen's shelter**, built in 1911 and now standing next to four red phone boxes. The square is the scene of a ceremony that tradition claims dates back to 886, when Alfred the Great granted a town charter – at 9pm every evening the **Wakeman**, or **Ripon hornblower**, blows his horn at each corner of the central obelisk. It's well worth coming to see this, since he also gives a thirty-minute talk on Ripon's history, peppered with jokes, and hands out little wooden coins to bring good luck. Look out for the list of all the hornblowers from 1814 to 2004 attached to the obelisk and, on the south side of the square, the **Georgian Town Hall** (with an inscription about the Wakemen) and the half-timbered sixteenth-century **Wakeman's House**.

Ripon Cathedral

Minster Rd • Daily 8.30am–6pm • Free • ☎01765 602072, ⓦriponcathedral.info

Following curved Kirkgate from the Market Place brings you to the impressive **Ripon Cathedral** – your first view will be of the splendid early English west front, bare and unadorned compared with many large ecclesiastical buildings. Established by St Wilfrid in 672, most of the cathedral, including the central crossing, north and south transepts, chapter house and vestry, dates from the late twelfth century, early thirteenth century (the west end of the nave), late thirteenth and early fourteenth centuries (the east end of the chancel) and the early sixteenth century (most of the nave). Look out for the **Ripon Jewel**, a beautiful Saxon gold and semi-precious stone roundel about an inch across (ask one of the attendants where it might be – it seems to move around a lot).

Choir

The most satisfying part of the cathedral is the **choir**, whose stalls date from the late fifteenth century. There's a wealth of late medieval detail in the **carvings** on the misericords, including a man wheeling a woman in a barrow, a pig playing bagpipes, a mermaid brushing her hair as she admires herself in the mirror and, most famously, a griffon chasing a rabbit down a rabbit hole. This image is said to have inspired Lewis Carroll to write *Alice in Wonderland* – his father was a canon here from 1852. Incidentally, high up in the south transept there's another nod towards this story – representations of the Queen of Hearts and the Cheshire Cat put there by Sir George Gilbert Scott, who renovated the cathedral in the nineteenth century. Before leaving the choir notice the wooden hand that sticks out of the panelling above the entrance to the choir – it could be moved up and down to beat time for the choristers.

Crypt

The only part of St Wilfrid's original church to survive, the **crypt** lies beneath the cathedral's central crossing. It is said to be modelled on Christ's tomb, and it's certainly tomb-like, with a tiny tunnel-vaulted chamber less than 12ft by 8ft down a sloping passage – not suitable if you're claustrophobic. There's also a narrow "eye" through which, it is said, maidens had to crawl to prove their chastity.

Nave

In the south aisle of the **nave** is a rough-hewn stone font with a lid that could be locked (to prevent the theft of holy water for curing livestock and such), and in the nave itself, about halfway down, a wonderful 1913 Art Deco **pulpit** whose sounding board hanging above it disappeared between the wars and was replaced in 1960 by another – which some claim actually started life as a dining table.

Courthouse Museum

Minster Rd • Feb–Nov daily 1–4pm • £3, combined ticket with Prison and Police Museum & Workhouse Museum £9.50; family £22.50 • ☎ 01765 690799, ⓦ riponmuseums.co.uk

The Georgian **Courthouse Museum**, directly across the road from the cathedral, was in the 1800s the Quarter Sessions courthouse. Today you can see the rooms that housed the jury and the justices, and the courtroom itself with its two docks, witness box, seating for the advocates and so on, all looking much as they would have during the nineteenth century. A short audiovisual presentation outlines a number of actual cases tried in the court.

Prison and Police Museum

St Marygate • Feb–Nov daily 1–4pm • £4.50, combined ticket with Courthouse Museum & Workhouse Museum £9.50; family £22.50 • ☎ 01765 690799, ⓦ riponmuseums.co.uk

Occupying part of the former Ripon Prison (1816–78), just north of the cathedral on St Marygate, the **Prison and Police Museum** traces the history of policing. In the courtyard you can see a pillory, some stocks, a whipping post and a Tardis-like police phone box, while inside you can see (and sit in) the cells, learn about the various punishments meted out to lawbreakers, see a variety of old uniforms, enjoy lots of interactive displays and watch a short video.

Workhouse Museum

75 Allhallowgate • Feb–Nov daily 11am–4pm • £4.50, combined ticket with Courthouse Museum & Prison and Police Museum £9.50; family £22.50 • ☎ 01765 690799, ⓦ riponmuseums.co.uk

The **Workhouse Museum**, set in a Victorian workhouse, is a stark illustration of how the poor were treated after the Poor Law Amendment Act of 1832. Those who couldn't support themselves, whether through old age or unemployment, had to enter the workhouse, where families were broken up and housed in spartan accommodation. Men and women were separated, and all able-bodied adults were expected to do hard physical work such as chopping wood or breaking up stones for the roads.

Newby Hall

Four miles southeast of Ripon • **House** April–June & Sept Tues–Sun noon–5.30pm; July & Aug daily noon–5.30pm; 1hr guided tours on the hour • £22, including gardens; family £68 (tickets valid for 1 year) **Gardens** April–June & Sept Tues–Sun 11am–5.30pm; July & Aug daily 11am–5.30pm • £9.40 not including house admission; family £31 • ☏ 0845 450 4068, ⓦ newbyhallandgardens.com

One of England's great houses, **Newby Hall** was built "under the guidance of Sir Christopher Wren" in the 1690s, and its interior was largely designed by John Carr and Robert Adam in the 1760s for its then-owner William Weddell.

Home now to his descendants, Mr and Mrs Richard Compton, both house and gardens are open to the public, who can enjoy the Roman motifs of the blue entrance; the airy drawing room at the end of the red passage; the yellow dining room; the often droll contents of the chamber-pot room; the motto room adorned with French sayings; the almost unchanged tapestry room, designed to show off tapestries obtained from the famous Gobelins workshop in Paris; the Adam library; and the Grand Tour gallery containing a miscellany of classical statuary. The grounds include formal **gardens** along with woodland walks, a sculpture park and an imaginative children's playground.

Lightwater Valley Theme Park

North Stanley (a 10min drive northwest of Ripon) • June–Aug daily; April, May, Sept & Oct Sat & Sun from 10am (gates open 9.45am), closing from 4.30pm, depending on time of year and visitor numbers • £24; family tickets available • ☏ 0871 720 0011, ⓦ lightwatervalley.co.uk • Bus #159 from Ripon

Lightwater Valley Theme Park consists of an array of white-knuckle rides including the Eagle's Claw, White River Rapids, Raptor Attack and, what is claimed to be Europe's longest roller coaster, the Ultimate, together with more traditional and gentler fairground rides for all ages. There's also a rather good **Birds of Prey** centre and a **shopping village** with bar, restaurant and coffee shop. The whole park is on a more human scale than many, and is therefore both less expensive and less exhausting.

ARRIVAL AND INFORMATION   RIPON

By bus The bus station is just off the Market Place. Destinations Harrogate (every 15min; 35min); Leeds (every 15min; 1hr 24min); Richmond (2 daily; 1hr 20min).

Tourist office Old Market Place (April–Oct Mon–Sat 10am–5pm, Sun 10am–1pm; Nov–March Thurs & Sat 10am–4pm; ☏ 0845 389 0178, ⓦ visitripon.org).

ACCOMMODATION AND EATING

The Old Deanery Minster Rd ☏ 01765 600003, ⓦ theold deanery.co.uk. Luxurious contemporary hotel opposite the cathedral. The innovative menu (main courses from £15.95) features dishes such as belly of pork or fried stone bass. Mon–Sat noon–2pm & 7–9pm, Sun 12.30–2.30pm. **£125**

The Royal Oak 36 Kirkgate ☏ 01765 602284, ⓦ royal oakripon.co.uk. An eighteenth-century coaching inn that combines pub, restaurant and hotel, with six stylish rooms. Pub Sun–Thurs 11am–11pm, Fri & Sat 11am–midnight. **£80**

Fountains Abbey and Studley Royal

Fountains, 4 miles southwest of Ripon off the B6265 • **Abbey** April–Oct daily 10am–6pm; Oct–Jan Sat–Thurs 10am–5pm; Feb–March daily 10am–5pm; free guided tours April–Oct daily • £9.50; family £23.75; NT & EH **Deer park** All year dawn–dusk • Free; NT & EH • ☏ 01765 608888, ⓦ fountainsabbey.org.uk • Bus #139 from Ripon

Recognized as a World Heritage Site because of its unique combination of medieval abbey, Cistercian water mill and Georgian gardens, **Fountains Abbey and Studley Royal** is one of Yorkshire's top visitor attractions. At the heart of the property lie three distinct historic sights – the twelfth-century abbey itself, the ancient Fountains Mill and the eighteenth-century water gardens that stretch down river, all sitting pretty in the steep-sided and picturesque **Skell Valley**. And the modern **visitor centre** takes nothing away from this historical tranquillity: it offers restaurant, gift– and bookshops, toilets and a children's play area well away from and above the site itself. If you pay the full admission fee and enter via the visitor centre (recommended), there's a fair amount of walking involved – across a sheep-dotted field before you get to the steep paths down to the abbey, then down the valley on either or both sides of the river.

In addition to the big three attractions, there are two other features worth having a look at: the Jacobean **Fountains Hall**, at the top of the site, a mansion built partly from masonry scavenged from the Abbey; and, in the deer park, the quirky Gothic-revival **St Mary's Church** (Easter–Sept daily noon–4pm).

Fountains Abbey

3

Fountains Abbey is a Cistercian monastery established in 1132 when thirteen disaffected monks, expelled from a monastery in York for rioting, were granted land in the valley to start their own community. It grew to be one of the wealthiest and largest monasteries in Europe, but was, like all others in England, destroyed by Henry VIII's dissolution of the monasteries in the 1530s for its riches, and plundered locally for its masonry. It now consists of atmospheric **ruins** – a large L-shape created by the church and the cellarium and, within the L, cloisters, a refectory, the abbot's house, the chapter house and, across a little bridge, the guesthouse. At quiet times the sound of cawing rooks and running water gives the whole site a pleasantly melancholy feel.

Fountains Mill

Fountains Mill, across an attractive medieval bridge, is the oldest building on the estate. It's surprising that so little fuss is made of it, but this is probably because renovation, by the National Trust and English Heritage in partnership, started relatively recently. The only twelfth-century Cistercian corn mill in the country, it started out grinding corn and storing flour, but later powered a sawmill, a stone mason's workshop, even an electricity power station. A number of excellent displays tell the story.

Studley Water Gardens

Downriver from the abbey and the mill, and following the contours of the valley, the 800-acre **Studley Water Gardens** comprises a succession of lakes, rills, bridges and little waterfalls, the waters reflecting the beauties of the medieval buildings and the surrounding countryside. A triumph that emerged from disaster, they were largely the work of John Aislabie, who inherited the estate in 1693, became MP for Ripon in 1695 and Chancellor of the Exchequer in 1718, then was disgraced during the great financial disaster of the South Sea Bubble. Banned from public office for life, he spent the rest of his days on the water gardens, a project that was continued after his death by his son William. As you walk along the numerous paths that weave through the water features, look out for the Temple of Piety overlooking the Moon Pond, the lake below the dam, the rock-cut Serpentine Tunnel, the Temple of Fame and Anne Boleyn's Seat. The last was originally named the Surprise View, but took on its nickname in honour of a decapitated statue of Henry VIII's second wife that stood nearby.

The Yorkshire Dales

THEAKSTON BREWERY, MASHAM

The Yorkshire Dales

The Yorkshire Dales present a wonderful area of countryside: pastoral and idyllic in the river valleys, austere and grand in the limestone uplands. Together the Yorkshire Dales National Park and the Nidderdale Area of Outstanding Natural Beauty cover a large upland area on the western edge of the county of North Yorkshire, which boasts the county's three highest mountains – Pen-y-Ghent, Ingleborough and Whernside – and is scored by dozens of rivers and streams. Because it is made up largely of carboniferous limestone, and especially where this abuts the much harder millstone grit, there are numerous potholes, caves and waterfalls.

The Dales area can be confusing to newcomers, with more than twenty valleys apparently scattering in all directions, but it doesn't take long to find your way about. The Dales straddle the Pennine watershed, with most of the rivers draining east into the Vale of York and eventually the North Sea, but some draining west into the Irish Sea. The most interesting and attractive of them, including **Nidderdale**, **Wharfedale**, **Malhamdale** and **Ribblesdale**, run roughly from north to south, two (**Swaledale** and **Wensleydale**) run west to east, and one (**Dentdale**) runs southeast to northwest. The majority of them are named after the rivers that run along them (such as Swaledale and Wharfedale), while some take their name from a village (Dentdale, Wensleydale). And very roughly, the southern dales run longitudinally and the northern dales latitudinally.

Those who know the Dales well can attest to the individual identity of each one. However, to visitors they seem to have certain characteristics in common. **Lower dales** tend to be green and pastoral, with prosperous and picturesque villages, **upper dales** harsher, with spartan settlements, isolated farms and great tracts of open heathland. Main roads run along the valley bottoms beside main rivers, side roads along tributaries, and valley roads are usually bound on both sides by dry-stone walls. Dales either peter out, or are connected to other nearby dales by narrow roads that climb onto the open land between them. These are normally unfenced, with grazing animals confined to the uplands by cattle grids. Each dale has at least one **village**, most of which seem to feature a number of things that have died out elsewhere in the country – public conveniences, red telephone boxes, churches that are open to the public.

Many visitors come for the range of **outdoor activities** offered by this distinctive terrain – walking, cycling, potholing, caving, climbing, hang-gliding and canoeing and other water-based sports. Around nine hundred miles of footpaths, including two major cross-country paths, the **Pennine** and **Dales Ways**, cross the region, as does a new loop of the **Pennine Bridleway** and the **Yorkshire Dales Cycle Way**. But there's much, too, for the less hearty – attractive villages, exhilarating driving, tearooms, country pubs, museums, castles, fine houses, show caves, waterfalls and numerous festivals. Notable too are the number of workplaces where you can see things being made, and then buy them to take home (cheese, beer, chocolate, rope, teapots), and the many **heritage attractions** including farm parks, agritourism B&Bs, canal trips and steam train rides. And while the

GORDALE SCAR, MALHAM

Highlights

❶ The Settle to Carlisle railway This train line is famous for its beauty and for the heroic tale of its construction and survival. **See p.186**

❷ Malham A walk from this pretty two-pub village takes in a waterfall, a ravine, a limestone amphitheatre and lake. God's own country indeed. **See p.191**

❸ Auction Mart Theatre, Skipton A heady mix of art and agriculture – the local theatre uses the animal mart for its productions. See **p.197**

❹ Bolton Priory In the village of Bolton Abbey, picturesque ruins in a beautiful setting

and mile upon mile of gentle country walking. See p.198

❺ How Stean Gorge A chasm that you can either peacefully admire or actively tackle by walking, wading and climbing – and which boasts the fearsome Via Ferrata **See p.205**

❻ Masham's breweries Producers of two of Yorkshire's best-loved beers try to outdo each other with their visitor centres, in a village of outstanding beauty. **See p.213**

❼ Richmond Castle Spectacularly set on cliffs above the Swale, with unrivalled views of the river, the countryside and the town. **See p.216**

HIGHLIGHTS ARE MARKED ON THE MAP ON PP.182–183

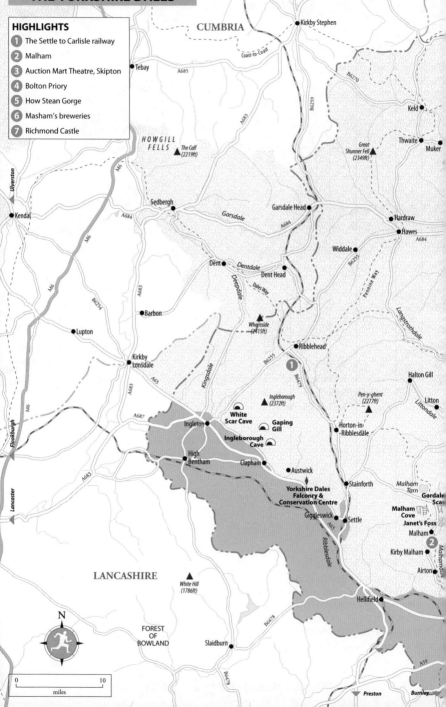

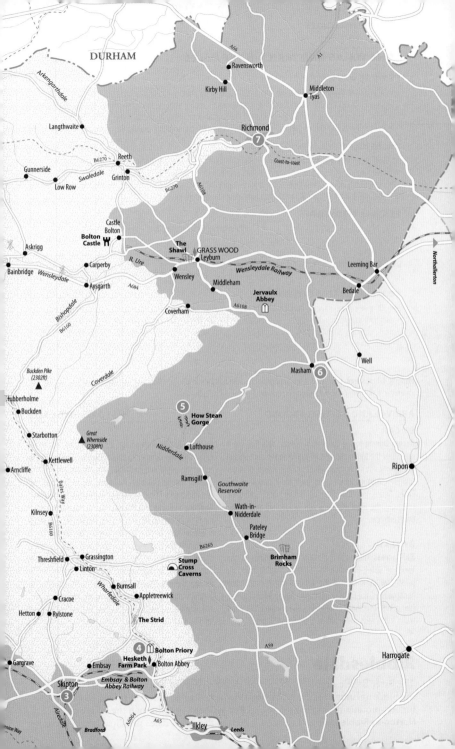

LONG WALKS AND TRAILS IN THE DALES

PENNINE WAY NATIONAL TRAIL

The **Pennine Way** is a 268-mile, long-distance walk that starts in Derbyshire, finishes in the Cheviot Hills on the Scottish borders, and takes in, on its way, Calderdale in West Yorkshire and Malham, Horton-in-Ribblesdale, Hawes, Thwaite and Keld in the Yorkshire Dales. The whole walk is likely to take from two to three weeks (see ⓦ nationaltrail.co.uk).

DALES WAY

At 82 miles the **Dales Way** is much shorter than the Pennine Way. It begins at Ilkley, follows Wharfedale right up to its source, crosses the watershed near Ribblehead, then passes down Dentdale to Sedbergh (inside the national park, although officially in Cumbria), ending at Windermere in the Lake District (see ⓦ thedalesway.co.uk).

PENNINE BRIDLEWAY

With 120 miles or so currently open, the **Pennine Bridleway** is the first purpose-built trail designed for horseriders, mountain-bikers and walkers. As such, therefore, it is notable for not having any stiles to negotiate. The bridleway dips into West Yorkshire along Calderdale, and further north at the Settle Loop, which includes Ribblesdale and Malhamdale (see ⓦ nationaltrail.co.uk).

YORKSHIRE DALES CYCLEWAY

A 130-mile circular route starting and finishing at Skipton (though obviously you can start and finish anywhere you like along the route), the **Yorkshire Dales Cycleway** falls into six roughly equal sections: Skipton to Malham, Malham to Ingleton, Ingleton to Hawes, Hawes to Grinton, Grinton to Kettlewell and Kettlewell to Skipton via Bolton Abbey (see ⓦ cyclethedales.org.uk).

major Dales get most of the attention, don't ignore those that are lesser known – there are many of them, often little visited and generally unspoilt.

ARRIVAL AND GETTING AROUND   THE YORKSHIRE DALES

BY CAR

Access Driving to the Dales from outside Yorkshire you'll use either the M6 to the west or the A1 to the east. Within the county, the main approaches are from a circle of larger towns – Skipton, which styles itself the Gateway to the Dales, Settle, Ingleton, Richmond, Ripon and Harrogate. Certainly, the most effective way of getting around the Dales is by car.

BY TRAIN

Rail access There are a number of rail options in the Yorkshire Dales, including the Settle to Carlisle line (see p.186), which is part of the national rail network; two heritage lines, the Embsay and Bolton Abbey Steam Railway (see p.198) and the Wensleydale Railway (see p.211); and trains from Leeds and Bradford to Ilkley and Skipton.

BY BUS

Getting to the Dales Buses are most frequent between Easter and mid-October. The best plan would be to head for one of the larger towns within striking distance of the Dales – Leeds, Bradford, Skipton, Harrogate, Ripon, Northallerton and Richmond – then proceed into the Dales from there.

Getting around the Dales If you're hoping to explore the Dales by bus, you'll need to plan in advance, as coverage is patchy and services labyrinthine – for comprehensive timetables see ⓦ traveldales.org.uk and ⓦ dalesbus.org. Useful hubs include Settle, Ilkley, Grassington, Pateley Bridge, Bedale, Leyburn and Hawes.

Rover tickets "Dales Rover" tickets are available on Sundays and bank holidays (obtainable from the driver), and many bus operators offer rover tickets for their own services for a day or a week.

Ribblesdale

The River Ribble runs south along the western edges of the Yorkshire Dales, starting in the bleak uplands near the **Ribblehead Viaduct**, flowing between two of Yorkshire's highest mountains, **Ingleborough** and **Pen-y-Ghent**, and through the village of **Horton-in-Ribblesdale** and then on to **Settle**, the upper dale's principal town. Thereafter it meanders south and west across Lancashire, entering the North Sea at Preston. Although the stretch of the A65 between Settle and **Ingleton** is not in Ribblesdale, it is very much a part of the cluster of villages and attractions that mark this western edge of the Dales, including the popular village of **Clapham**. There are **tourist offices** at Settle and Ingleton.

Settle

The main town in Ribblesdale, **SETTLE** sits just off the Skipton to Kendal A65, at the foot of Castleberg, an impressive limestone outcrop from the top of which you can get fine views over the town and the surrounding countryside (to get to it, follow the **Tot Lord Trail** – it takes about ten minutes). A small market town that owed its existence to a 1249 charter, Settle continued to prosper first due to the Keighley to Kendal turnpike of 1753 and then the **Settle to Carlisle railway** of 1876 (see box, p.186). While it is probably still best known as the starting point for this beautiful stretch of railway line, the town itself boasts a few attractions and some interesting architecture, including the **market place**, the **Shambles**, the ornate 1853 Victoria Hall (now the Victoria Theatre) on Kirkgate, and, across the road, the beautifully simple 1678 Friends Meeting House. It also makes a good base for forays into the excellent walking and climbing country to the east.

The Shambles
Market Place

Settle's central market place contains the rather peculiar **Shambles**. A seventeenth-century market hall heavily altered in the eighteenth century, it has late Victorian cottages plonked on top, with a loggia added at the front to give access to them. The whole oddball assemblage now consists of shops and cafés below and private housing above, and it really seems, against all reason, to work.

Museum of North Craven Life
Victoria St • March–Oct Tues 10.30am–4.30pm, Thurs–Sun 12.30–4.30pm • £2.70 • ☎ 01729 822361, ⓦ ncbpt.org.uk

Settle has its fair share of oddball buildings, not least the Folly, south of the Market Place. **The Folly** is genuinely old – the oldest building in town, dating from the 1670s – but earns its name from the strange combination of styles, and the curiously upside-down look created by the fact that there are far more windows on the ground floor than on the first and second – it seems surprising that it hasn't fallen down. The Grade I listed building now houses the **Museum of North Craven Life**, which contains fairly random odds and ends from the history of the town – bits of furniture, farm implements, fragments of an eighteenth-century boot – and a section on the Settle to Carlisle railway, "Scenes from the Line".

Settle Railway Station
Off Station Rd • Mon–Fri 7.15am–4.40pm, Sat 9.15am–6pm, Sun 9.30am–6pm • ⓦ settle-carlisle.co.uk

Settle Railway Station marks the start of the Settle to Carlisle line, a railway enthusiast's dream (see box, p.186). The station is a good example of the "Derby Gothic" style favoured by the Midland Railway Company, and it is beautifully maintained, looking more like a volunteer-run tourist attraction than a working station.

ARRIVAL AND INFORMATION   SETTLE

By train The station is on the southern edge of town. **Destinations** Carlisle (hourly; 1hr 43min); Dent (every 2hr; 26min); Horton-in-Ribblesdale (every 2hr; 8min); Leeds (every 1–3hr; 1hr 5min).

By bus Buses arrive and depart from the Market Place.

Destinations Horton-in-Ribblesdale (every 2hr; 21min); Ingleton (every 2hr; 31min); Skipton (hourly; 46min).

Tourist office Town Hall, Cheapside (April–Oct daily 9.30am–4pm; Nov–March Mon–Sat 9.30am–4pm; ☎ 01729 825192, ⓦ settle.org.uk).

THE SETTLE TO CARLISLE RAILWAY

The story of the construction of the **Settle to Carlisle railway** in the nineteenth century, and its fight for survival in the twentieth, is truly epic. Opened in 1875 for goods traffic, and 1876 for passengers, the 72-mile line was built by the Midland Railway Company, employing an army of navvies and miners. Crossing extremely inhospitable countryside, the line was a feat of engineering – no fewer than seventeen viaducts had to be built and fourteen tunnels dug, with the longest viaduct (Ribblehead) being followed immediately by the longest tunnel (Blea Moor). The irony was that the company only proposed the line as a bargaining ploy in a dispute with the London and North Western Railway over access to their west coast line to Scotland, and when the dispute was resolved, wanted to abort it before work on it had started – only to be denied by Parliament. Honourably, the company bit the bullet and built it. Though moderately successful, it could not compete in price with the east coast line to Scotland, whose building was much cheaper, and it started to be run down, a process that continued after nationalization in 1948.

Many stations on the line were closed in 1970 as a result of the Beeching Report and its swingeing railway cuts, and British Rail planned to close the entire line in the early 1980s on the grounds that the maintenance costs of the tunnels and the Ribblehead Viaduct were prohibitive. This last threat created such a furore, and generated so much interest in the line, that some of the stations had to be re-opened in 1986 to meet growing demand, and the whole plan was shelved in 1989. Today the Settle to Carlisle line is shared by passengers and freight, with seven passenger services a day (five on Sundays) doing the full route, which now runs from Leeds to Carlisle. The principal stops in the Dales are at **Settle**, **Horton-in-Ribblesdale**, **Ribblehead** and **Dent**; return fares from Settle to Carlisle are upwards of £15.50.

ACCOMMODATION AND EATING

As well as in Settle itself, there are a couple of interesting and individual places to stay in **Austwick**, a couple of miles northwest, and one in **Hellifield** in the opposite direction.

Austwick Hall Austwick ☎ 01524 251794, ⊚ austwick hall.co.uk. Absolutely solid, old-fashioned but stylish place, in a beautiful stone, ivy-covered and historic manor house (once a Pele Tower, fortified to repel the Scots). A perfect balance of state-of-the-art comfort and plush traditionalism. **£125**

★**Hellifield Peel Castle** Peel Green, Hellifield ☎ 01729 850248, ⊚ peelcastle.co.uk. Off the A65 about halfway between Skipton and Settle, and like *Austwick Hall* originally a Pele tower (see above). The bulk of the current building dates from the fourteenth century. Its renovation was recorded in *Grand Designs* in 2007, and when costs soared its owners decided that the house needed to start paying its way. Hence the opportunity to stay in this wonderfully historic house with lovely rooms and all mod cons. Booking well in advance is recommended. **£165**

The Lion Duke St ☎ 01729 822203, ⊚ thelionsettle .co.uk. The *Lion* (previously the *Golden Lion*) has comfortable rooms and a restaurant serving a wide range of locally sourced fish, meats, pies and sausages, with a fine choice of cheeses (£7.95–17.95). Food served Mon– Thurs 8am–10pm, Fri & Sat 8am–10.30pm, Sun 8am–9pm. **£95**

The Traddock Austwick ☎ 01524 251224, ⊚ thetraddock.co.uk. Off the A65, about 2 miles northwest of Settle, the *Traddock* is a warm and friendly hotel in lovely surroundings, with an excellent restaurant, good but unobtrusive service and comfortable rooms. **£110**

★**Ye Olde Naked Man Café** Market Place, Settle ☎ 01729 823230. For non-alcoholic drinks and good plain food this café is the best bet. Don't be put off by the twee name – there is a reason for it. The building was once an undertaker's, and the name is a reference to the old Yorkshire saying, "you bring now't into't world and you take now't out". Daily 9am–5pm.

Yorkshire Dales Falconry and Conservation Centre

Crowns Nest Rd, 3.5 miles northwest of Settle • Daily 10am–4pm (displays April–Oct noon, 2pm & 3.30pm; Nov–March noon & 1.30pm) • £7; family £23 • ☎ 01729 822832, ⊚ hawkexperience.com

On the A65, well signposted and visible from the main road just northwest of Settle, the **Yorkshire Dales Falconry and Conservation Centre** occupies an old farmhouse and houses more than fifty birds. The centre puts on falconry displays, holds half- and full-day falconry courses, and offers flying displays of eagles, hawks, falcons, vultures and owls. They also breed birds and have an avian hospital. There's a tearoom, a gift shop and children's play area.

Clapham

The village of **CLAPHAM** is just off the main A65 between Settle and Ingleton, about 6.5 miles northwest of Settle. Part of the **Ingleborough Estate**, owned since the eighteenth century by the Farrer family, the village is strung out along the Clapham Beck, has a market cross and a lake. Lying on the **Craven Fault** – where millstone grit and limestone meet, creating potholes and caves as the water floods off the impermeable millstone grit and dissolves and erodes the limestone – Clapham, a starting point for the walk to Ingleborough, one of the area's **Three Peaks** (see p.190), is also the gateway to **Ingleborough Cave**.

Ingleborough Cave

Clapham • Feb half term to Oct daily 10am–5pm, tours on the hour, every 30min when busy; Nov to Feb half term Sat & Sun 9am–3pm (pre-booked groups only) • £8; family £20 • ⓦ ingleboroughcave.co.uk

Above the village of Clapham, on the slopes of Ingleborough – one of the Dales' famous Three Peaks – the Fell Beck stream disappears into a gigantic hole known as **Gaping Gill**, where it drops more than 300ft. Underground, it carved out the impressive 10.5-mile system that ends in **Ingleborough Cave**. Unknown until 1837, the cave was discovered when limestone formations that had built up at its entrance were washed away by a flood.

The cave is one of Yorkshire's premier show caves, and offers a 250-yard trip into the mountain, with all the calcite flows and stalactites and stalagmites you'd expect, interpreted by an expert guide. Tours take around fifty minutes.

Ingleborough Estate Nature Trail

Church Ave, Clapham • Daily dawn–dusk • 50p • Park in the Dales National car park and walk up past the church.

Opened in 1970 the **Ingleborough Estate Nature Trail**, which starts at the Dales National Car Park in Clapham, is a walk of just over a mile that passes old sawmills, electrical installations designed to take advantage of the river's power-generating potential, and heads through woodland and impressive limestone scars. During this walk, for which you should allow about thirty minutes, you will see many of the plants that Reginald Farrer, the most famous of the Farrers of Ingleborough Estate (known as the "patron saint of alpine gardening"), collected. He travelled extensively in China, Burma and Tibet gathering plants to bring home, and the descendants of many of them are still there.

ACCOMMODATION	**CLAPHAM**
New Inn Old Rd ☎ 01524 251203, ⓦ newinn-clapham .co.uk. Eighteenth-century establishment with one oak-panelled bar and an attractive dining room. In addition to its normal high-spec rooms, the *New Inn* also has a	superior bunkroom designed for between seven and ten walkers/families/cyclists (with secure storage for bikes) with two shower-rooms and bedding provided. Dorms **£45**; doubles **£105**

Ingleton

East of the A65 between Settle and Kirkby Lonsdale, ten miles from Settle, is **INGLETON**, famous for its waterfalls and its caves, and as one of the starting points for the ascent of 2372ft **Ingleborough**. Even more than Clapham to the southeast (see above), the village owes its character and much of its livelihood to its position on the **Craven Fault**. Perched high above the confluence of the Twiss and Doe rivers, with fine views of the Victorian viaduct (and not so fine ones of a static caravan park), Ingleton's winding Main Street has a good selection of small shops and cafés, with a pub at each end.

DRY-STONE WALLS AND FIELD BARNS

Throughout the Dales you will see **dry-stone walls** – hundreds of miles of them, following roads and swooping up hillsides onto the uplands. Picturesque as they are, these walls represent centuries of hard manual labour. They were built to fulfil several purposes – to mark boundaries between farms, to divide farms into fields so that farmers could separate animals (pregnant ewes from ewes with lambs, for example), and to keep grazing animals off the meadows while the grass was growing. You will also see numerous **field barns** – more than six thousand at a conservative estimate – that housed cattle during the winter months, and from where manure could be stored in middens, then spread across the meadows to help to produce the next winter's fodder.

This stock of walls and barns has been built up over centuries, largely between the seventeenth and the end of the nineteenth, and is now an essential part of the character of the Yorkshire Dales. Yet both dry-stone walls and field barns are under threat. If a wall falls down, it is cheaper to replace it with fencing. Field barns are no longer used for their original purpose, and many are now in a dilapidated condition, which is why various concerned bodies – the National Parks Authority, English Heritage, the National Trust, the Yorkshire Dales Society and others – are trying to address the problem by encouraging their renovation and repair.

St Mary's Church

Main St · ⓦ stmaryschurchingleton.org.uk

St Mary's Church, in the centre of Ingleton, was built in medieval times on compacted river boulders that continued to settle, causing considerable damage to the building – the current church is the result of a rebuild in 1886, since when it has continued to have structural problems. Inside, take a look at the elaborately decorated Norman font, rescued after being used in the eighteenth century for mixing plaster and whitewash, and the British Legion chapel in the south aisle, which features wood carving from the Robert Thompson school – Thompson, known as the "mouseman", was a Yorkshire man who worked in the Arts and Crafts tradition of the 1920s and 1930s (look out for the carving of the mouse on one of the posts). Don't miss the 1717 "vinegar bible" which gets its name from the mis-transcription of the "parable of the vineyard" as "the parable of the vinegar", and the splendid modern carving of the Last Supper (based on Leonardo da Vinci's painting) on the reredos below the east window.

Waterfalls Trail

Broadwood, across the river from Ingleton town centre · Daily 9am, closing times vary · £6; family £14 · ☎ 01524 241930, ⓦ ingletonwaterfallstrail.co.uk

On the edge of Ingleton is the start of the eight-mile-long **Waterfalls Trail**, set up by one Joseph Craven (his memorial is the pump next to the village centre Memorial Gardens) and his Improvement Company in 1885, and now one of the most accessible and beautiful sets of waterfalls in the country. A well-marked and surfaced footpath takes you through ancient oak woodland and pretty dales up the River Twiss, across farmland, then down the River Doe. There are fourteen waterfalls and a thousand steps on the trail – with no wheelchair accessibility (allow 2hr 30min–4hr). There's a gift shop, café and toilets at the Broadwood car park at the start, and at the time of writing a café/kiosk was being planned for the furthest point where the trail turns back. It can get very busy in the summer – set off early, to avoid the crowds.

White Scar Cave

Beside the B6255, 1.5 miles northeast of Ingleton · Feb–Oct guided tours (80min) daily 10am–5pm; Nov–Jan Sat & Sun only, weather permitting · £9.50; family £26 · ☎ 01524 241244, ⓦ whitescarcave.co.uk

Even if caves normally leave you cold, the **White Scar Cave**, northeast of Ingleton on the road to Ribblehead, is guaranteed to take your breath away. Discovered by student Christopher Long in 1923, the cave now has a steel-grid walkway that takes you from the entrance past waterfalls, great sheets of flowstone, cream and red stalactites and stalagmites, through "**the Squeeze**" and the **Bagshaw Tunnel** (not happy experiences if you're claustrophobic) before eventually bringing you to the colossal **Battlefield Cavern**, at 330ft one of the longest underground caverns in the country.

Hard hats are provided (roofs are low in parts of the cave) for the mile-long guided tour, during which the guide will point out the usual fanciful show-cave names for formations – the Witch's Fingers, the Judge's Head, the Sword of Damocles, the Crown of Thorns, the Face and so on. You should wear warm clothing, as the cave is a constant 8º C, and, because of the 97 steps and the steel grid underfoot, heels are not recommended. There's a café and shop above the car park – parking is strictly for people visiting the cave.

ARRIVAL AND INFORMATION — INGLETON

By bus There are a number of bus stops, including at the community centre and the *Bridge Inn*. Destinations Kirkby Lonsdale (every 2hr; 15min); Settle (every 2hr; 31min).

Tourist office Community Centre, Main St (daily: Easter–Sept 10am–4.30pm; Nov–March 11am–3pm, ☎01524 241049, ⓦ ingleton.co.uk).

ACCOMMODATION

Riverside Lodge 24 Main St ☎01524 241359, ⓦ riversideingleton.co.uk. One of several guesthouses along Main St and a cut above most. Eight rooms, all named after flowers, plus a lounge, sauna and games rooms, with pleasant gardens and views. **£68**

Stackstead Farm One mile south of Ingleton, off the minor road to High Bentham ☎01524 241386, ⓦ stacksteadfarm.co.uk. Simple bunkhouse barn accommodation and a campsite; a good option for walkers. Bunkhouse per person **£11**; camping per pitch **£12**

YHA Ingleton Sammy Lane ☎01524 241444, ⓦ yha .org.uk/hostel/ingleton. YHA hostel with nearly sixty beds in a Victorian stone house with its own grounds. Dorms **£20**; doubles **£49**

Horton-in-Ribblesdale and around

To **follow the Ribble** itself you need to head due north from Settle on the B6479. The first village you come to, after 2.5 miles, is **STAINFORTH**, with its bridge and old-fashioned pub right next to it. Just across the river and the railway line from the village is **Stainforth Force,** where the Ribble thunders down a series of limestone steps into a hollow created by the current.

Another eight miles north, **HORTON-IN-RIBBLESDALE** is a centre for walking and climbing (and potholing – Craven Pothole Club has a hut in the village). It is the most convenient starting point for the ascent of **Pen-y-Ghent**, one of the Three Peaks, which glowers off to the east, and the *Pen-y-Ghent Café* is the unofficial headquarters for the Three Peaks Walk (see box, p.190).

In itself the village isn't much to write home about. Its principal industry from time immemorial was stone-quarrying, greatly expanded by the arrival in the mid-nineteenth century of the Settle to Carlisle railway (see p.186). It straggles along for a mile or more, with a **pub** at each end, a train station, post office and church. What should be an attractive river crossing, with two stone bridges and one graceful footbridge next to the *Crown*, is spoilt by telegraph poles, pipes crossing the stream and general junk cluttering up the river bank.

Ribblehead Viaduct

From Horton the road climbs upwards through increasingly bleak moorland, and the river peters out. As you approach a T-junction in the middle of nowhere you'll get your first view of the famous and elegant **Ribblehead Viaduct**, a triumph of Victorian civil engineering, whose maintenance costs, together with those of the numerous tunnels, were almost successfully used as an excuse for shutting down the Settle to Carlisle railway (see p.186).

4

THE THREE PEAKS

You can't visit the western Dales without becoming aware of Yorkshire's famous **Three Peaks** – in descending order of height above sea level **Whernside** (2415ft), **Ingleborough** (2372ft) and **Pen-y-ghent** (2277ft). While to the people of the Himalayas or the Alps they might not seem very impressive, they dominate this part of Yorkshire completely – and you're soon able to identify them by their distinctive shapes. Geographically, they form a triangle around the iconic **Ribblehead Viaduct**, with Whernside near the source of the Ribble on the border with Cumbria, and Ingleborough and Pen-y-ghent on the western and eastern flanks respectively of Ribblesdale itself. Not only are the three mountains an integral part of the landscape, they play an important role in the activities of walkers and cyclists in the region – each is the focus of individual well-trodden walking routes, with walkers setting off for Whernside usually from **Ribblehead**, Ingleborough from **Clapham or Ingleton**, and Pen-y-ghent from **Horton-in-Ribblesdale**.

In addition, the three mountains together form one of the Yorkshire Dales National Park's best-known and most testing long circular walks – the nearly 25-mile **Three Peaks Walk**. Although the mountains can be climbed in any order, and from any starting point on the circular route, most people set off from Horton-in-Ribblesdale, with walkers following an anti-clockwise route to the summits of Pen-y-ghent, Whernside and Ingleborough, in that order.

As well as the constant stream of individual walkers embarking on the Three Peaks Walk, there are numerous **charity events** at various fixed times. In addition there are two big regular events – the **Three Peaks Race** for fell runners towards the end of April, and the **Three Peaks Cycle Race** at the end of September.

Incidentally, don't get the Yorkshire Three Peaks route confused with the National Three Peaks Challenge, which is a different thing altogether, involving the highest mountains in England, Wales and Scotland.

ARRIVAL AND INFORMATION

By train The train station is west of the B6479 on Station Rd. Destinations Carlisle (every 2–3hr; 1hr 35min); Settle (every 2–3hr; 8min).

By bus There are several bus stops along the main road through the village.

HORTON-IN-RIBBLESDALE AND AROUND

Destinations Settle (every 2hr; 31min).

Tourist information *Pen-y-Ghent Café* (Feb half-term hols to mid-Oct Mon & Wed–Fri 9am–5.30pm, Sat & Sun 8am–5.30pm; winter Mon & Wed–Sun 9am–5.30pm; ☎01729 860333) gives out information (see below).

ACCOMMODATION AND EATING

Craven Heifer Main St, Stainforth ☎01729 822435, ⓦcravenheiferstainforth.co.uk. The *Craven Heifer* pub offers seven bedrooms, mellow stone-floored and wood-panelled bars, and good-quality pub grub (mains £8.95–10.50; the "hiker special", soup and sandwich. £7.95). Pub daily noon–11pm. **£90**

Crown Hawes Rd, Horton-in-Ribblesdale ☎01729 860209, ⓦcrown-hotel.co.uk. At the northern end of the village, right on the Pennine Way, the *Crown* offers basic accommodation in ten rooms (singles, doubles and family) and a traditional pub atmosphere. No dogs. Pub daily noon–11.30pm. **£85**

Golden Lion Horton-in-Ribblesdale ☎01729 860206, ⓦgoldenlionhotel.co.uk. Pub/hotel in a sixteenth-century coaching inn, with three bars, real ale, pub food (mains £7.50–14.95) and a beer garden. Much used by hikers. Dorms **£12**; doubles **£70**

Pen-y-Ghent Café Horton-in-Ribblesdale ☎01729 860333. The *Pen-y-Ghent Café* has been fulfilling a vital role for more than forty years, supplying much-needed hot drinks, snacks and meals and offering local information and advice. They also provide a clocking in/clocking out system for anyone who wants to join the café's "Three Peaks of Yorkshire Club" by completing the route within a 12hr period. The café no longer provides automatic back-up should walkers fail to return, but may do so ad-hoc on request. Feb half-term hols to mid-Oct Mon & Wed–Fri 9am–5.30pm, Sat & Sun 8am–5.30pm; winter Mon & Wed–Sun 9am–5.30pm.

Malhamdale

Malhamdale, lying between Wharfedale and Ribblesdale, is the shortest of the most popular dales, but what it lacks in length it more than makes up for in quality. Travel writer Bill Bryson once lived in the valley (in Kirkby Malham), considering it the finest place in the world this side of heaven. And he should know. Prime limestone country, Malhamdale provides some of the most magnificent scenery in the Dales and some of the best walking and cycling in England. The big attraction is the spectacular triumvirate of **Malham Cove**, **Malham Tarn** and **Gordale Scar**, but the lesser-known **Janet's Foss** waterfall is also wonderful. The starting point for any exploration of the area has to be the dale's main village, **Malham**, which lies in the upper reaches of the valley.

Malham

A fetching stone village meandering along the banks of a stream, **MALHAM** has a photogenic bridge, two delightful pubs (see p.192) and a scattering of cafés and shops. It's busy all year and packed in high season, with visitors setting off for or returning from the numerous walks in the area, or just enjoying the village itself.

Malham Cove

Malham Cove is an impressive horseshoe-shaped limestone cliff less than a mile north of the village. Soaring 260ft above the surrounding countryside, it can be approached via a broad footpath from which there are fine views of the cliff from below (if there are climbers on the cliff, it gives a sense of the vast scale of the formation), or by bearing left and climbing to the top via rough steps at the western end; it's a slog of ten minutes or so. Views from the top – where the deeply scored limestone pavement, a patchwork of huge clints (the blocks of limestone) and grykes (the gaps in between) looks like the skin of some giant pachyderm – are spectacular.

Malham Tarn

A mile north of Malham Cove, 2 miles from Malham village • Ⓦ nationaltrust.org.uk/malham-tarn-estate • Bus #210 or #211 from Skipton (Mon–Sat), plus #883 or #884 summer Sun and bank holidays

From the top of Malham Cove a path strikes a mile north to **Malham Tarn**, a shallow upland lake – at 1237ft above sea level England's highest – of glacial origin that is said to have been the inspiration for Charles Kingsley's *The Water Babies*. Though it's of huge geological and scientific interest, and the location of a well-regarded field studies centre, for general visitors it can appear a little underwhelming. The popular walk from Malham, via Malham Cove, is, however a pleasant way to spend three hours or so. The whole area is owned by the National Trust, and provides excellent walking, cycling and birdwatching.

Janet's Foss

If, instead of heading north from Malham village towards Malham Cove and the Tarn you strike east, a clearly signposted path leads, in about a mile, to **Janet's Foss**, just across Gordale Lane. A pretty waterfall that plunges over a self-created tufa curtain into a tree-fringed pool, Janet's Foss was once used by local farmers for dipping sheep, and is now an ideal place to go for a dip yourself, or at least cool your feet. The name is thought to refer to Jennet, a fairy queen said to live in a cave behind the falls. There is certainly something magical about the Foss and the woodland walk that stretches back to Malham.

Gordale Scar

Around a mile northeast of Malham, off Gordale Lane, is a well-marked and surfaced path signposted to **Gordale Scar**, a craggy limestone ravine little more than half a mile from the road. At the beginning of the path an information board explains how this extraordinary gorge – the grandeur of which inspired J.M.W. Turner and William Wordsworth, among others – was formed. A million years of glacial scouring followed by deluges of limestone-dissolving meltwater resulted in the tortured chasm with overhanging 330ft-high cliffs and tumultuous waterfalls you see today. Note that there's a steep and tricky ascent about a quarter of a mile from the start of the path.

A WALK FROM MALHAM

This popular circular walk (7.5 miles) takes in all the main sights of the area, starting and finishing in Malham, and taking in Janet's Foss, Gordale Scar, Malham Tarn and Malham Cove. It's well signposted, but for most of the year, you simply have to follow the crowds.

Turn left out of the **Dales National Park car park**, then cross the stream by the footbridge on the opposite side of the road from the *Buck Inn* and walk south until you come to a signpost for Janet's Foss. Follow it along a heavily wooded, National Trust-owned ravine until you come to the **Foss** itself.

Taking the path up to the left of the Foss, you'll come to a road. Turn right, walk along it the short distance to a signpost for **Gordale Scar**, off the road to the left. A broad gravel path from the road leads 0.5 mile into the Scar itself, a narrow canyon with lofty cliffs either side, with the Gordale Beck tumbling down the rock face. If you're reasonably fit, you can climb up a path (in places rather obscure, in other places stepped) to the left of the waterfall which, after a scramble, levels out at the top. Continuing along the path will bring you to a signpost for Malham Tarn (2 miles). Follow it.

If you'd rather not face the scramble up Gordale Beck, you can retrace your steps to the road, and then turn right and right again off the road, following a signpost for Malham Cove. After passing through an ancient settlement and field system, and having rejoined the hardier souls who climbed up through Gordale Scar, you'll arrive at a junction of two paths at Street Gate. Continue straight, and after about twenty minutes you will be able to see the water of **Malham Tarn** in the distance. Several tracks link Street Gate to the lake. The birdlife around the Tarn is plentiful, though the landscape is a little drab.

From the car park on Malham Tarn, first follow the sign "Pennine Way Watersinks ¾ mile", then, having turned right onto the road signed "Malham Cove 1 ½ miles", continue south, following signs for **Malham Cove**. You will eventually find yourself on the impressive limestone pavement at the top of the natural amphitheatre of Malham Cove. Don't go too close to the edge – it's a 260ft drop. Cross the pavement, then take the steep steps down the western edge of the escarpment. The path back to Malham is clearly defined and well signposted.

ARRIVAL AND INFORMATION

MALHAM

By bus Buses pick up and disgorge at Malham's main car park.

Destinations Ilkley (6 daily; 1hr 10min); Skipton (2 daily Mon, Wed & Fri; 35min).

Tourist information In addition to its core purpose of offering information about the park, the National Park Centre at Malham's main car park is also a tourist office (daily: April–June, Sept & Oct 10am–5pm; July & Aug 9.30am–5pm; Nov, Dec, Feb & March Sat & Sun 10am–4pm; ☎ 01969 652380, ⌨ yorkshiredales.org.uk).

Walking and cycling The most heavily used paths in Malhamdale are surfaced to almost urban standard; however, some are pretty rough and ready, so proper footwear and clothing are recommended. Look out for the free and widely available *Malhamdale Walk Brochure*, which offers detailed instructions for five walks, from just over 3 to 8 miles, and the excellent *Malham Landscape Trail* and *Malham Village Walk*. If you're really keen, you could sign up for the inaptly named "Malhamdale Meander", covering a strenuous 23 miles in 10hr, which takes place in May and takes in most of the main sights. See ⌨ malhamdale.com for more.

ACCOMMODATION AND EATING

★**Buck Inn** Cove Rd ☎ 01729 830317, ⌨ buckinn malham.co.uk. Pleasant pub, popular with walkers. With good, locally sourced food – especially sausages, pies and steaks (main courses £10–22) – comfortable rooms, and a relaxed attitude to muddy boots, this is the ideal base for a walking holiday. Food served daily noon–3pm & 6–9pm. £80

Lister Arms Just across the bridge from the Buck Inn ☎ 01729 830330, ⌨ listerarms.co.uk. The *Lister Arms* has a good reputation locally for superior pub food (mains £8.95–24.95), and offers comfortable rooms. Pub daily 11am–11pm; food served Sun–Thurs noon–10pm, Fri & Sat noon–10.30pm. £95

YHA Malham Middle of the village ☎ 0845 371 9529, ⌨ yha.org.uk/hostel/malham. A purpose-built youth hostel lying in the heart of the village, it's a good bet for families and serious walkers. Open all year. Office open 7–10am & 5–10.30pm. Dorms £13; doubles £49

Wharfedale

The River Wharfe runs south from just below Wensleydale through picturesque **Bolton Abbey**, likeable **Ilkley** and the market town of Otley, eventually joining the Ouse south of York. The upper reaches of the river flow through **Wharfedale**, one of the most popular dales in the National Park, with a good cluster of characteristic Dales villages – among them **Hubberholme** with its pub parliament, **Kilnsey** and **Kettlewell** of *Calendar Girls* fame and pretty **Grassington**. The attractive market town of **Skipton**, while not actually on the Wharfe – it's about six miles west – is the gateway to all the Dales, and makes a good base for exploring Wharfedale.

Ilkley

The small town of **ILKLEY** holds a special place in the iconography of Yorkshire out of all proportion to its size, largely because it's the setting of the county's unofficial anthem *On Ilkley Moor baht 'at*. Lying on the banks of the River Wharfe between Leeds and the Dales, it boasts the best of both worlds. Vibrant and stylish, with a number of things to see and enough top-end and independent shops, bars and restaurants to keep visiting urbanites happy, it is also overlooked by the wild **Ilkley Moor**, scattered with reminders of both distant geological time and the dawn of human history.

Brief history

Ilkley has had its ups and downs. The **Romans** built a fort here to guard an important crossroads, but after the fifth-century departure of the occupying forces it settled back to become a small rural backwater. Although bathing had begun in the town (at White Wells) as early as 1703 (where it was the icy temperatures of the water that stimulated circulation, rather than any mineral content), the growing popularity of hydrotherapy and the discovery of mineral springs in the area in the mid-nineteenth century led to its development as a **spa town**, and several hydros were built. The fashion for water treatments was relatively short-lived, but then the coming of the **railway** in the late nineteenth century led to Ilkley becoming a dormitory town for the rapidly growing cities of Leeds and Bradford. More recently it has been given a new lease of life as a popular tourist destination, becoming one of the most appealing bases in the whole of the Dales.

All Saints Church

Church St • Office hours Mon, Tues & Thurs 9.15am–1.15pm, Wed 10–11.30am, Fri 9.15am–12.30pm • ☎ 01943 431126

Sitting on the main intersection in the centre of Ilkley, **All Saints Church** was established in 627 by King Edwin of Northumbria and Bishop Paulinus of York, whose carved heads you can see in the entrance porch. Among its many treasures are three impressive eighth-century Saxon crosses collected at the base of the tower, a complete family pew dating from 1633, a superb Norman font made of Ilkley Moor stone with a magnificent seventeenth-century font cover complete with pulley and counter-weight for raising and lowering it, and, on the south wall of the chancel, a group of memorial brasses commemorating members of the same family (the Hebers) who died of the plague within a few weeks during 1649.

Manor House Museum

Castle Yard, Church St • Tues 1–5pm, Wed–Sat 11am–5pm, Sun 1–4pm • Free • ☎ 01943 600066

Tucked in just behind All Saints Church, the **Manor House Museum** was originally known as the castle (hence its address) because the mainly seventeenth-century building stands on the site of the original Roman fort (you can see a section of the Roman wall at the rear of the building). Today the museum contains a collection of Roman artefacts from the fort and surrounding area, and exhibits and information about Ilkley's prehistory and its growth as a Victorian spa town.

Ilkley Moor

Dominating Ilkley's southern skyline is the famous **Ilkley Moor**, the town's great playground and somehow smaller yet more forbidding than one might expect. Far from being a remote wilderness, it is very much part of the town's infrastructure, a place where people can walk, climb or ponder the immensities of time reflected in its **ancient rock formations** and **prehistoric markings**. Look out for the Swastika Stone, the Twelve Apostles, the famous Cow and Calf and a host of cup-and-ring marked rocks. Excellent information boards adorn the Moor's car parks, and there's more information available at the **White Wells Spa Cottage Visitor Centre** on a path that climbs onto Ilkley Moor from Wells Road. The Spa baths, dating back to 1703 are still functioning – a dip in the icy plunge pool has become something of a New Year's Day tradition. Whatever the physical benefits, the waters clearly do nothing for insanity.

ARRIVAL AND INFORMATION   ILKLEY

By train Ilkley station, in the heart of the town, is the terminus of a line that links the town to Leeds and Bradford. Destinations Bradford (every 30min; 32min); Leeds (every 30min; 31min).
By bus The bus station is next to the train station. Destinations Bolton Abbey (7 daily; 15min); Grassington (4 daily on Sun; 42min); Keighley (6 daily; 45min); Leeds (every 20min; 1hr 7min); Malham (6 daily; 1hr 10min); Skipton (hourly; 25min).

Tourist office Opposite the train station on Station Rd (April–Sept Mon–Sat 9.30am–4.30pm; Oct–March Mon & Wed–Sun 10am–4pm, Tues 10.30am–4pm; ☎01943 602319, ⓦvisitilkley.com).

ACCOMMODATION

Crescent Inn Brook St ☎01943 811250, ⓦthecrescent inn.co.uk. Conveniently situated in the centre of Ilkley, the *Crescent Inn* is housed in a fine, mid-nineteenth century building with all the stately spaciousness that that implies. Rooms are comfortable and public areas are brightly decorated. **£80**

Rombalds Hotel West View, Wells Rd ☎01943 603201, ⓦrombalds.co.uk. A *Best Western* hotel, *Rombalds* occupies a handsome Georgian terrace on the road out of the town up onto Ilkley Moor, with easy access both to the town centre below and the moor above. Rooms are traditional and comfortably furnished. **£94.50**

EATING AND DRINKING

Bar t'at Ale and Wine Bar 7 Cunliffe Rd ☎01943 608888. Who could resist the name! Huge selection of wines and beers, a nice crossover pub/wine bar atmosphere, and a decent range of light lunches, sandwiches, tasting boards and main meals (£9.50–12.50). Food served Mon–Fri noon–2.30pm & 5.30–9pm, Sat noon–9pm, Sun noon–6pm.

Box Tree 35–37 Church St ☎01943 608484, ⓦtheboxtree.co.uk. One of Yorkshire's handful of Michelin-starred restaurants, offering inventive, top-notch French cuisine (garden pea *velouté* with roasted langoustine and confit pork belly, perhaps, or ravioli of caramelized veal sweetbreads with *morels*, onion puree and madeira jus) in mellow, old-fashioned surroundings. Four-course a la carte menu £60; *gourmand* menu £75; menu du jour (Tues–Thurs dinner) £40. Tues–Thurs 7–9.30pm, Fri & Sat noon–2pm & 7–9.30pm, Sun noon–2pm.

★ **Flying Duck** 16 Church St ☎01943 609587. A real ale brewpub, with its own brewery (Wharfedale Brewery) in a barn at the rear, this is the town's oldest pub building, with stone walls, beamed ceilings and stone-flagged and wooden-floored rooms renovated to feel airy and spacious. The beers are great, with guest ales in addition to their own offerings. Check out the sunny upstairs terrace on warm days. Sun–Thurs noon–11pm, Fri & Sat noon–midnight.

Piccolino 31–33 Brook St ☎01943 244 3220, ⓦindividualrestaurants.com. Large Italian restaurant in the centre of Ilkley, one of a chain of *Piccolinos* across the country, with antipasti and a good range of fresh pastas, pizzas, fish and steak dishes. Star attraction, though, is the roof terrace with terrific views across the town and (this is England after all) a retractable roof and space heaters. Mains £15.95–22.95. Mon–Sat 10am–11pm, Sun 10am–1.30pm.

Skipton

SKIPTON ("sheep town" in Anglo Saxon) bills itself as the gateway to the Dales, and with good reason. It sits on their southern edge, at the intersection of the two routes that between them cradle the National Park and Area of Outstanding Natural Beauty – the A65 to the western and the A59/61 to the eastern dales.

A pleasant market town with a long history, Skipton is defined by its **castle** and **church** and by its long, wide and sloping **High Street**. The town also gets a lot of character from a **water system** that includes the Leeds and Liverpool Canal, its spur the Springs Canal, and the Eller Beck. The high street is lined on each side with large cobblestones (or setts), upon which, on Mondays, Wednesdays, Fridays and Saturdays, **market stalls** are erected (the rest of the time they're used for parking). Along with the usual high-street shops, it also features the nicely done **Craven Court**, a recreation of a Victorian two-tier arcade, with small shops selling jewellery, clothes, shoes and gifts.

Diverging from the High Street on the right is pedestrianized **Sheep Street**, off which, through an archway, lies a cobbled precinct consisting of **Victoria Square**, **Victoria** and **Albert** streets and **Albert Terrace**. The innovative **Auction Mart Theatre**, meanwhile, lies on the outskirts of town.

Skipton Castle

High St • March–Sept Mon–Sat 10am–6pm, Sun noon–6pm; Oct–Feb Mon–Sat 10am–4pm, Sun noon–4pm • £7.30; family £23.50 • ☎ 01756 792442, 🌐 skiptoncastle.co.uk

The dominant feature of Skipton, sitting squat and threatening at the top of the sloping High Street, is **Skipton Castle**, one of England's best-preserved medieval fortifications. After entering the outer bailey through the massive gatehouse, you can visit the Tudor conduit court, where Lady Anne Clifford's yew tree stands (see below), along with the thirteenth-century chapel and certain parts of the house (the rest is a private residence) – the banqueting hall, the kitchen, the bedchamber, the privy, the dungeon and the watchtower. Though there are periodic historical reconstructions, there's otherwise little attempt to put flesh on the bones with furnishings or exhibits – it's the castle itself, its architecture and austere beauty that makes it worth visiting. There's a shop, café and picnic area.

Holy Trinity Church

Mill Bridge • Mon–Sat 9am–4pm • Free • ☎ 01756 793622, 🌐 holytrinityskipton.org.uk

Right next to Skipton Castle is the largely fourteenth-century **Holy Trinity Church**, repaired by the indefatigable Lady Anne (see below), and worth visiting for its numerous monuments to members of the **Clifford family** (the earliest is for the 1st Earl of Cumberland, who died in 1542), and for the view down Skipton High Street from the churchyard.

THE CLIFFORD CLAN

Originally Norman, Skipton Castle was granted by the crown to Robert de Clifford in 1310, and remained in the **Clifford family** for generations. Among the more famous of the clan were John Clifford (1435–61) who fought in the War of the Roses and earned the name "The Butcher" after the battle of Wakefield; George Clifford, 3rd Earl of Cumberland (1558–1605), a notorious Elizabethan buccaneer who attacked Spanish shipping in the Caribbean using a man o'war which he paid for himself; and, possibly the most renowned, his daughter **Lady Anne Clifford** (1590–1676), at different times Countess of Dorset, Pembroke and Montgomery.

Lady Anne, the last member of the family to own the castle, was a fervent royalist during the English Civil War. After the Battle of Marston Moor, **Skipton Castle** was the only remaining Royalist stronghold in the north, eventually falling to the Parliamentary forces in 1645 after a valiant three-year siege led by Lady Anne herself. Cromwell ordered that the castle be "slighted" by having the roofs removed. Within ten years Lady Anne was allowed to replace them, on condition that they were not strong enough to bear cannon. To celebrate, she planted a yew tree in the central courtyard. The castle remained in the hands of her descendants into the twentieth century, and the roofs and yew tree remain to this day.

Craven Museum and Gallery

17–21 High St • Mon & Wed–Sat 10am–4pm • Free • ☎ 01756 706407, ⓦ cravenmuseum.org

On the High Street, downhill from the church and castle, the Town Hall building contains the diverting **Craven Museum and Gallery**, chock-a-block with archeological and social history artefacts. Look out for the prehistoric bear skull, the iron age sword, the excellent half-sized reconstruction of a Roman hypocaust (sophisticated under-floor central heating), the hoard of silver medieval coins, the comprehensive costume collection and the domestic bits and pieces (penny farthing bicycle, gas stove) from the Victorian and Edwardian periods. Interesting information boards in the foyer recount the history of Skipton's canals, and there are occasional fun days for kids.

The canals

To the east of town is the boat-thronged **canal wharf**, at the intersection of the 1770-built trans-Pennine **Leeds and Liverpool Canal** and the **Springs Canal**, a spur added in 1773–74 to move limestone from quarries a quarter of a mile to the north of the town centre down to the main canal. As in many similar towns, the canals have been cleaned up and are now an essential part of Skipton's character. Even in the early days haulage companies sometimes used their boats for excursions, and today the recreational aspect of the canals is an important attraction. The Wharf itself is an attractive waterside area with the odd bar and bistro, while the canal towpaths provide pleasant walking and information boards. Try following the Springs Canal past the High Corn Mill then through the gorge below the castle into Skipton Woods – it's a pleasant way to spend an hour, and the views of the castle are spectacular.

Auction Mart Theatre

Gargrave Rd, 1.5 miles west of town, near the A59/A65 bypass roundabout • Mon–Fri 9.30am–5pm • ☎ 01756 709666, ⓦ themarttheatre.org.uk

Skipton's three-ring **Auction Mart** was erected in 1990 to replace the auction houses that dated back to 1894. Watching cows, sheep and pigs being paraded, listening to the staccato patter of the auctioneer and mingling with cloth-capped farmers down from the Dales would be diverting enough – but something of a minority taste, perhaps. What makes this place unique is that, when it's not being used for the animal mart, the main ring becomes the **Auction Mart Theatre**, in an uncanny echo of Elizabethan players putting on shows in straw-strewn coaching inn yards. On performance nights (see opposite) the tubular steel barriers are removed, the concrete apron scrubbed down, the stage erected, and the show goes on to an audience that sit on the seats vacated by the farmers. And how do arts and agriculture get on? Like a house on fire, apparently, with the farmers insisting on using the theatre lights during auctions – they make the animals look their best.

ARRIVAL AND INFORMATION

SKIPTON

By train The train station is on Broughton Rd, a 10min walk from the centre.

Destinations Leeds (every 10–15min; 43min).

By bus The bus station is on Keighley Rd, at the bottom of High St. Buses from Skipton run up Wharfedale to Hubberholme (1hr 24min–1hr 44min).

Destinations Grassington (Mon–Sat every 1–2hr; 33min); Ilkley (hourly; 25min); London (2 daily; 6hr 20min); Malham (2 daily Mon, Wed & Fri; 35min); Settle (hourly; 46min).

Tourist office Town Hall, High St (Mon–Sat 9.30am–4.30pm; ☎ 01756 792809).

TOURS AND ACTIVITIES

Pennine Boat Trips Waterside Court ☎ 01756 790829, ⓦ canaltrips.co.uk. A variety of canal experiences: private charter, public canal trips, theme nights (country and western and swing among others), and on-board food

(1hr trips £8; family £22).

Pennine Cruisers 19 Coach St ☎ 01756 795478, ⓦ penninecruisers.com. This narrow-boat rental company offers 30min canal trips (£4).

ACCOMMODATION

With several accommodation options, Skipton makes an excellent base for exploring the **southern dales** – not only Wharfedale, but Ribblesdale, Malhamdale and Nidderdale as well.

Herriot's Hotel Broughton Rd ☎01756 792781, ⓦherriotsforleisure.co.uk. A short walk along the canal towpath from the centre of Skipton, in a Victorian listed building, the boutique-style hotel and its restaurant, *Rhubarb* (see below) both offer cheerful decor and lots of original features. Rooms vary in size and price, and there are frequent packages available. **£125**

Rendezvous at Skipton Keighley Rd ☎01756 700100, ⓦrendezvous-skipton.co.uk. A modern hotel on the canal side less than a mile south of the town centre. With comfortable rooms, contemporary lines, a ballroom and restaurant, *The Baby Swan* (see below), the *Rendezvous* is

building up a good reputation. **£67.50**

★**Skipton Park Guest 'Otel** 2 Salisbury St ☎01756 700640, ⓦskiptonpark.co.uk. Just northwest of the town centre. Rates are eminently reasonable for a warm welcome, comfortable double room and great breakfast. **£70**

Woolly Sheep Inn 38 Sheep St ☎01756 700966, ⓦwoollysheepinn.co.uk. Pleasant town centre Timothy Taylor tavern that offers a good range of pub food (from £8) including sandwiches, steaks and pasta dishes. The nine rooms are comfortable and well furnished, though some are small. Convivial, but it can be noisy. **£80**

EATING

The Baby Swan Keighley Rd ☎01756 700100, ⓦrendezvous-skipton.co.uk. Located in a conservatory-type room in the *Rendezvous* hotel (see above). They advertise "straightforward, honest-to-goodness food" – roast turkey, pork fillet, lamb niçoise – and an a la carte menu (mainly steaks) at £15.95–20.95. Daily 6.30–9pm.

Rhubarb Broughton Rd ☎01756 792781,

ⓦherriotsforleisure.co.uk. The restaurant of *Herriot's Hotel* (see above) has a good, slightly offbeat selection of starters (house Scotch egg with artichoke, broad bean and spinach salad; duck spring rolls; goats cheese and roast fig), main courses (deep-fried hoi sin and sesame seeded beef salad), speciality pies and steaks. Mains £12–18.95. Daily noon–2.30pm & 6–9.45pm.

ENTERTAINMENT

Skipton is enlivened by several **festivals**: a Waterways Festival on the canal in May, Sheep Day and Clogfest in July, and, every two years, a wonderful international Puppet Festival (the next is in Sept 2015).

★**Auction Mart Theatre** Gargrave Rd, 1.5 miles west of town ☎01756 709666, ⓦthemarttheatre.org.uk. This unique, nonprofit theatre, held in an animal auction mart (see opposite), offers touring productions, workshops, events, comedy, opera, folk music and much else. Since it

opened in 2005, the Mart Theatre has hosted plays by the Hull Truck Theatre Company, *Cosi Fan Tutti* by performers from Opera North, comedy with Alan Carr, Rory Bremner and Jeremy Hardy and music with Kiki Dee, Norma Waterson and Martin Carthy.

Bolton Abbey Estate

Five miles east of Skipton • Daily: March–May, Sept & Oct 9am–7pm; June–Aug 9am–9pm; Nov–Feb 9am–6pm, last admission 1–3hr before closing (car park daily 9.30am–4pm) • £7/vehicle • ⓦboltonabbey.com • Buses from Grassington (28min), Ilkley (14min) and Kettlewell (Sun; 1hr) stop on the village green and at Strid Wood; By car, turn off the A59 and follow the B6160 (signposted Bolton Abbey); there are car parks at Bolton Priory, Cavendish Pavillion and Strid Wood

The **Bolton Abbey Estate**, owned by the Devonshire family since 1753, incorporates a spectacularly beautiful stretch of Wharfedale, much admired by, among others, John Ruskin, who wrote lovingly about it, and J.M.W. Turner, who painted it frequently. A major tourist attraction, it consists of 30,000 acres of wonderful countryside – woodland and landscaped grassland – and more than eighty miles of footpaths on both sides of the river. It includes the village of **Bolton Abbey**, and a number of small-scale but interesting attractions, including the picturesque ruins of **Bolton Priory**.

Bolton Abbey

Entering the estate, the first thing of note you come to is the spectacularly upmarket *Devonshire Arms Country House Hotel and Spa* (see p.199). Beyond lies the village of **BOLTON ABBEY** itself – little more than a cluster of houses, a bookshop, several tearooms and a village hall, and the first of the estate's three **car parks** – the closest to the priory ruins.

Bolton Priory

Bolton Priory, a gentle 1.5-mile walk from the Bolton Abbey village car park, is a twelfth-century Augustinian priory, established in 1154 and dissolved in the 1530s, when it met the fate common to all monastic houses in the country. However, the nave of the priory was allowed to continue as a parish church, so this survives in good condition. The rest of the priory, stripped of its roof lead and left open to the elements, began to deteriorate rapidly and was raided for building stone by the inhabitants of the valley, leaving the picturesque ruins you see today. Opposite the priory are much-photographed **stepping-stones** giving access to the opposite bank of the river.

Cavendish Pavilion

A mile or so up Wharfedale beyond Bolton Priory, a car park stretches along the bank either side of the **Cavendish Pavilion** (turn right at the Victorian ornamental fountain). Halfway up the estate, this car park gives access by footpath downriver back to Bolton Priory, and upriver to the Strid and Strid Wood. There's a café, restaurant, shop and toilets, and a footbridge across the Wharfe, so you can choose to follow either bank.

Strid Wood

Strid Wood, designated a Site of Special Scientific Interest (SSSI) because of its acidic oaks, home to many plants, animals and birds, has a car park and visitor centre, a refreshment kiosk and a Caravan Club site. A path leads through the woodland, high above the Wharfe, then down to the **Strid**, where the river's water squeezes with great force through a narrow chasm. The rocks are smooth and pitted with holes created by the rotary motion of small stones driven by the current, and though it's exhilarating to get down close to such elemental power, care needs to be taken – the rocks can sometimes be slippery, and as a notice at the site says "the Strid is dangerous, and has claimed lives in the past". From the car park it's a ten-minute walk down to the river, and a fifteen-minute walk back – about half a mile.

Barden Tower

Footpaths from Strid Wood continue north as far as **Barden Tower**, the ruins of a hunting lodge that was home to Henry Clifford, 10th Earl of Skipton (nicknamed the Shepherd Lord because of his gentle and pious personality but who, in old age, fought successfully at the Battle of Flodden Field against the Scots). Next to the ruins is the sixteenth-century **Priest's House**, built by the Shepherd Lord for his chaplain, and now a rather swish restaurant (see opposite).

Hesketh Farm Park

Bolton Abbey village • April–Aug Tues–Sun 10am–5pm; Sept–Oct Sat & Sun 10am–5pm • £5; family £20–35 • ☎ 01756 710444, ⓦ heskethfarmpark.co.uk

Just up the road from Bolton Abbey's main car park is **Hesketh Farm Park**, a 600-acre family-run farm that raises cattle and sheep, with lots of other animals – pigs, goats, hens, donkeys and ponies, many of which reside in a large, heated barn, useful in inclement weather. There are also tractor and trailer rides, a fine playground, pedal go-karts, a sand pit and a café.

Embsay and Bolton Abbey Railway

Bolton Abbey train station • From £6, depending on day • ☎ 01756 710614, ⓦ embsayboltonabbeyrailway.org.uk

Running between Bolton Abbey and Embsay, five miles to the west, is the dinky **Embsay and Bolton Abbey Railway**, a private heritage railway (once part of the Skipton to Ilkley line) that offers a forty-minute trip from one terminus to the other and back. Most trains are steam hauled, the dales scenery is terrific, and there's a shop and café at each station. Services are most frequent in summer; check the website for timetables and fares.

ACCOMMODATION AND EATING — **BOLTON ABBEY**

Bolton Abbey Estate Caravan Club Site Strid Wood ☎ 01756 710433. A pretty site set in a woodland glade. Closed early Jan to mid-March. **£24.30**

★**Devonshire Arms Country House Hotel and Spa** Bolton Abbey ☎ 01756 710441, ☻ thedevonshirearms .co.uk. The *Dev* is a top-end luxury hotel with designer rooms, two restaurants – one, the *Burlington*, with a Michelin star (fixed menu £65, including beautifully executed classic dishes like turbot, Hereford beef rib, or – £10 extra – butter poached lobster) – and a spa. Various offers can bring the rack rates down. **£160**

Devonshire Fell Hotel Burnsall, 6.5 miles north of Bolton Abbey ☎ 01756 718111, ☻ devonshirefell .co.uk. The sister hotel of the *Devonshire Arms Country House Hotel* (see above), the *Devonshire Fell*, on the very edge of the estate, offers similar luxury, individual rooms designed by the Duchess herself, and wonderful views across the village of Burnsall. And you get to use some of the older sister's bells and whistles, including the spa and the chauffeur service. **£125**

★**Priest's House** Barden Tower, 3 miles north of Bolton Abbey ☎ 01756 720616, ☻ thepriestshouse .co.uk. Beautifully set next to the Barden Tower, with terrific views back down Wharfedale, the *Priest's House* offers fine food (top quality standards like chicken supreme, sea bass and herb-crusted rack of lamb) in heraldic surroundings. Prices aren't bad either – two courses £23.95, three courses £26.95 Booking essential. Fri & Sat noon–2.30pm & 7–11pm, Sun noon–2.30pm.

Burnsall

The B6160, after it crosses Barden Moor, sweeps down into the quaint village of **BURNSALL** – the view of the village as you approach, dominated by the elegant 1884-built bridge across the Wharfe, is worth stopping for. On the left as you approach the village is the **Devonshire Fell Hotel** (see above). Just before the bridge is a wide green running down to the river – this is a good place to stop, with a shop, tearooms and a pub and that picturesque bridge. Beyond the pub is the seventeenth-century village school, established by the "Dick Whittington of the Dales" Sir William Craven (he was Lord Mayor of London between 1610 and 1612), the church of St Wilfrid, probably built in around 1520, but using parts of an earlier church, and the village hall. There's nothing spectacular to see, but pottering around villages like Burnsall is one of the pleasures of visiting the Dales.

Linton

The village of **LINTON**, about nine miles north of Skipton, is a gem. It comes in two parts – the village itself, clustered around a riverside **green**, and the **church** and **falls**, a ten-minute walk away along a well-signposted footpath. Linton (or to give it its full title, Linton-in-Craven) is largely a product of the seventeenth and eighteenth centuries. A charming pub, the *Fountaine Inn* (see p.200) sits at the top of the green, which slopes down to the **Linton Beck**. On sunny days, with the pub terrace packed with drinkers and diners, and the green thronged with people being mugged by marauding gangs of ducks and geese, the village is a picture.

Fountaine's Hospital

Chapel services Sun 8am & Tues 9.15am

Fountaine's Hospital lies close to Linton's village green. Grade II-listed almshouses, built in 1721, they were bequeathed to the village in the will of Richard Fountaine, an undertaker who made his fortune in London during the plague in 1665 and the Great Fire of London the following year (it's an ill wind, as they say). The almshouses provided accommodation for six poor men or women of the parish, maintained by the income from lands purchased at the same time for that purpose. In the centre of the building is a chapel (open to the public), at which attendance was compulsory for the occupants. Run by twelve trustees, the charity still operates, though beneficiaries no longer have to attend chapel – places are open to anyone over the age of 60 who has lived in the parish for more than two years.

Linton Beck

Linton Beck is crossed by no fewer than three **bridges**. The oldest is the flat "clapper" bridge, now the furthest upstream after being moved to make way for the 1892 road bridge. Between them is the elegantly arched "packhorse" bridge, built in the fourteenth century, but with parapets that were raised in the seventeenth century – before that, low parapets were necessary to allow for the panniers slung either side of the packhorses.

St Michael's church

☎ 01756 752575, ⓦ linton.localchurch.org.uk

St Michael's church, down by the River Wharfe and said to be the oldest in England still in use, is delightful, probably dating from the tenth or eleventh century, with further additions in the following three centuries. There's much of interest inside – a Norman font, a Lady Chapel partly furnished with pieces by Thompson of Kilburn, the "mouseman" (see p.229) and a medieval stone altar. Entrance to the churchyard is through a gate or over a stone-stepped stile.

Linton Falls

On the road from Linton church to Threshfield, a signposted path leads to the moderately impressive **Linton Falls** (which are also accessible from Grassington), crossed by a footbridge. The falls are notable for the startlingly white rocks with black patches of weed which the water thunders over and between.

ACCOMMODATION AND EATING   LINTON

★**Fountaine Inn** Lauradale Lane ☎ 01756 752210, ⓦ fountaineinnatlinton.co.uk. The *Fountaine Inn*, at the top of the green in Linton, offers very good food and drink and really appealing accommodation in idyllic surroundings. Mains, such as bacon loin, steak pie and lamb shank hotpot, go for £10.95–18.25. A lovely place to sit outside on a warm day. Pub Mon–Sat 11am–11pm, Sun noon–10.30pm; food served daily noon–9pm. **£99**

Grassington

GRASSINGTON is the pretty stone capital of Upper Wharfedale. A market town by the end of the thirteenth century, and a lead mining community in the eighteenth and nineteenth centuries, it is now a centre for walkers and a good stop for anyone wishing to explore the southern dales.

Grassington Folk Museum

6 The Square • April–Oct Tues–Sun 2–4.30pm • Free • ☎ 01756 753287, ⓦ grassingtonfolkmuseum.org.uk

Housed in two converted lead-miners' cottages on the cobbled village square, the intriguing **Grassington Folk Museum** contains a miscellany of everyday objects from the village's past, ranging from Iron Age bones found in the local area to domestic equipment, tools, road-signs, and furniture – and even a selection of vintage cameras – in a series of attractive stone-walled rooms.

Grassington Lead Mining Trail

1.5 miles northeast of Grassington village centre

Grassington Lead Mining Trail, on the moors to the northeast of the village, guides you through the remains of extensive lead workings. This monument to the village's industrial history is particularly well worth visiting – though the mineral agent's house, blacksmith shop, carpenter's shop and counting house are now private residences, there's an excellent general information board, and no fewer than eighteen stop-off

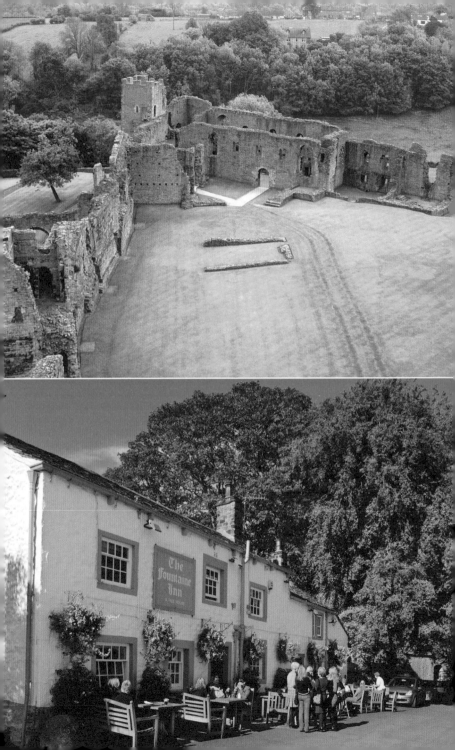

points with subsidiary boards giving clear explanations of what exactly you're looking at. If you visit each board you'll walk about five miles. But stick to the track – some of the mine shafts are uncapped and unrecorded.

ARRIVAL AND INFORMATION   GRASSINGTON

By bus The bus station is in the car park of the National Park Centre.
Destinations Ilkley (4 daily on Sun; 42min); Pateley Bridge (1 on Sun; 25min); Skipton (hourly; 33min).
National Park Centre Hebden Rd (April–Oct daily 10am–5pm; Nov–March check with centre; ☎01756

751690, ⓦyorkshiredales.org.uk).
Grassington Hub and Community Library Manor Hill Barn, 2 Garrs Lane (Mon–Fri 10am–6pm, Sat 10am–4pm; ☎01756 752222, ⓦgrassington.uk.com). This clearing house for local information, though designed for local residents, can be of use to visitors.

ACCOMMODATION AND EATING

Angel Inn Hetton, 5 miles southwest of Grassington ☎01756 730263, ⓦangelhetton.co.uk. Ivy-covered walls outside, oak beams and log fires within: a delightful old inn with an upmarket brasserie, just off the Grassington to Skipton road. Pick of the brasserie menu is the seven-week matured steak (mains £14.95–16.95). Top-end accommodation is offered in a barn conversion directly across the road. Mon–Fri noon–2.15pm & 6–9.30pm, Sat noon–2.15pm & 6–10pm, Sun noon–2.30pm & 6–8.30pm. **£150**
★**Ashfield House Hotel** 3 Summers Fold ☎01756 752584, ⓦashfieldhouse.co.uk. Top-end B&B in attractive converted lead miners' cottages just off the main square. Friendly welcome, lovely decor, excellent food cooked by the owner, Joe, and comfortable, quirky rooms. Guests often meet for drinks before dinner, and Joe is a fount of local knowledge. **£100**
Black Horse Hotel 4 Garrs Lane ☎01756 752770, ⓦblackhorsehotelgrassington.co.uk. In the centre of

the village, this seventeenth-century coaching inn has a nice carpeted bar with open fires and settles, and fifteen rooms with barely a right angle between them. There's a bar and restaurant with main courses at at £10–16. **£85**
★**The Devonshire Hotel** 25–27 Main St ☎01756 752525, ⓦthedevonshirehotel.co.uk. Pretty Dales pub with rooms on Grassington's main square. Good food (home-made steak and ale pie, crisp belly pork, caramelized red onion and Wensleydale tart) at reasonable prices (mains £8.95–14.25, two courses £12), clean rooms and a convivial atmosphere. This is the village's most popular pub, so it can get a bit noisy. Food served noon–9pm. **£80**
Old Hall Threshfield, 1 mile west of Grassington ☎01756 752441, ⓦoldhallinnandcottages.co.uk. Lovely old pub across the River Wharfe from Grassington, with four bedrooms on site and nearby self-catering cottages. Extensive a la carte menu covering all the usual pub favourites – main courses £11.95–19.95. **£90**

Kilnsey and around

Beyond Grassington, Wharfedale is more sparsely settled, with the river narrowing and the field barns proliferating. As you travel up the valley, the first village you come to is **KILNSEY**, a tiny village with a fish farm, a hotel and, just north of the village, **Kilnsey Crag**, a limestone cliff that sweeps down to the village and crouches over the main road, 165ft high with an overhang of 40ft. Mastiles Lane, which heads directly west from the centre of the village and peters out into a footpath, was once a Roman road (it passes through the remains of a Roman camp just south of Malham Tarn), and later became a drovers' route for taking Fountains Abbey sheep to the high summer pastures.

A mile or so further on, the road sweeps down into **KETTLEWELL**, where much of *Calendar Girls* was filmed. There are **pubs** in Kettlewell, all of which do **accommodation**, an old-fashioned **garage** and several shops.

ACCOMMODATION AND EATING   KILNSEY AND AROUND

Blue Bell Inn Middle Lane, Kettlewell ☎01756 760230, ⓦbluebellkettlewell.co.uk. Pretty seventeenth-century coaching inn that's very much a traditional pub and serves good, no-nonsense pub grub (lasagne, meat and potato pie and the like; main courses £10–15). Food served noon–5pm & 6–9pm. **£80**

Racehorses Hotel Southern end of Kettlewell ☎01756 760233, ⓦracehorseshotel.co.uk. Comfortable, recently refurbished hotel in what was once the *Blue Bell Inn*'s stables. The food is a cut above your standard bar food (home-made pate, for example, or rare breed belly pork); main courses start at £11. Food served noon–2pm & 6–9pm. **£90**

THE HUBBERHOLME PARLIAMENT

The lovely old **George Inn** (see below) in Hubberholme, built as a farm in the mid-seventeenth century, was once the vicarage, and the incumbent developed the habit of putting a lighted candle in the window as a sign of God's grace. A tradition developed that on the first Monday of the year, an auction would be held to decide who would get use of sixteen acres of church pasture land, the proceeds of which would be used to relieve the parish poor. The auction still goes on today. The vicar oversees the auction from the dining room (The House of Lords), the interested farmers make their bids in the bar (The House of Commons), and the highest bid when the candle goes out is the winner. And a good time, be assured, is had by all.

Tennants Arms Mastiles Lane, Kilnsley ☎ 01756 753946, ⓦ tennantsarms.co.uk. Nestled under Kilnsey Crag, the *Tennants Arms* offers pub food (mains £9.75–17.75) and accommodation in six nicely turned-out rooms. **£90**

Hubberholme

Upriver from Grassington and Kettlewell, beyond **Starbotton** and **Buckden**, is the peaceful village of **HUBBERHOLME**, sitting at the highest reaches of Wharfedale and at the entrance to Longstrathdale. A tiny place, the village has two main claims to fame. The first is the so-called **Hubberholme Parliament** (see box above); the second arises from its association with one of Yorkshire's greatest writers, **J.B. Priestley**. Hubberholme was one of his favourite haunts, and he mentions it fondly in *English Journey* ("a tiny hamlet that had a fine little old church and a cosy inn"). The pub – the *George* – is still cosy, with real fires and no gaming machines or piped music, and the church is still little and old. He liked Hubberholme so much, in fact, that his ashes are buried here – a plaque inside the church doesn't say where, simply that his ashes are "buried nearby".

ACCOMMODATION AND EATING   HUBBERHOLME

George Inn ☎ 01756 760223, ⓦ thegeorge-inn.co.uk. Occupying a lovely seventeenth-century farm building overlooking the river, this pretty spot, home to the famous Hubberholme Parliament (see box above) is all flagstone floors, thick stone walls and mullioned windows. The six guest rooms, in the main pub and in the coach house, are comfy and cosy; only five are en suite. Food is served, too, including home-made individual pies. Pub Mon 4–10.30pm, Wed & Thurs noon–10.30pm, Fri–Sun noon –11pm; food served noon–2.30pm & 6–8pm. **£80**

Littondale

If you've time, a detour up **Littondale** – which is named after the village of Litton, not its river (the Skirfare) – is well worth the effort. The road branches west from Wharfedale at Knipe Scar, between Kilnsey and Kettlewell, and is signposted for Arncliffe. As you travel up the dale, you come first to **ARNCLIFFE**, a pretty village with a medieval church next to a medieval bridge, and a long narrow green overlooked by the *Falcon Inn* (see below). If you continue straight you come to **LITTON**, with its own attractive little pub, the *Queens Arms* (see p.204). If, instead of going straight at Arncliffe you turn left, you soon climb up into the hills either side of a bleak but beautiful scree-dotted U-shaped valley created by the Cowside Beck, where the views back towards Arncliffe are magnificent. Eventually, having passed several hanging valleys and a waterfall on the left, the single-lane road goes around the top of Malham Tarn and drops down into Malham itself (see p.191).

ACCOMMODATION AND EATING   LITTONDALE

The Falcon Inn Arncliffe ☎ 01756 770205, ⓦ thefalcon inn.com. Quaint Dales pub with locally sourced food and five guest rooms. Lunches (sandwiches, pies, ploughman's) are available to all, but dinner is only for residents or if you've prebooked. Pub Mon–Thurs noon–3pm & 7–11pm, Fri & Sat noon–11pm, Sun noon–10.30pm. **£70**

4

Queens Arms Litton ☎ 01756 770096, ⓦ queensarms litton.co.uk. A traditional pub run by the local community, the *Queens Arms* does food (slow cooked belly pork in cider, for example, or baked tomato galette with goats cheese, with mains £10.95–17.95) and offers accommodation. It's popular with hikers. Pub Tues–Fri 11am–3pm & 6–11pm, Sat 11am–11pm, Sun 11am–10.30pm. **£89**

Nidderdale

The easternmost of the dales, **Nidderdale** is for some obscure bureaucratic reason not actually in the Dales National Park, but is an Area of Outstanding Natural Beauty instead. The River Nidd, after which the valley is named, rises on Little Whernside, flows south to the dale's main town, the charming **Pateley Bridge**, then wanders off across the Vale of York via Ripley, just outside Harrogate. Peaceful and relatively little-visited, with **How Stean Gorge** as its main visitor attraction, Nidderdale is sky-high on get-away-from-it-all potential. **Middlesmoor**, the hill village at the head of the dale, is worth a quick visit if only for the vistas – the views down the dale towards Gouthwaite Reservoir are out of this world. The **Nidderdale Rambler** bus service (ⓦ dalesbus.org) goes all the way up the valley.

Pateley Bridge and around

PATELEY BRIDGE, gateway to Nidderdale, is an extraordinarily pleasant little town, though its inhabitants must have strong legs to deal day in, day out with its hills. Sitting astride the B6265 Ripon to Skipton road, it owes its existence to the river crossing that gives it its name. Here the Nidd was forded from time immemorial and bridged in the fourteenth century, the original wooden bridge being replaced with a stone one in the eighteenth century. Today the main road drops steeply down to the river via the High Street, crosses the bridge, then climbs steeply up the other side of the valley. A footbridge keeps pedestrians and traffic apart. The main part of the town lies to the north of the Nidd, while south of the bridge lies pleasant **Bewerley Park** and a recreation ground complete with excellent children's playground, bandstand and war memorial. For some uplifting **views**, climb to the top of the High Street, turn right into the Ripon Road – the B6265 – and look out for the "Panorama Walk" sign that points off to the left. The walk loops north, then returns to the main road; it's a rewarding stroll of about 1.5 miles.

On either side of the town, not in Nidderdale itself but within Pateley Bridge's orbit, are the **Stump Cross Caverns**, about five miles to the west, and the **Brimham Rocks** about half as far to the east.

Nidderdale Museum

Old Workhouse, King St • Easter–Oct daily 1.30–4.30pm; Nov–Easter Sat & Sun 1.30–4.30pm • £2 • ☎ 01423 711225, ⓦ nidderdalemuseum.com

There's nothing wildly exciting to do in Pateley Bridge, but the town's history is well documented by the maroon plaques of its heritage trail, and in the **Nidderdale Museum**, housed in the Old Workhouse, with eleven rooms of exhibits covering local agriculture, industry, transport, costume and religion. There's a reconstructed cobbler's shop, a schoolroom, a Victorian parlour and a general store, together with costume exhibits, transport artefacts and much else.

Gouthwaite Reservoir

The seven-mile drive (or walk, along the Nidderdale Way) northwest from Pateley Bridge up Nidderdale is a delight. Passing a *pub*, *The Bridge Inn*, behind which is an old water mill with a huge wheel, you arrive, 1.5 miles after Pateley Bridge, at the 1899-built dam of **Gouthwaite Reservoir**, a nature reserve and a Site of Special

Scientific Interest (SSSI) owned by Yorkshire Water. There's a car park about halfway along the reservoir's two-mile length, and there are three viewing areas set aside for birdwatchers. At the upper end of the reservoir is the village of **Ramsgill**, most famous for the eighteenth-century **Yorke Arms** (see below).

Stump Cross Caverns

Five miles west of Pateley Bridge • Feb–Nov daily 10am–5.30pm (last admission 4.30pm); Dec–Feb Sat & Sun 10am–5.30pm (last admission 4.30pm) • £7.50 • ☎ 01756 752780, ⓦ stumpcrosscaverns.co.uk

Discovered by lead miners in 1860, and extended several times by further exploration, the four-mile-long **Stump Cross Caverns** have been a show cave now for more than 150 years. In addition to the usual stalactites and stalagmites, some of which have been at least 230,000 years in the making, you can also see the bones of reindeer, bison, wolves and wolverine, deposited more than ninety thousand years ago. The entrance to the caves includes an extensive shop and pleasant tearooms, and you can view an audiovisual presentation about the caves and the area.

Brimham Rocks

Summerbridge (2.5 miles southeast of Pateley Bridge) • Visitor centre Easter, June–Oct & half terms daily 11am–5pm; rest of year Sat & Sun 11am–5pm (except Nov & Dec; Sat & Sun 11am–4pm) • Free; NT • ☎ 01423 780688, ⓦ nationaltrust.org.uk/brimham-rocks

While Stump Cross Caverns (see above) give a taste of the region's underground delights, **Brimham Rocks**, spread across the moors east of Pateley Bridge, do the same for the surface. An extensive area (around 20 hectares, or 50 acres) of tortured rock formations created over three hundred million years ago by wind, water and ice erosion, the rocks are laced through with footpaths and opportunities for clambering among the surreal, nightmarish shapes – some of them seem to defy gravity.

ARRIVAL AND INFORMATION

By bus The easiest way to get to Pateley Bridge by bus is from Harrogate.

Destinations Harrogate (hourly; 47min); Middlesmoor (3 daily on Sun; 22–52min); Otley (1 daily; 40min); York

PATELEY BRIDGE AND AROUND

(1 weekly, on Sun; 1hr 20min).

Tourist office 8 High St (April–Oct Mon–Sat 10am–1pm & 1.30–5pm; Nov–March Fri & Sat 10am–4pm; ☎ 01423 711147, ⓦ nidderdale.co.uk).

ACCOMMODATION AND EATING

Lyndale Guesthouse King St, Pateley Bridge ☎ 01423 712657, ⓦ lyndaleguesthouse.com. Big stone Victorian house just off the High St, with spotless and nicely decorated rooms. **£85**

Roslyn House King St, Pateley Bridge ☎ 01423 711374, ⓦ roslynhouse.co.uk. Victorian guesthouse with attractive rooms, all en suite. They offer pick-up and take-out packages for walkers. **£79**

Sportsmans Arms Wath-in-Nidderdale, a mile north of Pateley Bridge ☎ 01423 711306, ⓦ sportsmans -arms.co.uk. The *Sportsmans Arms* is a fine old hotel with unpretentious food, cosy bars and lovely grounds. **£130**

★**Yorke Arms** Ramsgill-in-Nidderdale, just over 4 miles up the valley from Pateley Bridge, just beyond

Gouthwaite Reservoir ☎ 01423 755243, ⓦ yorke-arms .co.uk. Something of an institution in Nidderdale, and winning lots of press acclaim, the *Yorke Arms* is a very fancy restaurant-with-rooms. The chef is Frances Atkins, one of the few female Michelin-starred chefs in the country. It's in a beautiful old ivy-covered building, with luxurious decor and comfortable accommodation – and, of course, the food is top-quality fine dining, using lots of Yorkshire ingredients in delicate, imaginative combinations. Try the Wensleydale soufflé with sea scallops, vanilla and tomato, or the fillet of Yorkshire beef with wild mushrooms and foie gras (lunch £40 Mon–Sat, £50 Sun; eight-course taster menu £85, plus £55 if you want all the recommended wines). Restaurant daily noon–1.30pm & 7–8.30pm. Full board per person **£190**

How Stean Gorge

Lofthouse • Daily 10am–5pm • £5.75; family £16 • ☎ 01423 755666, ⓦ howstean.co.uk • Bus #825 or #25 from Pateley Bridge and Harrogate

Beyond **Lofthouse** at the northern end of Nidderdale, a road off to the left leads in a mile to Nidderdale's main attraction, **How Stean Gorge**, a ravine gouged out by the rushing waters of a tumultuous stream. Despite first appearances – it's 1000 yards long and up to 80ft deep – the gorge is remarkably easy to explore. The path that winds along above the river is manageable for most people (though you need to be relatively able-bodied if you want to take one of the paths or flights of steps down to the water) and excellent information boards tell you about the gorge's geology, history and wildlife. Though How Stean Gorge might not suit those with extreme claustrophobia, arachnophobia or vertigo, it is a lovely way to spend anything from a couple of hours to a whole day – real adrenaline junkies can explore it via the thrilling **Via Ferrata**.

Wear appropriate clothing and shoes; hard hats are provided at the ticket office and torches can be rented. The ticket office is in a café, which has a terrace (the cakes are delicious).

How Stean Tunnel and Tom Taylor's Cave

A hundred-yard walk upriver brings you to the **How Stean Tunnel**, from where the river that carved out the gorge emerges. Downstream there's an overhang that forces you to walk for 20 yards or so in a crouch, two footbridges across the gorge (one, a girder, flexes alarmingly as you cross, the other, made of wood, doesn't), and the entrance to **Tom Taylor's Cave**, a hundred-yard long bat- and spider-thronged tunnel that comes out at the top end of the car park (the fainthearted can skip this bit). At the bottom of the gorge there's access to huge flat rocks from which you can dangle your feet.

Via Ferrata

3hr guided walks £45 (prebooking necessary) • Ⓦ howstean.co.uk

You may notice in places fixed ladders, steel cables and beams crisscrossing the gorge. These are for the **Via Ferrata** ("Iron Way") courses that are put on in the gorge, which involve expert-accompanied wading through waterfalls, rock traversing, abseiling, scrambling up ladders and along beams, with, at the end, your very own DVD of the experience recorded on the guide's head-cam. Invigorating or insane, depending on your point of view.

Dentdale

Dentdale, at around ten miles, is one of the shorter of the Yorkshire Dales. It is also one of the most beautiful, named after its only village of any size – Dent – and not after the River Dee that runs through it, rising not far from the sources of the Ribble, but flowing in the opposite direction. The valley is a picture of rural peace and quiet, with the road running beside the river with its succession of waterfalls, crossing bridges to change banks. You're likely to see a lot of walkers, since the **Dales Way** also runs down the valley bottom. Finally the road crosses the river one more time and enters the delightful village of **Dent**.

Dent

DENT, accessible on the Dentdale Explorer bus (Ⓦ dalesbus.org), really is picture-postcard pretty, with cobbled streets, whitewashed stone cottages, two lovely pubs, a few shops and cafés and an interesting church. A good place to start a walk around the village is the car park, where context boards include an excellent relief plan of the village, information about its history and suggested walks in the area. Turning left out of the car park opposite the **Memorial Hall** (built as a Church of England elementary school in 1845) you come to a crescent – following it around brings you first to the *Sun Inn*, then to the *George and Dragon* (see opposite). Opposite the latter is a modern fountain, appropriately made of a giant rock, installed in honour of locally born geologist **Adam Sedgwick** (1785–1873), famous for his work on geological classification. The son of the local vicar, he became one of the founders of modern geology. He was an early influence on Charles Darwin, though strongly disagreed with his theory of evolution by natural selection.

St Andrew's Church

Daily, services 10.30am Sun

Within the centre of Dent crescent, **St Andrew's** parish church offers fascinating glimpses into the village's past. The first thing you see as you enter is a bicycle-wheeled hand-cart. Next (if walking clockwise), on the wall about halfway down the nave, is the Sill Memorial, dedicated to brothers who made a fortune in the West Indies and returned to Dent with slaves, causing a furore among local people. Also along this wall is a double row of the church's seventeenth-century box pews. The final two pillars in the nave are part of the original Norman church. Along the south aisle are a desk from the old village grammar school, what's left of a Jacobean three-decker pulpit, several windows dedicated to the Sedgwick family and a memorial to its most famous son, Adam (see opposite).

ACCOMMODATION AND EATING   DENT

★**George and Dragon** Main St ☎01539 625256, ⓦ thegeorgeanddragondent.co.uk. Opposite the fountain in the centre of the village, the *George and Dragon* is the bigger of Dent's two pubs, with slightly more of a hotel feel to it. They offer ten comfortable rooms (though some are small), good service and a convivial bar serving food.

Pub daily 11am–11pm; food served daily: June–Oct 6–9.30pm; Nov–May 6–8.30pm. **£90**

Sun Inn Main St ☎01539 625208, ⓦ suninndent .co.uk. Nice, old-fashioned little pub in the centre of the village, though perhaps in need of a little attention, with three basic rooms. **£42**

Wensleydale

The best-known and most populous dale in the National Park is **Wensleydale**, which slashes across the northernmost reaches of the southern dales and is named after the not-very-important village of **Wensley**. Its river, the Ure, heads east, joining the Nidd just northwest of York and becoming the Ouse. Wensleydale has the only main road in the north dales, the A684, which links Kendal in the Lake District with Northallerton on the edge of the North York Moors. It also has numerous towns and villages – the biggest and busiest being **Hawes**, where you'll find the information centre for the entire dale (see p.209) – and is therefore the easiest dale in which to find accommodation, and the best for even non-enthusiastic walkers to potter around in. And, of course, it is the source of one of the world's great **cheeses**, much beloved by claymation characters Wallace and Gromit, who once announced that the Moon was made of Wensleydale.

Public transport down Wensleydale from Hawes is not bad, but above Hawes is more problematic – where it exists, it involves a combination of bus and train, with some walking as well. Travel between Wensleydale and other places involves at least one change.

Hawes

Lying at the head of the valley, **HAWES**, Wensleydale's principal settlement, is accessible from the east and west via the A684, though its most attractive approach is from the south, over the top from the head of Wharfedale via beautiful, empty Langstrothdale and the 20° hill down into the town. As you'd expect of the region's main village, Hawes has a good range of shops, pubs and cafés, plenty of places to stay, and even a number of attractions, including a moderately impressive little waterfall just up from the bridge that crosses it. Thronged with walkers throughout the year, Hawes has an independent life of its own – a fact emphasized by its busy and venerable (established 1699) Tuesday **market**, always thronged with farmers as well as visitors, and the livestock mart at the eastern edge of the town (auctions are held on Tues, and sometimes Thurs and Sat).

Dales Countryside Museum

National Park Centre, Station Yard • Feb–Dec daily 10am–5pm; last admission 4pm • £4 • ☎ 01969 666210,
ⓦ www.dalescountrysidemuseum.org.uk

In the same building as the tourist office (see opposite) is the excellent **Dales Countryside Museum**, occupying the old railway station's buildings and three railway carriages attached to a tank engine, looking for all the world as if it has just steamed in. The imaginatively mounted displays cover the geology, wildlife, history, agriculture, industry, transport, domestic life, education and leisure of the region – in fact, of every conceivable aspect of life. You start in the main station building, continue through the railway carriages standing at the platform, and end in the railway shed. Look out for the simulated lead mine, the Roman soldier and milestone, the schoolroom equipment and the evocative children's toys.

Ropemakers of Hawes

Town Foot • Mon–Fri 9am–5.30pm • Free • ☎ 01969 667487, ⓦ ropemakers.co.uk

At the other side of the station car park from the Dales Countryside Museum, and well worth a look, is the **Ropemakers of Hawes**, a working rope manufacturer (Outhwaites

---

WALKS AND WATERFALLS AROUND HAWES

There are some excellent opportunities for **walking** around the village of Hawes. Visitors are requested to keep strictly to the paths, though – the revival in grass meadows is very welcome, and leads to wonderful displays of flowers in the spring and summer, but their principal function is to grow grass to be turned into winter fodder for the animals, not to set urban hearts aflutter. A couple of waterfalls make a good target for two short walks from the town:

AYSGILL FORCE (4 MILES)

Off the road south towards Langstrothdale, **Aysgill Force** is just upriver from Gayle Bridge and Gayle Mill, and is really impressive only when there's been a lot of rain. From the centre of Hawes take the footpath that starts directly across from the *White Hart* pub. Follow the path uphill behind the Wensleydale Creamery to **Gayle**, walk through the village, then continue along the path with the Gayle Beck to your left to the waterfall. If you want to return by a different route, continue along the Beck until you get to a green lane, then bear right, walking back towards Hawes. When you get to a tarmac road, carry on straight for about 550 yards, then turn right onto a fingerpost-marked path which brings you out back at the Wensleydale Creamery.

HARDRAW FORCE (3.5 MILES)

Northwest of the town, **Hardraw Force** is much more awe-inspiring than Aysgill Force, at nearly 100ft being the highest single-drop waterfall in England (above ground at least). From the **Dales Countryside Museum** car park in Hawes follow the Pennine Way north of the old platforms. About 100 yards beyond, follow the paved path off to the left which crosses two fields before rejoining the road. After crossing Haylands Bridge, turn right along a marked public footpath that climbs across a field towards Stone House. Cross the road, and continue up the path to the hamlet of **Sedbusk**. Here you can either cross the village green and follow the signposted path west to **Simonstone**, or if you'd prefer easier walking, take the lane parallel to the path. At Simonstone bear left down the hill to Hardraw, where access to the Falls is through the delightful *Green Dragon Inn* (see p.210). There's a charge of £2, payable at the pub, which gets you onto the path to the falls (it's on private land); it really is worth shelling out for.

OTHER WALKS

In addition to these two strolls, there are numerous waymarked walks all around Hawes; details can be picked up at the tourist office and National Park centres. For ramblers, Harvey's **Hawes Walks** (£2.50) manages to get eight relatively easy-to-follow walks and a lot of information onto a single sheet. More intrepid walkers might want to follow the seven-mile route through Gayle, up onto the Roman Road (Cam High Rd), around Wether Fell then down through Burtersett and back to Hawes, or the ten-mile walk through Gayle, along Gaudy Lane to Tarney Fors, then back via Appersett to Hawes.

Ltd). It's a good example of what the people of Wensleydale seem to excel at – going about their business all the while adding strings to their bows by opening up their establishments as visitor attractions. Most of us give ropes little thought, perhaps even assuming that they largely belong to the past, but a visit to Outhwaites soon puts this right. They make general-purpose rope and string, but also church bell ropes, banister ropes and everything from skipping ropes to carrier bag handles – the list seems endless.

Wensleydale Creamery

Gayle Lane • Daily 10am–4pm, best viewing times 10am & 2pm; winter opening times vary • Cheese Experience £2.50; family £7.50 •
☎ 01969 667664, ⓦ wensleydale.co.uk

The story of **Wensleydale Creamery**, which makes delicious traditional Wensleydale cheeses using milk from local farms, is a heart-warming one. Established in 1150 by Cistercian monks, the creamery made cheese continuously in the dale for more than eight hundred years. Having survived the 1930s Great Depression with the support of local people, it finally appeared to have bitten the dust in 1992. But then, following a successful management buy-out by a group of the creamery's ex-managers and a local businessman, the creamery was reopened, and a loss of 59 jobs was turned into the creation of more than two hundred. Following a major expansion, the creamery made a successful bid to secure Protected Geographical Indication (PGI) status, whereby no cheese made outside Wensleydale can call itself "Yorkshire Wensleydale". Today you can watch cheese being made and visit the museum of cheesemaking. Cheese lovers shouldn't miss the restaurant (daily 11am–4pm) and coffee shop (daily 9am–4.30pm) – with most of the dishes involving, of course, Wensleydale cheese – the gift shop, and the wonderful specialist cheese shop where you can stock up on all manner of sizes and flavours.

4

Gayle Mill

Mill Lane • Mid-April to early Oct Mon–Fri 1hr tours 1pm & 3pm • £6; 1st Sun of month 2hr demonstration tour 11.30am & 2.30pm £12 •
☎ 01969 667320, ⓦ gaylemill.org.uk

Just up the road from the Wensleydale Creamery is **Gayle Mill**, a restored mill that started life in 1784 as a textile mill but was converted into a sawmill in 1878, with the waterwheel being replaced by water turbines. In the early twentieth century the turbines were harnessed to generate electricity, and a gas engine installed as back up for when there wasn't enough water to drive the turbines. Abandoned in 1988, Gayle Mill is now a visitor attraction, education centre and a commercial sawmill, and sells green electricity to the National Grid. Viewing of the mill is by tour only and wooden products made on site – from fruit bowls to boot jacks – are on sale.

ARRIVAL AND INFORMATION   HAWES

By bus Public transport down Wensleydale from Hawes is fairly good.

Destinations Askrigg (1 daily; 10min); Aysgarth (1 daily; 20min); Bedale (hourly; 1hr 30min); Grassington (1 weekly; 1hr 18min); Leeds (Sun only; 2hr 43min); Leyburn (3 daily; 33min); Northallerton (Sun only; 1hr 13min); Ripon (3 weekly; 2hr 10min).

Tourist information Yorkshire Dales National Park Centre,

Station Rd (April–Oct daily 10am–5pm; Nov–March selected days 10am–4pm – phone for details; ☎ 01969 666210). An essential first stop when visiting the area is Hawes' recycled former railway station, which contains the National Park information centre and tourist office plus a museum (see opposite). Load up with information on what to do and where to go, and stock up with maps, walking guides, equipment and outdoor clothes.

ACCOMMODATION AND EATING

Caffé Curva Market Place ☎ 07523 981950. Stylish coffee bar/deli providing excellent coffee, breakfasts, lunches and snacks in a relaxed atmosphere. Tues–Sat 9am–5pm, Sun 9.30am–4.30pm.

Crown Market Place ☎ 01969 667212, ⓦ crownhawes .co.uk. Dog-friendly town-centre pub with a good

atmosphere, real ales and fires, pub food including steak and Old Peculier pie or Yorkshire gammon with egg (mains £5–12), outdoor seating and three attractive guest rooms. Pub 11am–11pm. **£70**

Fountain Market Place ☎ 01969 667206, ⓦ fountain hawes.co.uk. Substantial seventeenth-century pub/hotel that offers pub grub and real ale, plus eleven guest rooms including a couple of singles. Food served Sun–Fri noon–2.30pm & 6–8.30pm, Sat noon–8.30pm. **£75**

Green Dragon Hardraw Hawes, 1.5 miles north of Hawes ☎01969 667392, ⓦ greendragonhardraw.com. A pretty stone-built pub with stone flags, open fires, rag rugs, settles, comfortable rooms and suites. There are also facilities (though no hook-ups) for motor caravans, and an area for tents. Food on offer includes breakfasts, pies and game casseroles (mains £8.95–10.95). Food served daily 8am–10pm. Bunkhouse per person **£15**; doubles **£70**

Old Board Market Place ☎01969 667223, ⓦ theold boardinn.co.uk Pleasantly renovated town centre inn offering a warm atmosphere and hearty pub food. Much used by walkers. **£70**

Old Dairy Farm Widdale, 3 miles west of Hawes ☎01969 667070, ⓦ olddairyfarm.co.uk. Once the home of the original Wensleydale dairy herd, this farm, set in 5 acres. offers luxurious and contemporary accommodation, with classy dining – sea bass with roasted Mediterranean veg, lamb shank with spring onion mash, mint-marinated kangaroo fillet (two courses £24, three courses £29 at dinner, cheaper for Sun lunch). While non-residents are welcome to dine, there are no fixed opening hours – it is essential to phone first. **£140**

★**Stone House Hotel** Sedbusk, 2 miles north of Hawes ☎01969 667571, ⓦstonehousehotel.co.uk. Country house hotel in a stunning old building set in magnificent countryside. Old-fashioned decor, traditional food, welcoming bar – all you'd expect from a country house hotel. **£140**

YHA Hawes Lancaster Terrace ☎0845 371 9120, ⓦyha.org.uk/hostel/hawes. Modern hostel on the edge of town. Reception open 8.30–10am & 5–10pm. Dorms **£19**; doubles **£49**

Askrigg

Around five miles east of Hawes is **ASKRIGG**, best known as the setting for the TV adaptations of James Herriot's books *All Creatures Great and Small* – the real life *Kings Arms* made many appearances as the *Drover's Arms*. The vet himself, however, lived and worked in Thirsk (see p.226), on the edge of the North York Moors. The village's Grade I medieval church, **St Oswald's**, is worth a few minutes; take a look at the fine beamed nave ceiling, the very old font mounted on a millstone and the numerous seventeenth- and eighteenth-century memorials.

Aysgarth

AYSGARTH, ten miles east of Hawes on the A684, gives its name to **Aysgarth Falls**, its triple waterfall. The upper falls can be seen from the road where it crosses Yore Bridge, and there's an attractive eighteenth-century mill complex next to it which contains the *Mill-Race Teashop*, but the middle and lower falls to the east are even better. There's a fine **National Park Centre** and **café** with a large car park just off the A684 between the upper and middle falls, well placed for all three. A pleasantly wooded 0.5-mile walk along the bank high above the river gives access to the two lower falls – the middle falls via a flight of steps down to a viewing platform (which keeps you at arm's length), the lower falls down steps to extensive flat rocks beside the cascade. Don't expect Niagara – they're fairly low key – but the staircase of broken water and the continual roar were impressive enough to be used as a setting for Robin's fight with Little John in Kevin Costner's 1991 film *Robin Hood, Prince of Thieves*. Heed the warning signs telling you not to stray off the marked paths; if you fell into the river here you wouldn't stand much chance.

Castle Bolton

From Aysgarth, a ten-minute drive on a country lane that loops off the main A684 road to Leyburn brings you to the village of **CASTLE BOLTON** and its famous castle.

Bolton Castle

North Leyburn • Daily: Feb & March 10am–4pm; April–Oct 10am–5pm • £8.50; family £30 • ☎01969 623981, ⓦ boltoncastle.co.uk

Completed in 1399 for Richard le Scrope, **Bolton Castle** is a splendidly preserved medieval fortress set in sweeping Dales scenery and sitting halfway up a long slope. It's of particular interest to military architects, representing a time when the demands of defence were becoming balanced by those of domestic comfort. The castle saw Civil War action in 1645, was involved in the Pilgrimage of Grace in 1536 and served as a prison for Mary, Queen of Scots in 1569. It was also mentioned in three of Shakespeare's plays – *Henry IV, Henry V* and *Richard III*. Visitors get a real feel for what it must have been like to live in medieval times, and much has been done to cater for families with children – there are several family trails to follow, children can dress up in period costume, there's a medieval nursery with authentic toys for them to play with, and special events such as family fun days, falconry displays, medieval tournaments and wild boar feeding throughout the season. Interestingly, the castle is still owned by the original family – the current Lord Bolton is a direct descendant of le Scrope.

St Oswald's church
Morning prayer 3rd Sun of the month 9.30am

Although Bolton Castle is the main attraction in Castle Bolton, it's well worth popping into **St Oswald's church** (listed grade II) which stands next to it. For a start, it's older than the castle by about seventy years, and its bare simplicity, with small windows, no aisles and short tower, is pleasing. Note the very old font and the little window on the south side of the chancel, possibly a leper's window designed to allow those afflicted with the disease to participate in services without compromising the rest of the congregation.

Leyburn

The bracing market town of **LEYBURN**, one of Wensleydale's main settlements, lies sixteen miles east of Hawes, on a hillside astride three open squares – Market Place and the attached Commercial Square, and, along the short High Street, Grove Square. A handsome town whose prosperity during the great age of coaching has left it with a generous stock of Georgian houses, it's a useful centre for exploring mid-Wensleydale, with several banks with ATMs, numerous pubs and hotels, and a range of shops. Its main draw is the **Shawl** escarpment, but there are further attractions along the Harmby Road to the southeast of the centre. Leyburn also hosts the **Dales Festival of Food and Drink** (ⓦdalesfestivaloffood.org) early in May each year.

The Shawl

Just west of the centre is Leyburn's crowning glory, the **Shawl**, a limestone escarpment that penetrates right into the centre of the town. The Shawl has been used as a recreation area since Victorian times and offers open grassland, numerous benches and wonderful views across Wensleydale. Take Shawl Terrace, which leads from Commercial Square through a kissing gate out on to the grass.

Wensleydale Railway
Harmby Rd • Up to five trains a day, depending on the season • Adult single fare from £9; day rover £17 • ⓦ wensleydalerailway.com

Leyburn is a station on the scenic heritage **Wensleydale Railway**, a reopened section of the old Northallerton-Garsdale line. The sixteen-mile stretch from Leeming Bar on the A1 to Redmire is run by a private company, Wensleydale Railway PLC, not only as a visitor attraction, but also as a service to the people of the dale. In addition to the standard services through the fields, woodland and hills of beautiful Lower Wensleydale, they also mount a range of additional events – family fun days, murder mysteries, Christmas specials and so on.

ARRIVAL AND INFORMATION   **LEYBURN**

By bus Buses leave from and stop in the Market Place. Destinations Bedale (hourly; 20–30min); Hawes (3 daily; 32min); Northallerton (3 daily on Sun; 36min).
Tourist information *Dales Haven Guesthouse*, Market

Place (April–Oct Wed–Mon 10.30am–4pm; Nov–Christmas, Feb & March Fri–Sun 10.30am–4pm; ☎01748 622317, ⓦ welcometoleyburn.co.uk). A volunteer-run service.

Middleham

Around two miles south of Leyburn, across a castellated bridge which was originally a suspension bridge, built in 1829, is the fine market town of **MIDDLEHAM**. It centres on a sloping, cobbled **market square** that contains a cross dating back to the town's charter in 1388 and four good pubs, and offers good views of the surrounding countryside. Middleham is also at the hub of a major horse-training area, with around fifteen stables in the environs.

Middleham Castle

Castle Hill • April–Sept daily 10am–6pm; Oct daily 10am–5pm; Nov–March Sat & Sun 10am–4pm • £4.60; EH • ☎ 01969 623899, Ⓦ english-heritage.org.uk

Beyond the market place stands the impressive Norman **Middleham Castle**, which replaced an earlier motte-and-bailey some 550 yards away. Both were designed to protect the main road from Richmond to Skipton. The castle was built in the 1170s to be militarily functional, but was developed in the fourteenth and fifteenth centuries to provide more comfortable living accommodation, much in the same way as Bolton Castle (see p.210). This was the much-loved fortified palace where Richard III spent much of his childhood – hence the name of the pub in Middleham's main square. The connection with Richard III is marked, too, by the remains of Middleham's second market cross on Castle Hill, erected to commemorate the 1479 granting of a further market charter by Richard when he was still Duke of Gloucester.

Forbidden Corner

Tupgill Park Estate, Coverham, a couple of miles southwest of Middleham • April–Oct Mon–Sat noon–6pm, Sun 10am–6pm; Nov–Dec Sun only • £11; family £38 • ☎ 01969 640638, Ⓦ theforbiddencorner.co.uk • Note that entry is by pre-bought ticket only – you can't just turn up on the day (phone ahead, or go to Leyburn tourist office on the day, where a limited number of tickets are available on a first-come-first-served basis

Southwest of Middleham, in open countryside used by local stables as gallops, the **Forbidden Corner** is an attraction that is easier to enjoy than to describe. It's a sort of walk-through puzzle, a fantasy labyrinth of spirits, giants, monsters and much else. You walk from area to area via paths and tunnels, coming across follies, surprises and riddles at every turn, egged on by mysterious voices that talk to you in rhyme as you approach. In the garden of Tupgill Park, the Forbidden Corner was put together in the 1980s by the estate owner C.R. Armstrong for his children. After being opened up in 1993 for a charity event, it is now a popular and unique Wensleydale attraction. There's a café and gift shop, and a pleasantly wooded picnic area across the road.

ACCOMMODATION AND EATING   MIDDLEHAM

White Swan Hotel Market Place ☎ 01969 622093, Ⓦ whiteswanhotel.co.uk The pick of the four establishments on Middleham's market place, the *White Swan* has a contemporary look, with stripped pine or stone-flagged floors, nicely turned out bedrooms with cool decor, and a fashionable brasserie-style eating area. Pub Mon–Fri 11am–11pm, Sat 11am–midnight, Sun noon–11pm. **£65**

Jervaulx Abbey

Jervaulx • Visitor centre Feb–Nov 10am–4/5pm • Free, donations accepted • ☎ 01677 460391 (daytime) or ☎ 01677 460226 (evenings), Ⓦ jervaulxabbey.com

The remains of **Jervaulx Abbey** lie on the A6108 between Leyburn and Masham. Established in 1156, this was one of Yorkshire's three great Cistercian abbeys – the others being Fountains (see p.176) and Rievaulx (see p.234) – and today, beautifully sited and atmospheric to a fault, it's almost a one-stop-shop for serious students of ecclesiastical architecture, with "something of nearly everything monastic", as Pevsner's Architectural Guide has it.

A short walk from the main road, Jervaulx Abbey is privately owned. Looking very natural and un-buffed-up, it has no visitor centre, café or gift shop (there's a tearoom just across the main road). And yet it's a sort of do-it-yourself attraction, with information leaflets available that you pay for in an honesty box. Try to visit in spring, when the whole site is carpeted in wild flowers.

Masham

Between Jervaulx and Ripon stands the village of **MASHAM**, famous among tipplers for its two highly regarded **breweries** (the town's name is, alas, pronounced "Mass'm", whereas "Mash'em" would be much more appropriate). The production of industrial quantities of beer would, you'd have thought, dominate the town, but in fact, as you explore the large and attractive **Market Place** you wouldn't know that the two breweries are there – apart, perhaps, from the smell of hops. Try to visit the village on a Wednesday or Saturday, when the **Market Place** fills with stalls.

St Mary's church
Masham Vicarage • ☎ 01765 689255

St Mary's Church has monuments to members of the families who occupied Low Burton Hall (the splendidly named Sir Marmaduke Wyvill) and Swinton Park (the even more splendidly named Sir Abstrupus Danby). The former's tomb has Sir Marmaduke and his wife lying on their sides, heads propped on elbows as if they're lying on the beach. The church's most outstanding monument, though, is the early ninth-century **Anglo-Saxon shaft** that stands outside, just in front of the porch, which has detailed carvings of animals and legends in four tiers, alas heavily eroded.

4

ACCOMMODATION AND EATING
MASHAM

Bordar House Teas 13 Market Place ☎ 01765 689118. Sandwiches, hot and cold filled rolls, toasties and paninis (at around £2), cooked snacks (filled Yorkshire puddings, quiches) and cakes. Most sandwiches and snacks around £5. Daily 9am–5pm.

Kings Head Hotel Market Place ☎ 01765 689295, ⓦ chefandbrewer.com. A splendid late Georgian building right on the main square, the *Kings Head* has 27 renovated and cheerfully decorated rooms. Good pub grub is served (mains £7.99–15.99) with an evening set menu with two

---

MASHAM'S BREWERIES

Masham has almost iconic status among real-ale enthusiasts because it is home to not one but two famous traditional breweries whose output can be found issuing from hand-pumps in pubs across the land.

Theakston, makers of the famous Old Peculier bitter, is the original, built in 1875, while the **Black Sheep Brewery** is the newcomer, set up in 1992 by Paul Theakston, a member of the great brewery family who didn't agree with the takeover of the firm by big boys Scottish and Newcastle. The name Black Sheep speaks for itself. The breweries are overwhelmingly welcoming – both have pub-style bars in excellent visitor centres, offer guided tours (which include a beer or soft drink), and have shops overflowing with beer and branded goodies. You can imagine that there's keen competition between the two concerns – Theakston's flagship *White Bear Hotel* stands cheek-by-jowl with the Black Sheep Brewery. But for visitors this competition certainly seems to work – both breweries, and indeed Masham as a whole, make for a wonderful day (or more) out.

BREWERY TOURS
Black Sheep Brewery Gun Hill, Wellgarth, Masham ☎ 01765 680122, ⓦ blacksheepbrewery .com. In addition to its tours (£6.95; family £19.95) and its shop, the Black Sheep Brewery also has a large bistro with an extensive menu. Sun–Wed 10am–4.30pm, Thurs–Sat 10am–11pm.

Theakston Brewery Just off the Market Square,

Masham ☎ 01765 680000, ⓦ theakstons.co.uk. Theakston is hidden but signposted along a narrow lane – look out for the square, iron-strapped chimney. Tours (£6.95; family £18.40) include a glimpse into a genuine traditional cooper's workshop. No children under 10. Jan–June & Sept–Dec 10.30am–4.30pm (tours 11am, noon, 2pm & 3pm); July & Aug 10.30am–5.30pm (tours hourly from 11am).

courses for £12, three for £14. Pub Mon–Sat 11am–11pm, Sun noon–10pm; food served Mon–Sat 7am–11pm, Sun 8am–9.30pm. **£55**

★ **Swinton Park** Swinton Park, 1.5 miles south of Masham ☎01765 680900, ⓦ swintonpark.com. The ancestral home of the Cunliffe-Lister family, *Swinton Park* styles itself a "luxury castle hotel". Set in 200 acres of parkland, lakes and gardens, it offers fine dining, luxurious individually designed rooms with lovely views, a spa and service that is attentive without being intrusive. There are separate lunch, Sunday lunch and dinner menus, all of which focus on seasonal local produce; at dinner you can choose between a "classic" (£55) or "signature tasting" (seven courses; £65) menu. Non-residents are required to reserve tables for lunch and dinner, and there's a smart dress code in the evening. They also offer cookery courses and a host of special events including golf, kite flying, alfresco dining and fishing. Food served 7.30–10am, 12.30–2pm & 7–9.30pm. **£165**

White Bear Hotel Wellgarth ☎01765 689319, ⓦ thewhitebearhotel.co.uk. Theakston establishment sitting right next to the brewery of its competitor, Black Sheep, within walking distance of Masham town centre. Calm, cool decor. **£115**

Bedale

Just west of the A1, where the road from Northallerton to the Dales crosses it, is the handsome town of **BEDALE**. Tuesday markets have been held on its long, wide market place since 1251; the market place also features lots of independent shops, many with Georgian facades, and an ancient market cross. On North End First, the extension of the market place beyond the cross, is the church of **St Gregory** and **Bedale Hall**, home to the tourist office (see below) and the local **museum**, and behind which is a surviving ice house.

Constable Burton Hall

Leyburn, 7 miles northwest of Bedale • Grounds mid-March to Sept daily 9am–6pm • £4 • ☎ 01677 450428, ⓦ constableburton.com

On the A684 road from Bedale to Leyburn, **Constable Burton Hall** is one of England's most perfect, unaltered Georgian houses. Not to be confused with East Yorkshire's Burton Constable Hall, it was designed by John Carr of York, and built in 1762–68 for Sir Marmaduke Asty Wyville. The Wyville family are still in residence, and the grounds (though not the house) are open to the public. A printed sheet is available to help identify the plants, with ten marked stops.

INFORMATION AND ACTIVITIES   BEDALE

Tourist office Bedale Hall, North End (April–Oct Mon–Fri 10am–4pm, Sat 9am–2pm; Oct to mid-Dec & mid-Feb to Easter Tues 10am–4pm, Sat 10am–1pm; ☎01677 424604, ⓦ bedale.org).

Aerial Extreme Kirklington, 6 miles south of Bedale (Feb–Nov, days and times vary; £26; children £21; 20 percent discount for families; ☎0845 652 1736, ⓦ aerialextreme.co.uk). A must for adrenalin-junkies who like swinging around on ropes, wobbling across bridges, shooting along zipwires, climbing walls and generally defying gravity. There's also paintballing, quad-biking, archery and clay-pigeon shooting.

ACCOMMODATION AND EATING

Elmfield House Arrathorne, 6 miles northwest of Bedale ☎01677 450558, ⓦ elmfieldhouse.co.uk. Beautifully located in peaceful countryside south of the hamlet of Arrathorne, *Elmfield House* offers five beautifully appointed and spacious rooms, with 24 acres of gardens, paddocks and woodland for guests to explore. **£75**

Milbank Arms Bedale Rd, Well, 4 miles south of Bedale ☎01677 455041, ⓦ www.themilbankarms.co.uk. Traditional stone pub with good food, including curry, Cajun chicken, ham and eggs or home-made fishcakes, and a great selection of constantly changing pies. Mains £6.95–17.95. Tues–Sat noon–2pm & 6–11pm, Sun noon–2pm; food Tues–Sun noon–2pm, Tues–Sat 6.30–9pm.

Swaledale

Pretty **Swaledale**, the northernmost of the Yorkshire Dales, runs parallel to Wensleydale, and is linked to it by the **Buttertubs Pass** on the Hawes to Thwaite road. The pass is named after a number of deep potholes into which, legend has it, farmers on their way to market used to lower their butter to keep it cool. Swaledale has a few small villages, a large number of field barns, and, at its eastern end, the impressive town of **Richmond**.

Muker and around

The tiny villages of **Upper Swaledale** have little to offer the visitor except peace and quiet. **KELD**, for example, is the haunt of sheep and hardy walkers, with memories of a lead mining past. There are a few houses, a large United Reformed Church and a hotel – and that's about it. **MUKER**, however, has every claim to being the capital of Upper Swaledale. Its most distinctive building is the **Old School** (now a craft shop and gallery) – it's got a sheep sitting astride the roof ridge. Muker exudes a sense of community – its village hall is housed in the old Literary Institute (1868), which in its day had a stock of more than sixty books, a legacy of its nineteenth-century prosperity from lead mining. There's also St Mary's Church, a Public Hall dating back to 1922 and, of course, a pub. All in all, Muker appears, both in the past and nowadays, to punch well above its weight.

Ivelet bridge

Between Muker and Reeth, 1.5 miles west of the village of Gunnerside just north of the B6270, is the locally celebrated and very elegant medieval **Ivelet bridge**, a high single-span crossing the river Swale. The flat stone on the northern end of the bridge is a "coffin stone" where, it is said, pall bearers rested their burdens – until the consecration of a graveyard in Muker in 1580, corpses had to be carried to Grinton, ten miles to the east, for burial.

4

ACCOMMODATION AND EATING

MUKER AND AROUND

Farmers Arms Muker ☎01748 886297, ⓦfarmers armsmuker.co.uk. Traditional old pub, with the usual pub grub mains (£7.25–11.25) and a range of local real ales. Although it has no accommodation on site, the *Punch Bowl* does own a studio flat across the road. Mon–Fri 11am–11pm, Sat & Sun 11am–midnight; food served noon–2.30pm & 6–8.30pm. Weekly rental **£330**

Keld Lodge Keld, a mile north of Muker ☎01748 886259, ⓦkeldlodge.com. Once a shooting lodge, then a youth hostel, this is now a pleasant hotel "for the active and relaxed" with some singles as well as double

rooms. They offer food, too, from soy-marinated tuna steak with pak choi to lamb's liver with mash (mains £10.25–13.50). **£100**

★**Punch Bowl Inn** Low Row, 5 miles east of Muker ☎01748 886233, ⓦpunchbowl-swaledale.co.uk. Delicious, hearty English food – creamy cauliflower and stilton soup, say, or local loin of lamb with wild mushrooms and rosti – in pleasant surroundings at reasonable prices (mains £10.50–16.95). Also eleven nicely turned-out, individually designed guest rooms. Sun–Thurs 11am–11pm, Fri & Sat 11am–midnight. **£99**

Reeth

Swaledale's main village is **REETH**, which lies where Arkengarthdale joins Swaledale. On a hillside gathered around a large, sloping, triangular and partially cobbled green, which offers wonderful views of the surrounding hills, Reeth's village given over largely to walkers and other visitors. It's all stone cottages, Dales pubs, cafés and tearooms, with a few shops, a small, undistinguished church and a large war memorial with a flagpole.

Swaledale Museum

The Green • May–Oct daily 10am–5pm • £3 • ☎01748 884118, ⓦswaledalemuseum.org

Housed in what was built as a Methodist Day School in 1836, the **Swaledale Museum**, covering ordinary life in the valley, is a very good example of its kind, with displays, as you'd expect, about geology and prehistory, farming, lead mining and much else. There's a small café and a shop.

INFORMATION

Tourist information The National Park Centre, Hudson House (daily: May–Aug 10am–4pm; Sept–April 10am–3.30pm; ☎01748 884059, ⓦ yorkshiredales.org.uk), has a wealth of information on the area, including dry stone walls and barns, heather moorland, meadows, Swaledale sheep, lead mining and much else.

ACCOMMODATION AND EATING

Black Bull High Lane ☎01748 884213, ⓦ theblack bullreeth.co.uk. Reeth's oldest surviving pub, dating from 1680. Oddly, the pub sign is upside down – an eccentricity that dates back many years to a dispute between the then landlord and the Park Authority. Traditional pub food (mains £7.95–9.95) is on offer, along with no-frills accommodation. Many of the rooms have terrific views of the dale, but are in urgent need of some TLC. Daily 11am–2am. **£80**

Burgoyne Hotel The Green ☎01748 884292, ⓦ theburgoyne.co.uk. Comfortable hotel in the heart of the village, occupying a fine house built in 1783 and subsequently much extended. Good food (the fish is particularly tasty – perhaps a poached plaice fillet rolled in smoked salmon, or grilled Dover sole with sautéed fennel and brown shrimps) is served in an elegant dining room with great views (four-course dinner £40, two courses £27). Single sitting for dinner, with orders taken from 7pm, dinner starts 7.30–8pm, dining room closes 10pm. **£140**

Kings Arms High Row ☎01748 884259, ⓦ thekings arms.com Unpretentious 1734-built pub/hotel serving standard pub food (mains £7.95) and providing accommodation in rooms that are a little dated and tired. **£70**

Richmond

Below Reeth, Swaledale broadens out, with the hills getting lower and flatter, until finally you enter the jewel of the north dales, **RICHMOND**. Built high above a bend in the River Swale, the town centre is easy to get around – there's an imposing **castle** on a crag towering over the north bank of the river, beyond which the main streets radiate out north and west from the large, tinned-loaf shaped **Market Place**.

The town has a number of worthwhile attractions – the **Richmondshire Museum**, the **Greyfriars Tower** and the historic **Theatre Royal** among them – and just beyond the town limits is **Easby Abbey**. But it's the castle and the Market Place that give Richmond its great character.

Richmond Castle

Riverside Rd • April–Sept daily 10am–6pm; Oct–Nov daily 10am–5pm; Dec–March Sat & Sun 10am–4pm • £4.90; EH • ☎01748 822493, ⓦ english-heritage.org.uk

Richmond Castle is not only interesting in itself, but also has the most wonderful views from the top of the keep. Dating from as early as 1071, it is one of the oldest Norman stone fortresses in Britain, though the keep itself is later – between 1150 and 1180. Entry is through a well-stocked shop, there are walls and the cockpit garden to explore, the extensive interior lawns are ideal for kids to let off steam, there are picnic tables, and the whole castle has well-judged information boards. The star turn is, without doubt, the massive **keep**, with its stone staircases, spacious main rooms and fine battlements, from where the views down into the town, across the turbulent Swale, and out across the gentle surrounding countryside are out of this world. It's also well worth taking a stroll along **Castle Walk**, around the outside of the curtain walls: again, the views and the roar of the river far below are magical.

Richmondshire Museum

Ryder's Wynd, off the Victoria Rd roundabout at the top of King St • April–Oct daily 10.30am–4.30pm • £3 • ☎01748 825611, ⓦ richmondshiremuseum.org.uk

North of the Market Place, on Ryder's Wynd, is the **Richmondshire Museum**, a museum of local life set up by a branch of the Soroptimist Club (an association of professional and business women, since you ask), which covers lead mining, transport, village life, toys and so on, with reconstructed houses and shops, and even the set of James Herriot's surgery from the TV series *All Creatures Great and Small*.

Greyfriars Tower
Friary Gardens, Queens Rd

North of Victoria Road lies Friary Gardens, which contain the impressive **Greyfriars Tower**. A new Franciscan monastery was started in 1500 to replace an earlier thirteenth-century one, but the project was overtaken by events when the dissolution of the monasteries took place in the 1530s, so the tower was all that got completed.

Theatre Royal
Corner Victoria Rd and Friar's Wynd • Tours mid-Feb to mid-Dec Mon–Sat 10am–4pm, on the hour • £3.50 donation • ☎ 01748 825252, ⓦ georgiantheatreroyal.co.uk

Richmond's **Theatre Royal** is not only a venue for music and drama, but also a Grade I listed building dating from 1788 – the oldest unchanged working theatre in the country. It's beautifully restored, and you can either attend a performance or join a guided tour, during which you get to tread the boards on the stage and see Britain's oldest surviving painted scenery.

Easby Abbey
A mile southeast of Richmond centre • Daily: April–Sept 10am–6pm; Oct 10am–5pm; Nov –March 10am–4pm • Free; EH • ☎ 0870 333 1181, ⓦ english-heritage.org.uk

Easby Abbey was established in 1151 by Premonstratensian "white canons", a kind of radical splinter group of the Cistercians. Within pleasant walking distance from the centre of Richmond, the ruins are picturesque to a fault. Look out in particular for the thirteenth-century wall paintings in the **Church of St Agnes** in the grounds, the 1300 gatehouse and the impressive remains of the refectory. Often subjected to attack by the Scots, the abbey called in the English army for protection in 1346, an act that they came bitterly to regret. The drunken English soldiers, in an orgy of unrestrained violence, caused more damage than the Scots ever could have done.

ARRIVAL AND INFORMATION   RICHMOND

By bus Buses stop in the market square. Bus #159 runs between Masham, Leyburn and Richmond, while bus #30 (infrequent, not Sun) runs up the valley along the B6270 as far as Keld, 8 miles north of Hawes and at the crossroads of the Pennine Way and the Coast-to-Coast path.

Destinations Leyburn (every 2hr; 25min); Masham (every 2hr; 50min); Northallerton (4 daily; 52min); Ripon (every 2hr; 1hr 15min).
Tourist office 2 Queens Rd (daily 9.30am–5.30pm; ☎ 01748 850549, ⓦ richmond.org.uk).

ACCOMMODATION AND EATING

Frenchgate Hotel 59–61 Frenchgate ☎ 01748 822087, ⓦ thefrenchgate.co.uk. Georgian townhouse hotel with eight rooms and walled gardens. Its food (set menu £39) has an excellent reputation – spiced loin of Yorkshire rabbit, for example, or Reg's duck breast. Restaurant closed Mon. **£118**
Frenchgate House 66 Frenchgate ☎ 01748 823421, ⓦ 66frenchgate.co.uk. Three immaculately presented rooms, plus breakfast with the best – panoramic – view in town. **£85**
★**Millgate House** Millgate ☎ 01748 823571, ⓦ millgatehouse.com. Shut the big green door of this Georgian house and enter a world of books, antiques, embroidered sheets, handmade toiletries, scrumptious

breakfasts and the finest (and least precious) hosts you could wish for. No credit cards. **£110**
Rustique Finkle St ☎ 01748 821565, ⓦ rustiqueyork .co.uk. The clue to *Rustique*'s ambience lies in its name – it concentrates on rustic French food and wine in a bistro setting. The atmosphere is busy and cheerful, and the food – baked cod with horseradish mash, duck confit, French onion soup, mussels – is lovely, and very reasonably priced (two courses £13.95, three for £15.95). Daily noon–9pm.
★**Whashton Springs** Ravensworth Rd, near Whashton, 3 miles north of Richmond ☎ 01748 822884, ⓦ whashton springs.co.uk. This working Dales farm offers a peaceful night in the country in guestrooms (in the main house or round the courtyard) filled with family furniture. **£76**

The North York Moors

5

The North York Moors

A swathe of understated, almost unbroken beauty stretches along the eastern side of Yorkshire from the Tees in the north to the Humber in the south. Of this area, the North York Moors National Park, the Howardian Hills and the Vale of Pickering are all in North Yorkshire, and are covered in this chapter; the Wolds are largely in East Yorkshire, and appear in the next. Altogether, dotted as they are with towns and villages, stately homes and stone bridges, country churches and isolated farms, they represent one of England's largest and most attractive areas of open countryside. As a bonus, along the eastern edge of the National Park is one of the finest stretches of coast in Britain. Apart from the joys of driving, cycling or hiking across this landscape, sailing from it, gliding over it or skydiving into it, other pleasures abound.

From just below Middlesbrough, moors and dales stretch south across the Cleveland Hills and Hambleton Hills. A clutch of towns along the Moors' western edge make suitable bases, including **Great Ayton**, **Osmotherley**, **Northallerton**, **Thirsk** – with a broad market place and a James Herriot connection – and **Helmsley**, a delightful town that boasts a castle and stately home and, just to its west, the wonderful medieval/ Georgian double-whammy of **Rievaulx Abbey** and **Rievaulx Terrace**. Helmsley is also a good centre for visiting **Sutton Bank**, an escarpment overlooking the Vale of York, **Coxwold**, where Laurence Sterne, author of *Tristram Shandy*, lived and worked, **Kilburn**, with the only "chalk horse" in the north carved into the hillside above it, and **Ampleforth College**, Britain's greatest Roman Catholic school. Further south stretch the **Howardian Hills**, whose principal visitor attraction is one of the best of England's great stately homes, **Castle Howard**.

The central North York Moors and the Vale of Pickering are probably best explored from **Pickering** itself, the southern terminus of the **North Yorkshire Moors Railway**. Striking south from Pickering the A169 gives access to theme park and zoo **Flamingo Land**, the terrific **Eden Camp**, an imaginative museum located in an ex-POW camp, and the no-nonsense town of **Malton**.

North of Pickering lies a complicated network of country roads that meander hither and yon, through tiny hamlets, across stretches of moor, through woodland and across streams. **Hutton-le-Hole** is a pretty stone village set in a steep-sided valley around a sheep-dotted green, and is home to the **Ryedale Folk Museum**. Further north, the village of **Goathland**, the setting for TV's *Heartbeat*, still attracts diehard fans. To the east the **Dalby Forest** offers invigorating forest driving, walking, cycling and picnicking, whilst, on its edge, **Thornton-le-Dale** is one of the region's best-looking villages.

Across the north of the North York Moors lies one of the national park's most appealing valleys – that of the **River Esk**, which empties into the North Sea at Whitby. Its appeal lies not only in the beauty of its surrounding farmland and moors, but also in its lack of main roads – a skein of lanes and minor roads twist and climb between villages on either side of the river. Indeed, one of the best ways of seeing Eskdale isn't

<table>
<tr><td>The Cleveland Way p.225
Robert Thompson, "mouseman" of
  Kilburn p.229</td><td>Top ten Yorkshire abbeys p.234
Local lavender p.240
The Battle of Filey Bay p.265</td></tr>
</table>

CASTLE HOWARD

Highlights

❶ Rievaulx Terrace A walk between two eighteenth-century temples along a broad grassy way, with planned views through the trees of Rievaulx Abbey below. **See p.234**

❷ Castle Howard An impressive stately home, still occupied by descendants of the family who built it. **See p.236**

❸ Kirkham Priory Ruins of an Augustinian Priory also used during World War II to train soldiers for D-Day. **See p.238**

❹ Eden Camp A fascinating museum devoted largely to World War II, in a POW camp built by Italians captured in North Africa. **See p.241**

❺ Esk Valley Rolling countryside in an unspoiled valley that you can explore on foot, on two wheels or four, or by train. **See p.246**

❻ 199 steps, Whitby As the steps climb up onto the headland bearing St Mary's Church and Whitby Abbey, the picturesque town below slowly reveals itself. **See p.247**

❼ Scarborough Castle Interesting fortification of a commanding headland, with wonderful views out to sea and down across the town's two bays. **See p.260**

HIGHLIGHTS ARE MARKED ON THE MAP ON PP.222–223

5

by road at all, but via the **Esk Valley Railway**, which links Whitby to Middlesbrough, and passes right along the valley. More generally, you can explore the national park further by rail if you change onto the North Yorkshire Moors Railway at **Grosmont**.

Finally, along the **North Yorkshire Coast**, three seaside towns with virtually no urban sprawl between them, all very different in character, punctuate a wonderful coastline. **Filey** is genteel, like a breath of early twentieth-century air, **Scarborough** is big enough to be both brash and stately, while **Whitby** seems to have everything

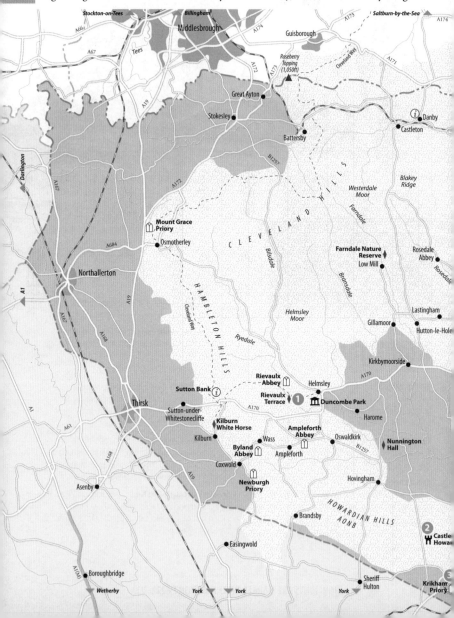

– the striking ruins of an abbey overlooking the town, links with Count Dracula and Captain Cook, and a fleet of busy fishing boats. All three resorts have fine blue-flag beaches. Along the coast in between, North Yorkshire sometimes flings itself into the sea from a great height, sometimes slips quietly beneath the waves, but always offers great vistas of beach, headland and sea. Don't miss wonderful little fishing villages like **Robin Hood's Bay** and **Staithes**, hidden away in the landscape's odd folds, nooks and crannies.

NORTH YORK MOORS

0   5
miles

HIGHLIGHTS

1 Rievaulx Terrace
2 Castle Howard
3 Kirkham Priory
4 Eden Camp
5 Esk Valley
6 199 steps, Whitby
7 Scarborough Castle

5

ARRIVAL AND GETTING AROUND

THE NORTH YORK MOORS

By car The North York Moors, Howardian Hills and Vale of Pickering are circumnavigated by a chain of main roads – imagine that they had been lassoed by the City of York. Thus the A19 and A172 head north on the western side up to Middlesbrough, the A171 curves eastwards from Middlesbrough to Scarborough, and the A64 strikes southwest back to York. This roughly kite-shaped area is bisected by one major route – the A170 Thirsk–Scarborough road. All the places in this chapter are easily accessible from these roads.

By train The Esk Valley Railway (☏ 01947 601987, ⓦ eskvalleyrailway.co.uk) and the North Yorkshire Moors Railway (☏ 01751 472508, ⓦ nymr.co.uk) allow you to explore large chunks of the northeastern part of the region by train.

By bus Public transport is remarkably good for a rural area. Several bus companies run routes in the region: for buses from Leeds, Tadcaster, York and Malton to Pickering, Thornton-le-Dale, Goathland and Whitby, go to ⓦ yorkshirecoastliner .co.uk; for buses in the northern area including Osmotherley, Cleveland and the North Yorkshire Coast, go to ⓦ arrivabus .co.uk; and for buses in the Scarborough area, including to Helmsley and throughout East Yorkshire, consult ⓦ eyms .co.uk. From April to October the Moorsbus Network (ⓦ moors.uk.net/moorsbus) provides an excellent service.

INFORMATION

North York Moors National Park Authority The best source of information for most of this area is the North York Moors National Park Authority (ⓦ www.northyorkmoors .org.uk), which has centres in Danby (see p.246) in the Esk Valley and Sutton Bank (see p.228) between Thirsk and Helmsley. The national park produces a host of publications and other information – have a look at their website or pick up one of their excellent free guides *Out and About in the North York Moors*, published annually. In addition, most towns have tourist offices.

The Western Moors and Howardian Hills

The western edge of the North York Moors is defined by and contained within a great bracket of hills – the **Cleveland Hills** to the north, the **Hambleton Hills** to the west (both within the national park), and the **Howardian Hills** to the south, an Area of Outstanding Natural Beauty outside the national park and most famous for the magnificent **Castle Howard**. The towns with the best claim to be the gateway to this area, with an adequate choice of accommodation and with tourist information, are **Great Ayton**, **Northallerton**, **Thirsk** and **Helmsley**, but other destinations on the western and southern edges are well worth visiting too.

Great Ayton

GREAT AYTON is an attractive little town that has links to **Captain Cook**, and which offers access to the Cleveland Hills. The heart of the town is the single, long High Street, strung out along the River Leven from High Green to Low Green. On High Green stands a statue of the young James Cook, stripped to the waist and looking like a member of a boy band.

Captain Cook Schoolroom Museum

101 High St · Daily: April–June, Sept & Oct 1–4pm; July & Aug 11am–4pm · Free · ☏ 01642 724296, ⓦ captaincookschoolroommuseum.co.uk

The **Captain Cook Schoolroom Museum** occupies the school, opened in 1704, that the explorer attended from 1736 to 1740. The museum includes a reconstruction of an eighteenth-century schoolroom, together with displays, many of them interactive, on his childhood, voyages, navigation methods and much else. While you're here, take a look, on the other side of the road in **Waterfall Park**, at the rather magnificent bright red Victorian urinal. You don't see one of those every day.

ARRIVAL AND INFORMATION

GREAT AYTON

By train The train station is about a mile east of the town centre, on Station Rd.

Destinations Middlesbrough (2 daily; 40min); Whitby (4 daily; 1hr 30min).

By bus Bus stops are spread along the main A173 through the town, most centrally at the Stone Bridge.

Destinations Middlesbrough (hourly; 47min).

Tourist information High Green (Mon–Sat 10am–4pm;

☎ 01642 722835). Lots of local info and walking guides in a little building at the end of a car park. Look out in particular for the walks to Roseberry Topping (4 miles) and to the Captain Cook memorial (5 miles).

Osmotherley

Southwest of Great Ayton, and eleven miles north of Thirsk, just off the A19, the village of **OSMOTHERLEY** is making a name for itself as a walking centre for the Cleveland and Hambleton hills. It's on the long-distance Cleveland Way (see box below) and is the starting point for the 42-mile **Lyke Wake Walk**, which follows a moorland "burial route" and ends at Ravenscar on the coast. The walk started as a bit of fun in 1955; if you complete it within 24 hours you are entitled to free membership of the Lyke Wake Club (see ⓦ lykewake.org). Anyone who finishes the walk three or more times may be granted a degree – Master (or Mistress) of Misery, Doctor of Dolefulness and Past Master or Mistress. The walk is also connected to the traditional song *Lyke Wake Dirge*, recorded by, among others, Pentangle and Steeleye Span.

On Osmotherley's small green – which has some good places to eat and drink – is an ancient **market cross** and a strange **barter table** made of stone, where John Wesley is said to have preached during one of his many tours of England. The church, hemmed in by houses and accessible from the green through a narrow alley, is worth a quick look for its lopsided interior – it has a south but no north aisle.

ARRIVAL AND DEPARTURE
OSMOTHERLEY

By bus Buses to and from Northallerton (every 35min– 1hr 40min; 18min) arrive at and leave from the green in the centre of the village.

ACCOMMODATION, EATING AND DRINKING

Golden Lion 6 West End ☎ 01609 883526, ⓦ golden lionosmotherley.co.uk. A mellow eighteenth-century pub whose menu has some interesting veggie options, with plenty of meat and poultry too (mains £9.95–19.95). Accommodation is offered in five attractive, cottagey rooms. **£95**

Queen Catherine Hotel 7 West End ☎ 01609 883209, ⓦ queencatherinehotel.co.uk. Very much a traditional stone-built village pub offering classic pub food (mains £7.95–8.95) and simple accommodation. Pub Mon–Thurs 11am–11pm, Fri–Sun 11am–1am. **£70**

Three Tuns 9 South End ☎ 01609 883301, ⓦ threetuns restaurant.co.uk. A restaurant-with-rooms-cum-pub, in a quaint stone cottage with a lovely garden. They serve traditional locally sourced food, such as local sea bream or wild sea trout, rack of Faceby lamb or confit Yorkshire chicken and leek terrine (mains £10.50–18.95) and have an interesting and relatively inexpensive wine list (from £16.95 a bottle). The four double guest rooms are all individually furnished. **£85**

Mount Grace Priory

Two miles north of Osmotherley (on the A19) • April–Sept daily 10am–6pm; Oct & Nov daily 10am–5pm; Dec–March Sat & Sun 10am–4pm • £5.60; NT & EH • ☎ 01609 883494, ⓦ nationaltrust.org.uk/mount-grace-priory

Fourteenth-century **Mount Grace Priory** is the best of ten Carthusian charterhouses in the country. Established in 1084 by St Bruno of Cologne, the order set up communities of

---

THE CLEVELAND WAY

One of England's twelve designated National Trails, the 110-mile-long **Cleveland Way** is distinctive in that it consists in almost equal parts of heather upland and coastal walking. It describes a great semicircle around the western, northern and eastern edges of the North York Moors, following the line of the Hambleton Hills, the Cleveland Hills and the Cleveland and Yorkshire coast. It starts at Helmsley, runs west along Sutton Bank, then swings north and east through Osmotherley and Great Ayton, before turning to follow the coast down through Staithes, Whitby, Robin Hood's Bay and Scarborough. It ends at Filey. For more information, see ⓦ nationaltrail.co.uk and ⓦ clevelandway.co.uk.

5

hermits – an oxymoron if ever there was one – where each monk (or in some cases nun) had their own cell, each of which consisted of several rooms on two floors and a small walled garden. Entrance to the priory is through the guesthouse, which was turned, after the Dissolution, into a rather grand manor house. There's a reconstructed cell, an exhibition on the history of the priory, a children's story box and, during school holidays, special children's trails. The **gardens** teem with wildlife, including the famous priory stoats – apparently they use the drainage system as a way of creeping up undetected on their prey.

Northallerton

NORTHALLERTON is the county town of North Yorkshire, though its residents seem to feel that not enough people realize this. Located in the Vale of York between the two great North Yorkshire national parks, and between the two main north–south routes (the A1 and the A19), and serving as the region's market town, it's an excellent base for exploring the area. Consisting largely of a long, broad Georgian High Street, it has a good range of independent shops, but actual tourist attractions are few. The site of the **Battle of the Standard**, which took place on August 22, 1138, is worth a look. Marked by an obelisk beside the A167 north of town, the battle between the English and the Scots was part of the chaotic struggle for supremacy between King Stephen, grandson of William the Conqueror, and his cousin, the Empress Matilda. Although outnumbered, the English won, largely thanks to their bowmen.

ARRIVAL AND INFORMATION
NORTHALLERTON

By train The train station is southwest of the town centre. **Destinations** Middlesbrough (hourly; 32min); York (every 5–50min; 25min).

By bus Buses stop on the High St, and at the Town Hall, the Post Office and the *Nag's Head*.

Destinations Bedale (every 30min; 21min); Ripon (every 2hr; 1hr 3min); Thirsk (every 30min; 31min).

Tourist office Applegarth car park (April–Oct Mon–Sat 10am–4pm; Nov–March Wed–Sat 10am–4pm; ☎ 01609 776864, ⓦ northallerton.info).

ACCOMMODATION

Golden Lion Hotel 114 High St ☎ 01609 777411, ⓦ golden-lion-hotel.co.uk. Solid old coaching inn, dating from the 1730s, right in the heart of Northallerton. It offers old-fashioned, if a little florid, comfort, and efficient, friendly service. Can be noisy when there are functions on. **£80**

★ **Solberge Hall Hotel** Newby Wiske, 5 miles south of Northallerton ☎ 01609 779191, ⓦ macdonaldhotels .co.uk. A handsome country house hotel, now part of the Macdonald group, in a beautiful setting. It's a fine building, with wonderful grounds and luxurious rooms. **£155**

EATING AND DRINKING

★ **Bettys** 188 High St ☎ 01609 775154, ⓦ bettys .co.uk. Occupying a handsome Georgian building, this is another in the top-end chain of Yorkshire tearooms (see p.158), offering delicious light meals, afternoon tea and cakes in a regal setting. Mon–Fri 9am–5pm, Sat 9am–5.30pm, Sun 10am–5pm.

★ **Lewis & Cooper** 92 High St ☎ 01609 766712, ⓦ lewisandcooper.co.uk. Famous for its deli and hampers, with a lovely tearoom, café and lounge on two floors of the store's estimable seventeenth-century building, in the rooms once occupied by founding partner George Lewis. Wonderful fresh cakes and light lunches.

Mon–Sat 9am–5pm, Sun 10am–4pm.

Tithe Bar and Brasserie 2 Friarage St ☎ 01609 778482, ⓦ markettowntaverns.co.uk. Pleasant little brasserie, just off the High St, in what was once the tithe barn (where the church's cut of the harvest was stored). There are three small bar areas downstairs, and a main dining room on the first floor. Food includes such dishes as charred avocado and pine nut salad, gourmet burgers, posh fish fingers and pie of the day. Bar Sun–Thurs noon–11pm, Fri & Sat noon–midnight; food served Mon–Fri noon–2.30pm & 6–9pm, Sat 6–9pm; restaurant Wed–Sat from 6pm, Sun noon–6pm.

Thirsk

Nine miles south of Northallerton, on the edge of the national park, the busy market town of **THIRSK** is a convenient centre for visiting not only the North York

Moors but also the Yorkshire Dales. Mentioned in the Domesday Book, it is generally associated nowadays with vet **James Herriot**, whose house (now a museum) is a key tourist attraction. Lying along the Cod Beck River, the town pleasantly clusters around a large cobbled square (markets Mon & Sat) where many of the buildings go back to the great days of coaching, when Thirsk was an important stopping place on the way to Scotland. Two main streets run north from the Market Place – Kirkgate and Millgate, from the northwest and northeast corners respectively – while south is the sister village of **Sowerby**. Well north of the Market Place, at the end of Kirkgate, stands **St Mary's**, a product of the fifteenth and sixteenth centuries, which many feel to be the most spectacular Perpendicular church in North Yorkshire. At the western edge of town is **Thirsk Racecourse** (☎01845 522276, ⓦthirskracecourse.net), which has been a horseracing venue for more than 150 years.

World of James Herriot
23 Kirkgate • Daily: March–Oct 10am–5pm; Nov–Feb 10am–4pm • £8.50 • ☎ 01845 524234, ⓦ worldofjamesherriot.org

Thirsk is now probably best known as James Herriot's Darrowby. Herriot (actual name Alf Wight; 1916–95) was a country vet here, and his series of affectionate and amusing tales about his life in the area, and his dealings with curmudgeonly farmers, won a huge following; the books, published from 1969 onwards, were followed by two feature films and the wildly popular TV series *All Creatures Great and Small*. The house where he lived and worked is now the popular **World of James Herriot**, which will delight fans of the books, especially – the rooms have been set up to match precisely the descriptions in the stories. It is also a diverting museum of the social history of Herriot's time, and the only veterinary science museum in the country. There's an interactive room for kids to learn about veterinary science, displays of props used during filming of the TV series, and a documentary made especially for the museum.

Thirsk Museum
14–16 Kirkgate • April–Oct Mon–Wed, Fri & Sat 10am–4pm • Free • ☎ 01845 527707, ⓦ thirskmuseum.org

The small **Thirsk Museum** displays a nostalgic jumble of objects of the type so often found in local museums – penny farthings and wash-day paraphernalia, dolls and butter-churns – located, interestingly enough, in the house where **Thomas Lord**, professional cricketer and founder of Lord's Cricket Ground, was born in 1755. One room is devoted to Lord and the history of cricket in the county.

ARRIVAL AND INFORMATION   THIRSK

By train The train station is a mile west of the town centre, beyond the racecourse.
Destinations Middlesbrough (hourly; 40min)
By bus Buses arrive at and depart from the Market Place.
Destinations Northallerton (every 15min–2hr; 14–30min); York (every 1hr–1hr 15min; 1hr).

Tourist office 93 Market Place (Jan–March Mon–Sat 10am–3pm; April–June & Sept–Dec Mon–Sat 10am–4pm; July & Aug 10am–4.30pm; ☎01845 522755, ⓦ visit-thirsk.org.uk). The North York Moors National Park Centre (see p.228) is at Sutton Bank, 5 miles to the east.

ACCOMMODATION AND EATING

Gallery 18 Kirkgate ☎01845 523767, ⓦgallerybed andbreakfast.co.uk. An award-winning B&B with three comfortable rooms and excellent breakfasts in an eighteenth-century Grade II-listed building. It's on a main street, and can get noisy at closing time. **£70**
Golden Fleece Market Place ☎01845 523108, ⓦgoldenfleecehotel.com. Good rooms and a nice busy atmosphere in this charming old coaching inn nicely

located on Thirsk's large cobbled square. They serve locally sourced food, too. Food served Mon–Sat noon–3pm & 6.30–9.15pm, Sun noon–2pm & 6.30–9pm. **£95**
The Poplars Carlton Miniott ☎01845 522712, ⓦ thepoplarsthirsk.com. Near the train station and the racecourse, this B&B offers clean rooms and "cottages" (actually cabins; three-night minimum). All have their own access. **£65**

5

Sutton Bank

Approximately five miles east of Thirsk, after passing through the village of **Sutton-under-Whitestonecliffe** – said to have the longest name in England – the road climbs to the top of **Sutton Bank**, a hill so high (978ft) and steep (1:3) that cars towing caravans are not allowed to use it. The bank itself is beautifully wooded, and from the top the views back across the Vale of York are inspiring.

The **Sutton Bank National Park Centre**, atop the escarpment, has details of walks and bike rides in the area. Sutton Bank's main **viewing point** is a two-minute walk away, and even the grounds of the centre have much of interest – you can watch birds feeding just outside the window through binoculars provided.

Yorkshire Gliding Club

Daily 9am–5pm • A test flight costs as little as £89.50, and this entitles you to three months' membership which allows you to take further flights at members' rates • ☎ 01845 597237, ⓦ ygc.co.uk

On the southern edge of Sutton Bank, the **Yorkshire Gliding Club** is well worth a stop, if only for the breakfasts, lunches and teas served at its clubhouse. There are splendid views – the escarpment faces west across the Vale of York, into the prevailing wind. Some visitors may be happy enough simply to watch the gliders; if you want to take part in this exhilarating activity yourself, bear in mind that you have to be over 4ft 7inches and under 6ft 2inches tall, and less than 16.5 stone in weight. The clubhouse has not only a bar and restaurant, but also rooms and self-catering kitchens for members. If you're not already an enthusiast, this could be the start of something big.

Kilburn White Horse

On the face of Sutton Bank's escarpment is the **Kilburn White Horse**. If you drive down the steep hill off to the right beyond the Gliding Club, you'll come to a car park. From here a footpath climbs steeply up to the right of the Horse – follow it to the top and along the escarpment and you'll arrive, after a couple of miles, back at Sutton Bank.

The Kilburn White Horse is not some ancient totem whose origins are lost in the mists of time. The horse was cut in 1857 on the initiative of a local man, Thomas Taylor, who had seen similar horses in the south of England and was determined to go one better in regard to size. By 1925 it had become badly overgrown, so the *Yorkshire Evening Post* ran a campaign to have it restored. Reader subscriptions paid for its restoration, and the £100 left over was invested to provide for its upkeep. It had to be covered up during World War II, apparently, to prevent it becoming an aid to navigation for German bomber pilots, and during protests against the 2004 hunting ban, a giant rider in full hunting pink suddenly appeared on the horse's back.

The horse is composed of whitewashed limestone chippings – visitors are asked not to walk on them, as the chippings get moved and the image of the horse degraded. As it is, gravity has already been causing slippage, so boards have been pegged across the steepest parts to stop the gravel moving downhill. A Kilburn White Horse Association exists to raise money for its continued maintenance (the money from the 1925 fundraising is presumably no longer enough).

INFORMATION   **SUTTON BANK**

Sutton Bank National Park Centre On top of the escarpment (April–Oct daily 10am–5pm; Nov, Dec & mid-Feb to March daily 11am–4pm; Jan to mid-Feb Sat & Sun 11am–4pm; ☎ 01439 770657, ⓦ www.northyorkmoors.org.uk). Pick up information here on the eight walks and six cycle rides of varying distances and difficulty that start here and head off to points of interest all over the area.

Kilburn

KILBURN village, less than two miles south of Sutton Bank, is attractive enough, with its collection of stone cottages gathered around a tiny village square. The person who has

5

ROBERT THOMPSON, "MOUSEMAN" OF KILBURN

Born in Kilburn village, **Robert Thompson** (1876–1955) followed in his father's footsteps as the local joiner and wheelwright. Using traditional tools, he developed an interest in the furniture styles of the seventeenth century, and by the 1920s had started to design pieces in a similar mould, using only naturally seasoned English oak. At some point one of the craftsmen he was working with said that they were all "as poor as a church mouse", and this gave him the idea of signing his work with a little carved mouse. From then on, the mouse adorned everything that he made. Nicknamed "the mouseman", he expanded his business after a commission for the headmaster of nearby **Ampleforth College** led him into ecclesiastical work for churches, convents and monasteries, though he continued to make domestic furniture as well.

Today furniture is still designed and made in the traditional way in **Robert Thompson's Craftsmen Ltd** in the centre of the village. The factory is run by the mouseman's descendants and sells furniture all over the world. Items range from, say, a cheese board at £80 to a display storage cupboard for £10,000.

put Kilburn on the map is **Robert Thompson**, the famous "mouseman", whose work you'll find in churches all over this part of the country (see box above).

Mouseman Visitor Centre

Kilburn village centre • Easter–Oct daily 10am–5pm; Nov & Dec Wed–Sun 11am–4pm • £4.50; family £12 • ☎ 01347 869102,
Ⓦ robertthompsons.co.uk

The **Mouseman Visitor Centre**, right in the centre of Kilburn, occupies what was originally Robert Thompson's workshop and the adjoining blacksmiths. Today it consists of a café and shop, displays on the history of the village and on the Kilburn White Horse (see opposite) and, in the **Shoeing Room**, an informative video about Robert Thompson, the "mouseman" of Kilburn (see box above), introduced by his great-grandson, who you'll see around the place. There's also a fine little **museum** stuffed with examples of Thompson's work and photos and documents concerning his life. Behind the centre, a garden climbs up the hillside and offers views over the village towards the White Horse.

Across the road is Robert's cottage, which now houses the showroom and offices, and the Robert Thompson's Craftsmen Ltd workrooms themselves, complete with viewing galleries where you can see the craftsmen working at the large benches. Behind, and in the garden of the visitor centre, you'll see lots of oak tree-trunks, sawn into planks and left out to weather naturally.

ACCOMMODATION, EATING AND DRINKING   KILBURN

The Forresters Arms The Square ☎ 01347 868386,   frequented by walkers, offering food (mains £10–19.95)
Ⓦ forrestersarms.fsnet.co.uk. A traditional pub, much   and accommodation. Daily 9am–11pm. **£80**

Coxwold and around

In the angle between the A19 and the A170 lies **COXWOLD**, a village with a considerable claim to fame. At the top of the sloping main street, two buildings associated with a single great man – eighteenth-century writer **Laurence Sterne** – draw your attention. On one side is **Shandy Hall**, where he lived. A hundred yards away, on the opposite side, is **St Michael's Church**, where he was vicar from 1760 until his death in 1768, and where he is buried in the churchyard.

Shandy Hall and Gardens

May–Sept Wed & Sun 2.30–4.30pm • £4.50 • ☎ 01347 868465, Ⓦ laurencesternetrust.org.uk

Shandy Hall and Gardens, a beautiful early fifteenth-century brick house, is where Sterne wrote his most famous works – *The Life and Opinions of Tristram Shandy, Gentleman* and *A Sentimental Journey* – and where he would wander out into the

5

garden between writing sessions "to weed, hack up old roots or wheel away rubbish". The house was rescued from neglect by a group of enthusiasts in the 1960s and is now a museum dedicated to the writer. All manner of Sterne memorabilia, including a huge collection of his novels and various prints and paintings relating to his works, are jumbled together in an intriguing manner throughout the study, dining room and kitchen. Though the lovely two-acre gardens are open every day during the summer (May–Sept), opening hours for the house are limited.

St Michael's Church

Main St • Morning prayer every second Sun 9am, Holy Communion every fourth Sun 9am

Standing on its hill at the top of the main street, **St Michael's Church** is an impressive sight, with an especially striking octagonal west tower. This was where **Laurence Sterne** worked as vicar, drawing big crowds with his sermons. It is also where he is buried – against the south wall, next to the porch. His internment was the last chapter of a fascinating story. Sterne (1713–68) died in London, and was buried in St George's, Hanover Square. Two days (or rather nights) after his burial, his body was dug up by graverobbers and sold to a surgeon, who used it for an anatomy lesson in Cambridge. Sterne's face was recognized, and his cadaver was returned to its original resting place. Then, in 1969, when the graveyard was due for development, the Laurence Sterne Trust arranged for his body to be exhumed and reburied where it now lies, in the cemetery here.

The interior

On entering the church, the first thing you'll notice is the impressive **arch** that separates the nave from the narrower chancel. Above it are George II's coat of arms, and on either side those of the Fauconberg family, local lords of the manor. Their motto is a pun on Belasyse, the family name (the first baron took the name Fauconberg when he received the title in 1627) – "Bonne et Belle Assez" "good and beautiful enough". Under the arch on the left is a wooden lectern carved, "to the glory of God" by Josef Heu, an Austrian sculptor who settled in Coxwold after fleeing from the Nazis in 1941. The box pews and pulpit were built during Laurence Sterne's incumbency, though both have been reduced in height since then. Look out for **mouseman** mice (see p.229) in various parts of the church (there's one on the base of the lectern). The **roof bosses** in the nave are worth getting a stiff neck for – in between the various arms of great families are some wonderfully hideous grotesques. The **monuments** in the chancel are all worth a look, but the most impressive, to the left of the altar, is that of Sir William and Lady Margaret Belasyse, lying in armour and long robes respectively, hands together in prayer, figures of their five children around the base, ornate canopies and decorations above. The whole edifice would originally have been painted in gold, black and red.

Newburgh Priory

Half a mile south of Coxwold • **Gardens** April–June Wed & Sun 2–6pm • £3 **House** April–June Wed & Sun 2.30–4.45pm • £6 including gardens • ☎ 01347 868372, ⊛ newburghpriory.co.uk

Newburgh Priory, just south of Coxwold village on the road to Easingwold, was built on the site of an 1150 Augustinian priory. It was bought by the Belasyse (or Bellasis) family from Henry VIII at the time of the dissolution of the monasteries – you'll see their coat of arms and motto over the main gate. The house, which has been in the same family (now the Fauconbergs) ever since, is a delightfully mellow melange of many styles – largely eighteenth century, but with a few survivals from the original Augustinian priory and an interesting two-storey Jacobean porch. An interesting tale associated with Newburgh Priory involves the daughter of Oliver Cromwell, who married into the family and who, to prevent her father's body being desecrated after the restoration of the monarchy in 1660, is said to have brought it here and hidden it in the roof.

Byland Abbey

Byland, 1.5 miles northeast of Coxwold • July & Aug daily 11am–6pm; Sept Wed–Sun 10am–6pm; Oct Wed–Sun 10am–5pm; Nov–
March Sat & Sun 10am–4pm • £4.60; EH • ☎ 01347 868614, ⓦ english-heritage.org.uk

The ruins of **Byland Abbey**, where Laurence Sterne (see p.229) liked to walk, lie south
of the A170 Thirsk to Pickering road. The third of the Cistercian "shining lights of the
north" – the other two are Fountains (see p.176) and Rievaulx (see p.234) – Byland
Abbey is not as impressive as the others in either remains or setting. This fact is
reflected at the entrance, where you will find not a handsome visitor centre, but instead
something that more resembles a garden shed. However, one way in which Byland wins
hands down is in the **Byland Abbey Inn** (see below) across the road.

ACCOMMODATION AND EATING   COXWOLD AND AROUND

Black Swan Oldstead, 4 miles north of Coxwold
☎ 01347 868387, ⓦ blackswanoldstead.co.uk. Michelin-
starred dining in a rural setting. In addition to the a la carte
menu, listing dishes such as turbot with potato, hen of the
woods and truffle, there are six-course lunch and nine-
course dinner tasting menus (£55/£80). The food is creative
yet traditional, using the best local ingredients. Mon–Fri
4–11pm, Sat & Sun noon–11pm; food served Mon–Fri
6–9pm, Sat & Sun noon–2pm & 6–9pm.

★ **Byland Abbey Inn** Byland, 1.5 miles northeast of
Coxwold, opposite Byland Abbey ☎ 01347 868204,
ⓦ bylandabbeyinn.co.uk. Owned by English Heritage,

this place, despite its name, is actually a tearoom and hotel.
It offers three palatial guest rooms in a building that was
originally part of the abbey precinct before being converted
first into a farmhouse, then a pub, and now a tearoom.
Wed–Sun 10am–5pm. **£95**

Fauconberg Arms Thirsk Bank, Coxwold ☎ 01347
868214, ⓦ fauconbergarms.com. This superb stone
building has a cool contemporary feel inside, eight rooms
(four luxury, four standard) and good traditional food
(mains £7.50–22.50). Many ingredients are sourced
locally, including home-bred meat and fresh fish. Food
served daily 10am–midnight. **£85**

Ampleforth Abbey and College

Ampleforth, 6 miles east of Coxwold • **Abbey** Matins 6am, through lauds, mass, vespers and others, to compline at 9pm; church tours
Thurs 12.15pm **Sports centre** Mon–Fri 7am–9.30pm, Sat 8am–7pm, Sun 9am–8pm • ☎ 01439 766000, ⓦ ampleforth.org.uk

Most monasteries and convents in England are, like Byland (see above), in a ruined
state, having been dissolved by Henry VIII in the 1530s, stripped of their wealth by the
king, then plundered of land and building stone by local people. **Ampleforth Abbey
and College** is a rare exception. Now a flourishing and fully functioning Benedictine
monastery, Ampleforth dates from the return of a group of English monks, forced out
of France by the French Revolution, who started a small house here in 1803. Alumni of
the **college**, a (now co-educational) Roman Catholic private school, include actor
Rupert Everett, actor/writer Julian Fellowes, sculptor Antony Gormley, rugby player
Lawrence Dallaglio and journalist Hugo Young.

The whole impressive complex stands in a beautiful valley, and offers wonderful
walking (there are details of a six-mile walk around the estate on the website), a
swimming pool, a **sports centre** and a **tearoom**. There's also a **shop** selling religious
gifts and bottles of the monastery's fierce cider and brandy, made with produce
from their own orchards. In keeping with the Rules of St Benedict, which include
"Let guests be received as Christ Himself", Ampleforth is the most extraordinarily
welcoming place.

EATING AND DRINKING   AMPLEFORTH

Ampleforth Abbey tearoom Ampleworth Abbey
complex ☎ 01439 766868, ⓦ visitors.ampleforth.org
.uk/tea-room. Not only drinks and cakes, but also more
substantial food (honey glazed ham, rump steak strips,
fish and chips) eaten from carved oak "mouseman"
tables (see p.229). Mon–Sat 10am–5.30pm, Sun
noon–5.30pm.

White Swan East End, Ampleforth village ☎ 01439
788239, ⓦ thewhiteswan-ampleforth.co.uk. Good, hearty
food in either a formal dining room, comfortable wood-
floored lounge or bar thronged with locals. Mains £10.20–
19.95. Pub Mon–Fri noon–3pm & 5.30–11/11.30pm, Sat
& Sun noon–11/11.30pm; food served Mon–Sat noon–
2pm & 6–9pm, Sun noon–2pm & 6–8.30pm.

5

Helmsley

East of Thirsk, about fourteen miles along the A170, is the appealing stone town of **HELMSLEY**, clustered around a market place and with a fascinating **castle**, a large country house, an interesting church, a number of good pubs, hotels and restaurants and a host of small, independent specialist shops.

Market Place

Dominating Helmsley's **Market Place** is a memorial to the second Baron Feversham (1797–1867), MP for various local constituencies from 1820 until his succession to the title in 1841, when he transferred to the House of Lords. Although he became the President of the Royal Agricultural Society, you still can't help feeling that his Prince Albert-style memorial is perhaps more prominent than his modest achievements deserve.

All Saints Church

Market Square • Daily; services Sun 8am, 9.30am, 11am & 6pm, Wed 9.30am • Free • ☎ 01439 770236, ⓦ helmsleyparish.org.uk

Just off the northwest corner of the Market Place is **All Saints Church**, an interesting structure which, though dating largely from the 1860s, has enough survivals from earlier periods to satisfy architecture detectives. It also features colourful early twentieth-century paintings (including a 20ft dragon) on the walls and ceilings, a wooden yoke from a freed slave, three halberds and church furniture sporting numerous "mouseman" mice (see p.229).

Helmsley Castle

Castlegate • April–Sept daily 10am–6pm; Oct daily 10am–5pm; Nov–March Sat & Sun 10am–4pm • £5.20; EH • ☎ 01439 770442, ⓦ english-heritage.org.uk

Helmsley Castle, west of the Market Place, was started in around 1120 by Walter L'Espec, a man whose large size and loud voice were by all accounts more impressive than his name, which means "Wally the Woodpecker". Most of the visible medieval fortifications, however, date from the time of crusader Robert de Roos and his descendants. The **medieval structures** – the barbican and gate, the large west tower and even larger D-shaped east tower – are easily distinguishable from later additions, made in **Tudor** times to make the castle more comfortable and user-friendly for the Manners family.

The only time the castle saw action was during the Civil War, when Parliamentary forces under Sir Thomas Fairfax successfully laid siege in 1644, securing the surrender of the Royalists in three months. The castle was subsequently slighted (made useless as a defence by blowing key bits up). Notice the east tower, facing the town, which had the whole of its outer wall brought down – the rubble from its destruction still lies drunkenly in the moat.

The interior

You enter the castle after walking along the bottom of the moat (never, incidentally, likely to have been filled with water) through the south barbican and south gate. Look inside the twelfth-century **west tower**, remodelled in the fourteenth and sixteenth centuries, which was used as accommodation – all the floors have gone, but you can see from the quality of the fireplaces and the size of the windows that the basement and top floor were used by servants, the middle two floors by the lord and his family. Beyond is the **West Range**, remodelled in the sixteenth century to provide greater comfort, and today housing a diverting exhibition telling the castle's story – it includes some impressive cannonballs hurled at it during the 1644 siege. Within the curtain walls and towers, look out for the outlines of the thirteenth-century chapel and the fourteenth-century hall and kitchen.

5

Helmsley Walled Garden

Cleveland Way • April–Oct daily 10am–5pm • £6 • ☎ 01439 771427, ⓦ helmsleywalledgarden.org.uk

Just behind Helmsley Castle, **Helmsley Walled Garden** was built as the kitchen garden to Duncombe Park when the original one was washed away by a great flood in 1759, and is now open to the public – heaven on earth if you're a keen gardener. Apart from the huge array of plants (many for sale), there's a vegetarian restaurant and an ethical gift shop.

Duncombe Park

Helmsley • April–Aug Sun–Fri 10.30am–5.30pm (gardens and parkland only – house closed except for special events) • £5; parkland only £1 • ☎ 01439 770213, ⓦ duncombepark.com

The driveway to **Duncombe Park** starts right in Helmsley, and if you proceed directly from Helmsley Castle to the house, you'll be doing exactly what the Duncombes themselves did. In 1689 City banker and Lord Mayor of London **Sir Charles Duncombe** bought the Helmsley and Rievaulx estates, which included Helmsley Castle and Rievaulx Abbey, for £90,000. His nephew Thomas had Duncombe Park built in the early eighteenth century as a more comfortable replacement for the castle, whose remains were eventually relegated to being romantic ruins. These rather enhanced the views from the house – many eighteenth-century landowners had to resort to building follies, but the Duncombes had their own genuine ruins, ready-made. Most of the house was destroyed by fire in 1879 and later rebuilt, so not a lot of the architecture you can see is original, but it's still worth an hour of your time.

The grounds

The grounds of Duncombe Park are spectacular. Particularly fascinating is **Duncombe Terrace** (completed in 1718), which stretches south and east of the house. A long grassy terrace laid out as a walk or ride from one temple (Ionic) to another (Tuscan), it offers views of a carefully designed landscape through the trees down into the valley. In the eighteenth century, competition to impress each other between the (often intermarried) wealthy was intense, and similar landscaping can be seen at Castle Howard (see p.236), Studeley Royal (see p.177) and Roche Abbey (see p.62).

ARRIVAL AND INFORMATION
HELMSLEY

By bus Most buses pass through the Market Place. Destinations Pickering (every 1hr 10min; 35min); Scarborough (every 1hr 10min; 1hr 36min).

Tourist information Contact the Pickering tourist office (daily 9.30am–5pm; ☎ 01751 473791).

ACCOMMODATION, EATING AND DRINKING

Black Swan Market Place ☎ 0870 400 8112, ⓦ blackswan-helmsley.co.uk. An interesting Tudor/Georgian ex-coaching inn right on the main square, with a comfortable bar, airy restaurant, award-winning tearoom and charming, attentive staff. Pub 11am–11pm (later at weekends); restaurant daily 7.30–9.30pm; tearoom daily 10am–5.30pm. **£144**

Feathers Hotel Market Place ☎ 01439 770275, ⓦ feathershotelhelmsley.co.uk. This pub serves restaurant food – all the staples, from £11.95 – and has a surprisingly large choice of rooms. Mon–Sat 11.30am–midnight, Sun 11.30am–11pm; food served Mon–Fri noon–2.30pm & 5.30–9pm, Sat & Sun noon–8.30pm. **£80**

★ Feversham Arms 1 High St ☎ 01439 770766, ⓦ fevershamarmshotel.com. One of Yorkshire's top

hotels: multi-award winning, luxurious yet unpretentious. It has the look of a country pub, yet it also has a pool, an underground car park, a spa and a terrific fine dining restaurant, and many of the rooms have hot tubs. Special deals bring down the rates. Restaurant Mon–Sat noon–2.30pm & 6.45–9.30pm, Sun 12.30–2.30pm & 6.45–9.30pm. **£196**

Gepetto's 8 Bridge St ☎ 01439 770479, ⓦ gepettos -helmsley.co.uk. Busy Italian restaurant just off Market Place, serving fresh pasta, pizza and risottos, along with meaty and fishy mains and daily specials. Tues–Sun 5–8.30pm.

Royal Oak 15 Market Place ☎ 01439 770450, ⓦ theoak -helmsley.co.uk. Plentiful bar food at reasonable prices in this sports-orientated Market Place pub with rooms. **£70**

5

★**Star Inn** Harome, less than 3 miles southeast of Helmsley ⓣ01439 770397, ⓦthestaratharome.co.uk. Not only a beautiful thatched inn, but also one of Yorkshire's best restaurants. The food defines itself as Modern Yorkshire, with a frequently changing menu listing such dishes as grilled black pudding with pan-fried foie gras; cured Hartlepool-landed octopus with quail eggs, deep-fried anchovies and black olive sorbet; and lots of veggie delights like twice-baked Blue Wensleydale and lovage soufflé with pickled cherries. It's surprisingly affordable (main courses £18.95–24, with a two-/three-course "market menu" at £20/£25), and the atmosphere is blessedly unpretentious. Accommodation is available in a separate building, and there's an associated shop/deli across the road. Food served Mon 6–9.30pm, Tues–Sat 11.30am–2pm & 6–9.30pm, Sun noon–6pm. **£150**

Rievaulx Terrace

On the B1257, a couple of miles northwest of Helmsley • Feb–Nov daily 11am–5pm • £5.95; NT • ⓣ01439 798340 (summer) or ⓣ01439 748283 (winter), ⓦnationaltrust.org.uk/rievaulx-terrace

Rievaulx Terrace was, like Duncombe Park's terrace (see p.233), built by the Duncombes, though thirty years later – its construction began in 1759 and it took eight years to complete. It's an exact match with Duncombe Terrace – both follow the Rye – and there is some speculation that the ultimate plan was to connect the two, bridging a small valley in between. The plan and purpose of Rievaulx Terrace is simple – it's a broad swathe of grass that drops and curves gently for more than half a mile along a ridge above the Rye, extending from an oblong Ionic temple at one end to a round Tuscan one at the other.

Rievaulx Terrace was built to impress visitors. The household would set out from Duncombe House with their carriages, horses and servants, and the visitors would be escorted along the terrace, on foot or horseback, to admire the views and, in due course, dine in the Ionic temple. You can still enjoy the views (though you've got to bring your own food nowadays), and although you're not allowed into the **Tuscan temple**, you can see the ornate tiled floor through the windows and the painted ceiling via mirrors set on the window ledges. The **Ionic temple**, which is open to the public, has a highly decorated upstairs dining room; the old kitchen below houses an interesting exhibition on the history of the terrace, and on the plants and animals to be seen on and from it.

Rievaulx Abbey

Follow signposts left off the B1257 a couple of miles northwest of Helmsley (the approach road drops down from the B1257 right next to the entrance to Rievaulx Terrace) • April–Sept daily 10am–6pm; Oct–Nov daily 10am–5pm; Nov–March Sat & Sun 10am–4pm • £6.20; EH • ⓣ01439 798228, ⓦenglish-heritage.org.uk

The extensive ruins of **Rievaulx Abbey** lie in the valley of the Rye ("Rievaulx" means "the abbey in Ryedale") directly below Rievaulx Terrace; there is no direct route between them. The roofless abbey itself dominates the site, but you can also see vestiges of the entire community. The first Cistercian monastery in the north of England, the abbey was established as a colony of Clairvaux in France by twelve Cistercian monks led by Abbot William in 1132.

From the ticket office and shop, a gravel path leads up to the right of the monastery ruins, where detailed information boards fill you in on the setting, explaining that the

TOP TEN YORKSHIRE ABBEYS

Bolton Abbey See p.197
Byland Abbey See p.231
Easby Abbey See p.217
Fountains Abbey See p.176
Jervaulx Abbey See p.212
Kirkstall Abbey See p.94
Rievaulx Abbey See p.234
Roche Abbey See p.62
St Mary's Abbey See p.149
Whitby Abbey See p.249

monks eventually diverted the Rye in order to give themselves more room for building, and to pursue the simple life that was part of their order. They established water meadows, fish ponds and a mill for metal working, and used the timber that surrounded them for building and for charcoal-burning. The abbey eventually owned land all over England, and traded with other Cistercian monasteries throughout Britain and Europe. By the middle of the twelfth century Rievaulx had grown to house 140 monks and five hundred lay brothers and servants.

The ruins

Before entering the **ruins**, have a look at the exhibition "The Work of God and Man", which has fascinating displays on the life of the Order – farming, raising animals, weaving cloth, tanning leather, working metal, producing tiles, illuminating books – as well as outlining the hierarchy of the monks and their functions. Once in the ruins themselves, it is relatively easy to follow the tour via the nave, south transept, presbytery, cloister, chapter house, refectory, kitchen, scriptorium, infirmary, abbot's house, lay-brothers' range and tannery, with the audio-guide creating a vivid picture of the life of the monastery as you go round.

Kirkbymoorside

Three miles along the A170 east of Helmsley, the village of **KIRKBYMOORSIDE** (W kirkbymoorside.com), while lacking the charisma of Helmsley, is worth considering as a base. Lining its sloping main street, the Market Place and the High Market Place, are a couple of nice hotels, and the town has a good variety of shops and pleasant cafés.

ACCOMMODATION AND EATING   **KIRKBYMOORSIDE**

George and Dragon 17 Market Place ☎ 01751 433334, W georgeanddragon.net. Cosy hotel with a formal restaurant (mains £12.50–21), a more relaxed bistro and a range of individualized rooms and suites. Daily 7.30am–11.30pm. **£90**

Kings Head 5 High Market Place ☎ 01751 431340, W thekingsheadkirkbymoorside.co.uk. This seventeenth-century coaching inn offers nicely decorated elegance and a really comfortable guest lounge, plus a sheltered, walled beer garden/terrace. Mon–Thurs & Sun 10am–11pm, Fri & Sat 10am–11.30pm. **£75**

Penny Bank 19 Market Place ☎ 01751 432606, W pennybankcafe.co.uk. Simple café offering a range of coffees, breakfasts, lunches, sandwiches and vegetarian options, using lots of local ingredients and with a slightly Mediterranean twist. Mon–Sat 8am–5pm, Sun 10am–3pm.

Nunnington Hall

Nunnington, 20 miles east of Thirsk • Feb–Oct daily 11am–5pm (closed some Mon – check website); Nov & Dec Sat & Sun 11am–4pm • £7.50; NT • ☎ 01439 748283, W nationaltrust.org.uk

Nunnington Hall, on the northern edge of the Howardian Hills, is a Yorkshire country house set in lush countryside by the river in Ryedale. With organic gardens thronging with peacocks and period rooms hosting art and photography exhibitions, it also has a collection of sixteen miniature rooms, a sort of deconstructed, one-eighth-scale doll's house created over forty years.

The house dates largely from the sixteenth, seventeenth and eighteenth centuries. It was damaged during the Civil War, and inherited by Richard Graham, 1st Viscount Preston in 1685, Charles II's ambassador to Louis XIV and master of the wardrobe to James II. He, alas, backed the wrong side during the Glorious Revolution in 1688, was put in the tower, and barely escaped execution. He lived the rest of his life quietly at Nunnington Hall, and with time on his hands, did a great deal of the remodelling of the house, the results of which you can see today.

5

Castle Howard

Thirteen miles southeast of Helmsley • **House** Late March to late Oct & late Nov to mid-Dec daily 11am–4pm • £14 including grounds **Grounds** Daily 10am–5pm • £9.50 • ☎ 01653 648333, ⓦ castlehoward.co.uk • The summer Moorsbus (see p.224) comes out here from Helmsley, while some Yorkshire Coastliner buses run from York, Malton or Pickering

In the heart of the Howardian Hills, and worth a day to itself, **Castle Howard** is one of England's greatest stately homes, famous for the exuberance of its architecture, the wealth of its interiors and the beauty of its grounds. There has been some dispute as to who designed it – some claim it was Nicholas Hawksmoor – but most experts now agree that it is Sir John Vanburgh's work, despite the fact that he was, until getting the Castle Howard commission, a writer. Hawksmoor was his assistant, which could explain his influences on the style. Conceived in 1699 for Charles Howard, 3rd Earl of Carlisle, and started in 1700, it took more than a century to complete.

The Avenue

Advance notice of the grandeur to come is given by the monument (1869–70) to the 7th earl with its gold-topped column set on a plinth, surrounded by four obelisks, which you pass long before arriving at Castle Howard itself, and by the subsequent five-mile drive along the beech- and lime-lined approach road – the **Avenue**, first laid out in the early eighteenth century.

The grounds

Access to the house and its grounds is through the handsome former **stables**, gathered around a paved courtyard. As you approach the house side on, there's a **walled garden** to the right, laid out in the early eighteenth century as a kitchen garden, now planted with roses and ornamental vegetables, and to the left, the **Boar Garden**, with a statue of a powerful looking wild boar at its centre.

At the house, an enormous lawn to the right – the South Parterre – surrounds the famous **Atlas Fountain**, which dates from 1853. Beyond this, in order, lie the South Lake (1720s) with its Prince of Wales fountain (1850s), the Cascade (1860s), the New River Bridge (1740s), the Temple of the Four Winds (1730s) and the mausoleum (1740s). The mausoleum, commissioned by the 3rd earl to be his burial place, continues to be used by the family, and is not open to the public. Beyond the house is Ray Wood, which contains the reservoir that powers the Atlas and Prince of Wales fountains, and to the north, overlooked by the massive north face of the house, the Great Lake (1790s), where there are boat trips, an adventure playground and a pleasant lakeside **café**. There's also a café on the west side of the house itself.

The house

The entrance to the **house** is in the west wing (the east wing is occupied by the family and isn't open to the public). On entering, immediately ahead is the Grand Staircase, which takes you up to the China Landing, then a succession of rooms groaning with priceless antiques, porcelain, furniture, sculpture and paintings. The most important room in the house, the huge, stately **Great Hall** soars 70ft upwards through two storeys and into the dome that gives the outside of the building its distinctive shape. Other rooms of great elegance succeed each other, and everywhere you look there are paintings by world-famous artists – Gainsborough, Holbein, Canaletto, Titian, Bellini and Rubens among them.

ACCOMMODATION   **CASTLE HOWARD**

Lakeside Holiday Park Across the Great Lake from the house ☎ 01653 648316, ⓦ castlehoward.co.uk /holiday-park.html. Caravan park and campsite in a tree-shaded area by the lake, with space for tourers and tents, and holiday homes for sale. Closed Nov–Feb. Two people and a pitch **£16**; caravan/motorhomes **£20**

CLOCKWISE FROM TOP SCARBOROUGH (P.257); NORTH YORKSHIRE MOORS RAILWAY (P.239); FLAMINGO LAND (P.242) >

5

Kirkham Priory

Whitwell on the Hill, around 4 miles south of Castle Howard • April–July & Sept Wed–Sun 10am–6pm; Aug daily 10am–6pm • £3.60; EH • ☎ 01653 618768, ✆ english-heritage.org.uk

At the very edge of the Howardian Hills, **Kirkham Priory** stands on a riverbank next to an attractive bridge, the serenity of the rolling wooded countryside broken only by the occasional train that clatters along on the opposite bank. The priory was founded in 1122 by Walter L'Espec, the founder of Helmsley Castle, for the Augustinian order. It had all the usual buildings – a large church, chapter house, dormitory, refectory, kitchen and storehouses – the remains of which are all clearly and fully described by excellent information boards around the site. One of them goes into detail about the unusual episode when parts of the priory were used during World War II for training soldiers in preparation for **D-Day**. The relatively flat land between the priory and the river was flooded to provide a shallow pool for testing the waterproofing of landing craft and amphibious tanks, while the wall of the western cloister was used to train soldiers in the use of the scrambling nets by which they would transfer from troop transports to landing craft.

EATING AND DRINKING   KIRKHAM PRIORY

Stone Trough Inn Whitwell on the Hill ☎ 01653 618713, ✆ stonetroughinn.co.uk. Just beyond Kirkham Priory, in a converted stone-and-tile cottage, the *Stone Trough Inn* offers pub food of a high standard, with main courses from £10.95 to £15.95 and a range of Yorkshire beers. Daily noon–11pm; food served Mon–Fri noon–2.30pm & 6–9pm, Sat noon–9pm, Sun noon–8pm.

Pickering

Set on the northern edge of the Vale of Pickering (see p.240), the market town of **PICKERING** is in an enviable position to act as a base for exploration of the surrounding countryside. The A170 Thirsk-to-Scarborough road and the A169 York-to-Whitby road intersect here, with the town centre lying to the north and west of the intersection, making it very easy to get into and out, while also allowing through traffic. The main streets of the town form a loop off the A170 – the Ropery, Market Place, Birdgate and Smiddy Hill. However, there's more to Pickering than its convenience as a base – it's a very convivial little town with a number of attractions of its own, notably the **Beck Isle Museum**, the **North Yorkshire Moors Railway** and the **castle**.

Beck Isle Museum

Bridge St • Feb–Nov daily 10am–5pm • £6 • ☎ 01751 473653, ✆ beckislemuseum.org.uk

Just off the town centre, prettily situated in gardens that slope down to the Pickering Beck next to a stone bridge, the **Beck Isle Museum** vividly conjures up a picture of life in Pickering and Ryedale over the centuries. The building itself is historic – its original owner, agricultural pioneer William Marshall, was adapting it into an agricultural college in 1818 when his death put an end to the project. Today the museum holds a huge collection of artefacts illustrating a variety of aspects of life and work in the area, all in an informal setting. Its rooms overflow with stuff that has drifted down through the centuries, including mock-ups of retail outlets (a chemist, a men's outfitters, the *Station Hotel*) plus displays on traditional occupations, such as cooper, cobbler, blacksmith, lacemaker and grocer, and a lovely ragbag of artefacts, photographs and documents on all sorts of subjects. Pickering was blessed with a fine high-street photographer in Sydney Smith, who documented ordinary life and special events, in landscapes, portraits and postcards, from 1914 to 1947; here you can see a unique record of life between the start of World War I and the end of World War II. You can also see a printer and blacksmith at work.

North Yorkshire Moors Railway

Park St • Days and hours vary: April– Oct steam trains daily, July & Aug trains hourly; Nov, Dec, Feb & March Sat & Sun only; check website for full timetables • Day rover tickets to Grosmont £19, Whitby £25 • ☎ 01751 472508, Ⓦ nymr.co.uk

Pickering is the southern terminus of the **North Yorkshire Moors Railway**, a lovely exercise in authenticity and aching nostalgia. Everything in the station speaks of the bygone steam age: the suitcases, luggage trolleys, advertising signs and station clock, the signage, porters and station master, the signals and gaslight fittings, and, above all, the great steam engines and carriages. And the station goes to great lengths to keep everything in period – a sign as you enter explains that, though you can't smoke inside, to maintain authenticity the usually compulsory "No Smoking" signs are not displayed. There's a refreshment room, a ticket office and shop, and you can catch trains north through the beautiful North York Moors, stopping at Levisham, Goathland and Grosmont. Grosmont is the terminus of this railway, but you can transfer there to trains on the **Esk Valley line** (Ⓦ eskvalleyrailway.co.uk) to Whitby.

Pickering Castle

Castlegate • Daily: April–Sept 10am–6pm; Oct 10am–5pm • £4.20; EH • ☎ 01751 474989, Ⓦ english-heritage.org.uk

At first **Pickering Castle**, a five-minute walk along Castlegate north of the town centre, doesn't look like much, but be patient. Though the castle was founded by William the Conqueror in 1069–70, most of what you see today dates from the thirteenth and fourteenth centuries. As you make your way through the entrance and into the outer then the inner bailey, you can learn all you need to know about early Norman military architecture.

Pickering Castle started as a rudimentary motte and bailey, the sort the Normans threw up immediately after the conquest by digging an enormous ditch and piling the earth in the centre to create a "motte", or artificial hill, which they would then top with a wooden fortification. The flat area around it became the "bailey" or enclosure (inner and outer), and the whole thing was surrounded by a wooden palisade. These fortifications could be built quickly, but were of course susceptible to attack by fire. So, following the immediate subjugation of the area, the castle was inevitably fortified in stone. Pickering Castle still has its artificial mound, topped now with the ruins of a stone castle, surrounded by a formidable stone curtain wall with towers enclosing the baileys, itself surrounded by a deep ditch. The castle doesn't appear to have figured in any great battles or sieges – its main job was to keep the locals cowed. It was, though, popular with several kings as a base for hunting in the surrounding forests. And, common to most castles (where a good vantage point was essential), the views in all directions are special.

Church of St Peter and St Paul

Hall Garth • Daily 9am–5pm • ☎ 01751 472983, Ⓦ pickeringchurch.com

Although the castle, the railway and the museum are the main reasons to visit Pickering, the **Church of St Peter and St Paul** is also of interest, not only for its position – at the highest point of the town centre, but surrounded by houses and with no access apart from up little stepped lanes – but also because it has some of the best **wall paintings** of any church in the country. Originating in the mid-fifteenth century, they bring home to modern eyes how colourful places of worship were in the Middle Ages, when murals and stained-glass windows would convey to a largely illiterate congregation, in considerable and sometimes gory detail, stories from the Bible and from early Christian history. Look out for St George and the Dragon, the Passion and Resurrection, and a couple of gory martyrdoms – John the Baptist and St Edmund. Note, too, the mid-fourteenth century effigy of a knight lying next to the lectern – legs nonchalantly crossed and two little angels poised like vampire bats at his neck.

5

By train The North Yorkshire Moors Railway station is just west of the town centre (see p.239).
By bus Buses run to Helmsley (every 1hr 10min; 35min) and Scarborough (every 1hr 10min; 56min).

Tourist office The Ropery (daily 9.30am–5pm; ☎01751 473 791), opposite a Co-op and a convenient short-stay car park. ⊕ pickering.uk.net is a useful website.

ACCOMMODATION AND EATING

Beckside Gifts and Tearoom Bridge St ☎01751 472845. A nice little teashop with a gift shop attached, serving simple sandwiches, cakes, savoury and sweet scones and light meals. Mon–Sat 9am–5pm.
White Swan Market Place ☎01751 472288, ⊕ white -swan.co.uk. A fine old coaching inn that is highly regarded for its well-executed, seasonal and locally sourced British food (dishes might include roast moorland grouse or potted Whitby crab; mains £12.95–25), the *White Swan* offers a choice of comfortable "vintage" or "contemporary" rooms. Daily 7.30am–11pm. **£125**

Vale of Pickering

To the south of **Pickering**, and separating the North York Moors from the Yorkshire Wolds, is the **Vale of Pickering**, a narrow neck of land that stretches from Helmsley in the west to Scarborough on the coast. Though this area isn't in a national park or an Area of Outstanding Natural Beauty, it is still attractive open country, with a couple of original attractions, notably **Eden Camp**, a gem of a museum that is not to be missed.

Malton

Eight miles south of Pickering lies **MALTON** which, together with sister town **Norton-on-Derwent** and the pretty **Old Malton**, is the principal market town for the Derwent Valley and the Vale of Pickering. It has had a chequered history. The **Romans** established a fort here – where Orchard Fields in town is today – to command the River Derwent. Later the Saxons settled at Old Malton where, in around 1150, Eustace Fitz John established the Gilbertine Priory of St Mary, and built a castle (now alas gone) next to the old Roman Fort. New Malton, to the west, was also established in the twelfth century. The town prospered, becoming the main market settlement and transport hub for the region.

An attractive yet refreshingly un-twee place, Malton is worth at least an hour's stopover, especially on market days (Sat) or during the animal auctions. It is centred on

---

LOCAL LAVENDER

Two fragrant, free and perhaps rather surprising attractions lie within easy reach of **Malton**: Wolds Way Lavender and Yorkshire Lavender.

Wolds Way Lavender Wintringham, just off the A64 Filey Rd ☎01944 758641, ⊕ woldsway lavender.co.uk. Eco-friendly farm shop, tearoom and plant centre with a little 7¼-inch gauge railway (£2). There's also a beehive (important for pollination), Yorkshire's only lavender oil distillery, complete with informative audiovisual presentation, and a raised platform that in summer offers spectacular views of the different hues of the lavender beds. You can buy a wide range of lavender-based products, and eat lavender scones in the tearoom. April–Aug daily 10am–4/5pm; Sept & Oct Sun–Thurs 10am–4/5pm.

Yorkshire Lavender and Howardian Herbs Terrington, signposted from Castle Howard ☎01653 648008, ⊕ yorkshirelavender.com. A gift shop selling lavender-based products, a tearoom/ restaurant, plant sales, a flower meadow and a maze, "probably the largest snakes and ladders in Yorkshire". An intriguing sculpture greets you as you enter – a group of life-sized metal cut-out cricketing figures represent the moment when a wicket has fallen. The owner Nigel Goodwill, a cricket fanatic, designed it himself and got the figures made locally. April–Oct daily 10am–5pm.

an eccentrically shaped, sloping **Market Place**, where you'll find the **church**; the Market Place is also used as a car park (free). Up the narrow Shambles, lined with small shops, is the **Cattle Market**, with metal-and-wooden pens, the premises of auctioneers Cundals. If you're in town on a Tuesday or Friday, it's well worth taking a look, with the market full of farmers and the pens full of animals.

St Michael's Church
Market Place • Daily 7am–5pm • Free • ☎ 01653 692089, ⓦ stmichaelsmalton.org.uk

St Michael's Church stands right in the centre of the Market Place, with no surrounding churchyard. Dating from 1150, the church is one of two new "chapels of ease" granted in that year to the Gilbertine Priory of Old Malton, and has been extensively altered and restored over the centuries. The most obvious survivals from Norman times are the pillars in both aisles, and possibly the font, though this might be Jacobean. The west tower is fifteenth century and, not being strong enough to stand up to the considerable stresses caused by swinging bells, contains ones that are struck rather than swung. Look out for the woodwork in the chancel by the mouseman's firm, Thompson of Kilburn (see p.229).

Malton Museum
Parish Rooms, Yorkersgate • Thurs–Sat 10am–4pm • Free • ☎ 01377 288497, ⓦ maltonmuseum.co.uk

Malton Museum, though it touches on most aspects of the town's history, concentrates mainly on one period – its Roman legacy. There are useful displays on the fort, army life, Roman artillery and many aspects of Roman life, including a poignant case devoted to an infant burial. At the time of writing, the museum was occupying temporary premises, with the aim of finding a permanent home in the future.

Eden Camp
Old Malton, a mile or so east of Malton • Daily 10am–5pm • £6.50 • ☎ 01653 697777, ⓦ edencamp.co.uk

Just north of the village of **Old Malton**, **Eden Camp** is a unique attraction whose own history is almost as interesting as that covered by its exhibits. Set up as a Prisoner of War camp in 1942, Eden Camp started as a complex of barbed wire and tents before its first inmates – Italians captured in North Africa – built more permanent accommodation. The Italians stayed until 1944, when they were replaced by Germans; the Germans remained until the last 1200 were repatriated in 1948, and the camp was closed. Nearly forty years later the derelict site was bought and refashioned into a museum.

The museum
The scene is set when you enter the **museum**, passing full-size replicas of a spitfire and a hurricane, and various big guns and military vehicles. Beyond are the rows of POW huts, which now house the exhibits; a simple progression takes you through Hut 1 ("The Rise of Hitler") to Hut 2 ("The Home Front"), Hut 3 ("The U-Boat Menace"), and all the way to Hut 22 ("Forces Reunion"). Each covers an aspect of the war, often in atmospheric detail. For example, in "The Blitz" in Hut 5 you walk past the mock-up of a bombed house – smoke, smashed furniture, burnt-out windows, ruptured water pipes. Elsewhere you'll see tableaux of prisoners digging a tunnel to escape, a family listening to Chamberlain's speech announcing the start of the war, land girls at work, staff in a bomber command ops room and so on. Huts 24 to 29 give a chronological account of the progress of the war. And though overwhelmingly about World War II, there is a hut dealing with trench warfare in World War I (Hut 11) and post-World War II conflicts (Hut 13).

Around the camp
Dotted around the **camp** are pieces of military hardware, including tanks, artillery and a VI "Doodlebug". There's a postwar "prefab" with a dig-for-victory garden, several air-raid shelters, sentry towers, a music hall where you can watch a puppet show of the great entertainers of the time, and, to help the kids let off steam, an adventure playground.

5

You can eat in the *Prisoners Canteen* and the *Officers Mess Tearoom* (where meals have appropriate names – Dambusters Stew, for example, or Submariners Feast) or drink Eden Camp bitter in the Garrison Cinema bar.

ARRIVAL AND INFORMATION   MALTON

By train The train station is a couple of hundred yards south of the town centre, just across the Derwent.
Destinations Scarborough (hourly; 22min); York (hourly; 24min).
By bus The bus station is in Railway St, next to the

train station.
Destinations Filey (every 2hr; 47min); Pickering (hourly; 24min); Scarborough (every 1–2hr; 50min); York (every 30min; 37min).
Useful website ⓦ malton.co.uk.

ACCOMMODATION AND EATING

Malton Relish 58 Market Place ☎ 01653 699389, ⓦ maltonrelish.co.uk. Excellent deli offering a wide range of cheese, cold meats, fish, pies and vegetables. They can put together hampers and picnics, too. Mon–Fri 9am–5.30pm, Sun 10am–4pm.

Suddaby's Crown Hotel 12 Wheelgate ☎ 01653 692038, ⓦ suddabys.co.uk. Early nineteenth-century, Grade II listed coaching inn with a microbrewery attached. It's very central, and friendly, though the rooms are a bit dated. **£77**

Flamingo Land

Kirby Misperton • March–Oct daily 10am–4/5/6pm • £35; family £110 • ☎ 0871 911 8000, ⓦ flamingoland.co.uk

Flamingo Land, off the A169 Malton-to-Pickering road, is a well-judged combination of theme park and zoo with something for children of all ages – a formidable collection of white-knuckle rides for the older ones, a group of smaller rides and activities for younger children and a rather good zoo for all ages, liberally sprinkled with places to eat and drink. Though it's not cheap, once you've paid your entrance fee only food and drinks aren't included. Rides and activities are roughly grouped together, so with the map provided it's easy to navigate. Most of the big, scary rides are grouped in **Metropolis**, water-based ones in **Splash**, little kids' attractions in **Muddy Duck Farm** and the zoo in the **Lost Kingdom**, but there's a fair bit of overlapping and intermixing. It's a large park, but tired legs can be rested by using the cross-park **monorail**, the **little train** or the **cable car**.

The **zoo**'s inhabitants generally look healthy, happy and in good condition, living in spacious enclosures. There's a good range of animals, mainly African, including big beasts like giraffes, camels, lions, tigers, white rhinos and zebras; smaller ones such as meerkats, lemurs, chimps, baboons and kangaroos, a variety of birds, including, of course, flamingos; reptiles, and an aquarium and a pool where you can see sea lions being fed.

The central and eastern Moors

The main route into the **central and eastern moors** is from Pickering in the south and Whitby in the north, along the A169 road that joins them. From the A170 either side of Pickering the moors stretch northward, with turbulent rivers and narrow valleys separated by heather upland. An alternative route into the area is the **North Yorkshire Moors Railway** (see p.239) which, together with the eastern end of the **Esk Valley Railway**, covers roughly the same ground. Whichever way you come, the region's moorlands, forests and pretty villages make it a delight to explore.

Hutton-le-Hole

One of the highlights of the central Moors is the pretty village of **HUTTON-LE-HOLE**, around four miles northeast of Kirkbymoorside. Set in the steep-sided valley of the Hutton Beck, surrounded by wooded hills and pastures, its houses spread either side

5

of an undulating, sheep-dotted common which is crisscrossed with footpaths and tidy white fencing. Through the common meanders the river, spanned by a little wooden footbridge.

Ryedale Folk Museum

Mid-Jan to March & Nov daily 10am–4.30pm; April–Oct 10am–5.30pm; winter closing time can vary • £7; family £22.50 • ☎ 01751 417367, ⓦ ryedalefolkmuseum.co.uk

The **Ryedale Folk Museum**, right in the centre of the village, offers a comprehensive collection of vernacular buildings assembled here from all over the dale. There are domestic houses, including a crofter's cottage and a manor house, workplaces (a blacksmith's, cobbler's, tinsmith's, cooper's and wheelwright's), farm buildings and shops, as well as reconstructions of an Iron Age settlement and a Victorian classroom. The museum also offers hands-on craft experiences for kids, a trail, and various special events, all in a stunningly beautiful setting.

ACCOMMODATION AND EATING   HUTTON-LE-HOLE

Barn Guest House and Tearooms ☎ 01751 417311, ⓦ thebarnguesthouse.com. A wide range of home-made cakes, scones, jams, pickles and so on, and functional accommodation. Tearoom March–Oct 10.30am–4.30pm. **£79**

Crown ☎ 01751 417343, ⓦ crownhuttonlehole.com. The *Crown* is a spacious real-ale-and-food pub; sit outside with your drink and enjoy the peace of the village. Good pub food (mains, such as steak and ale pie or seared lamb's liver, £9.50–13.95). Pub daily 11am–10pm/12.30am, depending on how busy they are; closed Mon & Tues in winter; food served Mon–Thurs 11.45am–2.15pm & 5.30–8.15pm, Fri & Sat 11.45am–2.30pm & 5.30–8.30pm, Sun 11.45am–6pm.

Lastingham

Less than two miles beyond Hutton-le-Hole lies **LASTINGHAM**, another pretty-as-a-picture village nestling in the steep-sided Hole Beck valley. It consists of a cluster of stone houses, a small green with benches and a bridge across the Beck, beyond which is a drinking fountain dedicated to **St Cedd**.

St Mary's of Lastingham

Holy Communion Wed 9.30am • ☎ 01653 658360

Lastingham's striking church, **St Mary's of Lastingham**, sits on its sloping churchyard overlooking the village. As early as 654 AD, a monastery was established here with St Cedd, an important Anglo-Saxon monk written about by the Venerable Bede, as its first abbot. It is said that, after he died of the plague, a group of monks from the south of England came to mourn his death, all but one of whom succumbed to the disease themselves. Nothing now remains of this early building, which was probably destroyed by the Vikings. However, in 1078 a new monastery was begun by Stephen of Whitby, first abbot of St Mary's of York.

From the outside, the **church** looks distinctly French, with its squat, square west tower and, at the east end, the apse – a semicircular extension beyond the end of the chancel – giving this end of the church its distinctive round shape. What makes this country church so very interesting is that the Norman crypt is still in place, and still used for worship. The steps down into the crypt start from the middle of the nave. The crypt itself mirrors the structure of the main church above it – nave, chancel, apse; the floor appears to be of compressed earth. Four thick, very short columns hold up the roof in the nave, a further two the chancel, and there's an archway, which starts at the floor level, beyond which is a simple stone altar. There's even a tiny stained-glass window set into the apse, made possible by the fact that the church is built into a steep slope. In the crypt are the remains of an Anglo-Saxon cross that must originally have been more than 20ft high, a hog-back gravestone with the carving of a bear, and several coffin lids.

5

★**Blacksmiths Arms** Anserdale Lane ☎01751 417247, ⓦwww.blacksmithslastingham.co.uk. A long, very appealing old pub, dating back to the seventeenth century and in a lovely spot opposite the church, with a friendly local atmosphere, open fires and tasty locally sourced pub food (don't miss the homemade steak and ale or lamb and mint pies). Three en-suite guest rooms upstairs. Daily noon–11pm; food served Mon–Sat noon–4.45pm & 6–8.45pm, Sun noon–4.45pm. **£75**

Thornton-le-Dale

THORNTON-LE-DALE, less than two miles east of Pickering, stands at the southern end of **Dalby Forest**, and is one of the prettiest villages in Yorkshire, despite the main Scarborough road (the A170) going right through it. Stone cottages line the Thornton Beck, there's a small triangular village green and a pond thronged with ducks, moorhens, dippers and kingfishers, and almost every house has its own little bridge. There are, too, several small independent shops and a couple of bakeries, cafés and tearooms.

Dalby Forest

Ten miles northeast of Thornton-le-Dale • Daily 7.30am–8.30pm • March–Oct £7 (7-day pass £20) • ☎01751 460295, ⓦforestry.gov.uk

Managed by the Forestry Commission, **Dalby Forest** boasts walking and cycle trails, a couple of adventure play areas, a visitor centre, and a **Go Ape** facility (Feb–Nov; £30; ⓦgoape.co.uk/days-out/dalby) with its thrilling rope bridges, tunnels, zipwires and segways.

Bridestones

Staindale, Dalby • Daily 24hr • Free; NT • ☎01723 870423, ⓦnationaltrust.org

Starting at Low Staindale, just north of the Dalby Forest Drive, is the Bridestones Trail. The **Bridestones**, owned by the National Trust, are huge sandstone formations that have been eroded into wildly tortuous shapes that get bigger the further north you go. Surrounded by heather moorland and ancient woodland, they are much loved by bouldering enthusiasts, though they are also of more general interest.

Levisham and around

Around five miles north of Thornton-le-Dale, and west of the main road lie two bucolic villages. **LOCKTON** has a tiny church and a youth hostel (see below), while **LEVISHAM**, a mile or so further on, offers access to the nearby national park-owned **Levisham Estate**, where more than five square miles of beautiful moors, valleys and woods form a microcosm of the whole national park. This is prime **walking** country – check ⓦgazetteherald.co.uk/leisure/countrywalks and ⓦnorthyorkmoors.org.uk for some good options.

By train You can get to Levisham on the North Yorkshire Moors Railway (see p.239) – it has its own station.

Useful website ⓦlocktonlevisham.co.uk.

★**Horseshoe Inn** Main St, Levisham ☎01751 460240, ⓦhorseshoelevisham.co.uk. Highly regarded family-run country inn with open fires, locally sourced pub food and nine comfortable B&B rooms. The meat dishes are good – famed meat producer The Ginger Pig is practically next door – with main courses at £10–16. Daily 11am–11pm. **£80**

Moorlands Country House Hotel Levisham ☎01751 460229, ⓦmoorlandslevisham.co.uk. An award-winning guesthouse with chintzy decor and nice gardens in a renovated Victorian building on the green. **£130**

YHA Dalby Forest Old School, Lockton ☎0845 371 9128, ⓦyha.org.uk/hostel/dalby-forest. Environmentally friendly hostel that's ideally placed for exploring the area on foot or on two wheels. Dorms **£18**; doubles **£69**

Hole of Horcum

Seven miles north of Pickering, on the A169, the **Hole of Horcum** is a gargantuan depression in the landscape (0.75 mile wide, 400ft deep), which looks as though it might have been caused by a primordial meteor strike. According to legend it was created by the Old English giant Wade scooping out earth to throw at his wife during an argument and missing, creating instead the nearby hill called Blakey Topping. Its actual origins are, alas, considerably more mundane – it's the result of erosion caused by the Levisham Beck, which you can see meandering along its bottom. There's also an ancient earthwork here – the **Horcum Dyke**; keep to the footpaths to avoid damaging it.

Goathland and around

Some twelve miles north of Pickering, to the west of the A169, is the unspoiled village of **GOATHLAND**. Easily accessible by road or rail (it's on the North Yorkshire Moors Railway), the village is strung out on a hillside along a sheep-dotted common (the sheep of the Duchy of Lancaster have long had common grazing rights). From here you can follow a footpath from the fine Victorian *Mallyan Spout Hotel* to the national park's most famous waterfalls – the 80ft-high **Mallyan Spout**. When you get to the beck, turn left, and the waterfall is a couple of hundred yards along the bank; it can be wet underfoot – allow twenty minutes there from the hotel, thirty on the way back.

Goathland attracts a fair number of *Harry Potter* fans – the station is the real Hogsmeade station – and also, although the last episode was broadcast in 2010, of the popular TV series **Heartbeat**, much of which was filmed here.

Roman Road

Two miles southwest of Goathland is one of the best-preserved stretches of **Roman Road** in Britain, though it's not easy to get to. If you drive west from the *Mallyan Spout Hotel* you'll arrive at a signpost giving you the choice of approaching the Roman Road on foot or by car. Either way, there's not much to see, since although the road was excavated, it is now fairly overgrown, but it does allow you to appreciate the amazing feat achieved by the Romans – the whole of Europe was crisscrossed by hundreds of miles of these wonderfully well-engineered roads.

Sleights

Five miles beyond Goathland along the A169 brings you to the village of **SLEIGHTS**, about three miles short of the coastal town of Whitby. Slung out on the hills either side of the River Esk, its main claim to fame is as the birthplace of Flint Jack, a famous nineteenth-century antique forger who made a living selling fake flint tools, arrows and fossils, along with "ancient" artefacts, to major museums for considerable amounts of money. Just before the village, a road heads west towards Grosmont, and the beautiful **Esk Valley**.

ARRIVAL AND INFORMATION   **GOATHLAND AND AROUND**

By train Goathland is a stop on the North Yorkshire Moors Railway (see p.239); the station is on the eastern edge of the village (ⓦ goathlandstation.org.uk).
Useful website ⓦ goathland.info.

ACCOMMODATION

La Rosa Campsite Between Goathland and Egton, 8 miles south of Whitby ☎ 01947 606981, ⓦ larosa.co.uk. Run by the same people who run the *La Rosa* hotel in Whitby (see p.252), and with a similar sense of aesthetics and humour, this 20-acre rural campsite features comfy beds in vintage and classic caravans, a funky camping barn, a converted truck and a tepee. It's quite basic, with low-energy lighting (candles and fairy lights) and compost loos. **£60**

Mallyan Spout Hotel Goathland ☎ 01947 896486, ⓦ mallyanspout.co.uk. This good-looking country house hotel, which combines an old-fashioned air with all modern comforts, caters for both passing walkers in search of a quick pint and pub grub and longer-term guests wanting comfort and good food – roast rump of Ryedale lamb with charred polenta and kale, say, or poached sole with wilted spinach (mains £14.95–24.95). **£120**

5

Esk Valley

Cutting right across the northern edge of the North York Moors, from west to east, the **Esk Valley** is an idyllic area of Yorkshire that remains largely undiscovered by many of the holidaymakers who visit the county. This is partly because there are no main roads in the valley itself – just a network of minor roads that meander from village to village through pasture and woodland.

Grosmont

At the heart of a farming area that became industrialized in the nineteenth century, first when the railway arrived, then when navvies digging tunnels discovered ironstone, the village of **GROSMONT** enjoyed great prosperity in the mid-nineteenth century by quarrying stone, smelting iron, making bricks and servicing the railway. Its iron industry was, however, destroyed by the wholesale production of steel in Sheffield and elsewhere from about the 1880s, and the village today is pleasantly rural, known largely for being the junction between the **North Yorkshire Moors Railway** (see p.239) and the **Esk Valley Line** from Whitby to Middlesbrough. There are numerous good **walks** in the vicinity – check the York Moors National Park Authority website (⊚www.northyorkmoors.org.uk/visiting/enjoy-outdoor).

Egton and around

In the pretty village of **EGTON** on the River Esk it's worth visiting the Catholic **St Hedda's Church**, noted for its wall paintings and for the shrine to martyr Father Nicholas Postgate, hung, drawn and quartered in York in 1679 for tending to Catholics in the area. Egton also has a station on the Esk Valley Line, and a fine moors **pub**. The village of **EGTON BRIDGE**, just down the road, climbs from the tree-filled valley on either side of the eponymous bridge and is known for its **stepping stones** (presumably pre-dating the bridge) and its fine **gooseberries** – the Egton Bridge Old Gooseberry Society holds its annual show in St Hedda's Church on the first Tuesday in August. Five miles northwest, **LEALHOLM** is another very pretty village with stepping stones across the river, and is the focus of numerous local walks (see ⊚northyorkmoors.org.uk /visiting/enjoy-outdoors).

Moors National Park Centre

Lodge Lane, Danby • April–July daily 10am–5pm; Aug daily 9.30am–5.30pm; Nov, Dec & March daily 10.30am–4pm; Jan & Feb Sat & Sun 10.30am–4pm • Free • ☎ 01439 772737, ⊚ www.northyorkmoors.org.uk

DANBY, an attractive moorland village with an Esk Valley Line railway station, also boasts the excellent **Moors National Park Centre**, one of just two National Park Centres for the North York Moors – the other is at Sutton Bank (see p.228). From the car park you can follow numerous **walks** – including the gentle quarter-mile **Crow Wood Trail** – enjoy the outside children's **play area** and lunch at the picnic site. The centre itself, housed in a row of stone cottages, offers interactive exhibitions, an audiovisual presentation about the national park, an indoor climbing wall for kids, tourist information, a well-stocked tearoom, a gift shop and toilets.

INFORMATION, ACCOMMODATION AND EATING ESK VALLEY

Tourist information Pick up useful local information at the Moors National Park Centre in Danby (see above).
The Wheatsheaf High St, Egton ☎01947 895271, ⊚wheatsheafegton.co.uk. Nineteenth-century inn with a cosy bar, attractive dining room – fish stew, vegetable tarts, nut roast, slow-braised belly pork – and four guest rooms (one of which is a children's bunk room). Pub hours Tues–Fri 11.30am–3pm & 5.30–11pm, Sat & Sun 11.30am–11pm; food served Tues–Sat noon–2pm & 6–8.30pm, Sun noon–2pm. **£85**

Whitby

Part fishing port, part seaside resort, picture-postcard-pretty **WHITBY** is the most interesting and atmospheric of Yorkshire's coastal towns. Rich in fossils and jet, both of which can be bought in the town, historically Whitby is important for its medieval **abbey** (where the pivotal Synod of Whitby is thought to have taken place), its long fishing and **whaling** traditions, its connections to **Captain Cook**, who came here as a lad to train as a ship's apprentice, and its shipbuilding. Its literary credentials include connections with medieval poet Cædmon, and with Elizabeth Gaskell, Lewis Carroll and Wilkie Collins. Above all, Whitby is associated with Bram Stoker's **Count Dracula**, who made landfall in the British Isles here – this pretty seaside town is a perennial Goth favourite.

The northernmost of the main North Yorkshire coastal towns, and the only one to face largely north, Whitby occupies the gorge created over millennia by the River Esk, which runs through the town and out between its famous twin piers and breakwaters into the North Sea. The town itself climbs up the gorge on either side. Whitby is thus divided into two clearly defined areas – the **East** and **West Cliffs**, the two joined by a century-old swing bridge.

The **old town** on the East Cliff is packed with history, with the narrow cobbled streets and tile-roofed houses of the fishing port dominated by the church and graveyard of **St Mary's** and the gaunt ruins of **Whitby Abbey**, high on the headland above. Here you will find the famed **199 steps**, joining the old town to the church and abbey, the shops selling **Whitby jet**, the old **Market Place** with its 1788-built **Town Hall**, and the **Captain Cook Memorial Museum**.

The West Cliff, mainly Georgian and Victorian, has the modern port and **fish quay**, a few amusement arcades, gift shops and souvenir stalls, the **Lifeboat Museum**, the **Whitby Museum** and **Pannett Art Gallery** (they're in the same building), the **Whitby Pavilion and Theatre** and, on the top of the cliff looking out across the town towards the abbey, the **Captain Cook Monument** and the dramatic **whalebone arch. Whitby Beach**, meanwhile, a wide expanse of fine sand partially lined by colourful traditional beach huts, stretches as far as Sandsend and offers safe bathing and attractive views of Whitby Abbey.

199 steps

Whether you're staying in Whitby for a few hours or a few weeks, you really must climb up the **199 steps** to St Mary's Church and Whitby Abbey. The 199 steps, or Church Stairs, which curve elegantly up from the end of Church Street onto the headland, are now stone-flagged and iron-railed, but once consisted of a wooden staircase constructed to help pallbearers carry coffins up to St Mary's churchyard. It's quite a climb, but there are benches at various points where you can take a breather. And if the climb doesn't take your breath away, the views across the roofs of the old town and Whitby harbour to West Cliff certainly will. If you're pushing a buggy or are in any other way restricted, you can take the steep cobbled ramp-like street beside the steps (Church Lane) or, if you want to drive, you can go the long way around – the abbey's signposted from the A171 southeast of town.

St Mary's Church

One of the most interesting churches in the country, Grade I listed **St Mary's Church**, on the headland next to the abbey, is worth a very long look. Though not perhaps one for the architectural purist, it's among the most extraordinary churches in the UK, battlemented, low and sprawling, a mixture of medieval and Georgian.

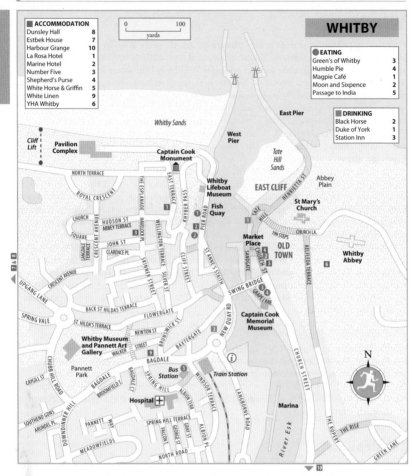

WHITBY

■ ACCOMMODATION	
Dunsley Hall	8
Estbek House	7
Harbour Grange	10
La Rosa Hotel	1
Marine Hotel	2
Number Five	3
Shepherd's Purse	4
White Horse & Griffin	5
White Linen	9
YHA Whitby	6

● EATING	
Green's of Whitby	3
Humble Pie	4
Magpie Café	1
Moon and Sixpence	2
Passage to India	5

■ DRINKING	
Black Horse	2
Duke of York	1
Station Inn	3

The tower is probably Norman, but the windows of the nave don't even pretend to be ecclesiastical – they're straightforward Georgian domestic windows. Inside, the stonework is a jumble of different dates and styles, but it's the furnishings that make this church unique. Everywhere there are wooden galleries and balconies, dating from the seventeenth century onwards, making it look more like a Nonconformist chapel than an Anglican church. Seventeenth-century too is the **Cholmley Pew**, one of the galleries that stands on four barley-sugar columns, built in the most conspicuous place right across the chancel arch to celebrate the local lord of the manor's importance, and with its own external wooden covered way to save the great man and his family from having to mix with the hoi polloi. Another external covered way gave access to some of the other galleries. Elsewhere in the church, look out for the parish chest, the great candelabra (there's no electric lighting, so the church has to be lit by candles) and the wonderful three-tier pulpit with two "vamping horns" – an early form of public address system. In the **churchyard**, near the top of the steps, you'll see **Cædmon's Cross**, erected at the end of the nineteenth century to celebrate the Anglo Saxon poet.

Whitby Abbey

Abbey Lane • Visitor centre April–Sept daily 10am–6pm; Oct & March daily 10am–5pm; Nov–Feb Sat & Sun 10am–4pm • £6.60; includes a useful audio-guide; EH • ☎ 01947 603568, ⓦ english-heritage.org.uk

Beyond St Mary's Church, crowning the top of the headland, stand the ruins of Benedictine **Whitby Abbey**, made famous by Bram Stoker in his novel *Dracula*. The abbey was established in 657 AD as a double monastery (home to monks and nuns) by King Oswy of Northumbria, who appointed a royal princess **Hild** (614–80) as first abbess. A formidable woman who had previously been the abbess of Hartlepool, she became advisor to kings and ordinary men alike – Cædmon was a cow-herd until, following a dream and encouraged by Abbess Hild, he became the first English poet. Because of her reputation for wisdom, Whitby Abbey was chosen as the venue for the **Synod of Whitby** in 664.

The abbey has suffered over the ages – from the ravages of time; from its position, exposed to the storms that blow in off the North Sea; from its dissolution at the hands of Henry VIII; and from a German naval bombardment in 1914. Nothing of the Anglo-Saxon monastery is now visible. The ruins are of a monastery built by the Normans in around 1220, and even then only of the monastery church. What it lacks in surviving remains, however, it more than makes up for in atmosphere, especially on stormy days – its skeletal remains dominate the skyline, and are visible from most parts of the town. It's easy to see why Bram Stoker would choose it as the backdrop for Count Dracula's arrival in Britain.

Next to the abbey, the **Abbey Visitor Centre** offers a detailed and hands-on introduction to the abbey and its history, including touch-screen computers via which Bram Stoker or a monk will answer a range of key questions.

Market Place and around

At the bottom of the 199 steps, the cobbled streets and "yards" of the **old town** – narrow Church Street, even narrower Sandgate Street, the **Market Place** – are worth exploring for their small independent shops, their cafés and pubs. There are lots of places where you can buy Whitby jet, minerals and fossils, plus an authentic Victorian jet workshop in the **Whitby Jet Heritage Centre** (123B Church St; ☎ 01947 821530, ⓦ whitbyjet.co.uk). There are also some great pubs backing on to the harbour, offering views that look like paintings – the **Board Inn** and the **Duke of York** (see p.253) in particular. The Market Place itself is dominated by the **Town Hall**, built in 1788 for Nathaniel Cholmley, with an open ground floor of Tuscan columns sheltering a couple of stalls selling clothes, a spiral staircase to the upper floor, Venetian windows and a rather fine clock.

Captain Cook Memorial Museum

Grape Lane • Daily: April–Oct 9.45am–5pm; March 11am–3pm • £4.80 • ☎ 01947 601900, ⓦ cookmuseumwhitby.co.uk

Beyond the Market Place both Church Street and Sandgate Street run into Bridge Street. Just before the swing bridge, down pretty flagstoned Grape Lane, is the **Captain Cook Memorial Museum**, housed in the well-preserved seventeenth-century house that the great man lodged in when he first came to Whitby as a 17-year-old to learn his trade as a seaman. It was the family home of the Quaker ship-owner John Walker, who used to lodge the apprentices from his ships in the attic between voyages. His ships hauled coal to London, and Cook learned everything he needed to know about seamanship and navigation on these colliers between 1746 and 1749. The collection includes maps, paintings and documents covering every aspect of Cook's life and times – apprenticeship, navigation, ship-building and cartography. The Green and Blue rooms convey a good idea of the austere decor in keeping with Walker's Quaker beliefs – simple furniture, no pictures – while the kitchen features its original seventeenth-century brick floor and a range of utensils used at the time.

5

It's not just the contents of the museum that recreate Cook's times. The views – out across the harbour on one side, into narrow Grape Lane on the other – give a tangible sense of what it must have been like in the seventeenth century.

Whitby Room

On the first floor, the **Whitby Room** displays a model of the type of ship owned by John Walker. Note the muster role of one of these ships – *Freelove* – from 1747, with Cook's name third from the bottom; a 1772 letter from Cook to Captain Hammond; Walker's copy of Cook's *A voyage towards the South Pole and Round the World*; and at the painting of the Whitby shipyards.

London, Voyages and Scientists rooms

The **London Room** covers Cook's early service in the Royal Navy and his subsequent career, when he lived in London, while the **Voyages Room** deals with his three great voyages (1758–63 to Australia, 1772–75 to the Antarctic, South Atlantic and Pacific, and 1776–79 to the North Pacific) in more detail. On the second floor the **Scientists Room** explores the huge contribution Cook's voyages made to eighteenth-century science – he was elected Fellow of the Royal Society in 1775, and during the American War of Independence, Benjamin Franklin ordered that, if American ships came into contact with Cook's vessels, they were not to interfere with them in any way, on the grounds that Cook and his men were "common friends to mankind".

Artists Room

The **Artists Room** contains a wealth of landscapes, botanical and ornithological studies and a portrait of Captain Bligh (of *Mutiny on the Bounty* fame), who captained the *Resolution* on Cook's third voyage. Finally, and most affectingly, is the humble top-floor **attic** where Cook slept as a youth, the scene recreated by a pinhole model.

The swing bridge, harbour and piers

Just beyond Grape Lane is the steel **swing bridge** that links the East and West Cliffs. There's been a bridge here for centuries, but the present structure, built by the same company that built Blackpool Tower, was inaugurated in 1908. After a warning bell, it swings open electrically to allow boats to move between the Upper and Lower harbours. Upriver is the **Upper Harbour** with the **Endeavour Wharf** on the west bank and, further up, the **marina**, while on the east bank is the Parkol Marine Engineering works where boats are still built. Downriver on either side of the **Lower Harbour** are fish quays, the Lifeboat Station and the Tate Hill pier.

Finally, like jaws at the mouth of the river, stand the **West Pier**, completed in 1831 and with a graceful 65ft-plus lighthouse at its tip, and the **East Pier**, which is shorter, newer (1854), and has a smaller, more functional-looking lighthouse. Look out for the capstans used to haul ships into port when the wind was in the wrong direction. Each pier is extended by concrete-and-wood structures, further protecting the harbour from the elements, their two tiers today often lined with anglers.

Most of the town centre lies to the west of the river. Look out, between the attractively simple 1847 train station and the swing bridge, for the bench in the shape of an ammonite, and the tribute to local sea captain, explorer and minister William Scoresby, inventor of the Crow's Nest.

West Cliff

The buildings of the **West Cliff** tell volumes about Whitby's Georgian heyday as a fishing and whaling port and its Victorian and Edwardian incarnation as a seaside resort. Right after the bridge, the dockside road (from New Quay Rd to Pier Rd) is

5

lined with cafés, restaurants, pubs, fish-and-chip shops, hot-dog stalls – even a clairvoyant's booth. Goths and gothic novel fans might enjoy the **Dracula Experience** (9 Marine Parade; Easter–Oct daily 9.45am–5pm; Nov–Easter Sat & Sun 9.45am–5pm; £3; family £9; ☎01947 601923, ⓦdraculaexperience.co.uk), with tableaux and special effects illustrating the story of Bram Stoker's *Dracula*.

Whitby Lifeboat Museum

Pier Rd • Easter–Oct daily 10am–5pm; Nov & Dec daily 11am–4pm (weather permitting); Jan–March Sat & Sun 11am–4pm (weather permitting) • ☎01947 606094, ⓦrnli.org.uk

Whitby Lifeboat Museum is stuffed with medals, photographs, paintings, models, lifeboat paraphernalia and artefacts from famous rescues. Stories from the archives of individual RNLI crew and survivors rub shoulders with evocative mementos from those involved in wrecks and rescues.

Fish quay and Whitby Sands

Opposite the Whitby Lifeboat Museum is the western **fish quay**, and beyond it the **bandstand** – a sight for sore eyes on a summer's evening, with the band playing against the backdrop of the East Cliff, its orange-roofed houses overlooked by St Mary's Church, with just the top of the abbey peeping out behind it. From Battery Parade next to it, its gun pointing out to sea, there is access to broad, clean **Whitby Sands**.

Royal Crescent

A stiff climb to the top of the West Cliff brings you to the main concentration of hotels and B&Bs, centring on the **Royal Crescent**. The whole area owes its existence to George Hudson ("the Railway King") who, determined to develop Whitby as a seaside resort, brought the railway to the town in 1839, and developed this part of the West Cliff as a typical Victorian resort, with handsome buildings and pleasant green areas, all with views across the sea or, in some cases, the town. At the end of the East Terrace is a commanding statue of **Captain Cook**, and the iconic **whalebone arch**, topped with the point of a harpoon. Though there's been a whalebone arch here since the middle of the nineteenth century, the present one (the jawbone of a bowhead whale killed under license by Inuits) was apparently donated to the town by Alaska in 2003.

Whitby Museum and Pannett Art Gallery

Pannett Park • Tues–Sun 9.30am–4.30pm • £5 • ☎01947 602908, ⓦwhitbymuseum.org.uk

On the western edge of Whitby is Pannett Park, with a state-of-the-art children's playground, extensive views over the town and the combined **Whitby Museum** and **Pannett Art Gallery** occupying the splendid building of the Whitby Literary and Philosophical Society. Deliberately retaining the atmosphere of an Edwardian museum, with mahogany cases mounted on sets of drawers, it covers local geology, the medieval background to the abbey, Whitby's heyday as a port, including Cook and the Scoresbys, and local industry (fishing, shipbuilding, jet, the coming of the railways, tourism). On show are some rather good collections of ceramics and glass, coins, seals, clocks and watches, weapons, toys, dolls and costume.

As one might expect, though, the museum's greatest strength is in its **fossil collection**, which includes a wide range of prehistoric life forms, and in particular massive marine reptiles. Indeed, the impetus for the formation of the Whitby Literary and Philosophical Society in 1823 came from concerns that the large numbers of fossils being found by alum quarrymen in nearby cliffs were being sold to collectors and therefore lost to the Whitby area. The **Art Gallery** has a collection of paintings of Whitby and around, and of the work of local artists.

5

By car Whitby is joined by the A171 to Middlesbrough to the west and Scarborough to the south. Motorists entering the town are likely to do so along one or other of the banks of the river – either way, there's plenty of parking along the riverside, especially around the marina. There's also considerable on-street parking on the hotel-lined streets of West Cliff. Once in town, everywhere is walkable – indeed, walking around Whitby is one of its great pleasures.

By train Whitby's train station is in the centre of town on Station Square, just south of the swing bridge, conveniently just across the road from the tourist office and near the bus station. Whitby is the terminus of the Esk Valley line, which runs to Middlesbrough and connects with the steam trains of the North Yorkshire Moors Railway at Grosmont, heading south to Pickering (see p.239).

Destinations Danby (4–5 daily; 40min); Great Ayton (4–5 daily; 1hr 5min); Grosmont (4–5 daily; 16min); Middlesbrough (4–5 daily; 1hr 30min).

By bus The bus station is next to the train station.

Destinations Robin Hood's Bay (hourly; 19min); Staithes (every 30min; 30min); York (4–6 daily; 2hr).

Tourist office Corner Langborne Rd and New Quay Rd, across the road from the train station (daily: Nov–March 9.30am–4.30pm; April–June, Sept & Oct daily 9.30am–6pm; July & Aug 9.30am–7pm; ☎01723 383636, Ⓦ discoveryorkshirecoast.com or Ⓦ visitwhitby.com).

ACCOMMODATION

Most of Whitby's accommodation is up on **West Cliff**, though a number of pubs and restaurants in the town centre also offer rooms.

HOTELS, B&BS AND GUESTHOUSES

Dunsley Hall Dunsley, a couple of miles west of town ☎01947 893437, Ⓦ dunsleyhall.com. This dignified Victorian country house hotel (the choice of visiting celebrities) has spacious, often oak-panelled, rooms, fine gardens, a pool, sauna and leisure club. **£125**

Estbek House Sandsend, two miles from Whitby ☎01947 893424, Ⓦ estbekhouse.co.uk. Georgian house beside the beck and close to the beach in the village of Sandsend. Four attractive rooms (called Alum, Florence, Eva and Nora – who could resist?) and a restaurant known for its fresh fish and seafood (mains from £19.95; reservations recommended). Daily 6–9pm. **£165**

★ **La Rosa Hotel** 5 East Terrace ☎01947 606981, Ⓦ larosa.co.uk. Eccentric B&B with eight rooms done out in extravagantly individual style – French naughty nineties courtesy of auctions, eBay and car boot sales – and terrific views of the harbour and the abbey. A breakfast picnic is delivered in a basket to your door. If you want slick modern accommodation with comprehensive facilities, perhaps go elsewhere. But for sheer exuberant fun and faded glory, try *La Rosa*. Street parking. **£86**

Marine Hotel 13 Marine Parade ☎01947 605022, Ⓦ the-marine-hotel.co.uk. Tiny hotel (more a restaurant with rooms) on the quayside, which has done wonders with very little space. There are four rooms here, two with balconies, and three with nice views across the harbour. A further three rooms are available at the *Moon and Sixpence* bar just along the road, with natty design and top-end fixtures. The restaurant specializes in fresh, largely locally sourced seafood (mains £9–24). Daily 8.30am–10pm. **£140**

Number Five 5 Havelock Place ☎01947 606361. West Cliff B&B that provides a good breakfast. Eight rooms with small but smart en-suite showers. No credit cards. **£66**

Shepherd's Purse 95 Church St ☎01947 820228, Ⓦ theshepherdspurse.com. Popular wholefood store-cum-clothes and gift shop that also offers guest rooms. Its best rooms (with brass bedsteads and pine furniture) are set around a galleried courtyard; the two pricier doubles on the upper level are nicest, and one has its own balcony. **£60**

White Horse & Griffin 87 Church St ☎01947 604857, Ⓦ whitehorseandgriffin.co.uk. Nicely renovated rooms (and several cottages) with many original features in the centre of Whitby's old town, with wonderful views of the harbour. The restaurant has a good range of fish and meat dishes, with vegetarian options. If you like character, this is a good option, but it can be noisy. **£70**

White Linen 24 Bagdale ☎01947 603635, Ⓦ white linenguesthouse.co.uk. Superior B&B in a restored Georgian house. Nine individually styled rooms with modern feel and good shower rooms. **£85**

HOSTELS

Harbour Grange Spital Bridge, Church St ☎01947 600817, Ⓦ whitbybackpackers.co.uk. Backpackers' hostel right on the river (eastern side) with 24 beds in five small dorms. Self-catering kitchen and lounge; 11.30pm curfew. **£18**

YHA Whitby Abbey House, East Cliff ☎0845 371 9049, Ⓦ yha.org.uk/hostel/whitby. Flagship YHA hostel in a Grade I listed building next to the Abbey Visitor Centre. Stunning views, good facilities and a Victorian conservatory, tearoom and restaurant. Rates include breakfast and entry to the abbey. Dorms **£15**; doubles **£59**

EATING, DRINKING AND ENTERTAINMENT

Whitby boasts a good range of pubs and restaurants, most of them gathered around both shores of the **harbour**. Nightlife is low-key, revolving around the pubs, but there are a handful of major **festivals**. At the end of August, **Whitby Folk Week** (ⓦ whitbyfolk.co.uk) offers a huge number of traditional artists and bands, gigs and workshops – more than 650 events in thirty venues across the town. The **Whitby Goth Weekends**, meanwhile (ⓦ whitbygothweekend.co.uk), in April and October, attract thousands of black-clad, ghost-white goths to town for all manner of music and events – including a charity football match between a local team and Real Gothic – along with undecidedly un-Goth activities such as sandcastle-building competitions, boat trips and picnics.

CAFÉS AND RESTAURANTS

★**Green's of Whitby** 13 Bridge St ⓣ 01947 600284, ⓦ greensofwhitby.com. A few yards from the swing bridge, and thought by many to be the best restaurant in Whitby, *Green's* offers great food in friendly, unpretentious surroundings, with a lively bistro downstairs and a fine dining restaurant on the first floor. Ingredients are locally sourced, so there are lots of great fish and meat dishes, including salt and pepper squid, fish pie, sea trout, slow-cooked belly pork and the like (bistro mains £10–20; restaurant two courses £34.95, three £41.95). Mon–Fri noon–2pm & 6.30–9.30pm, Sat & Sun noon–10pm.

★**Humble Pie** 163 Church St ⓣ 01947 606444, ⓦ humblepiemash.com. Tiny sixteenth-century building serving a range of pies cooked fresh to order – steak, stout and leek; Romany; Homity; haggis and neep, and many more – with mash and peas, amid 1940s decor with a soundtrack of World War II music. There's no license, so it's soft drinks only. Mon–Sat noon–8pm, Sun noon–4pm.

★**Magpie Café** 14 Pier Rd ⓣ 01947 602058, ⓦ magpiecafe.co.uk. Said by Rick Stein to be one of the best fish-and-chip shops in the country, the *Magpie* has served food from its 1750-built premises since the start of World War II. To call it a fish-and-chip shop is a bit misleading – although it provides the normal takeaway service, it also serves lesser-known fish like Woof and John Dory in its restaurant, and has an extensive wine list. Daily 11.30am–9pm.

Moon and Sixpence 5 Marine Parade ⓣ 01947 604416, ⓦ moon-and-sixpence.co.uk. Near the quay, with bistro-style ambience and good fish and meat dishes, from smoked haddock risotto with peas, spinach and poached egg to steak and chips (mains £9.90–16.90). There are rooms, too (see opposite). Daily 9am–midnight.

Passage to India 30–31 Windsor Terrace ⓣ 01947 606500, ⓦ passagetoindia.eu. Tandoori restaurant near the station, with great food and friendly and efficient service (mains £8–12). Mon–Thurs 5.30pm–midnight, Fri 5.30pm–1am, Sat noon–1am, Sun noon–midnight.

PUBS

Black Horse 91 Church St ⓣ 01947 602906, ⓦ the-black-horse.com. Lovely old pub (parts of which date from the seventeenth century) in the heart of the old town. Real ale, Yorkshire cheeses and seafood tapas on offer, along with twelve different varieties of snuff. Daily noon–11pm.

★**Duke of York** 124 Church St ⓣ 01947 600324, ⓦ dukeofyork.co.uk. In a great position at the bottom of the 199 steps, the *Duke of York* is warm and inviting, with black beams, nautical memorabilia (harpoons, propellers, photos), church pews and views across to the harbour and West Cliff. The pub food is good (no main course above £9); the only downside is the recorded music and TV, alas. Sun–Thurs 11am–11pm, Fri 11am–11.30pm, Sat 11am–midnight.

Station Inn New Quay Rd ⓣ 01947 603937, ⓦ stationinnwhitby.co.uk A real ale haunt, with a changing selection of guest beers and live music on Wednesdays, Fridays, Saturdays and Sunday afternoons. Mon–Sat 10am–midnight, Sun 10am–11.30pm.

VENUES

Pavilion Complex (aka the Spa Pavilion) West Cliff ⓣ 01947 820625, ⓦ www.whitby.uk.net. A glass-and-iron structure built as the *Westcliff Saloon* in 1880, much extended since, and now a complex that hosts pantomimes, comedy, drama and music, as well as events in various music festivals – folk, country, and the famous twice-yearly Goth Weekend. There's also the pleasant *Crystal Lounge* café, with views over the sea.

North of Whitby

North of Whitby the coast becomes increasingly rugged, with headlands, bays, a scattering of small villages and some wonderful views, especially after the road climbs up out of **Sandsend** and twists and swoops along the cliffs and headlands, with roads off to **Runswick Bay**, **Port Mulgrave** and **Staithes**, before heading inland and west towards Middlesbrough.

5

Sandsend

Two miles up the coast from Whitby, and accessible from it by road or along the beach, the village of **SANDSEND** is made up almost entirely of boarding houses and cafés lining the sea wall. The *Wits End Café* has a large car park from which people often fish. Sandsend is great fun when the sea's rough, because the water breaks over the sea wall.

Runswick

A North Yorkshire smuggling village, with houses stacked steeply up from the sea, the pretty village of **RUNSWICK** lies on Runswick Bay some ten miles from Whitby off the A174 towards Middlesbrough. Runswick has suffered badly over the years from the ravages of storm and sea, with a whole new village having to be built in the seventeenth century when a landslide destroyed the old one, and it continued to suffer storm damage until a sea wall was built in 1970. Today Runswick is an idyllic little place with café/tearoom (summer only), a pub, a chapel and a colossal **beach**. Look out for the last few remaining "binks" – standing stones outside front doors, where the laundry was traditionally done. You can also see one of the few remaining thatched houses on this stretch of coast – it was once the coastguard's cottage.

EATING AND DRINKING   RUNSWICK

Royal Hotel ☎01947 840215, ⓦroyalhotelrunswick .com. Appealing family-owned and -run pub in a stunning location, offering good food from £8.25–10.50. April–Oct | daily noon–10.45pm; Nov–March Fri–Sun noon– 10.45pm; food served daily 10am–2pm & 6–8.30pm.

Port Mulgrave

PORT MULGRAVE, once a thriving ironstone-mining settlement nine miles north of Whitby, is now uninhabited and owned by the National Trust. Opened in 1855, the mine had exhausted the reserves of ironstone by the turn of the century. The port continued to be used for ironstone from another pit, but eventually fell into disuse after World War I, and its facilities succumbed to the weather, to fire, and to the attentions of the Royal Engineers, who didn't want it to be used by the Germans during World War II. There's a steep path down to the remains of the port – a ruined jetty, the entrance to the adit mine – dotted now with corrugated iron sheds, fishing boats and lobster pots. It is also a fossil-hunter's paradise on a par with Dorset's Jurassic coast, its crumbling cliffs yielding **ammonites** and dinosaur remains, especially after winter storms.

Staithes

At one time one of the biggest fishing ports in England, the fishing village of **STAITHES,** on the A174 just before it bears inland towards Middlesbrough, has always depended on the sea for its livelihood – not only fishing, but boat-building, sail-making and even smuggling. The hill down to the village, most of which is on the east bank of the **Staithes Beck**, is seriously steep; there are benches dotted along its length where people toiling up it can catch their breath. The houses – the few on the west bank are joined to the rest by a footbridge – are painted in various pastel shades, and there are several independent shops and a couple of pubs on the High Street (see p.256). Courts and alleys, often stepped, head off the main street and there's a small, attractive **harbour** with a boat-launching slipway, steps down onto a small **beach** and a café/sandwich shop. Across the mouth of the Beck stands **Cowbar Nab**, a sombre, gull-dotted cliff.

5

Captain Cook and Staithes Heritage Centre

High St • Feb–Dec daily 10am–5pm; Jan Sat & Sun 10am–5pm • ☎ 01947 841454, ⓦ captaincookatstaithes.co.uk

Although Staithes would undoubtedly attract visitors for its beauty and quaintness alone, it also claims a connection to **Captain Cook**. As a young man the great explorer worked in a shop in the village – Sanderson's, which stood near today's *Cod and Lobster* pub and which was washed away during a storm. Today the **Captain Cook and Staithes Heritage Centre** offers a ragbag collection of photographs, paintings, models, books and manuscripts, with a reconstructed street and period rooms, all illustrating the history of the village in general and James Cook's stay here in particular.

ARRIVAL AND INFORMATION   STAITHES

By car Turn off the A174 and leave the car in the car park at the top of a hill, then walk down into the village.
By bus Bus #4 travels from Whitby to Staithes (every

30min; 28min).
Tourist information Staithes is covered by Whitby's tourist office (see p.252); see also ⓦ staithes-town.info.

EATING AND DRINKING

★**Cod and Lobster** Harbour Front ☎ 01947 840330. Small, no-frills real ale and pub grub establishment with a fabulous location perched on the sea wall, and great views; perfect on a sunny day. Try the cod and chips (£7.50) or the seafood platter – £40 gets you a huge selection. Regular guest ales. Daily 11am–midnight; food served Mon–Fri noon–

2.30pm & 5.30–8.30pm, Sat & Sun noon–8.30pm.
Royal George High St ☎ 01947 841432, ⓦ royal georgestaithes.co.uk. Tiny nineteenth-century village pub with an old-fashioned atmosphere, real fires, real ale and pub food. Mains £5.95–9.95. Daily noon–11.30pm; food served noon–2.30pm & 6–8pm.

South of Whitby

The twenty-mile stretch of coast **south of Whitby** down to Scarborough offers a succession of headlands, sea views and rocky and sandy bays. Take any of the minor lanes that strike east from the A171 and you're virtually guaranteed vistas to gladden the heart. **Robin Hood's Bay**, though undoubtedly a little twee, is irresistible, while the **Shire Horse Centre** and **Ravenscar** are worth a detour.

Robin Hood's Bay

Five miles south of Whitby, **ROBIN HOOD'S BAY** is one of the prettiest villages in the country. Known locally as "Bay Town" or "Bay", it is in two parts – the Victorian development at the top of the hill, and the more attractive original settlement at the bottom, best approached on foot. Descending into the village, down a steep hill with views across rose-coloured roofs to the sea, you come to a plaque commemorating heroic efforts to save the crew of the brig *Visitor*, which ran aground in the bay in 1881. Local boats couldn't be launched, so the Whitby lifeboat was dragged across the headland by eighteen horses over six miles, rising to 500ft, through seven snowdrifts, with the way being cleared by hundreds of men. It took two hours, and all the crew were saved.

Today there are many reasons to stop off at this lovely village. When the tide's out the flat rocks (scaurs) that appear, split by a geological fault, are a rich source of rock pool life and **fossils**. The village was also the setting for the **Bramblewick books**, a series of tales about local fishermen by local author Leo Walmsley (1892–1966), who lived here for most of his childhood – a blue plaque marks the house. It's a nice place for a wander, with lanes and flights of steps to explore, terraces with wonderful bay views, teashops, pubs and independent shops selling sweets, books and gifts.

Brief history

Probably originally settled by Saxons and Vikings, Robin Hood's Bay appears in records from Tudor times. Despite local legend, there's little likelihood that the village was ever visited by, or had anything to do with, Robin Hood of Sherwood Forest. If Dutch trading maps are anything to go by, Robin Hood's Bay was more important than Whitby – the former was identified on the maps, the latter wasn't. The village's great heyday was in the eighteenth century, when it supplemented its earnings from fishing and farming with a well-developed **smuggling industry**. Remote and difficult to get to, the village was ideal for smuggling, with virtually everybody in the village involved – not only the fishermen and their families, but also farmers, the clergy and the gentry, either directly or by providing finance and safe houses. Certainly, all took their share of the profits or of the tea, gin, rum, brandy and tobacco that was being smuggled. Frequent set-tos took place between excise cutters and smugglers' ships, and between excisemen and smugglers on land. It is said that a series of tunnels and passageways ensured that contraband could be moved from the quay to the top of the village without seeing the light of day.

Old Coastguard Station

The Dock • Late Feb daily 10am–4pm; April–Oct daily 10am–5pm; Jan, March, Nov & Dec Sat & Sun 10am–4pm • Free; NT • ☎ 01947 885900, ⓦ nationaltrust.org.uk

Following the main street down between terraced cottages and narrow lanes, continuing as it takes a sharp right at the *Laurel Inn*, you will eventually come to sea level at the **Old Coastguard Station**. Now a visitor centre, the station has a number of displays of local interest, with exhibits about the slipway and explaining how the local landscape was formed. The steps to the right of the Old Coastguard Station lead to a two-mile clifftop walk across to Boggle Hole and its youth hostel.

Robin Hood's Bay Museum

Fisherhead, south side of the village • June Wed & Sun 2–4pm; July & Aug Mon–Fri & Sun noon–4pm; also limited other days, check website • Free • ☎ 01947 881252, ⓦ museum.rhbay.co.uk

Set in an old house that has been used variously as a coroner's office and a library, **Robin Hood's Bay Museum** is on the south side of the village, and accessible only via one of its characteristic cobbled and stepped pathways. With just three rooms filled with displays on aspects of the village's geology and history, it focuses on fishing, shipwrecks and smuggling, with some exhibits on local friendly societies.

ARRIVAL AND INFORMATION   **ROBIN HOOD'S BAY**

By car The car park is at the top of the hill, and you'll need to walk down the steep incline to get to the interesting bit.
Tourist information Robin Hood's Bay is covered by the Whitby tourist office (see p.252) but the National Trust's Old

Coastguard Station (see above) is a source of information for the whole of this stretch of coast, and ⓦ robin-hoods -bay.co.uk is worth a look.

EATING AND DRINKING

Swell Old Chapel, Chapel St ☎ 01947 880180, ⓦ swell .org.uk. Café/bar and gift shop in a building erected in 1779 as a Wesleyan Chapel – John Wesley himself preached (and Leo Walmsley went to school) here. The café/bar offers breakfasts, soup, sandwiches, paninis, wraps, salads

and ploughman's lunches, with a variety of drinks, alcoholic and otherwise (food £4.75–7.50). There are super views from the tables on the terrace, while the gift shop has a good range of ceramics and art. Daily 10am–4.15pm; later if busy.

Ravenscar and around

On the coast about fourteen miles south of Whitby is the village of **RAVENSCAR**, which boasts spectacular views across Robin Hood's Bay from its steep access road – there's a line of benches beside the road, and you can quite see why they were put there. Notice the overgrown railway station platform with a long carved sign saying "Peak" (which was until 1897 the name of the village). This is all that remains of the highest (630ft above sea level) station on the Scarborough-to-Whitby **railway**, which was in operation

5

from 1885 to 1965. Because the gradient was so steep, trains had to take a run at it, sometimes several times. The whole area was bought by the Peak Estate Company in 1890, with plans to develop a new resort to rival Scarborough; new roads were built, plots of land sold, sewers laid, and works set up to make bricks for the anticipated building boom. The company had, however, misjudged the market, plots didn't sell, and in 1911 they went bankrupt. The beach here is rather stony, so today the village is frequented more by walkers on the Cleveland Way or finishing the Lyke Wake Walk, or by guests at the big hotel that overlooks the sea.

National Trust Centre

Ravenscar • April–Oct daily 10am–4.30pm • ☎ 01723 870423, ⓦ nationaltrust.org.uk

The **National Trust Centre**, just southeast of Ravenscar, has displays on the ten miles of National Trust-owned land on the beautiful stretch of coast between Saltburn and Filey. Exhibits focus on its geology, wildlife and early industrial history – especially the remains of the alum works, which extracted alum from the hillside to be used in dying cloth and tanning leather, and which you can walk to from the centre.

Shire Horse Centre

Staintondale, two miles south of Ravenscar, east of the A171 Whitby to Scarborough Rd • July & Aug Tues, Wed, Fri & bank hol Sun & Mon 10.30am–4.30pm • £5.50 • ☎ 01723 870458, ⓦ shirehorsefarm.co.uk

The **Shire Horse Centre**, well signposted off the main A171 south of Ravenscar, offers not only a chance to get close to these engaging gentle giants but also a variety of live horse and pony shows. You can visit the stables, see a forge and explore the small museum, and children may be able to stroke Shetland ponies. There's a café and a variety of walks, and the drive to the centre through a wooded glen with waterfalls is in itself a delight.

Scarborough

The undoubted queen of the North Yorkshire coast is **SCARBOROUGH**, located on a headland with a bay on either side, about halfway between Bridlington in the south and Whitby in the north. Its significance arose in the mid-twelfth century when a powerful royal **fortress** was built overlooking the town, and from the thirteenth century onwards Scarborough was also famous for its annual **fair**, which lasted from mid-August to late September, attracting merchants from all over Britain and abroad (and giving its name to the traditional ballad *Scarborough Fair*). In the seventeenth century, when mineral waters were discovered, Scarborough became popular as a **spa town** – especially after the 1660 publication of a book about the waters – and in the eighteenth century it increasingly became known as a seaside resort. As the crowds of visitors grew, other attractions were introduced – horseracing on the sands, boating and sea-bathing; Scarborough was one of the first resorts (in 1735) to use bathing machines to preserve modesty. When the railways arrived in 1845 the number of visitors attracted by the sea bathing rose to a flood. Today Scarborough is a large town with a fine collection of Victorian and Edwardian buildings and which, though still recognizably a seaside resort, is also a player in the corporate events market, a functioning fishing port and the regional capital, and has its share of light industry.

Of its two magnificent **beaches**, the South Bay beach in particular is perfect for families. The North Bay beach is further from the road and less crowded. Away from the sands the town has a lot to look at – a ruined **castle**, two interesting **churches**, several good **museums**, the **Sea Life Centre**, linked to the town by the miniature **North Bay railway**, a number of beautifully landscaped **public gardens**, an attractive **fishing port** and the largest **Open Air Theatre** in Europe. It also has all the elements of the

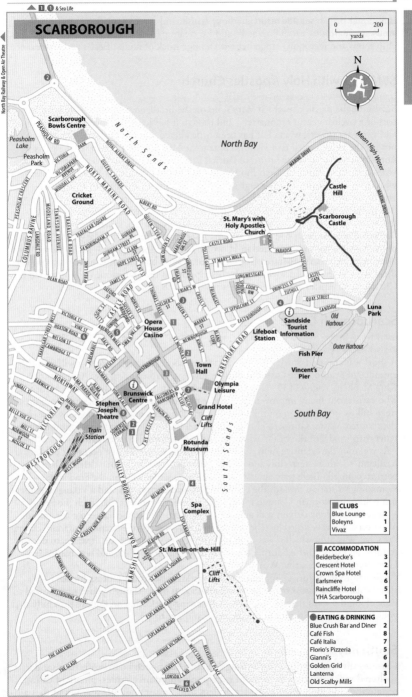

SCARBOROUGH

North Bay Railway & Open Air Theatre

▲ 🏠 **1**, **0** & Sea Life

0   200
yards

N

North Bay

Peasholm Lake

Peasholm Park

Scarborough Bowls Centre

North Sands

Castle Hill

Scarborough Castle

Cricket Ground

St. Mary's with Holy Apostles Church

Mean High Water

MARINE DRIVE

Opera House Casino

Luna Park

Sandside Tourist Information

Old Harbour

Town Hall

Lifeboat Station

Fish Pier

Outer Harbour

Brunswick Centre

Olympia Leisure

Vincent's Pier

Stephen Joseph Theatre

Grand Hotel

Cliff Lifts

South Bay

Train Station

Rotunda Museum

South Sands

Spa Complex

St. Martin-on-the-Hill

Cliff Lifts

■ **CLUBS**
Blue Lounge	2
Boleyns	1
Vivaz	3

■ **ACCOMMODATION**
Beiderbecke's	3
Crescent Hotel	2
Crown Spa Hotel	4
Earlsmere	6
Raincliffe Hotel	5
YHA Scarborough	1

● **EATING & DRINKING**
Blue Crush Bar and Diner	2
Café Fish	8
Café Italia	7
Florio's Pizzeria	5
Gianni's	6
Golden Grid	4
Lanterna	3
Old Scalby Mills	1

5

traditional British **seaside resort**: harbour cruises and speedboat rides, fairgrounds and amusement arcades, candyfloss stalls and ice cream parlours, donkey rides and cliff lifts, chip shops and tearooms – together with a huge stock of hotels, B&Bs and restaurants.

St Mary's with Holy Apostles Church

Castle Rd • ☎ 01723 500541, ⓦ scarborough-stmarys.org.uk

Scarborough's parish church, **St Mary's**, up on the headland, may originally have been part of a twelfth-century monastery, and though it has lost its chancel, north transept and two west towers, what's left has been little altered since it was built. However, it's not for the church itself that visitors come to St Mary's, but rather to see the grave of **Anne Brontë**. Anne was the third of Patrick Brontë's famous children to die within a year – after first Branwell, then Emily had passed away, the clearly very ill Anne was whisked off to breathe Scarborough's sea air by her sister Charlotte in a desperate attempt to avoid their fate. To no avail – four days after leaving her home at Haworth (see p.111) Anne died of tuberculosis at the *Grand Hotel*, which still stands above the South Bay. To spare her father yet another family funeral, Charlotte decided to "lay the flower where it had fallen" and had her sister buried at St Mary's, the only one of the Brontës not to be interred in Haworth church. Anne's grave – it's in the part of the churchyard that's separated from the church itself by Church Lane – looks out over the town and the sea. Incidentally, the inscription on the gravestone commissioned by Charlotte got Anne's age wrong – she was 29, not 28 years old.

Scarborough Castle

Castle Rd • April–Sept daily 10am–6pm; Oct daily 10am–5pm; Nov–March Sat & Sun 10am–4pm • £4.70; EH • ☎ 01723 372451, ⓦ english-heritage.org.uk

A short walk beyond St Mary's Church is a gatehouse; through here you will find the entrance to **Scarborough Castle**. Built illegally by a baron during the "Anarchy" of King Stephen's reign (1135–41), it was confiscated in 1154 by his successor Henry II, who carried out many improvements. Once over the barbican bridge, you climb up a steep hill to an exhibition on the history of the headland and the castle – it's here, in the restored Master Gunner's House, that you'll find the tearoom. Look out too for the relief map/model of the castle, which provides much-needed orientation.

As you tour the extensive **ruins**, note that the castle wasn't the first occupant of the headland – with its steep cliffs and narrow point of access, its natural defences had long been recognized. There were at least two prehistoric settlements on the headland: a Roman signal station towards the end of the Roman occupation, and a Viking settlement just before the Norman Conquest. But it's the medieval remains that catch the eye – especially the long curtain wall and the ruined keep. The castle has seen a fair amount of action – it was besieged by rebel barons in 1312, and twice by Parliamentarians during the Civil War, after which it was "slighted" to prevent its further use. It was partially restored and strengthened during the Jacobite Rebellion of 1745, and bombarded by German naval guns during World War I.

Apart from its historical importance, the castle is also worth visiting for the spectacular **views** across both the North and South bays. Though you're not allowed to walk along the walls themselves, there is a viewing platform, and the site is so hilly that you get numerous glimpses across the town and out to sea.

South Bay

Close to the town centre, Scarborough's **South Bay beach** boasts soft, firm sand, sheltered safe bathing, a number of rock pools and donkey rides, plenty of cafés, restaurants and amusement arcades, toilets, and, in summer, lifeguards and first aid and lost children posts. There are also many visitor attractions – the funfair, the **harbour** with speedboat rides, cruises and fishing trips, and lots of attractive **gardens** and open spaces – the Valley Gardens, Belvedere, Italian Gardens and, off to the west, Oliver's Mount Country Park. Access to the South Bay is via several streets at the northern end or, much more fun, via a couple of **cliff lifts** – there's one next to Olympia Leisure, another between the Spa complex and the Belvedere Gardens.

Scarborough Harbour
Scarborough Harbour is divided into the Old Harbour, full of fishing boats, and, beyond it, the narrow Outer Harbour, where leisure craft join yet more fishing boats. It's a vibrant and thriving place – any doubts that it's a fully functioning fishing harbour will be squashed after seeing the huge mounds of lobster and crab pots piled up on the quaysides, and the people working along the **Fish Pier** and on the fishing boats moored to the quays. Next to the Fish Pier there are detailed information boards about the harbour and, outside the **Lifeboat Station**, about Scarborough's RNLI, while, at the end of Vincent's Pier, which separates the Old from the Outer Harbour, you can see the **Diving Belle** – a modern statue of a young woman on tiptoe about to dive into the sea next to the lighthouse. Its sister statue – a Victorian woman dipping her toe in the water – stands on Westborough. There are pubs and restaurants in the harbour area too, and a small information kiosk.

The seafront
In the angle between the harbour and the headland, **Luna Park** (see p.263) is one of dozens of funfairs named after the original in Coney Island, USA. Heading south along the promenade – **Foreshore Road** – you'll come to Olympia Leisure (see p.263), the largest of numerous amusement arcades, while on the cliff top above, and dominating the South Bay, is the 1867 **Grand Hotel** (☎0871 222 0047, ⓦbritanniahotels.com), once the largest hotel in Europe, and the place where Anne Brontë died. Nearby is the old Town Hall, beside which a small paved garden features a statue of Queen Victoria and wonderful views across South Bay to the castle.

Spa Complex
South Bay • ☎01723 821888, ⓦscarboroughspa.co.uk
At the southern end of Scarborough's South Beach is the **Spa Complex** (see p.264). Now a theatre/performing arts venue, the complex owes its existence to the discovery of mineral waters by a Mrs Farrer in the 1620s – she saw spring water running from the cliff, noticed that it stained the rocks brown, tasted it and found it bitter and salty. She had soon recommended it to her friends as a cure for minor ailments, and over the years its popularity spread. By the early eighteenth century a building had been erected where the Spa Complex is today, to facilitate the "taking of the waters". The present building dates largely from 1880.

Rotunda Museum
Vernon Rd • Tues–Sun 10am–5pm • £3 • ☎01723 353665, ⓦrotundamuseum.co.uk
The **Rotunda Museum**, at the southern end of Vernon Road (you can't miss it – it's round), is the second oldest purpose-built museum in the country. Built in 1829 and constructed to the plans of William Smith, famed and influential English geologist, it's a fascinating building in its own right and includes in its venerable shell modern displays on geology and local history. The Dinosaur Coast Gallery is particularly child friendly.

5

St Martin-on-the-Hill

Albion Rd • Hours vary, so call in advance to confirm • ☎ 01723 363828, ⓦ st-martin-on-the-hill.org.uk

In the streets west of the Spa Complex, in the angle between Craven Street and Albion Road, is **St Martin-on-the-Hill**, a church that it is well worth visiting for its **Pre-Raphaelite decoration**. Look out for the "Mary" window, featuring the Virgin Mary by Edward Burne-Jones and Mary Magdalene and Mary of Bethany by William Morris, all three with the strong features and red hair typical of Pre-Raphaelite imagery. Mary of Bethany is said to have been modelled on Elizabeth Siddal, Rossetti's wife, and the Virgin Mary on Georgina MacDonald, who married Burne-Jones in 1860. Notice, too, the four chancel rose windows by Rossetti and Morris, the west windows by Burne-Jones and the King David window by Morris. The pulpit is particularly interesting, with Pre-Raphaelite panels designed (but not painted) by Rossetti, Ford Madox Brown and Morris as part of the first commission won by Morris's company in 1861.

North Bay

Overlooked by hotel-lined cliffs and some lovely **gardens**, blue flag **North Bay** is a great crescent of firm sand and safe, clean bathing – it is much frequented by surfers. A beach centre offers showers, first aid and lifeguards in season, and, at the northern end, there are numerous rock pools to explore. It's perfect for long walks and flying kites.

Peasholm Park

Daily 24hr • Free • ☎ 01723 500954, ⓦ peasholmpark.com

Just back from the seafront, **Peasholm Park** is, unlike many seaside municipal parks, attractive and naturalistic. Its Japanese theme goes right back to its inception in 1912, and the naval warfare displays with model boats originated in 1927. Throughout the interwar and immediate post-World War II period the gardens hosted open-air concerts and firework displays, but with visitor numbers falling in the cash-strapped 1970s and 1980s, they fell into neglect. However, the early years of the twenty-first century saw a National Lottery-fuelled renaissance, and the gardens are once again one of Scarborough's main attractions, with the concerts and fireworks back on the agenda, and the **reconstructed naval battles** taking place three times weekly in summer – check the website for dates and times. The replica ships and aircraft used in the reconstructions have been updated as the years have passed – at the time of World War I it was all dreadnoughts, after World War II British and German battleships, and from the 1960s more modern fighting craft including Ark Royal, an aircraft carrier. When it's not being used for battles, the boating lake has a good choice of boats to rent – swan pedaloes, rowing boats and Canadian canoes. Between Peasholm Park and the promenade is a skate park and the **Scarborough Bowls Centre**, while north of the park, in **Northstead Manor Gardens**, stands the **Scarborough Open Air Theatre** (see p.264).

North Bay Railway

Peasholm Park Station, Burniston Rd • Daily: June–Aug 10am–5.30pm; April, May & Sept 10.30am–5.30pm; Feb, March & Oct–Dec 11am–5.30pm • Single £2.60, return £3.30 • ☎ 01723 368791, ⓦ nbr.org.uk

The **North Bay Railway** linking Northstead Manor Gardens with the village of Scalby Mills is a 0.75 mile, 20-inch narrow-gauge railway that was opened in 1931. All four of its locomotives and all its coaches date from the 1930s – some were built specifically for the Scarborough set up, others for railways elsewhere which have since closed. At the southern terminus (Peasholm Park Station which, despite its name, is just inside Northstead Manor Gardens) there's a station building, with shop, ticket office, waiting room and bistro/café bar. The North Bay Railway Company also runs pedaloes on the Northstead Manor Gardens boating lake (£3.50) and a historic water chute (£2.20 for two rides).

Sea Life

Scalby Mills • Daily 10am–6pm • £16.20 • ☎ 01723 373414, ⓦ visitsealife.com

At the Scalby Mills end of the miniature railway is **Sea Life**, the Scarborough Sea Life Centre and marine sanctuary, part of a network of many such centres across the UK, Europe and the US. Under several conical white roofs a series of habitats introduces you to turtles, sharks, seals, jellyfish, otters, penguins and many other creatures. It's very accessible, with demonstrations, feeding times and an ocean tunnel, and has a serious conservation purpose – there's a seal rescue and rehabilitation programme on site, for example, and for £25 you can adopt a shark, turtle, seal or penguin. There's a soft play area, a gift shop and a restaurant – but if you want to escape the crowds try the *Old Scalby Mills* pub (see p.264), just beyond the entrance to the car park.

ARRIVAL AND DEPARTURE
SCARBOROUGH

By car There's a good choice of permanent and seasonal short- and long-stay car parks in the town, and two Park-and-Ride facilities south of the town centre (one on the A64, the other on the A165). The tourist offices have a comprehensive *Visitors Guide to Parking in Scarborough*.

By train The station is on the southwest edge of the town centre, halfway along Westborough.

Destinations Bridlington (every 1hr 30min; 36min); Hull (every 1hr–1hr 30min; 1hr 25min); Leeds (hourly; 1hr 15min); Manchester (hourly; 2hr 15min); York (hourly; 48min).

By bus Most buses arrive and depart in the streets surrounding the train station, while National Express coaches use the car park adjacent.

Destinations Bridlington (every 1hr–1hr 40min; 1hr–1hr 18min); Hull (every 1hr 50min; 2–3hr); Whitby (hourly; 57min).

GETTING AROUND AND INFORMATION

By bus Open-top seafront buses (Feb–Nov daily from 9.30am, every 12–20min; £2 return) run between North Bay and the Spa Complex in South Bay.

Tourist offices Brunswick Shopping Centre, Westborough (April–June & Sept Mon, Tues & Thurs–Sat 9.30am–5.30pm, Wed 10am–5.30pm, Sun 11am–4.30pm; July & Aug Mon, Tues & Thurs–Sat 9.30am–5.30pm, Wed 10am–5.30pm, Sun 10.30am–4.30pm; check for winter hours; ☎ 01723 383636, ⓦ discoveryorkshirecoast.com); also on Sandside by the harbour (daily: April–June, Sept & Oct 10am–5.30pm; July & Aug 9.30am–7pm, ☎ 01723 383636, ⓦ discover yorkshirecoast.com).

ACTIVITIES

Luna Park Sandside ☎ 01723 361984. Traditional funfair overlooking the harbour, more suitable for young families than gangs of thrill-seeking teenagers. All the things you'd expect – Ferris wheel, dodgems, helter-skelter, amusement arcades, fairground rides – together with toffee apples, candy floss and ice cream. Summer daily; rest of year Sat & Sun

10am–various closing times.

Olympia Leisure Foreshore Rd ☎ 01723 377960, ⓦ olympiascarborough.co.uk. Bowling alley, pool tables, amusement and video games, a kart track for 4–10 year olds, soft play area, snack bar – ideal when the weather's proving uncooperative. Daily 9am–11pm.

ACCOMMODATION

Scarborough has a wealth of **accommodation**. The largest Victorian and Edwardian hotels are ranged along the cliff tops of both bays, with hundreds of guesthouses and B&Bs in between and back from the front. The advantage of such competition is, of course, competitive prices – shop around.

★**Beiderbecke's** 1–3 The Crescent ☎ 01723 365733, ⓦ beiderbeckes.com. Boutique hotel in a sedate terrace (dating from 1832) on the South Cliff, with free parking. Rooms are comfortable and the bar is old-fashioned (in a good way), with live jazz on Saturday. They have a stylish, reasonably priced brasserie, too. **£130**

★**Crescent Hotel** The Crescent ☎ 01723 360929, ⓦ thecrescenthotel.com. A spacious, slightly old-fashioned hotel catering for holidaymakers and business folk alike, with friendly, helpful staff, comprehensive

facilities and a fine restaurant, all housed in mid-nineteenth century splendour. **£107**

★**Crown Spa Hotel** 7–11 Esplanade ☎ 01723 357400, ⓦ crownspahotel.com. Lovely Victorian building (opened in 1845) in a superb position on the cliff above South Shore, with all the facilities you'd expect from a four-star hotel – health club, spa, swimming pool, restaurant and café/bar. Accommodation is not as expensive as you might expect – and prices vary considerably depending on demand. **£172**

5

5

Earlsmere 5 Belvedere Rd ☎01723 361340, ⓦtheearlsmere.co.uk. A boutique guesthouse, on the cliff above South Shore, housed in an Edwardian terrace building that has retained many original features, in particular the staircase and stained-glass window. The decor of the five guest bedrooms is in keeping with the hotel's origins, but with up-to-date facilities. No children under 12. **£70**

Raincliffe Hotel 21 Valley Rd ☎01723 373541, ⓦraincliffehotel.co.uk. A high-quality traditional hotel/guesthouse in a Victorian building back from the South Cliff, with fifteen en-suite rooms. Good dinner available, too. No pets, no children under 8. Street parking. **£70**

YHA Scarborough Burniston Rd, 2 miles north of town ☎01723 361176, ⓦyha.org.uk/hostel/scarborough. In an early seventeenth-century water mill a 15min walk from the sea, this is a good hostel for families with kids. Dorms **£13**; family rooms **£60**

EATING AND DRINKING

Scarborough has a good mixture of places to eat and drink, with numerous seaside **pubs** and **fish-and-chip** shops and an above-average number of **Italian** restaurants.

Blue Crush Bar and Diner Peasholm Gap ☎01723 362450, ⓦbluecrushbar.com. Near the beach opposite Peasholm Park, the *Blue Crush* is a music bar in a contemporary glass-and-steel building, which does good food – burgers, pasta, salads, sandwiches (mains £8.50–9.95). Summer daily 10am–midnight; food served 10am–10pm.

★**Café Fish** 19 York Place, at the intersection with Somerset Terrace ☎01723 500301. More of a top-end fish restaurant than a fish-and-chip shop, where a two-course dinner with wine could feature fish curry, steamed mussels or Thai fishcakes, and will cost from about £30. It gets very busy at weekends. Daily 5.30–10pm.

Café Italia 36 St Nicholas Cliff ☎01723 501973. Enchanting, tiny, authentic Italian coffee bar. They stick to what they're good at: excellent coffee, ice cream and cakes. Daily 9am–9pm.

★**Florio's Pizzeria** 35–37 Aberdeen Walk ☎01723 351124, ⓦflorios-restaurant.co.uk. Highly rated restaurant, popular with locals – noisy, convivial, child-friendly, with cheerful service and authentic Italian food. Main courses start as low as £5, climbing to around £20 for steaks. Sun–Thurs 5–10pm, Fri & Sat 5–10.30pm.

Gianni's 13 Victoria Rd ☎01723 507388, ⓦgianni restaurant.co.uk. The most immediately welcoming of the town's Italian restaurants, where the good-natured staff bustle up and down stairs delivering quality pizzas, pastas and quaffable wine by the carafe. Pizzas £8–10, pasta £8–11.50, steaks around £18–24. Daily 5pm–late.

Golden Grid 4 Sandside ☎01723 360922, ⓦgolden grid.co.uk. The harbourside's choicest fish-and-chip establishment, "catering for the promenader since 1883". Offers grilled fish, crab and lobster, a *fruits de mer* platter and a wine list alongside the standard crispy-battered fry-up. Decent portions of fish from £7.80. Easter–Oct Mon–Thurs 10am–8.30pm, Fri 10am–9pm, Sat 10am–9.30pm, Sun 11am–6.30pm; Nov–Easter opens 11am, closing varies.

Lanterna 33 Queen St ☎01723 363616, ⓦlanterna -ristorante.co.uk. Long-established, special-night-out destination, featuring traditional, seasonal Italian cooking – chick pea stew with oxtail, venison ravioli, veal marsala, truffle dishes – in quiet, formal surroundings. Meat courses around £23, pasta and risotto £15–18. Booking recommended. Mon–Sat 7–9.30pm.

Old Scalby Mills Scalby Mills Rd ☎01723 500449, ⓦoldscalbymills.co.uk. Next to Sea Life, the *Old Scalby Mills* offers a good range of real ales, pub food (£5–8) and nice sea views. Daily 11am–4am (earlier if not busy); food served 11am–8pm.

NIGHTLIFE AND ENTERTAINMENT

Many of Scarborough's **nightclubs** are in and around St Thomas Street and its extension St Nicholas Street. There are also a number of excellent theatres.

THEATRES AND VENUES

Opera House Casino 56–64 St Thomas St ☎01723 357940, ⓦoperahousecasino.co.uk. Full range of gaming, plus bars and a restaurant and special events including live football, parties and tribute bands. Bars daily 10am–late; food served 6pm–2am; restaurant Sun–Thurs 7pm–2am, Fri 6pm–3am, Sat 6pm–2am.

Scarborough Open Air Theatre Burniston Rd, Northstead Manor Gardens ☎01723 383636, ⓦscarboroughopenairtheatre.com. Venue for live music, opera, sporting events, family shows and comedy. Originally opened in 1932, it was reopened in 2010, and its 6500 capacity makes it the largest of its kind in Europe. In addition to the main auditorium it has bars, restaurants, shops and funfair rides. Box office Mon–Thurs 11am–4pm, Fri–Sun & school holidays 11am–6pm.

Spa Complex South Bay ☎01723 376774, ⓦscarboroughspa.co.uk. A major venue for shows, concerts by the Scarborough Spa Orchestra, comedy, family entertainment and music from opera and ballet to folk and rock 'n' roll. The complex includes various theatre spaces, including the Suncourt for open-air concerts, plus cafés and bars. Box office Mon–Sat 9am–9pm, Sun 9am–8pm.

Stephen Joseph Theatre Westborough ☎01723 370541, ⓦsjt.uk.com. World-famous theatre-in-the-round associated with writer and, until he stepped down in 2009, artistic director Alan Ayckbourn, which opened in its current premises (an Odeon cinema) in 1996. Around ten plays a year are staged, mostly first productions, often including those written by Ayckbourn himself. Box office Mon–Sat 10am–8pm; Sun 2hr before performance (closed on non-performance days).

CLUBS

Blue Lounge 4 St Nicholas St ☎01723 367930. Popular bar with comedy, sport and a good range of music – funk, soul, r'n'b and disco classics. Daily 10.30am–4am.

Boleyns 17 St Thomas St ☎01723 500065, ⓦboleyns nightclub.com. Three rooms, five bars – playing mainly pop and house. Entry £1–5. Thurs–Sun until late.

Vivaz Huntriss Row ☎01723 368222, ⓦvivaz.co.uk. Just around the corner from St Nicholas St, *Vivaz* is the resort's main venue for alternative music, with resident DJs and live music – classic rock, blues, contemporary and retro pop, electro, indie, metal and dance. Daily 11am–4am.

Filey

Of North Yorkshire's three main resorts, **FILEY**, nine miles south of Scarborough, is by far the most genteel, offering few specific attractions but a vivid idea of what Victorian and Edwardian seaside resorts would have been like. Its success in attracting visitors after the arrival of the railway in 1846 wasn't simply a confluence of a nice stretch of coast and the means to get there – the worthies of the town set about developing it to meet the needs of visitors, and the result is a classic well-bred British seaside resort of the nineteenth and early twentieth century.

THE BATTLE OF FILEY BAY

In 1779, Scottish-born sea captain **John Paul Jones** became a hero of the American War of Independence when he was despatched to Britain with a squadron of five ships to attack British coastal shipping. Aboard his flagship, the **Bonhomme Richard**, he was heading for Bridlington when he encountered the British warships **HMS Serapis**, captained by Richard Pearson, and the **Countess of Scarborough**, captained by Thomas Piercy, which were escorting a merchant fleet along the east coast. At 7.15pm on September 23, 1779, the American and British ships began one of the most ferocious battles of naval history. Jones, realizing that his gaggle of converted merchantmen was no match for the Royal Navy's purpose-built warships, immediately set about getting to close quarters. To start with he failed, the *Serapis* using her superior speed to circle the *Bonhomme Richard*, firing continuously and causing massive damage. But then the two ships became entangled and collided. Locked together, they drifted, guns still firing at point-blank range, with individual hand-to-hand combat taking place all over this floating wooden island. Both ships caught fire. Called on to surrender, John Paul Jones refused (though his famous words "I have not yet begun to fight" have been doubted by some). An American sailor threw a grenade from high in the rigging of the *Bonhomme Richard* through an open hatch on the *Serapis*, its explosion igniting a magazine and killing many men. Finally, with both ships wrecked and the *Bonhomme Richard* sinking, Pearson decided that there was nothing to be gained by further fighting and surrendered. The Americans boarded and took command of the *Serapis*, and the struggle to keep the *Bonhomme Richard* afloat was lost – it sank 36 hours later. John Paul Jones sailed off south, to be showered with praise and honours by Benjamin Franklin, then United States Minister to France, and by Louis XVI. In England, Pearson was cleared of blame by a court martial, and in his own way, for saving the convoy, became a hero. He was declared a freeman of a number of east-coast towns, and received a knighthood from King George III.

The wreck of the *Bonhomme Richard* now lies somewhere off Flamborough Head, and its position is, of course, the subject of intense speculation, not least in the USA, and not least because it might contain the personal effects of John Paul Jones and much else of interest to historians of the War of Independence. The **American Ocean Technology Foundation** runs annual expeditions to search for it, but with hundreds of ships having been wrecked in this stretch of sea over the centuries, it's not going to be easy to identify.

5

Filey figures in the country's **aviation history** – its broad flat sands were used as an airstrip by pioneer Robert Blackburn in 1910 and 1911 as he tested the aircraft he was building for his Leeds company – and, on the evening of September 23, 1779, was witness to one of the great battles of the American War of Independence, the **Battle of Filey Bay**, sometimes called the Battle of Flamborough Head (see box, p.265). All evening throngs of people lined the coast from Scarborough to Flamborough Head to watch the US and British warships engaged in moonlit battle out in the bay, seeing the flashes and hearing the rumble of the guns.

Filey's town centre stands on the heights above the sea, with a long **promenade** just above the beach. Along and beyond the promenade is a series of **gardens**, and along the front too you'll find a bandstand, boating lake and paddling pool, shelters, cafés, the contemporary **Sculpture Trail** and access to the superb **beach** – quiet and sandy, with safe bathing and little of the brashness of many other holiday resorts. At the north end of the promenade is **Coble Landing**, with a slipway where Yorkshire cobles – small wooden fishing boats said to be descended from Viking longships – are still winched up.

Filey Museum

8–10 Queen St · Easter–Oct Sun–Fri 11am–5pm, Sat 2–5pm · £2.50 · ☎ 01723 515013, ⓦ fileymuseum.co.uk

In the compact town centre, the **Filey Museum**, housed in late seventeenth-century whitewashed cottages, traces the history of the town from its early days as a fishing and farming community to its heyday as a seaside resort. There are eight rooms on two floors, each with an audio commentary, covering the development of the town, rural and domestic crafts, the Victorian era, the Lifeboat service and much else, together with displays on the geology and marine life of the area.

Lifeboat Station

Cobble Landing · Daily 10am–5pm · Free · ☎ 01723 513197, ⓦ fileylifeboat.co.uk

If the Lifeboat service exhibit at the Filey Museum piques your interest, you could follow it up with a visit to the **Lifeboat Station** at the northern end of the promenade next to the Coble Landing. This station is kept busy by the danger to shipping represented by two rocky promontories that jut out into the North Sea: Flamborough Head to the south and Filey Brigg to the north.

Filey Brigg

The headland immediately north of the town, **Filey Brigg** was created by a geological fault whereby the southern edge slipped, bringing the soft clay overlay down to the level of the sea or below, creating a fascinating succession of flat rocks and rock pools teeming with life. The northern edge of the headland, which didn't slip, is made of steep cliffs deeply etched by the sea. The whole promontory protects the coast to the south from northeasterly gales, which is why the Romans probably had a harbour here, and which is certainly why Filey grew up where it did. A Sight of Special Scientific Interest, it is now a country park providing pleasant walking, benches to sit on, lots of rock pools to explore and fine views back across the town.

ARRIVAL AND INFORMATION   **FILEY**

By car Between Filey and Scarborough the A165 offers a pleasant drive through stone villages and rolling countryside. There are car parks behind the bus station and along Church Ravine on the northern edge of the town centre, and on-street parking in the town and along the promenade.

By train The train station is off Station Ave to the west of the town centre.

Destinations Bridlington (every 1hr 30min–2hr; 22min); Hull (every 1hr 30min; 1hr 12min); Scarborough (every 1hr 30min; 17min).

By bus The bus station is on Station Ave just east of the train station.

Destinations Bridlington (every 30min–1hr 30min; 25–47min); Hull (1 daily; 2hr 11min); Leeds (2 daily; 2hr 45min); Scarborough (every 10–20min; 30min); York (2 daily; 1hr 33min).

Tourist information Evron Centre, John St (Mon–Sat 9am–5pm; ☎01723 383636, ⓦdiscoverfiley.org.uk). The centre also stages plays, exhibitions and live music, screens movies and offers leisure and sports facilities.

ACCOMMODATION

★**5 Leys** 9–10 The Beach ☎07702 262509, ⓦ5leys .co.uk. Well-appointed self-catering accommodation in four apartments in a tall terrace overlooking the beach. Per week **£450**

All Seasons Guesthouse 11 Rutland St ☎01723 515321, ⓦallseasonsfiley.co.uk. A 2min walk from the beach, this award-winning guesthouse has spotless and nicely decorated rooms, and lifts seaside B&B standards to a new level. **£80**

EATING AND DRINKING

Bella Italia 20 Mitford St ☎01723 516001, ⓦbella italiaristorante.co.uk. Small and friendly family-run Italian restaurant (not part of the chain of the same name) with good food at very reasonable prices (mains around a tenner). Daily 6–10pm.

★**Bonhomme's Bar** Royal Crescent Court ☎01723 514054. Just off the Crescent (it's easy to miss – it's on the left as you enter Royal Crescent Court) and named after John Paul Jones' flagship (see box, p.265), this CAMRA favourite serves a good range of real ales. Mon–Fri 11am–12.30am, Sat 11am–1am, Sun noon–12.30am.

Filey Tandoori 16 Belle Vue Crescent ☎01723 515992, ⓦfileytandoori.co.uk. This good tandoori restaurant is BYOB, so customers are welcome to bring their own beer and wine. Mains £6–9.95 April–Sept daily 6–11pm; Oct–March Tues–Sun 6–11pm.

Ingham's Fish Restaurant 40 Belle Vue St ☎01723 513320. Excellent fish-and-chip shop known throughout the region. July & Aug Mon–Thurs 11.45am–7pm, Fri & Sat 11.45am–7.30pm; Sept–June Mon–Fri 11.45am–2pm & 4.15–6.30pm, Sat & Sun 11.45am–7.30pm.

East Riding of Yorkshire

SPURN HEAD

6

East Riding of Yorkshire

Think of Yorkshire and you think of the city of York and its surrounding countryside, the beautiful dales, moors and rugged coast to the north, the hilly nineteenth-century wool towns around Leeds and Bradford to the west, even the coal, iron and steel towns of South Yorkshire. Less well known is the rather remote-seeming East Riding of Yorkshire. Yet it has a character all of its own.

Its largest settlement is the maritime city of **Hull**, formally known as **Kingston-upon-Hull**, quietly making a lie of its rather rough reputation by remodelling its centre into a fine space dotted with references to its history, focused on a busy and colourful marina. Hull offers some of the best nautical and social museums in Yorkshire which, true to the city's long tradition of left-wing principles, are free. Many of its old lanes and alleys survive, and it is home to the **Deep**, a superb modern aquarium with a strongly conservationist ethos. Beyond Hull, the empty and atmospheric **Holderness** peninsula is skirted on one side by the North Sea and the other by the wide Humber estuary, separated by the unique sand-spit **Spurn Head**, which is lengthening by about 6ft every year. A low-lying land of villages and farms, of old-fashioned seaside towns and impressive churches, Holderness is attractively unobtrusive. North and northeast of Hull are pretty upmarket towns like **Beverley**, which has not one, but two of England's greatest ecclesiastical buildings, and **Driffield**, a busy farming town known, at least to itself, as the capital of the Wolds. The **Yorkshire Wolds** themselves – low, unspoiled chalk hills – lie like an eyebrow across the north of the county, with farms and tiny villages and short steep hills, great houses like **Sledmere** and **Burton Agnes Hall**, the tallest standing stone in the country at **Rudston** and the most famous abandoned medieval village at **Wharram Percy**. East of the Wolds, empty east-coast beaches stretch for miles up to the brash resort of **Bridlington** and the majestic **Flamborough Head** beyond. East Yorkshire is a land rich in ecclesiastical and domestic architecture, a land that looks outwards to Europe rather than just inwards to the rest of Britain. And it remains relatively undiscovered by modern tourism – at times it seems that the only foreign visitors it sees are the hordes stampeding from Hull docks towards the crowded, and expensive, streets of York.

Hull

Founded by King Edward I in 1293 as **Kingston-upon-Hull** (which is still its proper title), **HULL**, on the confluence of the River Hull and the Humber estuary, became the most important port on the east coast. Its stature was reflected by its parish church, **Holy Trinity**, the largest by area in the whole country, and by the fact that several of the great religious orders – the Whitefriars, the Greyfriars and the Austin Friars – had houses in the town (nothing remains of them, except in street names). Hull's **whaling industry**, whose heyday was in the early nineteenth century, was crucial to the city's

THE DEEP, HULL

Highlights

❶ The Humber Bridge Useful for getting across the Humber estuary, and beautiful in its own right – one of the world's great engineering feats. **See p.275**

❷ The Deep Fine modern aquarium in what is rapidly becoming an iconic building. **See p.280**

❸ Beverley Minster Cathedral-sized church stuffed with the fine and the fascinating. **See p.285**

❹ Nellies, Beverley Step back in time – a pub which is heated by open fires and lit by gas, where the local conversation is good and the beer is cheap. **See p.289**

❺ Burton Agnes Hall Stunning Jacobean mansion bursting with architectural detail and great works of art. **See p.292**

❻ Rudston Monolith Britain's tallest standing stone, so old it makes the medieval church in whose churchyard it stands seem positively contemporary. **See p.294**

❼ Spurn Head A geological phenomenon created by east-coast erosion, Spurn Head is home to a nature reserve, a famous lifeboat and the Humber pilots. **See p.301**

HIGHLIGHTS ARE MARKED ON THE MAP ON PP.272–273

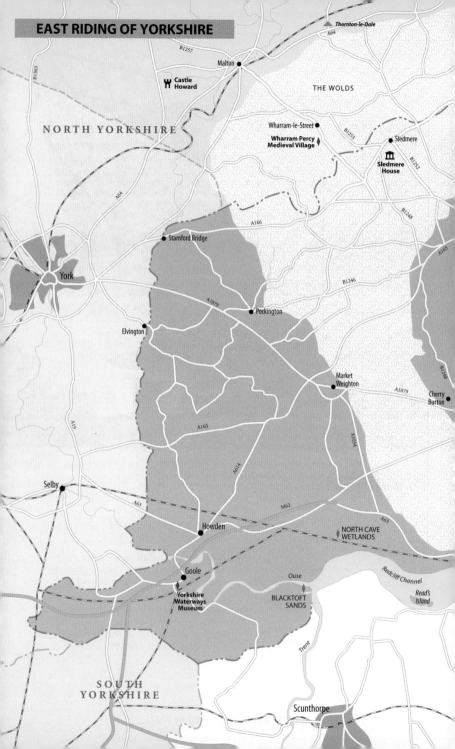

0   10
miles

N

HIGHLIGHTS

1. The Humber Bridge
2. The Deep
3. Beverley Minster
4. Nellies, Beverley
5. Burton Agnes Hall
6. Rudston Monolith
7. Spurn Head

Filey

Bempton

BEMPTON CLIFFS

British Skysport
Paracentre

B1253

FLAMBOROUGH
HEAD

Flamborough

Rudston
Monolith   6

Rudston

A165

Bridlington

Burton Agnes Hall   5

Burton
Agnes

Bridlington
Bay

B1249

Driffield

B1249

Skipsea

A165

NORTH SEA

**EAST
YORKSHIRE**

B1244

Hornsea

Hornsea
Mere

Mappleton

Great Cowden

B1242

4
3

Beverley

Aldbrough

B1238

B1240

Garton

B1239

Cottingham

A164

Tunstal

Ross

Hull

Preston

Withernsea

B1362

2

HOLDERNESS

Humber
Bridge

1

Fort
Paull

Thorngumbald

A1033

Queen of
Holderness

Patrington

Holmpton

B1445

A1077

River Humber

A25

A1173

Easington

LINCOLNSHIRE

A180

Immingham

Cleethorpes

SPURN HEAD   7   Spurn
Head

wealth and importance – in 1820 alone 62 whaling vessels were operating out of the city, bringing in a quarter of a million pounds.

Today, as you approach the city centre, Hull doesn't look too promising. It was one of the English cities most vigorously attacked by the Luftwaffe during World War II. As a major port and industrial centre it was always going to be a prime target, but it also had the misfortune to be close to German bomber stations on mainland Europe, and to be easily recognizable from the air because of its two rivers and its city-centre docks. In repairing bomb damage and erecting new buildings after the war, speed and economy were more important than quality and elegance. And much of what the German air force didn't destroy later fell to the developer's wrecking ball.

So, there's a lot of unsympathetic postwar architecture, but once you reach the city's centre and waterfront, starting at Queen Victoria Square, it's a different place, with a handful of excellent **museums**, the modern **Deep** aquarium, a first-class **theatre** in the

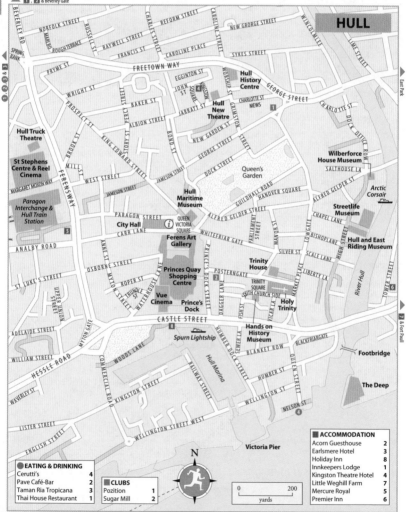

HULL

EATING & DRINKING
Cerutti's	4
Pave Café-Bar	2
Taman Ria Tropicana	3
Thai House Restaurant	1

CLUBS
Pozition	1
Sugar Mill	2

ACCOMMODATION
Acorn Guesthouse	2
Earlsmere Hotel	3
Holiday Inn	8
Innkeepers Lodge	1
Kingston Theatre Hotel	4
Little Weghill Farm	7
Mercure Royal	5
Premier Inn	6

THE HUMBER BRIDGE

The **Humber Bridge** across the estuary to the west of Hull is one of the major sights to be seen in the Hull area. Opened in 1981, it took eight years to build, is over a mile long between anchorages, with a main span between the two towers of 1500yd. Other gee-whiz statistics abound. The bridge contains 480,000 tonnes of concrete; it contains 44,000 miles of steel wire – almost enough to encircle the earth twice; in high winds the centre of the bridge flexes by 10ft; because of the curvature of the earth, its two towers are 1½ inches further apart at the top than at the bottom. When it opened, the Humber Bridge was the longest single-span suspension bridge in the world. Since then it has been superseded, and now lies seventh in the world rankings, while remaining the longest bridge that you can cross on foot.

At the time of its construction there was much debate as to how useful it would be, with suspicions that it arose more out of political expediency than economic necessity – it was sanctioned in 1966 to bolster Labour's chances in the Hull North by-election, when a defeat would have threatened Harold Wilson's slim House of Commons majority. In some ways these doubts have been borne out – numbers crossing the bridge never achieved a level high enough to pay off the building costs. Whatever the argument, the bridge certainly brought together the previously rather isolated East Riding and North and East Lincolnshire, and in doing so provided the region with one of the world's greatest, and most beautiful, structures.

The **Humber Bridge Country Park** offers nature trails on the Yorkshire side of the bridge, and there's a North Bank Viewing Area with a large car park, clearly signposted from the main road, from where you can walk out along the bridge to examine it and enjoy the spectacular views. There are public toilets, a **tourist office** (daily: May–Sept 9am–1pm & 1.30–5pm; March, April & Oct 9am–1pm & 1.30–4pm; Nov–Feb 10am–3pm; ☏01482 640852), a kiosk selling sweets and drinks and **Mrs B's Café** (daily 9am–5pm). There's a **toll** for driving across (cars £1.50).

Hull Truck and even a **Philip Larkin** trail. Hull feels, too, like a young city; with two large universities and Hull College, its streets are thronged with students, and its bars and clubs are vibrant and popular. It well deserves its status as the UK's City of Culture 2017.

A good place to start exploring is **Queen Victoria Square**, with its couple of museums. South of here stretches the water of **Princes Dock**, with twin fountains spouting out of its surface, and to the left cobbled and brick-paved quaysides and fashionable pavement cafés bustling with people. To the right is the imaginatively designed **Princes Quay Shopping Centre**, sitting on stilts over the water, looking like some latter-day Crystal Palace, clouds reflected in its acres of glass, the flags on its roof snapping in the North Sea breeze. Beyond the dock, across Castle Street, the **marina** is crowded with boats of all types, including the **Spurn lightship**. East of the Princes Dock are the main shopping streets, most of them branching off **Whitefriargate**.

There are some good museums in the **Museum Quarter** on and near the **High Street**. Narrow, cobbled and lined with many old buildings, this is one of the most attractive streets in the city, and is joined to the River Hull by several "staithes" – narrow cobbled lanes that allowed the ships in the river to be unloaded directly onto wagons. Look out for the remains of the merchants' grand houses and offices, the lowly courts in which ordinary workpeople lived, the pubs and the warehouses, all of which started to decline when the port activities moved elsewhere in the city, and which have been restored and reinvigorated since the 1980s. Finally, the city is blessed with a fine **river** frontage along which to wander.

Queen Victoria Square and around

Dominated by a statue of Queen Victoria mounted on a stepped island (it's not just decorative – there are listed public toilets, dating from 1925, underneath), **Queen Victoria Square** is a handsome triangular open area surrounded by fine buildings – the **City Hall**, the **Hull Maritime Museum** in what was once the Dock offices, the neoclassical **Ferens Art Gallery**, the ornate *Punch Hotel* and the Yorkshire Penny Bank building (now a *Caffè Nero*).

6

THE SEVEN SEAS FISH TRAIL

It's impossible to escape the seafaring and fishing theme as you walk around Hull. The witty **Seven Seas Fish Trail** is particularly fun, featuring life-size metal fish embedded in appropriate positions in the pavement – an electric eel outside an electricity sub-station, a plaice in the Market Place, a shark outside a bank and so on. There are 41 pieces in total, created by artist Gordon Young in 1992. The tourist office (see p.282) will provide a trail map, and will also issue a certificate if you complete the whole thing. They'll get you going by pointing out the first fish on the trail – a shoal of 36 chromed bronze anchovies set into the pavement outside the City Hall ticket office in Queen Victoria Square.

Between Queen Victoria Square and Whitefriargate is the end of **Princes Dock** and a paved excavation, liberally dotted with (slightly forlorn-looking) information boards, which was the site of the old Beverley Gate and the Monument Bridge. The **Beverley Gate** was the main entrance to the walled city, where the governor, Sir John Hotham, famously refused entry to King Charles I in 1642, thus sparking off the English Civil War. The **Monument Bridge** was built in 1829 to span the access to the Queen's Dock from the Princes Dock, with a bigger replacement erected in 1905 to accommodate trams. Both consisted of two halves that could be raised to allow ships to come and go. This second bridge was demolished in 1932 when the Queen's Dock was filled in, turning it into **Queen's Gardens**. Incidentally, the "monument" in question was a statue of William Wilberforce on top of a tall column, erected here in 1835. It now stands outside Hull College, at the other end of the Gardens.

Ferens Art Gallery

Little Queen St • Mon–Sat 10am–5pm • Free • ☎ 01482 613933, ⓦ hullcc.gov.uk

The **Ferens Art Gallery** houses Hull's collection of paintings and sculptures from the Middle Ages onwards, from Old Masters to twentieth-century British art; you'll see works by, among others, Frans Hals (*Portrait of a Young Woman*), Canaletto (*View of the Grand Canal*) and John Constable (a cloud study, though only "attributed to"). There's a children's area aimed at 6- to 10-year olds with lots of hands-on activities, free family activity boxes and events, placed in the centre of an upstairs gallery featuring images of Hull through the ages. The gallery hosts numerous one-off events and exhibitions.

Hull Maritime Museum

Queen Victoria Square • Mon–Sat 10am–5pm, Sun 1.30–4.30pm • Free • ☎ 01482 300300, ⓦ hullcc.gov.uk

Facing Queen Victoria Square, the former Dock Offices now house the **Hull Maritime Museum**, one of the best such museums you're likely to encounter anywhere. It covers three areas of maritime history – whaling, fishing and merchant shipping – with the emphasis on the part played by Hull from the late eighteenth century onwards. The standout exhibits are grouped together in the **whaling gallery**, with whale skeletons, fearsome exploding harpoons, the sort of flimsy boats in which whalers in the nineteenth century used to chase the leviathans of the deep, a crow's nest made of a barrel, and oddities such as a whalebone seat, a blubber cauldron and a group of narwhal tusks. As you move through the gallery, the ululating, unearthly song of the whale surrounds you, making for an eerie experience.

Other galleries cover various types of fishing and specialist ships – North Sea herring drifters, Flamborough long lines, Paull shrimpers, trawlers – the city's famous Wilson shipping line (see p.280) and sailing in general. Look out for the figurehead (a carved dog) of transatlantic paddle steamer *Sirius*, the magnificent model ships, a ship's wheel and binnacle and the carved whalebone (or scrimshaw). There's even a stuffed polar bear – some whalers would capture these huge beasts to sell when they got home.

The whole museum is a record of centuries of skill and expertise, not to mention courage and fortitude, now slowly fading into the past.

Hull and East Riding Museum

36 High St • Mon–Sat 10am–5pm, Sun 1.30–4.30pm • Free • ☎ 01482 300300, ⓦ hullcc.gov.uk

One of four museums clustered on the High Street, the **Hull and East Riding Museum**, in the old Corn Exchange building of 1856, emphasizes the archeology of the region. It gets off to a flying start with an impressive full-size model of a woolly mammoth, accompanied by information and dioramas covering early humankind. This is followed by superb displays on the Iron Age Celts who inhabited East Yorkshire before and during the Roman occupation, with a succession of realistic tableaux complete with sound effects (in ancient Welsh; pick up a leaflet for translations).

Next is a fascinating display of information about and photographs of the **Ferriby Boats**, three Bronze Age boats discovered between the 1930s and the 1960s on the shore of the Humber at North Ferriby, which were made of planks of wood sewn together with yew withies. The amazing thing about them is their great age – they have been carbon-dated as 4000 years old – and their impressive size. A later Iron Age boat, discovered at Hasholme in 1984, is preserved in a long glass case, constantly showered with water and wax, and as you walk beside it you can pace out the length – 41ft. These boats could negotiate estuaries and even go out to sea. Beyond this, a series of mosaics introduces the Romans, with further tableaux and mock-ups of rooms – a Roman bathhouse, for example, or a paymaster's office. Finally, smaller displays cover the Middle Ages (wooden coffin lids, a huge tub in which live fish were kept) and the Civil War.

Streetlife Museum

High St • Mon–Sat 10am–5pm, Sun 1.30–4.30pm • Free • ☎ 01482 300300, ⓦ hullcc.gov.uk

Across the courtyard next to the Hull and East Riding Museum, the **Streetlife Museum** outlines the history of transport through galleries focusing on bicycles, carriages, motor cars and railways. The first exhibit will bring a smile to many, especially to anybody who lived through the 1950s and '60s – a bubble car or, to give this one its proper title, the BMW Isetta 300. Similarly the Morris 8 of 1939 – there were plenty around right into the 1960s – and the Morris Minor 1000 van dating from 1969, pretty in its Hull City Council blue-and-yellow livery (though it's not an actual car, but one made up of bits of others). A balance of explanation and exhibit, and a succession of even older cars, do full justice to motoring history. A collection of trams (the Kitson steam tram is particularly impressive) and buses, a mock-up of a level crossing complete with signal box, a low-flying biplane, shops, penny arcade machines – the whole museum is stuffed with interest.

Wilberforce House Museum

23–25 High St • Mon–Sat 10am–5pm, Sun 1.30–4.30pm • Free • ☎ 01482 300300, ⓦ hullcc.gov.uk

The **Wilberforce House Museum**, in its own gardens next to the Streetlife Museum, occupies the house in which abolitionist William Wilberforce was born. It has a dual

---

HULL'S TELEPHONES

You may notice as you walk around Hull that the city's **phone boxes** are different from those you'll see in the rest of the country. They're similar in design to the old style that has largely disappeared in the rest of Britain, but are cream coloured rather than red and have no royal crown above the door. They were part of Hull's independent phone system, established in 1902 and owned by the city. Although now privatized, the unique cream phone kiosks have been retained.

focus: the life and times of Wilberforce himself (1759–1833), and details of the horrible trade in slaves that he successfully devoted his life to abolishing. So there are a number of his **possessions** – his journals and personal effects, including his court suit, a tea service he gave his sister as a wedding present in 1790, his collection of books, his inkwell and candlestick –which build up a remarkably human picture of the great man. There's even his waxwork likeness, made originally for Madame Tussauds. The campaign to outlaw slavery is recounted in detail, with information on the many who played a part in the struggle – the great Staffordshire potter **Josiah Wedgwood**, for example, who created a ceramic medallion of a kneeling slave with the slogan "Am I not a man and a brother?", and Thomas Clarkson, whose travelling chest of visual aids used in anti-slavery meetings is on show – including instruments of confinement and torture, from thumbscrews to shackles and chains, collected from slave ships. The fight against the slave trade was a long one – while the campaign gathered pace in the 1780s, the trade wasn't abolished in the British Empire until 1807, and even then the Slave Trade Act only got rid of the trade; slavery itself didn't become illegal until 1833. Further displays on the culture of **West Africa**, source of most of the slaves sold in the Americas, on the processes of enslavement and human trafficking and on the inhuman treatment meted out to the slaves make for harrowing viewing – neck shackles, the famous plan of the Brooks slave ship showing the barbarous overcrowding, and all the other obscene paraphernalia of control and punishment. The museum is an unflinching view of a brutal part of our history, and an uplifting homage to those who successfully fought it.

Arctic Corsair

Rear of Streetlife Museum, High St • Guided tours only (1hr–1hr 30min): April–Oct Wed & Sat 10.30am–4.30pm, Sun 1.30–4.30pm • Free • ☎ 01482 300300, ⓦ hullcc.gov.uk

The **Arctic Corsair** is a Hull sidewinder trawler moored in the River Hull directly behind the museums on the High Street. Built in 1960, she has had a chequered career – holed in a collision off the Scottish coast in 1967, hauling a world-record amount of cod and herring in the White Sea in 1973, rammed by an Icelandic gunboat during the Third Cod War of 1976, retired, brought out of retirement in the 1980s, and finally sold to Hull City Council in 1993, who moored her here as a museum ship. A ten-minute introductory film is shown in the Hull and East Riding Museum before the superb tours; whenever again you hear the shipping forecast on the radio, or hear of maritime disasters, you'll be reminded of this excellent visit.

Hull History Centre

Worship St • Tues–Fri 9.30am–5pm, 1st & 3rd Sat in the month 9am–4.30pm • Free • ☎ 01482 317500, ⓦ hullhistorycentre.org.uk

The **Hull History Centre** is an archive of documents, illustrations, photographs, maps and newspapers relating to the city's history and some of its most famous sons and daughters. A stylish modern building with similarities to Sheffield's Winter Garden (see p.46), the centre was set up by the city and the university to rationalize and make more accessible Hull's documentary archive. While designed principally for local people, the centre stages events, behind-the-scene tours and temporary exhibitions that visitors to Hull might usefully check out.

Trinity Square

West of the High Street, between the River Hull and Princes Quay, lies the attractive **Trinity Square** with its ensemble of church, historic buildings and statues, and the unspoilt **Prince Street** running off it. Down Trinity House Lane on the right as you walk away from the square is the entrance to the Trinity House **indoor market**.

ANDREW MARVELL

In Trinity Square stands a statue of **Andrew Marvell** (1621–78), the Metaphysical poet associated with George Herbert and John Donne, and friend of John Milton. Born in the Holderness village of Winestead, about fifteen miles east of Hull, he attended Hull Grammar School and, at the remarkably young age of 12, Trinity College, Cambridge. His most famous poem, *To His Coy Mistress* – "But at my back I always hear/Time's wingèd chariot hurrying near/ And yonder all before us lie/Deserts of vast eternity" – was published around 1681; during his lifetime he was better known for his political pamphlets than for his poetry. Although with distinctly Parliamentary leanings and Puritan sympathies (though not himself one), he seems to have sat out the English Civil War on a tour of Europe. After the war, for nearly twenty years until his death, he served as a conscientious local MP for the area.

6

Holy Trinity Church

Market Place • Tues–Fri 11am–3pm, Sat 9.30am–3pm • Free • ☎ 01482 324835, ⓦ holy-trinity.org.uk

Trinity Square is flanked on one side by **Holy Trinity Church**, the largest parish church in the country. When you're inside, it's difficult to believe that it's not a cathedral. The order of its building is pleasantly straightforward – the transepts (1300–20) came first, then the chancel (1320–60) and the nave (1389–1418), with the crossing tower being built last (around 1500). The transepts, the chancel and the lower parts of the tower are built of brick, the earliest use of brick on this scale in the country, giving it an odd, rather attractive two-tone look.

Hands on History Museum

South Church Side • Open selected Sat noon–4pm • Free • ☎ 01482 300300, ⓦ hullcc.gov. uk

Behind the statue of local poet and politician Andrew Marvell (see box above), his **Grammar School**, together with the Fish Street Day Schools building, added in 1871, now house the **Hands on History Museum**. Slightly incongruously, the museum combines an interesting series of displays on Hull's social history with one on the Egyptians, the latter presumably because the city happens to have a rather good Egyptian mummy. A large display area contains some of the most famous of King Tutankhamun's grave goods, but don't get too excited – they're replicas. Completely genuine, however, are the 2600-year-old mummy and its elaborately carved catafalque, which occupy a dimly lit room.

Trinity House

Trinity House Lane • ☎ 01482 324956, ⓦ trinityhousehull.org.uk

Trinity House is not, alas, open to the public. However, the lovely old building ("rebuilt 1753" it says over the door), with its carved pediment (a coat of arms and figures of Britannia and Neptune) above a doorway with Tuscan columns is worth a look. Trinity House started as a fourteenth-century religious guild, became a mariners' guild by the fifteenth century, and in the seventeenth and eighteenth centuries took increasing responsibility for shipping and navigation in the Humber, as well as becoming a charity for seamen. It retains its charity functions to this day, though it isn't part of the larger Trinity House organization responsible for lighthouses and navigation buoys.

Hull Marina and the riverside

From Trinity Square any of the attractive streets heading west will bring you to Princes Wharf. Just across the busy dual-carriageway Castle Street, in **Hull Marina** is moored the *Spurn Lightship* (see p.280). Beyond it, at the southern end of the marina, are a couple of heavy-duty lock gates with a swing bridge between them that allow boats to move in and out of the marina. A business-like naval gun on one side of the gates and a "Welcome to Hull Marina" sign on the other convey amusingly

6

IMMIGRATION THROUGH HULL

Between 1836 and 1914 more than 2.2 million people from Scandinavia, Germany and Russia landed at Hull and the other Humber ports, travelled by train across Britain to Glasgow, Liverpool, London and Southampton and there took ships for America, Canada, South Africa and Australia. The biggest shipping line involved in this mass migration was Hull's famous **Wilson Line**, which began steamship services from Norway and Sweden in 1843. By 1914 the flow of Northern European immigrants was so great that a special Wilson Line landing station, called Island Wharf, was built near where the statue of the man, woman and child (see below) stands today, with the Wilson Line becoming the largest privately owned shipping line in the world. The era of mass Victorian and Edwardian migration ended suddenly in 1914 with the start of World War I, and the introduction of immigration controls in a number of destination countries.

---

mixed messages. Beyond the gates the whole area has been redeveloped and landscaped, providing modern office space and a pleasant riverfront promenade. Alongside the naval gun, there's a **statue** of a man, woman and child, erected to commemorate European immigrants who entered Britain via Hull in the late nineteenth and early twentieth centuries (see box above), and an identification guide to the **birds** you're likely to see on the Humber estuary – ringed plover, redshank, curlew, dunlin, black-headed gull and turnstone.

Spurn Lightship

Castle St • Selected Sun 1.30–4.30pm • Free • ☎ 01482 300300, ⓦ hullcc.gov.uk

Though when riding mountainous seas it must have looked rather insignificant, the **Spurn Lightship**, built in 1927, appears impressively big – it's 100ft long and 24ft wide. Exhibits inside the boat explain what life was like on board during its almost fifty years service guiding ships through the mouth of the Humber. Opening hours are limited, but an interpretation board on the dockside fills you in with some of the information.

Victoria Pier

East across the swing bridge, the riverfront continues past an old muzzle-loading cannon to the Humber Ferry Terminal and **Victoria Pier**. The site of a port since medieval times, a new dock was built here at the start of the nineteenth century, and a ferry service to New Holland across the river started in 1825, with a booking office added in 1880 – it's still there, though now converted into flats. The pier itself has largely disappeared, but there's a wide wooden deck (beyond the *Café Gelato*) with benches facing south, east and west offering good views of the river, the Deep (see below) and the North Sea ferries coming and going.

Hull Tidal Barrier

North of its confluence with the Humber, the River Hull is crossed by a large and imposing structure. This is the **Hull Tidal Barrier**, opened in 1980 to prevent a recurrence of the flooding suffered by the city in 1969. In front of it is a modern **footbridge** that crosses the river to the Deep.

The Deep

Tower St • Daily 10am–6pm • £11.50; family £37.60 • ☎ 01482 381091, ⓦ thedeep.co.uk

A fitting attraction for a great seaport like Hull, the **Deep** calls itself, somewhat obscurely, "the world's only submarium", but the rest of us will recognize it as a varied, interesting and very hands-on aquarium. Sitting on the eastern bank of the River Hull where it flows into the Humber, it looks for all the world like the first view of the Great White Shark in *Jaws*, thrusting out of the water.

The best approach is to take the lift to the top of the building, then make your way down the sloping ramp that winds around the main tank through a series of areas dealing with different aspects of the world's oceans. Though everybody seems to head for the **sharks** and **rays**, don't be rushed – there are hundreds of wonders to see: "Spud", the potato grouper rescued from an Australian mall fish tank; the Pacific hagfish that tunnels into its prey then eats its way out; the horribly poisonous arrow frog; the giant African land snail, which grows to 10in long; the beautiful moon jellyfish; the curious, friendly, but rather frightening giant octopus; and the nightmarish fangtooth with teeth so huge it can't shut its mouth. At the very least a visit to the Deep will fill you with wonder at the multiplicity of life to be found in the world's oceans. At most, you'll learn a huge amount about the dynamics of our seas and oceans, of the dangers that threaten them and the work being done to protect them. The aquarium has one of the world's deepest underwater tunnels along the bottom of one of the world's deepest tanks, together with a magical glass lift in which you can ascend or descend surrounded by the denizens of the deep. You'll need at least three hours for the visit, but to make the most of it, go for the day. There's a restaurant and a café.

East Park

On the A165 Bridlington Rd • Daily: April–Oct 9.30am–4pm; Nov–March 9.30am–3.30pm • Free • ☎ 01482 300300, ⓦ hullcc.gov.uk • Bus #10, #56 or #57 from Paragon Interchange

Following the trajectory of many parks across the country, **East Park** was established to celebrate Queen Victoria's Golden Jubilee in 1887, became a Grade II listed park, saw reduced visitor numbers during the twentieth century, became dowdy and rundown, then enjoyed a new lease of life as Heritage Lottery money was pumped into it. It's now a little (or at 130 acres, not so little) gem. Together with everything you'd expect in a public park – model yacht pond, boating lake, flower beds and bowling greens – there's an "outdoor gym", a "youth zone" with skateboarding and climbing facilities, a pavilion with café, the Khyber Pass (a rock folly with waterfall, built from stones rescued during demolition work in the city), an excellent waterplay area and a more general playground, and the prewar (1929) Wicksteed Splash Boat or waterchute, one of only three in the country. A variety of activities for kids are organized throughout the year.

Fort Paull

Battery Rd, Paull, less than 5 miles east of Hull • March–Oct daily 10am–6pm • £6; family £18 • ☎ 01482 896236, ⓦ fortpaull.com

At the village of **Paull**, on the Humber shore, the pentagonal **Fort Paull** was built in 1864 as one of the Palmerston Forts (named after the Prime Minister at the time), a series of fortifications built around the coast of Britain. Shut down by the Ministry of Defence in 1960, it became a place of crumbling brickwork and weed-choked wasteland until it was renovated by a local group as a military museum and reopened in 2000.

TWO HULL STATUES

Hull has two interesting statues on the banks of the Humber, near the point where it meets the River Hull. One is a nineteenth-century likeness of Hull's first mayor – **Sir William De-la-Pole**. Nothing very startling about that, except how long ago he held the post – from 1332 till 1335. Another, nearby and directly across the mouth of the River Hull from the Deep, is **Voyage** – the figure of a man atop a tall column. It was erected to celebrate the links between Hull and Iceland – there's a corresponding statue at Vik, Iceland's southernmost village. Though it refers to a thousand years of sea trading between the two lands, it's actually a lot more to do with the Cod Wars of the 1950s to the 1970s, when Icelandic and British fishing boats and naval vessels were involved in a series of confrontations over territorial waters and fishing rights. The two statues represent a sort of burying of the hatchet between the two countries.

6

PHILIP LARKIN

Philip Larkin (1922–85), who was chief librarian at Hull University from 1955 until he died, was one of the twentieth century's greatest poets. He may have written cogently about his home town – "the widening river's slow presence/The piled gold clouds, the shining gull-marked mud" in *Here* – but only recently have Hull's powers that be realized that his wide popularity might be turned to the city's advantage. In 2010, the 25th anniversary of his death, the city staged theatrical, musical, literary and art events in his honour, raised a statue of him in the train station and launched a permanent **Larkin Trail** of places of significance in his life and work. The first eleven sites are in Hull city centre, with the trail starting at the *Royal Hotel*. It then heads out to the suburbs and university where he worked, and loops around places such as the Humber Bridge and Beverley, ending at Spurn Point. Check out ⓦ thelarkintrail.co.uk for more details and a downloadable podcast. One can only speculate what the famously acid-tongued poet would have made of all this fuss – despite his name and his mordant sense of humour, he wasn't the jolliest of men.

Today Fort Paull is an odd ragbag of guns, tank turrets, planes, wartime memorabilia and information about the Women's Land Army, POWs, carrier pigeons and the days when the fort was used for supplying ammunition to naval ships anchored in the river. There are several fascinating **planes** – a 1916 bi-plane, a Hawker Hunter and the colossal Blackburn Beverley troop transport which itself contains displays – and lots of cannons and field guns. Some of the exhibits are really interesting – a 3D viewer with which you can look at reconnaissance photos of German ground installations, the "corgi" motorbike used by paratroopers which folded into its own container for the drop – and some are bizarre. There are numerous tableaux, including a rather tasteless one of a man hanging in a cell (a miscreant, imprisoned for petty theft who took his own life), and others on child evacuees and Winston Churchill. While there seems to be no clear narrative thread behind Fort Paull's collection, it's still great fun – a bit like rummaging through an old attic.

You can let the kids have the run of the play area, picnic on the walls overlooking the estuary, or eat a snack in the *Berliner Tea Rooms* (a troop restaurant car) or the *Dukes of York Bar and Café* (where the counter is made of sandbags).

ARRIVAL AND INFORMATION HULL

By train There's an integrated train, bus and coach exchange – the Paragon Interchange – in the angle between Anlaby Rd and Ferensway, next to the St Stephen's Centre.

Destinations Bridlington (every 30min; 44min); Doncaster (every 30min; 53min); Driffield (every 30min; 26min); London Kings Cross (every 2hr; 2hr 50min); Scarborough (every 10min–1hr 30min; 1hr 30min); Sheffield (hourly; 22min).

By bus The principal bus operators serving Hull are East Yorkshire Motor Service (ⓦ eyms.co.uk) and Stagecoach (ⓦ stagecoachbus.com). All buses use the Paragon Interchange (see above).

Destinations Bridlington (4 daily; 1hr 42min); Driffield

(hourly; 1hr 5min); Leeds (hourly; 1hr 48min); London (2 daily; 6hr 15min–7hr 30min); Scunthorpe (every 30min; 1hr 23min); York (every 2hr; 1hr 49min).

By car The main road approaches to Hull are along the A63 (an extension of the cross-Pennine M62) or along the A15, which branches off the M180, and across the Humber Bridge (by far the best approach to the city). Motorists can either use the Park-and-Ride facility or park in the city centre – the most central of the numerous car parks is in the Princes Quay Shopping Centre.

Tourist office 1 Paragon St (Mon–Sat 10am–5pm, Sun 11am–3pm; ☎ 01482 223559, ⓦ visithullandeast yorkshire.com).

ACCOMMODATION

★ **Acorn Guesthouse** 719 Beverley Rd ☎ 01482 853248, ⓦ acornguesthousehull.co.uk. Suburban semi on the northwest edge of the city, about 2.5 miles from the centre, with regular buses into town. Seven comfortably old-fashioned rooms, with big hotel facilities at B&B prices and a nice back garden. Service is friendly and attentive. **£55**

★ **Earlsmere Hotel** 76–78 Sunny Bank, off Spring Bank West ☎ 01482 341977, ⓦ earlsmerehotel.co.uk. An old-fashioned, friendly guesthouse in a quiet street about a mile from the city centre. Most but not all rooms have en-suite facilities. **£50**

Holiday Inn Castle St North ☎ 0871 942 9043,

ⓦ hihullmarina.co.uk Standard *Holiday Inn* in an excellent position right in the city centre, overlooking the Marina. There's a health and fitness centre and a pool. **£116**

Innkeepers Lodge Beverley Rd, Cottingham, about 7 miles northwest of town ☎ 0845 155 1551, ⓦ innkeeperslodge.com. In Cottingham, on the main road from the Humber Bridge to Beverley (it's across the road from the *Ketch* pub), the *Innkeepers Lodge* is a good budget option for visits to Hull and Beverley. Big, clean rooms, and cheap food at the *Toby Carvery* next door. **£55**

★**Kingston Theatre Hotel** 1–2 Kingston Square ☎ 01482 225828, ⓦ kingstontheatrehotel.com. Nicely furnished rooms and the highly rated *Clapham* restaurant – serving good pies and fish dishes (mains £8.95–23) – on the premises. Just 5min from the city centre, yet quiet. **£90**

Little Weghill Farm Weghill Rd, Preston, about 5 miles east of town ☎ 01482 897650, ⓦ littleweghillfarm .co.uk. In a quiet location, this is a beautiful eighteenth-century farmhouse that has kept many original features, with good en-suite barn-conversion rooms. There are many good walks in the area. **£76**

Mercure Royal 170 Ferensway ☎ 01482 325087, ⓦ hotels-hull.co.uk. Large Victorian hotel near the station, offering fully refurbished, comfortable rooms, a leisure centre and pool. Many offers available. **£87**

Premier Inn Tower St ☎ 0871 527 8534, ⓦ premierinn .com. Modern building near the Deep and city centre, offering cheap rooms and inexpensive food. The surroundings aren't brilliant, but the hotel starts on the seventh floor so the views from the bar, and from rooms, are great. **£65**

EATING AND DRINKING

★**Cerutti's** 10 Nelson St ☎ 01482 328501, ⓦ ceruttis .co.uk. Facing the site of the Victoria Pier overlooking the river, this fish restaurant has been so successful since it opened in 1974 that another (*Cerutti 2*) was opened in Beverley train station. Main courses – halibut fromage, fish cakes, chargrilled scallops, seafood platter, pan-fried sea bass, monkfish – range from £13.25–22.95, but look out for special two- and three-course deals. Mon–Fri noon–2pm & 6.45–9.30pm, Sat 6.45–9.30pm.

★**Pave Café-Bar** 16–20 Princes Ave ☎ 01482 333181, ⓦ pavebar.co.uk. Nice laidback atmosphere with lots going on, including live jazz/blues and comedy (featuring such luminaries as Rich Fulcher, Tom Rosenthal and Terry Christian). Most main courses (from lentil and chickpea

stew to rib eye steak) £5.75–14.95, with lots of creative veggie options and a kids' menu. Sun–Thurs 11am–11pm, Fri & Sat 11am–11.30pm; food served till 7pm.

Taman Ria Tropicana 22 Princes Ave ☎ 01482 345640, ⓦ tropicana-hull.co.uk. Malay and Indonesian (rather than the more generic Malaysian) cuisine. All food is halal, and pork is never used – favourites include beef *rendang* and vegetarian *nasi*. Check with staff regarding how spicy different dishes are. Tues–Sat 5–10.30pm.

Thai House Restaurant 51 Princes Ave ☎ 01482 473473. Fairly Authentic Thai food and good service (though drink refills can be infuriatingly slow) amid slightly eccentric decor with lots of potted plants. Sun–Thurs 5.30–10.30pm, Fri & Sat 5.30–11pm.

NIGHTLIFE AND ENTERTAINMENT

Hull's flourishing pub and **club** scene, booze-fuelled and driven largely by the student population, is especially lively from Thursdays to Sundays. It also has a flourishing performing arts scene, attested to by its selection as UK City of Culture for 2017.

CLUBS

Pozition 135–141 George St ☎ 01482 323643, ⓦ pozition.co.uk. Colourfully lit venue with music on three floors – the Champagne Lounge, Mezz Bar and R'n'B room. Evenings include Big Student Socials (entry £3, all drinks £1) on Thursdays, Lemon Drizzle on Fridays and Freshly Squeezed on Saturdays. Thurs 10.30pm–3.30am, Fri 11pm–3am, Sat 11pm–5am.

Sugar Mill Dagger Lane ☎ 01482 227222, ⓦ sugar millhull.co.uk. Popular club in a beautiful old three-storey warehouse. Mon, Fri & Sat 10.30pm–3am.

THEATRES AND VENUES

City Hall Little Queen St ☎ 01482 300300, ⓦ hullcc .gov.uk. Music and comedy venue that shares a programme with Hull New Theatre. Performers have included John Cooper Clark, Steve Harley, Al Murray and

Paloma Faith. Box office Mon–Sat 8am–7pm.

Hull New Theatre Kingston Square ☎ 01482 300300, ⓦ hullcc.gov.uk. Sumptuous Grade II listed building which mounts touring plays, musicals, pantomimes, comedy and classical music concerts, with performers from Elkie Brooks to Sooty. Box office Mon–Sat 8am–7pm.

Hull Truck Theatre 50 Ferensway ☎ 01482 323638, ⓦ hulltruck.co.uk. Renowned theatre, known for its wide-ranging programme and for its cultural links with the community of the East Riding. The theatre has an impressive track record: previous writers and directors include Anthony Minghella and, the driving force behind its early development and writer of numerous hard-hitting comedies, John Godber. Box office: performance days Mon–Sat 10am–7.30pm, Sun 5.30–7.30pm; other times Mon–Sat 10am–5.30pm.

Yorkshire Waterways Museum

Dutch River Side, Goole, around 30 miles west of Hull • April–Oct Mon–Fri 9am–4pm, Sat & Sun 10am–4pm; Nov–March Mon–Fri 9am–4pm • Free • ☎ 01405 768730, ⓦ waterwaysmuseum.org.uk

Not known for its good looks, **GOOLE** is a determinedly workaday inland port in the area where the Ouse, the Don and the Trent come together to become the Humber. Though it's not near anywhere that holidaymakers are likely to fetch up, it is easy to get to, being in the angle formed by the M62 and the M18. There's only one reason for tourists to visit Goole, and that's to take in the Yorkshire Waterways Museum – for anybody interested in British inland waterways, it's a delight. Covering the Aire and Calder Navigation and the creation of the Port of Goole, the museum has displays on the life of barge families, the import/export trade, the carrying of coal through the Port of Goole, shipbuilding and much else, with interactive and audiovisual displays and a photographic archive. Best of all, the museum has boats, including the 1910-built Humber keel *Sobriety* and the *City of Hull*, built in 1995, both of which are available for trips, and a former grain barge which is now an art gallery (Room 58).

Beverley

The town of **BEVERLEY** lies about eight miles north of Hull – when you allow for Hull's urban sprawl, that means that there's barely three miles between the edges of the two. Daniel Defoe remarked of Beverley in the 1720s: "One is surprised to find so large and handsome a town within six miles of Hull", which still rings true. Being so close to a large city, you might expect Beverley to be a dormitory town with few shops and little character of its own, but this couldn't be further from the truth. Indeed, the people of

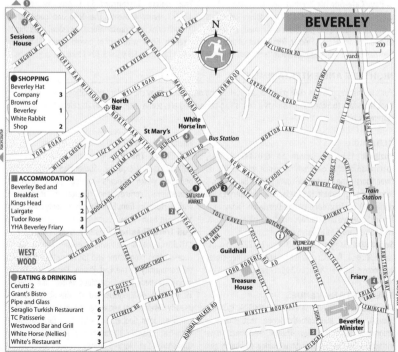

Beverley seem to regard its sprawling neighbour with considerable suspicion – historically, whenever there's been a choice, Beverley has chosen the other side. So, during the English Civil War where Hull supported Parliament, Beverley was Royalist, and today where Hull tends to be Labour or Lib-Dem, Beverley is Tory.

Though light on obvious stand-alone attractions (except its two churches), Beverley is certainly worth at least a day's visit, might well repay a longer stay, and makes an excellent centre for exploring the whole of East Yorkshire. It has a wonderfully quirky medieval layout, a stock of impressive Georgian houses, two magnificent churches – the **Minster** on the southern edge of the town centre and beautiful **St Mary's**, best known today for its "minstrels capital", to the north – along with a good selection of shops, restaurants and pubs and a large open-air **Saturday market**. It also has a strong reputation as a venue for musical events and for hosting more than its share of **music festivals**. To the west of the town centre is the large stretch of common land called the **Westwood** and Beverley's **racecourse** (❶01482 867488, ⓦbeverley-racecourse.co.uk) – wide open spaces for walking, flying kites and, on race days, having a flutter. To the east is **Beverley Beck**, a canal that leads from the River Hull to within a mile of the town centre; having once served a substantial industrial area, it has recently been cleared ready for development and is now lined with desirable housing.

6

Brief history

Beverley owes its birth to the building of a **Minster** here by St John of Beverley at the end of the seventh century, with a settlement developing to support pilgrims (John, and his tomb, had a reputation for miraculous cures). During the Middle Ages Beverley continued to prosper as an important regional capital, with a busy market, healthy woollen industry and flourishing trade guilds. Its religious credentials were further enhanced with the coming of Knights Hospitallers and Dominican and Franciscan establishments, and the town became a renowned place of pilgrimage across Roman Catholic Europe. The parish church of **St Mary's** was established in the twelfth century to serve people frequenting the town's market and the members of its many guilds.

When Henry VIII ended the pope's authority in Britain in order to get his hands on Anne Boleyn, and then dissolved the monasteries in order to get his hands on their wealth, Beverley was perhaps inevitably involved in the backlash – it contributed five hundred men to the Pilgrimage of Grace, the pro-Catholic rebellion against the King. One of the most prominent Roman Catholic martyrs executed by Henry VIII for his opposition to the break with Rome – St John Fisher – was from Beverley (not to be confused with St John of Beverley). The closing of the religious houses in Beverley, and the substantial reduction in the number of pilgrims, hit the town hard, and it became something of a backwater during the seventeenth century. A modest revival of its fortunes in the eighteenth century, when it became not only the main commercial centre for this part of Yorkshire but also the East Riding's county town, is reflected in the large number of Georgian buildings you see today. The nineteenth century saw continued prosperity, with the coming of the railway in 1846 and the establishment of a number of large factories, and having been spared the Luftwaffe pounding that Hull endured, Beverley has continued to do well since World War II, enjoying a healthy tourist industry.

Beverley Minster

Minster Yard North • May–Aug Mon–Sat 9am–5.30pm, Sun noon–4.30pm; March, April, Sept & Oct Mon–Sat 9am–5pm, Sun noon–4.30pm; Nov–Feb Mon–Sat 9am–4pm, Sun noon–4.30pm; parts of the building may be closed off for services, weddings or funerals • Free • ❶01482 868540, ⓦ beverleyminster.org.uk

Any tour of Beverley should start with the undoubted jewel in its crown: **Beverley Minster**, widely considered to be the best non-cathedral church in the country. Despite its architectural and historical importance, the Minster comes across as delightfully unstuffy. The verve of its carved musicians and misericords, the big box of toys to keep children occupied while their parents worship or sightsee, the welcoming friends of the Minster who are happy to show you round, all create a warm and welcoming atmosphere. If you've only time to do one thing while you're in town, visit the Minster.

Brief history

Beverley Minster has a long and complicated (and in many cases disputed) history. It starts with a monastery established by John, the Archbishop of Hexham (and later York), in around 690/700 AD. St John of Beverley – he was canonized in 1037 – was reputed to have performed a number of miracles both during his lifetime and after his death and burial in the church in 721. Pilgrims flocked to his tomb from all over the country, and the town grew up to provide for their needs. St John's church was destroyed by the Vikings, and rebuilt as part of a monastery by King Athelstan in 935 AD, reputedly in thanks for a vision of victory he experienced here before the Battle of Brunanburh. He also granted the church the right of sanctuary, and the people of Beverley a number of tax concessions that helped toward their subsequent prosperity. After the Norman invasion a new Minster replaced the Saxon one, and finally, after a fire in 1188, the present building was begun. Most of the current Minster dates from the thirteenth to the fifteenth centuries.

If you start from the **west doors** and walk the length of the building, you travel back in time from the Perpendicular west end (1380–1420) through the Decorated nave from the entrance onwards (1308–49) to the Early English chancel (1220–60).

Nave: north side

Having entered via the **Highgate Porch** and turned left, you'll see a wealth of **carvings** down the north aisle of people playing musical instruments – lute, lyre, drums, bagpipes, zither, fiddle, accordion, hunting horn, tambourine, guitar and many others – with angels playing instruments high up in the central part of the nave as well. At the crossing with the north and south transepts are the tomb of St John and ornate lectern, pulpit and organ. The splendid tomb and shrine that originally marked the saint's burial place was, alas, destroyed during Henry VIII's Reformation. Its location is marked by an understated plaque let into the nave floor.

North Choir Aisle

Beyond the transepts, in the **North Choir Aisle**, a double flight of steps meets at what was once a doorway halfway up the wall – this was the entrance to the Chapter House, pulled down following the Reformation. Beyond the steps, towards the end of the Minster, is one of its star attractions – the ornately Gothic fourteenth-century **Percy tomb** and canopy, thought to belong to Eleanor Percy, who died around 1340. The Percys were the foremost Roman Catholic family in the north of England – virtually every Catholic uprising after the Reformation had its Percy supporter.

Choir

To the right of the Chapter steps is the **Choir**, which has nice carved **misericords** (brackets placed on the underside of hinged choir seats, so that priests could take the weight off their feet while still seeming to stand). Though not medieval (they date from the sixteenth century), they follow the tradition that no two are alike, each illustrating a succession of everyday activities, animals or strange events – people dealing with a domestic fire, a hare riding a fox, woodcarvers quarrelling, a fox preaching to geese, geese hanging a fox, a man wheeling a woman in a wheelbarrow and so on. There are 68 of them – hours of fun. Also in the choir is the stone **Frith Stool**; by sitting on this a fugitive could claim the strongest form of sanctuary, the breach of which was an unpardonable sin.

East Window and retro choir

The **East Window** itself is the only window in the Minster that contains medieval stained glass – all the windows were blown out in a storm in 1608, and the surviving glass was eventually incorporated in the East Window in 1725. In front of the window the **retro choir** is where pilgrims would pray.

South transept

The Minster's **south transept** has three chapels dedicated to the East Yorkshire Regiment, the first of which contains the wooden **Henin Cross** erected on the Henin Hill on the Western Front in April 1917, where men of the 64th infantry brigade fell in battle. It was replaced by a stone memorial in 1931, and the original brought to Beverley Minster.

6

Nave: south side

On the **south side of the nave** are **statues** of King Athelstan and St John of Beverley. Though painted to look like stone, they are actually made of lead, and were cast in nearby Driffield in 1781. Beyond is the Norman **font** (about 1170 AD), with an ornate eighteenth-century canopy. This and the figures of the four Evangelists, Matthew, Mark, Luke and John, on the west doors were designed, it is thought, by Nicholas Hawksmoor, the great eighteenth-century architect and pupil of Sir Christopher Wren.

The markets

North of the Minster both Highgate and Eastgate lead to the first of Beverley's public squares – the small, triangular **Wednesday Market**, with several restaurants, shops and pubs. A handful of stalls sell fruit and vegetables, watches, rugs, mats and clothes. From here, pedestrianized **Butcher Row** and **Toll Gavel** (both crammed with shops) lead to the **Saturday Market**. Much bigger than the Wednesday Market, it would be square if it weren't for a large pub (the *Push*) and the red-brick-fronted **Corn Exchange** (1886, now Browns department store). It is, nevertheless a handsome open space, cluttered, alas, with cars and taxis during the week, but vibrant with market stalls on Saturdays. There's a fine **Market Cross** with eight Tuscan columns, coats of arms, urns and an ornate roof, erected in 1714. Notice the two cream phone boxes outside the *Push* and the Corn Exchange – Beverley's phones were part of the Hull municipal system (see box, p.277).

Guildhall

Register Square • May–Oct Wed & Fri 10am–4pm; Nov–April Fri 10am–4pm • Free • ☎ 01482 392783

Beverley's Grade I listed **Guildhall** has been the town's seat of government since 1501. Parts of the building date back to a fourteenth-century merchant's house, but after it was acquired by the town it was remodelled several times, most thoroughly in 1762 and the 1830s. The splendid architecture and interesting historical contents – minstrels' chains from the fifteenth century, a seventeenth-century mayor's bench, even

---

BEVERLEY TOWN TRAIL

The **Beverley Town Trail** traces a route through town via a number of public art works on the theme of its medieval guilds and the crafts they represented. Thus, slung high up between the *Beaver* pub and Barclay's Bank in North Bar Within is a jerkin, representing the Jerkin Makers' Guild; on top of the signpost where Lairgate comes into North Bar Within is a jester's hat (Hatters' Guild); there's a cut-out ox carcass next to the *Angel* pub in Butcher Row (Butchers' Guild), and a flight of arrows on the gable of HSBC bank in Old Waste, between the Saturday Market and Lairgate (Fletchers' Guild). The tourist office (see p.290) can provide you with a map.

eighteenth-century graffiti left by boys from the school next door, and a collection of silver and pewter used by a succession of mayors, together with paintings by Fred Elwell, make for an interesting half-hour.

Treasure House

Champney Rd • Mon, Wed & Fri 9.30am–5pm, Tues & Thurs 9.30am–8pm, Sat 9am–4pm • Free • ☎ 01482 392790, ⊕ eastriding.gov.uk

West of the Minster is the **Treasure House**, a distinctive modern building with a circular tower and two wings, the right-hand one attached to the old public library. The name says it all – this building contains much that the town treasures: library, archives, galleries and museum under one roof.

Heading upstairs from the ground floor, which offers access to the library and a research centre, you come to a number of galleries. Chief among them is the small but very well organized **East Riding Museums Collections**, with displays on Iron Age weapons found near the village of South Cave, geology, shipbuilding, religious history, archeology and much more, some of it very hands on and with questionnaires for kids. The **permanent art collection** (Gallery 3) has a number of works by prominent local artist Fred Elwell, and an ostrich made of leather on a metal frame by Karen Trower – it's 10ft high. In Gallery 2, one of two **temporary art spaces** on this floor, there's a café serving good coffee, excellent sandwiches and snacks, and delicious Yorkshire-produced crisps.

The top floor of the Treasure House features a circular **viewing platform** from where you can see the town's other treasures – the Minster, St Mary's and the jumbled rooftops of the centre.

St Mary's Church

North Bar Within • April–Sept Mon–Fri 10am–4.30pm; Oct–March Mon–Fri 10am–4pm (but it is worth phoning to check) • Free • ☎ 01482 869137, ⊕ stmarysbeverley.org.uk

On the northeast edge of the town centre, **St Mary's Church** – founded in the twelfth century though now mostly Georgian – has, if anything, more aesthetically pleasing external proportions than the Minster. The best viewpoint is from opposite the entrance, where one-way traffic sweeps into Hengate.

The interior

After entering the church through the south porch, look beyond the west door and large fifteenth-century west window to the intricately carved **font** made of solid Derbyshire stone dating from 1530. Look too down the length of the nave towards the chancel – the arch between them is truly colossal. At the eastern end of the nave is the **minstrels' capital**, the pillar nearest the pulpit, which bears the famous group of five carved minstrels, each painted in vivid colours with his own costume and hairstyle. This pillar was probably paid for by the town's musicians' guild; other pillars have donor inscriptions, but no carvings. Incidentally, there are 33 other musical carvings in the church – a recurring theme in Beverley – as the town was famous for music, even in the Middle Ages.

Proceeding beneath the tower (which collapsed in 1520 and had to be rebuilt), you come to the north transept organ with the vestry next to it (the **vestry ceiling**, with its sun and stars is worth a look), and beyond that St Michael's Chapel. Look out for the wonderfully vaulted roof and, on the right of the doorway, a **carving of a hare** or rabbit, dating from around 1330, with pilgrim's staff and scrip (a shoulder bag). It is said to have given Lewis Carroll the idea for the white rabbit in *Alice in Wonderland*, but then Ripon Cathedral makes the same claim for one of its woodcarvings. In the **choir**, notice the chancel ceiling, with its colourful paintings of forty English kings up to Henry VI, dating from 1445 (George VI was added during a 1939 restoration). As in the Minster (see p.285), an excellent set of 28 misericords features elaborate and sometimes satirical carvings – one depicts an ape dressed as a doctor, while others include foxes, eagles, dogs and monkeys, as well as numerous green men.

The exterior

Outside, look up at the octagonal **turrets** above the western end of the church. They were rebuilt in the mid-nineteenth century by famous Victorian architect Augustus Pugin. In particular, look at the weathervane on the nearest turret. This was the very last thing Pugin ever designed – he sketched it on the back of an envelope shortly before his death from a stroke.

If you turn left along Hengate, you'll spot an oval memorial plaque attached to the side of the church, just beyond the south transept. It tells the story of two Danish soldiers, part of a mercenary force that William of Orange was sending to Ireland to engage with the Roman Catholic supporters of James II, which landed at Hull. Just opposite, also on Hengate, is the **White Horse Inn**, known locally as *Nellies*, an essential stop on any visit to Beverley (see p.291).

North Bar and around

Beyond St Mary's lies the intriguingly named **North Bar Within**, lined with stately Georgian houses. At the end you will see the **North Bar** itself, a crenellated brick building with a pointed archway through which alternate streams of traffic have to squeeze. Built in 1409, this is Beverley's only surviving town gate (the position of the others is indicated by several street names – Keldgate, Highgate, Hengate, Eastgate, Lairgate). Beyond it lies the tree-lined **North Bar Without**, with its very large houses, and, just after it becomes New Walk, the **Sessions House**. Once the town's court building, it now houses a health and beauty spa, *Westwood* restaurant (see p.291) and the police station.

Beverley Beck

If you take the **footbridge** over the railway line on the south side of town you will see the chaotic results of the clearance of industrial land to the south – it looks like the aftermath of wartime bombing. This was once Beverley's industrial heartland, clustered around the navigation called **Beverley Beck**. To get to the Beck turn right along Armstrong Way beyond the footbridge, then left along Flemingate. A ten-minute walk (past the Leisure Centre on the right) brings you to the **Beck End**.

Originally, as the name suggests, a stream, the Beck was made navigable in medieval times, and a lock gate installed where it runs out into the River Hull in 1802, after which it became an important means of getting raw materials to and finished products from within half a mile of the centre of Beverley. Tiles, pottery, cloth, leather, flour, ships and later motor-vehicle parts were manufactured here, with the Beck becoming a major thoroughfare until the development of road and rail transport made it redundant. Heavily polluted for a time, it has since been cleaned up, and today desirable housing lines its banks, anglers trail their lines in the water and narrow boats and the Humber keel *Comrade* are often moored to its quays.

Skidby Mill and the Museum of East Riding Rural Life

Skidby, Cottingham, 4 miles south of Beverley • Daily 10am–5pm • £2.50 • ☎ 01482 848405, ⓦ museums.eastriding.gov.uk/skidby-mill • Bus #61, #X80 or #180 from Beverley

Skidby Mill, a pristine four-sail working tower-mill built in 1821, has been grinding grain ever since, and still does so from Wednesdays to Sundays, weather permitting. The whole mill creaks and groans as the four huge sails (1.25 tonnes each) drive the three pairs of millstones and all the ancillary machinery including the hoists and hoppers. The mill is set within a complex of warehouses that also houses the **Museum of East Riding Rural Life**, which covers the history of the Wolds. There's a café in the courtyard, a picnic area, a wildlife garden and a pond.

ARRIVAL AND INFORMATION BEVERLEY

By train The train station lies on the eastern edge of the town centre.

Destinations Bridlington (every 30min; 30min); Driffield (every 30min; 14min); Hull (every 25–35min; 17min); Scarborough (every 1hr 30min; 1hr 17min); Sheffield (hourly; 1hr 44min)

By bus The bus station is on the northern edge of the town centre.

Destinations Hull (every 25–35min; 35–45min); Scarborough (4 daily; 2hr 10min).

By car Beverley is easy to get to by road from the south and west, either via the M62/A63 into Hull, or the M180 across the Humber Bridge, both of which routes are linked to Beverley by the A164. From the north and east it's a bit more difficult, in that roads from York and Bridlington are not dual carriageway. The town centre is kept free of through traffic by an efficient bypass. There's ample parking in town, mostly to the northeast of the town centre.

Tourist office 34 Butcher Row (July & Aug Mon–Fri 9.30am–5.15pm, Sat 10am–4.45pm, Sun 11am–3pm, Sept–June Mon–Fri 9.30am–5.15pm, Sat 10am–4.45pm; ☎ 01482 391672, ⓦ visithullandeastyorkshire.com). Come here for copies of the Beverley Town Trail leaflet (see p.287) and details of guided tours including a ghost and history tour and a pub walk ("an intoxicating tour").

ACCOMMODATION

Beverley Bed and Breakfast 2 Keldgate ☎ 01482 882402, ⓦ beverleybedandbreakfast.com. Perfectly located right next to the Minster, facing the meadow from which it is usually photographed, this elegant Georgian guesthouse bills itself, for what it's worth, as Beverley's first boutique guesthouse. Rooms are varied in terms of decor and levels of luxury, and breakfasts are DIY in-room affairs. The Minster bells ring every 15min, but otherwise the location is quiet. **£69**

Kings Head 37–38 Saturday Market ☎ 01482 868103, ⓦ kingsheadpubbeverley.co.uk. Tucked into a corner of busy Saturday Market, this period building has contemporary decor inside. It's a Marston's pub, with food from £7, and it can be noisy, especially at weekends, but the rear rooms are quieter, and ear plugs are provided.

Mon–Thurs 9am–11pm, Fri & Sat 9am–1am, Sun 11am–11pm; food served Mon–Sat 10am–9pm, Sun 10am–8pm. **£80**

Lairgate 30–34 Lairgate ☎ 01482 882141, ⓦ bestwestern.co.uk. Attractive listed Georgian building with many period details (staircase, windows) and a pleasant courtyard, right in the town centre. It's part of the Best Western brand, with good food and friendly staff. **£112**

★ **Tudor Rose** 11 Wednesday Market ☎ 01482 882028, ⓦ thetudorrosehotelbeverley.co.uk. Nice little hotel/restaurant in the town centre. Rooms, all en suite, are pleasantly old-fashioned. The restaurant specializes in meat and fish with much use of sauces and also has some Polish food on offer (mains £10–15). **£95**

BEVERLEY'S MUSIC FESTIVALS

Though Beverley's reputation for music is unarguable, nobody seems to know quite why. Certainly it goes back a long way – both the Minster and St Mary's are rich in representations of musicians and their instruments. Today, the town's strong music connections are displayed in some excellent **festivals**.

Early Music Festival May ⓦ ncem.co.uk. Five-day festival of choral and instrumental music, held in May. Concerts and workshops are staged at churches around town, including Beverley Minster.

Folk Festival ⓦ beverleyfestival.com. Held over a weekend in June, the long-standing Beverley Folk Festival, based at the racecourse, showcases British and world folk music as well as blues, rock and classical music, Morris dancing, comedy, film, poetry and storytelling. Past festivals have starred the Watersons, Steeleye Span,

Eliza Carthy and Billy Bragg. Most events are held in marquees, but there are fringe events in local pubs.

Chamber Music Festival ⓦ beverleychamber musicfestival.org.uk. Held in late September in St Mary's Church, with soloists, trios and quartets (one performance per night Wed–Sat).

Blues Festival ⓦ beverleyblues.com. This three-day mid-October festival has featured headliners from the Dan Burnett Blues Band to Tom Attah and the Bad Man Clan and Ian Siegal.

★**YHA Beverley Friary** Friar's Lane ☎0845 371 9004, ⓦyha.org.uk/hostel/beverley-friary. Beautiful medieval monastic house in the shadow of the Minster. Established in 1240, the building is wonderfully mellow, showing its age with leaning walls, a hotchpotch of building materials (some brick, some stone), the carving of a woman that dates back to the early fourteenth century and attractive brick-walled gardens impressively overlooked by the Minster. What it lacks in luxury it makes up for in atmosphere, location and, of course, price. Dorms £18; triples £69

EATING AND DRINKING

Beverley has a good selection of **restaurants**, several of them outstanding, and, as you'd expect in an agricultural area, making use of locally sourced food. Later on in the evening, and during Saturday market, the **pubs** get packed out.

6

★**Cerutti 2** Station Square ☎01482 866700, ⓦceruttis.co.uk. Occupying what was once the station waiting rooms, Cerutti 2, run by the same family as Cerutti's in Hull (see p.283), specializes in fish, though there are meat and vegetarian options too (mains around £12–23). Popular with locals, so it's as well to book, especially at weekends. Tues–Sat noon–2pm & 6.45–9.30pm.

Grant's Bistro 22 North Bar Within ☎01482 887624, ⓦgrantsbistro.co.uk. In an eighteenth-century building on the corner between North Bar Within and Hengate, opposite St Mary's, Grant's Bistro offers a good range of grills, fish and meat dishes, in three small rooms. Strong on steaks, it also offers rarer meats including buffalo and wild boar (mains £15.50–24.95). Booking advised, especially for its "candlelit dinners" – a five-course meal for two for £54, including a bottle of house wine. Mon–Thurs 6–9.30pm, Fri & Sat noon–2pm & 6–9.30pm.

★**Pipe and Glass** 8 West End, Dalton, about 5 miles northwest of Beverley ☎01430 810246, ⓦpipeand glass.co.uk A fifteenth-century inn idyllically set in a pretty village, with nice views across open countryside, the Pipe and Glass is an outstanding Michelin-starred restaurant that hasn't lost its pub feel. Top-quality ingredients provide a range of delicious meals at amazingly reasonable prices – the most expensive main course on the lunch menu comes in at £26.95 (fillet of beef), but many are £10–12. The starters, in particular, are full of creative flair– guinea fowl and ham hock ballotine with a scampi fritter, pease pudding, air-dried ham and pea shoots, for example, or dressed white crab meat with carrot, pickled cucumber, coriander, brown crab and sea salt crisps. Pub Tues–Sat noon–11pm, Sun noon–10.30pm; food served Tues–Fri noon–2pm & 6.30–9.30pm, Sat noon–11pm, Sun noon–4pm.

Seraglio Turkish Restaurant 5 North Bar Within ☎01482 887878. Atmospheric, friendly restaurant tucked away down an alley off North Bar Within (there is a sign above Hawley's Auctioneers, but it's easy to miss). The decor is nicely understated, with delightful alfresco dining in a flagged area with potted plants. You can choose from a variety of grilled meats, of course, plus a fair choice of vegetarian options, all at reasonable prices (most mains around £10). Daily noon–2.30pm & 5–10pm.

TC Patisserie 101 Lairgate ☎01482 860884, ⓦtcpatisserie.co.uk. Unpretentious little patisserie, serving wonderful breakfasts, together with a mouthwatering range of tartlets and pastries. Mon 11am–2.30pm, Tues–Sat 9am–4.30pm.

Westwood Bar and Grill 4 New Walk ☎01482 881999, ⓦthewestwood.co.uk. Just 5min from the town centre along North Bar Without, in one wing of the lovely old Courthouse building (see p.289). High-quality, locally sourced food is presented in cool and elegant surroundings, with outdoor seating when the weather's good – or try the chef's table, overlooking the kitchen. The menu might include such dishes as wild halibut a la plancha, sweet soy-braised beef cheek or cep mushroom macaroni with soft poached egg, and there are some rather lovely desserts. A la carte mains run from £18.50 to £21.95; set menus £18.50 for two courses, £22.50 for three. Tues–Sat noon–2pm & 6–9.30pm, Sun noon–3pm.

★**White Horse (Nellies)** 22 Hengate ☎01482 861973, ⓦnellies.co.uk. Opposite St Mary's and an institution in Beverley, Nellies, a coaching inn since the seventeenth century, is a wonderful old pub. Dingy with exhaust fumes and with bulging walls, it doesn't look much from the outside, but entering it you encounter another world. A warren of small rooms surrounding a central bar, it has stone-slabbed, quarry-tiled and wooden floors, gas lighting, coal fires, smoke-blackened ceilings, embossed wallpaper and brass coal scuttles. It's like going back to Victorian times and, being a Sam Smith's pub, even the prices hark back to the past – a pint of bitter will cost you £1 less than anywhere else. Good selection of lunchtime pub grub as well. Daily 11am–11pm.

★**White's Restaurant** 12a North Bar Without ☎01482 866121, ⓦwhitesrestaurant.co.uk. With its clean simple decor, White's offers the delicious food of highly regarded chef John Robinson, who has earned rave reviews from top critics. The interesting, creative menu makes good use of fish like wild sea bass and monkfish, but you'll find anything from duo of crab "lasagne" to 54hr cooked pork belly with black pudding puree. There's a choice of two taster menus, with reasonable prices for these standards: nine courses (evenings) £55, or four courses (Tues–Thurs evenings & Sat lunch) £25 (£20 on Sat). Tues–Sat 6.45–8pm, also Sat noon–1.30pm.

SHOPPING

Beverley Hat Company 46 Lairgate ☎01482 861046, ⓦthebeverleyhatcompany.co.uk. Huge range off the peg or bespoke ladies and gents hats from top designers including Nigel Rayment, Vivienne Sheriff, Stetson and Bailey. Mon–Fri 10.30am–4.30pm, Sat 10am–5pm.

Browns of Beverley The Corn Exchange, Saturday Market ☎01482 860130, ⓦbrownsyork.co.uk. Something of a regional institution (there are stores in York and Helmsley as well), Browns stock a good range of clothing, beauty products and homeware. Mon–Sat 9am–5.30pm, Sun 10.30am–4pm.

White Rabbit Shop 16 Dyer Lane ☎01482 679325, ⓦwhiterabbitchocolate.co.uk. With a name that refers to Lewis Carroll's alleged inspiration in St Mary's Church (see p.288), the White Rabbit makes its own delicious and extensive range of chocolates on the premises, and offers a number of tasting events. Mon 11am–4pm, Tues–Sat 9.30am–5pm.

The Yorkshire Wolds

The swathe of countryside that stretches east from the city of York to the coast between Bridlington and Filey is known as the **Yorkshire Wolds** – rolling hills and broad farmland interspersed with hedgerows and stands of trees. It's pretty countryside, with good walking along two long-distance paths – the **Wolds Way**, which curves for nearly eighty miles from Hessle outside Hull through the Wolds to Filey, and the fifty-mile-long **Minster Way**, connecting Beverley and York minsters. There are also several sites of historical interest, including the **Rudston monolith**, **Wharram Percy Medieval village**, **Sledmere House** and **Burton Agnes Hall**, but little in the way of tourist infrastructure. **Driffield** is the nearest thing to a capital, but the nearby villages offer nicer places to stay.

Driffield

DRIFFIELD is very much a working market town, and significant because of its perceived role as the gateway to the Wolds, which spread out to the west and north. A bustling if low-key place, the town is easy to find your way around, because the street names are unashamedly geographical – Middle Street (north and south, separated by the Market Place), which stretches from the train station in the south to and beyond imposing **All Saints Church**, is the single main street, with numerous cafés, restaurants, pubs and shops. Its parallel streets are Eastgate and Westgate; all are crossed at the top by North Street.

There's not a lot to see in Driffield. A small stream – intriguingly called Water Forlorns – meanders through the centre, but the most attractive part of the town is **Riverhead**, behind the station, where converted canalside warehouses and cottages are reflected in the calm waters of the Driffield navigation. The canals and becks of the town offer pleasant walks and wildlife-spotting – pick up a copy of *Town Walks Guide* from the tourist office (see below). Driffield also has two weekly **markets** (Thurs & Sat), a monthly farmers' market (first Sat of the month) and the biggest one-day Agricultural Show in the country (July).

Burton Agnes Hall

Burton Agnes (6 miles northeast of Driffield along the A614 Bridlington Rd) • April–Oct daily 11am–5pm • £9; family £23; gardens only £6; family £16 • ☎01262 490324, ⓦburtonagnes.com

Begun in 1601, **Burton Agnes Hall** is one of the finest early Jacobean houses in the country. Just off the A614 (you can see it from the road) it's entered directly from the village through a pink brick, turreted gatehouse of 1610. The view through the gatehouse arch is out of this world, with a small central statue, clipped lawns and dark topiary yews against the beautiful red-brick, multi-windowed, perfectly symmetrical facade of the house itself.

Burton Agnes is something of a haven for artists. A series of artists in residence occupy the summerhouse, and there's an interesting gallery for local artists to display

their work in a red double-decker bus in the courtyard. Also in the courtyard are several shops, a café, a good children's play area and toilets. Various talks, tours, re-enactments, rallies and festivals are held here – check out the website for details.

The house

Inside Burton Agnes, enjoy the magnificent **Great Hall** with its ornate screen and chimneypiece, the complicated plaster decoration containing biblical references and celebrations of the Griffith family, who owned the house. The Hall also contains works of art commissioned by the family over four centuries. The **Drawing Room** beyond the Great Hall and the bedrooms above are equally sumptuous, but the rest of the house is a little more Georgian and restrained. The **Long Gallery**, which runs along the top floor, and which was restored in the 1950s and 1970s, is covered in priceless works of art by artists such as Cézanne, Corot, Gauguin, Matisse, Renoir and Pissarro.

Rudston monolith

Rudston, 3 miles north of Burton Agnes

The village of **RUDSTON** is worth visiting for its spectacular **monolith**, which dates from about 1600 BC. Standing in the churchyard of **All Saints Church**, on a hill above the village, it is 25ft high and nearly 6ft wide at the base. The nearest source of gritstone from which it could have come is ten miles north – given the technology available at the time, moving its forty tonnes must have been quite a feat. All Saints dates from Norman times, so when the church was built the stone must have already been standing there for two millennia, prompting the speculation that its site may have been chosen because it was already considered sacred. Eighteenth-century excavation turned up a number of human skulls, which gave rise to further theories that the stone might have been associated with human sacrifice. On the other hand, it is a churchyard, and churchyards are full of bones.

Sledmere

The village of **SLEDMERE**, seven miles northwest of Driffield and right in the centre of the northern Wolds, is a classsic example of a village that is dominated by one great family – the Sykes family – and its stately home, **Sledmere House**. Apart from a handful of cottages, the whole estate and village is currently owned by Sir Tatton Sykes (8th baronet). Although the great house is likely to be the principal reason for a visit, it's worth looking around the rest of the village, too. Much of it was built by Sir Tatton Sykes II in the half-century before World War I.

The **church** that lies in the grounds of the house is rather dull, but on the main road is a collection of **monuments** – a stone bench dedicated to Sir Richard Sykes, who died in 1978; a copy of an Eleanor Cross (one of those built by King Edward I in honour of his wife Eleanor), which was erected as a village cross in 1896/8, then modified to act as a war memorial after World War I; and a Waggoners Memorial, a cylinder with four columns with battle stories in relief, again in memory of those lost in the war.

Opposite the entrance to the house, occupying what was formerly a model farm, is **Triton House**, a venue for local artists to show their work.

Sledmere House

Sledmere • House 11.30am–4pm, gardens 10.30am–5pm: April Sun & Thurs; May & Sept Sun, Tues & Thurs; June Sun & Tues–Thurs; July & Aug Sun & Tues–Fri; Oct Sun • £9; family £22; park only £6.50 • ☎ 01377 236637, ⓦ sledmerehouse.com

Construction on **Sledmere House** was started in 1751 by Richard Sykes, with further parts being added by Sir Christopher Sykes in the late 1770s and 1780s, when the park was laid out partly from designs by Capability Brown. Despite a major fire in 1911, which led to comprehensive restoration, the house still has the feel of the eighteenth century and is worth visiting for its unfussy, almost austere design. The library is very impressive, and the Sledmere Grand Organ, built in the 1920s, is one of the finest pipe organs in the country.

In addition to the beautiful parkland, dotted with grazing deer, there's also a kitchen garden, the *Terrace Café* in the converted stable block and a shop. There are displays on Sledmere and on the history of the Waggoners Special Reserve, which was raised locally by Sir Mark Sykes at the outbreak of World War I and was one of the first units to enter the war, driving horse-drawn wagons to supply soldiers at the front. Regular events and organ recitals are held at Sledmere House – check the website for details.

6

Wharram Percy Medieval Village

Just off the Beverley to Malton Rd (the B1248), clearly signposted to the right about a mile south of the village of Wharram-le-Street • Open all year, any reasonable time • Free; EH • ⓦ english-heritage.org.uk • It's a pleasant 0.5-mile walk, steep in places, from the car park to the village

Wharram Percy Medieval Village is the best known and most thoroughly excavated of England's thousands of deserted medieval villages, discovered in 1948. It was established some time in the tenth to the twelfth centuries, suffered from the effects of the Black Death in 1348–49, flourished in the fourteenth and fifteenth centuries, and finally died in around 1500, probably because the local landowners, spurred on by high wool prices, evicted families in order to end cultivation and turn the whole area over to sheep-rearing. Today you can see the remains of St Martin's church, one or two cottages (and the floor plans of several more, outlined by footings, ditches or banks) and the village pond. Information boards around the site tell you exactly what you're looking at.

ARRIVAL AND INFORMATION

THE YORKSHIRE WOLDS

By train Driffield train station is on the southern edge of town.

Destinations Beverley (every 30min; 14min); Bridlington (every 30min–1hr; 16min); Hull (every 30min; 33min).

By bus Driffield bus station is in the Market Place.

Destinations Beverley (hourly; 28min); Bridlington (hourly; 34min); Hull (hourly; 1hr 8min).

Tourist office The only tourist office is in Driffield, in the town council offices, 2–4 Market Walk, just west of the Market Place (Mon–Fri 9am–12.30pm & 1–4pm; ☎ 01377 254160).

ACCOMMODATION AND EATING

Blue Bell Hotel Main Rd, Burton Agnes, 6 miles northeast of Driffield ☎ 01262 490050, ⓦ bluebell hotel.net. The *Blue Bell Hotel*, directly opposite Burton Agnes Hall, is a good place to eat or spend the night. With traditional English food (mains around £9.25–17.95) and a good selection of bar meals, it also puts on impressive entertainment evenings in the field behind the pub – performers have included Katherine Jenkins and Paul Young. Pub daily noon–late; food served Mon–Sat noon–9pm, Sun noon–8pm. **£83**

★**Triton Inn** Main St, Sledmere, 7 miles northwest of Driffield ☎ 01377 236078, ⓦ thetritoninn.co.uk. It's lucky that such an interesting village has such an excellent inn, making it a really good centre for exploring the Wolds. Hand-pulled cask ales usually include beer from the local Wold Brewery, and they serve hearty English pub food – sausage and mash, pies and the like. The five en-suite rooms are comfortable and quite smart. Mon–Sat noon–3pm & 6pm–midnight, Sun noon–9.30pm; food served Mon 6–9pm, Tues–Sat noon–2pm & 6–9pm, Sun noon–7.30pm. **£75**

Bridlington and around

In character **BRIDLINGTON** has more in common with North Yorkshire's Scarborough than with any of the rest of the East Yorkshire coast. Its two magnificent **beaches** – the reason for its growth as a resort in the first place – both have cafés, beach huts, gardens and pleasant walks, and at the point they collide is a busy fishing port, **harbour** and marina. Beyond the harbour, the seafront is dominated by traditional English seaside things – amusement arcades, fish-and-chip shops, candyfloss stalls, ice-cream parlours, bingo halls, funfair rides, while the town itself, somehow small and lacking in TLC, is undergoing much renovation. Less than a mile to the north is the historic **Old Town**, unexpectedly quaint and full of character.

The harbour

Bridlington's **harbour** is a busy, workaday and quite exhilarating place, thronged with fishing boats and pleasure craft, boat-launching slipways and quays piled high with lobster pots.

Bridlington Harbour Heritage Museum

Harbour Rd · Easter–Oct daily 10am–4pm · Free · ☎ 01262 809598

Devoted to the history of the harbour, **Bridlington Harbour Heritage Museum** is packed with memorabilia from model ships to nautical paintings, including a ship's bell and a figurehead. The museum is run by the Bridlington Sailing Coble Preservation Society, and the prize exhibit isn't in the museum at all, but floating in the harbour – it's the sailing coble *Three Brothers,* built in 1912.

South Bay

Bridlington exists because of its beaches. The broad and sandy beach of **South Bay** is the best, accessible via the South Promenade on foot, by car or on the land train service to the Belvedere jetty (approximately every 20min). Wide and clean, with fine sand, the beach stretches off into the distance, and is far too big ever to become really crowded, even at the height of summer. Added to the pleasures of bathing and sandcastle-building, there are donkey rides, kiddie rides and the **Spa Bridlington** (see p.298). As you explore the area around the Spa look out for the **Royal Yorkshire Yacht Club** just off South Cliff Road. Once the *Ozone Hotel*, this is where T.E. Lawrence (the future Lawrence of Arabia) stayed on and off between November 1934 and February 1935 while he was working on the boats of the RAF Marine Craft Unit based in the town. There's a memorial sundial dedicated to him in nearby Southcliff Gardens, in front of a block of flats known to locals as "The Carbuncle".

North Bay and around

While the South Bay simply disappears over the horizon into the haze, the **North Bay**, the beach to the north of the harbour, accessed from the North Promenade, has as its backdrop the escalating white cliffs that lead out to Flamborough Head (see opposite). There are lots of rock pools on the beach beyond the prom, and a pleasant clifftop walk.

Like the South Bay, North Bay has its own land train, which runs from just outside **Leisure World** (Ⓦbridlingtonleisureworld.co.uk) out to **Sewerby Hall** (daily 10am–5pm, some parts close at 4.30pm; £4.30; ☎01262 673769, Ⓦsewerby-hall.co.uk), a pleasant small country house with pretty gardens, a pitch-and-putt, a small children's zoo, craft units and a tearoom. Nearby, **Bondville Miniature Village** (daily: Easter–June & Sept 11am–4pm; July & Aug 10am–5pm; £3.25; ☎01262 401736) modestly claims to be a masterpiece and is certainly diverting for kids.

Bridlington Old Town

About a mile inland from the Bridlington town centre is the original market town, now called **Old Town**. With its narrow lanes, Georgian houses, Priory church (**St Mary the Virgin**) and Priory Green, the Old Town comes as a complete surprise to visitors who expected only a brash holiday resort. With its ancient pillory and stock, it has bags of character, with lots of pubs and many independent shops.

Bayle Museum

64 High St · Easter–Sept Mon–Fri 11am–4pm · £1 · ☎ 01262 674308, Ⓦ baylemuseum.moonfruit.com

The only part of the original Priory to survive apart from the church is the Grade I listed **Bayle**, or gatehouse. With a lower storey made of stone, and an upper storey of brick, and with a large entry for coaches and a smaller one for pedestrians, it now houses the **Bayle Museum**, which offers an eclectic, if a little hit-and-miss, collection of life-size figures – a monk sitting on a garderobe (a toilet), a female prisoner sitting in her cell, a farmer sitting at his table – scale models, interactive games and information points outlining some aspects of Bridlington's social history. You can also see, up a spiral staircase on the first floor, the courtroom in which local medieval miscreants were tried. There's a fine collection of dolls, a display about the North Yorkshire Green Howards regiment, a glove belonging to Henrietta Maria (wife of Charles I) and a breech-loading swivel gun dating from 1600.

Flamborough Head

North of Bridlington the cliffs of **Flamborough Head** sweep eastwards into the North Sea. These lofty chalk cliffs and the headland in general offer good clifftop walks, fossil hunting, fishing, diving and lots of sea views. Above all, this is **birdwatching** heaven – along the northern edge are two **nature reserves** –the Yorkshire Wildlife Trust's **Flamborough Cliffs Nature Reserve** and the **RSPB reserve at Bempton Cliffs**. Each has its own car park and access points (see p.321). The best place to park is at the lighthouse beyond the village of Flamborough on the B1259.

Flamborough Head Lighthouse

Around 1 mile from Flamborough on the B1259 • Opening hours are complicated; check the website or phone in advance • £3.50; family £10.50 • ☎ 01262 673769, ⊛ trinityhouse.co.uk

Flamborough Head Lighthouse, still operational, is open to the public, though opening hours vary. Visits start with a short introductory talk from one of the lighthouse keepers there for the purpose – the light is now fully automatic – followed by a steep climb up the spiral staircase to the top of the tower and then up a ladder into the light itself. It's not advised for the infirm or for vertigo sufferers – unlike offshore lighthouses, Flamborough has no intermediate floors. Although the first lighthouse was built here in 1669, the current one dates from 1806, when a light giving two white flashes followed by a red one was installed. This was the first time alternating white and red flashes had been used, an innovation that was quickly copied elsewhere.

The lighthouse sits on the cliff top above formidable chalk cliffs, and there are way-marked paths to take you down to the sea.

ARRIVAL AND INFORMATION   BRIDLINGTON

By train The train station is on Station Rd, just north of the town centre.

Destinations Beverley (every 30min; 25min); Driffield (every 30min; 12–15min); Hull (every 30min; 46min); Scarborough (every 1hr 30min; 40min).

By bus The bus station is on Marshall Ave, near the Promenade shopping centre.

Destinations London (1 daily; 6hr 55min); Scarborough (every 30min; 50min–1hr 20min).

By car Bridlington's road links with the rest of Yorkshire and England are fair but not brilliant, with the A165 striking south to Beverley and Hull and north to Filey and Scarborough, the A614 west to Driffield, and the A64 to

York. These are not fast roads, and you'd have to drive a long way to get to the nearest dual carriageway, even further to the nearest motorway. The town centre and seafront are well supplied with car parks.

By land train Hop-on-hop-off land trains run from Easter to September along North and South Parades, linking the town centre with car parks and South Cliff Caravan Park (from £1.50).

Tourist office Prince St, just above the harbour (April–Sept Mon–Sat 9.30am–5.30pm, Sun 9.30am–5pm; Oct–March Mon–Sat 9.30am–5pm, Sun noon–4pm; ☎ 01262 673474, ⊛ visithullandeastyorkshire.com).

ACCOMMODATION AND EATING

For a big seaside resort, Bridlington isn't well supplied with quality hotels. However, it does have a good choice of guesthouses.

★**Bluebell Guest House** 3 St Anne's Rd ☎01262 675163, ⓦthebluebellguesthouse.co.uk. A tall terraced house a minute's walk from the North Promenade, 5min from the centre of town, the *Bluebell* offers a warm welcome, clean accommodation and a good range of breakfasts. **£60**

★**Expanse Hotel** North Marine Drive ☎01262 675347, ⓦexpanse.co.uk. Big family-owned seaside hotel which looks like an ocean liner, with comfortable, if tired, rooms, a large bar and restaurant, many rooms with sea views, and a fine location on the seafront. **£64**

Oakwell Guest House 84 Windsor Crescent ☎01262 674238, ⓦoakwell-guesthouse-bridlington.co.uk. Off South Cliff Rd, a 2min walk from the town centre, *Oakwell Guest House* is small and family run. The spotless rooms are all en suite, with hot-drink making facilities and satellite TV. A good-value traditional seaside B&B. **£60**

Sewerby Grange 441 Sewerby Rd, Sewerby, just north of Bridlington ☎01262 673439, ⓦsewerbygrange.co.uk. Comfortable mid-Victorian vicarage converted into a privately owned, friendly hotel and restaurant with modern decor. Two-course lunches £10.95, three courses £11.95, table d'hote £18.95. Look out for good deals on rooms. **£100**

South Cliff Caravan Park Wilsthorpe, 3 miles south of Bridlington ☎01262 671051, ⓦsouthcliff.co.uk. Pleasant camping and caravan park with a bar, shop, chip shop, small leisure complex, amusement arcade and launderette. It's just a 5min walk to Bridlington's magnificent South Bay beach, from where there's a road train into town in summer. **£27**

EATING AND DRINKING

Ship Inn Cliff Rd, Sewerby, just north of Bridlington ☎01262 672374, ⓦshipinnsewerby.co.uk. Family pub offering food, a children's play area and open fires in winter. Tues & Wed 11.30am–7pm, Thurs & Fri 11.30am–11pm, Sat & Sun 11am–11pm; food served Tues & Wed noon–2.30pm, Fri & Sat noon–2.30pm & 5.30–8.30pm, Sun noon–4pm.

Supattra Thai Restaurant 29 Quay Rd ☎01262 678565, ⓦsupattrathairestaurant.com. Top-quality Thai restaurant about a mile from the front. Good range of Thai soups and salads, with mains at £8.95–11.95. May–Sept Wed–Sun 6–10pm; Oct–April Thurs–Sun 6–10pm.

Times Gone By Café 33 Hilderthorpe Rd ☎07729 367078. Stepping in here you're stepping into the past – oilcloth tablecloths, Tiffany-style lamps, memorabilia from the years after World War II. The menu also has a touch of nostalgia, from meat and two veg to lemon sponge and custard. The food is beautifully cooked and easy on the pocket. Daily 8am–3pm.

ENTERTAINMENT

Spa Bridlington South Marine Drive ☎01262 678258, ⓦthespabridlington.com. The Spa, with its Royal Hall and Spa Theatre, stages a full programme of films, comedy, music, dance, sport and variety, together with a series of summer shows and winter pantomimes. Previous performers have included everyone from Peter Andre to Jake Bugg and Paul Hollywood. It also has a plaque commemorating Wallace Hartley, the local bandleader whose eight-piece combo allegedly played as the *Titanic* sank. Mon–Sat 9am–5pm, Sun 10am–4pm (later on performance nights).

The Holderness peninsula

South of Bridlington lies the **Holderness peninsula**, the large hook of land that curls all the way down the coast and via the Humber River to Hull. Compared to the North Yorkshire coast, this East Yorkshire seaboard is undramatic and understated, consisting of slightly undulating and relatively empty countryside dotted with villages. As with many peninsulas, however, the area is defined more by its coasts than its interior. The eastern **coast** of Holderness suffers badly from erosion, with the tides scouring the sand off the beaches and depositing it on the eerie and ever-lengthening **Spurn Head** spit, which is increasing by about 2yd a year. Consequently, although there are numerous little seaside towns and villages along the North Sea coast, they tend to be disfigured by necessary, but ugly, concrete sea defences.

Hornsea

Fifteen miles south of Bridlington is **HORNSEA**, a typical small English seaside town, with a promenade, lots of amusement arcades and fish-and-chip shops, the Freeport Shopping Complex just south of the town, and a **beach** that is suffering particularly badly from erosion, despite all sorts of measures taken to combat it. South of Hornsea the coast is quietly attractive, with crumbling bluffs and wide empty beaches. A succession of small villages – Mappleton, Great Cowden, Aldbrough, Garton and Tunstall – dot the coast, while just inland the village of **Roos** has a nice Grade I listed church, and a notable ex-resident in J.R.R. Tolkien.

The Mere
If you approach Hornsea from the south, the views of the town and its church reflected in its large **Mere** are delightful. Said to be Yorkshire's largest natural freshwater lake, the Mere is a nice place to eat your sandwiches (watch out for the gangs of swans and geese), potter around in a rowing boat (£3/person/hour) or have a round on the putting green (£1.20). The road down to the Mere is easy to miss, so follow signs carefully.

The seafront
Despite the fight that the town has had with erosion in the past, the resulting **seafront** is extremely pleasant, with the old promenade sitting below a substantial sea wall, built in 1985 following serious flooding, topped with a second, modern promenade. There are numerous places to sit, and a kiosk/shop in what was a public shelter. The beach is an excellent place to hunt fossils, especially after the storms that lash this coast, and there are invigorating beach walks both north and south of the town (though be careful – even experienced walkers have found themselves cut off by the tide). The **Trans Pennine Trail** (⊚ transpenninetrail.org.uk), Britain's first long-distance multi-user trail, starts here, linking Hornsea with Southport on the west coast. There's an impressive marker and an information board.

Hornsea Museum
Burns Farm, 11–17 Newbegin • Mon–Fri 11am–5pm, Sat 10am–4pm, Sun 1–4pm • £3.50; family £10 • ☎ 01964 533443, ⊚ hornseamuseum.com

Though production ceased in 2000, Hornsea's main non-seaside claim to fame is for its **pottery**, produced here throughout the second half of the twentieth century. The most comprehensive collection in the world of the colourful, distinctive ware can be seen in the **Hornsea Museum**, housed in a row of cottages along the main street, Newbegin. The museum also has extensive displays on the social history of the area, including a series of residential and workplace rooms.

ARRIVAL AND INFORMATION   HORNSEA

By bus The town's bus station is in the market place. Destinations Beverley (hourly; 39min); Bridlington (6 daily; 59min); Hull (every 15–45min; 54min–1hr 19min).

Tourist office 11–17 Newbegin (☎ 01964 536404 – the number for the Humber Bridge Tourist Centre, which deals with enquiries about Hornsea).

SHOPPING

Freeport Outlet Shopping Village Rolston Rd, just outside the town centre, on the road to Withernsea ☎ 01964 534211, ⊚ hornseafreeport.com. Freeport claims to be the country's first discount retail village, and is certainly one of the most pleasant, with retail units in single low-rise buildings on a sloping, landscaped site. At the top of the site is Potters Square, with a small food court, ATMs and toilets – given the choice, park in Car Park 3, which is next to the square. Mon–Fri 10am–5.30pm, Sat 9.30am–5.30pm, Sun 11am–5pm.

Withernsea and around
WITHERNSEA has more about it than most of Holderness's windblown minor resorts. In particular, you can't miss the stately 124ft-high **lighthouse** that stands just back from the beach. Look out, too, for the pair of crenellated structures – the **Pier Towers** – on the promenade. They once formed the entrance to a splendid 1150ft Victorian pier,

built in 1877, which got shorter and shorter as boats kept crashing into it, until what was left was finally dismantled during the building of sea defences in the 1930s. The towers remain, squat sandstone buildings that look like chess pieces guarding something that's no longer there. Next to the towers are the **Valley Gardens**, which host free entertainment on Sundays and some Saturdays in summer.

Withernsea Lighthouse Museum

Hull Rd • June to mid-Sept Mon–Fri 11am–5pm, Sat 1–5pm, Sun noon–4pm; Easter–May & mid-Sept to Oct Sat 1–5pm, Sun noon–4pm • £2.50; family £6.50 • ☎ 01964 614834, 🌐 withernsealighthouse.co.uk

As its name implies, **Withernsea Lighthouse Museum** occupies a lighthouse. It has sections dealing with the RNLI, HM Coastguards and the history of the town, and, more intriguingly, with the town's most famous daughter – Kay Kendall, the glamorous 1950s film star. Containing tableaux, memorabilia, stills from her pictures and movie posters, it is not only unexpected but oddly moving. The lighthouse itself is, of course, the central exhibit – it may seem odd that it lies a quarter of a mile from the coast, with the town between it and the sea, but when it was built, in 1892, there was only sand and a mere where the town now stands. You can climb the 144 steps that spiral up to the lamp room, from where there are terrific views across the town and the coast. However, there are no intermediate floors and the steps are steep, so if you suffer from vertigo or ill health, stay at the bottom – you can see the views on CCTV. There's a tourist information point and a small café.

RAF Holmpton

Rysome Lane, Holmpton • Tours (90min) March–early July, Sept & Oct Tues–Thurs, Sat & Sun 2pm; July daily 2pm; Aug daily 11am & 2pm; Nov Sat & Sun 2pm • £7; family £20 • ☎ 01964 630208, 🌐 rafholmpton.com

Just outside Withernsea, **RAF Holmpton** – it's signposted **Underground Bunker** –is the site of a huge RAF and Military Command Bunker, built 80ft underground in 1951–52 as part of the Cold War Early Warning System. It consists of not only the military installation (a message centre, coding and encryption centre, computer and radar rooms, Command HQ offices, Royal Observer Corps operations room and more) but also all the backup services that turned it into an underground village – hospital, cinema, canteen, dormitories – together with the life-support systems that would have made the bunker self-sufficient in the event of an attack. Look out for the chilling Weapons of Mass Destruction room. Incidentally, poet Ted Hughes was once stationed at RAF Patrington (now Holmpton), and there are several references to the area in his work.

Patrington and around

The inland village of **PATRINGTON**, five miles southwest of Withernsea, is famous for one thing – the magnificent **St Patrick's Church**, widely known as the **Queen of Holderness**. Beyond Patrington, the road to the end of the peninsula – the B1445 – strikes south through a succession of villages – Welwick, Weeton, Skeffling (look out for its wind turbine), Easington (notable as the landfall for the mighty North Sea gas pipeline) and **Kilnsea**, which has a Grade II listed acoustic mirror dating from World War II, used to listen out for approaching enemy aircraft, and a rather nice pub outside which you can enjoy a drink and fine views of the ships coming and going on the Humber estuary.

Queen of Holderness

Church Lane • Daily 9am–5pm (dusk in winter) • Free • ☎ 01964 630327

Patrington's pride in St Patrick's Church, the **Queen of Holderness**, is obvious – a notice inside says simply "this is England's finest village church". Its rave reviews arise from its consistency: it was built quickly and was then little added to, so it represents a single

THE HUMBER PILOTS

The mouth of the Humber River, between Spurn Head and Cleethorpes in Lincolnshire, is a busy and dangerous seaway, and ships require **specialist pilots** to guide them through. Every few minutes one of the pilot cutters peels away from the pilot's jetty and ploughs out towards one of the anchored ships. Then, with the pilot on board, the ship will get under way and thrum through the gap between Spurn Head and Bull Fort (one of two built on sandbanks in the estuary), heading upriver towards Grimsby, Immingham, Hull, or the Trent and Ouse river ports. Similarly, when a ship needs to leave one of these ports for the high seas, a pilot will guide it through the estuary into the North Sea before returning to Spurn Point. A fleet of cars is available to pilots for the resulting to-ing and fro-ing (though since the road was damaged, the last leg out to the point itself has to be done in a specialist 4WD). When the British economy is booming, the straits get very busy, but during recession you might have to wait hours to see a ship – there's a summary of shipping movements on ⓦhumber.com.

style – early fourteenth-century Decorated – rather than the more usual extended muddle. Built of pale grey limestone, its exterior and interior are of a piece, its spire is pretty and in proportion, and its interior is uncluttered by too many monuments and memorials. Even the approach to the church has a lot to commend it – you can see it for miles across the rolling cornfields of Holderness in any direction, but when you get to the village, because of its position, it seems to disappear. Suddenly you're right on it, and there it is in all its beauty.

Spurn Head

Beyond Kilnsea it's edge-of-the-world stuff. The road heads out along **Spurn Head**, a narrow spit of land – more than three miles long (and getting longer by the year) and in places less than 50yd wide – that divides the Humber estuary from the North Sea. As you walk to **Spurn Point** you'll see several **lighthouses** (the newest was decommissioned in 1985), a lifeboat station and the facilities and pier of the Humber Pilots (see box above).

Spurn Point

Free; organized safari trips run by Yorkshire Wildlife Trust £10 • ☎ 01904 659570, ⓦ ywt.org.uk

Although **Spurn Point** is a nature reserve run by the Yorkshire Wildlife Trust (see p.319), it is also strategically important, dominating the Humber estuary and this part of the North Sea. As a result, it is littered with wartime defences, and is currently the home of the Humber lifeboat and pilot stations (see box above). Apart from the two lighthouses, other buildings include the homes of the lifeboatmen, and the radio-and radar-festooned **Humber Pilots' Control Tower**. It's well worth climbing up past this huddle of buildings to a vantage point on top of the ridge. From here to your left you can see the ships riding at anchor in the North Sea waiting their turn to enter the straits, while to the right the Humber Pilots' Jetty stretches out into the estuary, with, beyond it, the bright orange-and-black Humber lifeboat. The waters around Spurn Head are so dangerous that this RNLI station is the only one in England with a permanent professional crew.

ARRIVAL AND INFORMATION   SPURN POINT

Until recently access to Spurn Point was by a single-lane road built during World War II to supply the Spurn Head defences – before that, the only link was a railway, stretches of which can still be seen. However, a tidal surge in December 2013 carried away a substantial length of road, so that now visitor access is on foot only. The walk to the point involves parking at the visitor centre, about 0.25 miles beyond the **Blue Bell Café and Nature Reserve office** (☎ 01964 650533), then walking along beaches and sand dunes.

Contexts

History

Yorkshire has played an important part in the history of Britain as a whole, from the struggles between Celts, Anglo-Saxons and Vikings, via the English Civil War – when the county was mainly Royalist but with important Parliamentary enclaves – to the period from the mid-eighteenth century onwards when the Agricultural and Industrial revolutions changed the world. The region's attempt to find a response to the post-industrial decay that followed is shared by many other parts of Britain, with Yorkshire often taking a lead during that great upheaval.

Because of its size, however, it's worth bearing in mind that the historical experience of different parts of Yorkshire varies enormously – the Dales sheep-farmer had little in common with the South Yorkshire coal miner, the Whitby whaler with the Halifax clothier, the owner of the stately home with the occupant of the back-to-back. Secondly, far from being a succession of accepted facts, Yorkshire history abounds with the unknown and the disputed. So what appears below is inevitably a simplification, and focuses on the events that are most significant to the sights covered in this Guide.

Prehistoric times

Evidence from the early eras – the Old and New Stone Ages especially – is sparse, though many local museums across Yorkshire have displays of what there is. For the Bronze and Iron Ages, probably the best museum to visit is the **Hull and East Riding Museum** in Hull.

The Stone Ages

Remains from the **Old Stone Age** (up to 4500 BC), the period when people used roughly shaped flint tools, deer antlers, animal bones and wood, and survived by hunting wild animals and gathering wild fruit and seeds, have been found in many parts of Yorkshire. Antler points, mammoth, rhino and hippo bones, worked flints and wood and bone implements from the early Old Stone Age have been found in the Dales and in South Yorkshire, from the later Old Stone Age in the Dales, the Pennines, the Vales of York and Pickering, the Wolds and on the Holderness peninsula.

The big change from the Old to the **New Stone Age** (4500–2200 BC) was the development of agriculture. Instead of leading a nomadic life following the herds, people settled down, domesticating animals and sowing crops, rather than relying on the bounty of nature. From this period the evidence in Yorkshire includes grooved pottery, flint tools such as axe heads and weapons such as arrowheads, stone circles and the barrows that are marked as tumuli on OS maps. Finds have been particularly rich in the Yorkshire Wolds and the Vale of York. Specific artefacts dating from the New Stone Age include the **Rudston Monolith** (see p.294) and the **Devil's Arrows** (see p.172)

Earliest times–4500 BC	4500–2200 BC	2200–700 BC
Old Stone Age. Rough flint implements widely distributed across Yorkshire.	New Stone Age. Pottery, tools and weapons found, especially in Wolds and Vale of York.	Bronze Age. Bronze tools and weapons are made across the county. The North Ferriby boats are built – the earliest sewn-plank boats found in Europe.

– the three circular henges in Thornborough near Ripon, which have a slight kink in their alignment corresponding exactly to that of the stars in Orion's Belt – and rock art that has been found above Wharfedale near Ilkley.

The Bronze Age

The introduction of bronze – an alloy of copper and tin – led to a new **Bronze Age** (2200–700 BC) not only of sophisticated tools and weapons, but also of earthworks, tombs and presumed ceremonial centres. Dating from this period are the famous **North Ferriby boats** (see p.277); crop marks in the vales of Pickering and York; burial mounds on the North York Moors; low cairns, stone circles and walls in the Pennines; earthworks in Holderness and several lengthy boundary dikes, axes, tools and prestige ceremonial weapons.

The Iron Age

From 700 BC, when the much harder **iron** started to replace bronze as a material for making tools and weapons, serious clearing of woodland using iron axes and ploughing of land using iron ploughshares became possible, transforming the Yorkshire landscape. The two Iron Age tribes to dominate the area were the **Brigantes**, who settled what is today South, East and West Yorkshire, and the **Parisii**, who dominated East Yorkshire. Although, as you'd expect with farming people, the greatest population density was in the fertile lowlands, remains from those areas have been largely ploughed under by subsequent generations and most of the surviving remains have been found in the uplands. There are lots of Iron Age remains in the Dales (the settlement platforms of Wharfedale and Swaledale, for example) and also in the North York Moors. The Wolds, too, have their fair share, including the spectacular "carriage burials" where skeletons have been found accompanied by two-wheeled carriages or chariots. One of the most important finds was made in **Hasholme**, where a third-century BC 45ft-long log boat was unearthed (see p.277). There are lots of iron-smelting sites and evidence of coppicing, too, and a number of hill forts have been identified – the largest is the enormous site at **Ingleborough** (see p.190) – many of which were reinforced Bronze Age fortifications.

The Romans

Despite Julius Caesar's punishment/exploratory raids in 55 BC and 54 BC, the actual **Roman invasion** of Britain didn't begin until almost a hundred years later. From 43 AD the invading Roman armies worked their way inexorably northwards, probably reaching the Don, the southern edge of the Brigantes' homeland, around 45/46 AD. To start with, the Brigantes, under their **Queen Cartimandua**, became a Roman client state, with the queen gaining favour by handing over Celtic rebel Caradoc to the conquerors. When Cartimandua divorced her husband Venutius and he responded with armed rebellion, the Romans sent powerful forces to support her. The second time this happened, however, they didn't have the soldiers to spare and sent only auxiliaries. They rescued her, leaving Venutius in charge. Losing patience in 69 AD, the Romans conquered the Brigantes and incorporated them into the Roman Empire.

During Rome's almost four-hundred-year rule, Roman roads spread across Yorkshire and forts were established in various places. In due course, **York (Eboracum)** became the

700BC–45 AD	45 AD	63 AD	63–410 AD
Iron Age. Tools and weapons made of iron start to transform the landscape. Two tribes, the Brigantes and Parisii, dominate the region.	The Romans arrive in the area nowadays known as Yorkshire.	Yorkshire is incorporated into the Roman Empire.	Roman rule consolidates. York, as Eboracum, becomes the capital of the north of Roman Britain.

undisputed Roman capital of the North, but other Roman sites were important at different times – Aldborough, Malton, Doncaster, Castleford, Tadcaster, Catterick and Brough. In each case a fort was built to protect a river crossing or an important road intersection, then a "vicus" or civilian settlement would grow up nearby. There are numerous Roman remains to be seen in Yorkshire, not only in towns like York and Malton, but also out in the country – the piece of Roman road called Wade's Causeway, for example, or the Military Camps at Cawthorne. York has a statue of Emperor Constantine the Great near the Minster – Constantine was in York when he was proclaimed Emperor. Towards the end of the Roman period, attacks from the sea along the east coat led to the building of signal towers, for example, at Scarborough, Filey, Flamborough and Holderness, though much of the evidence has since been washed away by the sea.

The Anglo-Saxons

The traditional story of what happened after the Roman legions left Britain around 410 AD is that hordes of Germanic **Angles**, **Saxons** and **Jutes** flooded across the North Sea and drove the native **Celts** out of England into what is today Wales, Scotland, Cornwall and Brittany. The story involved British chief Vortigern inviting Anglo-Saxon mercenaries to help him against rival Celtic chieftains, only for the mercenaries to rebel and seize the territory for themselves. It is, however, very difficult in reality to know what went on, since so little evidence has survived – the account of what happened taught in most schools until recently was based almost exclusively on *The Ecclesiastical History of the English People*, written in around 731 by the monk known as the Venerable Bede.

Modern research, however, indicates that the process was a great deal more gradual and more confused than this, with Angles coming in and settling down alongside the native Celts. Any warfare, it's now believed, was limited to a small number of warriors, with most of the population unaffected. If there was a major change during the fifth to the seventh centuries, it was that a Celtic aristocracy was probably replaced by an Anglo-Saxon one. In Yorkshire the infiltration of the **Angles** started on the western edges of the Wolds, then spread through the Vale of York and across to the coast. In around 600 AD Aethelfrith formed the new kingdom of Northumbria and, although he was killed at the Battle of the Idle near Bawtry in 616 AD, the English conquest of the region continued under Edwin, with struggles between Northumbria and Mercia. The new kingdom's capital was set up in **Eoforwic**, or **York**. Roman fortifications were renewed and strengthened. Internecine troubles continued, with kings being killed in battle, assassinated or exiled until the beginning of the Viking invasion in 867 AD.

The story of the **growth of Christianity** is, of course, dealt with in great detail by Bede – he was, after all, a monk. The Roman Empire had become Christian under Constantine, and remnants of Christianity remained among the Celts after the Roman evacuation. The stronghold of this **Celtic church** was across the sea in Ireland, from which Columba had set up a monastery on Iona off the Scottish coast in 563 AD, with the Celtic church making inroads in the north of England. Then, Augustine landed in Kent in 597 AD and began a campaign to convert the English to the **Roman** version of

410–793 AD	563 AD	597 AD	637 AD
Angles, Saxons and Jutes slowly infiltrate and mix with the native Brigantes and Parisii tribes.	Columba establishes a Celtic monastery on Iona, from where Celtic Christianity starts to spread east towards Yorkshire.	Augustine lands in Kent and Roman Christianity starts to spread north towards Yorkshire.	The first stone version of what was to become York Minster is built.

Christianity as it had survived in Rome itself. As this was going on, King Oswald of Northumbria invited Aidan to set up a Celtic monastery on Lindisfarne and, shortly afterwards, established an abbey at Whitby. The spread of Christianity of both types continued apace: the Celtic church from the north, the Roman church from the south. Eventually, in 663 at the **Synod of Whitby**, King Oswy of Northumberland heard the arguments of both sides regarding the differences between the two churches – specifically, the date of Easter – and ruled that the Roman Church should prevail.

In the eighth century, **York** became the major Christian religious centre for the region. New monasteries were established by members the Northumbrian royal family, and Christianity was imposed top-down. Great efforts were made to suppress surviving pagan beliefs among ordinary people, and where they stubbornly persisted, they were incorporated into the Christian church – the **Rudston Monolith** almost certainly has pagan religious significance, so the church for the village was built right next to it, and it was incorporated into the churchyard (see p.294). Survivals from the Anglo-Saxon period are uncommon, but you can visit **Ripon Cathedral crypt**, look at the carved column in the churchyard at **Masham**, or go down into the crypt of **Lastingham church** – actually the remains of the monastery of St Cedd established there in 659 AD (see p.243). Look out too for the many Anglo-Saxon **place names** – those that end in ...ton, ...ley, ...burgh and ...field.

The Vikings

In the 1970s, knowledge of the **Vikings** in Yorkshire took a big leap forward when the Coppergate excavations in York revealed evidence of a large Viking city. Imaginatively developed by the York Archaeological Trust into the **Jorvik** attraction (see p.151), and with complementary **Dig** (see p.150) dealing with the processes and methods of archeology, we now have a remarkably vivid idea of what Viking life was like shortly before the Norman Conquest.

The first sign of the imminent Viking storm came in 793 AD, when Lindisfarne was attacked. Subsequent raids became increasingly frequent until successive waves of Viking attacks started in 866. York was taken in 867, East Anglia was conquered in 870, Mercia fell in 874. Monasteries were sacked, monks killed or dispersed and their lands confiscated, though many minsters seem to have survived. In due course, though, Viking leaders started to adopt Christianity. Warfare continued between the Vikings and the Anglo-Saxons until, in 886, Alfred the Great of the Saxons and Guthrum of the Vikings signed a treaty fixing the borders between Wessex and the Danelaw. Towards the end of the Viking period Christianity flourished and many parish churches were built, sometimes incorporating elements of their Saxon predecessors – take a look, for example, at **St Peter's Church** in Kirkgate, Leeds. The term **Yorkshire** itself was first used in 1065, the year before the Battle of Hastings.

The main evidence for the Viking occupation of the region was until fairly recently the spread of Viking **place names** – those ending in ...by, ...thorpe and ...thwaite. The word **"Riding"** itself, which was attached to Yorkshire's three areas, is derived from the Danish "thrithing" or third. There are also Viking carvings in parts of Yorkshire, including the crosses at St Andrew's Church, Middleton (just outside Pickering) carved with warriors and scenes from Scandinavian mythology.

663	793	866–867	886
The Synod of Whitby decides to adopt Roman rather than Celtic Christianity.	The Viking invasion of Britain starts with an attack on Lindisfarne in the northeast of England.	The Viking invasion intensifies until eventually York is taken.	The borders of Saxon Wessex and Viking Danelaw are agreed by Alfred the Great (Saxon) and Guthrum (Viking).

The Normans

Yorkshire played a crucial part both in the events preceding and following the **Norman Conquest**. While **King Harold of England** was waiting for the expected invasion by William of Normandy in the south of England, news arrived that a force under his disaffected brother Tostig, supported by Harald Hardrada of Norway, had attacked Scarborough, then sailed up the Humber, and started on their way to York. King Harold sped northwards, and destroyed the invaders at **Stamford Bridge**, east of the city, on September 25, 1066. Three days later, William and his invading Normans landed on the south coast. So King Harold and his exhausted soldiers had to rush back south, only to be beaten at the **Battle of Hastings** on October 14, 1066. King Harold, as every schoolchild knows, was killed, William seized the throne, and his Norman commanders and supporters were granted extensive estates in return for their support, going on to replace the top level of Anglo-Saxon aristocracy as the country's ruling class.

From the start, Yorkshire was at the heart of **resistance** to William the Conqueror, and it was to pay dearly for it. The ruling class in the area was largely Danish in origin, the language spoken a combination of Anglo-Saxon and Danish, which the southern English couldn't understand (no change there then), and the hold of the Anglo-Saxon kings of England over the area was at best tentative. It might even have seemed to the people of Yorkshire themselves that the area could, with the help of Scottish and Scandinavian allies, remain independent of Norman England. William the Conqueror, of course, didn't see it this way. A series of northern rebellions caused him increasing frustration, until in 1069–70 he undertook a series of ferocious attacks on the area which has since gone down in history as the **Harrying of the North**. Whole populations

---

THE NORMAN MONASTERY-BUILDING BOOM

Yorkshire is renowned for the number and beauty of its **monasteries** and **convents**. Most of these were established between the Norman Conquest and the mid-twelfth century, in phases when the different main orders seemed to be favoured in turn. The dates when religious houses were established are often unclear – they are sometimes only rough approximations, or several dates could be given depending on when the original monastery was established, when it changed orders, or when it was restored.

BENEDICTINE

Selby Abbey (1069)
Whitby (1078)
Lastingham (1078)
York: St Mary's (1088)
Holy Trinity, Micklegate (1089)

AUGUSTINIAN

Nostell Priory (1114)
Bridlington (1114)
Kirkham Priory (1122)
Bolton Priory (1154/5)

GILBERTINE

Old Malton (1150)

CISTERCIAN

Rievaulx Abbey (1132)
Fountains Abbey (1135)
Roche Abbey (1138)
Byland Abbey (1143)
Kirkstall Abbey (1152)
Jervaulx Abbey (1138)

PREMONSTRATENSIAN

Easby Abbey (1151)

CLUNIAC

Pontefract (1154)
Monk Bretton Priory (1154)

886–1066	1065	1066–69	1069–70
Yorkshire firmly established as part of the Danelaw.	The term "Yorkshire" first appears in records.	Yorkshire fiercely resists the Norman Conquest.	The "Harrying of the North" by William the Conqueror begins in an attempt to subjugate the rebels.

were ruthlessly cut down, villages destroyed and survivors deprived of food by a scorched earth policy. His soldiers even salted the land to make it barren. It has been estimated that up to one hundred thousand people died directly or indirectly as a result of this pitiless campaign. The action was followed by the wholesale division of Yorkshire into "honours" ruled over by William's most trusted, competent and ruthless lieutenants. Castles sprang up across Yorkshire, with pressed labour building first the quickly erected earthen motte and bailey castles, then, when the county was secure, more permanent and less easily attacked stone castles with powerful keeps, gatehouses and curtain walls (**Richmond Castle**, for example). Castles of increasing power and sophistication were built during the following centuries, at first for purely military reasons, but becoming more comfortable and residential as the threat of rebellion receded. Today, **castles**, or what's left of them, can be seen in Conisbrough, Pontefract, Tickhill, Richmond, Middleham, Skipton, Skipsea, Scarborough, Pickering and Helmsley.

Meanwhile, the new Norman overlords were also building and restoring numerous **monasteries** (see box, p.307), and from the thirteenth century onwards many of them, especially those of the Cistercians, expanded their wealth, power and influence both in Yorkshire and elsewhere. They were known for their entrepreneurial spirit – Fountains Abbey, for example, became a major sheep owner with huge flocks in the Dales, while Rievaulx, Kirkstead and Byland abbeys were involved in mineral extraction. Another feature of the time was the increase in the number of friars who preached, lived off charity and owned no property beyond their churches and monastery buildings. Thus the Dominicans (Blackfriars) had houses in York, Beverley, Scarborough and Pontefract; the Franciscans (Greyfriars) in York, Beverley, Doncaster, Hull, Richmond and Scarborough; the Carmelites (Whitefriars) in York, Hull, Scarborough, Doncaster and Northallerton; and the Augustinians (Austin Friars) in York, Tickhill and Hull.

As well as the big monastic houses that made their appearance at this time were many **parish churches**. A good number survive today, with recognizably Norman features – among them St Mary's in Armthorpe, St Helen's in Austerfield and many more. In addition, virtually every **market town** in Yorkshire can trace its origins to the early Norman period, though some, like Bradford, Halifax, Rotherham and Barnsley, came to prominence much later as Victorian industrial centres. In the countryside royal forests and deer parks were established, and many field patterns and town layouts that were to last for centuries can trace their origin to the Normans.

The Wars of the Roses

A series of dynastic struggles fought between 1455 and 1485, the **Wars of the Roses** are often mistakenly thought of as a simple battle between Yorkshire and Lancashire. They were in fact a struggle between two branches of the **Plantagenet** royal house, the descendants of two of the younger sons of Edward III in the previous century. A tangled web of plots, rebellions and battles, the struggle was between the **House of York** (emblem, the White Rose) and the **House of Lancaster** (the Red Rose). Geographically, support for the two houses was by no means cleanly divided between Yorkshire and Lancashire – most of the great families in the East and West Ridings of Yorkshire supported Lancaster, and in the North Riding allegiance was divided. Two of the major

1069–1154	1220	1455–85
A great monastery building boom in Yorkshire.	Building begins on York Minster, which is to become the largest Gothic cathedral in Europe.	Wars of the Roses between the royal houses of York and Lancaster.

battles of the Wars of the Roses were fought in Yorkshire. On December 30, 1460, in the **Battle of Wakefield**, Richard Duke of York was killed, beheaded, and his head displayed on Micklegate Bar in York. Three months later, on March 29, 1461, the bloodiest battle ever to have been fought on British soil took place at **Towton**, south of Tadcaster, when – although they outnumbered the Yorkists – the Lancastrians were defeated. Estimates of the size of the armies and the number of casualties varies – somewhere between sixty thousand and eighty thousand soldiers took part, with perhaps 28,000 losing their lives. Lancastrian heads replaced the Yorkist ones on Micklegate Bar, and **Edward IV** of York, who had been crowned shortly before the battle, emerged as undisputed king.

However, the Wars of the Roses continued, ending only on August 22, 1485, at the **Battle of Bosworth** when the Lancastrian Henry Tudor, Duke of Richmond, defeated King Richard III, who had succeeded his brother Edward IV two years earlier. **Henry VII** was crowned on the battlefield. This might well have been just the latest battle in the Wars of the Roses had it not been for Henry's exceptional ability as king. He cut through the York/Lancaster tit-for-tat of the preceding thirty years by being merciful during subsequent rebellions, by using taxation and legislation to bring the overmighty barons to their knees, and by marrying Elizabeth of York, uniting the red and white roses into the new two-colour Tudor Rose – as seen in the rose window in the south transept of York Minster. In so doing, he laid the foundations for a Tudor dynasty that ruled England for more than a century.

The Dissolution of the monasteries

Henry VII built up a fortune during his 24-year reign, making the monarch by far the richest and most powerful man in England. His son **Henry VIII** had spent all the money within two years of his 1509 succession. This set the scene for years of financial problems for the crown. An issue of succession also emerged as Henry's wife, Catherine of Aragon, failed to provide a son and heir. Famously, the two problems were solved during the 1530s by related events – Henry pressed for a divorce from Catherine so that he could marry Anne Boleyn, and when the pope refused to grant it (he had problems of his own), the train of events was set in motion that led to England's break with Rome, the establishment of the Church of England, and the start of the English **Reformation**. Once the pope's authority in England had been denied, it gave Henry the excuse to dissolve the monasteries, whose money, lands and treasure went some way towards stopping up the hole in the royal finances.

All these events had important consequences for Yorkshire. Being one of the regions with the most monasteries and convents, it was most affected by the **Dissolution** between 1536 and 1540. Commissioners had earlier been sent around the religious houses to gather evidence of their wrongdoing (the excuse) and taking an inventory of their wealth (the real reason), and now the monasteries were closed, their abbots, monks and nuns expelled, their gold and silver carted off to London, their lands rented out or sold to local people, their buildings partially dismantled to become sources of free dressed stone for construction. At a stroke, Henry's financial problems were eased and a whole class of people had been created with a vested interest in the continuation of the break with Rome.

1460

1461

The Battle of Wakefield sees a rousing victory for the Lancastrians. The Yorkist army is destroyed and claimant to the throne the Duke of York dies.

In the Battle of Towton, said to be the bloodiest battle ever to be fought on English soil, the Yorkist Edward IV seizes the throne at the expense of the Lancastrian Edward VI.

However, though the Dissolution was supported in Yorkshire by those who benefited from it, it was deeply unpopular with others in what was largely a conservative, Catholic area, and in October 1536 a rebellion against the changes and in favour of the Roman Catholic church started in Lincolnshire and spread to Beverley, the Wolds, Holderness and York. This was the **Pilgrimage of Grace**, led by lawyer Robert Aske. Tenants who had newly taken over monastic lands were expelled, dispersed monks and nuns were returned to their monasteries and the Roman Catholicism restored. Further rebellions occurred around Ripon and Richmond, and these fresh rebels joined the movement. By the end of October, almost the whole of Yorkshire was up in arms. Though with hindsight it seems likely that the rebellion had little chance of success, at the time it was perceived as a serious challenge to the king's authority. Henry at first played it softly, promising to consider the rebels' grievances and demands. Aske naively accepted the king's word and stood his forces down. Early in 1537 Henry had Aske arrested and executed, and his body displayed on the walls of York Castle. His leading noble supporters, together with numerous abbots, monks and priests, were also executed – in all 216 died.

The English Reformation

The break with Rome was political and financial. But despite Henry's innate religious conservatism, he couldn't prevent the arguments that were raging on the continent between Protestants and Roman Catholics, which started with Martin Luther in 1517 and spread to England. The disagreements – over the power of priests, the authority of the pope, corrupt practices such as nepotism, simony and the selling of indulgences, the disapproval of "idolatry" and pomp in churches and services – started to lead to piecemeal change in the English church.

Conservative Yorkshire had little enthusiasm for this **Reformation**. It is significant that no Protestant martyrdoms occurred here during Roman Catholic Bloody Mary's reign, but twenty Roman Catholics were martyred, in the 1580s alone, during Protestant Elizabeth I's – including Margaret Clitherow of York, pressed to death at the age of 30 for harbouring priests. Many of the county's upper-class families, like the **Nevilles** and the **Percys**, were famously Roman Catholic – it is said that there wasn't a Catholic rebellion that didn't involve at least one member of the Percy family. The Wakefield Plot (1541), the Seamer Rising (1549), and in particular the Rebellion of the Northern Earls (1569–70), all involved members of the great Catholic families. The Rebellion of the Northern Earls was by far the most serious, but it failed: one of its leaders, Neville, fled into exile, another, a Percy, ended up with his head on a spike at Micklegate Bar in York. The focus of many Catholic rebellions was, of course, **Mary Queen of Scots**, who spent a considerable proportion of her long imprisonment in England under the control of the Earl of Shrewsbury in various places, including Sheffield (see p.47) and Bolton Castle (see p.210). Yorkshire disaffection with the growing Protestantism continued into the reign of James I – **Guy Fawkes**, one of the leaders of the Roman Catholic Gunpowder Plot to blow up king and parliament, was from York.

Economically, however, Yorkshire flourished during the Tudor years. In the countryside the early harbingers of the Agricultural Revolution can be detected, with considerable enclosure of open fields in Holderness to help with the growing of grain

1485–1603	1530s	1536
Tudor rule begins with Lancastrian Henry VII, Earl of Richmond seizing the throne from Yorkist Richard III. He marries Elizabeth of York, thus finally uniting the red and white roses.	Henry VIII splits with Rome, sets up the Church of England, and marries Anne Boleyn.	Much of Yorkshire rises in rebellion against the religious changes of Henry VIII during what is known as the Pilgrimage of Grace.

and cattle, and in the Wolds to facilitate the changeover to more profitable sheep. In addition, the early shoots of industries that were to flourish during the later Industrial Revolution can be seen – cutlery in Sheffield, woollen cloth in Wakefield and Halifax, even liquorice in Pontefract.

The English Civil War

During the **English Civil War** (1642–51), when Parliament rose up in rebellion against the king, Yorkshire as a whole remained true to the county's conservative traditions by staying firmly **Royalist**. That said, Hull supported **Parliament** throughout – and indeed, it can be claimed that it was the refusal of the burghers of Hull to allow Charles I into their city that sparked off the war in the first place. There was much fighting between the forces of both sides across the county, with sieges of York, Hull, Pontefract, Skipton and Bradford. Parliamentarians from Hull captured Bridlington and Whitby for a time, and the biggest battle of the Civil War was fought at **Marston Moor**, just west of York, in 1644. When the war ended with a Parliamentary victory, many of Yorkshire's castles were destroyed, such as Sheffield and Pontefract, or "slighted" – made unusable by partial destruction – including Helmsley and Scarborough.

Yorkshire's response to the **Commonwealth** – the constitutional experiment of rule without a monarch – is little recorded, but being a largely royalist county, it is likely that it bore it with grudging acquiescence. Though Oliver Cromwell, from 1653 Lord Protector, introduced many far-seeing reforms in government, the puritanism that accompanied it held little attraction for most Yorkshire folk. The **restoration** of the monarchy in 1660 was welcomed in most of Yorkshire – although again, Hull, a stronghold of Parliament, was less keen.

The population explosion

Up to the eighteenth century, **population**, both in Yorkshire and in England as a whole, generally remained fairly static. Good times would be reflected in moderate increase, bad times in moderate (or in the case of the Black Death, catastrophic) decline. From the restoration of the monarchy in 1660 until the beginning of the eighteenth century, there was little change. But throughout the **eighteenth century** population grew increasingly quickly. Bearing in mind that until the coming of the census in 1801 population estimates are little more than informed guesswork, the population of England seems to have risen from five million in 1700 to 5.8 million in 1750 and then to nine million in 1800. From then on it doubled to eighteen million by 1850 and doubled again to 36 million by 1911.

The rapidly industrializing north grew in comparison with the relatively rural south, except for London. It was long thought that this implied a mass migration of people from the countryside to the towns, from the farm to the factory. This didn't actually happen – people seemed, rather, to move in concentric circles, with those near the towns moving into them, those a bit further away moving in to replace the migrants, and so on. And a great deal of the population increase in the industrial cities and towns of the north appears to have been self-generated, with families having more children.

This population increase was the single most important fact of the period. It created an expanding market for food and finished goods, and at the same time provided a

1536–40	1540s–70s	1605
Many monasteries are dissolved and destroyed by Henry VIII, their wealth redistributed to the king and the aristocracy.	Yorkshire is heavily involved in a succession of Catholic plots against Henry's religious reforms. All of them fail.	The Roman Catholic Gunpowder Plot attempts to blow up the Houses of Parliament. One of its leaders, Guy Fawkes, is a native of York.

rapidly increasing workforce. The needs of the growing population were met by the improved agrarian and industrial methods that were being introduced – that is, by the agricultural and industrial revolutions.

The Agricultural Revolution

Small-scale changes in **land management** could be detected in Yorkshire as early as Tudor times. These changes gathered pace during the seventeenth and eighteenth centuries, whereby villages would move from the open-field system where each family held strips on open fields, and also had grazing and fuel gathering rights on the common, to the consolidation of land-holding into separate farms. This was not only more efficient but also reduced the spread of animal diseases. Enclosure could only be carried out with the agreement of everybody in the village, though, and as the eighteenth century progressed, the need for a unanimous decision to enclose in each village became increasingly onerous. Parliament started to intervene, a process that culminated in the 1845 **General Enclosure Act**, which implemented procedures for any village to enclose with the minimum of fuss. Though there was a great deal of opposition to the enclosure movement, it is hard to see what alternative there was if the growing population was to be fed.

The other development in farming, very noticeable in Yorkshire, was the introduction of **new methods** and new machinery. Crops such as turnips and clover were introduced (in Hatfield, for example), the practice of spreading lime on acid soils was more widely adopted, potatoes were introduced in the Dales, rape was cultivated to feed sheep and produce oil. New **machines**, too, became popular – the Rotherham plough, for example, patented in 1730, became the precursor of many future metal ploughs. As the century wore on, Yorkshire farmers largely adopted the new ways and the new machines (though the enthusiasm wasn't universal). Symptomatic of this enthusiasm is the story of **William Marshall** (1745–1818), an enlightened agricultural reformer and writer who was instrumental in setting up the British Board of Agriculture, and who established an agricultural college in Pickering (see p.238).

The Industrial Revolution

In industry, too, small changes detectable in Tudor times gathered pace during the seventeenth and eighteenth centuries. Coal mining, iron smelting, glass manufacture and pottery production were all under way by the end of the seventeenth century, while woollen manufacture had been long established in West Yorkshire. Road and river transport was being improved piecemeal – new packhorse bridges were built, rivers were made more navigable. With hindsight, one can almost imagine that Yorkshire was waiting for the **Industrial Revolution** with bated breath.

From the middle of the eighteenth century, in common with other industrial areas like Lancashire, the West Midlands and northeast England, Yorkshire towns and cities grew, and improvements in transport, extraction and manufacturing processes accelerated at such an unprecedented rate that what was happening was not just an industrial revolution – it was a world-changing revolution in human life that was to sweep the planet.

1642–51	**18th and 19th centuries**
The English Civil War is fought between supporters of Charles I (Royalists, or Cavaliers) and of Parliamentarians (Roundheads). The biggest battle of the war is fought at Marston Moor near York, in 1644.	Yorkshire experiences massive population growth and the agricultural and industrial revolutions. The wool trade, factory system, coal mining, steel production and road, canal and rail transport all grow.

Textiles

At the forefront of this revolution was West Yorkshire's **textile industry**. Organized loosely in a domestic system, it was uniquely suited to fast and widespread change. Across the hills of **West Yorkshire**, families lived on smallholdings where they grew food part-time, the rest of their year being spent making **woollen** cloth. The head of the household would weave cloth on a loom in the house, the other processes – preparing the wool, spinning and finishing – being done by the women and children. Each household financed and produced its own cloth and sold it in the town wool markets. Here then was a great stock of small entrepreneurs ready to innovate when the chance came, and with time available – when necessary, they could simply spend less time farming and more time spinning and weaving. Furthermore, a wide variety of types of cloth was produced – worsteds, kerseys, woollens, broad cloths and narrow cloths – so that production could be switched easily from one to the other as prices and fashions changed.

Following mechanical innovations in Lancashire, a number of places on the western edge of West Yorkshire took that county's lead and started to produce **cotton** cloth. Innovations in the cotton areas were then quickly adopted by the much bigger Yorkshire woollen industry, which meant that, from being just one of the UK's wool producing regions (the others were East Anglia and the West Country), West Yorkshire shot ahead to become supreme: the area, with Lancashire, that clothed the world.

Towards the end of the eighteenth century, large woollen **mills** started to be built, first powered by water and then by steam. **Machines** took over: Hargreaves's spinning jenny, Arkwright's water frame and Crompton's mule on the spinning side, bracketed by Kay's flying shuttle and Cartwright's power loom in weaving. The new social and geographical landscape – giant factories, the chimneys of their engine rooms belching smoke; the back-to-back housing that snaked along the valley floors and up onto the hills; the horrendous overcrowding and lack of sanitation; the use of child labour; the long hours and dangerous working conditions – presented a whole raft of problems that the world had never faced.

Coal

As steam replaced water power and increasing amounts of iron and steel were needed for making machinery and building factories, the demand for **coal** grew rapidly. The existing coal mines in South and West Yorkshire had to expand – old-fashioned bell-pits and adit mines were not enough, and deep mining had to go progressively deeper to extract the necessary coal. Although there were innovations – such as steam winding and ventilation, and the use of underground tramways and safety lamps – rock falls, the build-up of poisonous gas, flooding and methane explosions began to make coal mining one of the most dangerous jobs in the country. Thirty men died in Barnsley in 1803, 73 at the Oaks colliery in 1847 and 75 at Darley Main in 1849. Children as young as 7 or 8 were employed as "trappers", though the practice of using young girls to pull trucks of coal like tethered animals was not common in the Yorkshire pits. Output did rise quickly, and some coal owners developed reputations for being good employers, but others were grasping and incompetent and in general conditions remained appalling, safety standards poor, hours long, wages low and relations between management and workers dreadful.

1768	1833
Yorkshire man Captain James Cook (1728–79) embarks on his first great voyage of discovery for the Royal Society, exploring and mapping New Zealand and Australia's east coast.	The slave trade is abolished throughout the British Empire, partly as the result of the efforts of Hull's great abolitionist William Wilberforce.

Iron and steel

The building material of the early Industrial Revolution was iron; that of the late Industrial Revolution steel. South Yorkshire was the region's great iron-and-steel-producing area. There were, broadly, three types of iron, each with its own properties and uses. **Cast iron**, as it emerged from the furnace in which it was extracted from the ore, had a high carbon content and was very hard but relatively brittle. It was cast into moulds in foundries to make such things as kitchen ranges, gutters, downpipes and manhole covers – anything where it wouldn't be put under lateral stress. **Wrought iron**, made by heating cast iron and beating out the carbon and other impurities, was softer, more malleable and less brittle than cast iron. Able to stand up to stress without shattering, wrought iron was widely used during the early Industrial Revolution for such things as bridges and machinery, as well as in ornamental ironwork. **Steel**, with a higher carbon content than wrought iron but lower than cast iron, was tough and malleable, with excellent edge-retaining properties. It was initially very difficult to make – cast iron was turned into wrought iron, and then the carbon content had to be raised to a precisely calculated level: too much and it reverted to cast iron, too little and it remained as wrought iron. This long and tedious process ensured that steel was prohibitively expensive, and was only used for things like clock springs, surgical instruments, cutlery, weapons and razors. However, with the invention of the Bessemer process in the 1850s and the open-hearth process in the 1870s, steel could be mass produced, and it replaced wrought iron as the engineering material of choice during the later Industrial Revolution, produced in vast quantities in Sheffield in particular (see box, p.50).

Transport

The rapid development in the production of textiles, coal, iron and steel made massive demands on the region's **transport system**. In the eighteenth century each parish was responsible for the repair and maintenance of its own roads, a system that resulted in many roads that were impassably muddy in winter and dusty and rock-hard in summer. Wherever possible, heavy goods were moved on navigable rivers.

Attempts were made to improve things during the early eighteenth century – stone packhorse bridges replaced wooden ones, way-markers were set up to guide travellers across moorland (on the North York Moors for example) and attempts were made to improve existing rivers by means of "navigations" – straightening and deepening hitherto non-navigable stretches. However, from the 1740s onwards, as the Industrial Revolution really took off, the need for better transport became critical. A series of Turnpike Trusts were set up whereby local businessmen could raise capital, improve an existing road or build a new one, then cover the costs, and possibly make a profit, by charging for its use. Many roads were turnpiked – especially those across the Pennines to Lancashire, where five routes were opened between 1751 and 1772. Yorkshire's greatest native road builder was **John Metcalf** – Blind Jack of Knaresborough – who built roads across Yorkshire, Lancashire and elsewhere (see p.168). His first road, between Minskip and Ferrensby, was opened in 1752. The new turnpike roads were not popular with local people who had to use them often, but they did improve transport between industrial areas, though carrying heavy goods by road was still slow and expensive. The new roads did have an impact, however, in speeding up

1847	1850–World War I
First novels published by the three Brontë sisters – *Jane Eyre* by Charlotte, *Wuthering Heights* by Emily, and *Agnes Grey* by Anne – forever change the way that Yorkshire is viewed both inside and outside its borders.	Yorkshire clothes the world. The Municipal Reform Act of 1835 and the County Councils Act of 1888 create elected councils and enforce urban improvements in an attempt to clean up the mess created by industrialization.

long-distance coach travel and also in carrying mail. The growth of (relatively) fast passenger and mail transport was certainly important to the new class of entrepreneur that was developing in Yorkshire.

The search for a cheap way of carrying heavy raw materials and finished goods was still on. When, in Lancashire in 1761, the opening of the Bridgewater Canal from the coal mines of Worsley to the city of Manchester led to an immediate drop in the price of coal in the latter, it was not lost on businessmen elsewhere in England. Canals started to be built in many parts of the country, a process that became known as "canal mania" from the 1790s onwards. In Yorkshire the most ambitious canal scheme was to link Leeds with the industrial centres of Lancashire – ambitious because of the technical problems presented by the intervening Pennines. Though started in the mid-1770s, the **Leeds and Liverpool canal** wasn't completed until 1816.

When the Stockton to Darlington **railway** was opened in 1825, and even more so when the Liverpool to Manchester railway was opened in 1830, it was obvious that the holy grail of the Industrial Revolution had been found. Rail transport with steam locomotives pulling wagons or coaches could provide industry with a fast way of moving heavy goods around, passengers could get anywhere in the country in a day and mail trains sped up communications to an unbelievable extent – the impact was similar to that of computers in the late twentieth century. A frantic "railway mania" was sparked with schemes to build railways starting up all over the country, the economy got a huge injection of capital and whole towns grew up to service the new wonder of the age. Even the previous rather slapdash approach to time had to be standardized as, in 1840, the Great Western Railway introduced "railway time" along its length. It was such a good idea that within a couple of years all companies had done the same, and time throughout the country was standardized to "London time" controlled from Greenwich. And the influence of the railways wasn't confined to the UK – they spread all over the world.

1850–World War I

By 1850 the expansion of industry in Yorkshire had left a terrible **mess**. Cities like Leeds, Bradford and Sheffield existed under a pall of smoke, untreated sewage and uncollected refuse built up in the streets and people lived in overcrowded hovels with poor sanitation, their lives threatened by epidemic diseases like cholera. **Working conditions** were no better – instead of toiling in their own homes, in small workshops, or in relatively safe bell-pits, people now had to cope with colossal factories or dangerous deep mines. Things that had gone unnoticed in small pre-industrial towns and villages, or were considered at least acceptable, now became not only unpleasant but life-threatening. The Victorians have got a bad press ever since, attacked by social commentators, authors like Charles Dickens and left-wing activists alike. Yet what is perhaps remarkable is not how little was done to solve the problems, but how much and how quickly.

Across Yorkshire the **clean up** progressed – patchy and piecemeal, certainly, but increasingly effective. Cities set up improvement societies and commissions (in Sheffield, for example, in 1818) which started the work, Parliament set up properly constituted local councils with the Municipal Reform Act of 1835 and the County

1857	1895	1897
Sheffield FC, the oldest Association Football (soccer) team in the world still playing, is established.	The Rugby League is created at a meeting in the *George Hotel*, Huddersfield.	Publication of *Dracula*, a novel by Bram Stoker, set partly in Whitby, which comes to define the vampire forever.

Councils Act of 1888. Fresh water supplies were created, sewers built, roads paved, refuse collected, streets lit, trams laid out, building regulations drawn up and enforced, police and fire services instituted. Great outbursts of civic pride led to the building of magnificent town halls, libraries, museums, baths, art galleries, indoor markets, colleges and public parks. Schools, hospitals, churches and chapels sprang up across Yorkshire. Architects like Broderick Crawford in Leeds, and Lockwood and Mawson in Bradford, vied with each other in the magnificence of their designs. Other developments arose because of the improvement in transport and travel. Towns became entertainment centres, with concert halls, theatres, music halls, racecourses and sports grounds attracting people from miles around. And coastal resorts like Bridlington, Filey and Scarborough flourished as trippers flooded in from the rest of Yorkshire.

Despite attempts by Parliament to insist on improvements in working conditions, life for many in Yorkshire continued to be hard. Working in the West Yorkshire textile mills or Sheffield's steel works was no picnic, but it was in the **coal mines** that the worst conditions were to be found. The coal owners were renowned for their obduracy, the miners for their militancy. And as the mines went deeper and deeper, the death toll climbed – 189 miners died in a disaster at Lundhill in 1857, 59 died in Edmunds Main in 1864, and a staggering 361 died in the Oaks colliery in 1866, 27 of them rescue workers killed by a second explosion. This last horrific disaster occurred just nineteen years after another at the same colliery, in which 73 miners had died and the subsequent enquiry had made recommendations, which were ignored, regarding ventilation. The country was horrified, but the deaths continued – 140 at Swaithe Main in 1875, ninety in Cadeby in 1912. Coal miners responded by uniting. In 1889 the **Miners Federation of Great Britain** was founded, and a series of strikes and lockouts took place right up to, and indeed after, World War I.

The two World Wars: 1914–45

Thousands of Yorkshiremen volunteered for service when **World War I** broke out in 1914, especially though not exclusively in the York and Lancaster, West Yorkshire, East Yorkshire, Yorkshire and Duke of Wellington's regiments, and the King's Own Yorkshire Light Infantry. As with recruits from elsewhere in the country, they were fed into the mincing machine that was the Western Front.

Despite the attack on Scarborough and Whitby by German naval vessels at the end of 1914, Yorkshire in general had a good war. The South Yorkshire iron and steel industry worked at full blast making steel and armaments and tools, the West Yorkshire textile industry fulfilled orders for uniforms and blankets, factories all over the county turned their hands to armaments and ammunition, and gaps in the labour force created by recruitment for the armed forces were filled by women, for the first time taking on work that had always been done by men. Farming and coal mining too flourished as a result of wartime demand.

The good times continued to 1921, but then a severe **postwar depression** hit, and unemployment soared. Though textile workers and steel workers were struggling, the depression hit the coal industry hardest of all, and the bitter struggle between owners and unions resumed, with a strike in 1921 followed by the **General Strike** in

1914–18	1926	1939–45
Yorkshire prospers during World War I by adapting its industrial output to the needs of a wartime economy.	During serious postwar depression the General Strike is sparked by problems in the coal industry, but lasts only nine days.	Yorkshire again prospers during World War II, but Sheffield, Hull and other towns and cities suffer severe German bombing.

1926. Although West Yorkshire was also hard hit, seeds were sown in Leeds during this period that would grow into household names – Burton, John Collier and Hepworth's in clothing, Arnold in school equipment and notebooks, Waddington in board games and playing cards. And the Town Planning Act, together with the growth of the Labour Party in Leeds and Sheffield led to further advances in road- and house-building.

During the years running up to **World War II**, and during the war itself, Yorkshire's ailing industry was given a new lease of life as it responded to wartime demand. Civilian life was, however, affected much more than during World War I. Everybody experienced rationing, blackouts and all the other effects of wartime legislation. Numerous fighter and bomber airfields appeared around the county – have a look at the signatures of allied aircrew on the mirror in the basement of *Bettys* in York (see p.158). Hull and Sheffield were particularly hard hit by the Luftwaffe.

Postwar years

After the war the decline of the county's traditional industries resumed, and during the 1960s and 1970s many old firms ceased trading. The Hull fishing industry went into decline, and Sheffield cutlery and West Yorkshire's textile industry suffered from fierce competition from the Far East. Above all, two of Yorkshire's great staple heavy industries, **steel** and **coal**, went into a free fall. Although there were real underlying economic reasons for their problems (especially competition from elsewhere in the world), these two industries also became an ideological battleground between the recently elected (1979) Conservative prime minister **Margaret Thatcher** and organized labour. Intent on reorganizing British industry and breaking the power of the trade unions, Thatcher put in Scottish-American hard man Ian MacGregor to take on the unions, first in the steel industry, where he was appointed Chairman of the British Steel Corporation in 1980, then in the coal industry, where he became leader of the National Coal Board in 1983. In both, MacGregor's uncompromising restructuring, with minimal consultation, swingeing plant closures and mass redundancies provoked the expected national **strikes**, led respectively by Bill Sirs of the Iron and Steel Trades Federation in 1980 and firebrand **Arthur Scargill** of the National Union of Mineworkers in 1984–85. Convinced that it was the unions who had cost the Conservatives the election in 1974, Thatcher had prepared carefully before deliberately provoking the strikes. Both were defeated, with much bitterness and hardship, especially in traditionally militant South and West Yorkshire. Thatcher's furious reaction to the miners' strike of 1984–85 in particular, in confrontations between police and pickets such as that at the **Orgreave Colliery** (the "Battle of Orgreave") just outside Rotherham, led to a loathing towards her and hostility and suspicion towards the police which has survived in many areas of Yorkshire to this day. Employment in the South Yorkshire steel industry fell from sixty thousand in 1971 to sixteen thousand in 1987 and less than ten thousand by the mid-1990s, whilst the Yorkshire coal mining industry virtually disappeared, surviving in only a handful of privatized pits. The industrial changes in Yorkshire might best be represented by the Meadowhall Shopping complex – once the site of a great steelworks, it is now one of the country's largest shopping malls.

1950s	1984–85
Successive waves of immigration from the Commonwealth substantially change the ethnic profile of many towns and cities.	The miners' strike, a showdown between Conservative Prime Minister Margaret Thatcher and the National Union of Mineworkers, leads to bitter industrial strife across the Yorkshire coalfields. The miners are defeated, and the industry begins a terminal decline.

Just as the industrial profile of Yorkshire has changed beyond all recognition since World War II, so too the **urban environment** in many of Yorkshire's towns and cities has been transformed. The Town and Country Planning Act of 1947 gave local councils the power to clear away urban slums and bomb-damaged buildings, increase the housing stock and refashion town and city centres, not always with fortunate results. Understandably, there was more emphasis during the rebuilding on speed and economy than on heritage and aesthetics, but a lot of damage was done – in Leeds and Bradford, for example, a large number of fine Victorian buildings were lost, replaced by unimaginative, anodyne and flimsy modern constructions, and huge council estates were built that later became crime-infested and down-at-heel. Labour shortages started to be met by recruitment abroad, and **immigration** from Commonwealth countries grew rapidly across South and West Yorkshire, especially in places like Bradford and Rotherham. This led to vibrant new communities in industrial towns and cities in the region, but also to social problems of overcrowding and racial tension.

The new millennium

Since the 1990s the situation has to some degree been retrieved, with the attractive development of canal basins (Leeds and Sheffield), the adapting of old buildings to new uses (Leeds Corn Exchange, Salt's Mill, Halifax's Dean Clough Mill, for example), and the cleaning up and remodelling of city centres, particularly in Sheffield, Leeds and Hull. Sterling work has been done, too, by local councils in attracting new industries and inward investment, including EU funds. Despite the drastic cuts imposed on local councils by the coalition government's policy of **austerity**, introduced from 2010, the success of such initiatives is reflected in triumphs such as the Grand Départ of the Tour de France being held in Yorkshire in 2014, and of Hull being declared UK City of Culture for 2017.

2006	**2011**	**2014**
Fred Trueman, controversial firebrand Yorkshire and England fast bowler and famous wit, dies.	The £35 million Hepworth Gallery opens in Wakefield. It attracts half a million visitors during its first year.	The start of the Tour de France (Le Grand Départ) takes place in North Yorkshire. Hull is announced as the UK's City of Culture 2017.

Wildlife

There are plenty of chances to see wildlife in Yorkshire. And whether you're a dyed-in-the-wool amateur naturalist or would simply like to see some of the birds, insects and plants of the county, perhaps with a bit of help with identification, there are many sources of useful and lively information. Nature reserves, run either by the Yorkshire Wildlife Trust or by the RSPB, dot the county, and both Yorkshire's National Parks offer a great deal of information and help.

Yorkshire Wildlife Trust

The best way to see the most wildlife in the least amount of time is to go to a **Yorkshire Wildlife Trust** (ⓦywt.org.uk) nature reserve. The YWT has 83 reserves across Yorkshire with 33 in North Yorkshire, 18 in East Yorkshire, 11 in South Yorkshire and 21 in West Yorkshire. Some have no facilities, others are well endowed with hides, toilets, cafés and information boards, and have free parking and access for wheelchairs and pushchairs. They cover a range of habitats – grassland, heathland, wetland, woodland and coast. Unless stated, reserves are free and are open all hours every day throughout the year. We've detailed some of the major YWT sites below; for the full list, check their website.

Askham Bog

Lying just southwest of the city of York, just off the A1036, **Askham Bog** (daily 24hr) was the reserve which started it all off – the Yorkshire Wildlife Trust was set up in 1946 specifically to protect it. A circular boardwalk with a spur off to a pond makes negotiating the bog a doddle, and there are interpretation boards to tell you what to look out for. The amazing thing about this site is the breadth of **plant life** that's found here – great fen sedge, more commonly seen in East Anglia, growing near bog myrtle which is usually found on the west coast; marsh orchids, yellow flag irises and water violets; yellow loosestrife, which attracts dentated pug moths; and alder buckthorn, which is fed on by brimstone butterflies. **Birds** commonly seen on the site include redpoll, siskin, woodcock and lesser spotted woodpeckers, while **mammals** include roe deer and water voles. There's free parking, and access for wheelchairs and buggies is good, courtesy of the boardwalk. Dogs must be kept on leads.

Grass Wood

Just outside Grassington, **Grass Wood** (daily 24hr) consists of an ancient ash wood and later beech plantation with lovely views of Wharfedale. Under its woodland canopy you'll find lily-of-the-valley, wood sorrel, bloody cranes-bill, rock-rose, melancholy thistle and the rare bird's nest orchid, and see willow warblers, nuthatches, tree creepers, a variety of tits and green and spotted woodpeckers. The wood is best visited in late spring, or for a wealth of fungi, in autumn. There are interpretation boards and parking. Visitors should keep to the paths (which are not really suitable for wheelchairs) and **dogs** must be kept on a lead.

Spurn Head

A long finger of sand that has been drawn out by erosion between the North Sea and the Humber estuary, the **Spurn National Nature Reserve** (see p.301) is a wonderfully windswept three miles of sand dunes, marram grass, sea buckthorn, lyme-grass, sea-holly, cord grass and sea rocket, with a variety too of butterflies and moths. But it is for its **birds** that Spurn Head is famous – the thousands of migrating swallows and house martins that pass through in spring and autumn, the great flocks of wintering wildfowl and waders, the rare visitor blown in by storms. With luck you might, too, see grey seal or minke whales out at sea. There is parking, toilets, a refreshment caravan, hides and information boards, along with some wheelchair access, but **dogs** are not allowed.

North Cave Wetlands

Just off the M62 between Hull and Goole, **North Cave** (daily 24hr) is a former gravel quarry and an excellent example of what can be achieved by careful management – in this case by controlling the water levels to create a variety of habitats. The result is that in this one reserve you can see 170 species of **birds**, 200 plant species and 24 species of butterfly. There can't be many places in the country that you might see, at different times of the year, reed warblers, reed buntings, ringed plover, little ringed plover, oystercatchers, redshank and avocet, goldeneye, pochard and smew, sand martins and kingfishers, skylarks, meadow pipits and redshank, goldfinch, redpoll and siskin, buntings and tree sparrows, hobby, merlin and peregrine falcons. **Insect** life includes common blue, small skipper and wall brown butterflies, and hawker and four-spotted chaser dragonflies. The reserve has parking, toilets, a mobile café and interpretation boards, and is wheelchair-friendly. No **dogs** are allowed.

Potteric Carr

Just two miles south of Doncaster, **Potteric Carr** (daily 9am–5pm; £3) is one of the largest urban nature reserves in the country. It has a mixture of habitats – woodland, grassland, marsh and open water – which ensures a wide range of birds, insects and plants. Over 158 species of **bird** have been recorded, including bittern, kingfisher, reed and sedge warblers, all three woodpeckers and woodcock, 28 species of butterfly, including comma, gatekeeper, white-letter hairstreak, purple hairstreak and brown argus, and twenty species of dragonfly, including black-tailed skimmer, banded demoiselle, hairy dragonfly, broad-bodied chaser and ruddy darter. **Plants** include orchids, great spearwort, lesser water-plantain, lesser reedmace, greater tussock sedge, purple small reed, great water dock, yellow-wort and traveller's-joy, and there are five species of bats. The full range of services are on offer, including fifteen hides and a splendid café that serves hot meals. Wheelchair users need a permit, because of problems associated with Network Rail lines within the reserve. No **dogs** are allowed.

Adel Dam

East of Leeds-Bradford airport, next to Golden Acre Park, **Adel Dam** (daily 24hr) is a small reserve based on a lake created by the damming of a beck to create a mill pond about 250 years ago. Good for **bluebells** in the spring and **fungi** in the autumn, it has seen more than one hundred species of **bird** since its establishment in 1968, and there are two hides, though it is the more common woodland and lake birds that dominate – kingfishers, herons and all three species of woodpecker. There are car parking, toilets and refreshment facilities in Golden Acre Park, and the site is wheelchair friendly, but **dogs** are not allowed.

The Royal Society for the Protection of Birds (RSPB)

The **Royal Society for the Protection of Birds** (ⓦrspb.org.uk) has four reserves in Yorkshire – two in East Yorkshire and one each in West and South Yorkshire. We've given a general rundown of the reserves here, but for full details and maps you should check the website – which also details the numerous special events that most reserves put on.

Bempton Cliffs

The top site in England for watching seabirds, **Bempton Cliffs** (open all year; visitor centre daily: March–Oct 9.30am–5pm; Nov–Feb 9.30am–4pm; £5/car) is on the north coast of Flamborough Head, just outside Bridlington. The most northerly chalk cliff expanse in the UK, this is seabird watching heaven – so much so that not only does the RSPB have a reserve here, but so does the Yorkshire Wildlife Trust, just along the headland. From April to August the towering cliffs are home to two hundred thousand birds: gannets, guillemots, razorbills, kittiwakes, fulmars and puffins, which set up a deafening roar – you can hear the colony long before you see it. There are five cliff-top viewing platforms (one is wheelchair accessible), and it's easy for even total beginners to learn to identify the main species. In spring the birds are nesting, in summer you'll see fledglings taking to the air for the first time, in the autumn large flocks of birds get ready to migrate, and in winter the remaining birds mass to feed and roost.

Blacktoft Sands

On the largest tidal reed beds in England, at the confluence of the Ouse and the Trent in east Yorkshire, **Blacktoft Sands** (reserve 9am–9pm or dusk if earlier, reception hut April–Oct daily 9am–4pm; Nov–March Sat & Sun 10am–3pm; £4; family £7) boasts no fewer than 270 species of birds, including avocet, bearded tit, bittern, hen harriers and marsh harriers. There are seven hides, all but one of which are easily accessible.

Dearne Valley Old Moor

In the heart of the Dearne Valley, not far from Doncaster in South Yorkshire, the **Dearne Valley Old Moor** reserve (visitor centre daily: Feb–Oct 9.30am–5pm; Nov–Jan 9.30am–4pm; April–Sept reserve open until 8pm; £5; family £11) has kingfisher, little owl, lapwing, golden plover and tree sparrows, together with lots of ducks, geese and swans. But it's not just birds you need to look out for – there's a wide variety of butterflies, dragonflies and orchids, too. Accessibility is good, and there's a café.

Fairburn Ings

Boasting three trails through a variety of habitats near Castleford, **Fairburn Ings** (daily: March–Oct 9am–5pm; Nov–Feb 9am–4pm; free, but parking costs £2.50) offers the opportunity to see see chiffchaff, green sandpiper, kingfisher, little ringed plover, reed warbler, tree sparrows and willow tits. There's a visitor centre and four hides.

Books

Included below is a subjective selection of the many books written about Yorkshire, penned by Yorkshire authors, or set in Yorkshire. Read them all, and you'll get a good feeling for the county – though you may not have time to actually visit. Those marked with ★ are especially recommended.

NOVELS, DRAMA AND POETRY

★**Kate Atkinson** *Behind the Scenes at the Museum*; *Started Early, Took My Dog*. Born in York, Kate Atkinson writes clever, exciting and often funny novels that fuse whodunnit and mainstream fiction. *Behind the Scenes...* (set in York) won the Whitbread prize in 1995, while *Started Early...* (which travels through Yorkshire from Leeds to Whitby) is the latest of a series featuring ex-police inspector Jackson Brody. **Brontës – Charlotte** (*Jane Eyre*), **Emily** (*Wuthering Heights*) and **Anne** (*Agnes Grey*). The writing of the three world-famous sisters was strongly influenced by the landscape (both natural and human) they saw around their Haworth home. Their novels in turn influenced the way in which Yorkshire is still perceived in the rest of the world.

John Godber *Bouncers*, *Up 'n' Under*, *Teechers* and many more. Founder and director of the Hull Truck Theatre Company, John Godber is a dramatist whose plays, in performance or on the page (they're published singly and in collections), are wonderfully entertaining.

Tony Harrison *Collected Poems*. A poet born and educated in Leeds, Tony Harrison has wide-ranging interests. However, it is for the wonderful poems describing his working-class 1940s childhood, his parents, family and ancestors, that he's included here.

James Herriot *All Creatures Great and Small*. A Scottish vet who settled in Thirsk in North Yorkshire, James Alfred ("Alf") Wight, writing under the pen name James Herriot, wrote a series of books based on his experiences (*If Only They Could Talk*, or *It Shouldn't Happen to a Vet* for example), which have collectively come to be known as *All Creatures Great and Small*. A huge success, they were turned into much-loved films and a television series, and offer pictures of Yorkshire folk which, while stereotypical, are sympathetic and amusing.

Ted Hughes *Birthday Letters*. Widely felt to be one of the best poets of the twentieth century, Poet Laureate for the last fourteen years of his life, and controversial because of his relationship with his wife Sylvia Plath, Ted Hughes is often seen as a typical Heathcliff-like Yorkshireman. He developed a love and healthy respect for nature during his upbringing in the Calder Valley, and his poems about animals and birds (in his *Collected Poems*) can be read as a way of developing an insight into the area's natural world. *Birthday Letters*, on the other hand, is more about his relationship with Plath, and includes several poems set in Yorkshire – *Wuthering Heights* and *Stubbing Wharfe* for example. Poignant, especially if combined with a visit to his birthplace (see p.119) and Plath's grave (see p.122).

★**Philip Larkin** *Collected Poems*. Though not born a Yorkshireman, Larkin was the librarian for Hull University for the last thirty years of his life. Many of the poems in the collected works are set in East Yorkshire and although they are not overtly about the area, and there's little detail, between them they create a picture of Hull and the region. Try *Arrivals, Departures* ("Tame water lanes, tall sheds"), *Friday Night at the Royal Station Hotel*, *Whitsun Weddings*, *Show Saturday* and more.

Ian McMillan *The Best of Ian McMillan* and others. The bard of Barnsley's poetry is local, graphic and very funny, though you only get the full flavour when you hear it read by the poet himself. *101 Uses for a Flat Cap*, illustrated by Tony Husband's charming cartoons, gives a typically tongue-in-cheek view of a quintessentially Yorkshire garment.

Bram Stoker *Dracula*. So overlaid by more recent books and films has the famous vampire story become that many people may not have read the book that started it all. This is a shame – it's a beautifully written and wonderfully readable story, with accounts of places (the Carpathians, and particularly relevant here, Whitby) that would put the attempts of specialist travel writers to shame. The long section set in Whitby is extraordinarily graphic – although it was written well over a century ago, you can still see everywhere mentioned in the book, and follow the action on the ground.

Arctic Monkeys *Whatever People Say I Am, That's What I'm Not*. Though not a book, or even strictly a poetry collection, Alex Turner's lyrics on this Arctic Monkeys album are works of genius – as an evocation of the life of young clubbers in Sheffield, it's unmatched.

MEMOIRS, BIOGRAPHY AND TRAVEL

Simon Armitage *All Points North*. From his home in the Pennines, close to the border with Lancashire, Yorkshire poet Simon Armitage dissects the characteristics of his home county (and other parts of the north) in a collection that is part travel journalism, part autobiography and part diary. It's acute, observant and witty.

Beryl Bainbridge *English Journey*. To mark the fiftieth anniversary of J.B. Priestley's *English Journey*, Liverpudlian writer Beryl Bainbridge, with a team from BBC Bristol, set out to follow in his footsteps. Only part of the journey was through Yorkshire, but this book of the series captures a vivid and amusing snapshot of the county in the 1980s. She visits a number of places described in *The Rough Guide to Yorkshire*, including Bradford and the Dales.

Alan Bennett *Writing Home* and *Untold Stories*. Prose collections including many autobiographical pieces that build up a picture of Alan Bennett's childhood in Leeds. Hilarious, sad, touching – Bennett is incapable of writing a dull sentence.

Dickie Bird *My Autobiography*. Not really an autobiography, more like sitting with the great cricket umpire as he reminisces over a pint of Barnsley Bitter. And absolutely none the worse for that.

Daniel Defoe *A Tour through the Whole Island of Great Britain*. Based on a tour of Britain that the great writer made between 1724 and 1726, here Defoe describes Yorkshire's towns, villages and countryside in fine and fascinating detail. There are descriptions of early eighteenth-century Sheffield, Bawtry and Doncaster, Huddersfield, Wakefield, Leeds and Pontefract, and there's a particularly detailed account of Halifax. Dip in and enjoy.

Lee Hanson (ed) *Edge of Heaven: the Yorkshire Coast*. Different aspects of Yorkshire's coastline described by a variety of writers, some of them, like Blake Morrison and Margaret Drabble, literary big-hitters. Nice photos, too.

Arnold Kellet *Blind Jack of Knaresborough*. A short and readable biography of the very long and eventful life of John Metcalf (1717–1810) – road builder, musician, drinker, gambler, smuggler, horse trader, tourist guide and

blind from the age of 6. If you're staying anywhere near Harrogate or Knaresborough, get your hands on this book.

Anne Lister *The Secret Diaries of Anne Lister 1791–1840*. Fascinating and candid ("I love and only love the fairer sex") diary of the famous early nineteenth-century lesbian, who lived at Shibden Hall in Calderdale (see p.116).

★ **Stuart Maconie** *Pies and Prejudice: In Search of the North*. A brilliant, laugh-out-loud book that, although covering the whole of the north, and although written by a Lancastrian, gives an excellent picture of Yorkshire. The prejudice of the title isn't that of Lancashire against Yorkshire or vice versa – it's more a common cause book aimed at southern views of the north, his attempt, as he puts it, to "discover both the north itself and my own inner northerner". Fans of Maconie's wry voice on radio and TV will love it.

Mike Pannet *Mike Pannet's Yorkshire*. A photographic tour of Yorkshire with one of the stars of the BBC's *Country Cops* documentary series. Pannet has also written a series of comic memoirs of his life as a country policeman in North Yorkshire (*Now Then, Lad*; *Not on My Patch, Lad* and so on).

Michael Parkinson *Parky*. The autobiography of one of Yorkshire's many national treasures. Michael Parkinson, TV superstar, journalist, film critic, chat show host, cricket enthusiast and all-round good egg was born in Barnsley and never lost his accent (though he did tone it down, otherwise viewers wouldn't have understood a word he said).

J.B. Priestley *English Journey*. The full title says it all – "English Journey, being a rambling but truthful account of what one man saw and heard and felt and thought during a journey through England during the Autumn of the Year 1933". Being one of Yorkshire's most famous writers and journalists, Priestley devotes a chunk of the book to his home city of Bradford in the chapter "To the West Riding".

HISTORY, ARCHITECTURE AND SPORT

★ **Catherine Bailey** *Black Diamonds – the Rise and Fall of a Great English Dynasty*. An absolutely riveting account of the social history of one small part of South Yorkshire, of the paternalistic relationship between the Fitzwilliams of Wentworth and the farm workers and miners who lived on their estate, and of the vicious manoeuvring among family members in the nineteenth and twentieth centuries, the effect of which can still be seen today. Read it, and you'll never look at a coal-mining area in the same way again.

Harry Gration *Yorkshire Sporting Heroes*. By sports commentator and much-loved co-host of BBC's regional news programme *Look North*, Harry Gration, this account of his thirty top Yorkshire sportsmen, written with a journalist's flair, is a good introduction to Yorkshire's sporting prowess. He doesn't limit himself to Yorkshire men and women either – his top player is John Charles, the great Welsh centre forward who played for Leeds United. Including his favourite sports grounds, traditions and quotes, it's like eavesdropping on a discussion between knowledgeable locals in a Yorkshire pub.

★ **David Hey** *A History of Yorkshire*. Detailed, well-written and with lots of excellent photographs, this book offers a history of the county from prehistoric times to the start of the twenty-first century. Probably on the heavy side for casual visitors to the county, but residents shouldn't be without it.

Simon Jenkins *England's Thousand Best Churches* and *England's Thousand Best Houses*. Many of Yorkshire's great houses and churches are included in these accessible architectural guides.

Nikolaus Pevsner *The Buildings of England*. Yorkshire is well served in this remarkable series, with three volumes covering "The North Riding", "York and the East Riding" and "The West Riding", together with two *Pevsner Architectural Guides* to Sheffield and Leeds. Virtually every building of note in the county is covered in detail. Providing probably more than the casual visitor needs to know, these books are invaluable for anybody interested in architecture, and for any long-term resident of the county.

Small print and index

Rough Guide credits

Editor: Samantha Cook
Layout: Nikhil Agarwal
Cartography: Lokamata Sahu, James Macdonald
Picture editors: Marta Bescos, Raffaella Morini, MIchelle Bhatia
Proofreader: Anita Sach
Managing editors: Mani Ramaswamy, Andy Turner
Assistant editor: Sharon Sonam

Production: Janis Griffith
Cover design: Nicole Newman, Marta Bescos, Nikhil Agarwal
Editorial assistant: Rebecca Hallett
Senior pre-press designer: Dan May
Programme manager: Gareth Lowe
Publisher: Joanna Kirby
Publishing director: Georgina Dee

Publishing information

This second edition published April 2015 by
Rough Guides Ltd,
80 Strand, London WC2R 0RL
11, Community Centre, Panchsheel Park,
New Delhi 110017, India
Distributed by Penguin Random House
Penguin Books Ltd,
80 Strand, London WC2R 0RL
Penguin Group (USA)
345 Hudson Street, NY 10014, USA
Penguin Group (Australia)
250 Camberwell Road, Camberwell,
Victoria 3124, Australia
Penguin Group (NZ)
67 Apollo Drive, Mairangi Bay, Auckland 1310,
New Zealand
Penguin Group (South Africa)
Block D, Rosebank Office Park, 181 Jan Smuts Avenue,
Parktown North, Gauteng, South Africa 2193
Rough Guides is represented in Canada by Tourmaline
Editions Inc. 662 King Street West, Suite 304, Toronto,
Ontario M5V 1M7
Printed in Singapore

336pp includes index
A catalogue record for this book is available from the
British Library
ISBN: 978-1-40937-104-5
The publishers and authors have done their best to
ensure the accuracy and currency of all the information in
The Rough Guide to Yorkshire, however, they can accept
no responsibility for any loss, injury, or inconvenience
sustained by any traveller as a result of information or
advice contained in the guide.
1 3 5 7 9 9 8 6 4 2

Help us update

We've gone to a lot of effort to ensure that the second
edition of **The Rough Guide to Yorkshire** is accurate
and up-to-date. However, things change – places get
"discovered", opening hours are notoriously fickle,
restaurants and rooms raise prices or lower standards. If
you feel we've got it wrong or left something out, we'd like
to know, and if you can remember the address, the price,
the hours, the phone number, so much the better.

Please send your comments with the subject line
"**Rough Guide Yorkshire Update**" to mail@uk
.roughguides.com. We'll credit all contributions and send
a copy of the next edition (or any other Rough Guide if you
prefer) for the very best emails.

Find more travel information, connect with fellow
travellers and plan your trip on Ⓦroughguides.com.

ABOUT THE AUTHOR

Jos Simon was raised on the Llŷn Peninsula in North Wales and settled in Yorkshire after teaching in Suffolk, Staffordshire, Derbyshire and Lincolnshire. Having come late to travel writing, he freelanced for a variety of magazines before embarking on several guidebooks to Mediterranean destinations – mainly Greek, since he's married to a Greek Cypriot. A long-held ambition to describe the county that he lived in and grew to love over twenty years was achieved by the commission to write this *Rough Guide to Yorkshire*.

Acknowledgements

Jos Simon would like to thank English Heritage and the National Trust for access to their many Yorkshire properties; Tourist Information Centres and holiday and tourism professionals throughout the county for information and help; editor Samantha Cook for meticulous editing and moral support; John and Jenny Deans for further visits to some of their favourite places, especially Doncaster Racecourse and numerous pubs and restaurants; and Farrah Holmes for her local knowledge of Pontefract. As ever, thanks too to my family (Doulla, Daniel, Catherine, Matt, Lazaros, Eliza, Arianwen and Chris) for help, forbearance and the loss of a summer holiday.

Readers' updates

Thanks to all who have offered comments and suggestions on how to improve the first edition (and apologies to any who have been omitted or whose names have been misspelt). In particular, for letters and emails: Gonzalo Arroyo, David Brooks, Jessica Haigh, Lara Lambert, Sue Leffman, Anita O'Donovan and John Weetman (Vicar of Selby Abbey). Thanks also to the readers who have offered positive feedback through Amazon, and in particular those who have made constructive suggestions or corrected mistakes: AJR45, Mazza, Moorsman, Nu Drover and SBLB1.

Index

Maps are marked in grey

E

F

H

I

Map symbols

The symbols below are used on maps throughout the book

✈	International airport	✝	Church	⌒	Cave	⊞	Christian cemetery
★	Transport stop	⊙	Statue	▨	Escarpment	☐	Beach
✉	Post office	♕	Castle	⚘	Waterfall	▬	Wall
@	Internet access	⊤	Garden	⚲	Gorge	▬▬	Motorway
✚	Hospital	✿	Country park	⋈	Bridge	⋯	Road
(i)	Information centre	◆	Nature reserve	▦	Building	⋯	Pedestrian road
◆	Place of interest	⚐	Lighthouse	☐	Market	- - - -	Path
∴	Ruin	⛴	Boat	⛪	Church (town maps)	⊶⊷	Railway
🏛	Stately home	⊠	Gate	◯	Stadium		
⌂	Abbey/priory/monastery	▲	Mountain peak	☐	Park		

Listings key

■	Accommodation
●	Eating & Drinking
■	Nightlife
●	Shopping

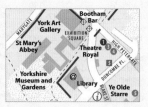

ROUGH GUIDES
A CHRONOLOGY

1982 The first *Rough Guide to Greece* – written and researched by Mark Ellingham, John Fisher and Nat Jansz – is published, shortly followed by Spain and Portugal **1983** *Amsterdam* – written by Martin Dunford – is published **1986** The first Rough Guides' offices set up in Kennington, south London **1987** Rough Guides set up as independent company **1988** BBC2 commission a Rough Guides TV series presented by Magenta Devine and Sankha Guha

1990 Rough Guides first published in the US under the name The Real Guides **1994** The first reference titles – *World Music*, *Classical Music* and *The Internet* – are published • World Music Network starts selling Rough Guides compilation CDs **1995** roughguides.com is launched **1997** New York office set up

2001 First ebooks launched **2002** Rough Guides moves to Penguin headquarters at 80 Strand, London • Delhi office established • Rip-proof city maps series launched **2003** New colour sections added to the guides • First commissioned photographic shoots take place **2004** *The Rough Guide to a Better World* published in association with DFID **2006** First full-colour Rough Guide – *World Party* – is published **2007** 25s series launched in honour of the 25th anniversary • *Make the Most of Your Time on Earth* becomes best-selling Rough Guide and is nominated in Richard and Judy Book Club awards **2008** A new Rough Guides TV series is broadcast on Channel 5 in the UK **2009** The first hardback picture book – *Earthbound* – featuring Rough Guides' commissioned photography goes on sale

2010 All guides are printed on FSC approved paper **2011** The new full-colour Pocket Guides series is launched • The first city guide iPhone/iPad apps are released **2012** Rough Guides' travel books are relaunched in time for our 30th anniversary, using full colour throughout • The first Rough Guide ebooks made specifically for the iPad go on sale **2013** roughguides.com is relaunched

A ROUGH GUIDE TO
ROUGH GUIDES

Published in 1982, the first Rough Guide – to Greece – was a student scheme that became a publishing phenomenon. Mark Ellingham, a recent graduate in English from Bristol University, had been travelling in Greece the previous summer and couldn't find the right guidebook. With a small group of friends he wrote his own guide, combining a highly contemporary, journalistic style with a thoroughly practical approach to travellers' needs.

The immediate success of the book spawned a series that rapidly covered dozens of destinations. And, in addition to impecunious backpackers, Rough Guides soon acquired a much broader and older readership that relished the guides' wit and inquisitiveness as much as their enthusiastic, critical approach and value-for-money ethos.